Second Edition

CONCEPTS OF PROGRAMMING LANGUAGES

ROBERT W. SEBESTA

University of Colorado, Colorado Springs

The Benjamin/Cummings Publishing Company, Inc.
Redwood City, California • Menlo Park, California
Reading, Massachusetts • New York • Don Mills, Ontario
Wokingham, U.K. • Amsterdam • Bonn • Sydney
Singapore • Tokyo • Madrid • San Juan

Sponsoring Editor: John Carter Shanklin
Editorial Assistant: Vivian McDougal
Production Coordinator: Andrew Marinkovich
Copy Editor: Barbara Conway
Proofreader: Kathy Lee
Cover Design: Michael Rogondino
Text Designer: Wendy Calmenson
Compositor: GTS Graphics

To Jake and Darcie

Library of Congress Cataloging-in-Publication Data

Sebesta, Robert W.
    Concepts of programming languages / Robert W. Sebesta. — 2nd ed.
      p.   cm.
    Includes bibliographical references and index.
    ISBN 0-8053-7130-3
    1. Programming languages (Electronic computers)   I. Title.
QA76.7.S43   1992   92-3219
005.13—dc20   CIP

3 4 5 6 7 8 9 10 -AL- 95 94 93

Preface

The principal goal of this book is to provide the reader with the necessary tools for the critical evaluation of existing and future programming languages and programming language constructs. An additional goal is to prepare the reader for a study of the design and construction of compilers.

There are two ways in which a book on the concepts of programming languages can be organized: a horizontal approach and a vertical approach. In the horizontal approach, languages are selected and each is presented in some depth. With the vertical approach, the general concepts and constructs of programming languages are described using some particular sequence. For each concept, examples from a variety of languages are presented. Both methods have merit. In order to accurately describe individual language concepts it is important to concentrate on the concepts and define their impact on programming and the evolution of languages. However, a chronological analysis of language developments necessitates the study of specific languages and their origins and development. Furthermore, the design of a specific facility of a particular language is often influenced by other characteristics of the language. Because of these considerations, this book uses the vertical approach for the majority of the material, but the horizontal approach is used when it is advantageous.

In this book I describe the fundamental concepts of programming languages by defining the design issues of the various language constructs, examining the design choices for these constructs in some of the most common languages, and critically comparing the design alternatives.

Doing this effectively requires studying a collection of closely related topics. To discuss languages and language constructs, descriptive tools are vital. I discuss in detail the most effective and widely used methods of syntax description. I also introduce the most common methods for describing the semantics of programming languages. To understand some of the reasons why the particular design choices for existing languages were made, I describe the historical context and specific needs that spawned them. Because ease of implementation is often a significant influence on language design, discussions of implementation methods and issues are integrated throughout the book.

Chapter 1 begins with a rationale for studying programming languages. It then discusses the criteria for evaluating programming languages. I recognize that defining these criteria is risky; however, evaluation principles are essential to any serious study of the design of programming languages. The primary influences on language design, common design trade-offs, and the basic approaches to implementation are also examined in Chapter 1.

Chapter 2 uses the horizontal approach to chart the chronological evolution of the most important languages discussed in this book. While no language is described completely, the origins, purposes, and contributions of each are discussed. This historical overview is valuable because it provides the background necessary to understanding the practical and theoretical basis for contemporary language design. It also motivates the further study of language design and evaluation. However, since none of the remainder of the book depends on Chapter 2, it can be skipped in its entirety.

Chapter 3 describes the primary formal methods for describing the syntax of programming languages: EBNF and syntax graphs. This is followed by a description of attribute grammars, which play a prominent role in compiler design. The difficult task of semantic description is then explored, including brief introductions to three of the most common methods: operational, axiomatic, and denotational semantics.

In Chapters 4–12 I use the vertical approach to describe in detail the design issues for the primary constructs of the imperative languages. In each case, the design choices for several example languages are presented and evaluated. Specifically, primitive data types and variables are covered in Chapter 4; more complicated data types in Chapter 5; expressions and assignments statements in Chapter 6; control statements in Chapter 7; subprograms and their implementation in Chapters 8 and 9; data abstraction facilities in Chapter 10; concurrent program units in Chapter 11; exception handling in Chapter 12. I use the vertical approach because it is inappropriate to describe and evaluate the details of a particular construct in several different parts of the book, which is what the horizontal approach requires. Discussing in a single chapter the various methods for providing concurrency, for example, allows for a concise comparison and evaluation of those methods.

Languages such as Pascal, Ada, FORTRAN, ANSI C, and C++ are frequently used to exemplify the concepts and constructs of the imperative languages.

The last three chapters briefly describe three of the most important alternative programming paradigms, functional programming, logic programming, and object-oriented programming. Each is discussed as a programming methodology, and then exemplified through a brief introduction to a specific language. The primary chosen languages are pure LISP, Prolog, and Smalltalk. However, Scheme and COMMON LISP are briefly described as functional languages, and C++ is discussed as an example of an imperative language with object-oriented features. In these three chapters, the horizontal approach is used again, because the languages for these paradigms have few basic concepts in common.

This book does not teach any complete programming language. We do not even introduce any particular imperative language. However, the three chapters on nonimperative languages introduce the fundamentals of programming in pure LISP, Prolog, and Smalltalk, and the reader will be able to write simple programs in these languages based on the contents of these chapters.

Use of the Book

In the junior-level programming language course at the University of Colorado at Colorado Springs, the book is used as follows. We typically cover Chapters 1 and 3 in detail. Our experience is that Chapter 2 requires little lecture time, because of its lack of hard technical content. Students, however, find it interesting and beneficial reading. Because no material in subsequent chapters depends on Chapter 2, it can, as noted earlier, be skipped entirely.

Chapters 4–8 and 10 should be relatively easy for students with extensive programming experience in Pascal, C, Modula-2, or Ada. Chapters 9, 11, and 12 are more challenging and require careful and detailed lectures.

Chapter 13–15 are entirely new to most students at the junior level. Ideally, language processors for LISP and PROLOG should be available for Chapters 13 and 14. Sufficient material is included in these chapters to allow students to dabble with some simple programs. Use of Smalltalk requires, beyond the material in Chapter 15, an introduction to its user interface, which is not included here.

Undergraduate courses will probably not be able to cover all of the last three chapters in detail. Graduate courses, however, by skipping over parts of the early chapters on imperative languages will be able to completely discuss the nonimperative languages.

Acknowledgments

The quality of this book was significantly improved as a result of the extensive suggestions, corrections, and comments provided by its reviewers. The first edition was reviewed by Andrew Oldroyd, Henry Bauer, Mary Louise Soffa, and Jon Mauney. The second edition was reviewed by:

- Henry R. Bauer, University of Wyoming
- L. Andrew Oldroyd, Washington University
- Robert McCoard, California State University, Northridge
- Peter Brouwer, SUNY College at Potsdam
- Jeffery Popyack, Drexel University
- John Crenshaw, Western Kentucky University
- Hamilton Richard, University of Texas at Austin
- Vicki Allan, Utah State University
- Mary Lou Haag, University of Colorado at Colorado Springs

Alan Apt, a former editor at Benjamin/Cummings, was instrumental in the development of the first edition of this book, and therefore deserves my thanks, especially for his insistence on high standards of quality by everyone involved.

Carter Shanklin, sponsoring editor, Vivian McDougal, editorial assistant, and Andy Marinkovich, production coordinator, each deserve my gratitude for their efforts to make this second edition significantly better than the first.

Finally, I thank my wife, Joanne, and our children, Jake and Darcie, for their patience in enduring my absence from them throughout the endless hours of effort I invested in writing the two editions of this book.

Contents

1

Preliminaries

Konrad Zuse

Konrad Zuse designed a series of electro-mechanical computers between 1936 and 1944 in Germany. In 1945, he designed a complete algorithmic programming language, Plankalkül, which was never implemented, and its complete description was not even published until 1972.

Key Concepts

- Programming domains
- Readability
- Simplicity
- Orthogonality
- Writability
- Reliability
- Language cost

- Machine architecture
- Program design methodologies
- Language design trade-offs
- Compilation
- Pure interpretation
- Hybrid implementation systems
- Software production environments

The intent of this book is to provide the reader with a detailed critique of the designs of the major programming languages of the past 35 years. The insight to be gained from the book will allow the reader to critically evaluate languages and language features, both old and new, from several important viewpoints.

Before we begin our exposition of the concepts of programming languages, we need to consider a few preliminaries. First we discuss some reasons why computer science students and computer professionals should study general language design concepts. This discussion is valuable for those who believe that a working knowledge of one or two programming languages is sufficient for computer scientists. The major programming domains are then briefly described. Next, because the book evaluates language features, we present a list of criteria by which judgments can be made. The major influences on language design, machine architecture, and program design methodologies are then discussed. Next we describe a few of the major trade-offs that must be considered during language design.

Because this book is also about implementation of programming languages, this chapter includes an overview of the most common approaches to implementation. Finally we briefly describe a few examples of programming environments, along with the impact that such environments have on software production.

1.1 Reasons for Studying Concepts of Programming Languages

It is reasonable for students to wonder how they will benefit from the study of programming language concepts. After all, there is an abundance of other topics in computer science that are worthy of serious study. The following is what we believe to be a compelling list of potential benefits of studying language concepts.

1. *Increased capacity to express ideas.* It is widely believed that the depth at which we can think is influenced by the expressive power of the language in which we communicate our thoughts. Those with a limited grasp of natural language are limited in the complexity of their thoughts, particularly in depth of abstraction. In other words, it is difficult for people to conceptualize structures that they cannot describe verbally. Programmers in the process of developing software are similarly constrained. The language in which they develop software places limits on the kinds of control structures, data structures, and abstractions they can use; thus the forms of algorithms they can construct are also limited.

   Awareness of a wider variety of programming language features can reduce such limitations in software development. Programmers can increase the range of their software development thought processes by learning new language constructs.

   It could be argued that learning the capabilities of other languages does not help a programmer who is forced to use a language that lacks those capabilities. That argument does not hold up, however, because there are often ways in which language facilities can be simulated in other languages that do not support those features.

   For example, having learned of the string manipulation functions of FORTRAN 77 (ANSI, 1978a), a Pascal (Ledgard, 1984) programmer naturally would be led to building process abstractions for those operations in the form of subprograms. The same is true for many other more complex constructs that are discussed in depth in this book.

   The study of programming language concepts builds an appreciation for valuable language features and will encourage programmers to use those features.

   The fact that many features of languages can be simulated in other languages does not lessen significantly the importance of designing languages with the best collection of features. It is always better to use a feature whose design has been integrated into a language than to use a simulation of that feature, which will often be less elegant and more cumbersome in a language that does not include it.

2. *Improved background for choosing appropriate languages.* Many professional programmers have had little formal education in computer science and were trained on the job or through in-house training programs. Such training programs often teach one or two languages that are directly relevant to the current work of the organization. Many other programmers received their formal training in the early days of computer science education, when few languages were taught and many features now available in programming languages were not

widely known. The result of this narrow background is that many programmers, when given a choice of languages for a new project, continue to use the language with which they are most familiar, even if it is poorly suited to the new project. If these programmers were familiar with the other languages available and the particular features of those languages, they would be in a better position to make informed language choices.

3. *Increased ability to learn new languages.* The process of learning a new programming language can be lengthy and difficult, especially for someone who is comfortable with only one or two languages and has never examined programming language concepts in general. Once a thorough understanding of the fundamental concepts of languages is acquired, it becomes far easier to see how these concepts are incorporated into the design of the language being learned.

For example, programmers who understand the concept of data abstraction will have a much easier time learning how to construct abstract data types in the Ada language (Goos and Hartmanis, 1983) than those who are not at all familiar with data abstraction.

4. *Better understanding of the significance of implementation.* In learning the concepts of programming languages, it is both interesting and necessary to touch on the implementation issues that affect those concepts. In some cases, an understanding of implementation issues leads to an understanding of why languages are designed the way they are. This in turn leads to the ability to use a language more intelligently, as it was designed tc be used. It is true that one can become a better programmer by understanding the choices among programming language constructs and the consequences of those choices.

Another benefit of understanding implementation issues is that it allows visualization of how a computer executes various language constructs. This in turn fosters an understanding of the relative efficiency of features chosen for a program.

5. *Increased ability to design new languages.* To a student, the possibility of being required at some future time to design a new programming language may seem remote. However, most professional programmers occasionally do design languages of one sort or another. For example, most software systems require the user to interact in some way, even if only to enter data and commands. In simple situations, only a few data values are entered, and the input format language is trivial. On the other hand, the user might be required to traverse several levels of menus and enter a variety of commands, as in the case of a word processor. In such systems, the user interface is quite elaborate. The form of that interface is designed by the system designer, and the criteria for judging it are similar to the criteria used to judge the design of a programming language. A critical examination of programming languages, therefore, will help in the design

of such complex systems, and more commonly, it will help users examine and evaluate such products.

6. *Overall advancement of computing.* Finally, there is a global view of computing that can justify the study of programming language concepts. Although it is usually possible to determine why a particular programming language became popular, it is not always clear, at least in retrospect, that the most popular languages are the best available. In some cases, it might be concluded, a language became widely used, at least in part, because those in positions to choose languages were not sufficiently familiar with programming language concepts.

For example, many believe it would have been better if ALGOL 60 (Backus et al., 1962) had displaced FORTRAN in the early 1960s, because it was more elegant and had much better control statements than FORTRAN, among other reasons. That it did not is due partly to the programmers and software development managers of that time, many of whom did not clearly understand the conceptual design of ALGOL 60. They found its description difficult to read (which it was) and even more difficult to understand. They did not appreciate the benefits of block structure, recursion, and well-structured control statements, so they failed to see the benefits of ALGOL 60 over FORTRAN.

Of course, many other factors, such as lack of support by IBM and the cost of change, contributed to the lack of acceptance of ALGOL 60. However, the fact that computer users were generally unaware of the benefits of the language played a significant role.

In general, if those who choose languages are better informed, better languages will more quickly squeeze out poorer ones.

1.2   Programming Domains

Computers have been applied to a myriad of different areas, from controlling nuclear power plants to storing the records of personal checkbooks. Because of this great diversity in computer use, programming languages with very different goals have been invented. In this section, we briefly discuss a few areas of computer application and their associated languages.

1.2.1   Scientific Applications

The first digital computers, which appeared in the 1940s, were used and in fact invented for scientific applications. Scientific applications typically have simple data structures but require large amounts of floating-point arithmetic computations. High-level programming languages invented for scientific applications were designed to provide for those needs. The competition was assembly language, so execution efficiency was a primary concern. The first language for scientific applications was FORTRAN. ALGOL 60 and most of its descendants were also intended for use in this area, although they were designed to be used in other related areas also. For some scientific applications where efficiency is the primary concern, like those that were common in the 1950s and 1960s, no subsequent language is better than FORTRAN.

1.2.2   Business Applications

The use of computers for business applications began in the 1950s. Special computers for this purpose were developed, along with special languages. The first successful high-level language for business was COBOL, which appeared in 1960. It is still the most commonly used language for these applications. Business languages are characterized, according to the needs of the application, by elaborate input and output facilities and decimal data types.

With the advent of microcomputers came new ways for businesses, especially small businesses, to use computers. Specifically two tools, spreadsheet systems and database systems, were developed for business and now are widely used.

There have been only limited developments in business application languages other than COBOL. Therefore, this book does not deal with business application languages other than to provide a history of the development of COBOL in Chapter 2.

1.2.3   Artificial Intelligence

Artificial intelligence (AI) software is meant to carry out some activity that is often thought to require intelligence. The first widely used programming language developed for AI applications was the functional language LISP (McCarthy, et al. 1965), which appeared in 1959. Until recently, most AI applications were written in LISP or one of its close relatives. During the early 1970s, an alternative approach to these applications appeared: logic programming using the Prolog (Clocksin and Mellish, 1984) language. LISP and Prolog are described briefly in Chapters 13 and 14, respectively.

AI application languages are characterized by symbolic processing and the use of lists as the primary data structure.

1.2.4   Systems Programming Languages

The operating system and all the programming support tools of a computer system are collectively known as its **systems software.** Systems software is used almost continuously and therefore must have execution efficiency. A language for this domain must have low-level features that allow peripheral device driver software to be written.

Some computer manufacturers, such as IBM, Digital, and Burroughs (now UNISYS), have developed special machine-oriented high-level languages for systems software on their machines. For IBM mainframe computers, the language is PL/S, for Digital it is BLISS, and for Burroughs it is Extended ALGOL.

UNIX is written almost entirely in C, which has made it relatively easy to port, or move, to different machines. Some of the characteristics of C make it applicable to systems programming. It is low level, it is execution efficient, and it does not burden the user with an overwhelming number of safety restrictions. Systems programmers are often excellent programmers and do not believe they need such restrictions. Others, however, find C to be too dangerous to use on large, important software systems.

1.2.5 Special-Purpose Languages

A host of special-purpose languages have appeared over the past 40 years. They range from RPG, which is used to produce business reports, to APT, which is used for automatically programmed tools, to GPSS, which is used for systems simulation. This book does not discuss special-purpose languages, primarily because of their narrow applicability and the difficulty of comparing them with other languages.

1.3 Language Evaluation Criteria

As noted previously, the purpose of this book is to examine carefully the underlying concepts of the various constructs and capabilities of programming languages. We will also evaluate these features, focusing on their impact on computer design and software development methodologies. To accomplish this, we need a set of evaluation criteria. However, a list of such criteria is necessarily controversial since it is virtually impossible to get even two computer scientists to agree on the value of a given language characteristic relative to others. In spite of these differences, most computer scientists would agree that the criteria discussed in the following subsections are important.

The hierarchy of these criteria is shown in Figure 1.1 on the following page and the criteria themselves are discussed in the following sections.

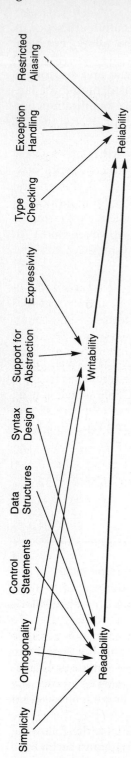

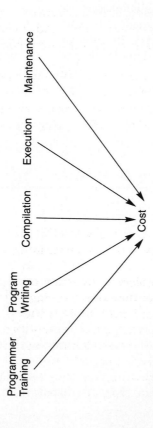

Figure 1.1
Programming language evaluation criteria

1.3.1   Readability

One of the most important criteria for judging a programming language is the ease with which programs can be read and understood. Before 1970, software development was largely thought of in terms of writing code. In the 1970s, however, the software life cycle concept (Booch, 1987) was developed; coding was relegated to play a much smaller role, and maintenance was recognized as a large part of the cycle, particularly in terms of cost. Because ease of maintenance is determined in large part by the readability of programs, readability became an important measure of the quality of programs and programming languages.

The following subsections describe the characteristics of a programming language that contribute to its readability.

1.3.1.1   Overall Simplicity

The overall simplicity of a programming language strongly affects its readability. A language that has a large number of elementary components is usually more difficult to learn than one with a small number of elementary components. Programmers who must use a large language have a tendency to learn a subset of the language and then ignore its other features. This learning pattern is sometimes used to excuse the large number of language components, but that argument is not valid. Readability problems occur if the program's author has learned a different subset from that subset with which the reader is familiar.

Having too many features is not the only detriment to language simplicity. Another problem is feature multiplicity—that is, having more than one way to accomplish a particular operation. For example, in the C language (Kernighan and Ritchie, 1978), a user can increment a simple integer variable in four different ways:

```
count = count + 1
count += 1
++count
count++
```

Although the last statement has slightly different semantics from the others in some uses, all four have the same meaning when used as stand-alone expressions.

A third potential problem is operator overloading, in which a single operator symbol has more than one meaning. Although this is a useful feature, it can lead to reduced readability if users are allowed to create their own overloading and they do not do it sensibly. For example, it is clearly acceptable to overload + by using it for both integer and floating-point addition. In fact, this overloading simplifies a language by reducing the number of operators. However, suppose the programmer defined + used between single-dimensioned arrays to mean the sum of all elements of both arrays. Because the usual meaning of vector addition is quite different from this, it would make the program more confusing for both the author and its readers. An even more extreme example of program confusion would be a user defining + used between two vectors to mean the difference between their respective first elements. Operator overloading is discussed again in Chapter 6.

Language statements can also be simplified too much. For example, the syntax and meaning of most assembly language statements are models of simplicity, as you can see when you consider the statements that appear in the next section. This very simplicity, however, makes assembly language programs less readable. Because they lack more complex control statements, their structure is more subtle; because their statements are simple, far more of them are required than equivalent programs in a high-level language.

1.3.1.2   Orthogonality

Orthogonality in a programming language means that there is a relatively small set of primitive constructs that can be combined in a relatively small number of ways to build the control and data structures of the language. Furthermore, every possible combination of primitives is legal and meaningful. Thus, orthogonality follows from a symmetry of relationships among primitives.

The use of orthogonality as a design concept can be illustrated by comparing one aspect of the assembly languages of the IBM mainframe computers and the VAX series of superminicomputers. We consider only a single simple situation, that of adding two 32-bit integer values that reside in either memory or registers and replacing one of the two values with the sum. For this purpose, the IBM mainframes have two instructions that have the forms

```
A      Reg1, memory_cell
AR     Reg1, Reg2
```

where Reg1 and Reg2 represent registers. The semantics of these are

Reg1 ← contents(Reg1) + contents(memory_cell)
Reg1 ← contents(Reg1) + contents(Reg2)

The VAX addition instruction for 32-bit integer values is

```
ADDL  operand_1, operand_2
```

whose semantics is

operand_2 ← contents(operand_1) + contents(operand_2)

In this case, either operand can be a register or a memory cell. The VAX instruction design is orthogonal in that there is a single instruction that can use either registers or memory cells as the operands. There are two ways to specify operands, which can be combined in any conceivable way. The IBM design is not orthogonal. Only two operand combinations are legal out of four possibilities, and the two require different instructions, A and AR. The IBM design is more restricted and therefore less writable. For example, you cannot add the value in a register to the value in a memory location. Furthermore, the IBM design is more difficult to learn because of the restrictions and the additional instruction.

Orthogonality is closely related to simplicity: The more orthogonal the design of a language, the fewer exceptions the language rules require. Fewer exceptions means a higher degree of regularity in the design, which makes the language easier to learn, read, and understand. Anyone who has learned a significant part of the English language can testify to the difficulty of learning its multitude of rule exceptions (for example, i before e except after c).

Although Pascal is a relatively modern language, its design has a large number of inconsistent type rules that must be followed. Procedures can have both "var" and "value" type parameters, unless the procedure itself is passed as a parameter. Functions can return only unstructured types. Formal parameter types must be named; they cannot be complete type descriptions. Files cannot be passed by value. The list of rules goes on and on. In other words, the type rules of Pascal are not orthogonal.

Too much orthogonality can also cause problems. Perhaps the most orthogonal programming language is ALGOL 68 (van Wijngaarden et al., 1969). Every language construct in ALGOL 68 has a type, and there are no restrictions on those types. In addition, most constructs produce values. This combinational freedom allows extremely complex constructs. For example, conditionals can appear as the left sides of assignments, along with declarations and other assorted statements, as long as the result is a location. This extreme form of orthogonality leads to unnecessary complexity. Furthermore, because languages require a large number of primitives, a high degree of orthogonality results in an explosion of combinations. So, even if the combinations are simple, their sheer numbers lead to complexity.

Simplicity in a language, therefore, is at least in part a result of a combination of a relatively small number of primitive constructs and limited use of the concept of orthogonality.

Some believe that functional languages offer a good combination of simplicity and orthogonality. A functional language is one in which computations are made primarily by applying functions to given parameters. In contrast, in the imperative languages, such as C and Pascal, computations are specified primarily with variables and assignment statements. LISP is currently the most widely used language that supports functional programming. LISP is not a purely functional language, for it also contains some imperative language features. Functional languages offer potentially the greatest overall simplicity because they can accomplish everything with a single construct, the function call, which can be combined with other function calls in simple ways. This simple elegance is the reason why many language researchers are attracted to functional languages as the primary alternative to complex nonfunctional languages, such as PL/I (ANSI, 1976) and Ada.

1.3.1.3 Control Statements

The structured programming revolution of the 1970s was a reaction to the poor readability caused by the limited control statements of some of the languages of the 1950s and 1960s. In particular, it became widely recognized that indiscriminate use of goto statements severely reduces program readability. Programs that can be read from top to bottom are much easier to understand than programs that require the reader to visually jump from one statement to some nonadjacent statement in order to follow the execution order. However, in certain languages, gotos that branch upward are sometimes necessary; for example, they are required to construct WHILE loops in FORTRAN 77. Nevertheless, restricting gotos in the following ways can make programs far more readable:

1. They must precede their targets, except when used to form loops.
2. Their targets must never be too distant.
3. Their numbers must be limited.

The versions of BASIC and FORTRAN that were available in the early 1970s lacked the control statements that allow strong restrictions on the use of gotos, so writing highly readable programs in those languages was difficult. Most programming languages designed since the late 1960s, however, have included sufficient control statements that the need for the goto statement has been nearly eliminated.

Thus, the control statement design of a language can be an important factor in the readability of programs written in that language.

1.3.1.4 Data Structures

The presence of adequate facilities for defining data types and data structures in a language is another significant aid to readability. For example, suppose a numeric type is used for an indicator flag because there are no Boolean types in the language. In such a language, we might have an assignment such as

```
sum_is_too_big := 1
```

whose meaning is unclear, whereas in a language that includes Boolean types, we would have

```
sum_is_too_big := true
```

whose meaning is perfectly clear. Similarly, record data types provide a method for representing employee records that is more readable than using a collection of arrays: one array for each data item in an employee record, which is what must be used in a language without records.

1.3.1.5 Syntax Considerations

The syntax, or form, of the elements of a language has a significant effect on the readability of programs. The following are three examples of syntactic design choices that affect readability.

1. *Identifier forms.* Restricting identifiers to very short lengths detracts from readability. If identifiers can have at most six characters, as in FORTRAN 77, it is often not possible to use connotative names for variables. A more extreme example is the original American National Standards Institute (ANSI) BASIC (ANSI, 1978b), in which an identifier could consist of only a single letter or a single letter followed by a single digit.

   The availability of connector characters, such as the underscore, in identifiers is a great aid to readability. SUM_OF_SQUARES is certainly clearer than SUMOFSQUARES.

   Other design issues concerning identifier forms are discussed in Chapter 4.

2. *Special words.* Program appearance and thus program readability are strongly influenced by the forms of a language's special words (for example, **begin**, **end**, and **for**). Especially important is the method of forming compound statements, or statement groups, primarily in control constructs. Several languages use matching pairs of special words or symbols to form groups. Pascal requires **begin–end** pairs to form groups for all control constructs except the **repeat** statement, in which they can be omitted (another example of Pascal's lack of orthogonality). C uses braces for the same purpose. Both of these languages suffer because statement groups are always terminated in the same way, which makes it difficult to determine which group is being ended when an **end** or } appears. FORTRAN 77 and Ada make this clearer by using a distinct closing syntax for each type of statement group. For example, Ada uses **end if** to terminate a selection construct and **end loop** to terminate a loop construct. This is an example of the conflict between simplicity that results from using reserved words, as in Pascal, and greater readability that results from using more reserved words, as in Ada.

   Another important issue is whether the special words of a language can be used as names for program variables. If so, the resulting programs can be very confusing. For example, in FORTRAN 77, special words such as DO and END are legal variable names, so the appearance of these words in a program may or may not connote something special.

3. *Form and meaning.* Designing statements so that their appearance at least partially indicates their purpose is an obvious aid to readability. Semantics, or meaning, should follow directly from syntax, or appearance. In some cases, this principle is violated by two language

constructs that are similar in appearance but have different meanings. In FORTRAN 77, for example, there are two statements, the assigned GOTO and the computed GOTO, whose appearances are very similar but whose meanings are different, although both are multiple-way branches. For example, the statements

```
GO TO (10, 20, 30), I
GO TO I, (10, 20, 30)
```

are used quite differently. In the first, the variable I is INTEGER type; in the second, it stores label values. The semantics of these two statements are described in Chapter 7.

One of the primary complaints about the shell commands of UNIX (Kernighan and Pike, 1984) is that their appearance does not always suggest their function. For example, the UNIX command grep can be deciphered only through prior knowledge, or perhaps cleverness and familiarity with the UNIX editor, ed. Its appearance connotes nothing to UNIX beginners. (In ed, the command /regular_expression/ searches for a substring that matches the regular expression. Preceding this with g makes it a global command, making the scope of the search the whole file being edited. Following the command with p specifies that lines with the matching substring are to be printed. So g/regular_expression/p, which can obviously be abbreviated as grep, prints all lines in a file that contain substrings that match the regular expression.)

1.3.2 Writability

Writability is a measure of how easily a language can be used to create programs for a chosen problem domain. Most of the language characteristics that affect readability also affect writability. This follows directly from the fact that the process of writing a program requires the programmer frequently to reread portions of the existing program.

Writability must be considered in the context of the target problem domain of a language, for it is not reasonable to compare the writability of two languages in the realm of a particular application when one was designed for that application and the other was not. For example, the writabilities of COBOL (ANSIC, 1985) and APL (Gilman and Rose, 1976) are dramatically different for creating a program to deal with two-dimensional data structures, for which APL is ideal. Their writabilities are also quite different for producing reports with complex formats, for which COBOL was designed.

The following subsections describe the most important factors influencing the writability of a language.

1.3.2.1 Simplicity and Orthogonality

If a language has a large number of different constructs, some programmers may not be familiar with all of them. This can lead to a misuse of some features and a disuse of others that may be either more elegant or more efficient, or both, than those that are used. It may even be possible, as noted by Hoare (1973), to use unknown features accidentally, with bizarre results. Therefore, a smaller number of primitive constructs and a consistent set of rules for combining them (that is, orthogonality) is much better than simply having a large number of primitives. A programmer can design a solution to a complex problem after learning only a simple set of primitive constructs.

In the same vein, too much orthogonality can be a detriment to writability. Errors in writing programs can go undetected when nearly any combination of primitives is legal. This can lead to absurdities in code that cannot be discovered by the compiler.

1.3.2.2 Support for Abstraction

Briefly, **abstraction** means the ability to define and then use complicated structures or operations in ways that allow many of the details to be ignored. Abstraction is a key concept in contemporary programming language design. This is a reflection of the central role that abstraction plays in modern program design methodologies. The degree of abstraction allowed by a programming language and the naturalness of its expression are therefore very important to its writability. As the reader will discover in exploring this book, a large amount of space here is filled with discussions of abstraction.

A simple example of process abstraction is the use of a subprogram to implement a sort algorithm that is required several times in a program. Without the subprogram, the sort code would have to be replicated in all places where it was needed, which would make the program much longer and more tedious to write. More importantly, if the subprogram were not used, the code that used the sort subprogram would be cluttered with the sort algorithm details, greatly obscuring the flow and intent of that code.

As an example of data abstraction, consider a binary tree that stores integer data in its nodes. Such a binary tree would usually be implemented in FORTRAN 77 as three parallel integer arrays, where two of the integers are used as subscripts to specify offspring nodes. In Pascal, these trees can be implemented by using an abstraction of a tree node in the form of a simple record unit with two pointers and an integer. The naturalness of the latter representation makes it much easier to write a Pascal program that uses a binary tree than to write one in FORTRAN. It is a simple matter of the problem solution domain of the language being closer to the problem domain.

The overall support for abstraction is clearly an important factor in the writability of a language.

1.3.2.3   Expressivity

Expressivity in a language can refer to several different characteristics. In a language like APL, it means that there are very powerful operators that allow a great deal of computation to be accomplished with a very small program. It more commonly means that a language has relatively convenient, rather than cumbersome, ways of specifying computations. For example, in C, the notation count++ is more convenient and shorter than count = count + 1. Also, the **and then** Boolean operator in Ada is a convenient way of specifying short-circuit evaluation of a Boolean expression. The inclusion of the **for** statement in Pascal makes writing counting loops easier than the use of **while**, which is also possible. All of these increase the writability of a language.

1.3.3   Reliability

A program is reliable if it performs to its specifications under all conditions. Although a desirable goal of programming language design is to allow and encourage reliable programs, it is not completely clear how this characteristic can be measured and compared among languages.

The following subsections describe several language features that have a significant effect on the reliability of programs in a given language.

1.3.3.1   Type Checking

Type checking is testing for type compatibility between two variables or a variable and a constant that are somehow related with one another. Two of the most common forms of such involvement are as the operands of an arithmetic operator and as the left and right sides of an assignment statement. Type checking is an important factor in language reliability. Because run-time type checking is expensive, compile-time checking is more desirable. Furthermore, the earlier errors in programs are detected, the less expensive it is to make the required repairs. The design of one contemporary language, Ada, requires type checks of nearly all variables at compile time, except when the user explicitly states that type checking is to be suspended. This nearly eliminates type compatibility errors at run time in Ada programs. Types and type checking are discussed in depth in Chapter 5.

One example of how failure to type check, at either compile time or run time, has led to countless program errors involves the parameters of subprograms in the original C language. In this language, the type of an actual parameter in a function call is not checked to determine whether its type matches that of the corresponding formal parameter in the function. An **int** type variable can be used as an actual parameter in a call to a function that expects a **float** type as its formal parameter, and neither the compiler nor the run-time system will detect the inconsistency. This naturally leads to problems, the source of which is often difficult to determine. (In response to this problem, the UNIX system includes a utility program named `lint` that checks C programs for such problems.) Subprograms and parameter-passing methods are discussed in Chapter 8.

In Pascal, the subscript range of an array variable is part of the variable's type. Therefore, subscript range checking is part of type checking, although it must be done at run time. Because most types are checked in Pascal, subscript ranges are also checked. Such checking is extremely important to program reliability, because out-of-range subscripts often cause errors that do not appear until long after the actual violations.

1.3.3.2   Exception Handling

The ability of a program to intercept run-time errors, as well as other unusual conditions, to take corrective measures, and to continue is a great aid to reliability. This facility is called **exception handling.** The Ada language includes extensive capabilities for exception handling, but such facilities are practically nonexistent in many widely used languages, such as Pascal, C, and FORTRAN. Exception handling is discussed in Chapter 12.

1.3.3.3   Aliasing

Aliasing is, loosely, having two distinct referencing methods, or names, for the same memory cell. It is now widely accepted that aliasing is a dangerous feature in a programming language. Most programming languages do allow some kind of aliasing—for example, equivalenced variables in FORTRAN and pointers in Pascal. In both cases, two different program variables can refer to the same memory cell. Some kinds of aliasing, as described in Chapters 4 and 8, can be prohibited by the design of a language.

In some languages, aliasing is used to overcome deficiencies in the language's data abstraction facilities. Other languages greatly restrict aliasing to increase their reliability.

1.3.3.4   Readability and Writability

Both readability and writability influence reliability. A program written in a language that does not support natural ways to express the required algorithms will necessarily use unnatural methods. Unnatural methods are less likely to be correct for all possible situations. The easier a program is to write, the more likely it is to be correct.

Readability affects reliability in both the writing and maintenance phases of the life cycle. Programs that are difficult to read are difficult both to write and to modify.

1.3.4 Cost

The total cost of a programming language is a function of many of its characteristics.

First there is the cost of training programmers to use the language. This is a function of the simplicity and orthogonality of the language, its closeness in purpose to the particular application, and the experience of the programmers. Though more powerful languages need not be harder to learn, they often are.

Second is the cost of writing programs in the language. This is a function of the writability of the language. The original efforts to design and implement high-level languages were driven by the desire to lower the costs of creating software.

Both the cost of training programmers and the cost of writing programs in a language can be significantly reduced in a good programming environment. Programming environments are discussed in Section 1.7.

Third is the cost of compiling programs in the language. A major impediment to the early use of Ada was the prohibitively high cost of running the first-generation Ada compilers. This problem is becoming less severe as Ada compilers become better.

Fourth, the cost of executing programs written in a language is greatly influenced by that language's design. A language, such as PL/I, that requires many run-time type checks will prohibit fast code execution, regardless of the quality of the compiler.

A simple trade-off can be made between compilation cost and execution speed of the compiled code. Optimization is the name given to the collection of methods that compilers may use to decrease the size and/or increase the execution speed of the code they produce. If little or no optimization is done, compilation can be done much faster than if a significant effort is made to produce optimized code. The extra compilation effort results in much faster code execution. The choice between the two alternatives is determined by the environment in which the compiler will be used. In a laboratory for beginning programming students, who use a great deal of compiling time but little code execution time (their programs are small and they must execute correctly only once), little or no optimization should be done. In a production environment, where completed programs are executed many times, it is better to pay the extra cost to optimize the code.

Finally there is the cost of maintaining programs, which includes both corrections and modifications to add new capabilities. The cost of software maintenance depends on a number of language characteristics, but primarily readability. Because maintenance is often done by people other than the original author of the software, poor readability can make the task extremely challenging.

The importance of maintainability of software cannot be overstated. It has been estimated that, for large software systems with relatively long lifetimes, maintenance costs can amount to from two to four times as much as development (Sommerville, 1989).

Of all these contributions to language costs, two are most important: program development and maintenance. Because these are functions of writability and readability, these two evaluation criteria are, in turn, the most important.

A final note on evaluation criteria: Most criteria, particularly readability and writability, are neither precisely defined nor exactly measurable. They are useful concepts, however, and they provide valuable insight into the design and evaluation of programming languages.

There are, of course, a number of other criteria for evaluating programming languages, for example, portability (the ease with which a program can be moved from one implementation to another); generality (the applicability of a language to a wide range of applications); and well-definedness (the completeness and precision of a language's official defining document). Those described above, however, are those that we believe to be most important.

1.4 Influences on Language Design

Several factors influence the basic design of programming languages. The most important of these are computer architecture and program design methodologies.

1.4.1 Computer Architecture

The basic architecture of computers has a large effect on language design. Most of the popular languages of the past 35 years have been designed around the prevalent architecture, called the von Neumann architecture after one of its originators, John von Neumann (pronounced "von Noyman"). These languages are called imperative languages. In a von Neumann computer, both data and programs are stored in the same memory. The central processing unit (CPU), which actually executes instructions, is separate from the memory. Therefore, instructions and data must be piped, or transmitted, from memory to the CPU. Results of operations in the CPU must be moved back to memory. Nearly all digital computers built since the 1940s have been based on the von Neumann architecture. The overall structure of a von Neumann computer is shown in Figure 1.2 on the following page.

Because of the von Neumann architecture, the central features of imperative languages are variables, which model the memory cells; assignment statements, which are based on the piping operation; and the iterative form of repetition, which is the most efficient method on this architecture, as

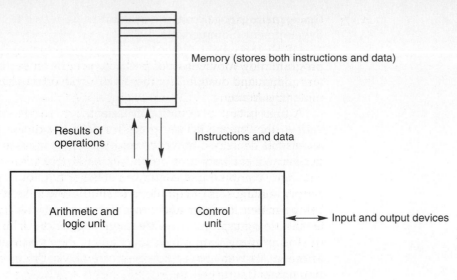

Figure 1.2
The von Neumann
computer architecture

Memory (stores both instructions and data)

Results of operations

Instructions and data

Arithmetic and logic unit

Control unit

Input and output devices

Central processing unit

explained later. Operands in expressions are piped from memory to the CPU, and the result of evaluating the expression is piped back to the memory cell represented by the left side of the assignment. Repetition in imperative languages is done by iteration, because the instructions in a von Neumann computer are stored in adjacent cells of memory, making iteration very efficient. However, it discourages the use of recursion for repetition, although recursion is often more natural.

As stated earlier, a functional, or applicative, language is one in which the primary means of making computations is by applying functions to given parameters. Programming can be done in a functional language without the kind of variables that are used in imperative languages, without assignment statements, and without iteration. Although many computer scientists have expounded on the myriad benefits of functional languages such as LISP, it is unlikely that they will displace imperative languages until a non–von Neumann computer is designed that will allow efficient execution of programs in functional languages. Among those bemoaning this fact, the most eloquent has been John Backus, the principal designer of the original version of FORTRAN (Backus, 1978).

It simply has proven to be difficult to invent an architecture for the efficient implementation of functional languages. The parallel architecture machines that appeared in the past ten years hold some promise for speeding the execution of functional programs, but so far that promise has not been enough to make them competitive with imperative programs. In fact, although there are elegant ways of using parallel architectures to execute functional programs, most parallel machines are used for imperative programs, particularly those written in dialects of FORTRAN.

1.4.2 Programming Methodologies

The 1970s brought an intense analysis, begun in large part by the structured programming movement, of both the programming process and programming language design. The results of these efforts have been consolidated under the heading "software engineering."

An important reason for the research in software engineering was the shift in the major cost of computing from hardware to software, as hardware costs decreased and programmer costs increased. Increases in the productivity of software were relatively small. In addition, progressively larger and more complex problems were being solved by computers. Rather than simply solving sets of equations to simulate satellite tracks, programs were being written for large and complex tasks, such as controlling large petroleum refining facilities and providing worldwide airline reservation systems.

The primary programming language deficiencies that were discovered in the 1970s were incompleteness of type checking, inadequacy of control statements (requiring the extensive use of goto's), and lack of facilities for exception handling.

In the area of program design methodologies, there has been a shift from process orientation to data orientation over the past 15 years. Simply put, data-oriented methods emphasize data design, concentrating on the use of logical, or abstract, data types to solve problems.

For data abstraction to be used effectively in software system design, it should be supported by the languages used to implement the system. The first language to provide even limited support for data abstraction was SIMULA 67 (Birtwistle et al., 1973), although that language certainly was not propelled to popularity because of it. The benefits of data abstraction were not widely recognized until the early 1970s. More recently, Mesa (Mitchell et al., 1979), CLU (Liskov et al., 1981), Modula-2, C++ (Ellis and Stroustrup, 1990), and Ada all support some degree of data abstraction. Even FORTRAN 77 provides a clumsy way to build partial data abstractions (through subprograms, functions, and globally accessible data). It is likely that any general-purpose language designed over the next decade will provide support for this important idea. Data abstraction is discussed in detail in Chapter 10.

The latest step in the evolution of data-oriented software development, which is taking place now, is object-oriented design. Object-oriented methodology begins with data abstraction, which encapsulates processing with data objects and hides access to data, and adds inheritance and dynamic type binding. Inheritance is a powerful concept that greatly enhances the possibility of reusing existing software. Dynamic type binding allows abstract data types to be type generic, but it has the drawback of conflicting with static type checking.

The development of object-oriented programming came along with that of a language that supported its concepts: Smalltalk (Goldberg and Robson, 1984). Although Smalltalk may never become widely used, support for object-oriented programming has made its way into several imperative languages, at least one of which will probably become widely used. These are Objective C (Cox, 1986), Eiffel (Meyer, 1988), and C++. Eiffel is a new language. Both Objective C and C++ are versions of C that have been extended to provide support for object-oriented programming. Object-oriented concepts have also found their way into functional programming in CLOS (Bobrow et al., 1988), and logic programming in Prolog++.

Object-oriented programming, Smalltalk, and C++ are discussed in some detail in Chapter 15.

Process-oriented programming is, in a sense, the opposite of data-oriented programming. Although process-oriented methods were used before data-oriented methods, they have not been abandoned. On the contrary, a good deal of research has occurred in process-oriented programming in recent years, especially in the area of concurrency. These research efforts brought with them the need for language facilities for creating and controlling concurrent program units. The Ada language includes such capabilities. So programming evolution is again requiring new language capabilities. Concurrency is discussed in detail in Chapter 11.

1.5   Language Design Trade-offs

The programming language evaluation criteria described in Section 1.3 provide a framework for language design. Unfortunately, the framework is self-contradictory. In his widely read paper on language design, Hoare (1973) states that "there are so many important but conflicting criteria that their reconciliation and satisfaction is a major engineering task."

Two criteria that conflict are reliability and cost of execution. For example, the Ada language definition demands that all references to array elements be checked to ensure that the index or indices are in their legal ranges. This checking adds a great deal to the cost of execution of Ada programs that contain large numbers of references to array elements. The FORTRAN language does not require index range checking, so FORTRAN programs execute faster than semantically equivalent Ada programs, although Ada programs are more reliable. The designers of Ada traded execution efficiency for reliability.

For another example of conflicting criteria, which will lead directly to a discussion of design trade-offs, consider the case of APL. The APL language includes a very powerful set of operators for array operands. Because of the large number of operators, a significant number of new symbols had to be included in APL to represent the operators. Also, in APL many operators can be placed in single, long, complex expressions. One result of this high degree of expressivity is that, for applications involving many array operations, APL is very writable. Indeed, a huge amount of computation can be specified in a very compact program. Another result is that APL programs have very poor readability. The compact and concise expressions have a certain mathematical beauty but are difficult to understand, particularly for someone other than the person who wrote it. The well-known author Daniel McCracken once noted that it took him four hours to read and understand a four-line APL program (McCracken, 1970). The designers of APL traded readability for writability.

The conflict between flexibility and safety is a common one in language design. Pascal variant records allow a memory cell to contain different type values at different times. For example, a cell may contain either a pointer or an integer. This provides a loophole in Pascal's type checking that allows a program to do arithmetic on pointers, which is sometimes necessary. However, this unchecked use of memory cells is, in general, a dangerous practice.

Examples of conflicts among language design (and evaluation) criteria abound; some are subtle while others are obvious. It is therefore clear that the task of choosing constructs and features when designing a programming language involves a collection of compromises and trade-offs.

1.6   Implementation Methods

As described in Section 1.4.1, a computer has two primary components, internal memory and a processor. The internal memory is used to store programs and data. The processor is a collection of circuits that provides a realization of a set of primitive operations, or machine instructions, such as those for arithmetic, logic, and data moves. In most computers, some of these instructions, which are sometimes called macroinstructions, are actually implemented with an even lower-level set of instructions called microinstructions. The machine language of the computer is its set of macroinstructions. Because microinstructions are never seen by software or programmers, they usually are not included in any discussion of software. Therefore, they will not be discussed further here.

In the absence of other supporting software, its own machine language is the only language that most hardware computers "understand." A few computers have been designed and built with a particular high-level language as their machine language, but such computers are very complex and expensive. Furthermore, they are highly inflexible, because it is difficult (though not impossible) to use them with other high-level languages. A more practical machine design implements in the hardware a very low-level language that provides the most commonly needed primitive operations and requires system software to create an interface to programs in other languages.

The software that provides the high-level language interface to a computer can take several different forms—compilers, pure interpreters, and hybrid implementation systems—as discussed later. This software depends not only on the computer's machine language but also on a large collection of programs, called the operating system, that supplies higher-level primitives than those of the machine language. These primitives provide system resource management, input and output operations, a file management system, text and/or program editors, and a variety of other commonly needed functions. Because high-level language implementations need many of the operating system facilities, they interface to the operating system rather than directly to the processor (in machine language).

The operating system and language implementations are layered over the machine language interface of a computer. These layers can be thought of as virtual computers, providing interfaces to the user at higher levels. For example, an operating system and a Pascal compiler provide a virtual Pascal computer. With other compilers, a machine can become other kinds of virtual computers; most computers provide several different virtual computers. User programs form another layer on top of the layer of virtual computers.

The layered view of a computer is shown in Figure 1.3. The software implementations of the first high-level programming languages, constructed in the late 1950s, were among the most complex software systems of that time. In the 1960s, widespread research efforts were made to understand and formalize the process of constructing these high-level language implementations. The greatest success of those efforts was in the area of syntax analysis, primarily because that part of the implementation process is an application of parts of automata theory and formal language theory that were then very well understood.

1.6.1   Compilation

Programming languages can be implemented by any of three general methods. At one extreme, programs can be translated to machine code, which then can be executed directly on the computer. We call this a compiler implementation. This method has the advantage of very fast program execution, once the translation process is complete. Most production implementations of languages such as C, COBOL, and Ada are by compilers.

The language that a compiler translates is called the source language. The process of compilation involves several phases, the most important of which are shown in Figure 1.4 on page 26.

The lexical analyzer gathers the characters of the source program into lexical units. The lexical units of a program are identifiers, special words, operators, and punctuation symbols. The lexical analyzer ignores comments in the source program because the compiler has no use for them.

Figure 1.3
Layered interface, on virtual computers, provided by a typical computer system

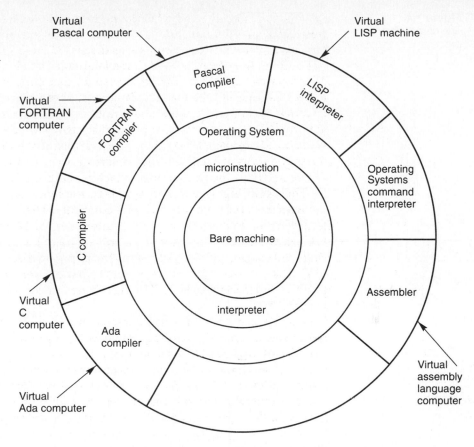

The syntax analyzer takes the lexical units from the lexical analyzer and from them constructs hierarchical structures called parse trees. These parse trees represent the syntactic structure of the program. Both lexical units and parse trees are further discussed in Chapter 3.

The intermediate code generator produces a program in a different language, at an intermediate level between the source program and the final output of the compiler, the machine code program. Intermediate languages sometimes look very much like assembly languages, and in fact sometimes are actual assembly languages. In other cases, the intermediate code is at a level somewhat higher than an assembly language.

Optimization is often an optional part of compilation. In fact, some compilers are incapable of doing any significant optimization. These compilers would be used in situations where execution speed is far less important than compilation speed. In most commercial and industrial situations, execution speed is more important than compilation speed, so optimization is routinely desirable. Because of the difficulty of optimizing machine code, optimization is usually done on the intermediate code.

Figure 1.4
The compilation
process

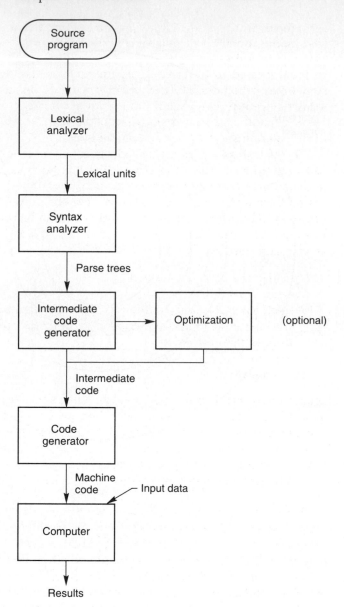

As stated above, although the machine code generated by a compiler can be executed directly on the hardware, it nearly always must be run along with some other code. Most user programs also require programs from the operating system. Among the most common of these are programs for input and output. The compiler builds calls to required system programs when they are needed by the user code. Before the machine language programs produced by a compiler can be executed, the required programs from the operating system must be found and "linked" to the user program. The linking operation connects the user code to the system programs by placing the addresses of the entry points of the system programs in the calls to them located in the user code. The user and system code together are sometimes called a load module, or executable image. The process of collecting system programs and linking them to user programs is called linking and loading, or sometimes just linking. It is accomplished by a program in the operating system called the linker.

The execution of a machine code program on a von Neumann architecture computer occurs in a process called the **fetch-execute cycle.** As stated in Section 1.4.1, programs reside in memory but are executed in the processor. Each instruction to be executed must be moved from memory to the processor. The address of the next instruction to be executed is maintained in a register named the program counter. The fetch-execute cycle can be simply described by the following:

> initialize the program counter
> **repeat** forever
>   fetch the instruction pointed to by the program counter
>   increment the program counter to point at the next instruction
>   decode the instruction
>   execute the instruction
> **end repeat**

This process terminates when a stop instruction is executed, although on an actual computer a stop instruction is rarely executed. Rather, control simply transfers from the operating system to a user program for its execution and then goes back to the operating system when the user program execution is completed. In a computer system in which more than one user program may be in memory at a given time, this process is far more complex.

The speed of the connection between a computer's memory and its processor usually determines the speed of the computer, because instructions often can be executed faster than they can be moved to the processor for execution. This connection is called the von Neumann bottleneck; it is the primary limiting factor in the speed of von Neumann architecture computers. The von Neumann bottleneck has been one of the primary motivations for the research and development of parallel computers.

1.6.2 Pure Interpretation

At the opposite extreme of implementation methods, programs can be interpreted by another program called an interpreter, with no translation whatever. The interpreter program acts as a software simulation of a machine whose fetch-execute cycle deals with high-level language program statements rather than machine instructions. This software simulation obviously provides a virtual machine for the language.

This technique, called **pure interpretation** or simply interpretation, has the advantage of allowing easy implementation of many source-level debugging operations, because all run-time error messages can refer to source-level units. For example, if an array index is found to be out of range, the error message can easily indicate the source line and the name of the array. On the other hand, this method has the serious disadvantage that execution is many times slower than in compiled systems. The primary source of this slowness is the decoding of the high-level language statements, which are far more complex than machine language instructions (although there may be fewer statements than instructions in equivalent machine code). Therefore, statement decoding, rather than the connection between the processor and memory, is the bottleneck of a pure interpreter.

Interpretation is a difficult process on programs written in a complicated language because the meaning of each expression and statement must be determined directly from the source program at run time. Languages with simpler structures lend themselves to pure interpretation. For example, APL and LISP are sometimes implemented as pure interpretive systems. Conversely, more complex languages such as FORTRAN and Ada rarely are.

The process of pure interpretation is shown in Figure 1.5.

1.6.3 Hybrid Implementation Systems

Some language implementation systems are a compromise between compilers and pure interpreters; they translate high-level language programs to an intermediate language designed to allow easy interpretation. This

Figure 1.5
Pure interpretation

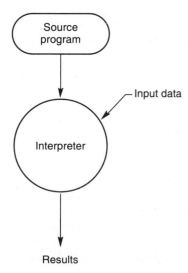

method is faster than pure interpretation because the source language statements are decoded only once. Such implementations are called **hybrid implementation systems.**

The process used in a hybrid implementation system is shown in Figure 1.6. Instead of translating intermediate language code to machine code, it simply interprets the intermediate code.

Sometimes an implementor may provide both compiled and interpreted implementations for a language. In these cases, the interpreter is used to develop and debug programs. Then, after a bug-free state is reached, the programs are compiled to increase their execution speed.

We describe implementation models for several different language constructs as we discuss those constructs later in the book.

Figure 1.6
Hybrid implementation system

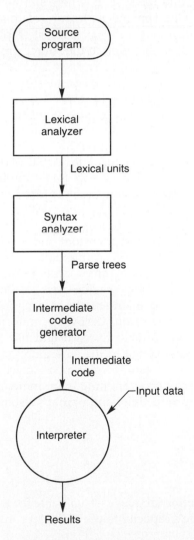

1.7 Programming Environments

A programming environment is the collection of tools used in the production of software. This collection may consist of only a file system, a text editor, a linker, and a compiler. Or it may include a large collection of integrated tools, each accessed through a uniform user interface. In the latter case, the writability and maintenance of software is greatly enhanced. Therefore, the characteristics of a programming language are not the only measure of the software development capability of a system. We now briefly describe several programming environments.

Turbo Pascal is a programming environment that runs on IBM-PC/XT/ AT microcomputer systems and their clones. It provides an integrated compiler, editor, debugger, and file system, where all four are accessed through a graphical interface. One convenient feature of this environment is that when the compiler encounters a syntax error, it stops and switches to the editor, leaving the cursor at the point in the source program where the error was detected.

Smalltalk is another integrated programming environment, but it is more elaborate, complex, and powerful than Turbo Pascal. Smalltalk makes use of a windowing system and a mouse pointing device to provide the user with a uniform interface to all tools. Smalltalk is an object-oriented language, which is discussed in Chapter 15.

A programming environment for Ada, APSE (Ada programming support environment), was specified even before compilers for the language appeared. The Ada designers obviously recognized the importance of support tools to the successful use of Ada. The APSE requirements document, named Stoneman (Department of Defense, 1980b), specifies a uniform interface among all tools and between each tool and a central database, which contains program units, data, and documentation files.

UNIX is an older programming environment built around a time-sharing operating system. It provides a wide array of powerful support tools for software production and maintenance in a variety of languages. The most important feature absent from UNIX is a uniform interface among its tools. This makes it more difficult to learn and use. It is also oriented to command lines and is less suited to the emerging graphical interfaces.

It is clear that most software development, at least in the near future, will make use of powerful programming environments. This will undoubtedly increase software productivity and perhaps also raise the quality of the produced software.

SUMMARY

The study of programming languages is valuable for a number of important reasons. It increases one's capacity to use different constructs in writing programs, enables one to choose languages for projects more intelligently, and makes learning new languages easier.

Computers are used in a wide variety of problem-solving domains. The design and evaluation of a particular programming language is highly dependent upon the domain in which it is to be used.

Among the most important criteria for evaluating languages are readability, writability, reliability, and overall cost. These criteria are the basis on which we examine and judge the various language features discussed in the remainder of the book.

The major influences on language design have been machine architecture and software design methodologies.

Designing a programming language is primarily an engineering feat, in which a long list of trade-offs must be made among features, constructs, and capabilities.

The major methods of implementing programming languages are compilation, pure interpretation, and hybrid inplementation.

Programming environments have become important parts of software development systems, in which the language is just one of the components.

PROBLEM SET

1. Do you believe our thinking capabilities are influenced by our language? Support your opinion.

2. What are some features of programming languages you know whose rationale is a mystery to you?

3. What arguments can you make for the idea of a single language for all programming domains?

4. What arguments can you make against the idea of a single language for all programming domains?

5. Name and explain another criterion by which languages can be judged (in addition to those in this chapter).

6. What common programming language statement, in your opinion, is most detrimental to readability?

7. Modula-2 uses END to mark the end of all compound statements. What are the arguments for and against this design?

8. Some languages, notably C and Modula-2, distinguish between uppercase and lowercase letters in identifiers. What are the pros and cons of this design decision?

9. Explain the different aspects of the cost of a programming language.

10. What are the arguments for writing efficient programs even though hardware is relatively inexpensive?

11. Describe some design trade-off between efficiency and safety in a language you know.

12. What major features would a perfect programming language include, in your opinion?

13. Was the first high-level programming language you learned implemented with a pure interpreter, a hybrid implementation system, or a compiler? (You would not necessarily know this without research.)

14. What arguments can you make for and against the inclusion of the **const** declarative statement in Pascal?

15. Compare **const** in Pascal to **define** in C, using the criteria of this chapter.

16. Describe the advantages and disadvantages of some programming environment you have used.

17. How do type declaration statements for simple variables affect the readability of a language, considering that some languages do not require them?

18. Write an outline for the design of a pure interpreter for a subset of Pascal in which there are no subprograms, no **char**, **file**, or **boolean** types, no user-defined types, no **case** statements, and no input and output.

19. Write an evaluation of some programming language you know, using the criteria described in this chapter.

2

Evolution of the Major Programming Languages

John Backus

John Backus, employed by IBM, designed the Speedcoding pseudocode system for IBM's 701 computer in the early 1950s. Between 1954 and 1957, he led the design team that produced FORTRAN, from which nearly all imperative languages evolved. In the 1958–1960 period, he was a principle member of the ALGOL design team.

Key Concepts

- Programming language evolution
- Language design environments
- Programming problems with machine code
- Interpretive pseudocodes
- Compiled high-level languages
- Scientific languages
- Business applications languages

- Interactive languages
- General-purpose languages
- Simulation languages
- Logic languages
- Requirements specifications for a language
- Object-oriented languages

This chapter follows chronologically the development of a collection of programming languages, with emphasis on the environment in which each was designed. In each case, we emphasize the contribution of the language and the motivation for its development. Overall language descriptions are not included; rather, we focus on the new features introduced by each language. Of particular interest are the features that most influenced subsequent languages or the fields of computing and computer science.

This chapter does not include an in-depth discussion of any language feature or concept; that is left for later chapters. Brief, informal explanations of features will suffice for our trek through the development of these languages.

The choice as to which languages to discuss here was subjective, and many readers will unhappily note the absence of one or more of their favorites. However, to keep this historical coverage to a reasonable size, it was necessary to leave out several languages that some regard highly. The choices were based on our estimate of each language's importance to language development and the computing world as a whole.

This chapter includes listings of nine complete example programs, each in a different language. None of these are described in this chapter—they are meant simply to illustrate the appearance of programs in these languages. Readers with familiarity with any of the common imperative languages should be able to read and understand most of the code in these programs, except those in LISP, COBOL, and Smalltalk. The LISP example is discussed in Chapter 13; the Smalltalk example is discussed in Chapter 15. The same problem is solved by the FORTRAN, ALGOL 60, PL/I, Pascal, C, and Ada programs.

Figure 2.1 is a chart of the genealogy of the high-level languages discussed in this chapter.

Figure 2.1
Genealogy of high-level programming languages

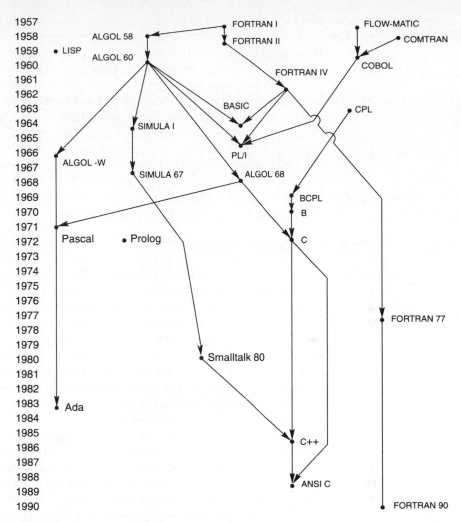

2.1 Zuse's Plankalkül

The first programming language discussed in this chapter is highly unusual in several respects. For one thing, it was never implemented, for a variety of reasons. Furthermore, although developed in 1945, its description was not published until 1972. As a result of the general ignorance of the language, some of its capabilities did not appear in other languages until 15 years after Plankalkül's development (1960).

2.1.1   Historical Background

Between 1936 and 1945, the German scientist Konrad Zuse (pronounced "Tsoo-zuh"), built a series of complex and sophisticated computers from electromechanical relays. By 1945, the war had destroyed all but one of his latest models, the Z4, so he moved to a remote Bavarian village, Hinterstein, and his research group members went their separate ways.

Working alone, Zuse embarked on an effort to develop a language for expressing computations, a project he had begun in 1943 as a proposal for his Ph.D. dissertation. He named this language Plankalkül, which means program calculus. In a lengthy manuscript dated 1945 but not published until 1972 (Zuse, 1972), Zuse defined Plankalkül and wrote algorithms in the language for a wide variety of problems.

2.1.2   Language Overview

Plankalkül was remarkably complete, with some of its most advanced features in the area of data structures. The simplest type in Plankalkül was the single bit. From the bit type were built types for integer and floating-point numeric types. The floating-point type used twos-complement notation and the "hidden bit" scheme currently used to avoid storing the most significant bit of the normalized fraction part of a value. Special representations were used for "infinite," "very small," and "undefined" quantities.

In addition to these usual scalar types, Plankalkül allowed arrays and record structures. Further, the record structures could use recursion to include other records as elements.

Although the language had no explicit goto, it did include an iterative structure similar to the Pascal **for**. It also had the command Fin, with a superscript, that indicated a jump out of a specified number of iteration loop nestings or to the beginning of a new iteration cycle. Plankalkül also had a conditional, but it did not allow an else clause.

One of the most interesting features of Zuse's programs was the inclusion of mathematical expressions showing the relationships between program variables. These expressions stated what would be true during execution at the points in the code where they appeared. These are very similar to the invariants used today in axiomatic semantics to prove the correctness of programs. Axiomatic semantics is discussed in Chapter 3.

Zuse's manuscript contained programs of far greater complexity than any written prior to 1945. Included were programs to sort given lists of numbers; test the connectivity of a given graph; carry out integer and floating-point operations, including square root; and perform syntax analysis on logic formulas that had parentheses and operators in six different levels of precedence. Perhaps most remarkable were his 49 pages of algorithms for playing chess, a game in which he was not an expert.

If a computer scientist had found Zuse's description of Plankalkül in the early 1950s, the single aspect of the language that would have hindered its implementation as defined would have been the notation. Each statement consisted of two or three lines of code. The first line was most like the statements of contemporary languages. The second line, which was optional, contained the subscripts of the array references in the first line. It is interesting to note that the same method of indicating subscripts was used by Charles Babbage in programs for his Analytical Engine in the mid-nineteenth century. The last line of each Plankalkül statement contained the type names for the variables mentioned in the first line. This notation is quite intimidating when first seen.

The following example assignment statement, which assigns the value of the expression A(4) + 1 to A(5), demonstrates this notation. The row labeled v is for subscripts and the row labeled s is for data types. In this example, 1.n means an integer of n bits.

```
    | A  +  1 => A
v   | 4           5
s   | 1.n         1.n
```

One can only speculate on the speed and direction that programming language design and computer development might have taken if Zuse's work had been widely known in 1945 or even 1950. It is also interesting to consider how his work might have been different had he done it in a peaceful environment surrounded by other scientists, rather than in Germany in 1945 in virtual isolation.

2.2 Minimal Hardware Programming: Pseudocodes

The computers that became available in the late 1940s and early 1950s were far less usable than those of today. In addition to being slow, unreliable, and expensive and having extremely small memories, the machines of that time were difficult to program due to the lack of supporting software.

There were no high-level programming languages or even assembly languages, so programming was done in machine code, which is both tedious and error-prone. Among its problems is the use of numeric codes for specifying instructions. For example, an ADD instruction might be specified by the code 14 rather than a connotative textual name, even if only a single letter. This makes programs very difficult to read. A more serious problem is absolute addressing, which makes programs very difficult to modify. For example, suppose we have a machine language program that is stored in memory. Many of the instructions in such a program refer to other locations within the program, usually to reference data or the targets of branch instructions. Inserting an instruction at any position in the program other than at the end invalidates the correctness of all instructions that refer to addresses beyond the insertion point, because those addresses must be increased to make room for the new instruction. To make the addition correctly, all those instructions that refer to addresses that follow the addition must be found and modified. A similar problem occurs with deletion of an instruction. In this case, however, machine languages often include a "no operation" instruction that can replace deleted instructions, thereby avoiding the difficulty.

These are standard problems with all machine languages and were the primary motivations for inventing assemblers and assembly languages. In addition, most programming problems of that time were numerical and required floating-point arithmetic operations and indexing of some sort to allow the convenient use of arrays. Neither of these capabilities, however, was included in the architecture of the computers of the late 1940s and early 1950s. These deficiencies naturally led to the development of somewhat higher-level languages that did include them.

2.2.1   Short Code

The first of these new languages, named Short Code, was developed by John Mauchly in 1949 for the BINAC computer. Short Code was later transferred to a UNIVAC I computer, and for a number of years was one of the primary means of programming those machines. Although little is known of the original Short Code because its complete description was never published, a programming manual for the UNIVAC I version did survive (Remington-Rand, 1952). It is safe to assume that the two versions were very similar.

The UNIVAC I had words that consisted of 72 bits, grouped as 12 six-bit bytes. Short Code consisted of coded versions of mathematical expressions that were to be evaluated. The codes were byte-pair values, and most equations fit into a word. Some of the codes were

01	$-$	06	abs value	1n	(n+2)nd power
02	)	07	+	2n	(n+2)nd root
03	=	08	pause	4n	if $<=$ to n
04	/	09	(	58	print and tab

Variables, or memory locations, were named with byte-pair codes, as were locations to be used as constants. For example, X0 and Y0 could be variables. The statement

```
X0 = SQRT(ABS(Y0))
```

would be coded in a word as 00 X0 03 20 06 Y0. The initial 00 was used as padding to fill the word. Interestingly, there was no multiplication code; multiplication was indicated by simple juxtaposition of the operands, as in algebra.

Short Code was not translated to machine code; rather, it was implemented with a pure interpreter. This process was called automatic programming at the time. It clearly simplified the programming process, but at the expense of execution time. Short Code interpretation was approximately 50 times slower than machine code.

2.2.2 Speedcoding

In other places, interpretive systems were being developed that extended machine languages to include floating-point operations. The Speedcoding system developed by John Backus for the IBM 701 is an example of such a system (Backus, 1954). The Speedcoding interpreter effectively converted the 701 to a virtual three-address floating-point calculator. The system included pseudoinstructions for the four arithmetic operations on floating-point data, as well as operations such as square root, sine, arc tangent, exponent, and logarithm. Conditional and unconditional branches and input/output conversions were also part of the virtual architecture. To get an idea of the limitations of such systems, consider that the remaining usable memory after loading the interpreter was only 700 words and that the add instruction took 4.2 milliseconds to execute. On the other hand, Speedcoding included the novel facility of automatically incrementing address registers. This did not appear until 1970 in the hardware of the PDP-11 computers. Because of such features, matrix multiplication could be done in 12 Speedcoding instructions. Backus claimed that problems that could take 2 weeks to program in machine code could be programmed in a few hours using Speedcoding.

2.2.3 The UNIVAC "Compiling System"

Between 1951 and 1953, a team led by Grace Hopper at UNIVAC developed a series of "compiling" systems named A-0, A-1, and A-2 that expanded a pseudocode into machine code in the same way as macros are expanded into assembly language. The pseudocode source for these "compilers" was still quite primitive, although even this was a great improvement over machine code because it made source programs much shorter. Wilkes (1952) independently suggested a similar process.

2.2.4 Related Work

Other means of easing the task of programming were being developed at about the same time. At Cambridge University, David J. Wheeler developed a method of using blocks of relocatable addresses to partially solve the problem of absolute addressing (Wheeler, 1950), and later, Maurice V. Wilkes (also at Cambridge) extended the idea to design an assembly program that could combine chosen subroutines and allocate storage (Wilkes et al., 1951, 1957). This was indeed an important and fundamental advance.

We should also mention that assembly languages, which are quite different from the pseudocodes mentioned, evolved during the early 1950s. However, they had little impact on the design of high-level languages.

2.3   The IBM 704 and FORTRAN

A great leap forward in computing came with the introduction of the IBM 704, in large measure because its capabilities prompted the development of FORTRAN. One could argue that if it had not been IBM with the 704 and FORTRAN, it would soon thereafter have been some other organization with a similar computer and related high-level language. However, IBM was the first with both the foresight and the resources to undertake these developments.

2.3.1   Historical Background

One of the primary reasons why interpretive systems were tolerated through the late 1940s to the mid-1950s was the lack of floating-point hardware in the available computers. All floating-point operations had to be simulated in software, a very time-consuming process. Because so much processor time was spent in software floating-point processing, the overhead of interpretation and the simulation of indexing were considered insignificant. As long as floating-point operations had to be done by software, interpretation was an acceptable expense. However, many programmers of that time never used interpretive systems, preferring the efficiency of hand-coded machine language. The announcement of the IBM 704 system in 1954, with both indexing and floating-point instructions in hardware, heralded the end of the interpretive era, at least for scientific computation.

Although FORTRAN is often credited with being the first compiled high-level language, the question of who deserves credit for implementing the first such language is somewhat open. Knuth and Pardo (1977) give the credit to Alick E. Glennie for his Autocode compiler for the Manchester Mark I computer. Glennie developed the compiler at Fort Halstead, Royal Armaments Research Establishment, in England. The compiler was operational by September 1952. However, according to John Backus (Wexelblat, 1981, p. 26), Glennie's Autocode was so low level and machine oriented that it should not be considered a compiled system. Backus gives the credit to Laning and Zierler at the Massachusetts Institute of Technology.

The Laning and Zierler system (Laning and Zierler, 1954) was the first algebraic translation system to be implemented. By algebraic we mean that it translated arithmetic expressions, used function calls for mathematical functions, and included subscripted variable references. The system was implemented on the MIT Whirlwind computer, in prototype experimental form, in the summer of 1952, and in a more usable form by May 1953. The translator generated a subroutine call to code each formula, or expression, in the program. The source language was easy to read, and the only actual machine instructions included were for branching. Although this work preceded the work on FORTRAN, it never escaped MIT.

In spite of these earlier works, the first widely accepted, compiled high-level language was FORTRAN. The following subsections chronicle this important development.

2.3.2 Design Process

Even before the 704 system was announced in May 1954, plans were begun for FORTRAN. By November 1954, John Backus and his group at IBM had produced the report entitled "The IBM Mathematical FORmula TRANslating System: FORTRAN" (IBM, 1954). This document described the first version of FORTRAN, which we refer to as FORTRAN 0, prior to its implementation. It also boldly stated that FORTRAN would provide the efficiency of hand-coded programs and the ease of programming of the interpretive pseudocode systems. In another burst of optimism, the document stated that FORTRAN would eliminate coding errors and the debugging process. Based on this premise, the first FORTRAN compiler included little syntax error checking.

The environment in which FORTRAN was developed was as follows: (1) Computers were still small, slow, and relatively unreliable. (2) The primary use of computers was scientific computations. (3) There were no existing acceptable ways to program computers. (4) Because of the high cost of computers compared to the cost of programmers, speed of the generated object code was the primary goal of the first real compilers. The characteristics of the early versions of FORTRAN follow directly from this environment.

2.3.3 FORTRAN I Overview

FORTRAN 0 was modified during the implementation period, which began in January 1955 and continued until the release of the compiler in April 1957. The implemented language, which we will call FORTRAN I, is described in the first FORTRAN *Programmer's Reference Manual*, published in October 1956 (IBM, 1956). The changes from FORTRAN 0 included the following: input/output formatting was added; the maximum length of variable names was increased from two to six characters; user-defined subroutines were added, although they could not be separately compiled. FORTRAN 0 included a logical IF statement whose Boolean expression used relational operators in their algebraic form—for example, >. The 704 character set did not include characters such as >, so these relational operators had to be dropped. Because the machine had a three-way branch instruction based on the comparison of the value in a storage location with the value in a register, the original logical IF was replaced with the arithmetic selection, which has the form

    IF (arithmetic expression) N1, N2, N3

where N1, N2, and N3 are statement labels. If the value of the expression is negative, the branch is to N1; if zero, it is to N2; if greater than zero, to N3. This statement is still part of FORTRAN.

The form of the FORTRAN I iterative statement was

    DO N1 variable = first, last

where N1 was the label of the last statement of the loop, and the statement on the line following the DO was the first.

The FORTRAN I DO loop was posttest, which means that the test for completion was at the bottom rather than the top of the loop. The disadvantage of posttest loops is that they always execute their loop statements once. For example,

    DO 10 K = 5, 1

causes the statements between the DO and the statement labeled 10 to be executed once, in spite of the fact that "last" is greater than "first."

As with the IF statement, the 704 had a single instruction to implement the DO. Because the instruction was designed for posttest loops, FORTRAN I's DO was designed in that way. A pretest loop could have been implemented on the 704, but that would have required one additional machine instruction, and since efficiency was the overriding concern in the design of FORTRAN, it was not done.

All of FORTRAN I's control statements were based on 704 instructions. It is not clear whether the 704 designers dictated the control statement design of FORTRAN I, or whether the designers of FORTRAN I suggested these instructions to the 704 designers.

There were no data-typing statements in the FORTRAN I language. Variables whose names began with I, J, K, L, M, and N were implicitly integer type, and all others were implicitly floating-point. The choice of the letters for this convention was based on the fact that at that time, integers were used primarily as subscripts, and scientists usually used i, j, and k for subscripts. To be generous, they threw in the three additional letters.

The most audacious claim made by the FORTRAN development group during the gestation period of the language was that the machine code produced by the compiler would be about as efficient as what could be produced by hand. This, more than anything else, made skeptics of potential users and prevented a great deal of interest in FORTRAN before its actual release. To almost everyone's surprise, however, the FORTRAN development group nearly achieved its goal in efficiency. The largest part of the 18 worker-years of effort used to construct the first compiler had been spent on optimization, and the results were remarkably effective.

2.3.4 FORTRAN II Overview

FORTRAN II was distributed in the spring of 1958. It fixed many of the bugs in the FORTRAN I compilation system and added some significant features, the most important being the independent compilation of subroutines. Without independent compilation, any change in a program requires that the entire program be recompiled. FORTRAN I's lack of independent compilation capability, coupled with the poor reliability of the 704, placed a practical restriction on the length of programs to about 300–400 lines (Wexelblat, 1981, p. 68). Longer programs had a poor chance of being compiled completely before a machine failure occurred. The capability of including precompiled binary versions of subprograms shortened the compilation process considerably.

The early success of FORTRAN is shown by the results of a survey made in April 1958. At that time, roughly half of the code being written for 704s was being done in FORTRAN—this in spite of the extreme skepticism of most of the programming world only a year earlier.

2.3.5 FORTRAN IV, FORTRAN 77, and FORTRAN 90

There was a FORTRAN III, although it was never widely distributed. FORTRAN IV, however, became one of the most widely used programming languages of its time. It evolved over the period 1960–1962 and was the standard version until 1978, when the FORTRAN 77 report (ANSI, 1978a) was released. FORTRAN IV was an improvement over FORTRAN II in many ways. Among its most important additions were type declarations, a logical IF construct, and the capability of passing subprograms as parameters to other subprograms.

FORTRAN 77 retains most of the features of FORTRAN IV and adds character string handling, logical loop control statements, and an IF with an optional ELSE clause.

FORTRAN 90 is the name of the latest version of FORTRAN (ANSI, 1990). FORTRAN 90 is dramatically different from FORTRAN 77. The most significant changes are briefly described in the following paragraphs.

A collection of functions are built-in for array operations. These include DOTPRODUCT, MATMUL, TRANSPOSE, MAXVAL, MINVAL, PRODUCT, and SUM, whose meanings are obvious from their names. These are just a few of the most commonly used functions among those available.

Arrays can be dynamically allocated and deallocated on command if they have been declared to be ALLOCATABLE. This is a radical departure from earlier FORTRANs, which all had nothing but static data. A form of records, called derived types, are included. Pointers are also part of FORTRAN 90.

New control statements have been added: CASE is a multiple selection statement, EXIT is used to depart prematurely from a loop, and CYCLE is used to transfer control to the bottom of a loop but not out.

Procedures can be recursive and also have optional and keyword parameters.

A module facility has been added that is similar to those of Ada and Modula-2. Modules can contain data declarations and subprograms, each of which can be either PRIVATE or PUBLIC to regulate external access.

A large number of other features have also been added to FORTRAN 90.

One new concept that is included in the FORTRAN 90 definition is that of removing language features from earlier versions. While FORTRAN 90 includes all of the features of FORTRAN 77, it has two lists of features that may be eliminated in future versions of FORTRAN. The **obsolescent** features list has features that may be eliminated in the next version of FORTRAN after 90. Included in this list are such things as the arithmetic IF and the assigned GOTO statements. The **deprecated** features list has features that may be eliminated in the second subsequent version after 90. Included in this list are the COMMON, EQUIVALENCE, and computed GOTO statements as well as statement functions.

2.3.6 Evaluation

The original FORTRAN design team thought of the language design only as a necessary prelude to the critical task of designing the translator. Further, it never occurred to them that FORTRAN would be used on computers not manufactured by IBM. Indeed, they were forced to consider building FORTRAN compilers for other IBM machines only by the fact that the successor to the 704, the 709, was announced before the 704 FORTRAN compiler was released. The effect that FORTRAN has had on the use of computers, along with the fact that all subsequent programming languages owe a debt to FORTRAN, are indeed impressive in light of the modest goals of its designers.

One of the features of FORTRAN I, and all of its successors except 90, that allows highly optimizing compilers is the fact that the types and storage for all variables are fixed before run time. No new variables or space can be allocated during run time. This is a sacrifice of flexibility to simplicity and efficiency. It eliminates the possibility of recursive subprograms and makes it difficult to implement data structures that grow or change shape dynamically. Of course, the kinds of programs that were being built at the time of the development of the early versions of FORTRAN were primarily numerical in nature and were simple in comparison with recent software projects. Therefore, the sacrifice was not a great one.

The overall success of FORTRAN is difficult to overstate: It dramatically changed forever the way computers are used. This is, of course, partially due to its being the first widely used high-level language. In comparison with concepts and languages developed later, early versions of FORTRAN suffer in a variety of ways, as should be expected. After all, Model T Fords are not to be compared across the board with 1993 Ford Thunderbirds. Nevertheless, in spite of the inadequacies of FORTRAN, the momentum of the huge investment in FORTRAN software, among other factors, has kept it one of the most widely used of all high-level languages.

Alan Perlis, one of the designers of ALGOL 60, said of FORTRAN in 1978, "FORTRAN is the *lingua franca* of the computing world. It is the language of the streets in the best sense of the word, not in the prostitutional sense of the word. And it has survived and will survive because it has turned out to be a remarkably useful part of a very vital commerce" (Wexelblat, 1981, p. 161).

The following is an example program in FORTRAN 90:

```
C   FORTRAN 90 EXAMPLE PROGRAM
C      INPUT: AN INTEGER, LIST_LEN, WHERE LIST_LEN IS LESS
C             THAN 100, FOLLOWED BY LIST_LEN-INTEGER VALUES
C      OUTPUT: THE NUMBER OF INPUT VALUES THAT ARE GREATER
C             THAN THE AVERAGE OF ALL INPUT VALUES
      INTEGER INTLIST(99)
      INTEGER LIST_LEN, COUNTER, SUM, AVERAGE, RESULT
      RESULT = 0
      SUM = 0
      READ *, LIST_LEN
      IF ((LIST_LEN .GT. 0) .AND. (LIST_LEN .LT. 100)) THEN
C   READ INPUT DATA INTO AN ARRAY AND COMPUTE ITS SUM
         DO 10 COUNTER = 1, LIST_LEN
            READ *, INTLIST(COUNTER)
            SUM = SUM + INTLIST(COUNTER)
10       CONTINUE
C   COMPUTE THE AVERAGE
         AVERAGE = SUM / LIST_LEN
C   COUNT THE VALUES THAT ARE GREATER THAN THE AVERAGE
         DO 20 COUNTER = 1, LIST_LEN
            IF (INTLIST(COUNTER) .GT. AVERAGE) THEN
               RESULT = RESULT + 1
            END IF
20       CONTINUE
C   PRINT THE RESULT
         PRINT *, 'NUMBER OF VALUES > AVERAGE IS:', RESULT

      ELSE
         PRINT *, 'ERROR--LIST_LEN VALUE IS NOT LEGAL'
      END IF
      STOP
      END
```

2.4   Functional Programming: LISP

The first functional programming language was invented to provide language features for list processing, the need for which grew out of the first applications in the area of artificial intelligence (AI).

2.4.1   The Beginnings of Artificial Intelligence and List Processing

Interest in AI began to appear in the mid-1950s in a number of places. Some of this interest grew out of linguistics, some from psychology, and some from mathematics. Linguists were concerned with natural language processing. Psychologists were interested in modeling human information storage and retrieval, along with other fundamental processes of the brain. Mathematicians were interested in mechanizing certain intelligent processes, such as theorem proving. All these investigations arrived at the same conclusion: Some method must be developed to allow computers to process symbolic data in lists (collections of noncontiguous memory cells that are chained together with pointers). At the time, nearly all computation was on numeric data in arrays.

The concept of list processing was developed by Allen Newell, J. C. Shaw, and Herbert Simon. It was first published in a classic paper that describes one of the first AI programs, the Logical Theorist, and a language in which it could be implemented (Newell and Simon, 1956). The language, named IPL-I (Information Processing Language I), was never implemented. The next version, IPL-II, was implemented on a Rand Corporation Johnniac computer. Development of IPL continued until 1960, when the description of IPL-V was published (Newell and Tonge, 1960). The low level of the IPL languages prevented their widespread use. They were actually assembly languages for a hypothetical computer, implemented by interpreters, in which list-processing instructions were included. The fact that the first implementation was on the obscure Johnniac machine was another factor that kept the IPL languages from becoming popular.

The contributions of the IPL languages were in their list design and their demonstration that list processing was feasible and useful.

IBM became interested in AI in the mid-1950s and chose theorem proving as a demonstration area. At the time, the FORTRAN project was still under way. The high cost (18 worker-years) of the FORTRAN I compiler convinced IBM that their list processing should be attached to FORTRAN, rather than in the form of a new language. Thus, the FORTRAN List Processing Language (FLPL) was designed and implemented as an extension to FORTRAN. FLPL was used to construct a theorem prover for plane geometry, which was then considered the easiest part of mechanical theorem proving.

2.4.2 Design Process

John McCarthy of MIT took a summer position at the IBM Information
Research Department in 1958. His goal for the summer was to investigate
symbolic computations and develop a set of requirements for doing such
computations. As a pilot example problem area, he chose differentiation of
algebraic expressions. From this study came a list of perceived language
requirements. Among them were the control flow methods of mathematical
functions: recursion and conditional expressions. The only available high-
level language of the time, FORTRAN I, had neither of these.

Another requirement that grew from the symbolic differentiation inves-
tigation was the need for some kind of implicit erasure of abandoned lists.
McCarthy simply would not allow his elegant algorithm for differentiation
to be cluttered with explicit statements to place list structures that were no
longer needed back into a pool of available storage.

Because FLPL did not support recursion, conditional expressions, or
implicit erasure, it was clear to McCarthy that a new language was
required.

When McCarthy returned to MIT in the fall of 1958, he and Marvin Minsky formed the MIT AI Project, with funding from the Research Laboratory
for Electronics. The first important effort of the project was to produce a
system for list processing. It was to be initially used to implement a program proposed by McCarthy called the Advice Taker. This application
became the impetus for the development of the list processing language
LISP. The first version of LISP is sometimes called pure LISP because it is
a purely functional language. In the following section we describe the
development of pure LISP.

2.4.3 Language Overview

2.4.3.1 Data Types and Structures

Pure LISP has only two kinds of data objects: atoms and lists. Atoms, which
have the form of identifiers, are the symbols of LISP. Numeric constants are
also considered atoms.

The concept of storing symbolic information in linked lists is natural and
was used in IPL-II. Such structures allow insertions and deletions at any
point, which was then thought to be a necessary part of list processing. As
it eventually developed, however, LISP rarely requires these operations.

Lists are specified by delimiting their elements with parentheses. The
elements of simple lists are restricted to atoms, as in

    (A B C D)

Nested list structures are also specified by parentheses. For example, the
list

(A (B C) D (E (F G)))

is composed of four elements. The first is the atom A; the second is the sub
list (B C); the third is the atom D; the fourth is the sublist (E (F G)), which
has as its second element the sublist (F G).

Internally, lists are usually stored as single-linked list structures, in
which each node has two pointers and represents an element. A node for
an atom has its first pointer pointing to some representation of the atom,
such as its symbol or numeric value. A node for a sublist element has its
first pointer pointing to the first node of the sublist. In both cases, the second pointer of a node points to the next element of the list. A list is referenced by a pointer to its first element. The internal representations of the
two lists above are shown in Figure 2.2.

Note that the elements of a list are shown horizontally. The last element
of a list has no successor, so its link is NIL. Sublists are shown with the
same structure.

2.4.3.2 Processes in Functional Programming

All computation in a functional program is accomplished by applying functions to arguments. There need not be any assignment statements or even
variables that are used the way those of the imperative languages are used
(to store values that change during program execution). Furthermore, iterative processes can be specified with recursive function calls—loops are
unnecessary. These basic concepts of functional programming makes it significantly different from programming in an imperative language.

Figure 2.2
Internal representation
of two LISP lists

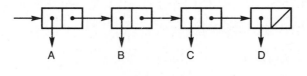

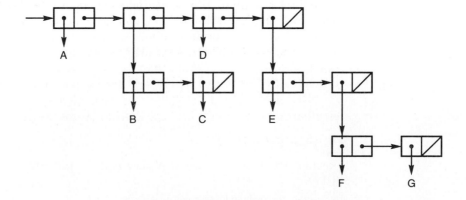

2.4.3.3 The Syntax of LISP

LISP is very different from Pascal (and the other imperative languages) because not only is it a functional programming language but also it is completely different in appearance. While the syntax of Pascal is a complicated mixture of English and algebra, LISP's syntax is a model of simplicity. Program code and data have exactly the same form: parenthesized lists. For example, consider the list

```
(A B C D)
```

When interpreted as data, it is a list of four elements. When viewed as code, it is the application of the function named A to the three parameters B, C, and D.

2.4.4 Evaluation

LISP totally dominated AI applications for a quarter of a century. It is still the most widely used language for AI. Much of the cause of LISP's reputation for being highly inefficient has been eliminated. Many contemporary implementations are compiled, and the resulting code is much faster than when the source code is interpreted. In addition to its success in AI, LISP pioneered the process of functional programming, which has proven to be a lively area of research in programming languages. As stated in Chapter 1, many programming language researchers believe functional programming is a much better approach to software development than the use of imperative languages.

LISP and functional programming are discussed at length in Chapter 13. The following example program is explained there:

```
;   LISP Example function
;   The following code defines a LISP predicate function,
;   which takes two lists as arguments and returns T (true)
;   if the two lists are equal, and NIL (false) otherwise
(DEFINE (
  '(equal (LAMBDA (lis1 lis2)
  (COND
     ((ATOM lis1) (EQ lis1 lis2))
     ((ATOM lis2) NIL)
     ((equal (CAR lis1) (CAR lis2))
          (equal (CDR lis1) (CAR lis2)))
     (T NIL)
   )
  ))
))
```

2.5 The First Step Toward Sophistication: ALGOL 60

ALGOL 60 has had a great influence on subsequent programming languages and is therefore of central importance in any historical review of languages.

2.5.1 Historical Background

ALGOL 60 came into being as a result of efforts to design a universal language. By late 1954, the Laning and Zierler algebraic system had been in operation for over a year, and the first report on FORTRAN had been published. FORTRAN became a reality in 1957, and several other high-level languages were being developed. Most notable among them were IT, which was designed by Alan Perlis at Carnegie Tech, and the two languages MATH-MATIC and UNICODE for the UNIVAC computers. The proliferation of languages was making communication among users difficult. Furthermore, the new languages were all growing up around single architectures, some for UNIVAC computers and some for IBM 700 series machines. In response to this language proliferation, several major computer-user groups in the United States, including SHARE (the IBM scientific user group) and USE (UNIVAC Scientific Exchange, the large-scale UNIVAC scientific user group), submitted a petition to the Association for Computing Machinery (ACM) on May 10, 1957, to form a committee to study and recommend action to create a universal programming language. Although FORTRAN might have been a candidate, it could not become a universal language because at the time it was solely owned by IBM.

Previously, in 1955, GAMM (a German acronym for Society for Applied Mathematics and Mechanics) had also formed a committee to design one universal, machine-independent, algorithmic language for use on all kinds of computers. The desire for this new language was in part due to the Europeans' fear of being dominated by IBM. By late 1957, however, the appearance of several high-level languages in the United States convinced the GAMM subcommittee that their effort had to be widened to include the Americans, and a letter of invitation was sent to ACM. In April 1958, after Fritz Bauer of GAMM presented the formal proposal to them, the two groups officially agreed to a joint language design project.

2.5.2 Early Design Process

GAMM and ACM decided that the joint design effort should be made at a meeting to which each group would send four members. The meeting was held in Zurich from May 27 to June 1, 1958.

The committee began with the following goals for the new language:

1. The language should be as close as possible to standard mathematical notation, and programs written in it should be readable with little further explanation.

2. It should be possible to use the language for the description of computing processes in publications.

3. Programs in the new language must be mechanically translatable into machine language.

The first goal indicates that the new language was to be used for scientific programming, which was the primary computer application area at that time. The second was something entirely new to the computing business. The last goal is an obvious necessity for any programming language.

Depending on how it is viewed, the Zurich meeting either produced momentous results or endless arguments. Actually, it did both. The meeting itself involved innumerable compromises, both among individuals and between sides of the Atlantic. In some cases, the compromises were difficult. The question of whether to use a comma (the European method) or a period (the American method) for a decimal point was not decided, at least not directly. From this small point grew the concept of having three separate language representations, which effectively sidestepped the problem.

The first of the three representations was the reference language, which made absolutely no assumptions about computers, character sets, or implementations. This was the only representation that was designed at the 1958 Zurich meeting. The second representation was the publication language, which was meant to be used in publishing algorithms. In this case, whatever characters were printable were allowed if they clarified programs; the character set was allowed to vary from country to country. So, Europeans could use commas and Americans could use periods. The last representation was the hardware language, of which there would be one per implementation. The hardware language would use whatever character set was available on the machine, and each implementation was required to include a set of rules for transliterating from the reference language to the hardware language.

2.5.3 ALGOL 58 Overview

The language designed at the Zurich meeting was named the International Algorithmic Language (IAL). It was suggested during the design that the language be named ALGOL, for ALGOrithmic Language, but the name was rejected because it did not sufficiently reflect the international scope of the committee. During the following year, however, the name was changed to ALGOL, and the language subsequently became known as ALGOL 58.

In many ways, ALGOL 58 was a descendant of FORTRAN, which is quite natural. It generalized many of FORTRAN's features and added several new constructs and concepts. Some of the generalizations had to do with the goal of not tying the language to any particular machine, and others were attempts to make the language more flexible and powerful. A rare combination of simplicity and elegance emerged from the effort.

ALGOL 58 formalized the concept of data type, although only variables that were not floating-point required explicit declaration. It added the idea of compound statements, which most subsequent languages incorporated. Some of the features of FORTRAN that were generalized were the following: Identifiers were allowed to have any length, as opposed to FORTRAN's restriction to six or fewer characters; any number of array dimensions was allowed, unlike FORTRAN's limitation to no more than three; the lower bound of arrays could be specified by the programmer, whereas in FORTRAN it was implicitly 1; nested IF statements were allowed, which was not the case in FORTRAN; a **for** statement was included to do what FORTRAN's DO does, but then a **do** statement was added to allow a sort of subprogram process, complete with parameters.

ALGOL 58 procedure calls had the form

name(input parameters) =: (output parameters)

Because of this form, it was and remains the only language to clearly separate the two kinds of parameters into different lists.

ALGOL 58 and all of its successors acquired the assignment operator in a rather unusual way. Zuse used the form

expression => variable

for the assignment statement in his Plankalkül. Although Plankalkül had not yet been published, some of the European members of the ALGOL 58 committee were familiar with the language. The committee dabbled with the Plankalkül assignment form but, because of arguments about character limitations, the greater-than symbol was changed to a colon. Then, largely at the insistence of the Americans, the whole statement was turned around to the form

variable := expression

The Europeans preferred the opposite form.

2.5.4   Reception of the ALGOL 58 Report

Publication of the ALGOL 58 report (Perlis and Samelson, 1958) in December 1958 was greeted with a good deal of enthusiasm. In the United States, the new language was viewed more as a collection of ideas for programming language design than as a universal standard language. Actually, the ALGOL 58 report was not meant to be a finished product but rather a preliminary document for international discussion. Nevertheless, three major design and implementation efforts used the report as their basis. At the University of Michigan, the MAD language was born (Arden et al., 1961). The

U.S. Naval Electronics Group produced the NELIAC language (Huskey et al., 1963). At System Development Corporation, JOVIAL was designed and implemented (Shaw, 1963). JOVIAL, an acronym for Jules' Own Version of the International Algebraic Language, represents the only language based on ALGOL 58 to achieve widespread use (Jules was Jules I. Schwartz, one of JOVIAL's designers). JOVIAL became widely used because it was the official scientific language for the U.S. Air Force for a quarter of a century.

The rest of the U.S. computing community was not so kind to the new language. At first, both IBM and its major scientific user group, SHARE, seemed to embrace ALGOL 58. IBM began an implementation shortly after the report was published, and SHARE formed a subcommittee, SHARE IAL, to study the language. The subcommittee subsequently recommended that ACM standardize ALGOL 58 and that IBM implement it for all of the 700 series computers. The enthusiasm was short-lived, however. By spring 1959, both IBM and SHARE, through their FORTRAN experience, had had enough of the pain and expense of getting a new language started, both in terms of developing and using the first-generation compilers and in terms of training users in the new language and persuading them to use it. By the middle of 1959, both IBM and SHARE had developed such a vested interest in FORTRAN that they decided to retain it as *the* scientific language for the IBM 700 series machines, thereby abandoning ALGOL 58.

2.5.5 ALGOL 60 Design Process

During 1959, ALGOL 58 was debated endlessly in both Europe and the United States. Large numbers of suggested modifications and additions were published in the European *ALGOL Bulletin* and in *Communications of the ACM*. One of the most important events of 1959 was the presentation of the work of the Zurich committee to the International Conference on Information Processing, for it was there that Backus introduced his new notation for describing the syntax of programming languages, which later became known as BNF (for Backus-Naur form). BNF is described in detail in Chapter 3.

In January 1960, the second ALGOL meeting was held, this time in Paris. The work of this meeting was to debate the 80 suggestions that had been formally submitted for consideration. Peter Naur of Denmark had become heavily involved in the development of ALGOL, even though he had not been a member of the Zurich group. It was Naur who created and operated the *ALGOL Bulletin*. He spent a good deal of time studying Backus's paper that introduced BNF and decided that BNF should be used to describe formally the results of the 1960 meeting. After making a few relatively minor changes to BNF, he wrote a description of the new proposed language in BNF and handed it out to the members of the 1960 group at the beginning of the meeting.

2.5.6 ALGOL 60 Overview

Although the 1960 meeting lasted only six days, the modifications made to ALGOL 58 were dramatic. Among the most important new developments were the following:

1. The concept of block structure was introduced. This allowed the programmer to localize parts of programs by introducing new data environments, or scopes. For example, consider the following code segment:

```
...
begin
  integer sum, count;
  ...
end;
...
```

The **begin-end** pair delimits a block in which the variables sum and count are local. They are not visible, nor do they have storage associated with them when control is outside the block.

2. Two different means of passing parameters to subprograms were allowed: pass by value and pass by name (they are referred to as call by value and call by name in the ALGOL documentation).

3. Procedures were allowed to be recursive. The ALGOL 58 description was unclear on this issue.

4. Semidynamic arrays were allowed. A semidynamic array is one for which the subscript range or ranges are specified by variables, so that the size of the array is set at the time storage is allocated to the array, which happens when the declaration is reached during execution. For example, consider the following ALGOL 60 procedure skeleton:

```
procedure insert (listlen, newvalue);
  value listlen;
  integer listlen, newvalue;
  begin
  integer array [1:listlen] list;
  ...
  end insert;
```

In this procedure, the array list is a local array of integer elements declared to have a subscript range of 1..listlen, where listlen is a parameter to the procedure. The size of list is not known until the procedure is called, so its storage cannot be allocated until then. Note that this is different from Pascal local array variables, which must have subscript ranges that are known at compile time.

Several features that might have had a dramatic impact on the success or failure of the language were proposed but rejected. Most important among these were input and output statements with formatting, which were omitted because they were thought to be too machine dependent.

The ALGOL 60 report was published in May 1960 (Naur, 1960). A number of ambiguities still remained in the language description, and a third meeting was scheduled for April 1962 in Rome to address the problems. At this meeting the group dealt only with problems; no additions to the language were allowed. The results of this meeting were published under the title "Revised Report on the Algorithmic Language ALGOL 60" (Backus et al., 1962).

2.5.7 ALGOL 60 Evaluation

In some ways ALGOL 60 was a great success; in other ways it was a dismal failure. It succeeded in becoming, almost immediately, the only acceptable formal means of communicating algorithms, and it remained for over 20 years the sole language for publishing algorithms. Every imperative programming language designed since 1960 owes something to ALGOL 60. In fact, most are direct or indirect descendants; examples are PL/I, SIMULA 67, ALGOL 68, C, PASCAL, Modula-2, and Ada.

The ALGOL 58/ALGOL 60 design effort included a long list of firsts. It was the first time that an international group attempted to design a programming language. It was the first language that was designed to be machine independent. It was also the first language whose syntax was formally described. This successful use of the BNF formalism initiated several important fields of computer science: formal languages, parsing theory, and compiler design. Finally, the structure of ALGOL 60 affected machine architecture. In the most striking example of this, an extension of the language was used as the systems language of a series of large-scale computers, the Burroughs B5000, B6000, and B7000 machines, which were designed with a hardware stack to efficiently implement the block structure and recursive procedures of the language.

On the other side of the coin, ALGOL 60 never achieved widespread or even significant use in the United States. Even in Europe, it never became the dominant language. There are a number of reasons for its lack of acceptance. For one thing, some of the features of ALGOL 60 turned out to be too flexible; they made understanding difficult and implementation inefficient. The best example of this is the pass-by-name method of passing parameters to subprograms, which is explained in Chapter 8. The difficulties of implementing ALGOL 60 are evidenced by Rutishauser's statement in 1967 that few if any implementations included the full ALGOL 60 language (Rutishauser, 1967, p. 8).

The lack of input and output statements in the language was another major reason for its lack of acceptance. Implementation-dependent input/output made programs difficult to port to other computers.

One of the most important contributions to computer science that is associated with ALGOL 60, BNF, was also a factor in its lack of acceptance. Although BNF is now considered a simple and elegant means of syntax description, to the world of 1960 it seemed strange and abstruse.

The character set of ALGOL 60 was also a problem, in spite of the option in the hardware versions that allowed users to alter the implemented character set. Most problematic was the method of representing reserved words. The publication version of ALGOL 60 uses boldface for reserved words. Some compilers delimited reserved words with apostrophes, and others simply used normal characters. Unfortunately, these differences made programs difficult to port between implementations.

Finally, although there were many other problems, the entrenchment of FORTRAN among users and the lack of support by IBM were probably the most important factors in ALGOL 60's failure to gain widespread use.

The ALGOL 60 effort was never really complete, in the sense that ambiguities and obscurities were always a part of the language description (Knuth, 1967). It has been noted that the ALGOL 60 report was meant to be like the Bible: It was to be interpreted, not merely read. Those who studied the report carefully and interpreted it for the rest of the world became known as ALGOL theologians.

The following is an example ALGOL 60 program:

```
comment ALGOL 60 Example Program
    Input: An integer, listlen, where listlen is less than
           100, followed by listlen-integer values
   Output: The number of input values that are greater than
           the average of all the input values    ;
begin
  integer array intlist [1:99];
  integer listlen, counter, sum, average, result;
  sum := 0;
  result := 0;
  readint (listlen);
  if (listlen > 0) ∧ (listlen < 100) then
    begin
comment Read input into an array and compute the average;
      for counter := 1 step 1 until listlen do
        begin
        readint (intlist[counter]);
        sum := sum + intlist[counter]
        end;
comment Compute the average;
      average := sum / listlen;
comment Count the input values that are > average;
      for counter := 1 step 1 until listlen do
        if intlist[counter] > average
          then result := result + 1;
comment Print result;
```

```
        printstring("The number of values > average is:");
        printint (result)
        end
    else
        printstring ("Error--input listlen is not legal");
    end
```

The ancestry of ALGOL 60 is shown in Figure 2.3.

Figure 2.3
Genealogy of ALGOL
60

FORTRAN I (1957)

FORTRAN II (1958)

ALGOL 58 (1958)

ALGOL 60 (1960)

2.6 Computerizing Business Records: COBOL

The story of COBOL is strange indeed. Although it has been used more than any other programming language, COBOL has had little effect on the design of subsequent languages, except for PL/I. It may still be the most widely used language, although it is very difficult to be sure one way or the other. Perhaps the most important reason why COBOL has had little influence is that few have attempted to design a new language for business applications since it appeared. That may be a tribute to how well COBOL's capabilities meet the needs of its application area. Another reason is that a great deal of growth in business computing over the past ten years has occurred in small businesses. In these businesses, very little software development has taken place. Instead, most of the software used is purchased as off-the-shelf packages for various business applications.

2.6.1 Historical Background

The beginning of COBOL is somewhat similar to that of ALGOL 60, in the sense that the language was designed by a committee of people meeting for relatively short periods of time. The state of business computing at the time, which was 1959, was similar to the state of scientific computing several years earlier, when FORTRAN was being designed. One compiled language for business applications, FLOW-MATIC, had been implemented in 1957, but it belonged to one manufacturer, UNIVAC, and was designed for that company's computers. Another language, AIMACO, was being used by the U.S. Air Force, but it was a only a minor variation of FLOW-MATIC. IBM had designed a programming language for business applications, COM-TRAN (COMmercial TRANslator), but it had not yet been implemented. Several other language design projects were being planned.

2.6.2   FLOW-MATIC

The origins of FLOW-MATIC are worth at least a brief discussion, because it was the primary progenitor of COBOL. In December 1953, Grace Hopper at Remington-Rand UNIVAC produced a budget request that was indeed prophetic. It suggested that "mathematical programs should be written in mathematical notation, data processing programs should be written in English statements" (Wexelblat, 1981, p. 16). Unfortunately, it was impossible in 1953 to convince nonprogrammers that a computer could be made to understand English words. It was not until 1955 that a similar proposal had some hope of being funded by UNIVAC management, and even then it took a prototype system to do the final convincing. Part of this selling process involved compiling and running a small program, first using English keywords, then using French keywords, and then using German keywords. This demonstration was considered remarkable by UNIVAC management and was a prime factor in their acceptance of Hopper's proposal.

2.6.3   COBOL Design Process

The first formal meeting on the subject of a common language for business applications, which was sponsored by the Department of Defense, was held at the Pentagon on May 28–29, 1959 (exactly one year after the Zurich ALGOL meeting). The consensus of the group was that the language, then named CBL (for Common Business Language) should have the following general characteristics. Most agreed that it should use English as much as possible, although a few argued for a more mathematical notation. The language must be easy to use, even at the expense of being less powerful, in order to broaden the base of those who could program computers. In addition to making the language easy to use, it was believed that the use of English would allow managers to read programs. Finally, the design should not be overly restricted by the problems of its implementation.

One of the overriding concerns at the meeting was that steps to create this universal language should be taken quickly, as a lot of work was already being done to create new business languages. In addition to the existing languages, RCA and Sylvania were working on their own business applications languages. If a universal language was not designed soon, its later acceptance would be more difficult. On this basis, it was decided that there should be a quick study of existing languages. For this task, the Short Range Committee was formed.

Initially, the goal of the Short Range Committee was not clearly understood: Was it only to evaluate existing languages, or was it to design a new language? Whichever was intended, the committee chose the latter. The language design it initially produced, most of which is still part of COBOL, would probably have been significantly different had members known how long it would endure. Committee members operated under the assumption that they were designing an interim language for short-range use and that a different committee would have the time and resources to produce a high-quality language for the long term.

There were early decisions to separate the statements of the language into two categories—data description and executable operations—and to have statements in these two categories reside in different parts of programs. One of the great debates of the Short Range Committee was over the inclusion of subscripts. Many committee members argued that subscripts were too complex for the people in data processing, who were thought to be mathematically naive. Similar arguments evolved around whether arithmetic expressions should be included. The final report of the Short Range Committee was completed in December 1959.

The language specifications for COBOL 60, published by the Government Printing Office in April 1960 (Department of Defense, 1960), were described as "initial." Revised versions were published in 1961 and 1962 (Department of Defense, 1961, 1962). The language was standardized by the American National Standards Instutute (ANSI) group in 1968. The next two revisions were standardized by ANSI in 1974 and 1985. The language continues to evolve today.

2.6.4 Evaluation

The COBOL language originated a number of novel concepts, some of which eventually appeared in other languages. For example, the DEFINE verb of COBOL 60 was the first high-level language construct for macros. More important, hierarchical data structures, which first appeared in Plankalkül, were first implemented in COBOL. They have since been included in the structured types of PL/I and the record types of ALGOL 68, Pascal, C, Modula-2, and Ada. COBOL was also the first language that allowed names to be truly connotative, because it allowed both long names (up to 30 characters) and word-connector characters (dashes).

Overall, the data division is the strong part of COBOL's design, whereas the procedure division is relatively weak. Every variable is defined in detail in the data division, including the number of decimal digits and the location of the implied decimal point. File records are also described with this level of detail, as are lines to be output to a printer, which makes COBOL ideal for printing accounting reports. Perhaps the most important weakness of the procedure division lies in its lack of functions. Versions of COBOL prior to the 1974 standard also did not allow subprograms with parameters.

Our final comment on COBOL: It was the first programming language whose use was mandated by the Department of Defense (DoD). This mandate came after its initial development, since COBOL was not designed specifically for the DoD. In spite of its merits, COBOL probably would not have survived without that mandate. The poor performance of the early compilers simply made it far too expensive to use. Eventually, of course, people learned more about producing compilers and computers became much faster, larger, and cheaper. Together, these factors have made COBOL a great success, inside and outside DoD. Its appearance led to the electronic mechanization of accounting, an important revolution by any measure.

The following is an example of a COBOL program:

```
IDENTIFICATION DIVISION.
PROGRAM-ID. PRODUCE-REORDER-LISTING.

ENVIRONMENT DIVISION.
CONFIGURATION SECTION.
SOURCE-COMPUTER.   DEC-VAX.
OBJECT-COMPUTER.   DEC-VAX.
INPUT-OUTPUT SECTION.
FILE-CONTROL.
     SELECT BAL-FWD-FILE        ASSIGN TO READER.
     SELECT REORDER-LISTING     ASSIGN TO LOCAL-PRINTER.

DATA DIVISION.
FILE SECTION.
FD   BAL-FWD-FILE
     LABEL RECORDS ARE STANDARD
     RECORD CONTAINS 80 CHARACTERS.

01   BAL-FWD-CARD.
     02   BF-ITEM-NO               PICTURE IS 9(5).
     02   BF-ITEM-DESC             PICTURE IS X(20).
     02   FILLER                   PICTURE IS X(5).
     02   BF-UNIT-PRICE            PICTURE IS 999V99.
     02   BF-REORDER-POINT         PICTURE IS 9(5).
     02   BF-ON-HAND               PICTURE IS 9(5).
     02   BF-ON-ORDER              PICTURE IS 9(5).
     02   FILLER                   PICTURE IS X(30).

FD   REORDER-LISTING
     LABEL RECORDS ARE STANDARD
     RECORD CONTAINS 132 CHARACTERS.

01   REORDER-LINE.
     02   RL-ITEM-NO               PICTURE IS Z(5).
     02   FILLER                   PICTURE IS X(5).
     02   RL-ITEM-DESC             PICTURE IS X(20).
```

```
      02   FILLER                               PICTURE IS X(5).
      02   RL-UNIT-PRICE                        PICTURE IS ZZZ.99.
      02   FILLER                               PICTURE IS X(5).
      02   RL-AVAILABLE-STOCK                   PICTURE IS Z(5).
      02   FILLER                               PICTURE IS X(5).
      02   RL-REORDER-POINT                     PICTURE IS Z(5).
      02   FILLER                               PICTURE IS X(71).


  WORKING-STORAGE SECTION.
  01   SWITCHES.
      02   CARD-EOF-SWITCH                      PICTURE IS X.
  01   WORK-FIELDS.
      02   AVAILABLE-STOCK                      PICTURE IS 9(5).


  PROCEDURE DIVISION.
  000-PRODUCE-REORDER-LISTING.
      OPEN INPUT  BAL-FWD-FILE.
      OPEN OUTPUT REORDER-LISTING.
      MOVE "N" TO CARD-EOF-SWITCH.
      PERFORM 100-PRODUCE-REORDER-LINE
          UNTIL CARD-EOF-SWITCH IS EQUAL TO "Y".
      CLOSE BAL-FWD-FILE.
      CLOSE REORDER-LISTING.
      STOP RUN.


  100-PRODUCE-REORDER-LINE.
      PERFORM 110-READ-INVENTORY-RECORD.
      IF CARD-EOF-SWITCH IS NOT EQUAL TO "Y"
          PERFORM 120-CALCULATE-AVAILABLE-STOCK
          IF AVAILABLE-STOCK IS LESS THAN BF-REORDER-POINT
              PERFORM 130-PRINT-REORDER-LINE.


  110-READ-INVENTORY-RECORD.
      READ BAL-FWD-FILE RECORD
          AT END
              MOVE "Y" TO CARD-EOF-SWITCH.
  120-CALCULATE-AVAILABLE-STOCK.
      ADD BF-ON-HAND BF-ON-ORDER
          GIVING AVAILABLE-STOCK.


  130-PRINT-REORDER-LINE.
      MOVE SPACE               TO REORDER-LINE.
      MOVE BF-ITEM-NO          TO RL-ITEM-NO.
      MOVE BF-ITEM-DESC        TO RL-ITEM-DESC.
      MOVE BF-UNIT-PRICE       TO RL-UNIT-PRICE.
      MOVE AVAILABLE-STOCK     TO RL-AVAILABLE-STOCK.
      MOVE BF-REORDER-POINT    TO RL-REORDER-POINT.
      WRITE REORDER-LINE.
```

The ancestry of COBOL is shown in Figure 2.4.

Figure 2.4
Genealogy of COBOL

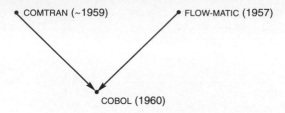

2.7   The Beginnings of Timesharing: BASIC

BASIC (Mather and Waite, 1971) is another programming language that has enjoyed widespread use but has gotten little respect. Like COBOL, it has been largely ignored by computer scientists. Also like COBOL, it is inelegant and has not led to successor languages.

Nevertheless, BASIC has strongly influenced programmers because for many of them it was their first language. This is due to its popularity on microcomputers, which follows directly from two of the main characteristics of BASIC: It is very easy for beginners to learn, especially those who are not science-oriented, and its smaller dialects can be implemented on computers with very small memories. The latter characteristic was very important in the early years of microcomputers (the late 1970s and early 1980s).

2.7.1   Design Process

BASIC was designed at Dartmouth College in New Hampshire by two mathematicians, John Kemeny and Thomas Kurtz, who were involved in the early 1960s in producing compilers for a variety of dialects of FORTRAN and ALGOL 60. Their science students had little trouble learning or using those languages in their work.

However, Dartmouth was primarily a liberal arts institution, where science and engineering students made up only about 25% of the student body. It was decided in the spring of 1963 to design a new language that would use terminals as the method of computer access. The goals of the system were

1. It must be easy for nonscience students to learn and use.
2. It must be pleasant and friendly.
3. It must provide fast turnaround for homework.
4. It must allow free and private access.
5. It must consider user time more important than computer time.

The last goal was indeed a revolutionary concept. It was based at least partly on the belief that computers would become significantly cheaper as time went on, which, of course, they did.

The combination of goals 2, 3, and 4 led to the time-shared aspect of BASIC. Only with individual access through terminals by numerous simultaneous users could these goals be met in the early 1960s.

In the summer of 1963, Kemeny began work on the compiler for the first version of BASIC, using remote access to a GE 225 computer. Design and coding of the operating system for BASIC began in the fall of 1963. At 4 A.M. on May 1, 1964, the first program using the time-shared BASIC was typed in and run. In June, the number of terminals on the system grew from 3 to 11, and by fall it had ballooned to 20.

2.7.2   Language Overview

The original version of BASIC was very small and, oddly, was not interactive: There was no means of getting input data from the terminal. Programs were typed in, compiled, and run in a sort of batch-oriented way. The original BASIC had only 14 different statement types and a single data type, floating-point. Because it was believed that few of the targeted users would appreciate the difference between integer and floating-point types, the type was referred to as "numbers." Overall, it was a very limited language, though quite easy to learn.

2.7.3   Evaluation

The most important aspect of the original BASIC was that it was the first widely used method of remote terminal access to a computer. Terminals had just begun to be available at that time. Before then, most programs were entered into computers through either punched cards or paper tape.

Much of the design of BASIC came from FORTRAN, with some minor influence from the syntax of ALGOL 60. Later it grew in a variety of ways, with little or no effort made to standardize it. The American National Standards Institute issued a Minimal BASIC standard (ANSI, 1978b), but this represented only the bare minimum of language features. In fact, the original BASIC was very similar to Minimal BASIC.

Although it may seem surprising, Digital Equipment Corporation used a rather elaborate version of BASIC named BASIC-PLUS to write significant portions of their largest operating system for the PDP-11 minicomputers, RSTS, in the 1970s.

BASIC has been criticized for the poor structure of programs written in it, among other things. By our evaluation criteria, the language does indeed fare very poorly. Clearly it was not meant for and should not be used for serious programs of any significant size.

The most probable reasons for BASIC's success are the ease with which it can be learned and the ease with which it can be implemented, even on very small computers. The ancestry of BASIC is shown in Figure 2.5.

Figure 2.5
Genealogy of BASIC

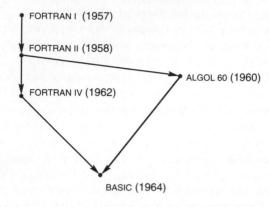

2.8   Everything for Everybody: PL/I

PL/I represents the first large-scale attempt to design a language that could be used for a broad spectrum of application areas. All previous and most subsequent languages have focused on one particular application area, such as science, artificial intelligence, or business.

2.8.1   Historical Background

Like FORTRAN, PL/I was developed as an IBM product. By the early 1960s, the users of computers in industry had settled into two separate and quite different camps. From the IBM point of view, scientific programmers could use either the large-scale 7090 or the small-scale 1620 IBM computers. This group used the floating-point data type and arrays extensively. FORTRAN was the primary language, although some assembly language was also used. They had their own user group, SHARE, and had little contact with anyone who worked on business applications.

For business applications, people used the large 7080 or the small 1401 IBM computers. They needed the decimal data type as well as elaborate and efficient input and output facilities. They used the COBOL language, although in early 1963, where the PL/I story begins, the conversion from assembly language to COBOL was only beginning. This category of users also had its own user group, GUIDE, and seldom had contact with scientific users.

In early 1963, IBM planners perceived the beginnings of a change in this situation. The two widely separated groups were moving toward each other in ways that were thought certain to create problems. Scientists began to gather large files of data to be processed. This data required more sophisticated and more efficient input and output facilities. Business applications people began to do things such as regression analysis, which required floating-point data and arrays. It began to appear that computing facilities would soon require two separate computers, supporting two very different programming languages.

These perceptions quite naturally led to the concept of designing a single universal computer that would be capable of doing both floating-point and decimal arithmetic, and therefore both scientific and business applications. Thus was born the concept of the IBM System/360 line of computers. Along with this came the idea of a programming language that could be used just as easily for both business and scientific applications. For good measure, systems programming and list processing were thrown in as capabilities. Therefore, the new language was to replace FORTRAN, COBOL, LISP, and the systems applications of assembly language.

2.8.2   Design Process

The design effort began when IBM and SHARE formed the Advanced Language Development Committee of the SHARE FORTRAN Project in October 1963. This new committee quickly met and formed a subcommittee called the 3×3 Committee, so named because it had three members from IBM and three from SHARE. The 3×3 Committee met for three or four days every other week to design the language.

As with the Short Range Committee for COBOL, the initial design was scheduled for completion in a remarkably short time. Apparently, regardless of the scope of a language design effort, the prevailing belief was that it could be done in three months. The first version of PL/I, which was then named FORTRAN VI, was supposed to be completed by December, less than three months after the committee was formed. The committee actually pleaded successfully on two different occasions for extensions, moving the due date back to January and then to late February 1964.

The initial design concept was that the new language would be an extension of FORTRAN IV, maintaining compatibility, but that goal was dropped quickly along with the name FORTRAN VI. Until 1965, the language was known as NPL, an acronym for New Programming Language. The first published report on NPL was given at the SHARE meeting of March 1964. A more complete description followed in April, and the version that would actually be implemented was published in December 1964 (IBM, 1964) by the compiler group at the IBM Hursley Laboratory in England, whose members were chosen to do the implementation. In 1965, the name was changed to PL/I to avoid the confusion of the name NPL with the National Physical Laboratory in England. If the compiler had been developed outside the United Kingdom, the name might have remained NPL.

2.8.3 Language Overview

Perhaps the best single-sentence description of PL/I is that it included what were then considered the best parts of ALGOL 60 (recursion, block structure), FORTRAN IV (separate compilation with communication through global data), and COBOL 60 (data structures, input/output, and report-generating facilities), along with a few new constructs, all somehow blended together. We will not attempt, even in an abbreviated way, to discuss all the features of the language, or even its most controversial constructs. Instead, we will mention briefly some of the language's contributions to the pool of knowledge of programming languages.

PL/I was the first programming language to have the following facilities:

1. Programs were allowed to create concurrently executing tasks. Although this was a good idea, it was poorly developed in PL/I. For example, no effective means were included for the synchronization of concurrently executing tasks.

2. It was possible to detect and handle 23 different types of exceptions, or run-time errors. Unfortunately, the design was too complex to be either understood by programmers or easily implemented.

3. Procedures were allowed to be used recursively, but the capability could be disabled, allowing more efficient code for nonrecursive procedures.

4. Pointers were included as a data type, although they were not as safe to use as those in later languages.

5. Cross sections of arrays could be referenced. For example, the third row of a matrix could be referenced as if it were a vector.

2.8.4 Evaluation

Any evaluation of PL/I must begin by recognizing the ambitiousness of the design effort. In retrospect, it appears naive to think that so many constructs could have been combined successfully. However, that judgment must be tempered by acknowledging that there was little language design experience at the time. Overall, the design of PL/I was based on the premise that any construct that was useful and could be implemented should be included, with insufficient concern about how the many features would behave when thrown together. Edsgar Dijkstra, in his Turing Award Lecture (Dijkstra, 1972), made one of the strongest criticisms of the complexity of PL/I: "I absolutely fail to see how we can keep our growing programs firmly within our intellectual grip when by its sheer baroqueness the programming language—our basic tool, mind you!—already escapes our intellectual control."

In terms of usage, PL/I must be considered at least a partial success. It has seen significant use in both business and scientific applications. It has also been widely used as an instructional vehicle, primarily in several subset forms, such as PL/C (Cornell, 1977) and PL/CS (Conway and Constable, 1976).

The following is an example of a PL/I program:

```
/* PL/I PROGRAM EXAMPLE
   INPUT: AN INTEGER, LISTLEN, WHERE LISTLEN IS LESS THAN
          100, FOLLOWED BY LISTLEN-INTEGER VALUES
  OUTPUT: THE NUMBER OF INPUT VALUES THAT ARE GREATER THAN
          THE AVERAGE OF ALL INPUT VALUES        */
PLIEX: PROCEDURE OPTIONS (MAIN);
   DECLARE INTLIST (1:99) FIXED.
   DECLARE (LISTLEN, COUNTER, SUM, AVERAGE, RESULT) FIXED;
   SUM = 0;
   RESULT = 0;
   GET LIST (LISTLEN);
   IF (LISTLEN > 0) & (LISTLEN < 100) THEN
      DO;
/* READ INPUT DATA INTO AN ARRAY AND COMPUTE THE SUM */
      DO COUNTER = 1 TO LISTLEN;
         GET LIST (INTLIST (COUNTER));
         SUM = SUM + INTLIST (COUNTER);
         END;
/* COMPUTE THE AVERAGE */
         AVERAGE = SUM / LISTLEN;
/* COUNT THE NUMBER OF VALUES THAT ARE > AVERAGE */
         DO COUNTER = 1 TO LISTLEN;
            IF INTLIST (COUNTER) > AVERAGE THEN
               RESULT = RESULT + 1;
            END;
/* PRINT RESULT */
         PUT SKIP LIST ('THE NUMBER OF VALUES > AVERAGE IS:');
         PUT LIST (RESULT);
         END;
      ELSE
         PUT SKIP LIST ('ERROR--INPUT LISTLEN IS NOT LEGAL');
   END PLIEX;
```

The ancestry of PL/I is shown in Figure 2.6.

Figure 2.6
Genealogy of PL/I

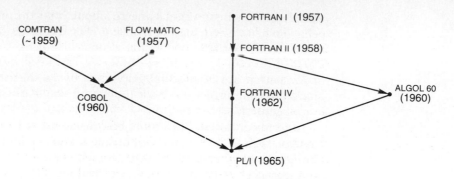

2.9 The Beginnings of Data Abstraction: SIMULA 67

Although SIMULA 67 never achieved widespread use and had little impact on the programmers and computing of its time, it is important for some of the concepts it introduced.

2.9.1 Design Process

Two Norwegians, Kristen Nygaard and Ole-Johan Dahl, developed the language SIMULA I during 1962–1964 at the Norwegian Computing Center (NCC). They were primarily interested in using computers for simulation and were also involved in operations research. SIMULA I was designed exclusively for system simulation and was first implemented by late 1964 on a UNIVAC 1107 computer.

As soon as the SIMULA I implementation was completed, Nygaard and Dahl began efforts to extend the language by adding entirely new features and modifying some existing constructs in order to make the language useful for more general-purpose applications.

The result of this continued effort was SIMULA 67, whose design was first presented publicly in March 1967 (Dahl and Nygaard, 1967). We will discuss only SIMULA 67, although some of the features of interest in SIMULA 67 are also in SIMULA I.

2.9.2 Language Overview

SIMULA 67 is an extension of ALGOL 60, taking both block structure and the control statement structure from that language. The primary deficiency of ALGOL 60 (and other languages at that time) for simulation applications is the design of its subprograms. Simulation requires subprograms that are allowed to restart at the position where they previously stopped. Subprograms with this kind of control are known as coroutines because the caller and called subprograms have a somewhat equal relationship with each other, rather than the rigid hierarchical relationship they have in ALGOL 60 and FORTRAN.

To provide the coroutine concept in SIMULA 67, the class construct was developed. This was a very important development because our ideas of data abstraction began with it. The basic idea of a class is that a data structure and the routines that manipulate that data structure are packaged together. Furthermore, a class definition is distinct from a class instance, so a program can create and use any number of instances of a particular class. Class instances can contain local data that are static, which means they are allocated at the time the instance is created. They can also include code that is executed at creation time, which can initialize some data structure of the class instance.

A more thorough discussion of classes and class instances is presented in Chapter 10. It is interesting to note that the important concept of data abstraction was not developed and attributed to the class construct until 1972, when Hoare (1972) recognized the connection.

The ancestry of SIMULA 67 is shown in Figure 2.7.

Figure 2.7
Genealogy of
SIMULA 67

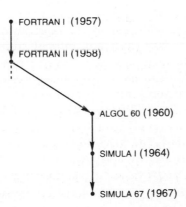

FORTRAN I (1957)

FORTRAN II (1958)

ALGOL 60 (1960)

SIMULA I (1964)

SIMULA 67 (1967)

2.10 Orthogonal Design: ALGOL 68

ALGOL 68 was the source of several new ideas in language design, some of which were subsequently adopted by other languages. We include it here for that reason, even though it never achieved widespread use in either Europe or the United States. Because some ALGOL 68 constructs are discussed in later chapters, we discuss in this chapter only two of its most important contributions.

2.10.1   Design Process

The development of the ALGOL family did not end when the revised report (Backus et al., 1962) appeared in 1962, although it was six years until the next design iteration was published. The resulting language, ALGOL 68 (van Wijngaarden et al., 1969), was dramatically different from its predecessor.

One of the most interesting innovations of ALGOL 68 is one of its primary design criteria: orthogonality. Recall our discussion of orthogonality in Chapter 1. The use of orthogonality results in several innovative features of ALGOL 68.

2.10.2   Language Overview

The following subsections describe two of the most significant innovations of ALGOL 68.

2.10.2.1   User-Defined Data Types

One important result of orthogonality in ALGOL 68 is its inclusion of user-defined data types. Earlier languages, such as FORTRAN, included only a few basic data structures. PL/I included a large number of data structures, which made it harder to learn and very difficult to implement, but it obviously could not provide an appropriate data structure for every application.

The approach of ALGOL 68 to data structures was to provide a few primitive types and structures but to allow the user to combine those primitives into a large number of different structures. This provision for user-defined data types was carried over to some extent into all of the major imperative languages designed since then: Pascal, C, Modula-2, and Ada. User-defined data types are valuable because they allow the user to design data abstractions that fit particular problems very closely. All aspects of data typing are discussed in Chapter 5.

2.10.2.2   Dynamic Arrays

As another first in the area of data types, ALGOL 68 introduced dynamic arrays. A dynamic array is one in which the declaration does not specify subscript bounds at all. Assignments to the dynamic array cause allocation of required storage. In ALGOL 68, dynamic arrays are called **flex** arrays. For example, the declaration

```
flex [1:0] int list
```

states that `list` is a dynamic array of integers with a single subscript whose lower bound is 1, but it allocates no storage. The aggregate assignment

```
list := (3, 5, 6, 2)
```

causes `list` to be allocated sufficient storage for four integers, effectively changing its bounds to [1:4].

2.10.3 Evaluation

ALGOL 68 is one of the most innovative of the imperative languages; it includes a significant number of features that had not been previously used. Its use of orthogonality, which some may argue was overdone, was nevertheless revolutionary. Many of the features that were introduced in ALGOL 68 became part of subsequent languages.

ALGOL 68 repeated one of the sins of ALGOL 60, however, and it was an important factor in its lack of widespread acceptance. The language was described using an elegant and concise but also unknown metalanguage. Before one could read the language-describing document (van Wijngaarden et al., 1969), he or she had to learn the new metalanguage, called van Wijngaarden grammars. To make matters worse, the designers invented a collection of words to explain the grammar and the language. For example, keywords are called indicants, substring extraction is called trimming, and the process of procedure execution is called a coercion of deproceduring, which might be meek, firm, or something else.

It is natural to contrast the design of PL/I with that of ALGOL 68. ALGOL 68 achieved complexity by the principle of orthogonality: a few primitive concepts and the unrestricted use of a few combining mechanisms. PL/I achieved complexity by simply including a large number of fixed constructs. ALGOL 68 extended the elegant simplicity of ALGOL 60, whereas PL/I simply added together the features of several languages to attain its goals. Of course, it must be kept in mind that the goal of PL/I was to provide a unified tool for a broad class of problems; ALGOL 68 was targeted to a single class: scientific applications.

PL/I achieved far greater acceptance than ALGOL 68, due largely to IBM's promotional efforts and the problems of understanding and implementing ALGOL 68. Implementation was a difficult problem for both, but PL/I had the resources of IBM to apply to constructing a compiler. ALGOL 68 enjoyed no such benefactor.

The ancestry of ALGOL 68 is shown in Figure 2.8.

2.11 Two Important Descendants of the ALGOLs: Pascal and C

All imperative languages designed since 1960 owe some of their design to ALGOL 60 and/or ALGOL 68. The most widely used of these are Pascal and C. The Ada language, discussed in Section 2.13, is a second-generation

Figure 2.8
Genealogy of ALGOL
68

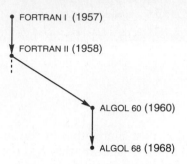

descendant of ALGOL 60, being based on Pascal. Neither Pascal nor C added important new features to the collective constructs of previous languages, but both have enjoyed wide popularity and thus deserve some attention in this chapter.

2.11.1   Simplicity by Design: Pascal

2.11.1.1   Historical Background

Niklaus Wirth was a member of the International Federation of Information Processing (IFIP) Working Group 2.1, which was created to continue the development of ALGOL in the mid-1960s. As a contribution to that effort, Wirth and C.A.R. Hoare in August 1965 presented to the group a somewhat modest proposal for additions and modifications to ALGOL 60 (Wirth and Hoare, 1966). The majority of the group rejected the proposal as being too small an advance over ALGOL 60. Instead, a much more complex proposed revision was developed, which eventually became ALGOL 68. Wirth, along with a few other group members, did not believe that the ALGOL 68 report should have been released, based on the complexity of both the language and the metalanguage used to describe it. This position later proved to have some validity because the ALGOL 68 documents, and therefore the language, were indeed found by the computing community to be very difficult to understand.

The modified version of ALGOL 60 proposed by Wirth and Hoare was implemented at Stanford University and named ALGOL-W. It was used primarily as an instructional vehicle at a few universities. The primary contributions of ALGOL-W were the value-result method of passing parameters and the **case** statement for multiple selection. The value-result method is another technique for implementing the two-way communication provided by ALGOL 60's pass-by-name method. Both methods are discussed in Chapter 8.

Wirth's next major design effort, again based on ALGOL 60, was his most successful: Pascal. The original published definition of Pascal appeared in 1971 (Wirth, 1971). This version was modified somewhat in the implementation process and is described in Wirth (1973). The features that are often ascribed to Pascal in fact came from earlier languages. For example, user-defined data types were introduced in ALGOL 68, the **case** statement in ALGOL-W, and Pascal's records are like the structured variables of COBOL and PL/I.

2.11.1.2   Evaluation

The largest impact of Pascal has been on the teaching of programming. In 1970, most students of computer science, engineering, and science were introduced to programming with FORTRAN, although some universities used PL/I, languages based on PL/I, and ALGOL-W. By the mid-1970s, Pascal had become the most widely used language for this purpose. This was quite natural, although perhaps not completely predictable, because Pascal had, in fact, been designed specifically for teaching programming.

Because Pascal was designed as a teaching language, it lacks several features that are essential for many kinds of applications. The best example of this is the impossibility of writing a subprogram that takes as a parameter an array of variable length. Another example is the lack of any separate compilation capability. These deficiencies naturally led to many nonstandard dialects.

Pascal's popularity, for both teaching programming and other applications, is based primarily on its remarkable combination of simplicity and expressivity. Although there are some insecurities in Pascal, as we discuss in later chapters, it is still a relatively safe language, particularly when compared with FORTRAN or PL/I.

The following is an example of a Pascal program:

```
{Pascal Example Program
   Input: An integer, listlen, where listlen is less
          than 100, followed by listlen-integer values
  Output: The number of input values that are greater
          than the average of all input values   }
program pasex (input, output);
   type intlisttype = array [1..99] of integer;
   var
     intlist : intlisttype;
     listlen, counter, sum, average, result : integer;
   begin
   result := 0;
   sum := 0;
   readln (listlen);
   if ((listlen > 0) and (listlen < 100)) then
     begin
{ Read input into an array and compute the sum }
     for counter := 1 to listlen do
       begin
       readln (intlist[counter]);
```

```
              sum := sum + intlist[counter]
            end;
        { Compute the average }
            average := sum div listlen;
        { Count the number of input values that are > average }
            for counter := 1 to listlen do
                if (intlist[counter] > average) then
                    result := result + 1;
        { Print the result }
            writeln ('The number of values that are > average is:',
                        result)
            end { of the then clause of if (( listlen > 0 ... }
        else
            writeln ('Error--input listlen is not legal')
        end.
```

The ancestry of Pascal is shown in Figure 2.9.

Figure 2.9
Genealogy of Pascal

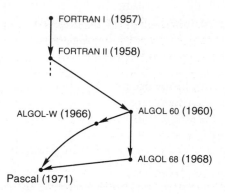

2.11.2   A Portable Systems Language: C

Like Pascal, C contributed little to the previously known collection of language features, but it has been very successful in terms of use. Although originally designed for systems programming, C is actually well suited for a wide variety of applications.

2.11.2.1   Historical Background

C's ancestors include CPL, BCPL, B, and ALGOL 68. CPL was developed at Cambridge University in the early 1960s. BCPL is a simple systems language developed by Martin Richards in 1967 (Richards, 1969).

The first work on the UNIX operating system was done in the late 1960s by Ken Thompson at Bell Laboratories. The first version was written in assembly language. The first high-level language implemented under UNIX was B, which was based on BCPL. B was designed and implemented by Thompson in 1970.

Neither BCPL nor B is a typed language, which is an oddity among high-level languages, although both are much lower level than a language such as Pascal. Being untyped means that all data are considered machine words, which, although extremely simple, leads to many complications. For example, there is the problem of specifying floating-point rather than integer arithmetic in an expression. In one implementation of BCPL, the operands of a floating-point operation were preceded by periods. Operands not preceded by periods were considered to be integers. An alternative to this would have been to use different symbols for the floating-point operations.

This problem, along with several others, led to the development of a new typed language based on B. Originally called NB but later named C, it was designed and implemented by Dennis Ritchie at Bell Laboratories in 1972 (Kernighan and Ritchie, 1978). In some cases through BCPL, and in other cases directly, C was influenced by ALGOL 68. This is seen in its **for** and **switch** statements, in its assigning operators, and in its treatment of pointers.

The only "standard" for C in its first decade and a half was the book by Kernighan and Ritchie (1978). Over that time span the language slowly evolved, with different implementors adding different features. Between 1982 and 1988, ANSI produced a new official description of C (ANSI, 1989), which included many of the features that implementors had already incorporated into the language.

A new version of C named C++ was developed in the middle and late 1980s (Ellis and Stroustrup, 1990). Its history and most significant features are briefly described in Section 2.15. Details of C++ support for data abstraction are discussed in Chapter 10. Details of C++ support for object-oriented programming are discussed in Chapter 15. The evolution of C++ is discussed in Section 2.15.

2.11.2.2 Evaluation

C has adequate control statements and data-structuring facilities to allow its use in many application areas. It also has a rich set of operators that allow a high degree of expressiveness.

One of the most important reasons why C is both liked and disliked is its lack of complete type checking. For example, functions can be written for which parameters are not type checked. Those who like C appreciate the flexibility; those who do not like it find it too insecure. A major reason for its great popularity is that it is part of the widely used UNIX operating system. This inclusion in UNIX provides an inexpensive (often free with UNIX) and quite uniform compiler that is available to programmers on many different kinds of computers.

The following is a C program example:

```
/* C Example Program
   Input: An integer, listlen, where listlen is less than
          100, followed by listlen-integer values
  Output: The number of input values that are greater than
          the average of all input values   */
main ()
  {
  int intlist[98], listlen, counter, sum, average, result;
  sum = 0;
  result = 0;
  scanf ("%d", &listlen);
  if ((listlen > 0) && (listlen < 100))
    {
/* Read input into an array and compute the sum */
    for (counter = 0; counter < listlen; counter ++)
      {
      scanf ("%d", intlist[counter]);
      sum = sum + intlist[counter];
      }
/* Compute the average */
    average = sum / listlen;
/* Count the input values that are > average */
    for (counter = 0; counter < listlen; counter ++)
      if (intlist[counter] > average) result ++;
/* Print result */
    printf ("Number of values > average is:%d\n", result);
    }
  else
    printf ("Error--input listlen is not legal\n");
}
```

The ancestry of C is shown in Figure 2.10.

2.12 Programming Based on Logic: Prolog

Simply put, **logic programming** is the use of a formal logic notation to communicate some computational process to a computer. Predicate calculus is the notation used in current logic programming languages.

Programming in logic programming languages is nonprocedural. Programs in such languages do not state exactly *how* a result is to be computed, but rather describe the form of the result. What is needed to provide this capability for logic programming languages is a concise means of supplying the computer with both the relevant information and a method of inference for computing desirable results. Predicate calculus supplies the basic form of communication to the computer, and the proof method named resolution, developed first by Robinson (1965), supplies the inference technique.

2.12.1 Design Process

During the very early 1970s, Alain Colmerauer and Phillippe Roussel of the Artificial Intelligence Group at the University of Aix-Marseille, together with Robert Kowalski of the Department of Artificial Intelligence at the University of Edinburgh, developed the fundamental design of Prolog, which amounts to a syntax for predicate calculus propositions and an implementation of a restricted form of resolution. The first Prolog interpreter was developed at Marseille in 1972. The version of the language that was implemented is described in Roussel (1975). The name Prolog is from *programming logic.

2.12.2 Language Overview

Prolog programs consist of collections of statements. Prolog has only a few kinds of statements, but they can become complex.

One common use of Prolog is as a kind of intelligent database. This application provides a simple framework for discussing the Prolog language.

The database of a Prolog program consists of two kinds of statements, facts and rules. An example of a fact statement is

```
mother (joanne, jake).
```

Figure 2.10
Genealogy of C

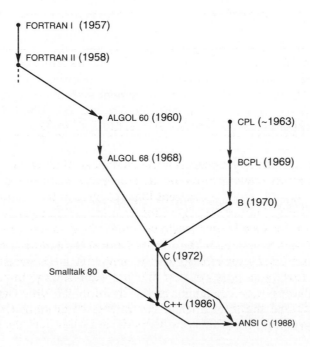

which states that joanne is the mother of jake.

An example of a rule statement is

```
grandparent (X, Z) :- parent (X, Y), parent (Y, Z).
```

which states that it can be deduced that X is the grandparent of Z if it is true that X is the parent of Y and Y is the parent of Z, for some specific values for the variables X, Y, and Z.

The Prolog database can be interactively queried with goal statements, an example of which is

```
father (bob, darcie).
```

which asks if bob is the father of darcie. When such a query, or goal, is presented to the Prolog system, it uses its resolution process, which is called unification, to attempt to determine the truth of the statement. If it can conclude that the goal is true, it displays "true." If it cannot prove it, it displays "false."

2.12.3 Evaluation

There is a relatively small group of computer scientists who believe that logic programming provides the best hope for escape from the imperative languages, and also from the enormous problem of producing the large amount of reliable software that is currently needed. So far, however, there are two major reasons why logic programming has not become more widely used. First, as with some other nonimperative approaches, logic programming thus far has proven to be highly inefficient. Second, it has been shown to be an effective method for only a few relatively small areas of application: certain kinds of database management systems and some areas of AI.

Logic programming and Prolog are described in greater detail in Chapter 14.

2.13 History's Largest Design Effort: Ada

The Ada language is the result of the most extensive and most expensive language design effort ever launched. It is the most recently designed imperative language that is likely to have a large impact on the language landscape. The Ada language was developed for the Department of Defense (DoD), so the state of their computing environment was instrumental in determining its form.

2.13.1 Historical Background

By 1974, over half of the applications of computers in DoD were embedded systems. An embedded system is one in which the computer hardware is embedded in the device it controls or for which it provides services. Software costs were rising rapidly, primarily because of the increasing complexity of systems. More than 450 different programming languages were in use for DoD projects, and none of them was standardized by DoD. Every defense contractor could define a new and different language for every contract. Because of this language proliferation, application software was rarely reused. Furthermore, no software development tools were created (because they are usually language dependent). A great many languages were in use, but none was actually suitable for embedded systems applications. For these reasons, the Army, Navy, and Air Force each independently proposed in 1974 the development of a high-level language for embedded systems.

2.13.2 Design Process

Noting this widespread interest, Malcolm Currie, Director of Defense Research and Engineering, in January 1975 formed the High-Order Language Working Group (HOLWG), initially headed by Lt. Col. William Whitaker of the Air Force. The HOLWG had representatives from all of the military services and liaisons with England, France, and West Germany. Its initial charter was to

1. Identify the requirements for a new DoD high-level language.
2. Evaluate existing languages to determine whether there was a viable candidate.
3. Recommend adoption or implementation of a minimal set of programming languages.

In April 1975, the HOLWG produced the Strawman requirements document for the new language (Department of Defense, 1975a). This was distributed to military branches, federal agencies, selected industrial and university representatives, and interested parties in Europe.

The Strawman document was followed by Woodenman (Department of Defense, 1975b) in August 1975 and Tinman (Department of Defense, 1976) in January 1976. The Tinman document was considered a complete set of requirements for a language with the desired characteristics. The principal author of these documents was David Fisher of the Institute for Defense Analysis. The group of participants in the effort was large, numbering over 200, with representatives from over 40 organizations outside DoD. In January 1977, the Tinman document was replaced by the Ironman requirements document (Department of Defense, 1977), which was nearly equivalent in content but had a somewhat different format.

While the requirements documents were being developed, a parallel effort was under way to evaluate existing languages in terms of the requirements. The report on this work was released in January 1977 (Amoroso et al., 1977). It contained 2800 pages of comments on the 26 languages that had been studied. The conclusions of the report were that no existing language met the requirements but that a single language for all embedded systems applications was both possible and desirable. The report suggested that the new language be based on Pascal, ALGOL, or PL/I.

In April 1977, the Ironman document was used as the basis for an unrestricted request for proposals, which was then made public, thereby making Ada the first language to be designed by competitive contract. In July 1977, four of the proposing contractors—Softech, SRI International, Cii Honeywell/Bull, and Intermetrics—were chosen to produce, independently and in parallel, Phase 1 of the language design. All four of the resulting design proposals were based on Pascal.

When the six-month Phase 1 was completed in February 1978, there was a two-month evaluation by 400 volunteers in 80 review teams scattered around the world. The result of this evaluation was that two finalists— Intermetrics and Cii Honeywell/Bull—were chosen to go on to Phase 2 of the development.

In June 1978, the next iteration of the requirements document, Steelman, was released (Department of Defense, 1978).

At the end of Phase 2, another two-month evaluation was done, and in May 1979 the Cii Honeywell/Bull language design was chosen as the winner. Interestingly, the winner was the only foreign competitor among the final four. The Cii Honeywell/Bull design team was led by Jean Ichbiah.

In the spring of 1979, Jack Cooper of the Navy Material Command recommended the name for the new language, Ada, which was then adopted. Augusta Ada Byron (1815–1851), Countess of Lovelace, mathematician and daughter of poet Lord Byron, is generally recognized as being the world's first programmer. She worked with Charles Babbage on his first mechanical computers, the Difference and Analytical Engines, writing programs for several numerical processes.

Phase 3 of the Ada design project began with the selection of the winning design. The design and the rationale for it were published by ACM in its *SIGPLAN Notices* (ACM, 1979) and distributed to a readership of over 10,000 people. A public test and evaluation conference was held in October 1979 in Boston, with representatives from over 100 organizations from the United States and Europe. By November, more than 500 language reports had been received from 15 different countries. Most of the reports suggested small modifications rather than drastic changes and outright rejections. Based on the language reports, the next version of the requirements specification, the Stoneman document (Department of Defense, 1980a), was released in February 1980.

A revised version of the language design was completed in July 1980 and was accepted as MIL-STD 1815, the standard *Ada Language Reference Manual*. The number 1815 was chosen because it was the year of the birth of Augusta Ada Lovelace. Another revised version of the *Ada Language Reference Manual* was released in July 1982. In 1983, the American National Standards Institute standardized Ada. This "final" official version is described by Goos and Hartmanis (1983). The Ada language design was then frozen for at least five years. There is currently under way a large project, named Ada 9X, to revise Ada. One of the focal points of this effort is the tasking model of the language.

2.13.3 Language Overview

This section briefly describes four of the major features of the Ada language. Because we use the language as a major source throughout the remainder of the book, other features will be described along the way.

Packages in the Ada language provide the means for encapsulating specifications for data types, data objects, and procedures. This, in turn, provides the support for the use of data abstraction in program design, as described in Chapter 10.

The Ada language includes excellent facilities for exception handling, which allows the programmer to gain control after a wide variety of exceptions, or run-time errors, have been detected. There is, thus, a good deal of flexibility in handling possible errors. Exception handling is discussed in Chapter 12.

Program units can be generic in Ada. For example, it is possible to write a sort procedure that uses an unspecified type for the data to be sorted. Such a generic procedure must be instantiated for a specified type before it can be used. This is done with a statement that causes the compiler to generate a version of the procedure with the given type. The availability of such generic units increases the range of program units that might be reused, rather than duplicated, by programmers. Generics are discussed in Chapters 8 and 10.

The Ada language also provides for concurrent execution of special program units, named tasks, using the rendezvous mechanism. Rendezvous is the name of a method of intertask communication and synchronization. Concurrency is discussed in Chapter 11.

2.13.4 Evaluation

Perhaps the most important aspects of the design of the Ada language to consider are the following:

1. Because the design was competitive, there was no limit on participation.
2. The Ada language embodies most of the concepts of software engineering and language design of the late 1970s. Although one can

question the actual methods used to include these features, as well as the wisdom of including such a large number of features in a language, most agree that the features are valuable.

3. Although many contractors did not initially realize it, the development of a compiler for the Ada language is an extremely difficult task. Only in 1985, almost four years after the language design was completed, did truly usable Ada compilers begin to appear. Not only is the sheer size of the language a burden on the compiler writer, but also such features as generic units and tasking pose problems that are not amenable to quick or easy solutions.

It is still too early to assess the value or impact of the Ada language. It has certainly been controversial—and was so even before any compilers existed to provide a base of experience. The most serious criticism is that it is too large and too complex. In particular, Hoare has stated that it should not be used for any application where reliability is critical (Hoare, 1981), which is precisely the type of applications for which it was designed. On the other hand, others have praised it as the epitome of language design.

Largely because of the length of Ada's definition (331 pages) and its inherent complexity, a subculture of computer scientists has appeared whose chosen occupation is the interpretation of the Ada definition. These people, in the tradition of ALGOL 60, are called Ada lawyers.

The following is an Ada example program:

```
-- Ada Example Program
--   Input: An integer, LIST_LEN, where LIST_LEN is less
--          than 100, followed by LIST_LEN-integer values
-- Output: The number of input values that are greater than
--          the average of all input values
with TEXT_IO;   use TEXT_IO;
procedure ADA_EX is
  package INT_IO is new INTEGER_IO (INTEGER);
  use INT_IO;
  type INT_LIST_TYPE is array (1..99) of INTEGER;
  INT_LIST : INT_LIST_TYPE;
  LIST_LEN, SUM, AVERAGE, RESULT : INTEGER;
  begin
  RESULT := 0;
  SUM := 0;
  GET (LIST_LEN);
  if (LIST_LEN > 0) and (LIST_LEN < 100) then
-- Read input data into an array and compute the sum
    for COUNTER := 1 .. LIST_LEN loop
      GET (INT_LIST(COUNTER));
      SUM := SUM + INT_LIST(COUNTER);
    end loop;
-- Compute the average
    AVERAGE := SUM / LIST_LEN;
```

```
    -- Count the number of values that are > average
       for COUNTER := 1 .. LIST_LEN loop
         if INT_LIST(COUNTER) > AVERAGE then
           RESULT := RESULT + 1;
         end if;
       end loop;
    -- Print result
       PUT ("The number of values > average is:");
       PUT (RESULT);
       NEW_LINE;
     else
       PUT_LINE ("Error--input LIST_LEN is not legal");
     end if;
     end ADA_EX;
```

The ancestry of Ada is shown in Figure 2.11.

Figure 2.11
Genealogy of Ada

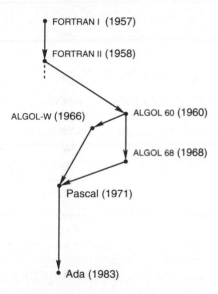

2.14 **Object-Oriented Programming: Smalltalk**

As discussed in Chapter 1, object-oriented programming includes data abstraction as one of its three fundamental characteristics, the other two being inheritance and dynamic type binding.

Inheritance appeared in a limited form in SIMULA 67, whose classes can be defined in hierarchies. Inheritance provides an effective method of code reuse.

Dynamic type binding allows abstract data types to be truly generic. This is one of the key positive features of object-oriented programming.

The unit control concept of object-oriented programming is loosely modeled on the idea that programs simulate the real world. This concept grew from the origins of SIMULA 67, which was designed for simulation applications. Because much of the real world is populated by objects, a simulation of such a world must include simulated objects. In fact, a language based on the concepts of real-world simulation need only include a model of objects that can send and receive messages and react to the messages it receives.

The essence of object-oriented programming is solving problems by identifying the real-world objects of the problem and the processing required of those objects, and then creating simulations of those objects, their processes, and the required communications between the objects. Abstract data types, dynamic type binding, and inheritance are the concepts that make object-oriented problem solving not only possible but also convenient and effective.

2.14.1 Design Process

The concepts that led to the development of Smalltalk originated in the Ph.D. dissertation work of Alan Kay in the late 1960s at the University of Utah (Kay, 1969). Kay had remarkable foresight in predicting the future availability of very powerful desktop computers. Recall that the first microcomputer systems were not marketed until the mid-1970s, and they were only distantly related to the machines envisioned by Kay, which were seen to execute a million or more instructions per second and contain several megabytes of memory.

Kay believed that such computers would be used by nonprogrammers and thus would need very powerful human interfacing capabilities. The computers of the late 1960s were largely batch oriented, and were used exclusively by professional programmers and scientists. For use by nonprogrammers, Kay determined, a computer would have to be highly interactive and use sophisticated graphics in its interface to users. Some of the graphics concepts came from the LOGO experience of Seymour Papert, in which graphics was used to aid children in the use of computers (Papert, 1980).

The original Kay concept was a system he called Dynabook, which was meant to be a general information processor. It was based in part on the Flex language, which he had helped design. Flex was based primarily on SIMULA 67. Dynabook was based on the paradigm of the typical desk, on which there are typically a number of papers, some partially covered. The top sheet is often the focus of attention, with the others temporarily out of focus. The display of Dynabook would model this scene, using the concept of screen windows. The user would interact with such a display both through a keyboard and by touching the screen with his or her fingers. After the preliminary design of Dynabook earned him a Ph.D., Kay's goal became to see such a machine constructed.

Kay found his way to the Xerox Palo Alto Research Center (Xerox PARC) and presented his ideas on Dynabook. This led to his employment there and the subsequent birth of the Learning Research Group at Xerox. The first charge of the group was to design a language to support Kay's programming paradigm and implement it on the best personal computer then available. These efforts resulted in an "Interim" Dynabook, consisting of the Xerox Alto hardware and the Smalltalk-72 software. Together, they formed a research tool for further development. A number of research projects were conducted with this system, including several experiments to teach programming to children. Along with the experiments came further developments, leading to Smalltalk-74, Smalltalk-76, Smalltalk-78, and eventually Smalltalk-80, which is the version discussed in this book. As the language grew, so did the power of the hardware on which it resided. By 1980, both the language and the Xerox hardware nearly matched the early vision of Alan Kay.

2.14.2 Language Overview

The program units of Smalltalk are objects. Objects are structures that encapsulate local data and a collection of operations called methods that is available to other objects. A method specifies the reaction of the object when it receives the particular message that corresponds to that method. The Smalltalk world is populated by nothing but objects, from integer constants to large complex software systems.

All computing in Smalltalk is done by the same uniform technique: sending a message to an object to invoke one of its methods. A reply to a message is an object, which returns the requested information, or simply notifies the sender that the requested processing has been completed. The fundamental difference between a message and a subprogram call is this: A message is sent to a data object, which then is processed by code associated with the object; a subprogram call usually sends the data to be processed to a subprogram code unit.

From the simulation point of view, which is never far away, Smalltalk is a simulation of a collection of computers (objects) that communicate with each other (through messages). Each object is an abstraction of a computer in the sense that it stores data and provides processing capability for manipulating that data. In addition, objects can send and receive messages. In essence, those are the fundamental capabilities of computers: to store and manipulate data and to communicate.

In Smalltalk, object abstractions are **classes**, which are very similar to the classes of SIMULA 67. Instances of the class can be created and are then the objects of the program. Each object has its own local data and represents a different instance of its class. The only difference between two objects of the same class is the state of their local variables.

As in SIMULA 67, class hierarchies can be formed in Smalltalk. Subclasses of a given class are refinements of it, inheriting the functionality and local variables of the parent class, or superclass. Subclasses can add new local memory and functionality and can modify or hide inherited functionality.

As briefly discussed in Chapter 1, Smalltalk is not just a language, it is also a complete software development environment. The interface to the environment is highly graphical, making heavy use of multiple overlaid windows and pop-up menus, and using a mouse pointing device and a high-resolution, bit-mapped monitor.

2.14.3   Evaluation

Smalltalk has done a great deal to promote two separate aspects of computing. The windowing systems that are now becoming the dominant method of user interfaces to software systems all grew out of Smalltalk. The most significant changes now taking place in program design methodologies and in programming languages fall under the object-oriented heading. Although the origin of some of the ideas of object-oriented languages came from SIMULA 67, they reached maturation only in Smalltalk. While Smalltalk may never achieve widespread use, its effect on the computing world may be long-lived.

The following is an example of a Smalltalk class definition:

```
"Smalltalk Example Program"
"The following is a class definition, instantiations
 of which can draw equilateral polygons of any number
 of sides"
class name                      Polygon
superclass                      Object
instance variable names         ourPen
                                numSides
                                sideLength
"Class methods"
 "Create an instance"
 new
      ^ super new getPen

 "Get a pen for drawing polygons"
 getPen
     ourPen <- Pen new

 "Instance methods"
 "Draw a polygon"
 draw
     numSides timesRepeat: [ourPen go: sideLength;
                                turn: 360 // numSides]

 "Set length of sides"
 length: len
     sideLength <- len
```

```
"Set number of sides"
sides: num
    numSides <- num
```

The ancestry of Smalltalk is shown in Figure 2.12.

Figure 2.12
Genealogy of Smallt

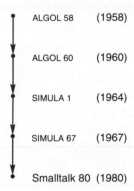

ALGOL 58   (1958)

ALGOL 60   (1960)

SIMULA 1   (1964)

SIMULA 67   (1967)

Smalltalk 80 (1980)

2.15 Combining Imperative and Object-Oriented Features: C++

The origins of C were discussed in Section 2.11; the origins of Smalltalk were discussed in Section 2.14. C++ builds language facilities on top of C to provide much of what Smalltalk pioneered. It is probable that C++ will eventually replace C in most if not all of its applications. C++ has evolved from C through a sequence of modifications to improve its imperative features and additions to support object-oriented programming.

2.15.1 Design Process

The first step from C toward C++ was made by Bjarne Stroustrup at Bell Laboratories in 1980. Modifications included the addition of function parameter type checking and conversion and, more significantly, classes, which are related to those of SIMULA 67 and Smalltalk. The resulting language was called "C with Classes" and is described in Stroustrup (1983). In 1983/84, the class feature of this language was extensively modified, with the resulting language being named C++. (Recall that ++ is C's increment operator.) These modifications added virtual functions, which support inheritance, and operator overloading. This first version of C++ is described in Stroustrup (1984). The evolution of C++ continued during 1984–85, and the first widely available implementation appeared in 1985. This implemented version is described in Stroustrup (1986). Between 1985 and 1990, C++ continued to evolve, based largely on user reaction to the first distributed implementation. Added during those five years were support for multiple inheritance (classes with more than one parent class) and abstract classes, along with some other enhancements. This version of the language is described in Ellis and Stroustrup (1990) and Stroustrup (1991). At the time of this writing, several other additions were being considered; among these are exception handling and parameterized types.

2.15.2   Language Overview

Because much of C++ is the same as ANSI C, only a few of the additional features of C++ will be mentioned here.

The most essential part of support for object-oriented programming is the class/object mechanism, which originated in SIMULA 67 and is the central feature of Smalltalk. C++ provides a collection of predefined classes, along with the capability of user-defined classes. The classes of C++ are data types, which, like Smalltalk classes, can be instantiated any number of times. Such instantiations in C++ are merely object, or data, declarations. Class definitions specify data objects (called data members) and functions (called member functions). Classes can name one or more parent classes, providing inheritance and multiple inheritance, respectively. Classes inherit the data members and member functions of the parent class that are specified to be inheritable.

Operators in C++ can be overloaded, meaning the user can create operators for existing operators on user-defined types. C++ functions can also be overloaded, meaning the user can define more than one function with the same name, provided either the numbers or types of their parameters are different.

Dynamic type binding in C++ is provided by virtual class functions. These functions define type-dependent operations, using overloaded functions, within a collection of classes that are related through inheritance. A pointer to an object of class A can also point to objects of classes that inherit class A. When this pointer points at an overloaded virtual function, the function of the current type is chosen dynamically.

2.15.3   Evaluation

C++ has an excellent chance to become a very popular language. Its evolution has taken place in an orderly way. There are good compilers available for it, the most important of which may be Turbo C++. This one is important because it is an inexpensive but high quality compiler/environment. Furthermore, it runs on the most common computers in the world, the IBM PC/XT/AT microcomputers and their clones.

Another factor in favor of the future popularity of C++ is that it is almost completely downward compatible with C (meaning that C programs can be, for the most part, compiled as C++ programs), and in most implementations it is possible to link C++ code with C code. This will allow it to replace C, which is currently a very popular language. Finally, there is currently intense interest in object-oriented programming. It now appears that C++ will be the vehicle by which most programmers will begin using object-oriented programming methodology.

The object-oriented features of C++ are described in far more detail in Chapter 15.

SUMMARY

We have investigated the development and development environments of a number of the most important programming languages. This chapter should have given the reader a good perspective on current issues in language design. We hope we have set the stage for an in-depth discussion of the important features of contemporary languages.

Chapters 13, 14, and 15 describe three different programming paradigms and several languages that were designed to support those paradigms.

BIBLIOGRAPHIC NOTES

Perhaps the most important source of historical information about the development of programming languages is *History of Programming Languages*, edited by Richard Wexelblat (Wexelblat, 1981). It contains the developmental background and environment of each of 13 important programming languages, as told by the designers themselves.

The paper "Early Development of Programming Languages" (Knuth and Pardo, 1977), which is part of the *Encyclopedia of Computer Science and Technology*, is an excellent 85-page work that provides a large amount of detail about the development of languages up to and including FORTRAN. The paper includes example programs to demonstrate the features of many of those languages.

Another book of great historical interest is *Programming Languages: History and Fundamentals*, by Jean Sammet (Sammet, 1969). It is a 785-page work filled with details of 80 programming languages of the 1950s and 1960s. Sammet has also published several updates to her book, such as Sammet (1976).

PROBLEM SET

1. What features of Plankalkül do you think would have had the greatest influence on FORTRAN 0 if the FORTRAN designers had been familiar with Plankalkül?

2. Determine the capabilities of Backus's 701 Speedcoding system, and compare them with those of a contemporary programmable hand calculator.

3. Write a short history of the A-0, A-1, and A-2 systems designed by Grace Hopper and her associates. (This will require some library research.)

4. Which class of languages found in every operating system is implemented as a pseudocode?

5. As a research project, compare the facilities of FORTRAN 0 with those of the Laning and Zierler system.

6. What argument would you make to support the removal from FORTRAN 0 of the DO statement form that allowed the loop body to be elsewhere?

7. Which of the three original goals of the ALGOL design committee, in your opinion, was most difficult to achieve at that time?

8. Choose one of three languages—MAD, NELIAC, or JOVIAL—and compare it feature by feature with ALGOL 58.

9. Make an educated guess of the most common syntax error in LISP programs.

10. LISP began as a pure functional language but gradually acquired more and more imperative features. Why?

11. Describe in detail the three most important reasons, in your opinion, why ALGOL 60 did not become a very widely used language.

12. Why, in your opinion, did COBOL allow long identifiers when FORTRAN and ALGOL did not?

13. What is the primary reason you have heard why computer scientists seldom use BASIC?

14. Outline the major motivation of IBM in developing PL/I.

15. Was IBM's major motivation for developing PL/I correct, given the history of computers and language developments since 1964?

16. Describe, in your own words, the concept of orthogonality in programming language design.

17. What is the primary reason, in your opinion, why PL/I became more widely used than ALGOL 68?

18. Describe the connection between the development of ALGOL 68 and Pascal.

19. What are the arguments both for and against the idea of a typeless language?

20. Are there any logic programming languages, other than Prolog?

21. What do the Ada and COBOL languages have in common?

22. What is your opinion of the argument that languages that are too complex are too dangerous to use and we should therefore keep all languages very small and simple?

23. Do you think language design by committee is a good idea? Support your opinion.

24. Languages continually evolve. What sort of restrictions do you think are appropriate for changes in programming languages? Compare your answers with the evolution of FORTRAN.

25. Build a table identifying all of the major language developments, together with when they occurred, in what language they first appeared, and the identities of the developers.

3

Describing Syntax and Semantics

Grace M. Hopper

Grace M. Hopper, a Naval officer and formerly employed by UNIVAC, designed a series of "compiler" systems in the early to mid-1950s that were used for business applications programming. By 1958, these systems evolved to the first high-level programming language for business applications, FLOW-MATIC, on which COBOL was, to a large degree, based. She was also involved with the COBOL design effort, serving as an advisor to the executive committee of CODASYL.

Key Concepts

- Syntax versus semantics
- Recognition and generation devices
- Backus-Naur form
- Syntax abstractions
- Rules
- Derivations
- Parse trees
- Ambiguity

- Operator precedence and associativity
- Extended BNF
- Syntax graphs
- Operational semantics
- Axiomatic semantics
- Weakest preconditions
- Denotational semantics
- Attribute grammars

The study of programming languages, like the study of natural languages, can be divided into examinations of syntax and semantics. The primary formal methods of describing the syntax of programming languages are context-free grammars—a formalism that is also known as Backus-Naur form—and syntax graphs. For semantics specification, the most common formal techniques are the operational, axiomatic, and denotational methods. Because of the inherent complexity of the semantics description methods, our discussion of them will be brief. Many books have been devoted to just a single one of the three methods.

The chapter also includes a section on attribute grammars, which can describe both the syntax and some aspects of the semantics—called the static semantics—of programming languages.

3.1 Introduction

The task of providing a concise yet understandable description of a programming language is difficult but essential to the language's success. ALGOL 60 and ALGOL 68 were first presented using concise descriptions; in both cases, however, the descriptions were not readily understandable, partly because each used a new notation. The levels of acceptance of both languages suffered as a result.

One of the problems in describing a language is the diversity of the people who must understand those descriptions. Most new programming languages are subjected to a period of public scrutiny before their designs are completed. The success of this feedback cycle depends heavily on the clarity of the description.

Programming language implementors obviously must be able to determine how the expressions, statements, and program units of a language are formed, and also their intended effect when executed. The difficulty of the job of implementors is in part determined by the clarity and complexity of the language description.

Finally, language users must be able to determine how to encode software systems by referring to a language reference manual. Textbooks and courses enter into this process, but language manuals are usually the only authoritative printed information source about a language.

The **syntax** of a programming language is the form of its expressions, statements, and program units. Its **semantics** is the meaning of those expressions, statements, and program units. For example, the syntax of a Pascal **if-then** statement is

> **if** <logic_expr> **then** <statement>

The semantics of this statement form is that if the current value of the logic expression is true, the embedded statement is selected for execution.

Although they are often separated for discussion purposes, syntax and semantics are closely related. In a well-designed programming language, semantics should follow directly from syntax; that is, the form of a statement should strongly suggest what the statement is meant to accomplish.

Describing syntax is easier than describing semantics, partly because a concise and universally accepted notation is available for syntax description, but none has yet been invented for semantics.

3.2 The General Problem of Describing Syntax

Languages, whether natural (such as English) or artificial (such as Ada), are sets of strings of characters from some alphabet. The strings of a language are called sentences or statements. The syntax rules of a language specify which strings of characters from the language's alphabet are in the language. English, for example, has a large and complex collection of rules for specifying the syntax of its sentences. By comparison, even the largest and most complex programming languages are syntactically very simple.

Language syntax descriptions, for simplicity's sake, often do not include descriptions of the lowest level language units. These small syntactic units are called **lexemes.** The description of lexemes can be given by a lexical specification, which can be separate from the syntactic description of the language. The lexemes of a programming language include its identifiers, constants, operators, and special words. One can think of programs as strings of lexemes rather than of characters.

A **token** of a language is a category of its lexemes. For example, identifier is a token in Pascal that can have lexemes, or instances, such as sum and total. In some cases lexemes and tokens are the same. For example, the arithmetic operator symbols of a programming language are both lexemes and tokens.

The example language descriptions in this chapter are very simple, and most include lexeme descriptions.

3.2.1 Language Recognizers

Languages can be formally defined in two distinct ways: by **recognition** and by **generation.** Suppose we have a language L that uses the alphabet A of characters. To formally define L using the recognition method, we would need to construct a mechanism R, called a recognition device, capable of inputting strings of characters from the alphabet A. R would need to be designed so that it indicated that a given input string was or was not in L. In effect, R would either accept or reject the given string. Such devices are like filters, separating correct sentences from those that are incorrectly formed. If R, when fed all possible strings of characters from A, accepts exactly those that are in L, then R is a description of L. Because most useful languages are, for all practical purposes, infinite, this might seem like a lengthy and ineffective process. Recognition devices, however, are not used to enumerate all of the sentences of a language.

The syntax analysis part of a compiler is a recognizer for the language the compiler translates. In this role, the recognizer need not test all possible strings of characters from some set to determine whether each is in the language. Rather, it need only determine whether given programs are in the language. In effect then, the syntax analyzer determines whether the given programs are syntactically correct.

3.2.2 Language Generators

A language generator is a device that can be used to generate the sentences of a language. One can think of the generator, or generation device, as having a button that, when pushed, produces a sentence of the language. Because it is unclear which sentence will be produced by a generator when its button is pushed, a generator seems to be a device of limited usefulness as a language descriptor. However, for people, certain forms of generators are better than recognizers because they are more easily read and understood. By contrast, the syntax-checking portion of a compiler is not as useful a language description for a programmer because it can only be used in trial-and-error mode. For example, to determine the correct syntax of a particular statement using a compiler, one can only submit a guessed-at version and see if the compiler accepts it.

There is a close connection between formal generation and recognition devices for the same language. This was one of the seminal discoveries in computer science, and it led to much of what is now known about formal languages and compiler design theory. We return to the relationship of generators and recognizers in the next section.

3.3 Formal Methods of Describing Syntax

This section discusses the formal language generation methods that are commonly used to describe the syntax of programming languages.

3.3.1 Backus-Naur Form and Context-Free Grammars

In the middle to late 1950s, two men, John Backus and Noam Chomsky, in unrelated research efforts, invented the same notation, which has since become the most widely used method for formally describing programming language syntax.

3.3.1.1 Chomsky's Hierarchy

In the mid-1950s, Chomsky, a noted linguist, described generative devices that define four classes of languages (Chomsky, 1956, 1959). These four language classes are called recursively enumerable, context-sensitive, context-free, and regular. Regular is the smallest class, and each successively larger class completely contains the smaller ones. It was discovered later that the languages of tokens of programming languages are in the class of regular languages. Also, programming languages are nearly completely contained in the class of context-free languages. Because Chomsky was a linguist, his primary interest was the theoretical nature of natural languages. He had no interest at the time in the artificial languages used to communicate with computers. Chomsky's hierarchy of language classes are shown graphically in Figure 3.1.

3.3.1.2 Origins of Backus-Naur Form

Shortly after Chomsky's work on language classes, the ACM-GAMM group began designing ALGOL 58. A landmark paper describing ALGOL 58 was presented by Backus, a prominent member of the ACM GAMM group, at an international conference in 1959 (Backus, 1959). This paper introduced a new formal notation for specifying programming language syntax. The new notation was later modified slightly by Peter Naur for the description of ALGOL 60 (Naur, 1960). This revised method of syntax description became known as the Backus-Naur form, or simply BNF.

BNF is a very natural notation for describing syntax. In fact, something similar to BNF was used to describe the syntax of Sanskrit by Panini several hundred years before Christ (Ingerman, 1967).

Although the use of BNF in the ALGOL 60 report was not readily accepted by computer users, it soon became and still remains the most popular method of concisely describing programming language syntax.

Figure 3.1
Chomsky's hierarchy of
language classes

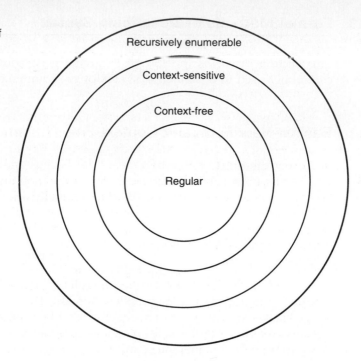

It is remarkable that BNF is nearly identical to Chomsky's generative devices for context-free languages, called context-free grammars. In the remainder of the chapter we refer to context-free grammars simply as grammars. Furthermore, the terms BNF and grammar will be used interchangeably.

3.3.1.3 Fundamentals

A **metalanguage** is a language that is used to describe another language. BNF is a metalanguage for programming languages.

BNF uses abstractions for syntactic structures. A Pascal assignment statement, for example, might be represented by the abstraction <assign>. (Pointed brackets are often used to delimit names of abstractions.) The actual definition of <assign> may be given by

<assign> → <var> := <expression>

The symbol on the left side of the arrow, which is aptly called the left-hand side (LHS), is the abstraction being defined. The text to the right of the arrow is the definition of the LHS. It is called the right-hand side (RHS) and consists of some mixture of tokens, lexemes, and references to other abstractions. Altogether, the definition is called a **rule,** or production. In the example rule just given, the abstractions <var> and <expression> must be defined before the <assign> definition becomes useful.

This particular rule specifies that the abstraction <assign> is defined as an instance of the abstraction <var>, followed by the lexeme :=, followed by an instance of the abstraction <expression>. One example sentence whose syntactic structure is described by the rule is

```
total := sub1 + sub2
```

The abstractions in a BNF description, or grammar, are often called **nonterminal symbols,** or simply **nonterminals,** and the lexemes and tokens of the rules are called **terminal symbols,** or simply **terminals.** A **grammar** is simply a collection of rules.

Nonterminal symbols can have two or more distinct definitions, representing two or more possible syntactic forms in the language. Multiple definitions can be written as a single rule, with the different definitions separated by the symbol |, meaning logical OR. For example, a Pascal **if** statement can be described with

<if_stmt> → **if** <logic_expr> **then** <stmt>
<if_stmt> → **if** <logic_expr> **then** <stmt> **else** <stmt>

or with

<if_stmt> → **if** <logic_expr> **then** <stmt>
    | **if** <logic_expr> **then** <stmt> **else** <stmt>

3.3.1.4 Describing Lists

Variable-length lists in mathematics are often written using an ellipsis (. . .); 1, 2, . . . is an example. BNF does not include an ellipsis, so an alternative method is required for describing lists of objects in programming languages. The most common technique used is recursion. A rule is **recursive** if its LHS appears in its RHS. For example, the list of identifiers on a data declaration in Pascal can be described as follows:

<ident_list> → identifier
    | identifier , <ident_list>

This defines <ident_list> as either a single token (identifier) or an identifier followed by a comma followed by another instance of <ident_list>.

3.3.1.5 Grammars and Derivations

BNF is a generative device for defining languages. The sentences of the language are generated through a sequence of applications of the rules, beginning with a special nonterminal of the grammar called the start symbol. Such a generation is called a **derivation.** In a grammar for a complete language, the start symbol represents a complete program and is usually named <program>. The following simple grammar is used to illustrate derivations:

Example 3.1   **A grammar for a small language**

$$
\begin{aligned}
\langle program \rangle &\rightarrow \textbf{begin } \langle stmt\_list \rangle \textbf{ end} \\
\langle stmt\_list \rangle &\rightarrow \langle stmt \rangle \\
&\mid \langle stmt \rangle \; ; \; \langle stmt\_list \rangle \\
\langle stmt \rangle &\rightarrow \langle var \rangle := \langle expression \rangle \\
\langle var \rangle &\rightarrow \texttt{A} \mid \texttt{B} \mid \texttt{C} \\
\langle expression \rangle &\rightarrow \langle var \rangle + \langle var \rangle \\
&\mid \langle var \rangle - \langle var \rangle \\
&\mid \langle var \rangle \quad \blacksquare
\end{aligned}
$$

This language has only one statement form: assignment. A program consists of the special word **begin**, followed by a list of statements separated by semicolons, followed by the special word **end**. An expression is either a single variable, or two variables and either a + or – operator. The only variable names are A, B, and C.

A derivation of a program in this language follows:

$$
\begin{aligned}
\langle program \rangle \Rightarrow &\; \textbf{begin } \langle stmt\_list \rangle \textbf{ end} \\
\Rightarrow &\; \textbf{begin } \langle stmt \rangle \; ; \; \langle stmt\_list \rangle \textbf{ end} \\
\Rightarrow &\; \textbf{begin } \langle var \rangle := \langle expression \rangle; \langle stmt\_list \rangle \textbf{ end} \\
\Rightarrow &\; \textbf{begin } \texttt{A} := \langle expression \rangle \; ; \; \langle stmt\_list \rangle \textbf{ end} \\
\Rightarrow &\; \textbf{begin } \texttt{A} := \langle var \rangle + \langle var \rangle \; ; \; \langle stmt\_list \rangle \textbf{ end} \\
\Rightarrow &\; \textbf{begin } \texttt{A} := \texttt{B} + \langle var \rangle \; ; \; \langle stmt\_list \rangle \textbf{ end} \\
\Rightarrow &\; \textbf{begin } \texttt{A} := \texttt{B} + \texttt{C} \; ; \; \langle stmt\_list \rangle \textbf{ end} \\
\Rightarrow &\; \textbf{begin } \texttt{A} := \texttt{B} + \texttt{C} \; ; \; \langle stmt \rangle \textbf{ end} \\
\Rightarrow &\; \textbf{begin } \texttt{A} := \texttt{B} + \texttt{C} \; ; \; \langle var \rangle := \langle expression \rangle \textbf{ end} \\
\Rightarrow &\; \textbf{begin } \texttt{A} := \texttt{B} + \texttt{C} \; ; \; \texttt{B} := \langle expression \rangle \textbf{ end} \\
\Rightarrow &\; \textbf{begin } \texttt{A} := \texttt{B} + \texttt{C} \; ; \; \texttt{B} := \langle var \rangle \textbf{ end} \\
\Rightarrow &\; \textbf{begin } \texttt{A} := \texttt{B} + \texttt{C} \; ; \; \texttt{B} := \texttt{C} \textbf{ end}
\end{aligned}
$$

This derivation, like all derivations, begins with the start symbol, in this case $\langle program \rangle$. The symbol $\Rightarrow$ is read "derives." Each successive string in the sequence is derived from the previous string by replacing one of the nonterminals with one of its definitions. Each of the strings in the derivation, including $\langle program \rangle$, is called a **sentential form.** In this derivation, the replaced nonterminal is always the leftmost nonterminal in the previous sentential form. Derivations that use this order of replacement are called leftmost derivations. The derivation continues until the sentential form contains no nonterminals. That sentential form, consisting of only terminals, or lexemes, is the generated sentence.

In addition to leftmost, a derivation may be rightmost or in an order that is neither leftmost nor rightmost. Derivation order has no effect on the language generated by a grammar.

By choosing alternative RHSs of rules with which to replace nonterminals in the derivation, different sentences in the language can be generated. By exhaustively choosing all combinations of choices, the entire language can be generated. This language, like most others, is infinite, so one cannot actually generate *all* the sentences in the language in finite time.

The following is another example of a grammar for part of a typical programming language:

Example 3.2   **A grammar for simple assignment statements**

$$<assign> \rightarrow <id> := <expr>$$
$$<id> \rightarrow A \mid B \mid C$$
$$<expr> \rightarrow <id> + <expr>$$
$$\mid <id> * <expr>$$
$$\mid (<expr>)$$
$$\mid <id> \quad \blacksquare$$

This grammar describes assignment statements whose right sides are arithmetic expressions with multiplication and addition operators and parentheses. For example, the statement

```
A := B * ( A + C )
```

is generated by the following derivation:

$$<assign> \Rightarrow <id> := <expr>$$
$$\Rightarrow A := <expr>$$
$$\Rightarrow A := <id> * <expr>$$
$$\Rightarrow A := B * <expr>$$
$$\Rightarrow A := B * (<expr>)$$
$$\Rightarrow A := B * (<id> + <expr>)$$
$$\Rightarrow A := B * (A + <expr>)$$
$$\Rightarrow A := B * (A + <id>)$$
$$\Rightarrow A := B * (A + C)$$

3.3.1.6   Parse Trees

One of the most attractive features of grammars is that they naturally describe the hierarchical syntactic structure of the sentences of the languages they define. These hierarchical structures are called **parse trees.** For example, the parse tree in Figure 3.2 shows the structure of the assignment statement derived above.

Every internal node of a parse tree is labeled with a nonterminal symbol; every leaf is labeled with a terminal symbol. Every subtree of a parse tree describes one instance of an abstraction in the statement.

One of the primary tasks of the syntax analyzer portion of a compiler is to analyze programs that are input to the compiler to determine whether they are syntactically correct. This process often produces a parse tree for

Figure 3.2
A parse tree for a
simple assignment
statement

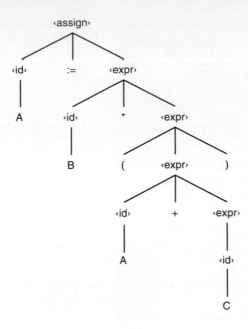

the program. The parse tree is used by subsequent parts of the compiler to perform the translation.

3.3.1.7   Grammars and Recognizers

It was suggested earlier in this chapter that there was a close relationship between generation and recognition devices for a given language. In fact, given a context-free grammar, a recognizer for the language generated by the grammar can be algorithmically constructed. A number of software systems have been developed that perform this construction. Such systems allow the quick construction of the syntax analysis part of a compiler for a new language and are therefore highly valued. One of the most widely used of these syntax analyzer generators is named yacc (yet another compiler-compiler) (Johnson, 1975).

Syntax analyzers for programming languages, which are often called parsers, construct parse trees for given programs. In some cases the parse tree is only implicitly constructed, but in all cases the information contained in the parse tree is created during the parse.

Parsers are categorized according to the direction in which they build parse trees. The two broad classes of parsers are top-down, in which the tree is built from the root downward to the leaves, and bottom-up, in which the parse tree is built from the leaves upward to the root.

3.3.1.8 Ambiguity

A grammar that generates a sentence for which there are two or more distinct parse trees is said to be **ambiguous.** Consider the following grammar, which is a minor variation of the grammar in Example 3.2.

Example 3.3   **An ambiguous grammar for simple assignment statements**

$$<assign> \rightarrow <id> := <expr>$$
$$<id> \rightarrow A \mid B \mid C$$
$$<expr> \rightarrow <expr> + <expr>$$
$$\mid <expr> * <expr>$$
$$\mid (<expr>)$$
$$\mid <id> \ \blacksquare$$

The grammar of Example 3.3 is ambiguous because the sentence

```
A := B + C * A
```

has two distinct parse trees, as shown in Figure 3.3.

The ambiguity occurs because the grammar specifies slightly less syntactic structure than does the grammar of Example 3.2. Rather than allowing the parse tree of an expression to grow only on the right, this grammar allows growth on both left and right.

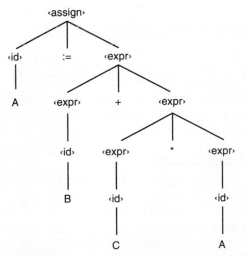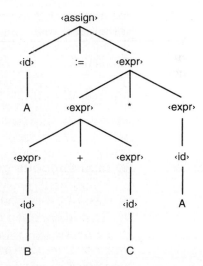

Figure 3.3
Two distinct parse trees for the same sentence
```
A := B + C * A
```

In general, syntactic ambiguity of language structures is a problem because compilers base the semantics of those structures on their syntactic structure. In particular, the compiler decides what code to generate for a statement by examining its parse tree. If a language structure has more than one parse tree, then the meaning of the structure cannot be determined uniquely. This problem is discussed in two specific examples in the following three sections.

3.3.1.9   Operator Precedence

As stated earlier, a grammar can describe a certain syntactic structure so that part of the meaning of the structure can follow from its parse tree. In particular, the fact that an operator in an arithmetic expression is generated lower in the parse tree (and therefore must be evaluated first) can be used to indicate that it has precedence over an operator produced higher up in the tree. In the first parse tree of Figure 3.3, for example, the multiplication operator is generated lower in the tree, which could indicate that it has precedence over the addition operator in the expression. The second parse tree, however, indicates just the opposite. It appears, therefore, that the two parse trees indicate conflicting precedence information.

Notice that although the grammar of Example 3.2 is not ambiguous, the precedence order of its operators is not the usual one. Rather, in this grammar, a parse tree of a sentence with multiple operators has the rightmost operator at the lowest point, with the other operators in the tree moving progressively higher as one moves to the left in the expression.

A grammar can be written to separate the addition and multiplication operators so they are consistently in a higher to lower ordering, respectively, in the parse tree. This ordering can be maintained regardless of the order in which the operators appear in an expression. It is done by using separate abstractions for the operands of the operators that have different precedence. This requires additional nonterminals and some new rules. The grammar of Example 3.4 is such a grammar.

Example 3.4   **An unambiguous grammar for expressions**

```
<assign>  →  <id> := <expr>
   <id>  →  A | B | C
  <expr>  →  <expr> + <term>
          |  <term>
  <term>  →  <term> * <factor>
          |  <factor>
<factor>  →  ( <expr> )
          |  <id>   ∎
```

This grammar generates the same language as the grammars of Examples 3.2 and 3.3, but it indicates the usual precedence order of multiply and add operators. The following derivation of the sentence A := B + C * A uses the grammar of Example 3.4:

$$
\begin{aligned}
\text{<assign>} &\Rightarrow \text{<id> := <expr>} \\
&\Rightarrow \text{A := <expr>} \\
&\Rightarrow \text{A := <expr> + <term>} \\
&\Rightarrow \text{A := <term> + <term>} \\
&\Rightarrow \text{A := <factor> + <term>} \\
&\Rightarrow \text{A := <id> + <term>} \\
&\Rightarrow \text{A := B + <term>} \\
&\Rightarrow \text{A := B + <term> * <factor>} \\
&\Rightarrow \text{A := B + <factor> * <factor>} \\
&\Rightarrow \text{A := B + <id> * <factor>} \\
&\Rightarrow \text{A := B + C * <factor>} \\
&\Rightarrow \text{A := B + C * <id>} \\
&\Rightarrow \text{A := B + C * A}
\end{aligned}
$$

The unique parse tree for this sentence using the grammar of Example 3.4 is shown in Figure 3.4.

The connection between parse trees and derivations is very close: Either can be easily constructed from the other. Every derivation with an unambiguous grammar has a unique parse tree, although that tree can be represented by different derivations. For example, the following derivation of the sentence A := B + C * A is different from the derivation of the same

Figure 3.4
The unique parse tree for A := B + C * A using an unambiguous grammar

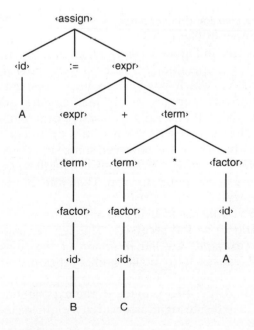

sentence given previously. This is a rightmost derivation, whereas the previous one is leftmost. Both of these derivations, however, are represented by the same parse tree.

$$
\begin{aligned}
\text{<assign>} &\Rightarrow \text{<id> := <expr>} \\
&\Rightarrow \text{<id> := <expr> + <term>} \\
&\Rightarrow \text{<id> := <expr> + <term> * <factor>} \\
&\Rightarrow \text{<id> := <expr> + <term> * <id>} \\
&\Rightarrow \text{<id> := <expr> + <term> * A} \\
&\Rightarrow \text{<id> := <expr> + <factor> * A} \\
&\Rightarrow \text{<id> := <expr> + <id> * A} \\
&\Rightarrow \text{<id> := <expr> + C * A} \\
&\Rightarrow \text{<id> := <term> + C * A} \\
&\Rightarrow \text{<id> := <factor> + C * A} \\
&\Rightarrow \text{<id> := <id> + C * A} \\
&\Rightarrow \text{<id> := B + C * A} \\
&\Rightarrow \text{A := B + C * A}
\end{aligned}
$$

3.3.1.10   Associativity of Operators

Another interesting question concerning grammars for expressions is whether operator associativity is also correctly described; that is, do the parse trees for expressions with two or more adjacent occurrences of operators with equal precedence have those occurrences in proper hierarchical order? An example of an assignment statement with such an expression is

```
A := B + C + A
```

The parse tree for this sentence, as defined with the grammar of Example 3.4, is shown in Figure 3.5.

The parse tree in Figure 3.5 shows the left addition operator lower than the right addition operator. This is the correct order if addition is meant to be left associative, which is typical. In most cases, the associativity of addition in a computer is irrelevant. (In mathematics, addition is associative, which means that left and right associative orders of evaluation mean the same thing. That is, $(A + B) + C = A + (B + C)$. Integer computer arithmetic is also associative. There are, however, some situations where floating-point addition is not associative.) Division is not mathematically associative, and this is reflected in computer division. Therefore, in general, correct associativity is essential.

When a BNF rule has its LHS also appearing at the beginning of its RHS, the rule is said to be **left recursive.** This left recursion specifies left associativity. For example, the left recursion of the rules of the grammar of Example 3.4 causes it to make both addition and multiplication left associative.

In most languages that provide it, the exponentiation operator is right associative. To indicate right associativity, right recursion can be used. A

Figure 3.5
A parse tree for A := B + C + A illustrating the associativity of addition

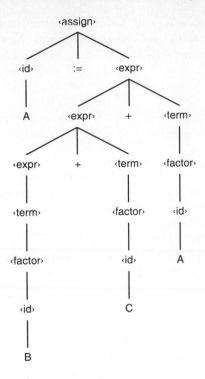

grammar rule is **right recursive** if the LHS appears at the right end of the RHS. Rules such as

$$<\text{factor}> \rightarrow <\text{exp}> \text{ ** } <\text{factor}>$$
$$| <\text{exp}>$$
$$<\text{exp}> \rightarrow (<\text{expr}>)$$
$$| <\text{id}>$$

could be used to describe exponentiation as a right-associative operator.

3.3.1.11 An Unambiguous Grammar for **if-then-else**

The BNF rules given in Section 3.3.1.3 for one particular form of the **if-then-else** statement are repeated here:

$$<\text{if\_stmt}> \rightarrow \text{if } <\text{logic\_expr}> \text{ then } <\text{stmt}>$$
$$| \text{ if } <\text{logic\_expr}> \text{ then } <\text{stmt}> \text{ else } <\text{stmt}>$$

If we also have `<stmt>` → `<if_stmt>`, this grammar is ambiguous, as the parse trees in Figure 3.6 show.

We will now develop an unambiguous grammar that describes this **if** statement. The rule for **if** constructs in most languages is that an **else** clause, when present, is matched with the closest previous unmatched **then**. Therefore, between a **then** and its matching **else**, there cannot be an **if** statement without an **else**. So, for this situation, statements must be distinguished between those that are matched and those that are unmatched, where unmatched statements are **else**-less **if**s, and all other statements are matched. The problem with the grammar above is that it treats all statements as if they had equal syntactic significance; that is, as if they were all matched.

To reflect the different categories of statements, different abstractions, or nonterminals, must be used. The unambiguous grammar based on these ideas follows:

$$
\begin{aligned}
\text{<stmt>} \;\rightarrow\; & \text{<matched>} \mid \text{<unmatched>} \\
\text{<matched>} \;\rightarrow\; & \textbf{if} \text{ <logic\_expr> } \textbf{then} \text{ <matched> } \textbf{else} \\
& \text{<matched>} \\
& \mid \text{ any non-if statement} \\
\text{<unmatched>} \;\rightarrow\; & \textbf{if} \text{ <logic\_expr> } \textbf{then} \text{ <stmt>} \\
& \mid \textbf{if} \text{ <logic\_expr> } \textbf{then} \text{ <matched> } \textbf{else} \\
& \text{<unmatched>}
\end{aligned}
$$

There is just one possible parse tree, using this grammar, for the sentence shown in Figure 3.6.

Figure 3.6

Two distinct parse trees for the same sentential form

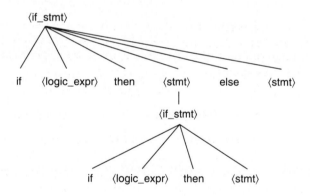

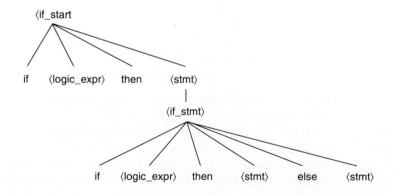

3.3.2 Extended BNF

Because of a few minor inconveniences in BNF, the method has been extended in several ways. Most extended versions are called Extended BNF, or simply EBNF, even though they are not all exactly the same. Note that the extensions do not enhance the descriptive power of BNF; they are only conveniences.

Three extensions are commonly included in the various versions of EBNF. The first of these denotes an optional part of an RHS, which is delimited by brackets. For example, a Pascal WRITELN statement can be described as

<writeln> → WRITELN [(<item_list>)]

Note that without the use of the brackets, the syntactic description of this statement would require two rules.

The second extension is the use of braces in an RHS to indicate that the enclosed part can be repeated indefinitely, or left out altogether. This extension allows lists to be built with a single rule, instead of using recursion and two rules. For example, lists of identifiers can be described by the following rule:

<ident_list> → <identifier> {, <identifier>}

This is a replacement of the recursion by a form of implied iteration; the part enclosed within braces can be iterated any number of times.

The third common extension deals with multiple-choice options. When a single element must be chosen from a group, the options are placed in parentheses and separated by the OR operator, |. For example:

<for_stmt> → **for** <var> := <expr> (**to** | **downto**) <expr> **do** <stmt>

Once again, it would require two BNF rules to describe this structure. Note that the brackets, braces, and parentheses in the EBNF extensions are metasymbols, which means they are notational tools and not terminal symbols in the syntactic entities they help describe. In cases where these metasymbols are also terminal symbols in the language being described, the instances that are terminal symbols can be underlined.

Example 3.5 is an expression grammar, first written in BNF and then in EBNF.

Example 3.5   **BNF and EBNF versions of an expression grammar**

BNF: <expr> → <expr> + <term>
              | <expr> – <term>
              | <term>
       <term> → <term> * <factor>

$$| \; \text{<term>} \; / \; \text{<factor>}$$
$$| \; \text{<factor>}$$

EBNF: $\text{<expr>} \; \rightarrow \; \text{<term>} \; \{(+ \; | \; -) \; \text{<term>}\}$
$\text{<term>} \; \rightarrow \; \text{<factor>} \; \{(* \; | \; /) \; \text{<factor>}\}$ ∎

Some versions of EBNF allow a numeric superscript to be attached to the right brace to indicate an upper limit to the number of times the enclosed part can be repeated. Also, some versions use a plus (+) super-script to indicate one or more repetitions. For example,

$\text{<block>} \; \rightarrow \; \textbf{begin} \; \text{<stmt>} \; \{\text{<stmt>}\} \; \textbf{end}$

and

$\text{<block>} \; \rightarrow \; \textbf{begin} \; \{\text{<stmt>}\}^{+} \; \textbf{end}$

are equivalent.

One more extension to BNF that is sometimes used is the ellipsis (. . .), which indicates, as in mathematics, more of the same. For example,

$\text{<ident\_list>} \; \rightarrow \; \text{<identifier>} \; [, \; \text{<identifier>}] \ldots$

3.3.3 Syntax Graphs

A **graph** is a collection of nodes, some of which are connected by lines, called edges. A **directed graph** is one in which the edges are directional; that is, they have arrowheads on one end to indicate a direction. A parse tree is a restricted form of directed graph.

The information in BNF rules can be represented in a directed graph. Such graphs are called **syntax graph**s, syntax diagrams, or syntax charts. A separate graph is used for each syntactic unit, in the same way a nonterminal symbol in a grammar represents such a unit.

In a syntax graph, there are two kinds of nodes which correspond to the terminal and nonterminal symbols of the right sides of a grammar's rules. A rectangle, which contains the name of a syntactic unit, or abstraction, represents a nonterminal. Circles or ellipses contain terminal symbols.

The Ada **if** statement syntax is described both in EBNF and with a syntax graph in Figure 3.7. Note that both the brackets and braces in the EBNF description are metasymbols rather than terminal symbols in the Ada language.

Using graphics to describe syntax offers the same advantage as using graphics to describe anything: it makes information easier to understand by allowing us to visualize it.

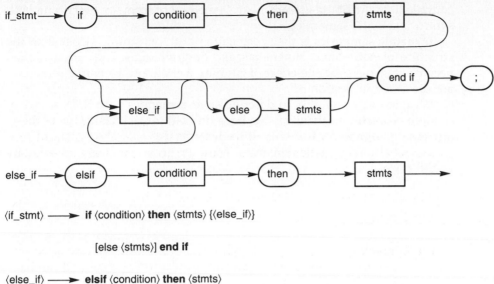

⟨if_stmt⟩ ————➤ **if** ⟨condition⟩ **then** ⟨stmts⟩ {⟨else_if⟩}

[else ⟨stmts⟩] **end if**

⟨else_if⟩ ————➤ **elsif** ⟨condition⟩ **then** ⟨stmts⟩

Figure 3.7
The syntax graph and EBNF descriptions of the Ada **if**
statement

3.4 Attribute Grammars

3.4.1 Static Versus Dynamic Semantics

There are some characteristics of the structure of programming languages
that are difficult to describe with BNF, and some that are impossible. As an
example of a language rule that is difficult to specify with BNF, consider
type compatibility rules. In Pascal, for example, a real type value cannot be
assigned to an integer type variable, although the opposite is legal.
Although this restriction can be specified in BNF, it requires additional nonterminal symbols and rules. If all of the typing rules of Pascal were specified
in BNF, the grammar would become too large to be useful.

As an example of a language rule that cannot be specified in BNF, consider the Pascal rule that all variables must be declared before they are referenced. It can be proven that this rule cannot be specified in BNF.

These two problems exemplify the category of language rules called
static semantics rules. The **static semantics** of a language has nothing to do
with the meaning of programs; rather it has to do with the legal forms of
programs (syntax rather than semantics). In many cases, the static semantic
rules of a language state its type constraints. Static semantics are so named
because the analysis required to check these specifications can be done at

compile time. Attribute grammars are a method of formally describing both syntax and static semantics.

Dynamic semantics is the specification of the meaning, rather than the structure, of expressions, statements, and program units. They are so named because they describe the effect of running a program. Dynamic semantics are discussed in Section 3.5.

Because of the inability to describe static semantics with BNF, a variety of more powerful mechanisms has been devised for that task. One of these, attribute grammars, was designed to describe not only the syntax of programs but also their static semantics. Attribute grammars were invented by Knuth (1968a).

3.4.2 Basic Concepts

Attribute grammars are grammars with sets of attribute values associated with the grammar symbols. **Attributes** are similar to variables and can have values assigned to them. **Attribute computation functions,** sometimes called semantic functions, are associated with grammar rules to specify how attribute values are computed. In addition, grammar rules may have associated **predicate functions** over the attribute values. Predicate functions state some of the syntax and static semantic rules of the language.

These concepts will become clearer after we formally define attribute grammars and provide an example.

3.4.3 Attribute Grammars Defined

An **attribute grammar** is a grammar with the following additions:

1. Associated with each grammar symbol X is a set of attributes A(X). The set A(X) consists of two disjoint sets, S(X) and I(X), called synthesized and inherited attributes, respectively. **Synthesized attributes** are used to pass information up a parse tree, while **inherited attributes** pass information down a tree.

2. Associated with each grammar rule is a set of semantic functions and a possibly empty set of predicate functions over the attributes of the symbols in the grammar rule. For a rule $X_0 \rightarrow X_1 \ldots X_n$, the synthesized attributes of X_0 are computed with a semantic function of the form $S(X_0) = f(A(X_1), \ldots, A(X_n))$. So, the value of a synthesized attribute on a parse tree node depends only on the values of the attributes on that node's children nodes. Inherited attributes of symbols X_j, $1 \leq j \leq n$ (in the rule above), are computed with a semantic function of the form $I(X_j) = f(A(X_0), \ldots, A(X_n))$. So, the value of an inherited attribute on a parse tree node depends on the attribute values of that node's parent node and those of its sibling nodes. Note

that to avoid circularity, synthesized attributes are often defined by functions of the form $I(X_j) = f(A(X_0), \ldots, A(X_{(j-1)}))$

Predicate functions have the form of a Boolean expression on the attribute set $\{A(X_0), \ldots, A(X_n)\}$. The only derivations allowed are those in which the predicates associated with every nonterminal are all true. A false predicate function value indicates a violation of the syntax or static semantics rules of the language.

A parse tree of an attribute grammar is the parse tree based on its underlying BNF grammar, with a possibly empty set of attribute values attached to each node. If all the attributes in a parse tree have values, the tree is said to be fully attributed. Although in practice it is not always done this way, it is convenient to think of attribute values as being computed after the complete unattributed parse tree has been constructed.

3.4.4 Intrinsic Attributes

Intrinsic attributes are synthesized attributes of leaf nodes, whose values are determined outside the parse tree. For example, the type of an instance of a variable in a program could come from a table—usually called a symbol table—used to store variable names and their types. The contents of such a table are determined from earlier declaration statements. Initially, assuming that an unattributed parse tree has been constructed and that attribute values are desired, the only attributes with values are the intrinsic attributes of the leaf nodes. Given the intrinsic attribute values on a parse tree, the semantic functions can be used to compute the remaining attribute values.

3.4.5 An Example Attribute Grammar

We now present an example of a simple attribute grammar and show how it can be used to check the static semantics of a simple assignment statement. The syntax and semantics of this assignment statement are as follows: The language consists entirely of simple assignment statements. The only variable names are A, B, and C. The right side of the assignments can either be a variable or an expression in the form of a variable added to another variable. The variables can be one of two types: int_type or real_type. When there are two variables on the right side of an assignment, they need not be the same type. The type of the expression when the operand types are not the same is always real_type. When they are the same, the expression type is that of the operands. The type of the left side of the assignment must match the type of the right side. So the types of operands in the right side can be mixed, but the assignment is valid only if the LHS and the value resulting from evaluating the RHS have the same type. The attribute grammar specifies how these semantic rules can be checked for correctness.

The syntax portion of our example attribute grammar is

$$\begin{aligned}
\text{<assign>} &\rightarrow \text{<var>} := \text{<expr>} \\
\text{<expr>} &\rightarrow \text{<var>} + \text{<var>} \\
&\mid \text{<var>} \\
\text{<var>} &\rightarrow A \mid B \mid C
\end{aligned}$$

The attributes are:

- *actual_type*   A synthesized attribute associated with the nonterminals <var> and <expr>. It is used to store the actual type, int_type or real_type in the example, of a variable or expression. In the case of a variable, the actual type is intrinsic. In the case of an expression, it is determined from the actual types of the child node or children nodes of the <expr> nonterminal.

- *expected_type*   An inherited attribute associated with the nonterminal <expr>. It is used to store the type, either int_type or real_type, that is expected for the expression, as determined by the type of the variable on the left side of the assignment statement.

- *lhs_type*   A synthesized attribute associated with <assign>. It is used to move the value of the synthesized actual_type of the LHS of an assignment statement to the inherited attribute expected_type for the <expr>.

- *env*   An inherited attribute associated with the nonterminals <assign>, <expr>, and <var>. It carries the reference to the correct symbol table entries to the instances of variables, where it is used for the lookup.

The environment attribute is inherited from above the root of the parse tree in this grammar. We assume that this grammar is embedded in a larger grammar that describes a complete language, which would include data declarations. These declarations would cause the compiler to generate a symbol table. The value for the environment attribute would be a pointer to that symbol table.

The complete attribute grammar follows. Notice that when there is more than one occurrence of a nonterminal in a syntax rule, the nonterminals are subscripted with brackets to distinguish them. Neither the subscript nor the brackets are part of the described language.

Example 3.6   **An attribute grammar for simple assignment statements**

1. Syntax rule: <assign> → <var> := <expr>
   Semantic rules: <var>.env ← <assign>.env
   <expr>.env ← <assign>.env
   <assign>.lhs_type ← <var>.actual_type
   <expr>.expected_type ← <assign>.lhs_type

2. Syntax rule: <expr> → <var>[2] + <var>[3]
  Semantic rules: <var>[2].env ← <expr>.env
      <var>[3].env ← <expr>.env
      <expr>.actual_type ←
        if (<var>[2].actual_type = int_type)
          and (<var>[3].actual_type = int_type)
            then int_type
            else real_type
        end if
  Predicate: <expr>.actual_type = <expr>.expected_type

3. Syntax rule: <expr> → <var>
  Semantic rule: <expr>.actual_type ← <var>.actual_type
  Predicate: <expr>.actual_type = <expr>.expected_type

4. Syntax rule: <var> → A | B | C
  Semantic rule: <var>.actual_type ←
        look-up (RHS, <var>.env) ∎

The look-up function looks up a given variable name in a given symbol table (or environment) and returns the variable's type.

An example of a parse tree of a sentence generated by this grammar is shown in Figure 3.8. As in the grammar, bracketed numbers are added after the repeated node labels in the tree so they can be referenced unambiguously.

3.4.6 Computing Attribute Values

Now consider the process of decorating the parse tree with attributes. This could proceed in a completely top-down order, from the root to the leaves, if all attributes were inherited. Alternatively, it could proceed in a completely bottom-up order, from the leaves to the root, if all the attributes were synthesized. Because our grammar has both synthesized and inherited attributes, and because of the interdependencies of the attributes, the eval-

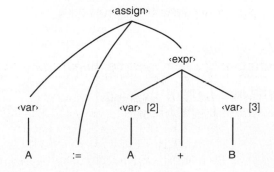

Figure 3.8
A parse tree for
A := A + B

uation process cannot be in any single direction. The following is an evaluation of the attributes, in an order in which those evaluations can be done. Each of the eight numbered steps in this evaluation depends on some attribute computation in a previous step. Note that determining attribute evaluation order for the general case of an attribute grammar is a complex problem, requiring the construction of a dependency graph to show all attribute dependencies.

1. <assign>.env ← inherited from the ancestor of <expr>
2. <var>.env ← <assign>.env (Rule 1)
   <expr>.env ← <assign>.env (Rule 1)
   <var>[2].env ← <var>[3].env ← <expr>.env (Rule 2)
3. <var>.actual_type ← look-up (A, <var>.env) (Rule 4)
4. <assign>.lhs_type ← <var>.actual_type (Rule 1)
5. <expr>.expected_type ← <assign>.lhs_type (Rule 1)
6. <var>[2].actual_type ← look-up (A, <var>[2].env) (Rule 4)
   <var>[3].actual_type ← look-up (B, <var>[3].env) (Rule 4)
7. <expr>.actual_type ← either int_type or real_type (Rule 2)
8. <expr>.expected_type = <expr>.actual_type is TRUE (Rule 2)

The tree in Figure 3.9 shows the flow of attribute values in the example of Figure 3.8. Solid lines are used for the parse tree; dashed lines show attribute flow in the tree.

The tree in Figure 3.10 shows the final attribute values on the nodes.

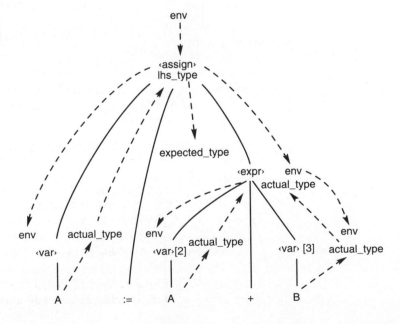

Figure 3.9
The flow of attributes in the tree

Figure 3.10
A fully attributed parse tree

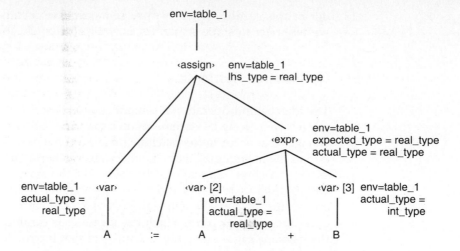

3.4.7 Evaluation

Attribute grammars have been used in a wide variety of applications. They have been used to provide complete descriptions of the syntax and static semantics of programming languages (Watt, 1979); they have been used as the formal definition of a language that can be input to a compiler generation system (Farrow, 1982); and they have been used as the basis of several syntax-directed editing systems (Teitelbaum and Reps, 1981; Fischer et al., 1984).

One of the main difficulties in using an attribute grammar for a real language is its size and complexity. The large number of attributes and semantic rules required for a complete programming language make such grammars difficult to write and to read. Furthermore, the attribute values on a large parse tree are costly to evaluate. On the other hand, less formal attribute grammars are a powerful tool for compiler writers, who are more interested in the process of producing a compiler than they are in formalism.

3.5   Describing the Meanings of Programs

We now turn to the difficult task of describing the dynamic semantics, or meaning, of the expressions, statements, and program units. Because of the power and naturalness of the available notation, describing syntax is a relatively simple matter. On the other hand, no universally accepted notation has been invented for dynamic semantics. In this section, we briefly describe several of the methods that have been developed. For the remainder of this section, when we say semantics we mean dynamic semantics; we will refer to static semantics as static semantics.

3.5.1 Operational Semantics

The idea behind operational semantics is to describe the meaning of a program by executing its statements on a machine, either real or simulated. The changes that occur in the machine's state when it executes a given statement define the meaning of that statement. To further explain this concept, consider a machine language instruction. Let the state of a computer be the values of all its registers and memory locations, including condition codes and status registers. If one simply records the state of the computer, executes the instruction for which the meaning is desired, and then examines the machine's new state, the semantics of that instruction are clear: It is represented by the change in the computer's state caused by the execution of the instruction.

3.5.1.1 The Basic Process

Describing the operational semantics of high-level language statements requires the construction of either a real or a virtual computer. Recall from Chapter 1 that the hardware of a computer is a pure interpreter for its machine language. A pure interpreter for any programming language can be constructed in software, which becomes a virtual computer for the language. The semantics of a high-level language can be described using a pure interpreter for the language. There are, however, two problems with this approach. First, the complexities and idiosyncrasies of the hardware computer and operating system that were used to run the pure interpreter would make the actions difficult to understand. Second, a semantic definition done this way would only be available to those with an identically configured computer.

These methodology problems can be avoided by replacing the real computer with a low-level virtual computer, implemented as a software simulation. The registers, memory, status information, and execution process would all be simulated. The instruction set would be designed so that the semantics of each instruction was easy to describe and understand. In this way, the machine would be idealized and thus highly simplified, making its changes of state easy to understand.

Using the operational method to describe the semantics of a programming language L requires the construction of two components. First, a translator is needed to convert statements in L to the chosen low-level language. The other component is the virtual machine for that low-level language. The state changes in the virtual machine brought about by executing the code that results from translating a given statement in the high-level language defines the meaning of that statement.

This basic process of operational semantics is not unusual. In fact, the concept is frequently used in programming textbooks and programming language reference manuals. For example, the semantics of the Pascal **for** construct can be described in terms of very simple instructions, as in:

```
Pascal Statement                Operational Semantics
for i := first to last do             i := first
   begin                    loop:  if i > last goto out
   ...                                  ...
   end                               i := i + 1
                                     goto loop
                             out:     ...
```

The human reader of such a description is the virtual computer and is assumed to be able to correctly "execute" the instructions in the definition and recognize the effects of the "execution."

A virtual machine for simple control statements, like the **for** example given above, could be constructed to "execute" the following instructions:

```
ident := var
ident := ident + 1
ident := ident − 1
goto label
if var relop var goto label
```

where relop is one of the relational operators from the set $\{=, <>, >, <, >=, <=\}$, ident is an identifier, and var is either an identifier or a constant. These are all simple and thus easy to understand and implement.

A slight generalization of the three assignments above allows general arithmetic expressions and assignment statements, where there is only a single data type, to be described. The new statements are

```
ident := var bin_op var
ident := un_op var
```

where bin_op is a binary arithmetic operator and un_op is a unary operator. Multiple arithmetic data types and automatic type conversions, of course, complicate this somewhat.

A few more relatively simple instructions allow the semantics of arrays, records, pointers, and subprograms to be described.

3.5.1.2 Evaluation

The first and most famous use of operational semantics was to describe the semantics of PL/I (Wegner, 1972). That particular abstract machine and the translation rules for PL/I were together named the Vienna Definition Language (VDL), after the city where it was devised by IBM.

Operational semantics provides an effective means of describing semantics for language users and language implementors, as long as the descriptions are kept as simple and informal as possible. The VDL description of PL/I, unfortunately, is so complex that it serves virtually no practical purpose.

Operational semantics is an informal method that depends on algorithms, not mathematics. In a very real sense, a programming language is being described by another programming language. This approach can lead to circularities, in which concepts are indirectly defined in terms of themselves. The methods described in the following two sections are formal, in the sense that they are based on logic and mathematics, not machines.

3.5.2   Axiomatic Semantics

The structure of axiomatic semantics was defined with the primary goal of developing a method to prove the correctness of programs. Each statement of a program is both preceded and followed by a logical expression that specifies constraints on and relationships among data values. These, rather than the entire state of an abstract machine (as with operational semantics), are used to specify the meaning of the statement. The notation used to describe constraints, indeed the language of axiomatic semantics, is predicate calculus. Although simple Boolean expressions are often adequate to express constraints, in some cases they are not.

3.5.2.1   Assertions

Axiomatic semantics is based on mathematical logic. The logical expressions are called predicates, or **assertions.** An assertion immediately preceding a statement describes the constraints on the program variables at that point in the program. An assertion immediately following a statement describes the new constraints on those variables (and possibly others) after execution of the statement. These assertions are called the **precondition** and **postcondition,** respectively, of the statement. Developing an axiomatic description of a given program requires that every statement in the program have both a precondition and a postcondition.

In the following sections, we examine assertions from the point of view that preconditions for statements are computed from given postconditions, although it is possible to consider these in the opposite sense. As a simple example, consider the following assignment statement and postcondition:

```
sum := 2 * x + 1    {sum > 1}
```

In this statement, `sum` and `x` are integer type variables. One possible precondition is {x > 10}. Pre- and postcondition assertions are presented in braces to distinguish them from program statements.

3.5.2.2 Weakest Preconditions

The **weakest precondition** is the least restrictive precondition that will guarantee the validity of the associated postcondition. For example, in the above statement and postcondition, {x > 10}, {x > 50}, and {x > 1000} are all valid preconditions. The weakest of all preconditions in this case is {x > 0}.

If the weakest precondition can be computed from the given postcondition for each statement of a language, then correctness proofs can be constructed for programs in that language. The proof is begun by using as the overall postcondition the desired results of the program's execution and by working backwards through the program, computing weakest preconditions for each statement until the start of the program is reached. At that point, the first precondition states the conditions under which the program will compute correct results.

For some program statements, the computation of the weakest precondition from the statement and a postcondition is simple and can be specified by an axiom. In most cases, however, the weakest precondition can be computed only by an inference rule. An **axiom** is a statement that is assumed to be true, and an **inference rule** is a method of inferring the truth of one statement on the basis of other true statements.

To use axiomatic semantics with a given programming language, whether for correctness proofs or for formal semantics specification, either an axiom or an inference rule must be defined for each kind of statement in the language. In the following subsections we present an axiom for assignment statements, and inference rules for statement sequences and logical pretest loops.

3.5.2.3 Assignment Statements

Let x := E be a general assignment statement and Q be its postcondition. Then its precondition, P, is defined by the axiom

$$P = Q_{x \to E}$$

which means that P is Q with all instances of x replaced by E. For example, if we have the assignment statement and postcondition

```
a := b / 2 - 1    {a < 10}
```

the weakest precondition is computed by substituting b / 2 - 1 in the assertion {a < 10}, to get:

```
b / 2 - 1 < 10
    b / 2 < 10 + 1
        b < 22
```

Thus, the weakest precondition for the given assignment and postcondition is {b < 22}. Note that this axiom is guaranteed to be true only in the absence of function calls in the expression that have side effects. Functional side effects are changes made by the function to program variables that are not local to the function. Such changes result from changes made in the function to reference parameters or globals.

The usual notation for specifying the axiomatic semantics of a given statement form is

{P} S {Q}

where P is the precondition, Q is the postcondition, and S is the statement form. In the case of the assignment statement, the notation is

$\{Q_{x \to E}\}$ x := E {Q}

As another example of computing a precondition for an assignment statement, consider the following:

    x := 2 * y - 3   {x > 25}

The precondition is computed as follows:

    2 * y - 3 > 25
        2 * y > 25 + 3
        2 * y > 28
          y > 14

So, {y > 14} is the weakest precondition for this assignment statement and postcondition.

Note that the appearance of the left side of the assignment statement in its right side does not affect the process of computing the weakest precondition. For example, for

    x := x + y - 3   {x > 10}

the weakest precondition is

    x + y - 3 > 10
        y > 10 - x + 3
        y > 13 - x

3.5.2.4   Sequences

The weakest precondition for a sequence of statements cannot be described by an axiom because the precondition depends on the particular kinds of statements in the sequence. In this case, the precondition can only be described with an inference rule. The general form of an inference rule is

$$\frac{\text{S1, S2, } \dots \text{, Sn}}{\text{S}}$$

which states that if S1, S2, ..., Sn are true, then the truth of S can be inferred.

Let S1 and S2 be adjacent program statements. If S1 and S2 have the following pre- and postconditions

{P1} S1 {P2}
{P2} S2 {P3}

then the inference rule for such a two-statement sequence is

$$\frac{\text{\{P1\} S1 \{P2\}, \{P2\} S2 \{P3\}}}{\text{\{P1\} S1; S2 \{P3\}}}$$

So, for the above example, {P1} S1; S2 {P3} describes the axiomatic semantics of the sequence S1; S2. If S1 and S2 are the assignment statements

    x1 := E1

and

    x2 := E2

then we have

$\{P3_{x2 \to E2}\}$ x2 := E2 {P3}
$\{(P3_{x2 \to E2})_{x1 \to E1}\}$ x1 := E1 $\{P3_{x2 \to E2}\}$

Therefore, the weakest precondition for the sequence x1 := E1; x2 := E2 with postcondition P3 is $\{(P3_{x2 \to E2})_{x1 \to E1}\}$.

For example, consider the following sequence and postcondition:

    y := 3 * x + 1;
    x := y + 3
    {x < 10}

The precondition for the last assignment statement is

    y + 3 < 10
        y < 7

{y < 7} is the precondition for the second assignment statement and also the postcondition for the first. The precondition for the first assignment statement is

    3 * x + 1 < 7
        3 * x < 6
            x < 2

3.5.2.5 Logical Pretest Loops

Another essential construct of an imperative programming language is the logical pretest, or **while** loop. Computing the weakest precondition for a **while** loop is inherently more difficult than for a sequence because the number of iterations is not statically known. If it were, the loop could be treated as a sequence. In general, however, the number of iterations cannot be determined from the text of the statement.

The problem of computing the weakest precondition here is similar to the problem of proving a theorem about all positive integers. In the latter case, induction is normally used, and the same inductive method can be used for **while** loops. The principal step in induction is finding an inductive hypothesis. The corresponding step in the axiomatic semantics of a **while** loop is finding an assertion called a **loop invariant,** which is crucial to the finding of the weakest precondition.

The mechanism for determining the precondition for a **while** loop is the following inference rule:

$$(I \text{ and } B) \ S \ \{Q\}$$

$$\overline{\{I\} \ \textbf{while} \ B \ \textbf{do} \ S \ \{I \text{ and } (\textbf{not } B)\}}$$

where I is the loop invariant.

The axiomatic description of a **while** loop is written as

$$\{P\} \ \textbf{while} \ B \ \textbf{do} \ S \ \textbf{end} \ \{Q\}$$

The loop invariant must satisfy a number of constraints to be useful. First, the weakest precondition for the **while** must guarantee the truth of the loop invariant. In turn, the loop invariant must guarantee the truth of the postcondition upon loop termination. These constraints move us from the inference rule to the axiomatic description. During execution of the loop, the truth of the loop invariant must be unaffected by the evaluation of the loop-controlling Boolean expression and the loop body statements.

Another complicating factor for **while** loops is the problem of loop termination. If Q is the postcondition that holds immediately after loop exit, then a precondition P for the loop is one that guarantees Q at loop exit and also guarantees that the loop terminates.

The complete description includes the following logic, in which $\Rightarrow$ means "implies" and I is the loop invariant:

```
P => I
{I} B {I}
{I and B} S {I}
(I and (not B)) => Q
the loop terminates
```

To compute a loop invariant, we can use a method used for determining the inductive hypothesis in mathematical induction; that is, the relationship for a few cases is computed, with the hope that a pattern emerges that will apply to the general case. If the loop body contains a single assignment statement, the axiom for assignment statements can be used to compute these cases. It is helpful to treat the process of producing a weakest precondition as a function, wp. In general

wp(statement, postcondition) = precondition

Our approach is to begin by using the loop postcondition, Q, to compute a precondition for the loop body. For the example

while y <> x **do** y := y + 1   {y = x}

we proceed as follows: For zero iterations, the weakest precondition is, obviously,

{y = x}

For one iteration, it is

wp(y := y + 1, {y = x}) = {y + 1 = x}, or {y = x − 1}

For two iterations, it is

wp(y := y + 1, {y = x − 1}) = {y + 1 = x − 1}, or {y = x − 2}

For three iterations, it is

wp(y := y + 1, {y = x − 2}) = {y + 1 = x − 2}, or {y = x − 3}

Through these calculations, it is clear that {y < x} will suffice for cases of one or more iterations. Combining this with {y = x} for the zero iterations case, we get {y ≤ x}, which can be used for the loop invariant. Now a precondition for the **while** statement can be determined from the loop invariant. In this example, P = I can be used.

We must ensure that our choice satisfies the five criteria for P for our example loop. First, because P = I, P ⇒ I. The second requirement is that I be unaffected by the evaluation of the loop Boolean expression, which is y <> x. This expression changes nothing, so it cannot affect I. Next, it must be true that

{I **and** B} S {I}

In our example, we have

{y ≤ x **and** y <> x} y := y + 1 {y ≤ x}

which is obviously true. Next, we must have

{I **and** (**not** B)} ⇒ Q

In our example, we have

{(y ≤ x) **and not** (y <> x)} ⇒ {y = x}

$$\{(y \le x) \text{ and } (y = x)\} \Rightarrow \{y = x\}$$
$$\{y = x\} \Rightarrow \{y = x\}$$

So, this is obviously true. Next, loop termination must be considered. In this example, the question is whether the loop

$$\{y \le x\} \text{ while } y <> x \text{ do } y := y + 1 \{y = x\}$$

terminates. It is easy to see that this loop does terminate. The precondition guarantees that y initially is not larger than x. The loop body increases y with each iteration, until y is equal to x. No matter how much larger y is than x initially, it will eventually become equal to x. So, the loop will terminate. Because our choice of P satisfies all five criteria, it is adequate for a precondition.

Finding loop invariants is not always easy. It is helpful to understand the nature of these invariants. First, a loop invariant is a weakened version of the loop postcondition, and also a precondition for the loop. So, I must be weak enough to be satisfied prior to the beginning of loop execution, but when combined with the loop exit condition, it must be strong enough to force the truth of the postcondition.

Because of the difficulty of proving loop termination, that requirement is often ignored. If loop termination can be shown, the axiomatic description of the loop is called total correctness. If the other conditions can be met, but termination is not guaranteed, it is called partial correctness.

In more complex loops, finding a suitable loop invariant, even for partial correctness, requires a good deal of ingenuity. Because computing the weakest precondition for a **while** loop depends on finding a loop invariant, the use of axiomatic semantics for **while** loops is difficult.

3.5.2.6   Evaluation

To define the semantics of a complete programming language using the axiomatic method, an axiom or an inference rule must be defined for each statement type in the language. It has proven to be a difficult task for some of the statements of programming languages. An obvious solution to this problem is to design the language with the axiomatic method in mind, so that only statements for which axioms or inference rules can be written are included.

Axiomatic semantics is a powerful tool for research into program correctness proofs, and it provides an excellent framework in which to reason about programs, both during their construction and later. Its usefulness in describing the meaning of programming languages to either language users or compiler writers is, however, limited.

3.5.3   Denotational Semantics

Denotational semantics is the most rigorous method of describing the meaning of programs. It is solidly based on recursive function theory. A thorough discussion of the use of denotational semantics to describe the semantics of programming languages is long and complex. It is our intent to introduce just enough to make the reader aware of how denotational semantics works.

The fundamental concept of denotational semantics is to define both a mathematical object for each language entity and a function that maps instances of that entity onto instances of the mathematical object. Because the objects are rigorously defined, they represent the exact meaning of their corresponding entities. The difficulty with this method lies in creating the objects and the mapping functions. The method is named denotational because the objects denote the meaning of their corresponding syntactic entities.

3.5.3.1   A Simple Example

We use a very simple language construct, binary numbers, to introduce the denotational method. The syntax of binary numbers can be described by the following grammar rules:

<bin_num> → 0
      | 1
      | <bin_num> 0
      | <bin_num> 1

A parse tree for an example binary number is shown in Figure 3.11.

To describe the meaning of binary numbers using denotational semantics and the grammar rules above, the actual meaning is associated with each rule that has a single terminal symbol as its RHS. The objects in this case are simple decimal numbers.

In our example, meaningful objects must be associated with the first two grammar rules. The other two grammar rules are, in a sense, computational rules because they combine a terminal symbol, to which an object can be associated, with a nonterminal, which can be expected to represent some construct. Presuming an evaluation that progresses upward in the parse tree, the nonterminal in the right side would already have its meaning

Figure 3.11
A parse tree of a binary number

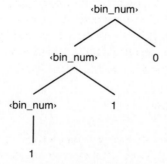

attached. Then such a syntax rule would require a function that computed the meaning of the LHS, which must then represent the meaning of the complete RHS.

Let the domain of semantic values of the objects be N, the set of non-negative decimal integer values. It is these objects that we wish to associate with binary numbers. The semantic function, named M_{bin}, maps the abstract syntax, as described in the grammar rules above, to the objects in N. The function M_{bin} is defined as follows:

M_{bin} (0) = 0
M_{bin} (1) = 1
M_{bin} (<bin_num> 0) = 2 * M_{bin} (<bin_num>)
M_{bin} (<bin_num> 1) = 2 * M_{bin} (<bin_num>) + 1

The meanings, or denoted objects (which in this case are decimal numbers), can be attached to the nodes of the parse tree above, yielding the tree in Figure 3.12.

This is syntax-directed semantics. Abstract syntactic entities are mapped to mathematical objects with concrete meaning.

In the following sections we present the denotational semantics of a few simple constructs. The most important simplifying assumption made here is that both the syntax and static semantics of the constructs can be assumed to be correct. Furthermore, we assume only two scalar types are included, integer and Boolean.

3.5.3.2   The State of a Program

The denotational semantics of a program could be defined in terms of state changes in an ideal computer. Operational semantics are defined in this way, and denotational semantics nearly are, too. In a further simplification, however, they are defined in terms of only the values of all the program's variables. The key difference between operational semantics and denotational semantics is that state changes in operational semantics are defined

Figure 3.12
A parse tree with denoted objects

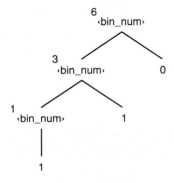

by coded algorithms, whereas in denotational semantics, state changes are defined by rigorous mathematical functions.

Let the state s of a program be represented as a set of ordered pairs, as follows,

$$\{<i_1, v_1>, <i_2, v_2>, \ldots, <i_n, v_n>\}$$

where each i is the name of a current variable and the associated v's are the current values of those variables. Any of the v's can have the special value, **undef,** which indicates that its associated variable is currently undefined. Let VARMAP be a function of two parameters, a variable name and the program state. The value of VARMAP(i_j, s) is v_j. Most semantics mapping functions for programs and program constructs map states to states. These state changes are used to define the meanings of program constructs and programs. Some language constructs, like expressions, are mapped to values, not states.

3.5.3.3   Expressions

Expressions are fundamental to most programming languages. The denotational semantics of expressions is quite simple, particularly under our assumptions. We now add the assumption that expressions have no side effects. The only error we consider in expressions is that a variable has an undefined value. Obviously other errors can occur, but most of them are machine dependent. Let Z be the set of integers and let **error** be the error value. Then, Z ∪ {error} is the set of values to which an expression can evaluate.

The required mapping function for a given expression E and state s follows. To distinguish between mathematical function definitions and the assignment statements of programming languages, we use the symbol $\triangleq$ to define mathematical functions.

M_e (E, s) $\triangleq$ if VARMAP(i, s) = **undef** for some i in E
                then **error**
                else E', where E' is the result of evaluating
                E after setting each variable i in E to VARMAP (i, s)

The evaluation process could, of course, be spelled out in more detail. This function definition, however, assumes that expression evaluation is sufficiently well understood so as to be left out.

3.5.3.4   Assignment Statements

An assignment statement is just an expression evaluation plus the setting of the left side variable to the expression's value. This can be described with the following function:

$$M_a(x := E, s) \triangleq \text{if } M_e(E, s) = \textbf{error}$$
$$\text{then } \textbf{error}$$
$$\text{else } s' \triangleq \{<i_1', v_1'>, <i_2', v_2'>, \ldots, <i_n', v_n'>\},$$
$$\text{where for } j = 1, 2, \ldots, n,$$
$$vj' = \begin{cases} \text{VARMAP}(i_j, s) \text{ if } i_j <> x \\ M_e(E, s) \text{ if } i_j = x \end{cases}$$

Note that the two comparisons in the last two lines above, $i_j <> x$ and $i_j = x$, are of names, not values.

3.5.3.5 Logical Pretest Loops

The denotational semantics of a simple logical loop is deceptively simple. To expedite the discussion, we assume that there are two other existing mapping functions, M_{sl} and M_b, that map statement lists to states and Boolean expressions to Boolean values (or error), respectively. The function is

$$M_1(\text{while B do L, s}) \triangleq$$
$$\text{if } M_b(B, s) = \textbf{undef}$$
$$\text{then } \textbf{error}$$
$$\text{else if } M_b(B, s) = \text{false}$$
$$\text{then } s$$
$$\text{else if } M_{sl}(L, s) = \textbf{error}$$
$$\text{then } \textbf{error}$$
$$\text{else } M_1(\text{while B do L}, M_{sl}(L, s))$$

The meaning of the loop is simply the value of the program variables after the statements in the loop have been executed the prescribed number of times, assuming there have been no errors. In essence, the loop has been converted from iteration to recursion, where the recursion control is mathematically defined by other recursive state mapping functions. Recursion is easier to describe with mathematical rigor than iteration.

One significant observation at this point is that this definition, like actual program loops, may compute nothing because of nontermination.

3.5.3.6 Evaluation

Objects and functions, such as those used in the statements above, can be defined for the other syntactic entities of programming languages. When a complete system has been defined for a given language, it can be used to determine the meaning of complete programs in that language. This provides a framework for thinking in a highly rigorous way about programming.

Denotational semantics can be used as an aid to language design. For example, statements for which the denotational semantic description is complex and difficult may indicate to the designer that such statements may also be difficult for language users to understand and that an alternative design may be in order.

A significant amount of work has been done on the possibility of using denotational language descriptions to automatically generate compilers (Jones, 1980; Milos et al., 1984; Bodwin et al., 1982). These efforts have shown that the method is feasible, but the work has not progressed to the point where it can be used to generate useful compilers.

Because of the complexity of denotational descriptions, they are of little use to language users. On the other hand, they provide an excellent method of concisely describing a language.

Although the use of denotational semantics is normally attributed to Scott and Strachey (1971), the general denotational approach to language description can be traced back to the nineteenth century (Frege, 1892).

SUMMARY

Backus-Naur form and context-free grammars are equivalent metalanguages that are almost ideally suited to the task of describing the syntax of programming languages. Not only are they concise descriptive methods, but the parse trees that can be associated with their generative actions give graphical evidence of the underlying syntactic structures. Furthermore, they are naturally related to recognition devices for the languages they generate, which leads to the relatively easy construction of syntax analyzers for compilers for these languages.

Syntax graphs are simply graphical representations of grammars.

An attribute grammar is a single formalism that can describe both the syntax and static semantics of a language.

In general, syntax description is a relatively easy task, whereas semantic description is very difficult. The only adequate formalisms of the latter are complex to learn and understand, so their usefulness is severely limited. If only static semantics is needed, attribute grammars are a useful syntax/semantic descriptive tool. Thus far, however, no standard form of such a grammar has been universally adopted, and they have only been widely used by compiler writers.

There are three primary methods of semantic description: operational, axiomatic, and denotational. Operational semantics is a method of describing the meaning of language constructs in terms of their effect on an ideal machine. Axiomatic semantics, which is based on formal logic, were devised as a tool for proving the correctness of programs. In denotational semantics, mathematical objects are used to represent the meanings of language constructs. Language entities are converted to these mathematical objects with recursive functions.

BIBLIOGRAPHIC NOTES

Syntax description using context-free grammars and BNF is thoroughly discussed in Cleaveland and Uzgalis (1976).

Syntax graphs were developed at Burroughs for a compiler development project to use as a compact description of ALGOL 60 syntax (Taylor et al., 1961). They were later modified by A. Schai, director of the computer center at ETH in Zurich. This modified version first appeared in print in a book on ALGOL 60 by Rutishauser (1967).

Research in axiomatic semantics was begun by Floyd (1967) and further developed by Hoare (1969). The semantics of a large part of Pascal was described by Hoare and Wirth (1973) using this method. The parts they did not complete involved functional side effects and goto statements. These were found to be the most difficult to describe.

The technique of using preconditions and postconditions during the development of programs is described (and advocated) by Dijkstra (1976), and also discussed in detail in Gries (1981).

Good introductions to denotational semantics can be found in Gordon (1979) and Stoy (1977). Introductions to all three semantics description methods discussed in this chapter can be found in Marcotty et al. (1976). Another good reference for much of the material of this chapter is Pagan (1981).

PROBLEM SET

1. There are two different mathematical models of language description: generation and recognition. Describe how each can define the syntax of a programming language.

2. Write EBNF and syntax graph descriptions of the Pascal procedure header statement.

3. Write EBNF and syntax graph descriptions of the Pascal procedure call statement.

4. Using the grammar in Example 3.2, show a parse tree and a leftmost derivation for each of the following statements:
   a. A := A * (B + (C * A))
   b. B := C * (A * C + B)
   c. A := A * (B + (C))

5. Using the grammar in Example 3.4, show a parse tree and a leftmost derivation for each of the following statements:
   a. A := (A + B) * C
   b. A := B + C + A
   c. A := (B + C) * A

6. Prove that the following grammar is ambiguous:

   S → A
   A → A + A
       | id

7. Modify the grammar of Example 3.4 to add unary plus and minus operators that have higher precedence than either + or *. Assume they can precede any operand.

8. Describe, in English, the language defined by the following grammar:

$$S \rightarrow A\ B\ C$$
$$A \rightarrow a\ A \mid a$$
$$B \rightarrow b\ B \mid b$$
$$C \rightarrow c\ C \mid c$$

9. Write a grammar for the language consisting of strings that have n copies of the letter "a" followed by the same number of copies of the letter "b," where $n \geq 0$. For example, the strings ab, aaaabbbb, and aaaaaaaabbbbbbbb are in the language but a, abb, ba, and aaabb are not.

10. Write a grammar that describes the floating-point constants of your favorite programming language.

11. Draw parse trees for the sentences aabcc and aaabbbc, as derived from the grammar of Problem 8.

12. Using the virtual machine instructions of Section 3.5.1.1, give an operational semantic definition of
    a. Pascal **repeat**
    b. Pascal **for-downto**
    c. FORTRAN 77 DO of the form: DO N K = start, end, step
    d. Pascal **if-then-else**

13. Compute the weakest precondition for each of the following assignment statements and postconditions:
    a. a := 2 * (b − 1) − 1 {a > 0}
    b. b := (c + 10) / 3 {b > 6}
    c. a := a + 2 * b − 1 {a > 1}
    d. x := 2 * y + x − 1 {x > 11}

14. Compute the weakest precondition for each of the following sequences of assignment statements and their postconditions:
    a. a := 2 * b + 1;
       b := a − 3
       {b < 0}
    b. a := 3 * (2 * b + a);
       b := 2 * a − 1
       {b > 5}

15. Write a denotational semantics mapping function for Pascal Boolean expressions.

16. Write a denotational semantics mapping function for a Pascal **for** statement.

17. Write a denotational semantics mapping function for a Pascal **repeat** statement.

18. What is the difference between an intrinsic attribute and a nonintrinsic synthesized attribute?

19. Write an attribute grammar whose BNF basis is that of Example 3.6 in Section 3.4.5 but whose language rules are as follows: Data types cannot be mixed in expressions but can be for the assignment operator.

20. Write an attribute grammar whose base BNF is that of Example 3.2 and whose type rules are the same as for the example of Section 3.4.5.

4

Primitive Data Types and Variables

Jean E. Sammet

Jean E. Sammet, employed by Sylvania at the time, was chair of two major subcommittees in the COBOL development process in 1959 and 1960. She also served on a 6-person subgroup that developed the detailed specifications. She is perhaps best known for her comprehensive book on the history of early programming languages. (Sammet, 1969).

Key Concepts

- Primitive data types
- Names
- Reserved words
- Keywords
- Variables
- Aliases
- Static versus dynamic binding
- Type inference
- Lifetime

- Strong typing
- Static versus dynamic scope
- Blocks
- Referencing environments
- Named constants
- Initialization
- Type compatibility by name and structure

Imperative programming languages are, to varying degrees, abstractions of the underlying von Neumann computer architecture. The architecture's two primary components are its memory, which stores both instructions and data, and its processor, which provides operations for modifying the contents of the memory. The abstractions in a language for the memory cells of the machine are variables. In some cases, the characteristics of the abstractions are very close to the characteristics of the cells; an example of this is an integer variable, which is usually represented exactly as in an individual hardware memory word. In other cases, the abstractions are far removed from the cells, as with a three-dimensional array, which requires a software mapping function to provide the abstraction.

A variable can be characterized by a collection of properties, or attributes, the most important of which is type, a fundamental concept in programming languages. The design of the data types of a language requires that a variety of issues be considered. Among the most important of these are the scope and lifetime of variables. Related to these are the issues of type checking and initialization. A knowledge of all these concepts is requisite to understanding the imperative languages.

The data types whose representations and operations are closely supported by hardware are called **primitive data types.** The variables of primitive data types, along with the related concepts mentioned above, are the topics of this chapter. In Chapter 5 we carry this discussion to the more complex data types.

Type compatibility is an important part of the data type design of a language and is therefore discussed in detail in this chapter.

In the remainder of this book, we will often refer to families of languages as if they were a single language. For example, when we refer to FORTRAN, we mean all the versions of FORTRAN. References to C include the original version of C, ANSI C, and C++. When we refer to a specific version of a language, it is because it is different from the other family members.

4.1   Primitive Data Types

Nearly all programming languages provide a set of primitive data types. Some of the primitive types are merely reflections of the hardware; for example, integer types. Others require only a little support for their implementation.

The primitive data types of a language are used, along with one or more type constructors, to provide more complex structured types such as arrays and records. Primitive types are abstract data types, for their implementation details are certainly hidden. Only when the purpose of the language is such that a given hardware-supported type is not useful does the language not include the type. An example is the decimal type of the VAX computers, for which a data type is provided only in COBOL (not in Pascal, C, or FORTRAN).

4.1.1   Numeric Types

4.1.1.1   Integer

The most common primitive numeric data type is **integer.** Many computers now support several sizes of integers. The DEC VAX-11 superminicomputers, for example, support four different sizes: byte, word (two bytes), longword (four bytes), and quadword (eight bytes). These capabilities are reflected in some programming languages. For example, Ada allows implementations to include up to three integer sizes: SHORT INTEGER, INTEGER, and LONG INTEGER. DEC's VAX Ada also includes a fourth size, SHORT SHORT INTEGER. Some languages, such as C, include unsigned integer types, which are simply integer types for integer values without signs.

4.1.1.2   Floating-Point

Floating-point data types model real numbers, but the representations are only approximations for most real values. For example, neither of the fundamental numbers π or e (the base for the natural logarithms) can be correctly represented in floating-point notation. Of course, neither of these numbers can be accurately represented in any finite space. On most computers, floating-point numbers are stored in binary, which exacerbates the problem. For example, even the value 0.1 in decimal cannot be represented by a finite number of binary digits.

Floating-point values are represented as fractions and exponents, with different implementations choosing different formats when hardware representations are different. An example of an implementation of a floating-point type is presented in Section 4.2.

Floating-point data types are included in most languages, although many small computers do not have hardware support for such types. Languages that are designed to support scientific programming generally include two floating-point types, often called **real** and **double-precision** after the original FORTRAN data type names. The real type is the standard size, and a value of real type is often stored in a single memory word. The double-precision type is provided for situations when larger fractional parts are needed. Double-precision variables usually occupy twice as much storage as real variables and provide at least twice the number of bits of accuracy.

4.1.1.3   Decimal

All mainframe and large minicomputers that are designed to support business systems applications have hardware support for **decimal** data types. Decimal data types store a fixed number of decimal digits, with the decimal point at a fixed position in the value. These are the primary data types for business data processing and are therefore essential to COBOL.

Decimal types have the advantage of being capable of precisely storing decimal values, at least those within a restricted range, which cannot be done in floating-point. The disadvantages of decimal types are that the range of values is restricted because no exponents are allowed, and their representation in memory is wasteful. The reason for this waste is explained in Section 4.2.

4.1.2   Boolean Types

Boolean types are perhaps the simplest of all types. Their range of values has only two elements, one for true and one for false. They were introduced in ALGOL 60 and have been included in most general-purpose languages designed since 1960. One popular exception is C, in which all numeric type variables and constants can be referenced in expressions used as conditionals as if they were Boolean. In such expressions, all operands with nonzero values are considered true, and zero is considered false.

Boolean types are often used to represent switches or flags in programs. Although other types, such as integers, can be used for these purposes, the use of Boolean types is more readable.

4.1.3 Character Types

Character data are stored in computers as numeric codings. The most commonly used coding is ASCII (American Standard Code for Information Interchange), which uses the values 0..127 to code 128 different characters. To provide the means of processing codings of single characters, many programming languages include a primitive type for them.

In C and C++, the **char** type is used for both character and small integer data. In FORTRAN 77, the CHARACTER type is used for both single characters and character strings. In Ada, the CHARACTER type is used exclusively for single character data.

Character strings, which are far more useful than single characters, are discussed in Chapter 5.

4.2 Implementing Primitive Data Types

An integer value is represented by a string of bits, with one of the bits, typically the leftmost, representing the sign. Integer types are supported directly by the hardware.

Floating-point values have been stored in a variety of different formats, although all have the same basic components. These are the fractional part, sometimes called the mantissa; the sign of the fractional part; the exponent, sometimes called the characteristic; and the sign of the exponent. If implemented in hardware, the format of floating-point variables is that chosen by the hardware designer. Figure 4.1 shows the widely used IEEE Floating-Point Standard 754 format for single- and double-precision representation (IEEE, 1985).

Figure 4.1
IEEE floating-point formats: (a) Single precision, (b) Double precision

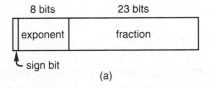

(a)

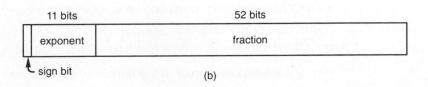

(b)

The sign bit of the two IEEE representations is the sign of the fraction. The exponent is stored in an **excess** notation. In the case of single precision, excess 127 notation is used; for double precision, it is excess 1023. Consider now the single-precision case. The eight bits could store the unsigned range of 0–255. A bias of 127 is added to the actual exponent before storing it in the format. Neither end value (0 or 255) is used for valid numbers. This leaves a range of −126 to 127 in the eight bits, without storing a sign. More details of the IEEE formats can be found in Tenenbaum (1990).

Decimal types are stored very much like character strings, using binary codes for the decimal digits. These representations are called binary coded decimal (BCD). In some cases they are stored one digit per byte, but in others they are packed two digits per byte. Either way, they take more storage than binary representations. It takes at least four bits to code a decimal digit. Therefore, to store a six-digit coded decimal number requires 24 bits of memory. However, it takes only 20 bits to store the same number in binary. This is the reason why we said (in Section 4.1.1.3) that decimal types waste storage. The operations on decimal values are done in hardware on machines that have such capabilities; otherwise, they are simulated in software.

A Boolean value could be represented by a single bit, but because a single bit of memory is difficult to access efficiently on many machines, they are usually stored in the smallest efficiently addressable cell of memory, typically a byte.

4.3 Names

Before we can begin our discussion of variables, we must discuss one of the fundamental attributes of variables, names, which have broader use than simply for variables. Names are also associated with labels, subprograms, and formal parameters, among other program entities.

4.3.1 Design Issues

The following are the primary design issues for names:

1. What is the maximum length of a name?
2. Can connector characters be used in names?
3. Are names case sensitive?
4. Are the special words reserved words or keywords?

These issues are discussed in the following two sections, which also include examples of several design choices.

4.3.2 Name Forms

A **name** is a string of characters used to identify some entity in a program. The earliest programming languages used single-character names. This was natural because early programming was primarily mathematical, and mathematicians have long used single-character names for unknowns in their formal notations.

FORTRAN I broke with the tradition of the single-character name, allowing up to 6 characters in its names. COBOL names can have up to 30 characters; FORTRAN 77 still restricts names to 6 characters; C allows them to have any length, but only the first 8 are significant; Ada names have no length limit, and all are significant; FORTRAN 90 limits names to 31 characters. Some languages do not specify a length limit on names, although implementors of those languages often do. They do this so the table in which identifiers are stored during compilation need not be too large and to simplify the maintenance of that table.

The ideal name form is a string with a reasonably long length limit, if any, with some connector character such as the underscore (_) allowed to provide the capability of building multiple-word names. The underscore serves the same purpose as a space in English text but without terminating the name string in which it is placed. Pascal, Modula-2, and FORTRAN 77 do not allow connector characters in names; C, COBOL, FORTRAN 90, and Ada do.

Some languages, notably C and Modula-2, recognize the difference between the cases of letters in names; that is, names in these languages are **case sensitive.** For example, the following three names are distinct in both C and Modula-2: Sum, SUM, and sum. To some, this is a serious detriment to readability because names that look highly similar in fact denote different entities. In that sense, case sensitivity violates the design principle that language constructs that look the same should have the same meaning.

Obviously, not everyone agrees that case sensitivity is bad for names, for if they did, C and Modula-2 would not have included the feature. In C, the problems of case sensitivity can be avoided by exclusive use of lowercase for names. In Modula-2, however, the problem cannot be escaped because many of the standard modules and functions have names that include both uppercase and lowercase letters. For example, the usual Modula-2 procedure for outputting an integer is WriteInt, and spellings such as WRITEINT are not recognized. This is a problem of writability rather than readability, because a need to remember odd spellings makes it more difficult to write correct programs. It is a kind of intolerance on the part of the language designer, which is enforced by the compiler.

In versions of FORTRAN prior to 90, only uppercase letters could be used in names, a needless restriction. Like FORTRAN 90, many implementations of FORTRAN 77 allow lowercase letters; they simply translate them to uppercase for internal use during compilation.

4.3.3 Special Words

Special words in programming languages are used to make programs more readable by naming actions to be performed. They also are used to separate the syntactic entities of programs. In most languages, these words are classified as reserved words, but in some they are only keywords.

A **keyword** is a word of a programming language that is special only in certain contexts. FORTRAN is one of the languages whose special words are keywords. In FORTRAN, the word REAL, when found at the beginning of a statement and followed by a name, is considered a keyword that indicates the statement is a declarative statement. However, if the word REAL is followed by the assignment operator, it is considered a variable name. These two uses are illustrated in the following:

```
REAL APPLE
REAL = 3.4
```

FORTRAN compilers must recognize the difference between names and special words by context.

A **reserved word** is a special word of a programming language that cannot be used as a name. In COBOL, Pascal, and most other common languages, the special words are reserved. As a language design choice, reserved words are better than keywords, because with keywords the ability to redefine special words can lead to readability problems. For example, in FORTRAN, one could have the statements

```
INTEGER REAL
REAL INTEGER
```

which declare the program variable REAL to be of INTEGER type and the variable INTEGER to be of REAL type. In addition to the strange appearance of these declaration statements, the appearance of REAL and INTEGER as variable names elsewhere in the program could be misleading to program readers.

ALGOL 60 took a different approach to the problem of recognizing the difference between names and special language words: Its definition specified that the reserved words be written with a different font. In computing literature, ALGOL 60 reserved words are usually printed in boldface, with the normal font being used for names. Computers of the time did not allow programmers to specify boldface, or italics, and often not even lowercase letters, so implementors had to invent alternatives. In some cases, the reserved words were delimited by apostrophes. Because the actual form of reserved words in programs was implementation dependent, porting ALGOL 60 programs was difficult.

In program code examples in this book, reserved words are presented in boldface.

4.4 Variables

A program variable is nothing more than an abstraction of a computer memory cell, or a collection of cells. Programmers often think of variables as names for memory locations, although there is much more to a variable than just a name. The great step from machine languages to assembly languages was largely one of replacing absolute numeric memory addresses with names, making programs far more readable, and thus easier to write and maintain. That step also provided an escape from the problem of absolute addressing, because the translator that converted the names to actual addresses also chose actual addresses, for both data operands and instructions.

A variable can be characterized as a sextuple of attributes: (name, address, value, type, lifetime, scope). Although this may seem too complicated for such a seemingly simple concept, it provides the clearest way to explain the various aspects of variables.

Our discussion of variable attributes will lead to examinations of the important related concepts of aliases, binding times, declarations, type checking, strong typing, scoping rules, and referencing environments.

The name, address, type, and value attributes of variables are discussed in the following subsections. The lifetime and scope attributes are discussed in Sections 4.5.3 and 4.8, respectively.

4.4.1 Name

Variable names are the most common names in programs. They were discussed at length in Section 4.3 in the general context of entity names in programs. Most variables have names, although nameless variables do exist, as discussed in Section 4.5.3.3. Names are often referred to as identifiers.

4.4.2 Address

The **address** of a variable is the memory address with which it is associated. This association is not as simple as it may at first appear. In many languages, it is possible for the same name to be associated with different addresses at different places in the program. For example, a Pascal program can have two procedures, p1 and p2, each of which defines a variable that uses the same name, say sum. A reference to sum in p1 is clearly unrelated to a reference to sum in p2. Similarly, some languages allow the same name to be associated with different addresses at different times during program execution. A recursive Pascal procedure can have multiple versions of each locally declared identifier, one for each activation of the procedure. Finally, if a Pascal procedure, p1, has a local variable, count, and is called by two different procedures, count will likely be associated with a different address in each of the activations of p1. The process of associating variables with addresses is further discussed in Section 4.5.3. An implementation model for procedures and their activations for ALGOL-like languages is discussed in Chapter 9.

4.4.2.1   Aliases

It is possible to have multiple identifiers reference the same address. When more than one variable name can be used to access a single memory location, the names are called **aliases.** Aliasing is a hindrance to readability because it allows a variable to have its value changed by an assignment to a different variable. For example, if variables A and B are aliases, any change to A also changes B, and vice versa. A reader of the program must always remember that A and B are different names for the same memory cell. This is very difficult in practice. Aliasing also causes difficulty for program verification methods.

Aliases can be created in programs in several different ways. In FORTRAN, aliases can be explicitly created with the EQUIVALENCE statement. Aliases can be created using the variant record structures of some languages, including Pascal. The aliases created by variant records are meant to save storage by allowing the same locations to be used by different types of data. They can also be used to circumvent the type rules of some of the languages in which they are provided. Variant records are discussed at length in Chapter 5.

Aliasing can be created in many languages through subprogram parameters. These kinds of aliases are discussed in Chapter 8.

In languages that have pointer variables, two pointer variables are aliases when they point to the same memory location. Aliasing with pointers is not meant to conserve storage but is simply a side effect of the nature of pointers. This and other characteristics of pointers are discussed in Chapter 5.

Some of the justifications for aliases no longer exist. When a language construct creates aliases for the purpose of reusing storage, it can be replaced by a dynamic storage management scheme, which will also allow reuse of storage but will not necessarily create aliases. Furthermore, computer memories are far larger now than when languages like FORTRAN were developed, so memory is now not such a scarce commodity.

The time when a variable becomes associated with an address is very important to an understanding of programming languages. This subject is discussed in Section 4.5.3.

4.4.3 Type

The **type** of a variable determines the range of values the variable can have and the set of operations that are defined for values of the type. For example, the type INTEGER in some FORTRAN implementations specifies a value range of −32,768 to 32,767, and arithmetic operations for addition, subtraction, multiplication, and division, along with some library functions for operations like absolute value.

Floating-point types have value ranges that are defined in terms of precision and range. Precision is the accuracy of the fractional part of a value. Range is a combination of the range of fractions and, more importantly, the range of exponents.

As we stated in Section 4.1.1.2, floating-point types model the real numbers of mathematics. There are several problems with this modeling. In addition to the inability to accurately represent many real values, there is the problem of not including all the integer values in the same implementation, because on many systems, integer values occupy the same amount of storage as floating-point values. Because integers do not have exponents, there is space for more digits. For this reason, in many implementations, the fraction of floating-point variables stores only about seven decimal digits of accuracy, whereas integers store about ten. Another problem with floating-point types is the loss of accuracy through arithmetic operations. For more information on the problems of floating-point notation, see Knuth (1981).

4.4.4 Value

The value of a variable is the contents of the memory cell or cells associated with the variable. It is convenient to think of computer memory in terms of *abstract* cells, rather than physical cells. The cells, or individually addressable units, of most contemporary computer memories are byte-sized, with a byte usually being eight bits in length. This size is too small for most program variables. We define an abstract memory cell to have the size required by the variable with which it is associated. For example, although floating-point values may occupy four physical bytes in a particular implementation of a particular language, we think of a floating-point value as occupying a single abstract memory cell. We consider the value of each simple nonstructured type to occupy a single abstract cell. Henceforth, when we say memory cell, we mean abstract memory cell. Sometimes we will use the term **object** to denote the combination of a memory cell and its contents.

The address of a variable is sometimes called its *l*-**value,** and the value is sometimes called its *r*-**value.** These names came about because the *l*-value of a variable is required when it is used on the left side of an assignment statement, and the *r*-value is required when a variable is used on the right side. To access the *r*-value, the *l*-value must be determined first. Such determinations are not always simple. For example, scoping rules can greatly complicate matters, as discussed in Section 4.8.

4.5   The Concept of Binding

In a general sense, a **binding** is an association, such as between an attribute and an entity or between an operation and a symbol. The time at which a binding takes place is called **binding time.** Bindings and binding times are very important concepts in the semantics of programming languages. Bindings can take place at language design time, language implementation time, compile time, link time, load time, or run time. For example, the asterisk symbol (*) is usually bound to the multiplication operation at language design time. A data type, such as INTEGER in FORTRAN, is bound to a range of possible values at language implementation time. At compile time, a variable in a Pascal program is bound to a particular data type. A call to a library subprogram is bound to the subprogram code at link time. A variable may be bound to a storage cell when the program is loaded into memory. That same binding does not happen until run time in some cases, as with variables declared in Pascal procedures.

A complete understanding of the binding times for the attributes of program entities is a prerequisite for understanding the semantics of a programming language. For example, to understand what a subprogram does, one must understand how the actual parameters in its call are bound to the formal parameters in its definition. To determine the current value of a variable, you may need to know when the variable was bound to storage.

4.5.1   Binding of Attributes to Variables

Because the focus of this chapter is primitive types and variables, the main concern here is the binding of attributes to variables.

A binding is **static** if it occurs before run time and remains unchanged throughout program execution. If it occurs during run time or can change in the course of program execution, it is called **dynamic.** Variables can be bound to attributes at a variety of times, such as compile time, load time, and run time. The physical binding of a variable to a storage cell in a virtual memory environment is complex, because the page or segment of the address space in which the cell resides may be moved in and out of memory many times during program execution. In a sense, such variables are bound and unbound repeatedly. These bindings, however, are maintained by computer hardware, and the changes are invisible to the program and the user. Because they are not important to the discussion, we are not concerned with these hardware bindings. The essential point is to distinguish between static and dynamic bindings.

4.5.2 Type Bindings

Before a variable can be referenced in a program, it must be bound to a data type. The two important aspects of this binding are how the type is specified and when the binding takes place. Types can be specified statically through some form of explicit or implicit declaration.

4.5.2.1 Variable Declarations

An **explicit declaration** is a statement in a program that lists variable names and declares them to be of a particular type. An **implicit declaration** is a means of associating variables with types through default conventions instead of declaration statements. In this case, the first appearance of a variable name in a program constitutes its implicit declaration. Both explicit and implicit declarations create static bindings to types.

Most programming languages designed since the mid-1960s require explicit declarations of all variables. Several earlier languages, notably FORTRAN, PL/I, and BASIC, have some kind of implicit declarations. For example, in FORTRAN, an identifier that appears in a program that is not explicitly declared is implicitly declared according to the following convention: If the identifier begins with one of the letters I, J, K, L, M, or N, it is implicitly declared to be INTEGER type; otherwise, it is implicitly declared to be REAL type.

Although they are a minor convenience to programmers, implicit declarations can be detrimental to reliability, because they prevent the compilation process from detecting some programmer errors. Variables that are accidentally left undeclared by the programmer are given default types and unexpected attributes, which could cause subtle errors that are difficult to diagnose.

4.5.2.2 Dynamic Type Binding

With dynamic type binding, the type is not specified by a declaration statement. Instead, the variable is bound to a type when it is assigned a value in an assignment statement. When the assignment statement is executed, the variable being assigned is bound to the type of the value, variable, or expression on the right side of the assignment.

Languages in which types are dynamically bound are dramatically different from those in which types are statically bound. The primary advantage of dynamic binding of variables to types is that it provides a great deal of programming flexibility. For example, a program to process a list of data in a language that uses dynamic type binding can be written as a generic program, meaning that it is capable of dealing with data of any type. Whatever type data is input will be acceptable, because the variables in which the data is to be stored can be bound to the correct type when the data is assigned to the variables after input. By contrast, because of static binding of types, one cannot write a Pascal program to process a list of data without knowing the type of that data, and then that program will process only data of that type.

In APL (Polivka and Pakin, 1975) and SNOBOL4 (Griswold et al., 1971), the binding of a variable to a type is dynamic. For example, an APL program may contain the following statement:

```
LIST ← 10.2 5.1 0.0
```

Regardless of the previous type of the variable named LIST, this assignment causes it to become a single-dimensioned array of length 3 of floating-point elements. If the statement

```
LIST ← 47
```

followed the assignment, LIST would then become a simple integer variable.

There are two disadvantages to dynamic type binding. First, the error detection capability of the compiler is diminished relative to a compiler for a language with static type bindings, because any two types can appear on opposite sides of the assignment operator. Incorrect types of right sides of assignments are not detected as errors; rather, the type of the left side is simply changed to the incorrect type. For example, suppose that in a particular program I and X are integer variables, and Y is a floating-point variable. Further suppose that the program needs the assignment statement

```
I := X
```

but because of a keying error, it has the assignment statement

```
I := Y
```

In a language with dynamic type binding, no error is detected by the compiler or run-time system. I is simply changed to floating-point type. But because Y was used instead of the correct variable X, the results are erroneous. In a language with static type binding (and in which it is illegal to assign a floating-point object to an integer variable, as in Pascal), the compiler would detect the error, and the program would not get to execution.

The other disadvantage of dynamic type binding is cost. The cost of implementing dynamic attribute binding is considerable, particularly in execution time. Type checking must be done at run time. Furthermore, every variable must have a descriptor associated with it to maintain the current type. The descriptors must also be of varying size, because more space is needed if the variable is a structured type than if it is a primitive type. Descriptors are discussed in Chapter 5.

Languages that have dynamic type binding for variables are often implemented using interpreters rather than compilers. This is partially because it is difficult to dynamically change the types of variables in machine code. Furthermore, the time to do dynamic type binding is nicely hidden by the overall time of interpretation, so it seems less costly in that environment. On the other hand, languages with static type bindings are seldom implemented by interpretation, because programs in these languages can be easily translated to very efficient machine code versions.

A somewhat different kind of dynamic type binding is included in some languages that include support for object-oriented programming. Chapter 15 includes a discussion of this particular kind of type binding.

4.5.2.3 Type Inference

ML is a relatively recent programming language that supports both functional and imperative programming (Milner et al., 1990). ML employs an interesting type inference mechanism, in which the types of most expressions can be determined without requiring the programmer to specify the types of the variables. For example, the function declaration

```
fun circumf r = 3.14159 * r * r;
```

specifies a function that takes a real argument and produces a real result. The types are inferred from the type of the constant in the expression. Likewise, in the function

```
fun times10 x = 10 * x;
```

the argument and functional value are inferred to be of type integer.

The ML system rejects the function

```
fun square x = x * x;
```

because the types of the argument and the function cannot be inferred. In such cases, the programmer can supply a hint, such as

```
fun square x : int = x * x;
```

The fact that the functional value is typed as an integer is sufficient to infer that the argument is also an integer. The following definitions are also legal:

```
fun square (x : int) = x * x;
fun square x = (x : int) * x;
fun square x = x * (x : int);
```

Type inference is also used in the purely functional language, Miranda (Turner, 1990).

4.5.3   Storage Bindings and Lifetime

The fundamental character of a programming language is in large part determined by the design of the storage bindings for its variables. It is therefore important to have a clear understanding of these bindings.

The memory cell to which a variable is bound must be somehow taken from a pool of available memory. This process is called **allocation**. **Deallocation** is the process of placing a memory cell that has been unbound from a variable back into the pool of available memory.

The **lifetime** of a program variable is the time during which the variable is bound to a specific memory location. So the lifetime of a variable begins when it is bound to a specific cell and ends when it is unbound from that cell. To investigate storage bindings of variables, it is convenient to separate primitive variables into four categories, according to their lifetimes. We call these categories static, semidynamic, explicit dynamic, and implicit dynamic. In the following sections, we discuss the meanings of these four categories, along with their purposes, advantages, and disadvantages.

4.5.3.1   Static Variables

Static variables are those that are bound to memory cells before execution begins and remain bound to those same memory cells until execution terminates. Variables that are statically bound to storage have several valuable applications to programming. Obviously, globally accessible variables are often used throughout the execution of a program, thus making it reasonable to have them bound to the same storage during that execution. Sometimes it is convenient to have variables that are declared in subprograms be **history sensitive;** that is, have them retain values between separate executions of the subprogram. This is a characteristic of a variable that is statically bound to storage.

The greatest advantage of static variables is efficiency. All addressing of static variables can be direct; other kinds of variables often require indirect addressing, which is more costly. Furthermore, no run-time overhead is incurred for allocation and deallocation.

The disadvantage of static binding to storage is reduced flexibility; in particular, in a language that has only variables that are statically bound to storage, recursive subprograms are not supported.

4.5.3.2   Semidynamic Variables

Semidynamic variables are those whose storage bindings are created when their declaration statements are elaborated, but whose types are statically bound. **Elaboration** of such a declaration refers to the storage allocation and binding process indicated by the declaration, which takes place when execution reaches the code to which the declaration is attached. Therefore, elaboration occurs during run time. For example, a Pascal procedure consists of a declaration section and a code section. The declaration section is elaborated just before execution of the code section begins, which happens when the procedure is called. The storage for the variables in the declaration section is allocated at elaboration time and deallocated when the procedure returns control to its caller. The variables declared in a procedure are called **local** variables.

The design of ALGOL 60 and its successor languages allow recursive procedures. To be useful, at least in most cases, recursive procedures require some form of dynamic local storage, so that each active copy of the recursive procedure has its own version of the local variables. These needs are conveniently met by semidynamic variables. Even in the absence of recursion, having semidynamic local storage for procedures is not without merit, because all procedures share the same memory space for their locals. The disadvantages are the run-time overhead of allocation and deallocation and the fact that locals cannot be history sensitive.

In versions of FORTRAN prior to FORTRAN 77, all variables were static. FORTRAN 77 and FORTRAN 90 allow implementors to use semidynamic variables for locals, but include the statement

SAVE list

that allows the programmer to specify that some or all of the variables (those in list) in the subprogram in which SAVE is placed will be static.

All attributes other than storage are statically bound to semidynamic variables of primitive types. That is not the case for some structured types, as discussed in Chapter 5. Implementation of allocation/deallocation processes for semidynamic variables is discussed in Chapter 9.

4.5.3.3 Explicit Dynamic Variables

Explicit dynamic variables are nameless objects whose storage is allocated and deallocated by explicit run-time instructions specified by the programmer. These variables can be referenced only through pointer variables.

An explicit dynamic variable is created by a call to a system routine provided for that purpose. This routine is sometimes in the form of a procedure (as in Pascal), sometimes it is in the form of an operator (as in Ada), and in other cases it has the form of a function (as in C).

In Pascal, the allocation procedure, named new, has a single parameter, which is a pointer variable. When called, an object, or explicit dynamic variable, of the type that the parameter can reference is created, and the parameter is set to reference it. Note that the type of the explicit dynamic variable can be determined at compile time. An explicit dynamic variable is bound to a type at compile time, but it is bound to storage at the time it is created, which is during run time.

In addition to a routine or operator for creating explicit dynamic variables, some languages include a means of destroying them.

As an example of explicit dynamic variables, consider the following Pascal code segment:

```
type intnode = ^integer;
var anode : intnode;
...
new(anode);
...
dispose(anode);
...
```

In this example, an explicit dynamic variable of integer type is created by the call to new. This variable is then referenced through the pointer, anode. Later, the variable is destroyed by the call to the system procedure, dispose.

Explicit dynamic variables are often used for dynamic structures, such as linked lists and trees, that need to grow and shrink during execution. Such structures can be conveniently built using pointers and explicit dynamic variables.

The disadvantages of explicit dynamic variables are the difficulty of using them correctly and the cost of references, allocations, and deallocations. These considerations, pointer data types, and implementation methods for explicit dynamic variables are discussed at length in Chapter 5.

4.5.3.4   Implicit Dynamic Variables

Implicit dynamic variables are bound to storage only when they are assigned values. In fact, all their attributes are bound every time they are assigned. In a sense, they are just names that adapt to whatever use they are asked to serve. The advantage of such variables is they have the highest degree of flexibility, allowing highly generic code to be written. The disadvantage is the run-time overhead of maintaining all the dynamic attributes, which could include array subscript types and ranges, among others. Another disadvantage is the loss of some error detection by the compiler, as discussed in Section 4.5.2.2. Examples of implicit dynamic variables in APL also appear in Section 4.5.2.2.

4.6   Type Checking

For our discussion of type checking, we generalize the concept of operands and operators to include subprograms and assignment statements. We will think of subprograms as operators whose operands are their parameters. The assignment symbol will be thought of as a binary operator, with its target variable and its expression being the operands.

Type checking is the activity of ensuring that the operands of an operator are of compatible types. A **compatible** type is one that is either legal for the operator or is allowed under language rules to be implicitly converted by compiler-generated code to a legal type. This automatic conversion is called a **coercion.**

A **type error** is the application of an operator to an operand of an inappropriate type.

If all bindings of variables to types are static in a language, then type checking can nearly always be done statically. Dynamic type binding requires type checking at run time, which is called dynamic type checking.

Type checking is complicated when a language allows a memory cell to store values of different types at different times during execution. This can be done with Pascal variant records and with FORTRAN EQUIVALENCE. In these cases, type checking, if done, must be dynamic and requires the run-time system to maintain the type of the current value of such memory cells. So, even though all Pascal variables are statically bound to types, not all type errors can be detected by static type checking.

4.7 Strong Typing

One of the new ideas in language design that became prominent in the so-called structured programming revolution of the 1970s is **strong typing.** Strong typing is widely acknowledged as being a highly valuable concept. Unfortunately, it is often loosely defined, and it is sometimes used in computing literature without being defined at all.

The following is one simple definition of a strongly typed language: A strongly typed language is one in which each name in a program in the language has a single type associated with it, and that type is known at compile time. The essence of this definition is that all types are statically bound. The weakness of this definition is that it ignores the possibility that, although a variable's type may be known, the storage location to which it is bound may store values of different types at different times. To take this possibility into account, we define a programming language to be **strongly typed** if type errors are always detected. This requires that the types of all operands can be determined, either at compile time or at run time. The importance of strong typing lies in its ability to detect all misuses of variables that result in type errors. A strongly typed language also allows the detection, at run time, of uses of the incorrect type values in variables that can store values of more than one type.

FORTRAN 77 is not strongly typed because the relationship between actual and formal parameters is not type checked. Also, the use of EQUIV-ALENCE between variables of different types allows a variable of one type to refer to a value of a different type, without the system being able to check the type of the value when one of the EQUIVALENCEd variables is referenced or assigned. In fact, type checking of EQUIVALENCEd variables would eliminate most of their usefulness.

Pascal is nearly strongly typed, but it fails in its design of variant records because it allows omission of the tag that stores the current type of a variable, which provides the means of checking for the correct value types. We discuss variant records and their potential problems in Chapter 5. Early versions of Pascal also fail in that the parameters of procedures and functions passed themselves as parameters cannot be statically type checked. This problem is discussed in Chapter 8.

Modula-2 is not a strongly typed language because its design of variant records is like that of Pascal. Furthermore, it has a type, WORD, that intentionally avoids type checking.

Ada is nearly strongly typed. References to variables in variant records are dynamically checked for correct type values. This is much better than Pascal and Modula-2, in which checking is not even possible, much less required. However, Ada allows programmers to breach the Ada type-checking rules by specifically requesting that type checking be suspended for a particular type conversion. This temporary suspension of type checking can be done only when the library function UNCHECKED_CONVERSION is used. This function, of which there can be a version for every data type, takes a variable of its type as its parameter and returns the bit string that is the current value of that variable. No actual conversion takes place; it is merely a means of extracting the value of a variable of one type and using it as if it were of a different type. This can be useful for user-defined storage allocation and deallocation operations, in which addresses are manipulated as integers but must be used as pointers. Because no checking is done in UNCHECKED_CONVERSION, it is the programmer's responsibility to ensure that the use of a value gotten from it is meaningful.

Original C, ANSI C, and C++ are not strongly typed languages because all allow functions for which parameters are not type checked.

The coercion rules of a language have an important effect on the value of type checking. For example, expressions are strongly typed in Pascal. However, an arithmetic operator with one floating-point operand and one integer operand is legal. The value of the integer operand is implicitly converted to floating-point, and a floating-point operation takes place. This is what is usually intended by the programmer. However, the coercion also results in a loss of part of the reason for strong typing—error detection. So, the value of strong typing is weakened by coercion. Languages with a great deal of coercion, like PL/I and, to a lesser degree, ANSI C and C++, are significantly less reliable than those with little coercion, such as Ada. The issue of coercion is examined in detail in Chapter 6.

Some languages, such as APL and SNOBOL4, because of their dynamic type binding, allow only dynamic type checking. It is much better to detect errors at compile time than at run time, because the earlier correction will always be less costly. The penalty for static checking is reduced programmer flexibility. Fewer shortcuts and tricks are possible. Such techniques, though, are now generally held in quite low esteem.

4.8   Scope

One of the most important factors having an effect on the understanding of variables is scope. The **scope** of a program variable is the range of statements in which the variable is visible.

A variable is **visible** in a statement if it can be referenced in that statement. The scope rules of a language determine how a particular occurrence of a name is associated with a variable. In particular, scope rules determine how references to variables declared outside the currently executing procedure are associated with their declarations, and thus their attributes. A complete knowledge of these rules for a language is therefore essential to being able to write or read programs in that language.

As defined in Section 4.5.3.2, a variable is local in a program unit if it is declared there. The **nonlocal variables** of a program unit are those that are visible within the program unit but are not declared in the unit.

4.8.1   Static Scoping

ALGOL 60 introduced a method of binding names to nonlocal variables called **static scoping,** which has been copied by most contemporary imperative languages. Static scoping is thus named because the scope of a variable can be statically determined—that is, determined prior to execution.

Individual static scopes in most imperative languages are associated with program unit definitions. In some languages, however, collections of statements within program units can also create new scopes, as explained later in this section. For now, however, we assume that all scopes are associated with program units. Furthermore, we assume that the program units are procedures. In this chapter, we also assume that static scoping is the only method of accessing nonlocal variables in the languages under discussion. This is not true for all languages that use static scoping, but the assumption simplifies the discussion here. Additional methods used in languages that have static scoping are discussed in Chapter 8.

In all common static-scoped languages except C, procedures are nested inside the main program, and procedures also can be nested inside other procedures. In these cases, the main program and all procedures create their own scopes. This creates a hierarchy of scopes in a program.

When a reference to a variable is found by a compiler for a static-scoped language, the attributes of the variable are determined by finding its declaration. In static scoped languages other than C, this process can be thought of in the following way. Suppose a reference is made to a variable x in procedure A. The correct declaration is found by first searching the declarations of procedure A. If no declaration is found for the variable there, the search continues in the declarations of the procedure that declared procedure A, which is called its **static parent.** If a declaration of x is not found there, the search continues to the next larger enclosing unit (the unit that declared A's parent), and so forth, until a declaration for x is found or the main program's declarations have been searched without success. In that case, an undeclared variable error has been detected. The static parent of procedure A, and its static parent, and so forth up to and including the main program, are called the **static ancestors** of A. Note that implementation techniques for static scoping, which are discussed in Chapter 9, are much more efficient than the process just described.

Consider the following Pascal procedure:

```
procedure big;
  var x : integer;
  procedure sub1;
    begin
    ... x ...
    end;
  procedure sub2;
    var x : integer;
    begin
    sub1
    end;
begin
sub2
end;
```

In this procedure, big calls sub2, which calls sub1.

Under static scoping, the reference to the variable x in sub1 is to the x declared in the procedure big. This is true because the search for x begins in the procedure in which the reference occurs, sub1, but no declaration for x is found there. The search thus continues in the static parent of sub1, big, where the declaration of x is found.

The presence of predefined names complicates this process somewhat. For example, Pascal systems include a library of predefined subprograms for commonly needed functions, such as sin, cos, and writeln. In some languages, these are like keywords and can be redefined by the user. In these cases, the library names are used only if the user program does not contain a redefinition. In other languages, the predefined names are reserved, which means the search for the meaning of a given name begins with the list of predefined names, even before the local scope declarations are checked.

In languages that use static scoping, some variable declarations can be hidden from some procedures. For example, consider the following skeletal Pascal program:

```
program main;
  var x : integer;
  procedure sub1;
    var x : integer;
```

```
        begin
        ..x..
        end;
      begin
      sub1
      end.
```

The reference to x in sub1 is to sub1's declared x. In some static-scoped languages, including Pascal, the x of the main program is hidden from the code of sub1. In these languages, a declaration for a variable effectively hides any declaration of a variable with the same name in a larger enclosing scope.

In Ada, hidden variables from ancestor scopes can be accessed with selective references, which include the ancestor scope's name. For example, in the preceding program, the x declared in the main program can be accessed in sub1 by the reference main.x.

Although C and C++ do not allow subprograms to be nested inside other subprogram definitions, they do have global variables. These variables are declared outside any subprogram definition. Local variables can hide these globals, as in Pascal. In C++, such hidden globals can be accessed using the scope operator (::). For example, if x is a global that is hidden in a subprogram by a local named x, the global could be referenced as ::x.

4.8.2 Blocks

Some languages allow new static scopes to be defined in the midst of executable code. This powerful concept, introduced in ALGOL 60, allows a section of code to have its own local variables whose scopes are minimized. Such variables are typically semidynamic, so they have their storage allocated when the section is entered and deallocated when the section is exited. Such a section of code is called a **block.**

In Ada, blocks are specified with **declare** clauses, as in

```
...
declare TEMP : integer;
  begin
  TEMP := FIRST;
  FIRST := SECOND;
  SECOND := TEMP;
  end;
...
```

Blocks provide the origin of the phrase **block-structured language.** Although Pascal and Modula-2 are called block-structured languages, they do not include these nonprocedure blocks.

C allows any compound statement (a statement sequence surrounded by matched braces) to have declarations and thus define a new scope. For example, if `list` were an integer array, one could write

```
if (list[i] < list[j])
  { int temp;
    temp = list[i];
    list[i] = list[j];
    list[j] = temp;
  }
```

4.8.3 Evaluation

Static scoping provides a method of nonlocal access that works well in many situations. However, it is not without its problems. Consider the program whose skeletal structure is shown in Figure 4.2. For this example, assume that all scopes are created by the definitions of the main program and the procedures.

This program contains an overall scope for `main`, with two procedures that define scopes inside `main`, A and B. Inside A, there are scopes for the procedures C and D. Inside B is the scope of procedure E. We assume that the necessary data and procedure access determined the structure of this program. The required procedure access is as follows: `main` can call A and B, A can call C and D, and B can call A and E.

It is convenient to view the structure of the program as a tree in which each node represents a procedure and thus a scope. A tree representation of the program of Figure 4.2 is shown in Figure 4.3.

The structure of this program may appear to be a very natural program organization that clearly reflects the design needs. However, a graph of the

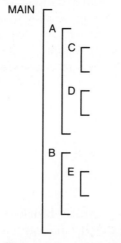

Figure 4.2
The structure of a program

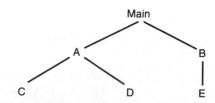

Figure 4.3
The tree structure of the program in Figure 4.2

potential procedure calls of this system, shown in Figure 4.4, shows that a great deal of calling opportunity beyond that required is possible.

Figure 4.5 shows the desired calls of the example program. The difference between Figures 4.4 and 4.5 illustrates the number of possible calls that are not necessary in this specific application. An erroneous call to a procedure that should not have been callable will not be detected as an error by the compiler. That delays detection of the error until run time, which makes its correction more costly. Therefore, access to procedures should be restricted to those that are necessary.

Too much data access is a closely related problem. For example, all variables declared in the main program are visible to all of the procedures, whether or not that is desired, and there is no way to avoid it.

To illustrate another kind of problem with static scoping, consider the following scenario. Suppose that after the program has been developed and tested, a modification of its specification is required. In particular, suppose

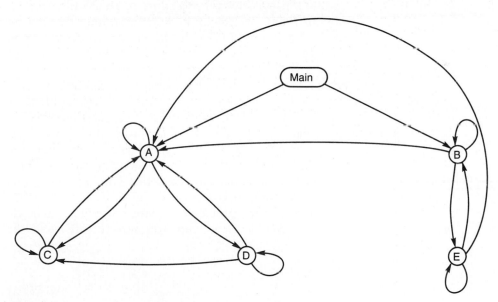

Figure 4.4
The potential call graph of the program in Figure 4.2

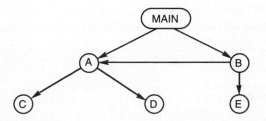

Figure 4.5
The graph of the desirable calls in the program in Figure 4.2

that procedure E must now gain access to some variables of the scope of D. One way to provide that access is to move E inside the scope of D. But then E can no longer access the scope of B, which it presumably needs (otherwise, why was it there?). Another solution is to move the variables defined in D that are needed by E into main. This would allow access by all the procedures, which would be more than is needed and thus creates the possibility of many incorrect accesses. For example, a misspelled identifier in a procedure can be taken as a reference to an identifier in some enclosing scope, instead of being detected as an error. Furthermore, suppose the variable that is moved to main is named x. x is needed by D and E. But suppose that there is a variable named x declared in A. That would hide the correct x from its original owner, D. One final problem with moving the declaration of x to main is that it is harmful to readability to have the declaration of variables so far from their uses.

A similar problem occurs because static scoping also determines procedure access. In the tree of Figure 4.3, suppose that, due to some specification change, procedure E needed to call procedure D. This could only be accomplished by moving D to nest directly in main, assuming that it was also needed by either A or C. It would then also lose access to the variables defined in A. This solution, when used repeatedly, results in programs that begin with long lists of low-level utility procedures.

Thus, getting around the restrictions of static scoping can lead to program designs that bear little resemblance to the original, even in areas of the program in which changes have not been made. Designers are encouraged to use far more globals than are necessary. All procedures can end up being nested at the same level, in the main program, using globals instead of deeper levels of nesting. Moreover, the final design may be awkward and contrived and may not reflect the underlying conceptual design. These and other defects of static scoping are discussed in detail in Clarke, Wileden, and Wolf (1980). One solution to the problems of static scoping is the module concept used by FORTRAN 90, C++, and Ada, which is discussed in Chapter 8.

4.8.4 Dynamic Scope

The scope of variables in APL, SNOBOL4, and some dialects of LISP is dynamic. **Dynamic scoping** is based on the calling sequence of subprograms, not on their spatial relationship to each other. Thus, the scope is determined at run time.

Consider again the procedure big from Section 4.8.1, which is shown again here:

```
procedure big;
  var x : integer;
```

```
      procedure sub1;
        begin
        ... x ...
        end;
      procedure sub2;
        var x : integer;
        begin
        sub1
        end;
      begin
      sub2;
      sub1
      end;
```

Assume that dynamic scoping rules apply to nonlocal references. The meaning of the identifier x referenced in sub1 is dynamic—it cannot be determined at compile time. It may reference the variable from either declaration of x, depending on the calling sequence.

The following describes one way the correct meaning of x can be determined at run time. As in the static case, the search begins with the local declarations, but that is where the similarity ends. When the search of local declarations fails, the declarations of the dynamic parent, or calling procedure, are searched. If a declaration for x is not found there, the search continues in that procedure's dynamic parent, and so forth, until a declaration for x is found. If none is found in any dynamic ancestor, it is a run-time error.

Consider the two different call sequences for sub1 in the example above. First, big calls sub2, which calls sub1. In this case, the search proceeds from the local procedure, sub1, to its caller, sub2, where a declaration for x is found. So the reference to x in sub1, in this case, is to the x declared in sub2. Next, sub1 is called directly from big. In this case, the dynamic parent of sub1 is big, and the reference is to the x declared in big.

4.8.5 Evaluation

The effect of dynamic scoping on programming is profound. The correct attributes of nonlocal variables visible to a program statement cannot be determined statically. Furthermore, such variables are not always the same. A statement in a subprogram that contains a reference to a nonlocal variable can refer to a different variable every time the statement is executed. Several kinds of programming problems follow directly from dynamic scoping.

First, during the time span beginning when a subprogram begins its execution and ending when that execution ends, the local variables of the subprogram are all visible to any other executing subprogram, regardless of its textual proximity. There is no way to protect local variables from this accessibility. Subprograms are always executed in the immediate environment of the caller; therefore, dynamic scoping results in less reliable programs than static scoping.

A second problem that results from dynamic scoping is the inability to statically type check references to nonlocals. This results from the inability to statically determine the declaration for a variable referenced as a nonlocal. Dynamic scoping also makes programs much more difficult to read, because the calling sequence of subprograms must be known in order to determine the meaning of references to nonlocal variables. This can be virtually impossible for a human reader.

On the other hand, dynamic scoping *can* be used to advantage in programming. For example, with dynamic scoping, subprograms inherit the context of their callers; that is, any variable declared in the caller that is not also declared in the called subprogram is visible in the called subprogram. This can be a convenient method of communication between program units, although it is less safe than other methods, such as parameter passing.

The disadvantages of dynamic scoping caused it to be replaced by static scoping in most current dialects of LISP.

Implementation methods for both static and dynamic scoping are discussed in Chapter 9.

4.9 Scope and Lifetime

Sometimes the scope and lifetime of a variable appear to be related. For example, consider a variable that is declared in a Pascal procedure that contains no procedure definitions. The scope of such a variable is from its declaration to the **end** reserved word of the procedure. The lifetime of that variable is the period of time beginning when the procedure is entered and ending when execution of the procedure reaches the **end** (Pascal has no return statement). Although the scope and lifetime of the variable are clearly not the same, because static scope is a textual, or spatial, concept whereas lifetime is a temporal concept, they at least appear to be related in this case.

This apparent relationship between scope and lifetime does not hold in other situations. In FORTRAN, for example, variables that are declared in subprograms are statically bound to the scopes of those subprograms, and usually are also statically bound to storage. So their scopes are static and local to the subprogram, but their lifetimes extend over the entire execution of the program of which they are a part.

Scope and lifetime are also unrelated when subprogram calls are involved. Consider the following Pascal-like program segment:

```
program example;
  procedure printheader;
    begin
    ...
    end;    {of printheader}
```

```
procedure compute;
  var sum : integer;
  begin
  ...
  printheader;
  ...
  end;    {of compute}
begin
...
end; {of example}
```

The scope of the variable sum is completely contained within the compute procedure. It does not extend to the body of the procedure printheader, although printheader executes in the midst of the execution of compute. The lifetime of sum does extend over the time during which printheader executes. Whatever storage location sum is bound to before the call to printheader, that binding will continue during and after the execution of printheader.

4.10   Referencing Environments

The **referencing environment** of a statement is the collection of all names that are visible in the statement. The referencing environment of a statement in a static-scoped language is the variables declared in its local scope plus the collection of all variables of its ancestor scopes that are visible. In such a language, the referencing environment of a statement is needed while that statement is being compiled, so code and data structures can be created to allow references to variables from other scopes during run time. Techniques for implementing references to nonlocal variables in both static- and dynamic-scoped languages are discussed in Chapter 9.

In Pascal, where scopes are created only by procedure definitions, the referencing environment of a statement includes the local variables, plus all of the variables declared in the procedures in which the statement is nested, plus the variables declared in the main program (excluding variables in nonlocal scopes that are hidden by declarations in nearer procedures). Each procedure definition creates a new scope and thus a new environment. Consider the following Pascal skeletal program:

```
program example;
  var a, b : integer;
  ...
  procedure sub1;
    var x, y : integer;
    begin    {of sub1}
    ...            <----------------------1
    end;    {of sub1}
```

```
procedure sub2;
  var x : integer;
    . . .

  procedure sub3;
    var x : integer;
    begin    {of sub3}
    ...      <---------------------2
    end;     {of sub3}
  begin    {of sub2}
  ...      <---------------------3
  end;     {of sub2}
begin    {of example}
...      <---------------------4
end.
```

The referencing environments of the indicated program points are as follows:

Point	Referencing Environment
1	x and y of sub1, a and b of example
2	x of sub3, (x of sub2 is hidden), a and b of example
3	x of sub2, a and b of example
4	a and b of example

Now consider the variable declarations of this skeletal program. First note that, although the scope of sub1 is at a higher level (it is less deeply nested) than sub3, the scope of sub1 is not a static ancestor of sub3, so sub3 does not have access to the variables declared in sub1. There is a good reason for this. The variables declared in sub1 are semidynamic, so they are not bound to storage if sub1 is not in execution. Because sub3 can be in execution when sub1 is not, it cannot be allowed to access variables in sub1, which would not necessarily be bound to storage during the execution of sub3.

A subprogram is **active** if its execution has begun but has not yet terminated. The referencing environment of a statement in a dynamically scoped language is the locally declared variables, plus the variables of all other subprograms that are currently active. Once again, some variables in active subprograms can be hidden from the referencing environment. Recent subprogram activations can have declarations for variables that hide variables with the same names in previous subprogram activations.

Consider the following example program. Assume that the only subprogram calls are the following: example calls sub1, which calls sub2.

```
program example;
  var a, b : integer;
  begin
  ...
  sub1;
  ...      <------------------------- 1
  end;   { of example }
```

```
procedure sub1;
  var b, c : integer;
  begin
  ...     <---------------------------2
  sub2;
  ...
  end;    { of sub1 }
procedure sub2;
  var c, d : integer;
  begin
  ...     <---------------------------3
  end;    { of sub2 }
```

The referencing environments of the indicated program points are as follows:

Point	Referencing Environment
1	a and b of example
2	a of example, b and c of sub1 (b of example is hidden)
3	a of example, b of sub1, c and d of sub2 (b of example and c of sub1 are hidden)

4.11 Named Constants

A **named constant** is a variable that is bound to a value only at the time it is bound to storage; its value cannot be changed by assignment or by an input statement. Named constants are useful as aids to readability and program reliability. Readability can be improved, for example, by using the name PI instead of the constant 3.14159.

Another advantageous use of named constants is in programs that process a fixed number of data values, say 100. Such programs usually use the constant 100 in a number of locations for declaring array subscript ranges, for loop control limits, and other uses. Consider the following skeletal Pascal program segment:

```
program example;
  type
    intarray = array [1..100] of integer;
    realarray = array [1..100] of real;
  ...
  begin
  ...
  for index := 1 to 100 do
    begin
    ...
    end;
  ...
```

```
    for count := 1 to 100 do
      begin
      ...
      end;
    ...
    average := sum div 100;
    ...
    end.
```

When this program must be modified to deal with a different number of data values, all occurrences of 100 must be found and changed. On a large program, this can be tedious and error-prone. An easier and more reliable method is to use a named constant, as in

```
program example;
  const listlen = 100;
  type
      intarray = array [1..listlen] of integer;
      realarray = array [1..listlen] of real;
  ...
  begin
  ...
  for index := 1 to listlen do
    begin
    ...
    end;
  ...
  for count := 1 to listlen do
    begin
    ...
    end;
  ...
  average := sum div listlen;
  ...
  end.
```

Now when the length must be changed, only one line must be changed, regardless of the number of times it is used in the program. This is another example of the benefits of abstraction. The name listlen is an abstraction for the number of elements in some arrays and the number of iterations in some loops. This illustrates how named constants can aid modifiability.

Pascal named constant declarations require simple values on the right side of the = operator. However, Modula-2 and FORTRAN 90 allow constant expressions to be used. These constant expressions can contain previously declared named constants, constant values, and operators. The reason for the restriction to constants and constant expressions in Pascal and Modula-2, respectively, is that both use static binding of values to named constants. Named constants in languages that use static binding of values are sometimes called **manifest constants.**

The Ada language allows dynamic binding of values to named constants. This allows expressions containing variables to be assigned to constants in the declarations. For example, the Ada statement

```
MAX : constant integer := 2 * WIDTH + 1;
```

declares MAX to be an integer type named constant whose value is set to the value of the expression 2 * WIDTH + 1, where the value of the variable WIDTH must be visible when MAX is allocated and bound to its value. Ada also allows named constants of enumeration and structured types, which are discussed in Chapter 5. C++ includes named constants that are similar to those of Ada.

4.12 Variable Initialization

The discussion of binding values to named constants naturally leads to the topic of initialization of variables, because binding a value to a named constant is the same process, except it is permanent.

In many instances, it is convenient for variables to have values before the code of the program or subprogram in which they are declared begins executing. The binding of a variable to a value at the time it is bound to storage is called **initialization.** If the variable is statically bound to storage, binding and initialization occur before run time. If the storage binding is dynamic, then initialization is also dynamic.

In FORTRAN, initial values of variables can be specified in a DATA statement, as in

```
REAL PI
INTEGER SUM
DATA SUM /0/, PI /3.14159/
```

which initializes SUM to zero and PI to 3.14159. The actual initializations take place at compile time, in this case. Once execution begins, SUM and PI are like any other variables.

In Ada, initial values of variables can be specified in the declaration statement, as in

```
procedure EXAMPLE is
  SUM : INTEGER := 0;
  ...
  begin
  ...
  end EXAMPLE;
```

FORTRAN 90 allows a similar kind of initialization.

In ALGOL 68, the only syntactic difference between the declaration of an initialized variable and that of a named constant is the = operator is used for constants and := is used for variables. The declarations

```
int first := 10;
int second = 10;
```

state that `first` is a variable with an initial value of 10, but `second` is a named constant with a fixed value of 10. This use of very similar symbols, `:=` and `=`, to specify two quite different meanings, is a violation of the design principle that constructs that look alike should have similar meanings.

In Ada, the syntactic difference between a named constant declaration and a variable declaration with initialization is the reserved word **constant**. For example, consider the following:

```
LIMIT : constant INTEGER := OLD_LIMIT + 1;
COUNT : INTEGER := OLD_COUNT + 1;
```

In both statements, the variables used in the expressions can be either named constants or variables that are visible when the declarations are elaborated. This use of the reserved word **constant** is a much better design than ALGOL 68's use of =, because it is syntactically very different and also connotative. C++ allows variable initialization that is similar to that of Ada.

Neither Pascal nor Modula-2 provides a way to initialize variables, except at run time with assignment statements.

In general, initialization occurs only once for static variables, but it occurs with every allocation for dynamically allocated variables, such as the local variables in an Ada procedure.

4.13 Type Compatibility

The idea of type compatibility was discussed when we discussed the issue of type checking. In this section, we investigate the type compatibility rules of languages that apply to structured types. The design of the type compatibility rules of a language is important, because it influences the design of the data types and the operations provided for objects of those types. Perhaps the most important result of two variables being of compatible types is that either one can have its value assigned to the other.

There are two primary type compatibility methods: name compatibility and structure compatibility. **Type compatibility by name** means that two variables have compatible types if they are in either the same declaration or in declarations that use the same type name. **Type compatibility by structure** means that two variables have compatible types if their types have identical structures.

Name type compatibility is easy to implement but is highly restrictive. Under a strict interpretation, a variable that is a subrange of the integers would not be compatible with an integer type variable. For example, suppose Pascal used strict name type compatibility, and consider the following:

```
type indextype = 1..100;
var
  count : integer;
  index : indextype;
```

The variables count and index would not be compatible; count could not be assigned to index or vice versa.

Another problem with name compatibility arises when a structured type is passed among procedures through parameters. Such a type must be defined only once, globally. A procedure cannot state the type of such formal parameters in local terms. This is the case with the original version of Pascal.

Structure type compatibility is more flexible than name type compatibility, but it is more difficult to implement. Under name type compatibility, only the two type names must be compared to determine compatibility. Under structure type compatibility, however, the entire structures of the two types must be compared. This comparison is not always simple. (Consider a data structure that refers to itself.) Other questions can also arise. For example, are two record types compatible if they have the same structure but different field names? Are two single-dimensioned array types compatible if they have the same element type but have subscript ranges of 0..10 and 1..11? Are two enumeration types compatible if they have the same number of components but spell the literals differently?

Another difficulty with structure type compatibility is that it disallows differentiating between types with the same structure. For example, consider the following:

```
type celsius = real;
     fahrenheit = real;
```

Variables of these two types are considered compatible under structure type compatibility, allowing them to be mixed in expressions, which is surely undesirable in this case. In general, types with different names are likely to be abstractions of different problem objects and should not be considered equivalent.

The original definition of Pascal (Wirth, 1971) does not specify clearly when name or structure type compatibility is to be used. This is highly detrimental to portability, because a program that is correct in one implementation could be illegal in another. The ISO Standard Pascal (ISO, 1982) clearly states the type compatibility rules of the language, which are neither completely by name nor completely by structure. Structure is used in most cases, while name is used for formal parameters and a few other situations. For example, consider the following declarations:

```
type
  type1 = array [1..10] of integer;
  type2 = array [1..10] of integer;
  type3 = type2;
```

In this example, type1 and type2 are not compatible, so structure equivalence is not used. Furthermore, type2 *is* compatible with type3, illustrating that name equivalence is not strictly used either.

The Ada language uses a restricted form of name compatibility. Ada provides a new construct for building types with identical structure that are not compatible. These are called **derived types.** Derived types inherit all the properties of their parent types. Consider the following example:

```
type celsius is new FLOAT;
type fahrenheit is new FLOAT;
```

Variables of these two derived types are not compatible, although their structures are identical. Furthermore, variables of neither type are compatible with any other floating-point type. Constants are exempt from the rule. A constant such as 3.0 has the type universal real and is compatible with any floating-point type. Derived types can also include constraints on the parent type.

C uses structural equivalence for all types except structures (C's records), for which C uses a form of name equivalence that is similar to that used by ISO Pascal. C++, on the other hand, uses name equivalence.

Variables can be declared in many languages without using type names. Consider the following Ada examples:

```
A : array (1..10) of INTEGER;
```

In this case, A has an anonymous type, though it is still unique. If we also had

```
B : array (1..10) of INTEGER;
```

A and B would be of anonymous but distinct and incompatible types, though they are structurally identical. The multiple declaration

```
C, D : array (1..10) of INTEGER;
```

creates two anonymous types, one for C and one for D, which are incompatible. This declaration is actually treated as if it were the following two declarations:

```
C : array (1..10) of INTEGER;
D : array  (1..10) of INTEGER;
```

The result of this is that C and D are not compatible. If we had written instead

```
type LIST_10 is array (1..10) of INTEGER;
  C, D : LIST_10;
```

then C and D would be compatible.

Type compatibility in expressions is discussed in Chapter 6; type compatibility for parameters is discussed in Chapter 8.

SUMMARY

The primitive data types of most imperative languages include numeric, character, and Boolean types. The numeric types are often directly supported by hardware.

The form of the names of a language can impact both the readability and writability of the language. The relationship of names to special words, which are either reserved words or keywords, is also a significant design decision.

Variables can be characterized by the sextuple of attributes: (name, address, value, type, lifetime, scope).

Aliases are two or more names bound to the same storage address. They are regarded as detrimental to reliability but are difficult to eliminate entirely from a language.

Binding is the association of attributes with program entities. Knowledge of the binding times of attributes to entities is essential to understanding the semantics of programming languages. Binding can be static or dynamic. Declarations, either explicit or implicit, provide a means of specifying the static binding of variables to types. In general, dynamic bindings allow greater flexibility but at the expense of readability, efficiency, and reliability.

Simple variables can be separated into four categories by considering their lifetimes. These are static, semidynamic, explicit dynamic, and implicit dynamic.

Strong typing is the concept of requiring that all type errors be detected. The advantage of strong typing is increased reliability.

Static scoping is a central feature of ALGOL 60 and all of its descendants. It provides an efficient method of allowing visibility of nonlocal variables and subprograms. Dynamic scoping provides more flexibility than static scoping but, again, at the expense of readability, reliability, and efficiency.

The referencing environment of a statement is the collection of all of the variables that are visible to that statement.

Named constants are simply variables that are bound to values only when they are bound to storage. Initialization is the binding of a variable to a value at the time the variable is bound to storage.

The type compatibility rules of a language have an important effect on the operations provided for the objects in the language. Type compatibility is generally defined in terms of name compatibility or structure compatibility. Name compatibility is better for several reasons, particularly because it is easiest to implement.

PROBLEM SET

1. Decide which of the following identifier forms is most readable, and then support that decision.

```
SumOfSales
sum_of_sales
SUMOFSALES
```

2. State the arguments for and against using reserved words instead of keywords in a programming language.

3. What are the arguments for and against representing Boolean values as single bits in memory?

4. Negative integer values are usually stored in either ones complement notation or twos complement notation. Ones complement is just the bitwise complement, in which each bit is changed. Twos complement is ones complement, except that 1 is added. What advantage does twos complement have over ones complement?

5. Why does a decimal value waste memory space?

6. COBOL uses several different methods of storing decimal numbers. Explain the format and purpose of each.

7. VAX minicomputers use a format for floating point numbers that is not the same as the IEEE standard. What is this format, and why was it chosen by the designers of the VAX computers?

8. One common use of FORTRAN's EQUIVALENCE is the following: A large array of numeric values is made available to a subprogram as a parameter. The array contains many different unrelated variables, rather than a collection of repetitions of the same variable. It is represented as an array to reduce the number of names that need to be passed as parameters. Within the subprogram, a lengthy EQUIVALENCE statement is used to create connotative names as aliases to the various array elements, which increases the readability of the code of the subprogram. Is this a good idea, or not? What alternatives to aliasing are available?

9. Dynamic type binding is closely related to implicit dynamic variables. Explain this relationship.

10. Describe a situation when a history-sensitive variable in a subprogram is useful.

11. Look up the definition of "strongly typed" as given in Gehani (1983) and compare it with the definition given in this chapter. How do they differ?

12. Consider the following Pascal skeletal program:

```
program main;
  var x : integer;
  procedure sub1;
    var x : integer;
    procedure sub3; forward
    procedure sub2;
      begin    { of sub2 }
      ...
      end;     { of sub2 }
    begin    { of sub1 }
    ...
    end;     { of sub1 }
```

```
procedure sub3;
  begin    { of sub3 }
  ...
  end;     { of sub3 }
begin      { of main }
...
end.
```

Assume that the execution of this program is in the following unit order:
```
main calls sub1
sub1 calls sub2
sub2 calls sub3
```

a. Assuming static scoping, which declaration of x is the correct one for a referenc to x in:
   i.   sub1
   ii. sub2
   iii. sub3

b. Repeat part a, but assume dynamic scoping.

13. Assume the following program was compiled and executed using static scoping rules. What value of **x** is printed in procedure **sub1**? Under dynamic scoping rules, what value of **x** is printed in procedure **sub1**?

```
program main;
  var x : integer;
  procedure sub1;
    begin    { of sub1 }
    writeln('x =', x)
    end;     { of sub1 }
  procedure sub2;
    var x : integer;
    begin    { of sub2 }
    x := 10;
    sub1;
    end;     { of sub2 }
  begin  { of main }
  x := 5;
  sub2
end. { of main }
```

14. Consider the following program:

```
program main;
  var x, y, z : integer;
  procedure sub1;
    var a, y, z : integer;
    procedure sub2;
      var a, b, z : integer;
      begin    { of sub2 }
      ...
      end;     { of sub2 }
    begin
    ...
    end;
```

```
      procedure sub3;
        var a, x, w : integer;
        begin   { of sub3 }
        ...
        end;    { of sub3 }
      begin     { of main }
      ...
      end. { of main }
```

List all the variables, along with the program units where they are declared, that are visible in the bodies of sub1, sub2, and sub3, assuming static scoping is used.

15. Consider the following program:

```
program main;
  var x, y, z : integer;
  procedure sub1;
    var a, y, z : integer;
    begin   { of sub1 }
    ...
    end;    { of sub1 }
  procedure sub2;
    var a, b, z : integer;
    begin   { of sub2 }
    ...
    end;    { of sub2 }
  procedure sub3;
    var a, x, w : integer;
    begin   { of sub3 }
    ...
    end;    { of sub3 }
  begin     { of main }
  ...
  end. {of main]
```

Given the following calling sequences and the fact that dynamic scoping is used, what variables are visible during execution of the last subprogram activated? Include with each visible variable the name of the unit where it is declared.

a. main calls sub1; sub1 calls sub2; sub2 calls sub3.
b. main calls sub1; sub1 calls sub3.
c. main calls sub2; sub2 calls sub3; sub3 calls sub1.
d. main calls sub3; sub3 calls sub1.
e. main calls sub1; sub1 calls sub3; sub3 calls sub2.
f. main calls sub3; sub3 calls sub2; sub2 calls sub1.

5

Data Types

Alan J. Perlis

Alan J. Perlis, who was at Purdue University at the time, was instrumental in the development of IT, which was a high-level language for which compilers were operational in 1957. Perhaps more significantly, he was a principle member of the ALGOL design team.

Key Concepts

- Character string types
- Enumeration and subrange types
- Arrays and their operations
- Records and their operations
- Discriminated and free unions
- Mathematical sets as a data type

- Dangling pointers
- Garbage
- Implementation methods for data types
- Array access functions
- Reference counters and garbage collection

The concept of a data type and the characteristics of some primitive data types were introduced in Chapter 4. We now investigate the design of the more complex data types in imperative languages.

For each of the various categories of data types, the design issues are stated, and the design choices made by the designers of the important imperative languages are explained. These designs are also evaluated.

Implementation methods for data types often have a significant, if not crucial, impact on their design. Therefore, implementation of the different data types is another important part of this chapter.

5.1   Introduction

Computer programs produce results by manipulating data. An important factor in determining the ease with which they can perform this task is how well the data types match the real-world problem space. It is crucial, therefore, that a language support the proper variety of data types and structures. The designers of PL/I included many data types, with the intent of supporting a large range of applications. A much better approach, introduced in ALGOL 68, is to provide a few basic types and a few flexible combining methods that allow a programmer to tailor a structure to the problem at hand. This approach, which results in an orthogonal data type design, was followed by the designers of most subsequent ALGOL-like languages.

The contemporary concepts of data typing have evolved over the last 30 years. In the earliest languages, all problem space data structures had to be modeled with only a few basic language-supported data structures. For example, in pre-90 FORTRANs, linked lists, nonlinked lists, and binary trees are all commonly modeled with arrays.

The data structures of COBOL took the first step away from the early FORTRAN model by allowing programmers to specify the accuracy of decimal data values, and also by providing a structured data type for records of information. PL/I extended the capability of accuracy specification to integer and floating-point types. This has since been incorporated in Ada and FORTRAN 90. As mentioned above, ALGOL 68 advanced data structure design by allowing programmers to construct new data types from the built-in types. This was clearly one of the most important advances in the evolution of data type design. User-defined types provide improved readability through the use of meaningful names for types. They allow type checking among the variables of a special category of use, which would otherwise not be possible. User-defined types also aid modifiability: a programmer can change the type of a category of variables in a program by changing only a type declaration statement.

The Ada language embodies the concepts in data type design that existed in the late 1970s, which resulted from a natural extension to the idea of user-defined types. The philosophy of this design is that the user should be allowed to create a unique type for each unique class of variables in the problem space. Moreover, the language must enforce the uniqueness of the types, which are in fact abstractions of the problem space variables. This is a powerful concept, and it has a significant impact on the overall process of software design. Taking this concept a step farther, one arrives at abstract data types, which are discussed in detail in Chapter 10.

5.2 General Design Issues for Data Types

Seven categories of data types are discussed in the following sections. Design issues particular to each are stated, and a number of example designs are discussed. One design issue is fundamental to all data types: What operations are provided for variables of types in the category, and how are they specified?

5.3 Character String Types

A **character string type** is one in which the objects consist of sequences of characters. Character string constants are used to label output, and input and output of all kinds is often done in terms of strings. Of course, character strings also are an essential type for all programs that do character manipulation.

5.3.1 Design Issues

The two most important design issues that are specific to character string types are

1. Should strings be a primitive type or simply a special kind of character array?
2. Should strings have static or dynamic length?

5.3.2   Strings and Their Operations

If strings are not defined as a primitive type, string data is usually stored in arrays of single characters. This is the approach taken by Pascal, Modula-2, C, and Ada. In Pascal, although strings are not a primitive type, **char** arrays that have the **packed** attribute can be assigned and compared with the relational operators. In Modula-2, strings in CHAR arrays can be assigned string constants, but that is the only operation provided by the language. However, Modula-2 implementations usually include a module that provides an abstract data type for character strings.

In Ada, STRING is a type that is predefined to be single-dimensioned arrays of CHARACTER elements. Substring reference, catenation, relational operators, and assignment are provided for STRING types. Substring reference allows any substring of a given string to be treated as a value in a reference or as a variable in an assignment. A substring reference is denoted by a parenthesized integer range, which indicates the desired substring by character position. For example,

```
NAME1(2:4)
```

specifies the substring consisting of the second, third, and fourth characters of the value in NAME1.

Character string catenation in Ada is an operation specified by the ampersand (&). The following statement catenates NAME2 to the right end of NAME1:

```
NAME1 := NAME1 & NAME2;
```

For example, if NAME1 has the string "CHRIST" and NAME2 has "MAS", then after the assignment statement is executed, NAME1 will have the string "CHRISTMAS".

FORTRAN 77, FORTRAN 90, and BASIC treat strings as a primitive type and provide assignment, relational operators, catenation, and substring reference operations for them.

Both assignment and comparison operations on character strings are complicated by the possibility of assigning and comparing operands of different lengths. Usually, simple and sensible choices are made for these situations, although users often have trouble remembering them.

Pattern-matching is another fundamental character string operation. Typically, it is provided by a library function rather than as an operation in the language. The exception is SNOBOL4 (Griswold et al., 1971), which has an elaborate pattern-matching operation built into the language. SNOBOL4 is probably the ultimate string manipulation language. Primarily because of the relative inefficiency of its implementations, however, SNOBOL4 never became a commercial success.

String patterns in SNOBOL4 are expressions that can be assigned to variables. For example, consider the following:

```
LETTER = 'abcdefghijklmnopqrstuvwxyz'
WORDPAT = BREAK(LETTER) SPAN(LETTER) . WORD
```

LETTER is a variable with the value of a string of all lowercase letters. WORDPAT is a pattern that describes words as follows: first skip until a letter is found, then span those letters until a nonletter is found. This pattern also includes a "." operator, which specifies that the string that matches the pattern is to be assigned to the variable WORD.

This pattern can be used in the statement

```
TEXT  WORDPAT
```

which attempts to find a string of letters in the string value of the variable, TEXT.

ICON (Griswold and Griswold, 1983) is a general purpose language that evolved from SNOBOL4 and includes the pattern matching facilities of that language.

5.3.3 String Length Options

There are several design choices regarding the length of string objects. First, the length can be static and specified in the declaration. Such a string is called a **static length string.** This is the choice in the FORTRAN 77, FORTRAN 90, COBOL, and Ada languages. For example, the following FORTRAN 90 statement declares NAME1 and NAME2 to be character strings of length 15:

```
CHARACTER(LEN = 15) NAME1, NAME2
```

The second option is to allow strings to have varying length up to a declared and fixed maximum, as exemplified by the strings in PL/I with the VARYING attribute. These are called **limited dynamic length strings.** Such string variables can store any number of characters between zero and the maximum.

The third option is to allow strings to have varying length with no maximum, as in SNOBOL4. These are called **dynamic length strings.** This option requires the overhead of dynamic storage allocation and deallocation but provides maximum flexibility.

5.3.4 Evaluation

String types are important to the writability of a language. Dealing with strings as arrays can be more cumbersome than dealing with a primitive string type. The addition of strings as a primitive type to a language is not costly, in terms of either language or compiler complexity. Therefore, it is difficult to justify the omission of primitive string types in some contemporary imperative languages. Of course, the availability of standard libraries of string manipulation subprograms can remove this deficiency when strings are not included as a primitive type.

String operations such as simple pattern matching and catenation are essential and should be included for string type objects. Although dynamic length strings are obviously the most flexible, the overhead of their implementation must be weighed against that additional flexibility.

5.4 User-Defined Ordinal Types

An **ordinal type** is one in which the range of possible values can be easily associated with a set of positive integers. In Pascal, for example, the primitive ordinal types are integer, char, and boolean. In many languages, users can define two kinds of ordinal types: enumeration and subrange.

5.4.1 Enumeration Types

An **enumeration type** is one in which all of the possible values, which are symbolic constants, are enumerated in the definition. A typical enumeration type is shown in the following Ada example:

```
type DAYS is (Mon, Tue, Wed, Thu, Fri, Sat, Sun);
```

The primary design issue that is specific to enumeration types is the following: Is a literal constant allowed to appear in more than one type definition, and if so, how is the type of an occurrence of that literal in the program checked?

5.4.1.1 Designs

In Pascal, a literal constant is not allowed to be used in more than one enumeration type definition in a given referencing environment. Enumeration type variables can be used as array subscripts, **for** loop variables, and **case** selector expressions, but can be neither input nor output. Two enumeration type variables and/or literals can be compared with the relational operators, with their relative positions in the declaration determining the result. For example, in

```
type colortype = (red, blue, green, yellow);
var color : colortype;
...
color := blue;
if (color > red) ...
```

the Boolean expression of the **if** will evaluate to true.

In ANSI C and C++, like Pascal, the same literal constant cannot appear in more than one enumeration type definition in a given referencing environment. Enumeration objects in ANSI C and C++ are implicitly converted to integer, so they are subject only to the rules of use of integers.

The enumeration types of Ada are similar to those of Pascal, except that the literals are allowed to appear in more than one declaration in the same referencing environment. These are called **overloaded literals.** The rule for resolving the overloading—that is, deciding the type of an occurrence of such a literal—is that it must be determinable from the context of its appearance. For example, if an overloaded literal and an enumeration variable are compared, the literal's type is resolved to be that of the variable.

In some cases, the programmer must indicate some type specification for an occurrence of an overloaded literal. Suppose, for example, that a program has the following two enumeration types:

```
type LETTERS is (A, B, C, D, E, F, G, H, I, J, K, L, M,
                 N, O, P, Q, R, S, T, U, V, W, X, Y, Z);
type VOWELS is (A, E, I, O, U);
```

Further suppose the program uses a **for** loop whose variable is to take on the values of the VOWELS type, as in

```
for LETTER in A..U loop
```

The problem is that the compiler cannot determine the correct type for LETTER, so the discrete range is ambiguous. (In Ada, the **for** variable is implicitly typed by the compiler. It has the type of the discrete range specified in the statement.) The solution is to use a type qualifier on the literals in the discrete range, as in

```
for LETTER in VOWELS'(A)..VOWELS'(U) loop
```

Enumeration variables can be output and enumeration literals can be input using Ada's TEXT_IO package. These operations require a generic instantiation of a built-in package for the specific enumeration type. Generic instantiations are discussed in Chapter 8.

In Ada, both the BOOLEAN and CHARACTER types are actually predefined enumeration types.

Common operations for enumeration types are for predecessor, successor, position in the list of values, and value for a given position number. In Pascal, these operations are provided by built-in functions. For example, pred(blue) is red. In Ada, they are attributes. For example, LETTER'PRED(B) is A.

5.4.1.2   Evaluation

Enumeration types provide greater readability in a very direct way: Named values are easily recognized, whereas coded values are not. Codings are meaningless to everyone except the program's author. For example, suppose a program being written in FORTRAN required a variable to store the days of the week. Most likely, the names of the days would be coded as integers, using the values 1, 2, . . . , 7. There are three distinct problems with this approach. First, any one of many arithmetic operations between the coded day and any integer would be legal, because their types would match. This eliminates compiler detection of many logic and typographical errors involving coded data. (Because ANSI C and C++ treat enumeration variables like integer variables, these languages do not provide this advantage.)

Second, the integer values used for codes are rarely connotative. If the constant 4, for example, denotes Wednesday and is assigned to a variable, that fact is not apparent to the reader of the program.

Third, if an integer variable is used by the programmer for a coding that used only a very small subrange of the integer values, range errors could occur but would not be detected by the run-time system.

So, using an enumerated type like the Ada LETTERS type defined above, rather than an integer, restricts the assignable values to a small range, is more readable, and provides type checking.

5.4.2   Subrange Types

A **subrange type** is a contiguous subsequence of an ordinal type. For example, 12..14 is a subrange of integer type. Subrange types were introduced by Pascal and are also included in Modula-2 and Ada. There are no design issues that are specific to subrange types.

5.4.2.1   Designs

In Pascal and Modula-2, typical subrange type declarations are

```
type
    uppercase = 'A' ..'Z';
    index = 1..100;
```

The connection of a subrange type to its parent type is established by matching the values in the subrange definition to those in previously declared or built-in ordinal types. In the example above, the type uppercase is defined to be a subrange of the built-in type for single characters. The type index is defined to be a subrange of the integers.

In Ada, subranges are included in the class of types called subtypes. **Subtypes** are not new types at all, but rather only new names for possibly restricted, or constrained, versions of existing types. For example, we could have the following:

```
subtype WEEKDAYS is DAYS range Mon..Fri;
subtype INDEX is INTEGER range 1..100;
```

In these examples, the restriction on the existing types is in the range of possible values. All of the operations defined for the parent type are also defined for the subtype, except assignment of values outside the specified range. For example, in the following,

```
DAY1 : DAYS;
DAY2 : WEEKDAYS;
...
DAY2 := DAY1;
```

the assignment is legal unless the value of DAY1 is Sat or Sun. As in Ada, the subrange types in Pascal and Modula-2 inherit all the operations of the parent.

One of the most common uses of user-defined ordinal types is for the indices of arrays, as will be discussed in Section 5.5. They can also be used for loop variables. In fact, subranges of ordinal types are the only way the range of Ada **for** loop variables can be specified. In this use, they are called discrete ranges.

Note that subrange types are very different from Ada's derived types. For example, consider the following type declarations:

```
type DERIVED_INT is new INTEGER;
subtype SUBRANGE_INT is INTEGER;
```

Variables of both types, DERIVED_INT and SUBRANGE_INT, inherit the value range and operations of INTEGER. However, variables of type DERIVED_INT are not compatible with any INTEGER type, whereas variables of type SUBRANGE_INT are compatible with variables and constants of INTEGER type and any subtype of INTEGER.

5.4.2.2 Evaluation

Subrange types enhance readability by making it clear to readers that variables of subtypes can store only certain ranges of values. Reliability is increased with subrange types, because assigning a value to a subrange variable that is outside the specified range is detected as an error by the run-time system.

5.5 Array Types

An **array** is a homogeneous aggregate of data elements in which an individual element is identified by its position in the aggregate, relative to the first element. A majority of computer programs need to model collections of objects, in which the objects are of the same type and must be processed in the same way. Thus, the universal need for arrays is obvious.

5.5.1 Design Issues

The primary design issues specific to arrays are the following:

1. What types are legal for subscripts?
2. When are subscript ranges bound?
3. When does array allocation take place?
4. How many subscripts are allowed?
5. Can arrays be initialized when they have their storage allocated?
6. What kinds of slices are allowed, if any?

In the following sections, examples of the design choices made for the arrays of the most common imperative languages are discussed.

5.5.2 Arrays and Indices

Specific elements of an array are referenced by means of a two-level syntactic mechanism, where the first part is the aggregate name, and the second part is a possibly dynamic selector consisting of one or more items known as **subscripts** or **indices**. If all of the indices in a reference are constants, the selector is static; otherwise, it is dynamic. The selection operation can be thought of as a mapping from the array name and the set of index values to an element in the aggregate. Indeed, arrays are sometimes called finite mappings. Symbolically, this mapping can be shown as

```
array_name[index_value_list] → element
```

The syntax of array references is fairly universal: The array name is followed by the list of indices, which is surrounded by either parentheses or brackets (as in the left side of the above mapping). A problem with using parentheses is that they often are also used to enclose the parameters in subprogram calls; this makes references to arrays appear exactly like those calls. For example, consider the following FORTRAN assignment statement:

```
SUM = SUM + B(I)
```

If parentheses are used for both subprogram parameters and array subscripts, as they are in FORTRAN, both program readers and compilers are forced to use other information to determine whether B(I) in this assignment is a function call or a reference to an array element. This can be frustrating for the reader.

The designers of pre-90 FORTRANs and PL/I chose parentheses for array subscripts because no other suitable characters were available at the time. When an identifier followed by a parenthesized expression or list of expressions is found in a pre-90 FORTRAN or PL/I program, the compiler determines whether it is an array reference or a function call by matching the name against all arrays declared in the referencing environment. If no match is found, such a reference is assumed to be a function call. If it is not found to be a locally defined subprogram, it is assumed to be defined externally. If the reference was to an array whose declaration is missing, this fact cannot be determined by the compiler, because these languages have separate compilation, and subprograms that are used in a program but defined elsewhere need not be declared external.

In Ada the compiler can always determine whether a reference is to an array or a function, because it has access to information (from previously compiled programs) about all names that can be referenced in a program unit that is being compiled. This is in contrast to pre-90 FORTRANs and PL/I, in which the compiler has access to no information about previously compiled programs.

The designers of Ada specifically chose parentheses to enclose subscripts so there would be uniformity between array references and function calls in expressions, in spite of potential readability problems. They made this choice based on the fact that both array element references and function calls are mappings. Array element references map the subscripts to a particular element of the array. Function calls map the actual parameters to the function definition and, eventually, a functional value.

Pascal, C, and Modula-2 use brackets to delimit their array indices.

Two distinct types are involved in an array type: the element type and the type of the subscripts. The type of the subscripts is often a subrange of integers, but Pascal, Modula-2, and Ada allow some other types to be used as subscripts, such as boolean, character, and enumeration.

5.5.3 Subscript Bindings and Array Categories

The binding of the subscript type to an array variable is usually static, but the subscript value ranges are sometimes dynamically bound.

In some languages, the lower bound of the subscript range is implicit. For example, in C, the lower bound of all index ranges is fixed at zero; in FORTRAN I, II, and IV, it was fixed at 1; in FORTRAN 77 and FORTRAN 90, it defaults to 1. In most other languages, subscript ranges are completely specified by the programmer.

Four categories of arrays can be defined based on the binding to subscript value ranges and the binding to storage. A **static array** is one in which the subscript ranges are statically bound and storage allocation is static (done before run time). The advantage of static arrays is efficiency: No dynamic allocation or deallocation is required.

A **semistatic array** is one in which the subscript ranges are statically bound, but the allocation is done at declaration elaboration time during execution. The advantage of semistatic arrays over static arrays is space efficiency. A large array in one procedure can use the same space as a large array in a different procedure, as long as both procedures are never active at the same time.

A **semidynamic array** is one in which the subscript ranges are dynamically bound and the storage allocation is dynamic (done during run time). Once the subscript ranges are bound and the storage is allocated, however, they remain fixed during the lifetime of the variable. The advantage of semidynamic arrays over static and semistatic arrays is flexibility. The size of an array need not be known until the array is about to be used.

A **dynamic array** is one in which the binding of subscript ranges and storage allocation is dynamic and can change any number of times during the array's lifetime. The advantage of dynamic arrays over the others is maximal flexibility: Arrays can grow and shrink during program execution as the need for space changes. Examples of the four categories are given in the following paragraphs.

In FORTRAN 77, the subscript type is bound to an array at language design time; all subscripts are integer type. The subscript ranges are statically bound, and all storage is statically allocated; therefore, FORTRAN 77's arrays are static.

Arrays that are declared in Pascal procedures are examples of semistatic arrays.

Ada arrays can be semidynamic, as in the following:

```
GET (LIST_LEN);
declare
  LIST : array (1..LIST_LEN) of INTEGER;
begin
...
end;
```

In this example, the user inputs the number of desired elements in the array list, which are then dynamically allocated when the declaration in the **declare** block is elaborated. When execution reaches the end of the block, the LIST array is deallocated.

C and FORTRAN 90 provide semidynamic arrays that can be used to simulate dynamic arrays. They can be allocated and deallocated on demand, but can only have their subscript ranges changed by a save, deallocate, reallocate process.

For example, in FORTRAN 90, one can declare an array to be semidynamic with

```
INTEGER, ALLOCATABLE, ARRAY (:,:) :: MAT
```

which declares that MAT is a matrix of INTEGER type elements that can be dynamically allocated. The allocation is specified with an ALLOCATE statement, such as

```
ALLOCATE (MAT(10, NUMBER_OF_COLS))
```

Note that the subscript ranges can be specified by program variables. Lower bounds of subscript ranges default to 1.

Dynamic arrays can be destroyed by the DEALLOCATE statement, as in

```
DEALLOCATE (MAT)
```

To make an existing dynamic array larger or smaller, its elements must be saved temporarily in another array, and the array must be deallocated and then reallocated in the new size.

C also allows this kind of semidynamic array. For example, consider a particular implementation of a neural network in which the network is represented in a four-dimensional array, but the sizes of the dimensions are not known until program execution. The four dimensions are named network, layers, outputs, and output_array_ptr. The network array can be created as follows:

```
double ****network;
double ***layers;
double **outputs;
double *output_array_ptr;
...
network = (double ****) malloc (num_layers *
               sizeof (double *));
layers = (double ***) malloc (num_outputs *
               sizeof (double *));
outputs = (double **) malloc (num_output_array_ptr
               * sizeof (double *));
output_array_ptr = (double *) malloc (num_locations
               * sizeof (double));
```

Note that malloc is a C function that allocates memory from the heap. Also, the parenthesized expressions that precede the calls to malloc in these assignments are explicit type specifications, called casts. Casts are discussed in Chapter 6. The element type of these arrays is **double**. Each asterisk in the object declarations specifies one level of indirection. For example, the variable outputs is a pointer to a pointer to a **double** object.

The most readable way to reference the elements of these arrays is to use normal array reference notation, rather than pointer notation, as in

```
network [0][0][0][index] = 0.0;
```

The trade-off in this design of the simulation of dynamic arrays is one of writability versus safety. None of the indices in references to the network can be range checked. On the other hand, this would be very difficult to implement in languages without this kind of semidynamic array.

ALGOL 68 has dynamic arrays. The assigning of aggregate values to an array type variable can change its subscript range and therefore its size. ALGOL 68's dynamic arrays are called **flex** arrays. The following ALGOL 68 code demonstrates how a **flex** array can change:

```
flex [1:0] int list;
...
list := (3, 5, 7);
list := 67
```

The declaration sets the type attributes of list to a single-dimensioned flexible array of integer type elements with an initial index range of [1:0], so that it has no storage. The first assignment statement causes the dynamic allocation of memory for three integers, binds list to that storage, and sets the index range to [1:3]. The last assignment causes the deallocation of the last two array elements, leaving an array with index range [1:1] and the single element with the value 67.

The index range of list could be converted back to [1:0] by assigning an "empty row display," as in

```
list := ()
```

To allow the program to determine the current index ranges of a flexible array, the binary operators **lwb** (lower bound) and **upb** (upper bound) are provided. For example,

```
upperbd := 1 upb list
```

sets the variable upperbd to the upper bound of the first dimension of list.

Ada has similar range capabilities for its arrays, although they are not dynamic. Rather than operations, in Ada they are attributes of variables. For example, LENGTH is an attribute of arrays. If a program has an array named LIST, LIST'LENGTH returns the number of elements in the first subscript range of LIST.

APL arrays, which are briefly discussed in Section 5.5.6, are dynamic.

In the original version of Pascal, the index range or ranges of an array were part of its type. This, along with the use of name equivalence for compatibility, disallowed the existence of a subprogram that processed arrays of different lengths. A procedure that sorted integer arrays, for example, could only be written for arrays with a single fixed subscript range. The ISO Standard Pascal (ISO, 1982) provides a loophole for this problem, **conformant arrays.** Conformant arrays are formal parameters that include the type definition of the array. Consider the following example:

```
procedure sumlist (var sum : integer;
    list : array [lower .. upper : integer]
                        of integer);
  var index : integer;
  begin
  sum := 0;
  for index := lower to upper do
    sum := sum + list[index]
  end;
```

An example call to this procedure is

```
var scores : array [1..100] of integer;
...
sumlist (sum, scores)
```

5.5.4 The Number of Subscripts in Arrays

FORTRAN I limited the number of array subscripts to three, because at the time of the design, execution efficiency was a primary concern. FORTRAN designers had developed a very fast method for accessing the elements of arrays of up to three dimensions, but not beyond three. FORTRAN 77 and FORTRAN 90 restrict the number of array dimensions to seven, but most other contemporary languages enforce no such limits. There is no justification for FORTRAN's limitation. A programmer who wishes to use a variable with ten dimensions and is willing to pay for the cost of references to the elements of such an array should be allowed to do it.

Arrays in C can have only one subscript, but arrays can have arrays as elements, thus supporting multidimensional arrays. This is an example of orthogonality. For example, consider the following C declaration:

```
int mat [5][4];
```

It creates an integer variable, mat, which is an array of five elements, each of which is an array of four elements. The difference between this and a matrix in another language, say FORTRAN, is minimal. The user can nearly always ignore the fact that mat is not really a matrix, except that the syntax for references requires a set of brackets for each subscript.

5.5.5 Array Initialization

Some languages provide the means to initialize arrays at the time their storage is allocated. In FORTRAN 77, all data storage is statically allocated, so load-time initialization using the DATA statement is allowed. For example, in FORTRAN 77, one could have

```
INTEGER LIST (3)
DATA LIST /0, 5, 5/
```

The array LIST is initialized to the values from the list delimited by slashes.

C also allows initialization of its static arrays, but with one new twist. In the declaration

```
int list[] = {4, 5, 7, 83}
```

the compiler sets the length of the array. This is meant to be a convenience, but it is not without cost. It effectively removes the possibility that the system could detect programmer errors, such as mistakenly leaving a value out of the list.

Character strings in C are implemented as arrays of **char**. Such arrays, when static (in C, arrays can be either static, semistatic, or semidynamic), can be initialized to string constants, as in

```
char name[] = "freddie"
```

The array name will have eight elements, because in C all strings are terminated with a null character (zero), which is implicitly supplied by the system for string constants. User-constructed strings require the user to supply the null characters.

Arrays of other types in C can also be initialized the same way. For example,

```
int list [] = {1, 3, 5, 7};
```

declares list to be an array of four integer elements initialized to the values 1, 3, 5, and 7.

Pascal and Modula-2 do not allow array initialization in the declaration sections of programs.

Ada provides two mechanisms for initializing arrays in the declaration statement: by listing them in the order in which they are to be stored, or by directly assigning them to an index position using the => operator. For example, consider the following:

```
LIST : array (1..5) of INTEGER := (1, 3, 5, 7, 9);
BUNCH : array (1..5) of INTEGER := (1 => 3, 2 => 4,
                                    others => 0);
```

In the first statement, all the elements of the array LIST have initializing values, which are assigned to the array element locations in the order in which they appear. In the second, the first and second array elements are initialized using direct assignment, and the **others** clause is used to initialize the remaining elements. These collections of values, delimited by parentheses, are called **aggregate values.**

5.5.6   Array Operations

Some languages provide operations that deal with arrays as units; this is not the case with FORTRAN 77, in which only individual elements of arrays can be manipulated.

Ada allows array assignments, including those where the right side is an aggregate value rather than an array name.

The only Ada operation on arrays is catenation, specified by the ampersand (&), which is defined between two single-dimensioned arrays and between a single-dimensioned array and a scalar. All types in Ada have the built-in relational operators for equality and inequality.

FORTRAN 90 includes a number of array operations that are called **elemental** because they are operations between pairs of array elements. For example, the add operator (+) between two arrays results in an array of the sums of the element pairs of the two arrays. The assignment, arithmetic, relational, and logical operators are all overloaded for arrays of any size or shape. FORTRAN 90 also includes intrinsic, or library, functions for matrix multiplication, matrix transpose, and vector dot product.

Arrays and their operations are the heart of APL; it is the most powerful array-processing language ever devised. Because of its relative obscurity and its lack of effect on subsequent languages, however, we present here only a glimpse into its array operations.

In APL, the four basic arithmetic operations are defined for vectors (single-dimensioned arrays) and matrices, as well as scalar operands. For example,

        A + B

is a valid expression, whether A and B are simple variables, vectors, or matrices.

APL includes a collection of unary operators for vectors and matrices, some of which are as follows (where V is a vector and M is a matrix):

⌽A	reverses the elements of V
⌽M	reverses the columns of M
⊖M	reverses the rows of M
⍉M	transposes M (its rows become its columns, and vice versa)
⌹M	inverts M

APL also includes several special operators that take other operators as operands. One of these is the inner product operator, which is specified with a period (.). It takes two operands, which are binary operators. For example,

        +.×

is a new operator that takes two arguments, either vectors or matrices. It first multiplies the corresponding elements of two arguments, and then it sums the results. For example, if A and B are vectors,

        A × B

is the mathematical inner product of A and B (a vector of the products of the corresponding elements of A and B). The statement

        A +.× B

is the sum of the inner product of A and B. If A and B are matrices, this expression specifies the matrix multiplication of A and B.

The special operators of APL are actually functional forms, which are described in Chapter 13.

5.5.7 Slices

A **slice** of an array is some substructure of that array. For example, if A is a matrix, the first row of A is one possible slice, as is the last row, and also the first column. It is important to realize that a slice is not a new data type. Rather, it is a mechanism for referencing part of an array as a unit. If arrays cannot be manipulated as units in a language, that language has no use for slices.

One of the design questions for slices is the syntax of specifying a reference to a particular slice. A reference to a particular element of a complete array is the array name and an expression for each subscript. Because a slice is a substructure of an array, a slice reference requires fewer subscript expressions than a reference to the whole array. Somehow, however, the missing subscript expressions must be denoted, so that the present expressions are associated with the correct subscripts. The missing subscript or subscripts of slice references are sometimes specified by asterisks. For example, consider the following FORTRAN 90 declarations. (The ampersand, &, specifies that the statement is continued.)

```
INTEGER VECTOR(1:10), MAT(1:3, 1:3), CUBE(1:3, 1:3, 1:4)
```

VECTOR(3:6) is a four-element array with the third through sixth elements of VECTOR; MAT(1:3, 2) refers to the second column of MAT; MAT(3, 1:3) refers to the third row of MAT. All of these references can be used as single-dimensioned arrays. References to all array slices are treated as if they were arrays of the remaining dimensionality. Thus a slice reference such as CUBE(1:3, 1:3, 2) could be legally assigned to MAT. Slices can also appear as the destinations of assignment statements. For example, a single-dimen-

Figure 5.1
Example slices in
FORTRAN 90

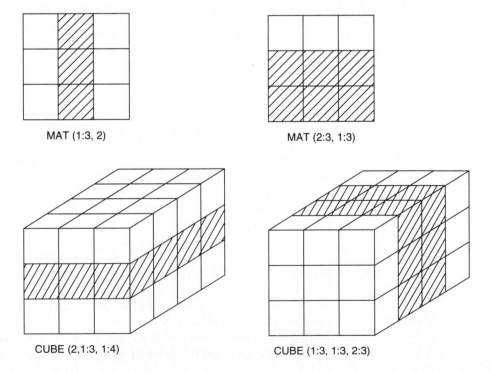

MAT (1:3, 2)

MAT (2:3, 1:3)

CUBE (2,1:3, 1:4)

CUBE (1:3, 1:3, 2:3)

sioned array could be assigned to a slice of a matrix. Figure 5.1 shows several slices of MAT and CUBE.

More complex slices can also be specified in FORTRAN 90. For example, VECTOR(2:10:2) is a five-element array consisting of the second, fourth, sixth, eighth, and tenth elements of VECTOR. Slices can also have nonregular arrangements of elements of an existing array. For example VECTOR((/3, 2, 1, 8/)) is an array of the third, second, first, and eighth elements of VECTOR.

In Ada, only highly restricted slices are allowed: those that consist of consecutive elements of a single-dimensioned array. For example, if LIST is an array with index range (1..100), LIST(5..10) is a slice of LIST consisting of the six elements indexed from 5 to 10. As discussed in Section 5.3.2, a slice of a STRING type is called a substring reference.

5.5.8 Evaluation

Arrays have been included in every imperative language. They are simple and have probably been developed to their optimum. The only significant advance since their introduction in FORTRAN I has been the inclusion of all ordinal types as possible subscript types and, of course, dynamic arrays. Although arrays are essential and fundamental, there is little controversy involved in their design.

Although it is sometimes convenient to allow the programmer to specify a particular substructure of a multidimensional array, the increased difficulty of implementation and readability are not necessarily worth the convenience.

5.6   Record Types

A **record** is a possibly heterogeneous aggregate of data elements in which the individual elements are identified by names.

There is frequently a need in programs to model collections of data that are not homogeneous. For example, information about a college student might include name, student number, grade point average, and so forth. A data type for such a collection might use a character string for the name, an integer for the student number, a floating-point for the grade point average, and so forth. Records are designed to meet this kind of need.

Records have been part of all the most popular programming languages, except pre-90 versions of FORTRAN, since the early 1960s when they were introduced by COBOL.

A discussion of the general design issues of the syntax of declarations and references and of the operation set will suffice to fully examine records.

5.6.1 The Structure of Records

The fundamental difference between a record and an array is the homogeneity of elements in arrays versus the possible heterogeneity of elements in records. One result of this difference is that record elements, or fields, are not usually referenced by indices. Instead, the fields are named with identifiers, and references are made using these identifiers. One more important difference between arrays and records is that records in some languages are allowed to include unions, which are discussed in Section 5.7.

The COBOL form of a record declaration, which is part of the data division of a COBOL program, is illustrated in the following example:

```
01   EMPLOYEE-RECORD.
     02   EMPLOYEE-NAME.
          05   FIRST      PICTURE IS X(20).
          05   MIDDLE     PICTURE IS X(10).
          05   LAST       PICTURE IS X(20).
     02 HOURLY-RATE       PICTURE IS 99V99.
```

The EMPLOYEE-RECORD record consists of the EMPLOYEE-NAME record and the HOURLY-RATE field. The numerals 01, 02, and 05 that begin the lines of the record declaration are **level numbers,** which indicate by their relative values the hierarchical structure of the record. Any line that is followed by a line with a higher level number is itself a record. The PICTURE clauses show the formats of the field storage locations, with X(20) specifying 20 alphanumeric characters and 99V99 specifying four decimal digits with the decimal point in the middle.

Pascal, Modula-2, and Ada use a different syntax for records; rather than using the level numbers of COBOL, they indicate record structures in an orthogonal way by simply nesting record declarations inside record declarations. Consider the following Ada declaration:

```
EMPLOYEE_RECORD :
  record
    EMPLOYEE_NAME :
      record
        FIRST : STRING (1..20);
        MIDDLE : STRING (1..10);
        LAST : STRING (1..20);
      end record;
    HOURLY_RATE : FLOAT;
  end record;
```

C also provides records, which are called structures. They are very much like the records of Pascal, except they do not include Pascal's record variants, or unions, which are described in Section 5.7.

FORTRAN 90 record declarations require that any nested records be previously defined as types. So, for the employee record above, the employee name record would need to be defined first, and then the employee record would simply name it as its first field.

5.6.2 References to Record Fields

References to the individual fields of records are syntactically specified by several different methods, two of which name the desired field and its enclosing records. COBOL field references have the form

```
field_name OF record_name_1 OF ... OF record_name_n
```

where the first record named is the smallest or innermost record that contains the field. The next record name in the sequence is that of the record that contains the previous record, and so forth. For example, the MIDDLE field in the COBOL record example above can be referenced with

```
MIDDLE OF EMPLOYEE-NAME OF EMPLOYEE-RECORD
```

Most of the other imperative languages use dot notation for field references, where the components of the reference are connected with periods. Names in dot notation have the opposite order of COBOL references: They use the name of the largest enclosing record first and the field name last. For example, the following is a reference to the field MIDDLE in the Ada record example above:

```
EMPLOYEE_RECORD.EMPLOYEE_NAME.MIDDLE
```

FORTRAN 90 field references have this form, except that percent signs (%) are used instead of periods.

A **fully qualified reference** to a record field is one in which all intermediate record names, from the largest enclosing record to the specific field, are named in the reference. Both the COBOL and the Ada field references above are fully qualified. As an alternative to fully qualified references, COBOL and PL/I allow **elliptical references** to record fields. In an elliptical reference, the field is named, but any or all of the enclosing record names can be omitted, as long as the resulting reference is unambiguous in the referencing environment. For example, FIRST, FIRST OF EMPLOYEE_NAME, and FIRST OF EMPLOYEE_RECORD are elliptical references to the employee's first name in the record declared above. Although elliptical references are a programmer convenience, they require a compiler to have elaborate data structures and procedures in order to correctly identify the referenced field. They are also somewhat detrimental to readability.

Pascal provides a mechanism that allows the user to avoid the necessity of using fully qualified field references. A segment of code can be placed in a **with** clause, wherein a portion of the qualification is implicit. For example, consider the following two code segments; the first is written without a **with** clause, and the second uses **with**.

```
employee.name := 'Bob';
employee.age := 42;
employee.sex := 'M';
employee.salary := 23750.0;

with employee do
  begin
  name := 'Bob';
  age := 42;
  sex := 'M';
  salary := 23750.0
  end; { with }
```

Note that the **with** clause is an aid to readability when its length is relatively small. But a **with** clause that spans several pages of code can be detrimental to readability.

5.6.3 Operations on Records

In Pascal and Modula-2, records can be assigned, but no other operations are defined for them. Furthermore, in such assignments, the types of the two sides must be the same.

Ada allows record assignment and comparison for equality and inequality as the only record operations. These operations are legal only if the two records have compatible types. Additional record operations can be defined as overloaded operators. User-defined operator overloading is discussed in Chapter 8.

In original C, the only record operations were address-of and field selection. ANSI C allows records to be assigned.

Record initialization at compile time is possible in Ada, where data aggregates are used as the initial values. Aggregate values can also be assigned to records by assignment statements.

COBOL provides the MOVE CORRESPONDING statement for moving records. This statement copies a field of the specified source record to the destination record only if the destination record has a field with the same name. This is frequently a useful operation in data processing applications, where input records are moved to output files after some modifications. Because input records often have many fields that have the same names and purposes as fields in output records, but not necessarily in the same order, the MOVE CORRESPONDING operation can save many statements. For example, consider the following COBOL structures:

```
01  INPUT-RECORD.
    02  NAME.
        05  LAST            PICTURE IS X(20).
        05  MIDDLE          PICTURE IS X(15).
        05  FIRST           PICTURE IS X(20).
    02  EMPLOYEE-NUMBER     PICTURE IS 9(10).
    02  HOURS-WORKED        PICTURE IS 99.
```

```
01 OUTPUT-RECORD.
   02 NAME.
      05 FIRST          PICTURE IS X(20).
      05 MIDDLE         PICTURE IS X(15).
      05 LAST           PICTURE IS X(20).
   02 EMPLOYEE-NUMBER   PICTURE IS 9(10).
   02 GROSS-PAY         PICTURE IS 999V99.
   02 NET-PAY           PICTURE IS 999V99.
```

The statement

```
MOVE CORRESPONDING INPUT-RECORD TO OUTPUT-RECORD.
```

copies the FIRST, MIDDLE, LAST, and EMPLOYEE-NUMBER fields from the input record to the output record.

5.6.4 Evaluation

Records are frequently valuable data types in programming languages. The design of record types is straightforward and their use is safe. The only aspect of records that is not clearly readable is the elliptical references allowed by COBOL and PL/I.

Records and arrays are closely related structural forms, and it is therefore interesting to compare them. Arrays are used when all the data objects have the same type and are processed in the same way. This processing is easily done when there is a systematic way of sequencing through the structure. Such processing is well supported by using dynamic subscripting as the addressing method.

Records are used when the collection of data objects is heterogeneous and the different fields are not processed in the same way. Also, the fields of a record often need not be processed in a particular sequential order. Field names are like literal, or constant, subscripts. Because they are static, they provide very efficient access to the fields. Dynamic subscripts could be used to access record fields, but it would disallow type checking and also would be slower.

Records and arrays represent thoughtful and efficient methods of fulfilling two separate but related applications of data structures.

5.7 Union Types

A **union** is a type that is allowed to store different type values at different times during program execution. As an example of the need for a union type, consider a table of constants for a compiler, in which are stored the constants found in a program being compiled. One field of each table entry is for the value of the constant. Suppose that for a particular language being compiled, the types of constants were integer, floating point, and Boolean.

In terms of table management, it would be convenient if the same location, a table field, could store a value of any of these three types. The type of such a location is, in a sense, the union of the three value types it can store.

5.7.1 Design Issues

The problem of type checking union types, which is discussed in Chapter 4, leads to one major design issue. The other fundamental question is the form of union types. In some cases, the forms are confined to be parts of record structures, but in others they are not. So, the primary design issues that are particular to union types are the following:

1. Should type checking be required? Note that any such type checking must be dynamic.
2. Should unions be embedded in records?

5.7.2 FORTRAN Union Types

The most primitive form of union is FORTRAN's EQUIVALENCE, with which one can have the following:

```
INTEGER X
REAL Y
EQUIVALENCE (X, Y)
```

This EQUIVALENCE declaration specifies that both X and Y are to cohabit the same storage location; that is, they are aliases. There is no mechanism in FORTRAN whereby the user program or the system can determine the type of the value currently stored in such a shared location, so no type checking is done.

5.7.3 ALGOL 68 Union Types

Although the merit of unions was recognized by the designers of ALGOL 68, they determined that it would be better if the run-time system could detect the current type value in a union. Thus was born the discriminated union.

A **discriminated union** is a union with which is associated an additional value called a **tag,** or **discriminant,** that identifies the current type value stored in the union. Consider the following example of an ALGOL 68 discriminated union:

```
union (int, real) ir1, ir2
```

In this case, the two variables ir1 and ir2 are declared to be of a **union** type that can have either **int** or **real** type values. Although it is legal to assign values of either of the possible types to such a variable, it is not so simple to reference them. For example, in the following,

```
union (int, real) ir1;
int count;
...
ir1 := 33;
...
count := ir1;
```

the first assignment statement is legal, but the second is not because the system cannot statically check the type of ir1. The compiler cannot guarantee that ir1 will actually contain an integer value. To alleviate this problem, ALGOL 68 provides **conformity clauses** for such references. For example, consider the following:

```
union (int, real) ir1;
int count;
real sum;
...
case ir1 in
  (int intval): count := intval,
  (real realval): sum := realval
esac
```

This **case** statement executes the assignment that is currently valid—that is, the one in which the value type of the union variable ir1 matches the type of the destination (count or sum). Therefore, the different types are handled individually. The correct choice is made by testing a type tag maintained by the run-time system for the variable. The parenthesized clauses that introduce the assignments specify the current type of ir1, and the following identifier is the means by which the value of ir1 is referenced. For example, (**int** intval) specifies that if the current type of the case variable (ir1) is **int,** the following statement is to be executed; the variable intval refers to the current value of ir1. This is a safe way of implementing discriminated union, because it allows static type checking of user code and dynamic checking of system discriminants in order to disallow erroneous uses of values. The dummy variables, intval and realval, can be thought of as implicitly declared variables whose scope is the statement following their specifications.

The only built-in operation provided for ALGOL 68 discriminated unions is assignment. Other operations can be constructed by user-defined overloaded operators.

5.7.4   Pascal Union Types

Pascal introduced the concept of integrating discriminated unions with a record structure. This design carried over into Modula-2 and Ada. In all of these, the discriminated union is called a **record variant**, or variant part of a record. The discriminant is a user-accessible variable in the record that stores the current type value in the variant. The following example illustrates a Pascal record with only a variant part:

```
type shape = (circle, triangle, rectangle);
     object =
       record
         case form : shape of
           circle:    (diameter : real);
           triangle:  (leftside : integer;
                        rightside : integer;
                        angle : real);
           rectangle: (side1 : integer;
                        side2 : integer)
       end;
var thing : object;
```

The structure of this variant record is shown in Figure 5.2.

The variable thing consists of the tag, which is named form, and sufficient storage for its largest variant. In this case, the largest variant is for triangle, which consists of two integers and a real. At any time during execution, the tag should indicate which variant is currently stored. If the variant must be printed, one could use the following:

```
case thing.form of
  circle:    writeln ('It is a circle; its diameter=',
                            thing.diameter);
  triangle: begin
            writeln ('It is a triangle');
            writeln ('its sides are:', thing.leftside,
                        thing.rightside);
            writeln ('angle between the sides is:',
                        thing.angle);
            end;
  rectangle: begin
            writeln ('It is a rectangle');
            writeln ('its sides are:', thing.side1,
                        thing.side2)
            end
end
```

There are two distinct problems with the Pascal and Modula-2 variant record design that can make their use unsafe. The first problem is that the user program can change the tag without making a corresponding change in the variant. Therefore, even if the run-time system checks the type of the variant by examining the tag before using the variant, it could not detect all type errors; the user program may have changed the tag so that its value is now inconsistent with the type of the current variant. This is one reason why implementors typically ignore type checking of variant record references in these languages.

Figure 5.2
A discriminated union
of three shape
variables

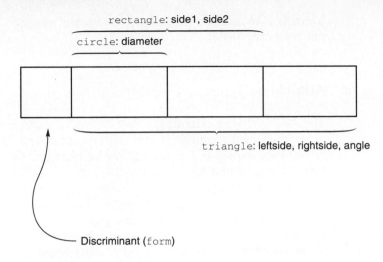

Discriminant (`form`)

The second problem is that the programmer can simply omit the tag from the variant record structure. Then the structure is no longer a discriminated union but is instead called a **free union.** For example, consider the following:

```
type
   object =
     record
       case shape of
          circle :   (diameter : real);
          triangle : (leftside : integer;
          ...
        end
```

With this structure, neither the user nor the system has any way to determine the current variant type. There is no way to guard against incorrect references such as

```
thing.diameter := 2.73;
side := thing.leftside;
```

in which the second assignment is rarely useful because there is currently a floating-point value in that part of the variant where `leftside` resides.

Variant records in Pascal are frequently used to get around some of the restrictions of the language. They provide a convenient loophole in the type-checking rules. For example, pointer arithmetic is not allowed in Pascal, although some applications need to manipulate pointer values. To circumvent the restrictions against pointer arithmetic, a pointer can be placed in a variant with an integer, and the integer form can be manipulated as desired. This particular application of variant records is not necessary in C,

Modula-2, or Ada, as they all provide other methods for doing pointer, or address, arithmetic.

5.7.5   Ada Union Types

The Ada language extends the Pascal form of variant records to make them safer. Both of the problems associated with Pascal and Modula-2 variant records are avoided. The tag cannot be changed without the variant also being changed, and the tag is required on all variant records. Furthermore, Ada systems are required to check the tag for all references to variants.

The Ada design allows the user to specify variables of a variant record type that will store only one of the possible type values in the variant. In this way the user can tell the system when the type checking can be static. Such a restricted variable is called a **constrained variant variable.**

The tag of a constrained variant variable is treated like a named constant. Unconstrained variant records are more like their Pascal counterparts in that the values of their variants can change types during execution. However, the type of the variant can be changed only by assigning the entire record, including the discriminant. This disallows inconsistent records because if the newly assigned record is a constant data aggregate, the value of the tag and the type of the variant can be statically checked for consistency. If the assigned value is a variable, its consistency was guaranteed when it was assigned, so the new value of the variable now being assigned is sure to be consistent.

The following example shows the Ada version of the Pascal variant record defined above:

```
type SHAPE is (CIRCLE, TRIANGLE, RECTANGLE);
type OBJECT (FORM : SHAPE) is
  record
    case FORM is
     when CIRCLE =>
       DIAMETER : FLOAT;
     when TRIANGLE =>
       LEFT_SIDE : INTEGER;
       RIGHT_SIDE : INTEGER;
       ANGLE : FLOAT;
     when RECTANGLE =>
       SIDE_1 : INTEGER;
       SIDE_2 : INTEGER;
    end case;
  end record;
```

The following two statements declare variables of type OBJECT:

```
THING_1 : OBJECT;
THING_2 : OBJECT (FORM => TRIANGLE);
```

THING_1 is declared to be an unconstrained variant record that has no initial value. Its type can change by assignment of a whole record, including the discriminant, as in the following:

```
THING_1 := (FORM => RECTANGLE,
            SIDE_1 => 12,
            SIDE_2 => 3);
```

The right side of this assignment is a data aggregate.

The variable THING_2 declared above is constrained to be a triangle and cannot be changed to another variant.

This form of discriminated union is perfectly safe, because it always allows type checking, although the references to fields in unconstrained variants must be dynamically checked.

5.7.6 Evaluation

Unions are potentially unsafe constructs in many languages. They are one of the reasons why Pascal and Modula-2 are not strongly typed: They do not allow type checking of references to variant parts of records. The unions of FORTRAN are one of the reasons why FORTRAN is more error-prone than some later languages.

On the other hand, unions provide programming flexibility; for example, their presence in Pascal allows pointer arithmetic. Furthermore, they can be designed so that they can be safely used, as in Ada. In most other languages, unions must be used with care.

5.8 Set Types

A **set** type is one whose variables can store unordered collections of distinct values from some ordinal type called its **base type.** Set types are often used to model mathematical sets. For example, text analysis often requires that small sets of characters, such as punctuation characters or vowels, be stored and conveniently searched.

A variable of a set type can store any subset of the range of the base type. The set of all subsets of a given base set is often called the **powerset** of that base set.

The only design issue that is particular to set types is, What should be the maximum number of elements in a set base type?

5.8.1 Sets in Pascal and Modula-2

Among the common imperative languages, only Pascal and Modula-2 include sets as a data type. We now briefly describe Pascal's set data type.

The maximum size of Pascal base sets is implementation dependent. Many implementations severely restrict it, often to much less than 100. They do so because sets and their operations are most efficiently implemented by representing set variables as bit strings that fit into a single machine word.

One problem with letting machine wordsize determine the maximum base set size is that users are restricted to modeling only very small sets. This is a deficiency in writability. Another problem is that different machines have different wordsizes, so programs developed on machines with larger wordsizes that use larger sets may not be portable to machines with smaller wordsizes. Both these problems result from letting maximum base set size be chosen by implementors, rather than making it part of the language design.

Pascal allows the following set operations:

:=	assignment of compatible set types
+	set union
*	set intersection
−	set difference
=	set equality
<>	set inequality
<=	set included in (subset)
>=	set includes (superset)
in	element inclusion in a set

The last five of these are predicate operations that return a Boolean value. The operations $=$, $<>$, $>=$, and $<=$ have two sets as operands, whereas the **in** operator has a set element as its first operand and a set as its other operand.

The following examples should help clarify the Pascal set operations. Suppose that the types colors and colorset and the variables set1, set2, and set3 are defined as

```
type colors = (red, blue, green, yellow, orange, white);
     colorset = set of colors;
var set1, set2, set3 : colorset;
```

Constant values can be assigned to set1 and set2, as in

```
set1 := [red, blue, yellow, white];
set2 := [blue, yellow];
```

The following assignments illustrate the union, intersection, and difference operations:

```
set3 := set1 + set2; {set3 is now [red,blue,yellow,white] }
set3 := set1 * set2; {set3 is now [blue, yellow] }
set3 := set1 - set2; {set2 is now [red, white] }
```

The following Boolean expressions illustrate the set predicates:

```
set1 = set2 is false
set1 <> set2 is true
```

```
set1 <= set2 is false
set1 >= set2 is true
red in set1 is true
red in set2 is false
```

Modula-2 includes the set type of Pascal, with a few minor changes in syntax and some additional operations. Set constants are enclosed in braces, {}, and constants may be preceded by the type name, which clarifies the type of such occurrences of those constants. For example, consider the following set type declarations:

```
TYPE setype1 = SET OF [red, blue, green, yellow];
     setype2 = SET OF [blue, yellow];
VAR  setvar1 : setype1;
```

In a program that includes these declarations, the constant {blue} may be ambiguous. However, the type of the constant, blue is the statement

```
setvar1 := setype1 {blue}
```

is very clear. In Pascal, the constant would simply be [blue], which does not specify its type.

Modula-2 includes two procedures for inserting and removing elements from sets: INCL and EXCL, respectively. If setvar1 were a variable of type setype1 as defined above, INCL (setvar1, green) would insert green into setvar1. Similarly, EXCL (setvar1, blue) would remove blue from setvar1. Of course, these procedures could easily be simulated in Pascal.

There is a predefined set in Modula-2 named BITSET, whose base type is the subrange 0..k, where k is one less than the wordsize (the number of bits per word) of the implementation computer. In some implementations, k is a small multiple of the wordsize, say 2 or 3. On most machines, the wordsize is either 16 or 32, so the subrange is often either 0..15 or 0..31. One purpose of BITSET is to provide a set type for which set operations can be efficiently implemented. If the wordsize of the machine is the set cardinality, then all operations can usually be done by using single machine instructions. Another application of the BITSET type is for referencing and assigning individual bits in a memory word.

Modula-2, like Pascal, does not specify a minimum cardinality of sets, so it is again implementation dependent. Set type variables, like enumeration type variables, can be neither input nor output in Pascal or Modula-2.

5.8.2 Evaluation

The Ada language does not include set types, although Ada was based on Pascal. Instead, Ada's designers added a set membership operator for its enumeration types. This provides for one of the most commonly needed set operations. Of course, the sets against which membership tests can be made are just enumeration values, which are constants.

In other languages without set types, set operations must be done with arrays, and the user must write the code to provide the operations. This is not difficult, although it is indeed more cumbersome and will most likely be far less efficient. For example, if the set of vowels were represented as a char array in Pascal, determining whether a given character variable stored a vowel would require a loop to search the vowel array. If the vowels were represented as a set, however, the same determination could be made with one application of the in operator. This is not only programmer efficient, but also will probably be computer efficient. In both cases, it is better because the whole set can be dealt with as a unit, whereas the array must be searched one element at a time.

Arrays are, of course, far more flexible than sets; they allow many more operations, more complex shapes, and more options for element types. In fact, if arrays were restricted to a maximum length of 32, as are sets in many Pascal implementations, users would not consider them acceptable. Sets provide an alternative that trades flexibility for efficiency for a certain class of applications.

5.9   Pointer Types

A **pointer** type is one in which the variables have a range of values that consists of memory addresses and a special value, nil. The value nil is not a valid address and is used to indicate that a pointer cannot currently be used to reference another object.

Pointers have been designed for two distinct kinds of uses. First, pointers provide some of the power of indirect addressing, which is heavily used in assembly language programming.

Second, pointers provide a method of dynamic storage management. A pointer can be used to access a location in the area where storage is dynamically allocated, which is usually called a **heap.** The name heap comes from the complex organization that may occur because of randomly ordered dynamic allocations and deallocations. It is only a historic accident that a particular kind of tree structure is also called a heap.

Variables that are dynamically allocated from the heap are called **dynamic variables.** They usually do not have identifiers associated with them and thus can be referenced only by pointer variables. Variables without names are called **anonymous variables.** It is in this latter application area of pointers that the most important design issues arise.

5.9.1   Design Issues

The primary design issues particular to pointers are the following:

1. What are the scope and lifetime of a pointer variable?
2. What is the lifetime of a dynamic variable?
3. Are pointers restricted as to the type of object to which they can point?

5.9.2   Pointer Operations

Languages that provide a pointer type usually include two fundamental pointer operations. The first operation sets a pointer variable to the address of some object. If pointer variables are used only to manage dynamic storage, the allocation mechanism, whether by built-in procedure or otherwise, serves to initialize the pointer variable. If pointers are used for indirect addressing to variables that are not dynamically allocated, then there must be an explicit operator or built-in procedure for fetching the address of a variable, which can then be assigned to the pointer variable.

A reference to a pointer variable in a program can be taken to be either a reference to the contents of the memory cell to which the variable is bound, which is an address, or a reference to the value in the memory cell whose address is in the memory cell to which the variable is bound. The former case is a normal pointer reference; the latter is the result of **dereferencing** the pointer. Dereferencing is the second fundamental pointer operation. To clarify dereferencing, consider a pointer variable, ptr, that is bound to a memory cell with the value 7080. Suppose that the memory cell whose address is 7080 has the value 206. A normal reference to ptr yields 7080, but a dereferenced reference to ptr yields 206.

Dereferencing can be either explicit or implicit. In ALGOL 68 and FORTRAN 90, it is implicit, but in most other contemporary languages, it occurs only when explicitly specified. In Pascal, it is explicitly specified with the circumflex (^), as a postfix unary operation. For example, if ptr is a pointer variable with the value 7080, as in the above example, and the cell whose address is 7080 has the value 206, then the assignment:

```
j := ptr^
```

sets j to 206. This process is shown in Figure 5.3.

Languages that provide pointers for the management of a heap must include an explicit allocation operation. Some also provide an explicit deallocation operation. These two operations are often in the form of built-in procedures, although Ada uses an allocator operator. For example, in Pascal, the allocation and deallocation procedures are called new and dispose,

Figure 5.3
The assignment operation $j := ptr\hat{}$

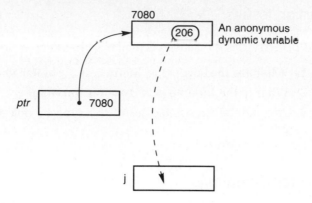

respectively. As we discuss later, only C includes more than these basic operations for pointer types.

5.9.3 Pointers and Pointer Problems in PL/I

The first high-level programming language to include pointer variables was PL/I, in which pointers can be used to refer to both dynamic variables and other program variables. The pointers of PL/I are highly flexible, but their use can lead to several kinds of programming errors.

Our primary purpose in discussing PL/I pointers is to introduce the main programming problems that can occur with pointers.

5.9.3.1 Type Checking

The type of object to which a pointer can point is called its **domain type.** For example, if a pointer is allowed to point only to integer type objects, its domain type is integer. A PL/I pointer is not restricted to a single domain type. The problem with this approach is that it makes static type checking of pointer references impossible, which thus lowers the reliability of PL/I programs that use pointers. All subsequent imperative languages that include pointers restrict them to single type domains, so this problem occurs only in PL/I.

5.9.3.2 Dangling Pointers

A **dangling pointer,** or **dangling reference,** is a pointer that contains the address of a dynamic variable that has been deallocated. Dangling pointers are dangerous because the location being pointed to either contains invalid data or is the value of a more recently allocated variable. However, because the system cannot detect the fact that the pointer is no longer pointing at useful data, it can still be used by the program—producing incorrect results.

In PL/I, there are two ways to create dangling pointers. First, a dangling pointer can be created if the scope of a pointer is larger than that of the object to which it points. This extends the lifetime of the pointer past the lifetime of the object to which it points. For example, consider the following PL/I code segment:

```
BEGIN;
DECLARE POINT POINTER;
...
  BEGIN;
  DECLARE SUM FIXED;
  POINT = ADDR(SUM);
  ...
  END;
...
END;
```

After exiting from the inner block, the pointer POINT still exists, but the object to which it pointed, SUM, has been deallocated. POINT is dangling after its exit from the inner block.

The second way a PL/I program can create dangling pointers is by including an explicit deallocation operation for dynamic variables. In PL/I, a dynamic variable, which is called a **based** variable, can be explicitly allocated with the ALLOCATE statement and deallocated with the FREE statement. Such a variable is declared to be BASED, and a pointer variable name to be used to reference it can be specified in the declaration.

The following code segment illustrates how dangling pointers can be created using FREE:

```
DECLARE SUM FLOAT BASED (POINT);
DECLARE POINT2 POINTER;
...
ALLOCATE SUM;
POINT2 = POINT;
FREE SUM;
```

The ALLOCATE operation implicitly sets POINT, which is SUM's pointer, to point at the new object.

After execution of the FREE statement that frees SUM, POINT2 is a dangling pointer. Because of the difficulty of the process, no attempt is made to find all pointers pointing to a dynamic variable when a FREE statement is executed.

5.9.3.3 Lost Objects

A **lost object** is an allocated dynamic object that is no longer accessible to the user program but may still contain useful data. Such variables are often called **garbage** because they are not useful to the user program that allocated them, and they also cannot be reallocated for some new use by the system. For example, consider the following code segment:

```
DECLARE SUM FLOAT BASED (POINT);
...
ALLOCATE SUM;
...
ALLOCATE SUM;
```

The first `ALLOCATE` dynamically allocates a `FLOAT` type anonymous variable that can be referenced through the pointer, `POINT`. After the second `ALLOCATE` is executed, however, the first anonymous variable still exists, but it is no longer accessible. If both versions of `SUM` are required, a second pointer variable can be used to store `POINT`'s value, which is the only access path to that first dynamic variable, before the second `ALLOCATE` is executed.

In the following sections we investigate how later language designers dealt with these problems.

5.9.4   Pointers in ALGOL 68

ALGOL 68 includes pointers that are less error-prone than those of PL/I. As a result of its orthogonal design, ALGOL 68 pointers are a natural part of the data-typing structure. A "normal" integer variable `X` is declared in ALGOL 68 with the following statement:

```
int X;
```

`X` is said to be of **ref int** type, because its usual use is as an address. In a sense, `X` is not an integer object; rather, it is a reference to an integer object. When `X` appears in an expression, its value is needed and it must be dereferenced. All variables that appear in expressions on the right sides of assignment statements are implicitly dereferenced whatever number of times is required to make their type match that of the left side of the assignment.

A variable `Y` that is to be used as a pointer to an integer is declared as follows:

```
ref int Y;
```

`Y` is said to be of **ref ref int** type. Consider the following example:

```
int X;
ref int Y;
```

Now, the assignments

```
X := 5;
Y := X;
```

require no implicit conversion or dereferencing. In the first case, the constant is of **int** type. In the second, no conversions are required because the types of both identifiers are exactly what is required. The address of X— not its value (5)—is moved to Y. A constant cannot be assigned to Y because constants cannot be of **ref** type.

In the assignment:

```
X := Y
```

Y is implicitly dereferenced twice. The integer at the address pointed to by Y is moved to the address specified by X. For example, if the other two assignment statements above (X := 5; Y := X) were executed, and then X := Y were executed, the 5 would again be assigned to X.

Another interesting result of the orthogonality of ALGOL 68's type structure is that one can easily declare pointers to pointers. For example,

```
ref ref int ptr;
```

declares ptr to be a pointer to a pointer to an integer variable.

Most occurrences of the dangling pointer problem are avoided in ALGOL 68 by the following restriction: When an assignment is made to a pointer, the scope of the object being pointed to must be at least as large as the scope of the pointer variable that points to it. This specifically disallows code like that in the PL/I example of dangling pointers in Section 5.9.3.2. The restriction can be statically checked, in most cases, because of the static scoping of ALGOL 68. One exception is when a pointer and an object are passed as parameters to a procedure, and then the object is assigned to the pointer. In this case, the legality of the assignment depends on the actual parameters that are passed. Although it is possible to check this dynamically, it is so costly that most ALGOL 68 implementations ignore the potential problem.

The other method of creating dangling pointers in PL/I—using explicit deallocation—is not a problem in ALGOL 68: ALGOL 68 has no explicit deallocation of heap-allocated objects.

The lost object problem is, in a sense, worse in ALGOL 68 than in PL/I. In ALGOL 68, data objects can be dynamically allocated from either the stack or the heap. The appearance of the reserved word **heap** causes a heap object to be allocated, and the appearance of the reserved word **loc** causes a stack object to be allocated. Lost objects can be created, therefore, in either the heap or the stack. For example, we could have

```
ref int ptr;
...
ptr := heap int;
ptr := heap int;
```

which creates a garbage object on the heap, or

```
ref int ptr;
...
```

```
ptr := loc int;
ptr := heap int;
```

which creates a garbage object on the stack.

A lost object on the stack is less of a problem than in a heap, for stack space is reclaimed when the current stack frame (for the current subprogram or block) is popped.

5.9.5 Pointers in Pascal

In Pascal, pointers are used only to access dynamically allocated anonymous variables.

Dangling pointers can be created easily in Pascal with explicit deallocation, as in PL/I. A Pascal programmer creates dynamic variables with new and destroys them with dispose. To destroy dynamic variables safely, the function dispose would be required to find and set all pointers pointing to the dynamic variable being destroyed to nil. Unfortunately, as is the case with PL/I's FREE, this process is complex and costly, and as a result it is rarely implemented that way. This is a problem for all explicit deallocation processes in programming languages.

Pascal implementors choose among the following four alternatives for explicit deallocation:

1. Simply ignore dispose, in which case no deallocation is done, and none of the pointers that were pointing at the dynamic object in question are changed.

2. Do not include dispose in the language, making dispose an illegal statement.

3. Actually deallocate the dynamic variable in question and set the pointer that is the parameter to dispose to nil, thus creating dangling pointers from any other pointers that happen to be pointing at the object.

4. Implement dispose completely and correctly, disallowing dangling pointers. The author knows of no Pascal implementation that chose this alternative.

Several dialects of Pascal provide an alternative method of deallocating dynamic variables. Instead of dispose, which is difficult to implement, two other procedures are provided: mark and release. Dynamic storage is allocated in sequential order from the heap, using a system pointer to point at the next available location. The mark procedure allows the user to access the value of the heap pointer. The release procedure resets the heap pointer to a previously saved value. At the beginning of a section of code that uses dynamic variables, a program can use mark to record the heap pointer. Then, after the section has completed execution, all dynamic storage allocated by the section can be returned by using `release` to set the heap pointer back to the value it had before the section began execution.

Although `mark` and `release` are easy to implement, they have their own problems. For one, they effectively turn the heap into a stack, thus lowering its flexibility. Indeed, heaps were invented to provide more flexibility than stacks by allowing allocation/deallocation sequences that are not nested. Furthermore, the necessity of releasing dynamic objects at the end of their usefulness is an easily forgotten task. Also, the use of the `mark/release` method can lead to dangling pointers by allowing the scope of dynamic objects to be smaller than pointers that point to them.

5.9.6 Pointers in Ada

Ada provides pointers, called **access** types, that are similar to those of Pascal. In Ada, however, the dangling pointer problem is partially alleviated by the language's design. A dynamic variable may be (at the implementor's option) implicitly deallocated at the end of the scope of its pointer type, thus dramatically lessening the need for explicit deallocation. Because dynamic variables can only be accessed by variables of one type, when the end of the scope of that type declaration is reached, no pointers can be left pointing at the object. This lessens the problem because improperly implemented explicit deallocation is the major source of dangling pointers. Unfortunately, the Ada language also has an explicit deallocation, `UNCHECKED_DEALLOCATION`. Its name is meant to discourage its use, or at least warn the user of its potential problems.

The lost object problem is not eliminated by Ada's design of pointers. Lost objects can be created in the same way as they can in PL/I.

One other small improvement in Ada pointers over those of Pascal and Modula-2 is the language's requirement that all pointers be implicitly initialized to **null** (Ada's version of `nil`). This prevents inadvertent accesses to random locations in memory because the user forgot to initialize a pointer before using it.

5.9.7 Pointers in C

In C, pointers can be used much like addresses are used in assembly languages. This means they are extremely flexible but must be used with great care. This design offers no solutions to the dangling pointer or lost object problems. However, the fact that pointer arithmetic is possible in C makes its pointers more interesting than those of the other imperative languages.

The asterisk (*) denotes the dereferencing operation, and the ampersand (&) denotes the operator for producing the address of a variable. For example, in the code

```
int *ptr;
int count, init;
...
ptr = &init;
count = *ptr;
```

the two assignment statements are equivalent to the following single assignment:

```
count = init;
```

The assignment to the variable `ptr` sets `ptr` to the address of `init`. The first assignment to `count` dereferences `ptr` to produce the value at `init`, which is then assigned to `count`. So the effect of the first two assignment statements is to assign the value of `init` to `count`. Notice that the declaration of a pointer specifies its domain type.

Pointers can be assigned the address value of any object of the correct domain type, or they can be assigned the constant zero, which is used for `nil`.

Pointer arithmetic is also possible in some restricted forms. For example, if `ptr` is a pointer variable that is declared to point at some object of some data type, then

```
ptr + index
```

is a legal expression. The semantics of such an expression is as follows. Instead of simply adding the value of `index` to `ptr`, the value of `index` is first scaled by the size of the object (in memory units) to which `ptr` is pointing. For example, if `ptr` points to an object four memory units in size, then `index` is multiplied by 4, and the result is added to `ptr`. The primary purpose of this sort of address arithmetic is array manipulation. The following discussion is related to single-dimensioned arrays only.

In C, all arrays use zero as the lower bound of their subscript ranges, and array names without subscripts always refer to the address of the first element. In fact, an array name without a subscript is treated exactly like a pointer, except that it is a constant and therefore cannot be assigned. Consider the following declarations:

```
int list [10];
int *ptr;
```

If there is the initializing assignment

```
ptr = list;
```

which assigns the address of `list[0]` to `ptr`, then

```
*(ptr + 1) is equivalent to list[1],
*(ptr + index) is equivalent to list[index], and
ptr[index] is equivalent to list[index]
```

So the pointer operations include the same scaling that is used in indexing operations.

Pointers can point to functions. This feature is used to pass functions as parameters to other functions. Pointers are also used for parameter passing, as discussed in Chapter 8.

In C, pointers that point to records can be used to reference fields of records. For example, if a pointer variable p points to a record with a field named age, `(*p).age` can be used to refer to that field. The form `p -> age` also references the same field.

5.9.8 Pointers in FORTRAN 90

Pointers in FORTRAN 90 are used to point to both dynamic variables and static variables. For example, in

```
INTEGER, POINTER :: INT_PTR
INTEGER, POINTER, DIMENSION (:) :: INT_LIST_PTR
```

INT_PTR can point at any object of type INTEGER, and INT_LIST_PTR can point at any single-dimensioned array of INTEGER elements.

FORTRAN 90 pointers are implicitly dereferenced in most uses. For example, when a pointer appears in a normal expression, it is always implicitly dereferenced. A special assignment statement form,

pointer => target

is used when dereferencing is not desired. This assignment is used both to set pointer variables to point at particular variables and to set them to have the address values of other pointer variables. Any variable that is to be pointed to by a pointer variable must have the TARGET attribute, which is set in its declaration. For example, in the following,

```
INTEGER, TARGET :: APPLE
INTEGER ORANGE
```

APPLE can be pointed to by INT_PTR, but ORANGE cannot.

FORTRAN 90 pointers can easily become dangling, because the DEALLOCATE statement, which takes a pointer as an argument, makes no attempt to determine if other pointers are pointing at a dynamic variable that is being deallocated.

5.9.9 Evaluation

The problems of dangling pointers and garbage have already been discussed at length. The problems of heap management are discussed in Section 5.10.7.

Pointers have been compared with the goto. The goto statement widens the range of statements that can be executed next. Pointer variables widen the range of memory cells that can be referenced by a variable. Perhaps the most damning statement about pointers was made by Hoare (Hoare, 1973): "Their introduction into high-level languages has been a step backward from which we may never recover."

In spite of the hazards, pointers are thought by many to be essential in imperative languages. They provide the means by which recursively defined data structures, such as linked lists and binary trees, can be represented. Although they have their problems, no one has yet suggested a retreat back to the old FORTRAN method of representing such structures, which is to use static arrays in place of heap management and indexing in place of pointer links between structure cells. Pointers also provide the mechanism for managing dynamic storage in a heap.

5.10   Implementing Data Types

We now take a brief look at implementation methods for the data types described in this chapter. The discussion will be general; it will not focus on language variations and specific implementation approaches.

It is convenient, both logically and concretely, to think of variables in terms of descriptors. A **descriptor** stores the attributes of a variable. If the attributes are all static, descriptors are required only at compile time. For dynamic attributes, however, part or all of the descriptor must be maintained during execution.

5.10.1   Character String Types

Character string types are sometimes supported directly in hardware. In other cases, software is used to implement string storage, retrieval, and manipulation. When character string types are actually character arrays, the language often supplies few operations. In C, for example, operations for string moves and string comparisons are provided outside the language, through a standard library of functions.

Static character string types usually require compile-time descriptors with a field for length, as shown in Figure 5.4.

Static strings require a descriptor only during compilation. Limited dynamic strings require a run-time descriptor to store both the fixed maximum length and the current length, as shown in Figure 5.5. Dynamic length strings require a simpler run-time descriptor because only the current length needs to be stored.

Static length and limited dynamic length strings require no special dynamic storage allocation. In the case of limited dynamic length strings, sufficient storage for the maximum length is allocated when the string variable is bound to storage, so only a single allocation process is involved. The maximum length is fixed at compile time.

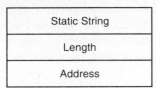

Static String
Length
Address

Figure 5.4
Compile-time descriptor for
static strings

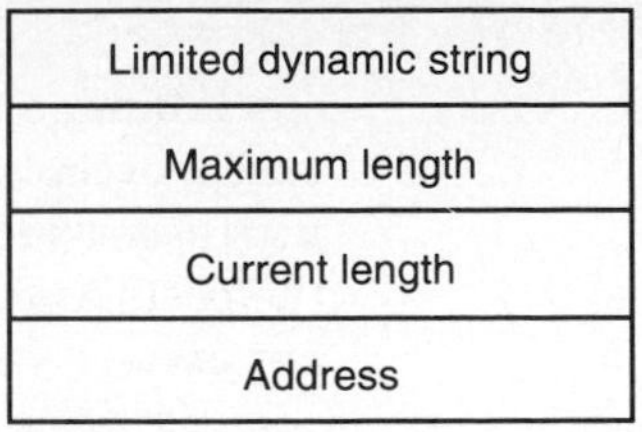

Limited dynamic string
Maximum length
Current length
Address

Figure 5.5
Run-time descriptor for limited
dynamic strings

Dynamic length strings require more complex storage management. The length of a string, and therefore the storage to which it is bound, must grow and shrink dynamically.

There are two possible approaches to the dynamic allocation problem. First, strings can be stored in a linked list, so that when a string grows, the newly required cells can come from anywhere in the heap. The drawback to this method is the large amount of storage occupied by the links in the list representation. The alternative is to store complete strings in adjacent storage cells. The problem with this method occurs when a string grows: How can storage that is adjacent to the existing cells continue to be allocated for the string variable? Frequently, such storage is not available. Instead, a new area of memory is found that can store the complete new string, and the old part is moved to this area. Then the memory cells used for the old string are deallocated.

Although the linked list method requires more storage, the associated allocation and deallocation processes are simple. However, some string operations are slowed by the required pointer chasing. On the other hand, using adjacent memory for complete strings results in faster string operations and requires significantly less storage. However, the allocation process is slower. The adjacency method involves the general problem of managing allocation and deallocation of variable size segments. This problem is discussed in Section 5.10.7.2.

5.10.2 User-Defined Ordinal Types

Enumeration types are usually implemented by associating a nonnegative integer value with each symbolic constant in the type. Typically, the first enumeration value is represented as 0, the second as 1, and so forth. As long as the association is constant, the integers can be used in place of the enumeration constants. Of course, the operations allowed are dramatically different from those of integers, except for the relational operators, which are identical. As stated earlier, in ANSI C and C++, enumeration types are treated exactly like integers.

Subrange types are implemented in exactly the same way as their parent types, except that range checks must be included in every assignment. This increases code size and execution time, but is usually considered well worth the cost. Also, a good optimizing compiler can optimize some of the checking away.

5.10.3   Array Types

Implementing arrays requires more compile-time effort than does implementing simple built-in types, such as integer. The code to allow accessing of array elements must be constructed at compile time. At run time, this code must be executed to produce element addresses. Accesses to array elements, especially in arrays with several subscripts, are more expensive than necessary if the access code is not carefully constructed. This is true regardless of whether the array is statically or dynamically bound to memory. There is no way to precompute the address to be accessed by a reference such as

```
list[k]
```

A single-dimensioned array is a list of adjacent memory cells. Suppose the array list is defined to have a subscript range lower bound of 1. The access function for list is often of the following form:

$$\text{address}(\texttt{list[k]}) = \text{address}(\texttt{list[1]}) + (k\text{-}1) *$$
$$\text{element\_size}$$

This simplifies to

$$\text{address}(\texttt{list[k]}) = (\text{address}(\texttt{list[1]}) - \text{element\_size}) +$$
$$(k * \text{element\_size})$$

where the first operand of the addition is the constant part and the second is the variable part.

If the element type is statically bound and the array is statically bound to storage, then the value of the constant part can be computed before run time. At run time, then, only the addition and multiplication operations remain to be done. If the base, or beginning address, of the array is not known until run time, the subtraction must be done when the array is allocated.

The generalization of this access function for arbitrary lower bound is

$$\text{address}(\texttt{list[k]} = (\text{address}(\texttt{list[lower\_bound]})) +$$
$$((k - \text{lower\_bound}) * \text{element\_size})$$

The compile-time descriptor for single-dimensioned arrays can have the form shown in Figure 5.6. This is the information required to construct the access function. If run-time checking of index ranges is not done and the attributes are all static, then only the access function is required during exe-

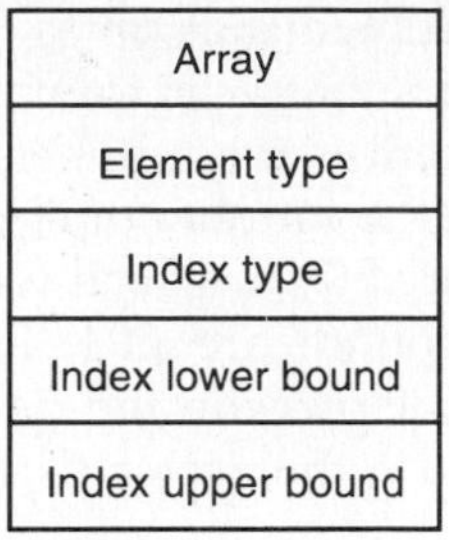

Figure 5.6

Compile-time descriptor for single-dimensioned arrays

Array
Element type
Index type
Index lower bound
Index upper bound

cution; no descriptor is needed. If run-time checking of index ranges is done, then those index ranges may need to be stored in a run-time descriptor. If any of the descriptor entries are dynamically bound, then those parts of the descriptor must be maintained at run time.

Multidimensional arrays are more complex to implement than single-dimensioned arrays, although the extension to more dimensions is fairly straightforward. There are two common ways in which multidimensional arrays can be implemented: row major order and column major order. In **row major order,** the elements of the array that have as their first subscript the lower bound value of that subscript are stored first, followed by the elements of the second value of the first subscript, and so forth. If the array is a matrix, it is stored by rows. For example, if the matrix had the values

3	4	7
6	2	5
1	3	8

it would be stored in row major order as

3, 4, 7, 6, 2, 5, 1, 3, 8

In **column major order,** the elements of an array that have as their last subscript the lower bound value of that subscript are stored first, followed by the elements of the second value of the last subscript, and so forth. If the array is a matrix, it is stored by columns. If the example matrix above were stored in column major order, it would have the following order in memory:

3, 6, 1, 4, 2, 3, 7, 5, 8

Column major order is used in FORTRAN, but the other imperative languages use row major order.

It is sometimes essential to know the storage order of multidimensional arrays; for example, when such arrays are processed using pointers in C programs, and when an array is EQUIVALENCEd to another array with a different shape in a FORTRAN program.

The access function for two-dimensional arrays stored in row major order can be developed as follows. The address of an element is the base address of the structure plus the element size times the number of elements that precede it in the structure. For a matrix in row major order, the number of elements that precedes an element is the number of rows above the element times the size of a row, plus the number of elements to the left of the element. This is illustrated in Figure 5.7, in which we make the simplifying assumption that subscript lower bounds are all 1. To get an actual address value, the number of elements that precede the desired element must be multiplied by the element size. Now, the access function can be written as

location(a[i,j]) = (address of a[1,1]) +
  ((((number of rows above the *ith* row) * (size of a row))
  + (number of elements left of the *jth* column))
    * element size)

or

location(a[i, j]) = (address of a[1, 1]) +
  ((((i − 1) * n) + (j − 1)) * element_size)

where *n* is the number of elements per row. This can be rearranged to the following form:

location(a[i, j]) = (address of a[1, 1]) −
        ((n + 1) * element_size) +
        ((i * n + j) * element_size)

where the first two terms are the constant part and the last is the variable part.

The generalization to arbitrary lower bounds results in the following access function:

location(a[i, j]) = (address of a[row_lb, col_lb]) +
        (((i − row_lb) * n) +
        (j − col_lb)) * element_size

Figure 5.7
The location of the [i, j] element in a matrix

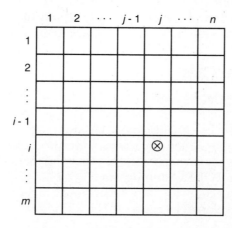

where row_lb is the lower bound of the rows, and col_lb is the lower bound of the columns. This can be rearranged to the form

$$location(a[i, j]) = (\text{address of } a[row\_lb, col\_lb]) - \\ ((row\_lb * n) + (element\_size * col\_lb)) + \\ (((i * n) + j) * element\_size)$$

where the first two terms are the constant part and the last is the variable part. This can be generalized relatively easily to an arbitrary number of dimensions.

For each dimension of an array, one add and one multiply instruction is required for the access function. Therefore, accesses to elements of arrays with several subscripts are costly. The compile-time descriptor for a multidimensional array is shown in Figure 5.8.

Slices add another layer of complexity to storage mapping functions. To illustrate this, consider a program in which there is a matrix and an array, and a column of the matrix is assigned to the array, as in

```
INTEGER MAT(1:10, 1:5), LIST(1:10)
...
LIST - MAT(1:3, 3)
```

The storage mapping function for the matrix, MAT, assuming row major order and an element size of 1, is

$$location(\text{MAT}(i, j)) = (\text{address of MAT}(1,1)) \\ + ((i - 1) * 5 + (j - 1)) * 1 \\ = ((\text{address of MAT}(1,1)) - 6) + ((5 * i) + j)$$

The storage mapping function for the slice reference MAT(1:3, 3) is

$$location(\text{MAT}(i, 3)) = (\text{address of MAT}(1,1)) \\ + ((i - 1) * 5 + (3 - 1)) * 1 \\ = ((\text{address of MAT}(1,1)) - 3) + (5 * i)$$

Figure 5.8
A compile-time descriptor for a multidimensional array

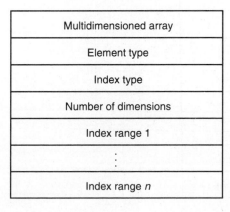

| Multidimensioned array |
| Element type |
| Index type |
| Number of dimensions |
| Index range 1 |
| ⋮ |
| Index range *n* |

Notice that this mapping has exactly the same form as any other single-dimensional array access function, although the form of the constant part is different because the basic array is two-dimensional.

The elements of MAT that are to be assigned to LIST are found by letting i take on the values in the subscript range of the first dimension of MAT.

5.10.4 Record Types

The fields of records are stored in adjacent memory locations. But because the size of the fields is not necessarily the same, the access method used for arrays is not used for records. Instead, the offset address, relative to the beginning of the record, is associated with each field. Field accesses are all handled using these offsets. The compile-time descriptor for a record has the general form shown in Figure 5.9. Run-time descriptors for records are unnecessary.

5.10.5 Discriminated Union Types

Discriminated unions are implemented by simply using the same address for every possible variant. Sufficient storage for the largest variant is allocated. In the case of constrained variants in the Ada language, the exact amount of storage can be used because there is no variation. The tag of a discriminated union is stored with the variant in a record-like structure.

At compile time, the complete description of each variant must be stored. This can be done by associating a case table with the tag entry in the descriptor. The case table has an entry for each variant, which points to a descriptor for that particular variant. To illustrate this arrangement, consider the following Ada example:

Figure 5.9
A compile-time descriptor for a record

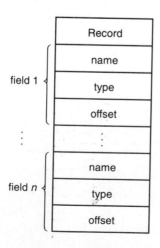

```
type NODE (TAG : BOOLEAN) is
  record
    case TAG is
      when true => COUNT : INTEGER;
      when false => SUM : FLOAT;
    end case;
  end record;
```

The descriptor for this type could have the form shown in Figure 5.10.

5.10.6 Set Types

Sets are usually stored as bit strings in memory. For example, if a set has
the ordinal base type

```
['a'..'o']
```

then variables of this set type can use the first 15 bits of a machine word,
with each set bit (1) representing a present element, and each clear bit (0)
representing an absent element. Using this scheme, the set value

```
['a', 'c', 'h', 'o']
```

would be represented as

```
101000010000001
```

The payoff in this approach is that a typical operation such as set union
can be computed as a single machine instruction, a logical OR. Set membership can also be done in a single instruction when the base set cardinality is less than or equal to the machine's wordsize. For example, if we
had a set variable named setchars, and the membership test was

```
'g' in setchars
```

Figure 5.10
A compile-time de-
scriptor for a discrimi-
nated union

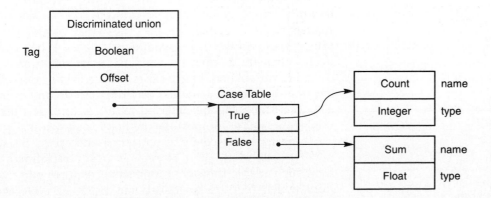

the process could be done with an AND operation between the bit string representations of the two operands.

5.10.7   Pointers and Heap Management

In most languages, pointers are used in heap management, so we cannot treat these two features separately. First, we briefly describe how pointers are represented. We then discuss two possible solutions to the dangling pointer problem. Finally, we describe the major problems with heap management techniques.

5.10.7.1   Representations of Pointers

In most larger computers, pointers are single values stored in either two- or four-byte memory cells, depending on the size of the address space of the machine. However, most microcomputers are based on Intel microprocessors, which use addresses with two parts: a segment and an offset. So, pointers are implemented in these systems as pairs of 16-bit words, one for each of the two parts of an address.

5.10.7.2   Solutions to the Dangling Pointer Problem

Dangling pointers are those that point to storage that has been deallocated. They are often created by explicit deallocation of dynamic variables. Explicit deallocation creates dangling pointers because the deallocation statement names only one pointer to the dynamic variable to be deallocated. Any other pointers to the disposed dynamic variable are made dangling by the process, because the run-time system does not determine that other such pointers exist.

Two separate but related solutions to the dangling pointer problem have been either proposed or actually implemented. First, there is the proposal that uses extra heap cells, called tombstones.

Tombstones were proposed by Lomet (1975). The idea is to have all dynamic variables include a special cell, called a tombstone, that is itself a pointer to the dynamic variable. The actual pointer variable points only at tombstones and never to dynamic variables. When a dynamic variable is deallocated, the tombstone remains but is set to `nil`, indicating that the dynamic variable no longer exists. This prevents a pointer from ever pointing to a deallocated variable. Any reference to any pointer that points to a `nil` tombstone can be detected as an error. The difference between the tombstone and nontombstone methods is shown in Figure 5.11.

Tombstones are costly in both time and space. Because tombstones are never deallocated, their storage is never reclaimed. Every access to a dynamic variable through a tombstone requires one more level of indirection, which requires an additional machine cycle on most computers.

Apparently none of the designers of the more popular languages have found the additional safety to be worth this additional cost, because no widely used language includes tombstones.

Tombstones have been found to be valuable outside programming languages, however. They are used extensively by Macintosh systems software to detect dangling pointer dereferences and to facilitate dynamic relocation of dynamically allocated objects.

An alternative to tombstones is the locks-and-keys approach used in the implementation of UW-Pascal (Fischer and LeBlanc, 1977, 1980). In this compiler, pointer values are represented as ordered pairs (key, address), where the key is an integer value. Dynamic variables are represented as the storage for the variable plus a header cell that stores an integer lock value. When a dynamic variable is allocated, a lock value is created and placed both in the lock cell of the dynamic variable and in the key cell of the pointer that is specified in the call to new. Every access to the dereferenced pointer compares the key value of the pointer to the lock value in the dynamic variable. If they match, the access is legal; otherwise, the access is treated as a run-time error. Any copies of the pointer value to other pointers must copy the key value. Therefore, any number of pointers can reference a given dynamic variable. When a dynamic variable is deallocated with dispose, its lock value is cleared to an illegal lock value. Then, if a pointer other than the one specified in dispose is dereferenced, its address value will still be intact, but its key value will no longer match the lock, so the access will not be allowed.

Figure 5.11
Implementing dynamic variables with and without tombstones

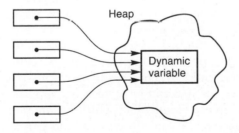

a. **Without tombstones**

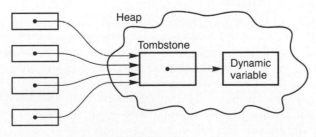

b. **With tombstones**

5.10.7.3 Heap Management

Heap management can be a very complex run-time process. We examine the process in two separate situations: one in which all heap storage is allocated and deallocated in units of a single size, and one in which variable-size segments are allocated and deallocated. Our discussion will be brief and far from comprehensive, since a thorough analysis of these processes and their associated problems is more appropriately found in books on data structures.

The simplest situation is when all allocation and deallocation is of a single-size cell. It is further simplified when every cell contains one or more pointers in fixed positions within the cell. This is the scenario of the implementation of LISP, where the problems of dynamic storage allocation were first encountered on a large scale. All LISP programs and most LISP data consist of cells connected into linked lists. Some string management processes also are involved, but we will ignore them here.

In a fixed-size allocation heap, all available cells can be linked together, forming a list of available space. Allocation is a simple matter of taking the required number of cells from this list when they are needed. Deallocation is a much more complex process. The basic problem with deallocation was discussed in Section 5.9.5, in connection with Pascal's `dispose` procedure. A dynamic variable can be pointed to by more than one pointer, making it difficult to determine exactly when the variable is no longer useful to the program. Simply because one pointer is disconnected from a cell obviously does not make it garbage.

In LISP, several of the most frequent operations in user programs create collections of cells that are no longer accessible to the program and therefore should be deallocated (put back on the list of available space). One of the fundamental design goals of LISP was to ensure that reclamation of unused cells would not be the task of the programmer but rather that of the run-time system. This left LISP implementors with the fundamental design question: When should deallocation be performed?

There are two distinct and in some ways opposite processes for reclaiming garbage: reference counters, in which reclamation is incremental and is done when inaccessible cells are created, and garbage collection, in which reclamation only occurs when the list of available space becomes empty.

The **reference counter** method of storage reclamation accomplishes its goal by maintaining a counter in every cell, which stores the number of pointers that are currently pointing at the cell. Embedded in the decrement operation for the reference counters, which occurs when a pointer is disconnected from the cell, is a check for a zero value. If the reference counter reaches zero, it means that no program pointers are pointing at the cell, and it has thus become garbage and can be returned to the list of available space.

There are three distinct problems with the reference counter method. First, if storage cells are relatively small, the space required for the counters is significant. Second, some execution time is obviously required to maintain the counter values. Every time a pointer value is changed, the cell to which it was pointing must have its counter decremented, and the cell to which it is now pointing must have its counter incremented. In a language like LISP, in which nearly every action involves changing pointers, that can be a significant portion of the total execution time of a program. Of course, if pointer changes are not too frequent, this is obviously not a problem. Third, complications arise when a collection of cells are connected circularly. The problem here is that each cell in the circular list has a reference counter value of at least 1, which prevents it from being collected and placed back on the list of available space. A solution to this problem can be found in Friedman and Wise (1979).

The primary alternative to reference counters is called **garbage collection** (obviously a poor name). With this method, the run-time system allocates storage cells as requested and disconnects pointers from cells as necessary, without regard for storage reclamation (allowing garbage to accumulate), until it has allocated all available cells. At this point, a garbage collection process is begun to gather all the garbage left floating around in the heap. To facilitate the garbage collection process, every heap cell has an extra indicator bit or field that is used by the collection algorithm.

The collection process consists of three distinct phases. First, all cells in the heap have their indicators set to indicate they are garbage. This is, of course, a good assumption for only some of the cells. The second part of the process is the most difficult. Every pointer in the program is traced into the heap, and all reachable cells are marked as not being garbage. After this, the third phase is executed: All cells in the heap that have not been specifically marked as not being garbage are returned to the list of available space.

To illustrate the flavor of algorithms used to mark the cells that are currently in use, we provide a simple version of a marking algorithm. We assume that all dynamic variables, or heap cells, consist of an information part, a part for the mark, named tag, and two pointers named llink and rlink. These cells are used to build directed graphs with at most two edges leading from any node. The marking algorithm traverses all spanning trees of the graphs, marking all cells that are found. Like other graph traversals, the marking algorithm uses recursion.

Marking Algorithm:

```
for every pointer r do
  mark(r)
procedure mark(ptr)
  if ptr <> null then
    if ptr^.tag is not marked then
      set ptr^.tag
      mark(ptr^.llink)
      mark(ptr^.rlink)
    end if
  end if
```

An example of the actions of this procedure on a given graph is shown in Figure 5.12. This simple marking algorithm suffers the problem of using a great deal of storage (for stack space to support recursion). A marking process that does not require additional stack space was developed by Schorr and Waite (1967). Their method reverses pointers as it traces out linked structures. Then, when the end of a list is reached, the process can follow the pointers back out of the structure.

The most serious problem with garbage collection can be summed up as follows: When you need it most, it works the worst. You need it most when the program actually needs most of the cells in the heap. Garbage collection in that situation takes a good deal of time, because most of the cells must be traced and marked as being useful. But in that case, the process yields only a small number of cells that can be placed on the list of available space. In addition to this problem, there is the cost of the additional space of the cell marks, which need be only a bit, and the execution time required to execute the collection process. However, these problems are not as serious as they sound, for two related reasons. First, memory is plentiful on most contemporary computers. Second, all larger computers use virtual memory, which makes their large memories appear much larger than they actually are.

Both the marking algorithms for the garbage collection method and the processes required by the reference counter method can be made more efficient by use of the pointer rotation and slide operations that are described by Suzuki (1982).

Managing a heap from which variable-size cells are allocated is more difficult than one from which only single-size cells are allocated. Unfortunately, this is the situation of the imperative languages. The additional problems posed by variable-size cell management depend on the method used. If garbage collection is used, the following additional problems occur:

Figure 5.12
An example of the actions of the marking algorithm

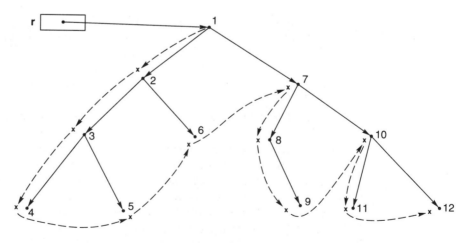

Dashed lines show the order of node_marking.

1. The initial setting of the indicators of all cells in the heap to indicate that they are garbage is difficult. Because the cells are different sizes, scanning them becomes a problem. One solution to this is to require each cell to have the cell size as its first field. Then the scanning can be done, although it takes slightly more space and somewhat more time than its counterpart for fixed-size cells.

2. The marking process is nontrivial. How can a chain be followed from a pointer if there is no predefined location for the pointer in the pointed-to cell? Cells that do not contain pointers at all are also a problem. Adding a system pointer to each cell will work, but it must be maintained in parallel with the user-defined pointers. This adds both space and execution time overhead to the cost of running the program.

3. Maintaining the list of available space is another source of overhead. The list can begin with a single cell consisting of all available space. Requests for segments simply reduce the size of this block. Reclaimed cells are added to the list. The problem is that before long, the list becomes a long list of various-size segments, or blocks. This slows allocation because requests cause the list to be searched for sufficiently large blocks. Eventually, the list may consist of a large number of very small blocks, which are not large enough for most requests. At this point, adjacent blocks may need to be collapsed into larger blocks. Alternatives to using the first sufficiently large block on the list can shorten the search but require the list to be ordered by block size. In either case, maintaining the list is additional overhead.

If reference counters are used, the first two problems are avoided, but the available space list maintenance problem remains.

SUMMARY

The data types of a language are a large part of what determines that language's style and use. Along with control structures, they form the heart of a language.

The user-defined enumeration and subrange types are convenient and add to the readability and reliability of programs.

Arrays are part of most programming languages. The relationship between a reference to an array element and the address of that element is given in an access function, which is an implementation of a mapping. Arrays can be either static, as in FORTRAN 77; semistatic, as in Pascal procedures; semidynamic, as in Ada blocks; or dynamic, as in ALGOL 68 **flex** arrays. Most languages allow only a few operations on complete arrays.

Records are now included in most languages. Fields of records are specified in a variety of ways. In the cases of COBOL and PL/I, they can be referenced without naming all of the enclosing records, although this is messy to implement and harmful to readability.

Discriminated unions are locations that can store different type values at different times. They include a tag to record the current value type. A free union is one without the tag. It has proven difficult to design discriminated unions safely, although the designers of the Ada language have succeeded in doing so.

Sets are sometimes convenient and are relatively easy to implement. The applications that usually use sets, however, can be done without too much difficulty using other data types.

Pointers are used for addressing flexibility and to control dynamic storage management. PL/I introduced pointers and allows maximum flexibility but minimum safety in their use. Pascal and Modula-2 offer less flexibility and more safety through restrictions. Pointers have some inherent dangers: Dangling pointers are difficult to avoid and garbage is difficult to collect.

The level of difficulty in implementing a data type has a strong influence on whether the type will be included in a language. Enumeration types, subrange types, and record types are all relatively easy to implement. Arrays are also straightforward, although array element access is an expensive process when the array has several subscripts. The access function requires one addition and one multiplication for each subscript.

Pointers are costly to implement if they are used for dynamic storage management and if steps are taken to avoid dangling pointers. Heap management is relatively easy if all cells have the same size, but it becomes more complicated with variable size-cell allocation and deallocation.

BIBLIOGRAPHIC NOTES

A wealth of computer science literature exists that is concerned with data type design, use, and implementation. Hoare gives one of the earliest systematic definitions of structured types in Dahl et al. (1972). Tenenbaum compares the type design of ALGOL 68 and Pascal (Tenenbaum, 1978). Feuer and Gehani (1982) compare C and Pascal, including their type structures. A discussion of the insecurities of the Pascal data type design is included in Welsh et al. (1977).

Implementing run-time checks on the possible insecurities of Pascal data types is discussed in Fischer and LeBlanc (1980). Most compiler design books, such as Fischer and LeBlanc (1988) and Aho et al. (1986), describe implementation methods for data types, as do the other programming language texts, such as Pratt (1984) and Ghezzi and Jazayeri (1987). A detailed discussion of the problems of heap management can be found in Tenenbaum et al. (1990). Garbage collection methods are developed by Schorr and Waite (1967) and Deutsch and Bobrow (1976). A comprehensive discussion of garbage collection algorithms can be found in Cohen (1981).

PROBLEM SET

1. What are the required entries in a Pascal array descriptor, and when must they be stored (at compile time or run time)?

2. What are the main advantages of user-defined enumeration types?

3. Differentiate clearly among static, semistatic, semidynamic, and dynamic arrays.

4. How is readability affected by dynamic binding of type?

5. What is an aggregate value?

6. What are the differences between the slices of FORTRAN 90 and those of Ada?

7. What is the worst aspect of elliptical references to fields of a record?

8. What is the main problem with designing discriminated union structures?

9. In what ways are the variant records of the Ada language safer than those of Pascal?

10. Why are there usually severe restrictions on the size of sets in Pascal implementations?

11. What problems can occur with Pascal pointers?

12. Why are the pointers of most languages restricted to pointing at a single type object?

13. Compare the tombstones and the locks-and-keys methods of avoiding dangling pointers, from the points of view of safety and implementation cost.

14. Design a set of simple test programs to determine the type compatibility rules of the Pascal compiler to which you have access. Write a report of your findings.

15. Determine whether some Pascal compiler to which you have access implements the `dispose` procedure.

16. Suppose that a language includes user-defined enumeration types and that the enumeration values could be overloaded; that is, the same literal value could appear in two different enumeration types, as in:

    ```
    type
      colors = (red, blue, green);
      mood = (happy, angry, blue);
    ```

    Use of the constant `blue` cannot be type checked. Propose a method of allowing such type checking without completely disallowing such overloading.

17. Multidimensional arrays can be stored in row major order, as in Pascal, or in column major order, as in FORTRAN. Develop the access functions for both of these arrangements for three-dimensional arrays.

18. In the Burroughs Extended ALGOL language, matrices are stored as a single-dimensional array of pointers to the rows of the matrix, which are treated as single-dimensional arrays of objects. What are the advantages and disadvantages of such a scheme?

19. Write a program that does matrix multiplication in some language that does subscript range checking and for which you can obtain an assembly language or machine language version from the compiler. Determine the number of instructions required for the subscript range checking and compare it with the total number of instructions for the matrix multiplication process.

20. Write a Pascal program that includes the following declarations:

```
var
   A, B : array [1..10] of integer;
   C : array [1..10] of integer;
   D : array [1..10] of integer;
```

Include code in the program that determines, for each array, which of the other three arrays are compatible with it.

21. If you have access to a compiler in which the user can specify whether subscript range checking is desired, write a program that does a large number of matrix accesses and times their execution. Run the program with subscript range checking and without it and compare the times.

6

Expressions and the
Assignment Statement

Friedrich (Fritz) L. Bauer

*Fritz Bauer, whose home is Munich, along
with Klaus Samelson in the early to
mid 1950s, designed an algebraic language
that could be directly implemented in
hardware. Bauer's more significant contributions to language design, however, came
as one of the principle members of the
ALGOL design team.*

Key Concepts

- Operator evaluation order
- Operand evaluation order
- Functional side effects in expressions
- Operator overloading
- Mixed-mode expressions
- Implicit and explicit type conversions
- Relational and Boolean expressions

- Short-circuit evaluation
- Multiple targets of assignments
- Conditional parts of assignments
- Assigning operators
- Unary operator assignments
- Assignment statements as operands
- Mixed-mode assignment

The essence of imperative programming languages is the dominant role of assignment statements. The purpose of assignment statements is to change the values of variables. So an integral part of all imperative languages is the concept of variables whose values change during program execution. (Nonimperative languages sometimes include variables of a different sort, such as the parameters of functions in functional languages.) Variables are discussed in Chapter 4.

To understand expression evaluation, it is necessary to be familiar with the orders of operator and operand evaluation. The operator evaluation order of expressions is governed by the associativity and precedence rules of the language. Although the value of an expression sometimes depends on it, the order of operand evaluation in expressions is often unstated by language designers, a situation that allows programs to produce different results in different implementations. Other issues in expression design are type mismatches, coercions, and short-circuit evaluation.

In the environment of von Neumann architecture, assignment is the most fundamental statement. An assignment statement can simply cause a value to be copied from one memory cell to another. But in many cases, assignment statements include expressions with operators, which cause values to be copied to the processor and to be operated upon, and the results to be copied back to memory.

Simple assignment statements specify an expression to be evaluated, the assignment operator, and a target location in which to place the result of the expression evaluation. As detailed in this chapter, there are a number of variations on this basic form.

6.1 Arithmetic Expressions

Automatic evaluation of arithmetic expressions similar to those found in mathematics was one of the primary goals of the first high-level programming languages. Most of the characteristics of arithmetic expressions in programming languages were inherited from conventions that had evolved in mathematics. Arithmetic expressions are constructions of operators, operands, parentheses, and function calls. The operators can be **unary,** meaning they have a single operand, or **binary,** meaning they have two operands. C includes a ternary operator, which we discuss in Section 6.1.3.

The purpose of an arithmetic expression is to specify an arithmetic computation. An implementation of such a computation must cause two actions: fetching the operands and executing the arithmetic operations on those operands. In the following sections we investigate the common design details of arithmetic expressions in the imperative languages.

6.1.1 Operator Evaluation Order

The evaluation order of an arithmetic expression depends on the order in which the operators and operands are evaluated. First, we investigate the order of evaluation of operators.

6.1.1.1 Precedence

The value of an expression depends, at least in part, on the order of evaluation of the operators in the expression. Consider the following expression:

    A + B * C

Suppose the variables A, B, and C have the values 3, 4, and 5, respectively. If evaluated left to right (the addition first and then the multiplication), the result is 35. If evaluated right to left, the result is 23.

Instead of simply evaluating the operators from left to right or right to left, mathematicians have developed the concept of placing operators in a hierarchy of evaluation priorities and basing the evaluation order of expressions partly on this hierarchy. For example, in mathematics, multiplication is considered to be of higher priority than addition, so if we follow that convention in our example expression, the multiplication would be evaluated first.

The **operator precedence** rules for expression evaluation define the order in which the operators of different precedence levels are evaluated. The operator precedence rules for expressions are based on the hierarchy of operator priorities, as seen by the language designer. The operator precedence rules of the common imperative languages are nearly all the same, because they are all based on those of mathematics. In these languages, exponentiation has the highest precedence, followed by multiplication and division on the same level, followed by addition and subtraction on the same level.

Many languages also include unary versions of addition and subtraction. Unary addition is called the **identity operator** because it has no associated operation and thus has no effect on its operand. Ellis and Stroustrup call it a historical accident and correctly label it useless (Ellis and Stroustrup,

1990, p. 56). Unary minus, on the other hand, does have an effect on its operand: It changes the sign of the operand's value.

In all the common imperative languages, the unary minus operator can appear in an expression either at the beginning or anywhere inside the expression, as long as it is parenthesized to prevent it from being adjacent to another operator. For example,

```
A + (- B) * C
```

is legal, but

```
A + - B * C
```

is not.

As we shall see in Section 6.1.1.2, the precedence of the unary operators is irrelevant in most languages.

APL is odd among languages because it has a single level of precedence, as illustrated in the next section.

The precedence of the arithmetic operators of a few of the most common programming languages are as follows:

	FORTRAN	*Pascal*	*ANSI C*	*Ada*
highest	**	*, /, **div**, **mod**	++, --, unary +, -	**, **abs**
	*, /	all +, -	*, /, %	*, /, **mod**
	all +, -		binary +, -	unary +, -
lowest				binary +, -

The / and **div** operators of Pascal are described in Section 6.2. The % operator of ANSI C is exactly like the **mod** operator of Pascal and Ada—it takes two integer operands and yields the remainder of the first after division by the second. The ++ and -- operators of ANSI C are described in Section 6.6.5. The precedence rules of C++ and those of ANSI C are the same. The **abs** operator of Ada is a unary operator that yields the absolute value of its operand.

Precedence accounts for only some of the rules for the order of operator evaluation—associativity rules also affect it.

6.1.1.2 Associativity

Consider the following expression:

```
A - B + C - D
```

If all the operators have the same level of precedence, the precedence rules say nothing about the order of evaluation of the operators in this expression.

When an expression contains two adjacent occurrences of operators with the same level of precedence, the question of which operator is evaluated first is answered by the **associativity** rules of the language. An operator can either have left or right associativity, meaning that the leftmost occurrence is evaluated first or the rightmost occurrence is evaluated first, respectively.

Associativity in common imperative languages is left to right, except that the exponentiation operator in some of the languages associates right to left. In the FORTRAN expression

```
A - B + C
```

the left operator is evaluated first. But exponentiation in FORTRAN is right associative, so in the expression

```
A ** B ** C
```

the right operator is evaluated first.

In Ada, exponentiation is nonassociative, which means that the expression

```
A ** B ** C
```

is illegal in Ada. Such an expression must be parenthesized to show the desired order, as in either

```
(A ** B) ** C
```

or

```
A ** (B ** C)
```

Let us now take another look at the question of why expression evaluation order is not affected by the fact that in FORTRAN unary and binary minus operations have the same precedence, but in Ada unary minus has precedence over binary minus. Consider the expression

```
- A - B
```

Because both FORTRAN and Ada use left associativity for both unary and binary minus, this expression is equivalent to

```
(-A) - B
```

in both languages. When unary operators appear at positions other than at the left end of expressions, they must be parenthesized in both languages, which gives those operators the highest precedence (see Section 6.1.1.3).

The associativity rules for a few of the most common imperative languages are given below:

```
FORTRAN:   left:   *, /, +, -
           right:  **
Pascal:    left:   all
ANSI C:    left:   *, /, %, binary +, binary -
           right:  ++, --, unary +, unary -
Ada:       left:   all except **
           nonassociative: **
```

As stated in Section 6.1.1.1, in APL, all operators have the same level of precedence. Thus, the order of evaluation of operators in APL expressions is determined entirely by the associativity rule, which is right to left for all operators. For example, in the expression

```
A × B + C
```

the addition operator is evaluated first, followed by the multiplication operator (× is the APL multiplication operator). If A was 3, B was 4, and C was 5, the value of this APL expression would be 27.

Many compilers make use of the fact that some arithmetic operators are mathematically associative, meaning that the associativity rules have no impact on the value of an expression containing only those operators. For example, addition is mathematically associative, so the value of the expression

```
A + B + C
```

does not depend on the order of operator evaluation. In some situations, if the compiler is allowed to reorder the evaluation of operators, it may be able to produce slightly faster code for expression evaluation. In C this is legal.

There are pathological situations in which integer addition on a computer is not associative. For example, suppose that a program must evaluate the expression

```
A + B + C + D
```

and that A and C are very large positive numbers, and B and D are negative numbers with very large absolute values. In this situation, adding B to A does not cause an overflow, but adding C to A does. Likewise, adding C to B does not cause overflow, but adding D to B does. Because of the limitations of computer arithmetic, addition is not associative in this case. Therefore, if the compiler reorders these addition operations, it affects the value of the expression. This is, of course, a problem that can be avoided by the programmer, assuming the approximate values of the variables are known: The programmer must simply parenthesize the expression to ensure that only the safe order of evaluation is possible. However, this situation can arise in far more subtle ways, in which the programmer is less likely to notice the order dependence.

6.1.1.3   Parentheses

Programmers can alter the precedence and associativity rules by placing parentheses in expressions. A parenthesized part of an expression has precedence over its adjacent unparenthesized parts. For example, although multiplication has precedence over addition, in the expression

```
(A + B) * C
```

the addition is evaluated first. Mathematically, this is perfectly natural. In this expression, the first operand of the multiplication operator is not available until the addition in the parenthesized subexpression is evaluated.

Languages that allow parentheses in arithmetic expressions could dispense with all precedence rules and simply associate all operators left to right or right to left. The programmer would specify the desired order of evaluation with parentheses. This would be simple, because neither the author nor the readers of programs would need to remember any precedence or associativity rules. The down side of this scheme is that it makes writing expressions more tedious, and it also seriously compromises the readability of the code. Yet this was the choice made by Ken Iverson, the designer of APL.

6.1.2 Operand Evaluation Order

A less commonly discussed design characteristic of expressions is the order of evaluation of operands. Variables in expressions are evaluated by fetching their values from memory. Constants are sometimes evaluated the same way. In other cases, a constant may be part of the machine language instruction and not require a memory fetch. If an operand is a parenthesized expression, then all operators it contains must be evaluated before its value can be used as an operand.

If neither of the operands of an operator has side effects, then operand evaluation order is irrelevant. Therefore, the only interesting case arises when the evaluation of an operand does have side effects.

6.1.2.1 Side Effects

A **side effect** of a function, called a **functional side effect,** occurs when the function either changes one of its parameters or a global variable. (A global variable is declared outside the function but is accessible in the function.)

Consider the expression

```
A + FUN(A)
```

If FUN does not have the side effect of changing A, then the order of evaluation of the two operands, A and FUN(A), has no effect on the value of the expression. Suppose it does, however, as in the following situation: FUN returns the value of its argument divided by 2 and changes its parameter to have the value 20. Suppose we have the following:

```
A := 10;
NEW := A + FUN(A)
```

Then, if the value of A is fetched first (in the expression evaluation process), its value is 10 and the value of the expression is 15. But if the second operand is evaluated first, then the value of the first operand is 20 and the value of the expression is 25.

The following Pascal code segment illustrates the same problem when a function changes a global variable that appears in an expression:

```
procedure sub1(...);
  var a : integer;
  function fun(x : integer): integer;
  ...
  a := 17;
  ...
  end;  { of fun }
  procedure sub2(...);
  ...
  a := a + fun(b);
  ...
  end;   { of sub2 }
...
end;   { of sub1 }
```

There are two distinct solutions to the problem of operand evaluation order. First, the language designer could disallow function evaluation from affecting the value of expressions by simply disallowing functional side effects. The second method of avoiding the problem is to state in the language definition that operands in expressions are to be evaluated in a particular order and demand that implementors guarantee that order.

Disallowing functional side effects is difficult, and it eliminates some flexibility for the programmer. It takes one of the tricks away from his or her bag. In fact, using access to global variables to avoid parameter passing is an important method of increasing execution speed. In compilers, for example, global access to data such as the symbol table is commonplace.

The problem with having a strict evaluation order is that some code optimization techniques used by compilers involve reordering operand evaluations. A guaranteed order disallows those optimization methods when function calls are involved. There is, therefore, no perfect solution, as is borne out by actual language designs.

The designers of FORTRAN 77 envisioned a third solution. The FORTRAN 77 definition states that expressions that have function calls are legal only if the functions do not change the values of other operands in the expression. Unfortunately, it is not easy for the compiler to determine the exact effect a function can have on variables outside the function, especially in the presence of COMMON and the aliasing provided by EQUIVALENCE. This is a case where the language definition specifies the conditions under which a construct is legal, but leaves it to the programmer to ensure that such constructs are legally specified in programs.

Pascal and Ada allow the operands of binary operators to be evaluated in any order chosen by the implementor. Furthermore, functions in these languages can have side effects, so the problems discussed above can occur. Functional side effects are further discussed in Chapter 8.

6.1.3   Conditional Expressions

Sometimes **if-then-else** statements are used to perform a conditional expression assignment. For example, consider

```
if (count = 0)
  then average := 0
  else average := sum / count
```

In C, this can be done more conveniently with an assignment statement with a conditional expression, which has the form

```
expression_1 ? expression_2 : expression_3
```

where expression_1 is interpreted as a Boolean expression (0 $\Rightarrow$ false, others $\Rightarrow$ true). If expression_1 evaluates to true, the value of the whole expression is the value of expression_2; otherwise it is the value of expression_3. For example, the effect of the **if-then-else** above can be achieved with the following assignment statement, using a conditional expression:

```
average = (count == 0) ? 0 : sum / count
```

In effect, the question mark denotes the beginning of the **then** clause, and the colon marks the beginning of the **else** clause. Both clauses are mandatory. Note that ? is used in conditional expressions as a ternary operator.

Conditional expressions can be used anywhere in a C program where any other expression can be used.

6.2   Overloaded Operators

Arithmetic operators are often used for more than one purpose. For example, + is frequently used for both integer and floating-point addition. In FORTRAN, it is used for INTEGER, REAL, COMPLEX, and DOUBLE PRECISION addition. Some languages, Turbo Pascal for example, also use it for string catenation. This multiple use of an operator is called **operator overloading** and is generally thought to be acceptable, as long as readability and/or reliability do not suffer. Some believe there is too much operator overloading in APL, where most operators are used for both unary and binary operations.

As an example of the possible dangers of overloading, consider the use of the ampersand, &, in C. As a binary operator, it specifies a bitwise logical AND operation. As a unary operator, however, its meaning is totally different. When used as a unary operator with a variable as its operand, the expression value is the address of that variable. In this case the ampersand is called the address-of operator. For example, the execution of

```
x = &y
```

causes the address of y to be placed in x. There are two problems with this multiple use of the ampersand. First, using the same symbol for two completely unrelated operations is detrimental to readability. Second, the simple keying error of leaving out the first operand for a bitwise AND operation can go undetected by the compiler, because it is interpreted as an address-of operator. Such an error may be difficult to diagnose.

Virtually all programming languages have some examples of a less serious, but similar, problem, which is often due to overloading of the minus operator. In the case of the minus operator, the problem is only that the compiler cannot tell if the operator was meant to be binary or unary. So, once again, failure to include the first operand when the operator is meant to be binary cannot be detected as an error by the compiler. However, the meanings of the two operations, unary and binary, are at least closely related, so readability is not seriously affected.

Distinct operator symbols not only increase readability; they are sometimes convenient to use for common operations. The division operator is an example. Consider the problem of finding the floating-point average of a list of integers. Normally the sum of those integers is computed as an integer. Suppose this has been done in the variable SUM, and the number of values is in COUNT. Now, if the floating-point average is to be computed and placed in the floating-point variable AVG, this computation could be specified in FORTRAN as

```
AVG = SUM / COUNT
```

But this assignment produces an incorrect result in most cases. Because both operands of the division operator are integer type, an integer division operation takes place, in which the result is truncated to an integer. Then, in spite of the fact that the destination (AVG) is floating-point type, its value from this assignment cannot have a fractional part. The integer result of division is converted to floating-point for the assignment *after* the truncation from division.

When a distinct operator symbol for floating-point division is available, the situation is simplified. For example, in Pascal, where / means floating-point division, the following assignment can be used

```
AVG := SUM / COUNT
```

where AVG is floating-point type and SUM and COUNT are integer type. Both operands will be implicitly converted to floating point, and a floating-point division operation is used. This kind of implicit conversion operation is further discussed in the following section. Integer division in Pascal is specified by the **div** operator, which takes integer operands and produces an integer result. When no distinct operator for floating-point division is provided, explicit conversions must be used. Such conversions are discussed in Section 6.3.

Ada allows the programmer to further overload operator symbols. For example, suppose a user wants to define the * operator between a scalar integer and an integer array to mean that each element of the array is to be multiplied by the scalar. This could be done by writing a function subprogram named * that performs this new operation. The Ada compiler will choose the correct meaning when an overloaded operator is specified, based on the types of the operands, as with language-defined overloaded operators. In our example situation, the Ada compiler will use the new definition for * whenever the * operator appears with a simple integer as the left operand and an integer array as the right operand.

When sensibly used, user-defined operator overloading can be a significant aid to readability. For example, if + and * are overloaded for a matrix data type, and A, B, C, and D are variables of that type, then

```
A * B + C * D
```

can be used instead of

```
MatrixAdd(MatrixMult(A, B), MatrixMult(C, D))
```

Implementing user-defined overloaded operators is discussed in Chapter 8.

C++ also allows user-defined operator overloading, as does FORTRAN 90.

6.3   Coercion in Expressions

One of the design decisions concerning arithmetic expressions is whether an operator can have operands of different types. Languages that do allow such expressions, called **mixed-mode** expressions, must define conventions for implicit operand type conversions, called coercions, because computers usually do not have operations that use operands of different types. (One exception is the VAX computers, in which longer integer values can be used as shorter integer operands.) Formally, as stated in Chapter 4, a **coercion** is an implicit type conversion that is initiated by the compiler. We refer to type conversions explicitly requested by the programmer as explicit conversions, or casts, not coercions.

Type conversions, whether implicit or explicit, are either narrowing or widening. A narrowing conversion is one that converts an object to a type that cannot include all of the values of the original type; for example, converting a double to a float. A widening conversion is one in which an object is converted to a type that can include at least approximations of all of the values of the original type; for example, converting a float to a double. Widening conversions are nearly always safe, whereas narrowing conversions are not.

As an example of a potential problem with a widening conversion, consider the following. In many language implementations, although integer to real conversions are widening conversions, some accuracy may be lost. For example, in VAX computers, integers are often stored in 32 bits, which allows at least nine decimal digits of accuracy. But floating-point values are also stored in 32 bits, with only about seven decimal digits of accuracy. So, integer to floating-point widening can result in the loss of two digits of accuracy.

Although some operator symbols may be overloaded, we assume that a computer system, either in hardware or in some level of software simulation, has an operation for each operand type and operator defined in the language. For overloaded operators in a language that uses static type binding, the compiler chooses the correct type of operation on the basis of the types of the operands. When the two operands of an operator are not of the same type and that is legal in the language, the compiler must choose one of them to be coerced and supply the code for that coercion. In the following discussion, we examine the coercion design choices of several common languages.

FORTRAN 77 has four numeric data types: INTEGER, REAL, DOUBLE PRECISION, and COMPLEX. For any of the four binary operators, *, /, +, and – in an arithmetic expression, the two operands can be any numeric types as long as DOUBLE PRECISION and COMPLEX are not both involved. The rules for the required coercions are given in the following table:

Operands	Coercions
INTEGER, REAL	Convert INTEGER to REAL
INTEGER, DOUBLE PRECISION	Convert INTEGER to DOUBLE PRECISION
INTEGER, COMPLEX	Convert INTEGER to COMPLEX
REAL, DOUBLE PRECISION	Convert REAL to DOUBLE PRECISION
REAL, COMPLEX	Convert REAL to COMPLEX
COMPLEX, DOUBLE PRECISION	Illegal

Notice that all coercions in FORTRAN 77 expressions are widening conversions.

FORTRAN 90 is similar to this, except that all combinations of numeric types over the arithmetic operators, including **, are legal.

The original C language includes the numeric types **int** (integer), **short int** (short integer), **long int** (long integer), **float** (floating-point), and **double** (double precision). The language definition dictates frequent coercions of operands. Although **float** and **short int** are legitimate data types, they are *always* coerced to **double** and **int**, respectively, when they appear in an expression or actual parameter list. For example, if x and y are **float** type variables in the expression x + y, regardless of where the expression occurs, both x and y are converted to **double**, and a double precision addition takes place.

ANSI C and C++ are much like the original C in their numeric types, except that float expressions are not automatically coerced to double.

Most of the other imperative languages followed the lead of FORTRAN by allowing mixed-mode expressions. However, in recent years, some people, the author included, have come to believe that the frequent coercions required by such mixing are not good because they allow the programmer to make errors that are not detectable by the compiler, thus lowering reliability.

To illustrate the problem, consider the following: Suppose a FORTRAN 77 program contains a function named FUN that has a single INTEGER parameter. Further suppose that FUN is incorrectly used as follows:

```
INTEGER A, B, C
REAL D
...
C = FUN(A + D)
...
```

The actual parameter expression in the call to FUN contains references to the variables A and D. The programmer's mistake is that the D was supposed to be B. A is declared to be INTEGER type and D is declared to be REAL. As a result of the mistake and the consequent mixing of types, A is coerced to REAL type. The expression value is then REAL type. So FUN is sent a REAL value instead of the INTEGER type it expects. Because parameter types are not checked in user-written FORTRAN 77 subprograms, FUN detects no error and carries out its operations on the parameter as if it were an INTEGER type. This cannot produce a sensible result.

This particular problem is the result of two design decisions: the lack of type checking of actual and formal parameters and the coercion of INTEGER to REAL in any expression that includes both types.

Because error detection is reduced when mixed-mode expressions are allowed, two languages, Ada and Modula-2, allow very few mixed type operands in expressions. Neither allows mixing of integer and floating-point operands in an expression, with one exception: In the Ada language, the exponentiation operator, **, can take either a floating-point or integer type for the first operand and an integer type for the second operand. Both languages allow a few other kinds of operand type mixing, usually related to subrange types.

As an example of the dangers and costs of too much coercion, consider PL/I's efforts to achieve flexibility in expressions. In PL/I, a character string variable can be combined with an integer in an expression. At run time, the string is scanned for a numeric value. If the value happens to contain a decimal point, it is assumed to be of floating-point type, the other operand is coerced to floating-point, and the resulting operation is floating-point.

This coercion policy is very expensive because both the type check and the conversion must be done at run time. It also eliminates the possibility of detecting programmer errors in expressions, because a binary operator can combine an operand of any type with an operand of virtually any other type.

Most languages provide some capability for doing explicit conversions, both widening and narrowing. In some cases, warning messages are produced when an explicit narrowing conversion results in a significant change to the value of the object being converted.

Both Modula-2 and Ada provide explicit conversion operations that have the syntax of function calls. For example, in Ada, we can have

```
AVG := FLOAT(SUM) / FLOAT(COUNT)
```

where AVG is floating-point type, and SUM and COUNT can be any numeric type. This assignment obviously produces the correct result when SUM and COUNT are integers, as in the examples in the previous section.

In C, explicit type conversions are called **casts.** The syntax of a cast is not that of a function call; rather, the desired type is placed in parentheses just before the expression to be converted, as shown in

```
(int) angle
```

One of the reasons for the parentheses in C conversions is that C has several two-word type names, such as **long int**.

In C++, both the syntax of Ada and that of C are acceptable.

6.4 Relational and Boolean Expressions

In addition to arithmetic expressions, programming languages include relational and Boolean, or logical, expressions.

6.4.1 Relational Expressions

A **relational operator** is an operator that compares the values of its two operands. A **relational expression** has two operands and one relational operator. The value of a relational expression is Boolean, except when Boolean is not a type in the language. The relational operators are usually overloaded for a variety of types. The operation that determines the truth or falsehood of a relational expression depends on the operand types. It can be simple, as for integer operands, or complex, as for character string operands. Typically, the types of the operands that can be used for relational operators are numeric types, strings, and other ordinal types.

The syntax of the relational operators available in some common languages is as follows:

Operation	Pascal	Ada	C	FORTRAN 77
equal	=	=	==	.EQ.
not equal	<>	/=	!=	.NE.
greater than	>	>	>	.GT.
less than	<	<	<	.LT.
greater than or equal	>=	>=	>=	.GE.
less than or equal	<=	<=	<=	.LE.

The FORTRAN I designers used English abbreviations because the symbols > and < were not on the card punches at the time of FORTRAN I's design. FORTRAN 90 allows both FORTRAN 77 relational operators and operators that are exactly like those of Pascal except that == is used for equality.

The relational operators always have lower precedence than the arithmetic operators, so that in expressions such as

```
a + 1 > 2 * b
```

the arithmetic expressions are evaluated first.

6.4.2 Boolean Expressions

Boolean expressions consist of Boolean variables, Boolean constants, relational expressions, and Boolean operators. The operators usually include those for the AND, OR, and NOT operations, and sometimes for exclusive OR and equivalence.

In most languages, the Boolean operators, like the arithmetic operators, are evaluated in a hierarchical precedence order. In most of the common imperative languages, the unary NOT has the highest precedence, followed by AND at a separate level, and OR at the lowest level. In Ada, NOT has higher precedence than AND and OR, but these two have equal precedence.

Because arithmetic expressions can be the operands of relational expressions, and relational expressions can be the operands of Boolean expressions, the three categories of operators must be placed in precedence levels relative to each other.

The precedence of all FORTRAN 77 operators is as follows:

> *Highest:* **
>   *, /
>   !, −
>   // (string catenation)
>   .EQ., .NE., .GT., .LT., .LE., .GE.
>   .NOT.
>   .AND.
>   .OR.
> *Lowest:* .EQV., .NEQV. (equivalent and not equivalent)

In the FORTRAN expression

```
A + B .GT. 2 * C .AND. K .NE. 0
```

multiplication is evaluated first, followed by addition, greater than, not equal, and finally AND.

The precedence of all Ada operators is

> *Highest:* **, **abs, not**
>   *, /, **mod, rem**
>   +, − (unary)
>   +, −, & (binary)
>   =, /=, <, >, <=, >=, **in, not in**
> *Lowest:* **and, or, xor, and then, or else**

Notice that Ada's Boolean operators, with the exception of **not**, share the same precedence level. All of these equal-precedence Boolean operators are nonassociative. If two or more different Boolean operators appear in an expression, parentheses must be used to show the order of evaluation. For example,

```
A > B and A < C or K = 0
```

is illegal in Ada. This expression can be legally written as either

```
(A > B and A < C) or K = 0
```

or

```
A > B and (A < C or K = 0)
```

The Ada Boolean operators **and then** and **or else** are discussed in the next section.

Boolean operators usually take only Boolean operands and produce Boolean values.

C is odd among the popular imperative languages in that it has no Boolean type and thus no Boolean values. Instead, numeric values are used to represent Boolean values. In place of Boolean operands, numeric variables and constants are used, with zero considered false and all nonzero values considered true. The result of evaluating such an expression is an integer, with the value 0 if false and 1 if true.

One odd result of C's design is that the expression

```
a > b > c
```

is legal. The leftmost relational operator is evaluated first because the relational operators of C are left associative, producing either 0 or 1. Then this result is compared with the variable c. There is never a comparison between b and c.

Readability dictates that a language should include a Boolean type, as we stated in Chapter 4, rather than simply use numeric types in Boolean expressions, as in C. Some error detection is lost in C's use of numeric types, because any numeric expression, whether intended or not, is a legal operand to a Boolean operator. In the other imperative languages, any non-Boolean expression used as an operand of a Boolean operator is detected as an error.

6.5 Short-Circuit Evaluation

A **short-circuit evaluation** of an expression is one in which the result is determined without evaluating all of the operands and/or operators. For example, the value of the arithmetic expression

```
(13 * A) * (B / 13 - 1)
```

is independent of the value of (B / 13 - 1) if A = 0, because 0 * x = 0 for any x. So when A = 0, there is no need to evaluate (B / 13 - 1) or perform the second multiplication. The value of the Boolean expression

```
(A >= 0) and (B < 10)
```

is independent of the second relational expression if A < 0, because FALSE **and** x is FALSE for all values of x. So, when A < 0, there is no need to evaluate B, the constant 10, the second relational expression, or the **and** operation. In discussing short-circuit evaluation, Boolean expressions are more interesting than the arithmetic expressions, as illustrated next.

Many Pascal programmers have encountered a problem when attempting to write a table look-up loop using the **while** statement. The Pascal code for such a look-up, assuming that list[1..listlen] is the array and value is the searched-for key, is

```
index := 1;
while (index <= listlen) and (list[index] <> key) do
    index := index + 1
```

The problem with this is that most (standard) Pascal implementations do not use short-circuit evaluation, so both relational expressions in the Boolean expression of the **while** statement are usually evaluated, regardless of the value of the first. Thus, if key is not in list, the program will terminate

with a subscript out-of-range error. The same iteration that has `index >`
`listlen` will reference `list[listlen+1]`, which causes the indexing error
because `list` is declared to have `listlen` as an upper-bound subscript
value.

If a language provides short-circuit evaluation of Boolean expressions
and it is used, this is not a problem. In the preceding example, a short-
circuit evaluation scheme would evaluate the first operand of the AND
operator, but it would skip the second operand if the first operand is false.

Short-circuit evaluation of expressions exposes the problem of allowing
side effects in expressions. Suppose that short-circuit evaluation is used on
an expression and part of the expression that contains a side-effect is not
evaluated; then the side effect will only occur in some evaluations of the
whole expression. If program correctness depends on the side effect, then
short-circuit evaluation can result in a serious error. The FORTRAN 77 definition recognizes this problem and simply states that the implementor may
choose not to evaluate any more of an expression than is necessary to determine the result. The relevant caveat is that if the unevaluated part of the
expression is a function reference that has the side effect of assigning a value
to any variable that is declared outside the function definition, that variable
must be set to "undefined" by the short-circuit evaluation. There are, however, problems in actually implementing the rule. For example, FORTRAN
77 provides no way of indicating an "undefined" value.

Ada allows the programmer to specify short-circuit evaluation of the
Boolean operators AND and OR by using the two-word operators **and then**
and **or else**. For example, again assuming that LIST is declared to have a
subscript range of `1..LISTLEN`, the Ada code

```
INDEX := 1;
while (INDEX <= LISTLEN) and then (LIST[INDEX] /= key)
  loop
  INDEX := INDEX + 1;
  end loop;
```

will not cause an error if INDEX becomes too large.

The inclusion of both short-circuit and ordinary operators, as in the Ada
design, is clearly the best design because it provides the programmer the
flexibility of choosing short-circuit evaluation for any or all Boolean
expressions.

In C and Modula-2, every evaluation of AND and OR expressions is
short-circuit. The decision to *always* do short-circuit evaluation of Boolean
expressions is an obvious trade-off made by the language designers. They
gain some efficiency at the expense of putting the responsibility of correct
evaluation on the programmer.

Also, in the C language, assignment statements can be the operands of
Boolean operators, so the side effect of the assignment operation can be lost
by short-circuit evaluation. The use of assignment statements as operands
in expression is discussed in Section 6.6.6.

6.6 The Assignment Statement

As we have previously stated, the assignment statement is one of the central constructs in imperative languages. It provides the mechanism by which the user can dynamically change the bindings of values to variables. In the following section, the simplest form of assignment is discussed. Subsequent sections describe a variety of alternatives.

6.6.1 The Simple Assignment

The general syntax of the simple assignment statement is

```
<target_variable> <assignment_operator> <expression>
```

FORTRAN, BASIC, PL/I, and C use the equal sign for the assignment operator. This can lead to confusion if the equal sign is also used as a relational operator, as it is in PL/I and BASIC. For example, the PL/I assignment

```
A = B = C
```

sets A to the Boolean value of the relational expression B = C, although it looks as though these variables are being set equal to each other. In the cases of FORTRAN and C, a different symbol is used for the relational operator for equality, which avoids the problem of overloading the assignment operator.

ALGOL 60 pioneered the use of := as the assignment operator, and many later languages have followed that choice.

The C assignment operator is treated much like a binary operator, and as such it can appear embedded in expressions. This operator is discussed in Section 6.6.6.

The design choices of how assignments are used in a language have varied widely. In some cases, such as in FORTRAN, Pascal, and Ada, it can appear only as a stand-alone statement, and the destination is restricted to a single variable. There are, however, many alternatives.

6.6.2 Multiple Targets

One alternative to the simple assignment statement is allowing assignment of the expression value to more than one location. For example, in PL/I, the statement

```
SUM, TOTAL = 0
```

assigns the value zero to both SUM and TOTAL. Multiple target assignment statements are a convenience for programmers, but not a significant one.

The effects of multiple-target assignments can also be achieved using C's assignment operator, as discussed in Section 6.6.6.

6.6.3 Conditional Targets

C++ allows conditional targets on assignment statements. For example, consider

```
flag ? count1 : count2 = 0
```

This is equivalent to

if flag **then** count1 = 0 **else** count2 = 0

6.6.4 Compound Assignment Operators

Compound assignment operators is a shorthand method of specifying commonly needed forms of assignments. The form of assignment that can be abbreviated with this technique has the destination variable also appearing as the first operand in the expression on the right side, as in

```
a = a + b
```

Compound assignment operators were introduced by ALGOL 68 and later adopted in a slightly different form by C. The syntax of C's compound assignment operators is the catenation of the desired binary operator to the = operator. For example,

```
sum += value;
```

is equivalent to

```
sum = sum + value;
```

C has versions of the compound assignment operators for most of its binary operators.

6.6.5 Unary Assignment Operators

The C language includes two special unary arithmetic operators that are actually abbreviated assignments. They combine increment and decrement operations with assignment. The operators, ++ for increment and −− for decrement, can be used either in expressions or to form stand-alone single-operator assignment statements. They can appear as either prefix operators, meaning they precede the operands, or as postfix operators, meaning they follow their operands. In the assignment statement

```
sum = ++ count;
```

the value of count is incremented by 1 and then assigned to sum. This could also be stated as

```
count = count + 1;
sum = count;
```

If the same operator were used as a postfix operator, as in

```
sum = count ++;
```

the assignment of the value of count to sum occurs first; then count is incremented. The effect is the same as that of the two statements

```
sum = count;
count = count + 1;
```

An example of the use of the unary increment operator to form a complete assignment statement is

```
count ++;
```

which simply increments count. It does not look like an assignment, but it certainly is one. It is precisely equivalent to the statement

```
count = count + 1;
```

When two unary operators apply to the same operand, the association is right to left. For example, in

```
- count ++
```

count is first incremented, and then negated. So it is

```
- (count ++)
```

not

```
(- count) ++
```

C's increment and decrement operators are frequently used to form array subscript expressions. In fact, their origin is in the autoincrement and autodecrement addressing modes of the PDP-11 computer, on which C was first implemented. These addressing modes are often used to implement array accesses efficiently.

6.6.6 Assignment Statements as Operands

In C, the assignment statement produces a result, which is the value assigned to the target. It can therefore be used as an operand in expressions. This design treats the assignment operator much like any other binary operator. Although this may seem odd to those unfamiliar with C, it is a very convenient capability. For example, in C it is common to write statements such as

```
while ((ch = getchar()) != EOF)
  { ... }
```

In this statement, the next character from the standard input file, usually the terminal keyboard, is gotten with `getchar` and assigned to the variable `ch`. The result, or value assigned, is then compared with the constant `EOF`. If `ch` is not equal to `EOF`, the compound statement `{...}` is executed. Note that the assignment must be parenthesized—in C the precedence of the assignment operator is lower than that of the relational operators. Without the parentheses, the new character would be compared with `EOF` first. Then the result of that comparison, which would be either 0 or 1, would be assigned to `ch`.

The disadvantage of allowing assignment statements to be operands in expressions is that it can lead to expressions that are very difficult to read and understand. An expression with any kind of side effect has this disadvantage. Such an expression cannot be read as an expression, which is a denotation of value, but only as an instruction string with a particularly bizarre order of execution.

Note that this interpretation of the assignment operator allows the effect of multiple-target assignments, such as

```
sum = count = 0;
```

in which `count` is first assigned the zero, and then `count`'s value is assigned to `sum`.

There is a loss of error detection in the C design of the assignment operation that frequently leads to program errors. In particular, if one types

```
if (x = y) ...
```

instead of

```
if (x == y) ...
```

which is an easy mistake to make, it is not detectable as an error by the compiler. Rather than testing a relational expression, the value that is assigned to `x` is tested (the value of `y` that reaches this statement). This is actually a result of two design decisions: allowing assignment to act as an ordinary binary operator and using arithmetic expressions as Boolean operands. This is another example of the relatively low safety of C programs.

6.7   Mixed-Mode Assignment

We discussed mixed-mode expressions in Section 6.3. A similar situation frequently arises in assignment statements. The design question is, does the type of the expression have to be the same as the type of the variable being assigned, or can coercion be used in some cases of type mismatch?

FORTRAN uses the same coercion rules for mixed type assignment that it uses for mixed type expressions; that is, many of the possible type mixes are legal, with coercion freely applied.

Pascal includes some assignment coercion; for example, integer expressions can be assigned to floating-point variables. Also allowed is some additional mixing involving subrange types. Ada and Modula-2 do not allow the coercion of integer to floating-point in their assignment, as Pascal does, but they do allow some type mixing in assignment, including subranges.

SUMMARY

Assignment statements include target variables, assignment operators, and expressions. Expressions consist of constants, variables, parentheses, function calls, and operators.

The associativity and precedence rules for operators in the expressions of a language determine the order of operator evaluation in those expressions. Operand evaluation order is important if functional side effects are possible. Coercion in expressions is common, although it eliminates some type checking, which in turn lowers reliability. Explicit type conversions are common, but when they are narrowing conversions, they can result in erroneous values.

Assignment statements have appeared in a wide variety of forms, including conditional left sides, conditional right sides, and assigning operators.

PROBLEM SET

1. When might you want the compiler to ignore type differences in an expression?

2. State your own arguments for and against allowing mixed-mode arithmetic expressions.

3. Do you think the elimination of overloaded operators in Pascal would be beneficial? Why or why not?

4. Would it be a good idea to eliminate all operator precedence rules and require parentheses to show the desired precedence in expressions? Why or why not?

5. Should C's assigning operations (for example, +=) be included in other languages? Why or why not?

6. Should C's single-operand assignment forms (for example, ++count) be included in other languages? Why or why not?

7. Describe a situation in which the add operator in Pascal would not be commutative.

8. Describe a situation in which the add operator in Pascal would not be associative.

9. Write a Pascal program segment, using a **while** construct to search an array of integers for a particular integer, that would work even if short-circuit evaluation of Boolean expressions were not done.

10. Assume the following rules of associativity and precedence for expressions:

    Precedence: Highest   `*`, `/`, **not**

    $\qquad\qquad\qquad$ `+`, `−`, `&`, **mod**

    $\qquad\qquad\qquad$ `−` (unary)

    $\qquad\qquad\qquad$ `=`, `/=`, `<`, `<=`, `>=`, `>`

    $\qquad\qquad\qquad$ **and**

    $\qquad\qquad$ Lowest: **or, xor**

    Associativity: left to right

    Show the order of evaluation of the following expressions by parenthesizing all subexpressions and placing a superscript on the right parenthesis to indicate order. For example, for the expression

    `a + b * c + d`

    show

    $((a + (b * c)^1)^2 + d)^3$

    a. `a * b − 1 + c`
    b. `a * (b − 1) / c` **mod** `d`
    c. `(a − b) / c & (d * e / a − 3)`
    d. `−` `a` **or** `c = d` **and** `e`
    e. `a > b` **xor** `c` **or** `d <= 17`
    f. `− a + b`

11. Show the order of evaluation of the expressions of Problem 10, assuming that there are no precedence rules and all operators associate right to left.

12. Write a BNF description of the expressions of Problem 10, assuming the only operands are the names a, b, c, d, and e.

13. Using the grammar of Problem 12, draw parse trees for the expressions of Problem 10.

14. Let the function FUN be defined as

    ```
    function FUN (var K : integer) : integer;
      begin
      K := K + 4;
      FUN := 3 * K - 1
      end;
    ```

    Suppose FUN is used in a program as follows:

    ```
    ...
    I := 10;
    SUM1 := (I / 2) + FUN(I);
    J := 10;
    SUM2 := FUN(J) + (J / 2);
    ```

    What are the values of SUM1 and SUM2?

15. What is your primary argument against (or for) the operator precedence rules of APL?

16. For some language of your choice, make up a list of operator symbols that could be used to eliminate all operator overloading.

17. Devise a situation in which mixed-mode expressions can lead to problems, such as that of Section 6.3, except without involving subprogram parameters.

18. Implement a simple version of the problem illustrated by the FORTRAN example of Section 6.3. Try the same program on a FORTRAN library function, such as MIN0.

19. Determine whether the narrowing explicit type conversions in two languages you know provide error messages when a converted value loses its usefulness.

7

Statement-Level Control Structures

Peter Naur

Peter Naur, whose home is Copenhagen, became heavily involved in language design after the first ALGOL report was issued in 1958. He became editor of the ALGOL Bulletin, a European discussion medium for people involved in the ALGOL development process. In 1960, he modified the notation that Backus used in 1959 and used it to present the latest version of ALGOL at the Paris ALGOL meeting in 1960.

Key Concepts

- Control statements and control structures
- Single- and two-way selection
- Problems with nesting selectors
- Multiple selectors
- Iteration constructs

- User location of control mechanisms
- Structure iterators
- Problems with unconditional branching
- Guarded commands

The flow of control, or execution sequence, in a program can be examined at several levels. In Chapter 6, we discussed the flow of control within expressions, which is governed by operator associativity and precedence rules. At the highest level is the flow of control among units, which is discussed in Chapters 8 and 11. Between these two extremes is the important issue of the flow of control among statements, which is the subject of this chapter.

Included are discussions of two-way and multiple selection statements, iterative statements, and unconditional branching statements. We will discuss the design issues, examine example designs, and evaluate the alternatives in each of these categories.

7.1 Introduction

Computations in imperative language programs are accomplished by evaluating expressions and assigning resulting values to variables. There are, however, very few useful programs that consist entirely of assignment statements. At least two additional linguistic mechanisms are necessary to make the computations in programs flexible and powerful: some means of choosing among alternative control flow paths (of statement execution) and some means of causing the repeated execution of certain collections of statements. Statements that provide these capabilities are called **control statements.**

The control statements of the first successful imperative language, FORTRAN, were, in effect, designed by the architects of the IBM 704. All were directly related to machine language instructions, so their form had more to do with instruction design than language design. At the time, little was known about programming, and as a result, the control statements of FORTRAN in the late 1950s were thought to be entirely acceptable. Subsequent sections of this chapter discuss FORTRAN's control statements and the reasons why they are now thought to be inadequate for contemporary software development.

A great deal of research and discussion was devoted to control statements in the ten years from the mid-1960s to the mid-1970s. One of the primary conclusions of these efforts was that, although a single control statement is obviously sufficient (a conditional branch, or goto), a language that is designed to *not* include a goto needs only a small number of different control statements. In fact, it was proven that all algorithms that can be expressed by flowcharts can be coded in a programming language with only two control statements: one for choosing between two control flow paths and one for logically controlled iterations (Bohm and Jacopini, 1966). An important result of this is the fact that unconditional branch statements are superfluous—possibly convenient but nonessential. This fact, combined with the problems of using the unconditional branches, or gotos, led to a great deal of debate about the goto, which is discussed in Section 7.5.1.

Programmers care less about the results of theoretical research on control statements than they do about writability and readability. All languages that have become widely used contain more control statements than the two that are minimally required, because writability is enhanced by a larger number of control statements. For example, rather than requiring the use of a **while** for all loops, it is easier to write programs when a **for** can be used to build loops that are naturally controlled by a counter. The primary factor that restricts the number of control statements in a language is readability, because the presence of a large number of statement forms demands that program readers learn a larger language. Recall that few people learn all of a very large language; instead, they learn the subset they choose to use, which is often a different subset from that used by the programmer who wrote the program they are trying to read. On the other hand, too few control statements can require the use of lower-level statements, such as the goto, which is far more harmful to readability.

The question of what is the best collection of control statements to provide the required capabilities and the desired writability has been widely debated for the past quarter century. It is essentially a question of how much should a language be expanded to increase its writability, at the expense of its simplicity and size.

A **control structure** is a control statement and the collection of statements whose execution it controls. The programming language research of the 1960s determined that control structures should have single entries and single exits. Multiple entries to iterative structures, in particular, make programs more difficult to read and understand.

Flowgraphs are useful methods of describing the actions of control statements. Figure 7.1 shows the flowgraph descriptions of the two fundamental structures: two-way selection and one form of logically controlled iteration.

Figure 7.1
Flowgraph of a two-way selector and a logically controlled loop

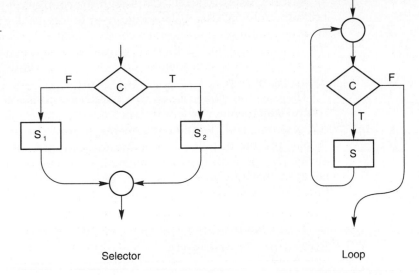

Selector   Loop

7.2 Compound Statements

One of the auxiliary language features that helps make control statement design easier is a method of forming statement collections. The primary reason for the inadequacies of the control statements of the early versions of FORTRAN was the lack of such a construct.

ALGOL 60 introduced the first statement collection structure, the **compound statement,** whose form is

```
begin
statement_1;
...
statement_n
end
```

Compound statements allow a collection of statements to be abstracted to a single statement. This is a powerful concept, which can be used to great advantage in control statement design.

Data declarations can be added to the beginning of a compound statement in ALGOL 60, making it a **block,** as in

```
begin
integer index, count;
...
end
```

The scope of the variables `index` and `count` is the block.

Pascal follows ALGOL 60's design for compound statements, but does not allow blocks. The C language uses braces to delimit both compound statements and blocks. Several recently designed languages have eliminated the need for specially delimited compound statements by integrating compound statements into their control structures. These are discussed in the following section.

There is one design issue that is relevant to all selection and iteration control statements: whether the control structure can have multiple entries. All selection and iteration statements control the execution of code segments, and the question is whether the execution of those code segments always begins with the first statement in the segment. It is now generally believed that multiple entries add little to the flexibility of control structures, relative to the decrease in readability caused by increased complexity.

7.3 Selection Statements

A **selection statement** provides the means of choosing between two or more execution paths in a program. Such statements are fundamental and essential parts of all programming languages, as was proven by Bohm and Jacopini.

Selection statements fall into two general categories, two-way and n-way, or multiple selection. Within the category of two-way selectors, there is a degenerate form called single-way selectors. We consider the FORTRAN three-way selector, the arithmetic IF, to be a primitive and degenerate multiple selector.

7.3.1 Two-Way Selection Statements

Although the two-way selection statements of contemporary imperative languages are quite similar, the variations in the evolution of them has been based on a collection of design considerations.

7.3.1.1 Design Issues

Perhaps the simplest design issue for two-way selectors is what type of expression controls the selector. In most cases, this is a Boolean expression. In C, however, because it does not have Boolean expressions, the selection is controlled by an arithmetic expression. A more interesting design issue is the question of whether single statements, compound statements, or statement sequences can be selected. A selector that can select only single statements is severely limited and usually leads to a heavy dependence on gotos. Allowing compound statements to be selected is a major step in the evolution of control statements. Allowing statement sequences to be selected requires that the selector include, for some cases, a syntactic entity to terminate such sequences. Another interesting and related issue is the question of how the meaning of selectors nested in **then** clauses is specified—by syntax or a static semantic rule.

These design issues are summarized as follows:

1. What is the form and type of the expression that controls the selection?

2. Can a single statement, a sequence of statements, or a compound statement be selected?

3. How should the meaning of selectors nested in **then** clauses of other selectors be specified?

7.3.1.2 Single-Way Selectors

All imperative languages include a single-way selector, in most cases as a subform of a two-way selector. Two exceptions are BASIC and FORTRAN, which include a selector form specifically for single-way selection. The flowgraph of a single-way selector is shown in Figure 7.2.

FORTRAN's single-way selector, called a logical IF statement, has the form:

IF (Boolean expression) statement

The semantics of this statement is that the selectable statement is executed only if the Boolean expression evaluates to true. The design choices for the FORTRAN logical IF statement are as follows: The selector control expression is Boolean type, and only a single statement is selectable. Nesting of logical IF statements is not allowed.

The logical IF statement is very simple and also highly inflexible. The fact that only a single statement can be selected promotes the use of goto statements, because usually more than one statement must be conditionally executed. The only reasonable way to conditionally execute a group of statements is to conditionally branch around the group. For example, suppose

Figure 7.2
Flowgraph of a single-way selector

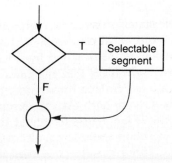

we wanted to conditionally initialize three variables to the values 1, 2, and 3. The typical way to do it in FORTRAN IV is

```
      IF(.NOT. condition) GO TO 20
      I = 1
      J = 2
      K = 3
  20  CONTINUE
```

The negative logic required by this form is especially harmful to readability. Also notice that this structure can have multiple entries, because any of the segment statements can be labeled and thus be the target of a GO TO anywhere in the program.

The compound statement provides the selection construct with a simple mechanism for conditionally executing groups of statements. This was one of the advances made by ALGOL 60 in selection constructs. It allowed either a single statement to be selected, as with FORTRAN's logical IF statement, or a compound statement to be selected, as in the following:

```
if (Boolean expression) then
  begin
  statement_1;
  ...
  statement_n
  end
```

Most of the languages that followed ALGOL 60, including FORTRAN 77 and 90, provide single-way selectors that can select a compound statement or a sequence of statements.

7.3.1.3 Two-Way Selectors

Two-way selectors allow one of two control paths to be selected. ALGOL 60 introduced the first two-way selector with the general form

```
if (Boolean_expression)
  then statement
  else statement
```

where either or both selectable statements can be compound. The statement following the **then** reserved word is called the **then clause,** and the statement following the **else** reserved word is called the **else clause.**

The semantics of a two-way selector is that the **then** clause is executed if the Boolean expression evaluates to true; otherwise, the **else** clause is executed. Under no circumstances are both clauses executed.

All of the important imperative languages designed since the mid-1960s have incorporated two-way selection statements, although the syntax has varied.

Although the two-way selectors of ALGOL 60 and C can have more than one entry, those of most other contemporary languages can have only one.

7.3.1.4   Nesting Selectors

An interesting problem arises when two-way selection constructs can be nested. Consider the following Pascal-like code:

```
if (sum = 0) then
  if (count = 0)
    then result := 0
else result := 1
```

This construct can be interpreted in two different ways, depending on whether the **else** clause is matched with the first **then** clause or the second. Notice that the indentation seems to indicate that the **else** clause belongs with the first **then** clause. However, indentation has no effect on semantics in most contemporary languages and is therefore ignored by their compilers.

The crux of the problem in this example is that the **else** clause follows two **else**-less **then** clauses, and there is no syntactic indicator to specify a matching of the **else** clause to one of the **then** clauses. Recall that in Pascal, as in most other imperative languages, the static semantics of the language specify that the **else** clause is always paired with the most recent unpaired **then** clause. A rule, rather than a syntactic entity, is used to provide the disambiguation. So, if the above example were Pascal, the **else** clause would be the alternative to the second **then** clause. The disadvantage of using a rule rather than some syntactic entity is that, although the programmer may have meant the **else** clause to be the alternative to the first **then** clause and the compiler finds the structure syntactically correct, its semantics is the opposite. To force the alternative semantics in Pascal, a different syntactic form is required, in which the inner **if-then** is put in a compound. This is an example of a lack of regularity in Pascal.

The designers of ALGOL 60 chose to use syntax, rather than a rule, to connect **else** clauses to **then** clauses. Specifically, an **if** statement is not allowed to be nested directly in a **then** clause. If an **if** must be nested in a **then** clause, it must be placed in a compound statement. For example, if the selection construct above were to pair the **else** clause with the second **then** clause, in ALGOL 60 it would be written as

```
if sum = 0 then
  begin
  if count = 0
    then result := 0
    else result := 1
  end
```

If the **else** clause were to be paired with the first **then** clause, it would be written as

```
if sum = 0 then
  begin
  if count = 0 then result := 0
  end
else result := 1
```

This is exactly what is necessary to get this meaning in Pascal. The difference between the two designs is that the Pascal version allows one to write the nested selector that looks like it pairs the **else** clause with the first **then** clause but does not, whereas this same form is syntactically illegal in ALGOL 60, thereby disallowing Pascal's subtle problem.

An alternative to ALGOL 60's design is to require special closing words for **then** and **else** clauses, as discussed in the following section.

7.3.1.5   Special Words and Selection Closure

Consider the syntactic structure of the Pascal **if** statement. The **then** clauses are introduced by the reserved word **then**, and the **else** clauses are introduced by the reserved word **else**. When the **then** clause is a single statement and the **else** clause is present, although there is no need to mark the end, the **else** reserved word in fact marks the end of the **then** clause. When the **then** clause is a compound, it is terminated by an **end**. However, if the last clause in an **if**, whether **then** or **else**, is not a compound, there is no syntactic entity to mark the end of the whole selection construct. The use of a special word for this purpose would resolve the question of the semantics of nested selectors and also add to the readability of the construct. This is the design of the selection construct in ALGOL 68, FORTRAN 77 and 90, Modula-2, and Ada. For example, consider the following Modula-2 constructs:

```
IF a > b
  THEN sum := sum + a
  ELSE sum := sum + b
END
```

or

```
IF a > b
  THEN
    sum := sum + a;
    acount := acount + 1
  ELSE
    sum := sum + b;
    bcount := bcount + 1
END
```

The design of these constructs is more regular than that of Pascal and ALGOL 60 selection constructs, because the form is the same regardless of the number of statements in the THEN and ELSE clauses. These clauses consist of statement sequences rather than compound statements. The first interpretation of the selector example at the beginning of Section 7.3.1.4 can be written in Modula-2 as follows:

```
IF sum = 0
  THEN IF count = 0
          THEN result := 0
          ELSE result := 1
       END
END
```

Because the END reserved word closes the nested IF, it is very clear that the ELSE clause is matched to the inner THEN clause.

The second interpretation of the selection construct can be written in Modula-2 as follows:

```
IF sum = 0
  THEN IF count = 0
          THEN result := 0
       END
ELSE result := 1
END
```

In FORTRAN 77, FORTRAN 90, and Ada, the closing special word for IF constructs is END IF. For other control constructs, different closing special words are used. Modula-2 closes all control constructs with the same reserved word, END. Although Modula-2 accomplishes the same result with fewer special words, Modula-2 programs are less readable than the same programs in Ada, especially when different control constructs are embedded in one another. When used to close an IF control construct, END carries only part of the information that END IF connotes.

7.3.2 Multiple Selection Constructs

The **multiple selection** construct allows the selection of one of any number of statements or statement groups. It is, therefore, a generalization of a selector. In fact, single-way and two-way selectors can be built with a multiple selector. The original forms of multiple selector are from FORTRAN, as you might have suspected.

The need to choose among more than two control paths in a program is common. Although a multiple selector can be built from two-way selectors and gotos, the resulting structures are cumbersome, difficult to write and read, and unreliable. Therefore, the need for a special structure is clear.

7.3.2.1 Design Issues

Some of the design issues for multiple selectors are similar to some of those for two-way selectors. For example, one issue is whether single statements, compound statements, or statement sequences may be selected. If the entire multiple selection structure is encapsulated, then all the selectable segments must be together; there can be no possibility of some being separated from the others, so encapsulation is certainly an issue. Another issue related to two-way selectors is the question of the type of expression upon which the selector is based. In this case, the range of possibilities is larger, in part because the number of possible selections is larger. A two-way selector only needs an expression with two possible values. Then there is the question of whether all control paths through the construct go through only a single selectable segment, or whether more than one can be included in a control path. This is not an issue for two-way selectors—every design allows only one of the clauses to be on a control path during one execution. As we shall see, the resolution of this issue for multiple selectors is a trade-off between reliability and flexibility. Finally, there is the issue of what should result from the selector expression evaluating to a value that does not select one of the segments. The choice here is between simply disallowing the situation from arising and having a rule that describes what happens when it does arise. Unrepresented selector expression values will be discussed in Section 7.3.2.3.

The following is a summary of these issues:

1. What is the form and type of the expression that controls the selection?

2. Can a single statement, a sequence of statements, or a compound statement be selected?

3. Should the entire construct be encapsulated in a syntactic structure?

4. Should execution flow through the structure be restricted to include just a single selectable segment?

5. How should unrepresented selector expression values be handled, if at all?

7.3.2.2 Early Multiple Selectors

As stated earlier, FORTRAN's **three-way selector,** which is called an arithmetic IF, is a special degenerate case of a multiple selection statement. Because only three or fewer statement collections can be selected, however, it is not, strictly speaking, a multiple selection statement.

The arithmetic IF is based on an instruction in the IBM 704, which chose among three branch target addresses based on the comparison of the value in a register with that in a memory cell. The branch is mathematically based on the trichotomy of numbers, which means that a given numeric value is either less than zero, equal to zero, or greater than zero. The arithmetic IF has the form

IF (arithmetic expression) N1, N2, N3

where N1, N2, and N3 are statement labels to which control is to transfer if the expression's value is negative, zero, or greater than zero, respectively. For example, if an arithmetic IF is used to select among three statement sequences, its general form is often the following:

```
    IF (expression) 10, 20, 30
10 ...
   ...
   GO TO 40
20 ...
   ...
   GO TO 40
30 ...
   ...
40 ...
```

Actually, this selector type could be much more harmful to readability than the example illustrates, because the statement sequences to be selected can literally be anywhere in the program unit that contains the GO TO. There is no syntactic encapsulation of the GO TO and its selectable sequences. Because the user is responsible for putting the GO TOs at the ends of the selectable segments, an execution of the construct can cause control flow to go through more than one selectable segment. The problem is that the mistake of leaving one of these branches out is not detected as an error by the compiler. Even when multiple segment execution is desired, the increase in complexity of the structure that results is highly detrimental to readability. This design is a trade-off of reliability for some added flexibility.

Finally, the arithmetic IF can be entered through any of its statements from anywhere in the program.

The first two actual multiple selection statements appeared in FORTRAN I and, like that language's other control statements, were based directly on IBM 704 instructions. Like the arithmetic IF, these statements are still part of FORTRAN. The FORTRAN computed GO TO has the form

GO TO (label 1, label 2, . . . , label n), expression

where the expression has an integer value and the labels are all defined as statement labels in the program. The semantics of the statement is that the expression's value is used to choose a label to which control will transfer. The first label is associated with the value 1, the second label with 2, and so forth. If the value is outside the range of 1 to n, the statement does nothing. There is no built-in error detection.

FORTRAN's other early multiple selector, the assigned GO TO, has the form

GO TO integer_variable, (label 1, label 2, . . . , label n)

In this form, the integer variable stores a label value, which it acquires only through an ASSIGN statement with the form

ASSIGN label TO integer_variable

In this case, the label must be defined in the program unit (main program or subprogram) of the ASSIGN statement.

Both of these multiple selectors suffer the same deficiencies of the arithmetic IF, the lack of encapsulation and possibly multiple entries. Furthermore, neither restricts a control flow to a single selectable segment.

7.3.2.3   Modern Multiple Selectors

A better form of multiple selector, named case, was suggested by Hoare and included in ALGOL-W (Wirth and Hoare, 1966). This structure is encapsulated and has single entry. Implicit branches to a single point at the end of the whole construct are also provided for each selectable statement or compound statement. This restricts the control flow through the structure to a single selectable segment.

The general form of Hoare's multiple selector is

```
case integer_expression of
   begin
   statement_1;
   ...
   statement_n
   end
```

where the statements could be either single statements or compound statements. The executed statement is the one chosen by the value of the expression. A value of 1 chooses the first and so forth.

Pascal's **case** is very much like that of ALGOL-W, except that the selectable segments are labeled. It has the form

```
case expression of
   constant_list_1: statement_1;
   ...
   constant_list_n: statement_n
   end
```

where the expression is of ordinal type (integer, Boolean, character, or enumeration type). As with most (but not all) of Pascal's control statements, the selectable statements can be either single statements or compound statements.

The semantics of the Pascal **case** is the following: The expression is evaluated, and the value is compared with the constants in the constant lists. If a match is found, control transfers to the statement attached to the matched constant. When statement execution is completed, control transfers to the first statement following the whole **case** construct.

The constant lists must be of the same type as the expression, of course. They must be mutually exclusive but need not be exhaustive; that is, a constant may not appear in more than one constant list, but not all values in the range of the expression type need be present in the lists.

Note that while the constant lists of the selectable segments have a form similar to that of labels, they are not the legal targets of branch statements.

Oddly, Pascal's first widely used definition (Jensen and Wirth, 1974) was not concerned with the possibility of unrepresented selector expression values (the expression taking on a value that did not appear in any of the constant lists). Such occurrences were said to cause undefined results. This vagueness, however, meant that the problem was simply ignored. The later ANSI/IEEE Pascal Standard (Ledgard, 1984) is more concrete; it specifies that such occurrences are errors, presumably to be detected and reported during execution by the code generated by Pascal compilers.

Many implementations of Pascal now include an optional clause to be executed when the expression value does not appear in any constant list in the **case**, as in the following:

```
case index of
  1, 3: begin
        odd := odd + 1;
        sumodd := sumodd + index
        end;
  2, 4: begin
        even := even + 1;
        sumeven := sumeven + index
        end;
  else writeln ('Error in case, index =', index)
end
```

If index is not in the range of 1 to 4 when this **case** statement is executed, the error message will be printed.

Note that the **else** clause need not be used exclusively for error conditions. Sometimes it also is convenient to use it for the normal condition and use the other cases for the unusual circumstances.

A flowgraph description of the preceding **case** statement is shown in Figure 7.3 on the following page.

The C multiple selector construct, **switch**, is a relatively primitive design. Its general form is

```
switch (expression)
  {
  case constant_expression_1: statement_1;
  ...
  case constant_expression_N: statement_N;
  [default: statement_N+1]
  }
```

where the control expression and the constant expressions are integer type. The selectable statements can be statement sequences, compound statements, or blocks.

Figure 7.3
Flowgraph of a Pascal
case statement

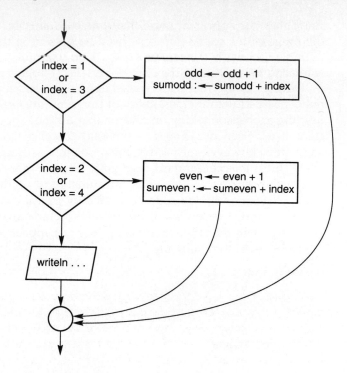

The **switch** encapsulates the selectable code segments, as does the Pascal **case**, but it does not disallow multiple entries and it does not provide implicit branches at the end of those code segments. This allows control to flow through more than one selectable code segment on a single execution. Consider the following example, which is similar to the Pascal **case** construct above:

```
switch (index)
  {
  case 1:
  case 3: odd += 1;
          sumodd += index;
  case 2:
  case 4: even += 1;
          sumeven += index;
  default: printf("Error in switch, index = %d\n", index);
  }
```

This code prints the error message on every execution. Likewise, the code for the 2 and 4 constants is executed every time the code for the 1 and 3 constants is executed. To logically separate these segments, an explicit branch must be used. C includes a **break** statement for exiting both **switch** and the bodies of C's loop structures. The **break** statement is actually a restricted goto.

The following C **switch** construct uses **break** and matches the semantics of the Pascal **case** example above:

```
switch (index)
  {
  case 1:
  case 3: odd += 1;
          sumodd += index;
          break;
  case 2:
  case 4: even += 1;
          sumeven += index;
          break;
  default: printf("Error in switch, index = %d/n",
                  index);

  }
```

Occasionally, it is convenient to allow control to flow from one selectable code segment to another. The reliability problem with this design arises when the mistaken absence of a **break** statement in a segment allows control to incorrectly flow to the next. The designers of C's **switch**, like those of FORTRAN's computed GO TO, chose to trade some decrease in reliability for some increase in flexibility.

The Ada **case** allows subranges, such as 10..15, and also OR operators specified by the symbol |, as in 10 | 15 | 20 in the constant lists. An **others** clause is available for unrepresented values. The additional Ada restriction that constant lists be exhaustive provides a bit more reliability, because it disallows the error of inadvertent omission of one or more constant values. Only integer and enumerated types are allowed for the **case** expression. Most Ada **case** statements include an **others** clause because that is the best way to ensure that the constant list is exhaustive.

The FORTRAN 90 CASE is similar to that of Ada.

In some situations, a **case** construct is inadequate for multiple selection. For example, when selections must be made on the basis of a Boolean expression rather than some ordinal type, nested two-way selectors can be used to simulate a multiple selector. To alleviate the poor readability of deeply nested two-way selectors, some languages, such as FORTRAN 90 and Ada, have been extended specifically for this use. The extension allows some of the special words to be left out. In particular, **else-if** sequences are replaced with a single special word, and the closing special word on the nested **if** is dropped. The nested selector is then called an **else-if** clause. Consider the following Ada selector construct:

```
if COUNT < 10 then BAG1 := TRUE;
elsif COUNT < 100 then BAG2 := TRUE;
elsif COUNT < 1000 then BAG3 := TRUE;
end if;
```

which is equivalent to the following:

```
if COUNT < 10
   then BAG1 := TRUE;
   else if COUNT < 100
           then BAG2 := TRUE;
           else if COUNT < 1000
                   then BAG3 := TRUE;
               end if;
       end if;
end if;
```

The **else-if** version is clearly the more readable of the two. Notice that this example is not easily simulated with a **case** statement, because each selectable statement is chosen on the basis of a Boolean expression. Therefore, the **else-if** construct is not a redundant form of **case**. In fact, none of the multiple selectors in contemporary languages are as general as the **if-then-else** simulation. A flowgraph description of a selector statement with **else-if** clauses is shown in Figure 7.4.

Figure 7.4
Flowgraph of a selector
with **else-if** clauses

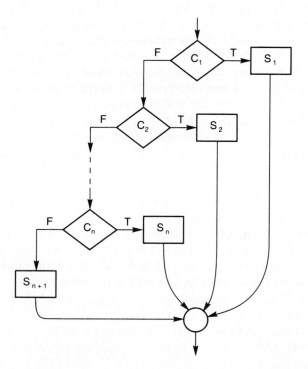

7.4 Iterative Statements

An **iterative statement** is one that causes a statement or collection of statements to be executed zero, one, or more times. Every programming language from Plankalkül on has included some method of repeating the execution of segments of code. Iteration is the very essence of the power of the computer. If iteration were not possible, programmers would be required to state every action in sequence; useful programs would be huge and take huge amounts of time to write.

The repeated execution of a statement is often accomplished in a functional language by recursion rather than by iterative constructs. Recursion in functional languages is discussed in Chapter 13.

The first iterative constructs in programming languages were directly related to arrays. This resulted from the fact that in the early years of the computer era, computing was overwhelmingly numerical in nature, making heavy use of loops to process data in arrays.

Several categories of iteration control statements have been developed. The primary categories are defined by how designers answered two fundamental design questions:

1. How is the iteration controlled?
2. Where should the control mechanism appear in the loop?

The primary possibilities for iteration control are logical, counting, or a combination of the two. The main choices for the location of the control mechanism are the top of the loop or the bottom of the loop. A third option, which allows the user to decide where to put the control, is discussed in Section 7.4.3. In this text, we use the term **pretest** to mean that the test for loop completion is at the top of the loop and the term **posttest** to mean it is at the bottom. The **body** of a loop is the collection of statements whose execution is controlled by the iteration statement. The iteration statement and the associated loop body together form an **iteration construct.**

In addition to the primary iteration statements, we discuss an alternative form that is in a class by itself: user-defined iteration control.

7.4.1 Counter-Controlled Loops

A counting iterative control statement has a variable, called the **loop variable,** in which the count value is maintained. It also includes some means of specifying the **initial** and **terminal** values of the loop variable and the difference between adjacent loop variable values, often called the **stepsize.** The initial, terminal, and stepsize specifications of a loop are called the **loop parameters.**

Although logically controlled loops are more general than counter-controlled loops, they are not necessarily more commonly used. Because counter-controlled loops are more complex, their design is more demanding.

Counter controlled loops are often supported by machine instructions. Unfortunately, machine architecture often outlives the prevailing approaches to programming at the time of the design. For example, VAX computers have an instruction that is very convenient for the implementation of posttest counter-controlled loops. But not even FORTRAN had such a loop by the time VAX computers became widely used.

7.4.1.1 Design Issues

There are many design issues for iterative counter-controlled statements. One of the fundamental design issues for any iterative statement is whether the control mechanism is at the top or bottom of the controlled code segment. The nature of the loop variable and the loop parameters provide a number of design issues. The type of the loop variable and that of the loop parameters obviously should be the same, but what types should be allowed? One apparent choice is integer, but what about enumeration, character, and floating-point types? Another question is whether the loop variable is a normal variable, in terms of scope, or should it have some special scope. Related to the scope issue is the question of the value of the loop variable after loop termination. Allowing the user to change the loop variable or the loop parameters within the loop can lead to very complex code, so another question is whether the additional flexibility that might be gained by allowing such changes is worth that additional complexity. A similar question arises about the number of times and the specific time when the loop parameters are evaluated. If they are evaluated just once, it results in simple but less flexible loops.

The following is a summary of these design issues:

1. What is the type and scope of the loop variable?
2. What value does the loop variable have at loop termination?
3. Should it be legal for the loop variable or loop parameters to be changed in the loop, and if so, does the change affect loop control?
4. Should the test for completion be at the top or the bottom of the loop?
5. Should the loop parameters be evaluated only once, or once for every iteration?

The length of this list is an indication of the relative complexity of counter-controlled loop constructs. All of these factors must be considered to produce a usable, efficient, and relatively safe statement.

7.4.1.2 The FORTRAN IV DO

FORTRAN I introduced the first iterative control statement, which remained the same in FORTRAN II and IV. We include a description of it here to illustrate the differences between it and the corresponding statement in FORTRAN 77. It is interesting to see how designs of constructs evolve, especially within a specific language. The FORTRAN IV counting posttest loop construct has the form

DO label variable = initial, terminal [, stepsize]

The label is that of the last statement in the loop body. The stepsize parameter is optional; when absent, it defaults to 1. The initial, terminal, and stepsize parameters are restricted to unsigned integer constants or simple integer variables with positive values. This disallows loops with descending loop variables. A flowgraph description of the FORTRAN IV DO statement is shown in Figure 7.5.

The FORTRAN IV DO design answers the above design questions as follows: The loop variable type is restricted to integer, and its scope is that of the program unit in which it appears. The value of the loop variable is undefined upon normal loop termination, because that sometimes makes it slightly easier to implement efficiently. The value of the loop variable upon abnormal termination (which can be caused by a goto statement) is its most recently assigned value. The loop variable and loop parameters cannot be

Figure 7.5
Flowgraph of the
FORTRAN IV DO

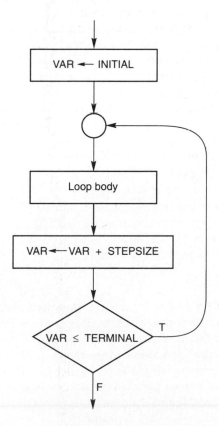

changed in the loop body, so there is no reason to evaluate the loop parameters more than once.

A DO construct can be exited and reentered from points outside the loop under certain circumstances. The acceptable circumstances are when a GO TO is used to exit the loop to a code segment called an **extended loop body.** At the end of the extended loop body, another GO TO transfers control back into the DO body. This is a dangerous capability. First, understanding such potentially complex control, which allows a direct violation of the concept of single-entry/single-exit control structures, can be difficult. Moreover, the capability poses a serious problem for compiler designers: How can illegal entries to loops be distinguished from legal entries from extended loop bodies? The answer is usually that no illegal entries are detected. When control transfers into a loop, the values used are those that the loop variable and loop parameters happen to have at that time.

Finally, as stated above, the DO is a posttest loop construct.

7.4.1.3   The DO Statement of FORTRAN 77 and FORTRAN 90

The basic form of the FORTRAN 77 DO statement is similar to that of FORTRAN IV but is generalized in several ways. The loop variable, for example, can be integer, real, or double-precision type. The loop parameters are allowed to be expressions and can have positive or negative values. They are evaluated at the beginning of the execution of the DO statement, and the value is used to compute an **iteration count,** which then has the number of times the loop is to be executed. The loop is controlled by the iteration count, not the loop parameters, so even if the parameters are changed in the loop, which is legal, those changes cannot affect loop control. The iteration count is an internal variable that is inaccessible to the user code. To eliminate a well-known problem with FORTRAN IV's DO syntax, a comma can be added following the label in the DO statement. The problem was that

```
DO 10 K = 1, 10
```

would be interpreted as an assignment statement if the comma happened to be mistyped as a period (because in FORTRAN, spaces are not used as token separators—with the spaces squeezed out, it is DO10K=1,10). In FORTRAN 77, the same can be written as

```
DO 10, K = 1, 10
```

This form is more different from an assignment statement than the FORTRAN IV version. The new comma, however, is not mandatory, so that backward compatibility is maintained with earlier versions of FORTRAN.

DO constructs can be entered only through the DO statement, thereby making the statement a single-entry structure. When a DO terminates—regardless of how it terminates—the loop variable has its most recently assigned value. Thus, the usefulness of the loop variable is independent of the method by which the loop terminates.

Perhaps the most significant change from one version of the language to another, however, was the move of the test for completion from the bottom to the top of the loop. FORTRAN I's DO loop was posttest because IBM 704 had a single machine language instruction to implement it that way. Placing the test at the top allows the loop body to be executed zero times (that is, skipped entirely). A flowgraph description of the FORTRAN 77 DO statement is shown in Figure 7.6.

FORTRAN 90 includes the FORTRAN 77 DO and adds a new form:

[name:] DO variable = initial, terminal [, stepsize]

    • • •

END DO [name]

Figure 7.6
Flowgraph of the
FORTRAN 77 DO

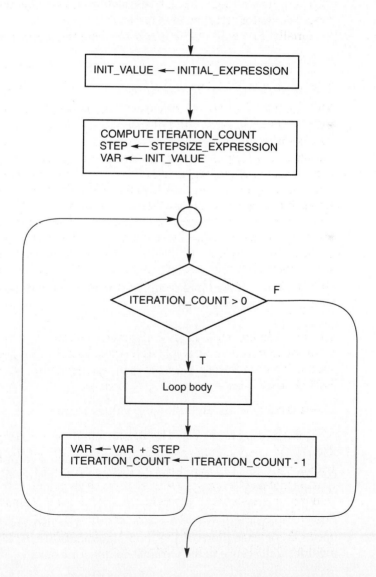

This DO again disallows any type but integer for the loop variable (like pre-77 FORTRANs). Another change is that it uses a specific closing special word (or phrase), END DO, instead of a labeled statement.

7.4.1.4   The ALGOL 60 **for** Statement

A description of the ALGOL 60 **for** statement is included here to show how the quest for flexibility can quickly lead to excessive complexity. ALGOL 60's **for** statement is a significant generalization of the FORTRAN DO, as shown in its EBNF description:

$$<\text{for\_stmt}> \rightarrow \textbf{for } \text{var} := <\text{list\_element}>$$
$$\{, <\text{list\_element}>\} \textbf{ do } <\text{statement}>$$
$$<\text{list\_element}> \rightarrow <\text{expression}>$$
$$| <\text{expression}> \textbf{ step } <\text{expression}>$$
$$\textbf{until } <\text{expression}>$$
$$| <\text{expression}> \textbf{ while } <\text{Boolean\_expr}>$$

The most significant difference between this and most other counter-controlled loops is that this construct can combine a counter and a Boolean expression for loop control. The three simplest forms are exemplified by the following:

```
for count := 1, 2, 3, 4, 5, 6, 7, 8, 9, 10 do
    list[count] := 0

for count := 1 step 1 until 10 do
    list[count] := 0

for count := 1, count + 1 while (count <= 10) do
    list[count] := 0
```

This statement is far more complex when its different simple forms are combined, as in the following:

```
for index := 1, 4, 13,
             41 step 2 until 47,
             3 * index while index < 1000,
             34, 2, -24   do
    sum := sum + index
```

The statement adds the following values to sum:

1, 4, 13, 41, 43, 45, 47, 141, 423, 34, 2, -24

Although there may be occasions when such a complicated statement is convenient, those occasions occur too rarely to justify the inclusion of such complexity in a language.

The ALGOL 60 **for** statement is even more difficult to understand than it first appears, since all expressions in the **for** lists are evaluated for every iteration, or execution, of the loop statements. Thus, if a **step** expression includes a reference to the variable count, for example, and if the loop statements change the value of count, the stepsize will change with each iteration. For example, consider the loop

```
i := 1;
for count := 1 step count until 3 * i do
   i := i + 1
```

This **for** statement causes the assignment (i := i + 1) to be executed with the values of count, which double with each iteration. Because count is increasing faster than the **until** clause expression (3 * i), the loop is not infinite, although that is not obvious at first glance.

The design choices of the ALGOL 60 **for** are the following: The loop variable can be either integer or real type, and it is declared like any other variable, so its scope is that of its declaration. As in FORTRAN 77, the loop variable has its most recently assigned value after loop termination, regardless of the cause of that termination. Loop parameters, but not the loop variable, can be changed in the loop body. It is illegal to branch into the loop body. It is a pretest loop, and, as stated above, the loop parameters are evaluated for every iteration.

It is not feasible to present a flowgraph of the complete ALGOL 60 **for** statement with all its options. In Figure 7.7 (p. 280), we present a flowgraph description of a general **for** statement with only the step-until form. Figure 7.8 (p. 281) is a flowgraph description of a more complex example of a **for** statement.

7.4.1.5 The Ada **for** Statement

The Ada **for** statement is a relatively simple counter-controlled pretest loop with the form

```
for variable in [reverse] discrete_range loop
   ...
end loop
```

A discrete range is a subrange of an integer or enumeration type, such as 1..10.

The most interesting feature of the Ada **for** statement is the scope of the loop variable, which is the range of the loop. The variable is implicitly declared at the **for** statement and implicitly undeclared after loop termination. For example, in

```
COUNT : FLOAT := 1.35;
for COUNT in 1..10 loop
   SUM := SUM + COUNT;
end loop
```

the FLOAT variable COUNT is unaffected by the **for** loop. Upon loop termination, the variable COUNT is still FLOAT type with the value of 1.35. Also, the FLOAT-type variable COUNT is hidden from the code in the body of the loop, being masked by the loop counter COUNT, which is implicitly declared to be the type of the discrete range, INTEGER.

Figure 7.7
Flowgraph of the
ALGOL 60 **step-
until-for**
statement

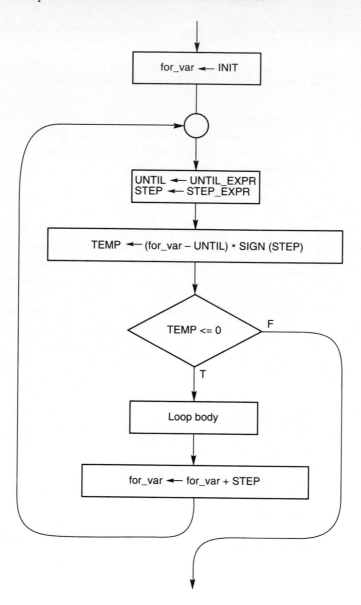

The Ada loop variable cannot be assigned a value in the loop body. Variables used to specify the discrete range can be changed in the loop, but because the range is evaluated only once, these changes do not affect loop control. The Ada **for** statement has a pretest control, and it is not legal to branch into the **for** loop body. Figure 7.9 (p. 282) is a flowgraph description of the Ada **for** loop.

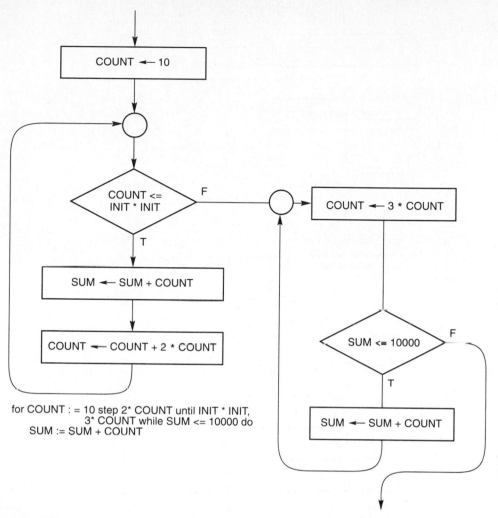

Figure 7.8
An example of an ALGOL 60 **for** statement

7.4.1.6 The C **for** Statement

The C language **for** statement forms a pretest counting loop structure. Its general form is

    for (expression_1; expression_2; expression_3)
      statement

The controlled statement can be a single statement, a compound statement, or a null statement.

Figure 7.9
Flowgraph of the Ada
for loop

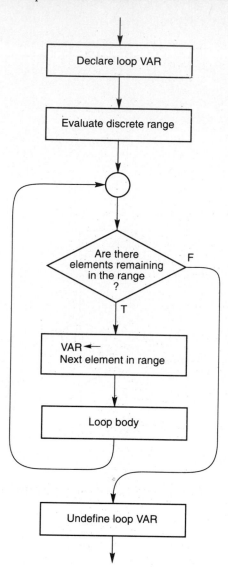

Because statements in C produce results and thus can be considered expressions, the expressions in a **for** statement are often statements. The first expression is for initialization and is evaluated only once, when **for** statement execution begins. The second expression is the loop control and is evaluated before each execution of the loop body. As usual in C, a zero value means false and all nonzero values mean true. Therefore, if the value of the second expression is zero, the **for** is terminated; otherwise, the loop statements are executed. The last expression in the **for** is executed after each execution of the loop body. It is often used to increment the loop

Figure 7.10
Flowgraph of the C
for statement

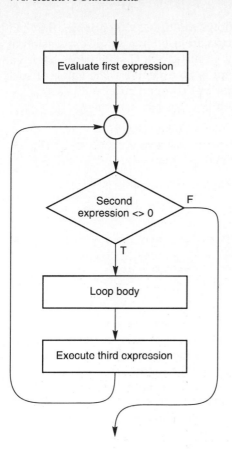

counter. A flowgraph describing the C **for** statement is shown in Figure 7.10.

A typical C counting loop is

```
for (index = 0; index <= 10; index++)
   sum = sum + list[index];
```

All of the expressions of C's **for** are optional. An absent second expression is considered true, so a **for** without one is potentially an infinite loop. If the first and/or third expressions are absent, no assumptions are made. For example, if the first expression is absent, it simply means that no initialization takes place.

The C **for** design choices are the following: There is no explicit loop variable or loop parameters. All involved variables can be changed in the loop body. The expressions are evaluated in the order stated above. Despite the fact that it can create havoc, it is legal to branch into a C **for** loop body.

C's **for** is more flexible than that of the other languages we have discussed, because each of the expressions can comprise multiple statements, which in turn allows multiple loop variables that can be of any type. When multiple statements are used in a single expression of a **for** statement, they are separated by commas. All C statements have values, and this form of multiple statement is no exception. The value of such a multiple statement is the value of the last component.

Consider the following **for** statement:

```
for (sum = 0.0, count = 0;
     count <= 10 && sum < 1000.0;
     sum = sum + count++);
```

The equivalent Pascal code for this is

```
sum := 0.0;
count := 0;
while (count <= 10) and (sum < 1000.0) do
  begin
  sum := sum + count;
  count := count + 1
  end
```

The C version of this **for** statement does not need and thus does not have a loop body. All the desired actions happen to be part of the **for** statement itself. The first expression is a multiple statement; its value is not used in this case. If the same two statements formed the second expression of the **for** statement, the value would be used for the loop control, and it would always be zero (false).

Note that C's **for** need not count. It can easily model counting *and* logical loop structures, as demonstrated in the next section.

7.4.2 Logically Controlled Loops

In many cases, collections of statements must be repeatedly executed, but the repetition control is based on a Boolean expression. In some of these cases a counter is needed, but in many others it is not. For the latter situation, a logically controlled loop is convenient. In fact, logically controlled loops are more general than counter-controlled loops. Every counting loop can be built with a logical loop, but the reverse is not true. Also, recall that only selection and logical loops are essential to express the control structure of any flowchart.

7.4.2.1 Design Issues

Because they are much simpler than counter-controlled loops, logically controlled loops have a relatively short list of design issues, one of which is also an issue for counter-controlled loops. There is little in this list that is either controversial or difficult.

1. Should the control be pretest or posttest?
2. Should the logically controlled loop be a special form of counting loop or a separate statement?

7.4.2.2 Examples

Some imperative languages—for example, Pascal, Modula-2, and C— include both pretest and posttest logically controlled loops that are not special forms of their counter-controlled iterative statements. In C, the pretest and posttest logical loops have the forms

    while (expression) statement

and

    do statement **while** (expression)

These two statement forms are exemplified by the following C code segments:

```
scanf ("%d", &indat);
while (indat >= 0)
  { sum = sum + indat;
    scanf ("%d", &indat);
  }

do
  { indat = indat / 10;
    digits = digits + 1;
  } while (indat > 0);
```

Note that all variables in these examples are integer type. The function scanf, called in the first code segment, inputs values from a keyboard.

In the pretest version (**while**), the statement is executed as long as the expression evaluates to true (nonzero). In the posttest version (**do**), the statement is executed until the expression evaluates to false (zero). In both cases, the statement can be compound. Flowgraph descriptions of both statements are shown in Figure 7.11 on the following page.

It is legal in C to branch into both **while** and **do** loop bodies.

FORTRAN 77 has neither a pretest nor a posttest logical loop. Ada and FORTRAN 90 have pretest logical loops, but no posttest version of the logical loop; Pascal and Modula-2 have both.

Pascal's posttest logical loop statement, **repeat-until**, is odd because its body can be either a compound statement or a statement sequence. It is the only control structure in Pascal with this flexibility. This is another example of the lack of orthogonality in the design of Pascal.

Posttest loops are infrequently useful and can also be somewhat dangerous in the sense that programmers sometimes forget that the loop body will *always* be executed at least once.

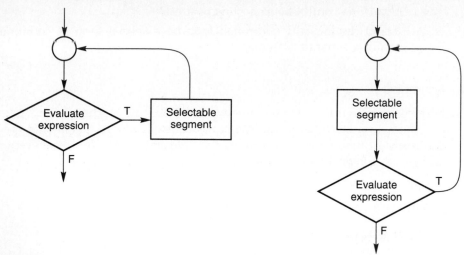

Figure 7.11
The pretest and posttest logical loops of C

7.4.3   User-Located Loop Control Mechanisms

In some situations it is convenient for a programmer to choose a location for loop control other than the top or bottom of the loop. As a result, some languages provide this capability. A syntactic mechanism for user-located loop control can be relatively simple, so its design is not difficult. Perhaps the most interesting question is whether a single loop or several nested loops can be exited. The design issues for such a mechanism are the following:

1. Should the conditional mechanism be an integral part of the exit?
2. Should the mechanism be allowed to appear in a controlled loop or only in one without any other control?
3. Should only one loop body be exited, or can enclosing loops also be exited?

Both FORTRAN 90 and Ada have loop statements that have no iteration control; they are infinite loops unless controls are added by the user. The form of the Ada infinite loop is

```
loop
    ...
end loop
```

The Ada **exit** can be either unconditional or conditional, and it can appear in any loop. Its general form is

```
exit [loop_label] [when condition]
```

With neither of the optional parts, **exit** causes the termination of only the loop in which it appears. For example, in

```
loop
  ...
  exit;
  ...
end loop;
```

the **exit**, when executed, transfers control to the first statement after the end of the loop.

An **exit** with a **when** condition exits its loop only if the specified condition is true, as in

```
loop
  ...
  SUM := SUM + INDEX;
  exit when sum >= 10000;
  ...
end loop;
```

Any loop can be labeled, and when a loop label is included on the **exit**, control is transferred to the statement immediately following the referenced loop. For example, consider the following code segment:

```
OUTER_LOOP:
   for ROW in 1 .. MAX_ROWS loop
INNER_LOOP:
      for COL in 1 .. MAX_COLS loop
         SUM := SUM + MAT(ROW, COL);
         exit OUTER_LOOP when SUM > 1000.0;
      end loop INNER_LOOP ;
   end loop OUTER_LOOP;
```

In this example, the **exit** is a conditional branch to the first statement after the outer loop. If the exit were instead

```
exit when SUM > 1000.0;
```

it would be a conditional branch to the first statement after the inner loop.

Note that **exit** statements are often used for handling unusual or error conditions.

FORTRAN 90 has an exit statement that is exactly like Ada's, except that it is unconditional. Both C and Modula-2 also have loop exit statements (C's **break** and Modula-2's EXIT). Both are unconditional and, as demonstrated in Section 7.3.2.3, **break** can also be used in the C multiple selection structure, **switch**.

C and FORTRAN 90 include a control mechanism that transfers control to the control mechanism of the smallest enclosing loop. This is not an exit but rather a way to skip the rest of the loop statements on the current iteration without terminating the loop structure. In C, it is named **continue**, and in FORTRAN 90, it is named CYCLE. For example, consider the following:

```
while(sum < 1000)
  {
  getnext (value);
  if (value < 0) continue;
  sum = sum + value;
  }
```

A negative value causes the assignment statement to be skipped, and control is transferred instead to the conditional at the top of the loop. On the other hand, in

```
while (sum < 1000)
  {
  getnext (value);
  if (value < 0) break;
  sum = sum + value;
  }
```

a negative value terminates the loop.

CYCLE, like FORTRAN 90's EXIT, can have a loop name operand, in which case the transfer is to the control mechanism of the named loop.

Both **exit** and **break** provide for multiple exits from loops, which is somewhat a hindrance to readability. However, unusual conditions that require loop termination are so common that such a construct is justified. Furthermore, readability is not seriously harmed, because the target of all such loop exits is the first statement after the loop, rather than a statement located just anywhere in the program.

7.4.4 Structure Iterators

Only one additional kind of looping structure remains to be considered here: structure iterators. Rather than have a counter or Boolean expression control the iterations, these loops use the number of elements in a user-defined data structure. Structure iterators are found only in certain experimental languages, such as CLU (Liskov et al., 1981).

A structure iterator construct is a loop construct similar to a **for**, except that the control mechanism is specified as a user-defined function. The function is called at the beginning of each iteration, and each time it is called, the function returns an element from a particular data structure in some specific order. For example, suppose a program has a linked list of data nodes, and the data in each node must be processed. A structure iterator loop for the list might successively set the loop variable to point to the nodes in the linked list, one for each iteration. The initial execution of the structure iterator construct needs to issue a special call to the function to get the first element. The user must provide the function to produce the next node address each time it is called. This routine must always remember which node it presented last so that it visits all nodes without visiting any node more than once. So this function must be history sensitive. A structure iterator loop terminates when the function that gets elements finds that the data structure has no more elements.

The C **for** construct, because of its great flexibility, can be used to simulate a structure iterator. For example, suppose the nodes of a binary tree are to be processed. If the tree root is pointed to by a variable named root, and if traverse is a function that sets its parameter to point to the next element of a tree in the desired order, the following could be used:

```
for (ptr = root; ptr; traverse(ptr))
  { ... }
```

Note that the second expression of this **for**, ptr, is a Boolean expression that compares ptr with zero. Its value is true if ptr is not zero. A pointer in C that is not currently pointing to any object has the value zero.

7.5 Unconditional Branching

An **unconditional branch statement** transfers execution control to a specified place in the program.

7.5.1 Problems with Unconditional Branching

The most heated debate in language design of the late 1960s was over the issue of whether unconditional branching should be part of any high-level language, and if so, whether its use should be restricted.

The unconditional branch, or goto, is the most powerful statement for controlling the flow of execution of a program's statements. However, although the goto has stunning power and great flexibility (all other control structures can be built with goto and a selector), it is this very power that makes its use dangerous. Without restrictions on use, imposed either by language design or programming standards, goto statements can make programs virtually unreadable and, as a result, highly unreliable and difficult to maintain.

These problems follow directly from a goto's capability of forcing any program statement to follow any other in execution sequence, regardless of whether that statement precedes or follows the first in textual order. Readability is best when the execution order of statements is nearly the same as the order in which they appear—this usually means top to bottom, which is the order to which we are accustomed. Thus, restricting gotos so they can transfer control only downward in a program partially alleviates the problem. It allows gotos to transfer control around code sections in response to errors or unusual conditions, but it disallows their use to build any sort of loop.

Although several thoughtful people had suggested them earlier, it was Edsgar Dijkstra who gave the computing world the first widely read expose on the evils of the goto. In his paper he noted, "The goto statement as it stands is just too primitive; it is too much an invitation to make a mess of one's program" (Dijkstra, 1968). During the first few years after publication of Dijkstra's views on the goto, a large number of people argued publicly for either outright banishment or at least restriction of the goto. Among those who did not favor complete elimination was Donald Knuth, who argued that there were occasions when the efficiency of the goto outweighed its harm to readability (Knuth, 1974).

A few languages have been designed without a goto—for example, Modula-2, Bliss (Wulf et al., 1971), and the experimental languages CLU, Euclid (Lampson et al., 1977), and Gypsy (Ambler et al., 1977). However, most currently popular languages include a goto statement. Kernighan and Ritchie (1978) call the goto infinitely abusable, but it is nevertheless included in Ritchie's language, C. Those languages that have eliminated the goto have provided additional control statements, usually in the form of loop and subprogram exits, to replace many of the typical applications of the goto.

7.5.2   Label Forms

Some languages, such as ALGOL 60 and C, use their identifier forms for labels. FORTRAN and Pascal use unsigned integer constants for labels. Ada uses its identifier form as the target part of its goto statement, but when the label appears on a statement, it must be delimited by the symbols << and >>. For example, consider the following:

```
        goto FINISHED;
          ...
    <<FINISHED>> SUM := SUM + NEXT;
```

The bracketing makes labels easier to find when one is reading a program. In most other languages, labels are attached to statements by colons, as in

```
    finished: sum := sum + next
```

In its design of labels, PL/I once again takes a construct to its limit of flexibility and complexity. Instead of treating labels as mere constants, PL/I allows them to be variables. In their variable form, they can be assigned values and used as subprogram parameters. This allows a goto to be targeted to virtually anywhere in a program. Although this flexibility is sometimes useful, it is far too detrimental to readability to be worthwhile. Imagine trying to read and understand a program that has branches whose targets depend on values assigned at run time. Consider a subprogram that has several labels and a goto whose target label is a formal parameter. To determine the target of the goto, one must know the calling program unit and the actual parameter value used in the call. The implementation of variable labels is also complex, primarily because of all the possible ways label variables can be bound to values.

7.5.3 ### Restrictions on Branches

Recognizing the problem inherent with gotos, most languages restrict their use. As an example of how the unconditional branch can be restricted, we examine the rules that Pascal applies to its **goto** statement. Pascal labels must be declared as if they were variables, but they cannot be passed as parameters, stored, or modified. The scope of a label is the same as that of the variables that are declared where the label is declared. As part of the **goto** statement, labels must be simple constants, not expressions or variables with labels as values.

Let a statement group be either a compound statement or the collection of statements in a **repeat** loop. Then the target of a Pascal **goto** must be one of the following:

1. The control statement that includes the **goto** or another statement in the statement group of which the **goto** is a part.

2. A statement in some statement group that contains the statement sequence that contains the **goto**.

3. Another statement in any enclosing subprogram scope, as long as the statement is not in a statement group.

What these rules mean is that a **goto** can never have as its target a statement in a compound statement of a control structure, unless execution of that compound statement has already begun and has not yet terminated. This means the target can never be in a compound statement or subprogram scope that is nested more deeply than the compound statement or scope of the **goto**. These rules prevent control structures from having more than one entry point. Consider the following Pascal skeletal code segment:

```
while ... do
  begin
  ...
  while ... do
    begin
    ...
100: ...
    ...
    end;
  while ... do
    begin
    ...
```

```
      goto 100;
      ...
      goto 200;
      while ... do
        begin
        ...
      200: ...
        ...
        end;
      ...
      end
   end
```

In the case of label 100, the compound statement that contains it completes its execution before the **goto** that references it can be executed. In the case of label 200, the **goto** that references it is executed before the compound statement that contains the label has begun its execution. Therefore, both label/**goto** pairs are illegal.

The **goto** in the following code segment is legal:

```
   while ... do
     begin
     ...
   100: ...
     ...
     while ... do
       begin
       ...
       goto 100;
       ...
       end
     end;
```

The major problem with Pascal's rules is that there still is no restriction on branching into a different procedure. The target procedure, because it must be enclosing, is already activated. So the **goto** can terminate one or more procedure activations, or executions, but cannot start one by branching into it. Of course, a branch to a procedure call indirectly causes the start of execution of a procedure.

Branching from one procedure to another is highly detrimental to program readability and is therefore an unreliable programming practice. Although Pascal's design attempts, through its restrictions, to prevent some problems with unconditional branching, it still allows what many consider unsafe use of the powerful **goto** control statement.

On the positive side—in defense of Pascal's **goto** target rules—the ability to branch from a procedure to its parent or other ancestor can be a convenient method of propagating error conditions to ancestor procedures for possible corrective action. This process is, of course, more properly done by an exception handling mechanism designed into the language. Exception handling is discussed in Chapter 12.

All the loop exit statements discussed in Section 7.4.3 are actually camouflaged goto statements. They are, however, severely restricted gotos and are not harmful to readability. In fact, it can be argued that they improve readability, because to avoid their use results in convoluted and unnatural code that would be much harder to understand.

7.6 Guarded Commands

Alternative and quite different forms of selection and loop structures were suggested by Dijkstra (1975). His motivation was to provide control statements that would support a program design methodology that ensured correctness during development, rather than relying on verification or testing of completed programs to ensure their correctness. This methodology is described in Dijkstra (1976).

Dijkstra's selection construct has the following form:

```
if  <Boolean expression> -> <statement>
[]  <Boolean expression> -> <statement>
[]  . . .
[]  <Boolean expression> -> <statement>
fi
```

The closing reserved word, **fi**, is the opening reserved word spelled backwards. This form of closing reserved word is taken from ALGOL 68. The small blocks, called fatbars, are used to separate the guarded clauses and allow the clauses to be statement sequences.

This selection construct has the appearance of a multiple selection, but its semantics is different. All the Boolean expressions are evaluated each time the construct is reached during execution. If more than one expression is true, one of the corresponding statements is nondeterministically chosen for execution. If none is true, a run-time error occurs that causes program termination. This forces the programmer to consider and list all possibilities, as with Ada's **case** statement. Consider the following example:

```
if  i = 0 -> sum := sum + i
[]  i > j -> sum := sum + j
[]  j > i -> sum := sum + i
fi
```

If i = 0 and j = 1, this construct chooses nondeterministically between the first and third assignment statements. If i is equal to j and is not zero, a run-time error occurs because none of the conditions is true.

This construct can be an elegant way of allowing the programmer to state that the order of execution, in some cases, is irrelevant. For example, to find the largest of two numbers, one can use

```
if x >= y -> max := x
[] y >= x -> max := y
fi
```

This computes the desired result without overspecifying the solution. In particular, if x and y are equal, it does not matter which is assigned to max. This is a form of abstraction provided by the nondeterministic semantics of the statement.

Another situation in which Dijkstra's selection construct is valuable is the following: Suppose we are writing a program that services interrupts, and the interrupts have the same priority. For this we need a construct that chooses among current interrupts in some random way.

Figure 7.12 is a flowgraph describing the approach used with Dijkstra's selector statement. Note that this flowgraph is different from those found

Figure 7.12
Flowgraph of the approach used with Dijkstra's selector statement

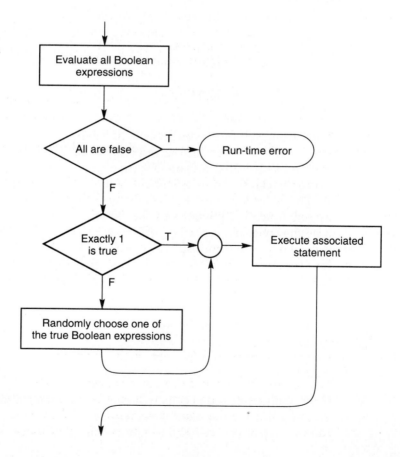

earlier in this chapter, for one cannot capture in a flowgraph the exact control flow operation of this construct.

The loop structure proposed by Dijkstra has the following form:

```
do  <Boolean expression> -> <statement>
[]  <Boolean expression> -> <statement>
[]  ...
[]  [Boolean expression> -> <statement>
od
```

The semantics of this construct is that all Boolean expressions are evaluated on each iteration. If more than one is true, one of the associated statements is nondeterministically chosen for execution, after which the expressions are again evaluated. When all expressions are simultaneously false, the loop terminates. Once again the programmer is forced to consider all possibilities.

Consider the following code, which appears in slightly different form in Dijkstra (1975). The four variables q1, q2, q3, and q4 are to be assigned the values of the four variables Q1, Q2, Q3, and Q4, so that q1 <= q2 <= q3 <= q4.

```
q1 := Q1;   q2 := Q2;   q3 := Q3;    q4 := Q4;
do q1 > q2 -> temp := q1;   q1 := q2;    q2 := temp;
[] q2 > q3 -> temp := q2;   q2 := q3;    q3 := temp;
[] q3 > q4 -> temp := q3;   q3 := q4;    q4 := temp;
od
```

A flowgraph describing the approach used with Dijkstra's loop statement is shown in Figure 7.13 (p. 296). Once again, note that the control-flow semantics of this construct cannot be depicted in a flowgraph.

A form of Dijkstra's **do** is used in the concurrency control in the Ada language, as discussed in Chapter 11.

Dijkstra's guarded commands, as these two constructs are known, are interesting in part because they illustrate how the syntax and semantics of statements can have an impact on program design methodologies, and vice versa. Program verification is virtually impossible when goto statements are used. Verification is greatly simplified if either only logical loops and selections, like those of Pascal, are used, or only guarded commands are used. The axiomatic semantics of guarded commands can be conveniently specified (Gries, 1981).

7.7 Conclusions

We have described and discussed a variety of statement-level control structures. A brief evaluation now seems to be in order.

First, we have the theoretical result that only sequence, selection, and pretest logical loops are absolutely required to express computations (Bohm and Jacopini, 1966). This result has been widely used by those who wish to ban unconditional branching altogether. Of course, there are already sufficient practical problems with the goto to condemn it without reliance on a theoretical finding. One application of goto that many feel is justified is its use to allow premature exits from loops in languages that do not have exit statements.

Figure 7.13
Flowgraph of the approach used with Dijkstra's loop statement

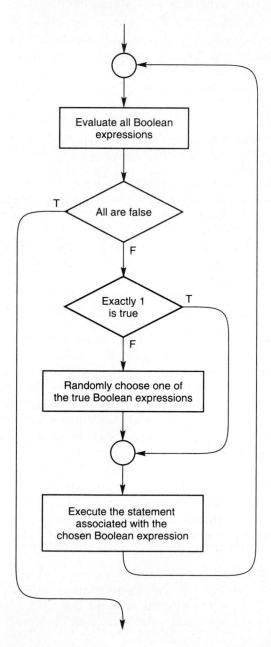

Perhaps the more interesting use of the Bohm and Jacopini result is to argue against the inclusion of *any* control structures beyond selection and pretest logical loop. No widely used language has yet taken that step; further, we doubt that any ever will because of the effect on writability and readability. Programs written with only selection and pretest logical loops are generally less natural in structure, more complex, and therefore harder to write and more difficult to read. For example, the Ada multiple selection structure is a great boost to Ada writability, with no clear negatives. Another example is the counting loop structure of many languages, especially when the statement is simple, as in Pascal and Ada.

It is not so clear that the utility of many of the other control structures that have been proposed is worth their inclusion in languages (Ledgard and Marcotty, 1975). This question is based to a large degree on the fundamental question of whether the size of languages must be minimized. Both Wirth (1975) and Hoare (1973) strongly endorse simplicity in language design. In the case of control structures, simplicity means that only a few control statements should be in a language, and they should all be simple.

The rich variety of statement-level control structures that have been invented shows the diversity of opinion among language designers. After all the invention, discussion, and evaluation, however, there is little unanimity on syntax design. No single set of control structures has been widely accepted. There is agreement that the set should be rather small and that there must be sufficient variety to make the goto rarely necessary. Beyond that, the debate continues.

One final note: The control structures of functional and logic programming languages, and those of Smalltalk, are all quite different from those described in this chapter. These mechanisms are discussed in some detail in Chapters 13, 14, and 15.

SUMMARY

The control statements of the imperative languages occur in several categories: two-way selection, multiple selection, iterative, and unconditional branching.

FORTRAN has a single-way single statement selector, the logical IF. ALGOL 60's selector is more advanced, allowing selection of compound statements and including an optional **else** clause. Many control structures benefited from the compound statement that ALGOL 60 introduced.

FORTRAN's arithmetic IF is a three-way selector that usually requires other unconditional branches.

FORTRAN introduced two forms of multiple selection statement: the computed GO TO and the assigned GO TO. True to their names, both are actually multiple-way branches. The Pascal **case** is representative of modern multiple selection statements; it includes both encapsulation of the selectable segments and implicit branches at the end of each to the single exit point.

A large number of different loop statements have been invented for high-level languages, starting with FORTRAN's counting DO. The **for** statement of ALGOL 60 was far too complex, combining logic and counter controls in a single statement. Pascal's **for** statement is, in terms of complexity, the opposite. It elegantly implements only the most commonly needed counting loop forms. C's **for** statement is the most flexible iteration construct.

The Modula-2, C, FORTRAN 90, and Ada languages have exit statements for their loops; these statements take the place of one of the most common uses of goto statements.

Structure iterators are user-defined loop constructs for processing user-defined data structures, such as linked lists and trees.

Dijkstra's guarded commands are alternative control constructs with positive theoretical characteristics. Although they have not been adopted as the control constructs of a language, part of the semantics appears in Ada's concurrency mechanism.

The unconditional branch, or goto, has been part of most imperative languages. Its problems have been widely discussed and debated. The current consensus is that it should remain in most languages but that its dangers should be minimized through programming discipline.

PROBLEM SET

1. Write a defense of the claim that the three-way selection statement of FORTRAN I was the best choice, given the circumstances of the time.

2. Devise a situation in which the label variable of PL/I would be a great advantage.

3. Describe three situations where a combined counting and logical looping construct is needed.

4. Compare the FORTRAN-computed GO TO with the Pascal **case** statement, especially in terms of readability and reliability.

5. What are the possible reasons why Pascal has a logical posttest loop while ALGOL 60 did not?

6. Study the iterator feature of CLU in Liskov et al.(1981), and determine its advantages and disadvantages.

7. Compare the set of Ada control statements with those of FORTRAN 77, and decide which are better and why.

8. What are the pros and cons of using unique closing reserved words on compound statements?

9. Analyze the potential readability problems with using closure reserved words for control statements that are the reverse of the corresponding initial reserved words, such as the **case-esac** reserved words of ALGOL 68. For example, consider common typing errors, such as the reversal of two adjacent characters.

10. Rewrite the following code segment using a loop structure in the following languages:
    a. Pascal
    b. FORTRAN 77
    c. Ada
    d. C

    ```
        k := (j + 13) / 27;
    loop:
        if k > 10 then goto out
        k := k + 1
        i := 3 * k - 1
        goto loop
    out: ...
    ```

    Assume all variables are integer type. Discuss which language, for this code, has the best writability, the best readability, and the best combination of the two.

11. Redo Problem 10, except this time make all the variables and constants floating-point type, and change the statement

    ```
    k := k + 1
    ```

    to

    ```
    k := k + 1.2
    ```

12. Rewrite the following code segment using a multiple selection statement in the following languages:
    a. Pascal
    b. FORTRAN 90 (you'll have to look this one up)
    c. Ada
    d. C

    ```
    if (k = 1) or (k = 2) then j :- 2 * k - 1
    if (k = 3) or (k = 5) then j := 3 * k + 1
    if (k = 4) then j := 4 * k - 1
    if (k = 6) or (k = 7) or (k = 8) then j := k - 2
    ```

    Assume all variables are integer type. Discuss the relative merits of the use of these languages for this particular code.

13. Consider the following ALGOL 60 **for** statement:

    for i := j + 1 **step** i * j **until** 3 * j **do** j := j + 1

    Assume that the initial value of j is 1. List the sequence of values for the variable i used, assuming the following semantics:
    a. All expressions are evaluated once at the loop entry.
    b. All expressions are evaluated before each iteration.
    c. **step** expressions are evaluated once at loop entry, and **until** expressions are evaluated before each iteration.
    d. **until** expressions are evaluated once at loop entry, and **step** expressions are evaluated before each iteration, just after the loop counter is incremented.

    In all cases, when more than one expression is evaluated at the same time, they are evaluated in left-to-right order. Also, the initial assignment to the loop variable is always done just once.

14. Use the *Science Citation Index* to find an article that refers to Knuth (1974). Read the article and Knuth's paper and write a paper that summarizes both sides of the goto argument.

15. Consider the following Pascal program segment. Rewrite it using only two-way selection.

```
case (expr)
  a, b: S1;
  c, d: S2;
  e: S3;
  else S4
end case
```

16. Consider the following program segment. Rewrite it using no **goto**s or **break**s.

```
j := -3;
for (i = 0; i < 10; i++) {
  switch (j + 2) {
    case 3:
    case 4: S1; break;
    case 0: S2; break;
    default: S3
    }
  if (E) goto out;
  j = j + 3 - i
  }
out: ...
```

8

Subprograms

Dennis Ritchie

Dennis Ritchie of Bell Laboratories was one of the principles involved with the development of UNIX. He was the designer of the first version of C, which was then used to rewrite UNIX for PDP-11 computers.

Key Concepts

- Process abstraction
- Local referencing environments
- Parameter-passing methods
- Aliasing with parameters
- Value versus access path transmission
- Nonlocal referencing environments

- Static versus dynamic scope
- Overloaded subprograms
- User-defined overloaded operators
- Generic subprograms
- Separate and independent compilation

Subprograms are the fundamental building blocks of programs and are therefore among the most important concepts in programming language design. We now explore the design of subprograms, including parameter-passing methods, local and nonlocal referencing environments, overloaded subprograms, generic subprograms, separate and independent compilation, and the aliasing and side effects problems that are associated with subprograms.

Coroutines and concurrent subprograms are not covered in this chapter; they are such important forms of subprograms that they have their own chapter, Chapter 11. Implementation methods for subprograms are discussed in Chapter 9.

8.1 Introduction

Two fundamental abstraction facilities can be included in a programming language: process abstraction and data abstraction. In the early history of high-level programming languages, process abstraction was held to be the more important of the two. It was the first of the two to be recognized and exploited, and it has been a central concept in all programming languages. In the 1980s, however, many people began to believe that data abstraction was equally important. Data abstraction is discussed in detail in Chapter 10.

The first programmable computer, Babbage's Analytical Engine, built in the 1840s, had the capability of reusing collections of instruction cards at any number of spots in a program where they were needed. In a modern programming language, a collection of statements is reused and ends up as a collection of machine instructions in memory. This reuse results in a variety of different kinds of savings, from memory space to coding time. Such reuse is also an abstraction if the collection is replaced in a program by a statement that "calls" that collection. Instead of explaining how some computation is to be done, that explanation (the collection of statements) is enacted by a "call" statement, effectively abstracting away the details. This increases the readability of a program by exposing its logical structure while hiding the small-scale details.

8.2 Fundamentals of Subprograms

8.2.1 General Subprogram Characteristics

Before discussing the fundamentals of subprograms, we must clarify the following basic characteristics of the kinds of subprograms that are discussed in this chapter:

1. Each subprogram has a single entry point.
2. The calling program unit is suspended during the execution of the called subprogram, which implies that there is only one subprogram in execution at any given time.
3. Control always returns to the caller when the subprogram execution terminates.

Although FORTRAN subprograms can have multiple entries, that particular kind of entry is relatively unimportant because it does not provide any fundamentally different capabilities. Therefore, in this chapter, we will ignore the possibility of multiple entries in FORTRAN subprograms.

Other alternatives to the above assumptions result in coroutines and concurrent units, which are explored in Chapter 11.

8.2.2 Basic Definitions

A **subprogram definition** describes the actions of the subprogram abstraction. A **subprogram call** is the explicit request that the subprogram be executed. A subprogram is said to be **active** if, after having been called, it has begun execution but has not yet completed that execution.

A **subprogram header,** which is the first line of the definition, serves several purposes. First, it specifies that the following syntactic unit is a subprogram definition of some particular kind. This specification is often accomplished with a special word. Second, it provides a name for the subprogram. Third, it may optionally specify a list of parameters. They are optional because not all subprogram definitions have parameters.

Consider the following header examples:

```
SUBROUTINE ADDER (parameters)
```

This is the header of a FORTRAN subroutine subprogram named ADDER. In Ada, the header for ADDER would be

procedure ADDER (parameters) **is**

No special word appears in the header of a C subprogram. C has only one kind of subprogram, the function, and the header of a function is recognized by context rather than by a special word. For example,

adder (parameters)

would serve as the header of a function named adder.

8.2.3 Parameters

Subprograms typically describe data computations. There are two ways that a subprogram can gain access to the data that it is to process: through direct access to nonlocal variables (declared elsewhere but visible in the subprogram), or through parameter passing. Data passed through parameters are accessed through names that are local to the subprogram. Parameter passing is more flexible than direct access to nonlocal variables. In essence, a subprogram with parameter access to the data it is to process is a parameterized computation. It can perform its computation on whatever data it receives through its parameters (presuming the types of the parameters are as expected by the subprogram). If data access is through nonlocal variables, the only way the computation can proceed on different data is to assign new values to those nonlocal variables between calls to the subprogram. Extensive access to nonlocals causes reduced reliability. Variables that are visible to the subprogram where access is desired often end up also being visible where access to them is not needed. This problem was discussed in Chapter 4 and is reviewed in Section 8.11.

In some situations, it is convenient to be able to transmit computations, rather than data, as parameters to subprograms. In these cases, the name of the subprogram that implements that computation may be used as a parameter. This form of parameter is discussed in Section 8.6. Data parameters are discussed in Section 8.5.

The parameters in the subprogram header are called **formal parameters.** They are sometimes thought of as dummy variables because they are not variables in the usual sense: In some cases they are only bound to storage when the subprogram is enacted, and that binding is often through some other program variables.

Subprogram call statements must include the name of the subprogram and a list of parameters to be bound to the formal parameters of the subprogram. These parameters are called **actual parameters.** They must be distinguished from formal parameters because the two can have different restrictions on their forms, and of course their uses are quite different.

In nearly all programming languages, the correspondence between actual and formal parameters—or the binding of actual parameters to formal parameters—is done by simple position: The first actual parameter is bound to the first formal parameter and so forth. Such parameters are called **positional parameters.** This is a good method for relatively short parameter lists.

When lists are long, however, it is easy for the program writer to make mistakes in the order of parameters in the list. One solution to this problem is to provide **keyword parameters,** in which the name of the formal parameter to which an actual parameter is to be bound is specified with the actual parameter. The advantage of keyword parameters is that they can appear in any order in the actual parameter list. Ada procedures can be called using this method, as in

```
SUMER (LENGTH => MY_LENGTH,
       LIST => MY_ARRAY,
       SUM => MY_SUM);
```

where the definition of SUMER has the formal parameters LENGTH, LIST, and SUM.

The chief disadvantage to keyword parameters is that the user of the subprogram must know the names of formal parameters.

In addition to keyword parameters, Ada allows positional parameters. The two can be mixed in a call, as in:

```
SUMER (MY_LENGTH,
       SUM => MY_SUM,
       LIST => MY_ARRAY);
```

The only restriction with this is that after a keyword parameter appears in the list, all remaining parameters must be keyworded. This is necessary because position may no longer be well defined after a keyword parameter has appeared.

In C++ and Ada, formal parameters can have default values. A default value is used if no actual parameter is passed to the formal parameter in the subprogram header. Consider the following partial Ada procedure header:

```
procedure COMPUTE_PAY (INCOME : FLOAT;
                       EXEMPTIONS : INTEGER := 1;
                       TAX_RATE : FLOAT;
                       ... ) is
```

The EXEMPTIONS parameter can be eliminated in a call to COMPUTE_PAY; when it is, the value 1 is used. No comma is included for an absent actual parameter in an Ada call, because the only value of such a comma would be to indicate the position of the next parameter, which in this case is not necessary because all actual parameters after an absent actual parameter must be keyworded. For example, consider the following call:

```
COMPUTE_PAY (20000.0, TAX_RATE => 0.8, ...);
```

In most languages that do not have default values for formal parameters, the number of actual parameters in a call must match the number of formal parameters in the subprogram definition header. However, in C this is not required. When there are fewer actual parameters in a call than formal parameters in a function definition, it is the programmer's responsibility to ensure that the parameter correspondence, which is always positional, and the subprogram execution are sensible.

Although this design, which allows a variable number of parameters, is clearly prone to error, it is also sometimes convenient. For example, the printf function of C can print any number of items (data values and/or literal strings). The restriction to a fixed number of parameters for such a function results in the Modula-2 design, in which only a single item can be printed with each call to a printing subprogram, which is far more cumbersome to use.

8.2.4   Procedures and Functions

There are two distinct categories of subprograms: procedures and functions, both of which can be viewed as methods of extending the language. Procedures are collections of statements that define parameterized computations. These computations are enacted by single call statements. Procedures define, in effect, new statements. When they are user defined, they are user-defined statements. For example, because Pascal does not have a sort statement, a user can build a procedure to sort lists of data and use that procedure in place of the unavailable sort statement.

Procedures can produce results in the calling program unit by two methods. First, if there are variables that are not formal parameters but are still visible in both the procedure and the calling program unit, the procedure can change them. Second, if the subprogram has formal parameters that allow the transfer of data to the caller, those parameters can be changed.

FORTRAN procedures are called **subroutines,** and we use that term when referring to those units.

Functions structurally resemble procedures but are modeled after mathematical functions. If a function is a faithful model, it produces no side effects; that is, it modifies neither its parameters nor any other variables declared outside the function.

Functions are called by appearances of their names, along with the required actual parameters, in expressions. The value produced by a function's execution is returned to the calling code, effectively replacing the call itself. For example, the value of the expression f(x) is whatever value f produces when called with the parameter x. For a function that does not produce side effects, the returned value is its only effect.

Functions define new user-defined operators. For example, if a language does not have an exponentiation operator, a function can be written that returns the value of one of its parameters raised to the power of another parameter. Its header in Pascal may be

```
function power (base, exp : real) : real;
```

which could be called, as in

```
result := 3.4 * power (10.0, x)
```

Compare this with the same operation in FORTRAN, in which exponentiation is a built-in operation:

```
RESULT = 3.4 * 10.0 ** X
```

8.3 Design Issues for Subprograms

Subprograms are complex structures in programming languages, and it follows from this that a lengthy list of issues are involved in their design. One obvious issue is the choice of parameter-passing method or methods that will be used. The wide variety of methods that have been used in various languages is a reflection of the diversity of opinion on the subject. A closely related issue is whether parameter types will be checked between calls and the called subprograms. Another related issue is whether the types of the parameters of subprograms, which are themselves passed as parameters, are checked.

The nature of the local environment of a subprogram dictates to some degree the nature of the subprogram. The most important question is whether local variables are statically or dynamically allocated. One important capability made possible by dynamically allocated local variables is recursion.

As mentioned earlier, some languages allow subprogram names to be passed as parameters. One design issue is simply whether this is to be allowed in a language. If it is, that raises the question of what should be the referencing environment of a subprogram that has been passed as a parameter.

A language that is meant to be useful for constructing significant software systems must allow the compilation of parts of programs (as opposed to being required to compile only complete programs). When some facility for this kind of compilation is provided, the next design issue is how flexible and reliable the mechanism should be. Two distinct approaches have been used, separate and independent compilation.

Finally, there are the questions of whether subprograms can be overloaded or generic. An overloaded subprogram is one that has the same name as another subprogram in the same referencing environment. A generic subprogram is one whose computation can be done on data of different types with different calls.

The following is a summary of these design issues for subprograms in general. Additional issues that are specifically associated with functions are discussed in Section 8.10.

1. What parameter-passing method or methods are used?
2. Are the types of the actual parameters checked against the types of the formal parameters?
3. Are local variables statically or dynamically allocated?
4. What is the referencing environment of a subprogram that has been passed as a parameter?
5. If subprograms can be passed as parameters, are the types of parameters checked in calls to the passed subprograms?
6. Can subprograms be overloaded?
7. Can subprograms be generic?
8. Is either separate or independent compilation possible?

These issues and example designs are discussed in the following sections.

8.4   Local Referencing Environments

Subprograms are generally allowed to declare their own variables, thereby defining local referencing environments. Variables that are declared inside subprograms are called **local variables,** because access to them is usually restricted to the subprogram in which they are declared.

Local variables can be either statically or dynamically bound to storage. In Chapter 4, variables of these two kinds were called static and semidynamic variables, respectively. If local variables are semidynamic, they are bound to storage when the subprogram begins execution and unbound from storage when that execution terminates. There are several advantages of semidynamic local variables, the primary one being the flexibility they provide the subprogram. It is essential that recursive subprograms have semidynamic local variables. Another advantage of semidynamic locals is that some of the storage for local variables of all subprograms can be shared. Such sharing obviously cannot take place among subprograms that are active at the same time. This is not as great an advantage as it was when computers had smaller memories.

The main disadvantages of semidynamic local variables are the following: First there is the cost of the time required to allocate, initialize (when necessary), and deallocate such variables for each call. Second, references to semidynamic local variables must be indirect, whereas references to static variables can be direct. On most computers, indirect references are slower than direct references. Finally, with semidynamic local variables, subprograms cannot be history sensitive; that is, they cannot retain data values of local variables between calls. It is sometimes desirable to be able to write history-sensitive subprograms. A very simple example of a need for a history-sensitive subprogram is one whose task is to cause a printer to move the paper to a new page and print the page number at the top. To avoid the need to pass the page number, a local variable can be used, but only if it is static. Coroutines (discussed in Chapter 11), and the subprograms used in iterator loop constructs (discussed in Chapter 7) are other examples of the need to be history sensitive.

The primary advantage of static local variables is that they are very efficient—they usually can be accessed faster because there is no indirection and no run-time overhead of allocation and deallocation. And, of course, they allow subprograms to be history sensitive. The greatest disadvantage is the inability to support recursion.

In ALGOL 60 and its descendant languages, local variables in a subprogram are by default semidynamic. In C functions, locals are semidynamic unless specifically declared to be **static**. For example, in the following C function, the variable sum is static and count is semidynamic:

```
adder (list, listlen)
  int list[], listlen;
  { static int sum = 0;
    int count;
    for (count = 0; count < listlen; count ++)
      sum = sum + list[count];
    return sum;
  }
```

Pascal, Modula-2, and Ada subprograms have only semidynamic local variables.

As discussed in Chapter 4, FORTRAN 77 implementors can choose whether local variables are to be static or semidynamic. Most implementors stay with the tradition of earlier FORTRANs and make them static. And actually, since pre-90 FORTRANs do not allow recursion, there is rarely a compelling reason to make them semidynamic. The savings in storage is not usually thought to be worth the loss in efficiency. FORTRAN 77 users can force one or more local variables to be static regardless of the implementation by listing their names on a SAVE statement.

In FORTRAN 90, a subprogram can be explicitly specified to be recursive, in which case its local variables are semidynamic.

8.5 Parameter-Passing Methods

Parameter-passing methods are the ways in which parameters are transmitted to and/or from called subprograms. We first focus on the primary semantics models of parameter-passing methods. Then we discuss the various implementation models invented by language designers for these semantics models. Next we survey the design choices of the various imperative languages and discuss the actual methods used to implement the implementation models. We finally consider the design considerations that face a language designer in choosing among the methods.

8.5.1   Semantics Models of Parameter Passing

Formal parameters are characterized by one of three distinct semantics models: (1) They can receive data from the corresponding actual parameter, (2) they can transmit data to the actual parameter, or (3) they can do both. These three semantics models are called **in mode, out mode,** and **inout mode,** respectively.

There are two conceptual models of how data transfers take place in parameter transmission: Either an actual value is physically moved (to the caller, to the callee, or both ways) or an access path is moved. Most commonly, the access path is a simple pointer. Figure 8.1 illustrates the three semantics models of parameter passing when physical moves are used.

8.5.2   Implementation Models of Parameter Passing

A variety of models has been developed by language designers to guide the implementation of the three basic parameter transmission modes. In the following sections, we discuss several of these and evaluate their strengths and weaknesses.

8.5.2.1   Pass-by-Value

When a parameter is **passed by value,** the value of the actual parameter is used to initialize the corresponding formal parameter, which then acts as a local variable in the subprogram, thus providing in-mode semantics.

Pass-by-value is normally implemented by actual data transfer, because accesses are usually more efficient with this method. It could be implemented by transmitting an access path to the value of the actual parameter in the caller, but that would require that the value be in a write-protected cell (one that can only be read). Enforcing the write protection is not always a simple matter. For example, suppose the subprogram to which the parameter was passed passes it in turn to another subprogram. This is another reason to use physical transfer.

The main disadvantage of the pass-by-value method, if physical moves are done, is that additional storage is required for the formal parameter, either in the called subprogram or in some area outside both the caller and the called subprogram. In addition, the actual parameter must be physically moved to the storage area for the corresponding formal parameter. The storage and the move operations can be costly if the parameter is a large object, such as a long array.

8.5.2.2   Pass-by-Result

Pass-by-result is an implementation model for out-mode parameters. When a parameter is passed by result, no value is transmitted to the subprogram.

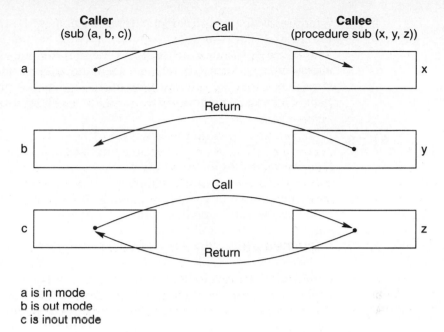

Figure 8.1
The three semantics models of parameter-passing when physical moves are used

a is in mode
b is out mode
c is inout mode

The corresponding formal parameter acts as a local variable, but just before control is transferred back to the caller, its value is passed back to the caller's actual parameter, which must be a variable. If values are returned (as opposed to access paths), as they typically are, pass-by-result also requires the extra storage and copy operations that are required by pass-by-value. As with pass-by-value, the complexity of implementing pass-by-result prevents transmitting an access path instead of a value. In this case, the problem is in ensuring that the initial value of the actual parameter is not used in the called subprogram.

One problem with the pass-by-result model is that there can be an actual parameter collision, such as the one created with the call

```
sub (p1, p1)
```

In sub, assuming the two formal parameters have different names, the two can obviously be assigned different values. Then whichever of the two is assigned to their corresponding actual parameter last becomes the value of p1. Thus the order in which the actual parameters are assigned determines their value. Because the order is usually implementation dependent, portability problems can occur that are difficult to diagnose.

Calling a procedure with two identical actual parameters can also lead to different kinds of problems when other parameter passing methods are used, as discussed in Section 8.5.2.4.

Another problem that can occur with pass-by-result is that the implementor may be able to choose between two different times to evaluate the addresses of the actual parameters: at the time of the call or at the time of the return. For example, suppose a subprogram has the parameter list[index]. If index is changed by the subprogram, either through global access or as a formal parameter, then the address of list[index] will change between the call and the return. This makes programs unportable between implementations that choose differently in this issue.

8.5.2.3   Pass-by-Value-Result

Pass-by-value-result is an implementation model for inout-mode parameters in which actual values are moved. It is in effect a combination of pass-by-value and pass-by-result. The value of the actual parameter is used to initialize the corresponding formal parameter, which then acts as a local variable. At subprogram termination, the value of the formal parameter is transmitted back to the actual parameter.

Pass-by-value-result is sometimes called pass-by-copy because the actual parameter is copied to the formal parameter at subprogram entry and then copied back at subprogram termination.

Pass-by-value-result shares with pass-by-value and pass-by-result the disadvantages of requiring multiple storage for parameters and time for copying values. It shares with pass-by-result the problems associated with the order in which actual parameters are assigned.

8.5.2.4   Pass-by-Reference

Pass-by-reference is a second implementation model for inout-mode parameters. Rather than transmitting data values back and forth, however, as in pass-by-value-result, the pass-by-reference method transmits an access path, usually just an address, to the called subprogram. This provides the access path to the cell storing the actual parameter. Thus the called subprogram is allowed to access the actual parameter in the calling program unit. In effect, the actual parameter is shared with the called subprogram.

The advantage of call-by-reference is that the passing process itself is efficient, in terms of both time and space. Duplicate space is not required, nor is any copying.

There are, however, several disadvantages to the pass-by-reference method. First, accesses to the formal parameters will most likely be slower because one more level of indirect addressing is needed than when data values are transmitted, as with pass-by-value-result. Second, if only one-way communication to the called subprogram is required, inadvertent and erroneous changes may be made to the actual parameter.

Another serious problem of pass-by-reference is that aliases can be created. This should be expected because pass-by-reference makes access paths available to the called subprograms, thereby broadening their access to non-local variables. There are several ways aliases can be created when parameters are passed by reference.

First, collisions can occur between actual parameters. Consider a Pascal procedure that has two parameters that are to be passed by reference, as in

```
procedure sub (var first, second : integer)
```

If the call to sub happens to pass the same variable twice, as in

```
sub (total, total)
```

then `first` and `second` in sub will be aliases.

Collisions between array elements can also cause aliases. For example, suppose the subprogram sub is called with two array elements that are specified with variable subscripts, as in

```
sub (list[i], list[j])
```

If `i` happens to be equal to `j`, then `first` and `second` are again aliases.

Collisions between array element parameters and elements of arrays passed as array name parameters are another possible cause of aliases. If two of the formal parameters of a subprogram are a scalar and an array of the same type, then a call such as

```
sub1 (list[i], list)
```

could result in aliasing in sub1, since sub1 can access all elements of `list` through the second parameter and access a single element through its first parameter.

Still another way to get aliasing with pass-by-reference parameters is through collisions between formal parameters and nonlocal variables that are visible.

These aliases are possible when a language provides more nonlocal access than is necessary, such as with static scoping. For example, consider the following Pascal code:

```
procedure bigsub;
  var global : integer;
  procedure smallsub (var local : integer);
    begin
    ...
    end;     { smallsub }
  begin
  ...
  smallsub (global);
  ...
  end;    { bigsub }
```

Inside smallsub, `local` and `global` are aliases. As stated above, the main reason for the aliasing is that static scoping provides too much access to nonlocal variables. The problem with these kinds of aliasing is the same as in other circumstances: It is harmful to readability and thus to reliability. It also makes program verification extremely difficult.

All these possible aliasing situations are eliminated if pass-by-value-result is used instead of pass-by-reference. However, in place of aliasing, other problems sometimes arise, as discussed in Sections 8.5.2.2 and 8.5.2.3.

Lastly, a subtle but fatal error can occur with pass-by-reference parameters if care is not taken in their implementation. Suppose a program contains two references to the constant 10, the first being as an actual parameter in a call to a subprogram. Further suppose that the subprogram mistakenly changes the formal parameter that corresponds to the 10 to the value 5. The compiler for this program may have built a single location for the value 10 during compilation, as compilers often do, and may use that location for all references to the constant 10 in the program. But after the return from the subprogram, all subsequent occurrences of 10 actually will be references to the value 5. This can happen in some systems, and it creates a programming problem that is very difficult to diagnose. This did in fact happen with many implementations of FORTRAN IV. Note that this problem cannot happen if pass-by-value-result is used rather than pass-by-reference.

8.5.2.5 Pass-by-Name

Pass-by-name is an inout-mode parameter transmission method that does not correspond to a single implementation model, as explained below. When parameters are passed by name, the actual parameter is, in effect, textually substituted for the corresponding formal parameter in all its occurrences in the subprogram. This is quite different from the methods discussed thus far. In those cases, formal parameters are bound to actual values or addresses at the time of the subprogram call. A pass-by-name formal parameter is bound to an access method at the time of the subprogram call, but the actual binding to a value or an address is delayed until the formal parameter is assigned or referenced.

The objective of the late binding in pass-by-name parameters is flexibility. This is consistent with other situations in which we have encountered differences in binding time. For example, binding a variable to a type occurs at a later point in APL than it does in FORTRAN, thus yielding more flexible uses of variables.

The form of the actual parameter dictates the implementation model of pass-by-name parameters. This distinguishes pass-by-name parameters from those passed by other methods. If the actual parameter is a scalar variable, then pass-by-name is equivalent to pass-by-reference. If the actual parameter is a constant expression, then pass-by-name is equivalent to pass-by-value. If the actual parameter is an array element, pass-by-name may be different from any other method, because the value of the subscript expression can change during execution between the times of various references. This allows different appearances of the formal parameter in the called subprogram to refer to different array elements. This is discussed in greater detail later in this section.

If the actual parameter is an expression that contains references to a variable, pass-by-name is again different from any other method. It is different because the expression is evaluated for each reference to the formal parameter at the time the reference is reached. If any of the variables in the expression are themselves accessible and are changed by the subprogram, the value of the expression can change with each reference to the formal parameter.

Consider the following example program, written in an ALGOL-like language:

```
procedure BIGSUB;
  integer GLOBAL;
  integer array LIST [1:2];
  procedure SUB (PARAM);
    integer PARAM;
    begin
    PARAM := 3;
    GLOBAL := GLOBAL + 1;
    PARAM := 5
    end;
  begin
  LIST[1] := 2;
  LIST[2] := 2;
  GLOBAL := 1;
  SUB (LIST[GLOBAL])
  end;
```

After execution, the array LIST has the values 3 and 5, both set in SUB. Access to LIST[2] is provided after GLOBAL is incremented to the value 2 in SUB.

Some rather clever tricks can be played with pass-by-name parameters. The most famous example of this was proposed by J. Jensen of the Regnecentralen in Copenhagen in 1960 and has since been called Jensen's Device. Jensen's idea involves passing an expression and one or more variables that appear in that expression as parameters to a subprogram. Whenever one of the variable form parameters is changed in the subprogram, that change can cause a change of the values of later occurrences of the formal parameter that corresponds to the expression actual parameter. Consider the following ALGOL 60 procedure:

```
real procedure SUM (ADDER, INDEX, LENGTH);
  value LENGTH;
  real ADDER;
  integer INDEX, LENGTH;
  begin
  real TEMPSUM;
  TEMPSUM := 0.0;
  for INDEX := 1 step 1 until LENGTH do
    TEMPSUM := TEMPSUM + ADDER;
  SUM := TEMPSUM
  end;
```

If A is a scalar, the call

```
SUM (A, I, 100)
```

simply produces the value 100 * A by adding A to an initially cleared location 100 times. Suppose that A is an array of 100 reals and SUM is called with

```
SUM (A[I], I, 100)
```

The **for** statement effectively becomes

```
for I := 1 step 1 until 100 do
   TEMPSUM := TEMPSUM + A[I]
```

So this call produces the sum of the array. If instead the sum of the squares of the elements of the A array is wanted, SUM can be called with

```
SUM (A[I]*A[I], I, 100)
```

The inner product of the two vectors in arrays A and B, each of length 100, can be gotten from

```
SUM (A[I]*B[I], I, 100)
```

These different uses of the procedure SUM show that the pass-by-name mechanism provides a large degree of flexibility: A single procedure can be used for a variety of different purposes. The cost of this flexibility lies in two areas: readability and execution speed. Procedures that use the pass-by-name feature to achieve the flexibility demonstrated above are difficult to understand. The many possible uses of such procedures are not always apparent from their listings. The cost of pass-by-name parameters, in terms of execution efficiency, is discussed in Section 8.5.5.

One surprising problem with pass-by-name is that it cannot be used to perform the simple task of interchanging the values of two given actual parameters. A simple implementation of the interchange is

```
procedure SWAP (FIRST, SECOND);
   integer FIRST, SECOND;
   begin
   integer TEMP;
   TEMP := FIRST;
   FIRST := SECOND;
   SECOND := TEMP
   end;
```

The procedure SWAP performs correctly if the two arguments are scalars, and in most other cases. However, if an array element and its subscript are sent, it fails. For example, if we called SWAP with the actual parameters I and A[I], the statements of SWAP become

```
TEMP := I;
I := A[I];
A[I] := TEMP;
```

The problem is that the new value of I is used to compute the address of the destination of the last assignment. The assignment to A[I] is to a different location than the value referenced in the second statement, which assigns the value of A[I] to I. It has been proven that it is not possible to write a general ALGOL 60 function that correctly interchanges the values of its two parameters.

In summary, the primary advantage of pass-by-name is the flexibility it affords the programmer. The main disadvantage is the slowness of the process, relative to other parameter-passing methods. Also, it is difficult to implement and may confuse both readers and writers of programs that use it.

The concept of late binding, on which pass-by-name is based, is by no means an odd or discredited one. The powerful mechanism of polymorphism, which is an integral part of object-oriented programming, is simply a late binding of calls to subprograms or messages to objects. (Polymorphism is discussed in Chapter 15.) Lazy evaluation is another useful mechanism that is a form of late binding. It is, briefly, the process of only evaluating parts of functional code when it becomes certain that the evaluation of that code is necessary. In the imperative languages, short-circuit evaluation of Boolean expressions is an example of lazy evaluation.

8.5.3   Parameter-Passing Methods of the Major Languages

FORTRAN implementations use the inout-mode semantics model of parameter passing. In most FORTRAN implementations before FORTRAN 77, parameters were passed by reference. In later implementations, however, pass-by-value-result has been frequently used for simple variable parameters.

As stated in the previous section, ALGOL 60 introduced the pass-by-name method. It also allows pass-by-value as an option. Primarily because of the difficulty in implementing pass-by-name parameters, they were not carried from ALGOL 60 to any subsequent languages that became popular, other than SIMULA-67.

The method used in ALGOL 68 is pass-by-value. A pointer type actual parameter can give the effect of pass-by-reference. ALGOL 68 introduced the syntax of attaching the type of a formal parameter to its name in the formal parameter list. For example, suppose there was a procedure named ADDER with three parameters, where the first and third were inout mode and the second was in mode. The ALGOL 68 header for ADDER could have the form

```
proc adder = (ref int a, int b, ref real c) ...
```

Both the a and c parameters are inout mode and are therefore passed as access paths, in this case simply pointers. The C language uses the same parameter-passing method as ALGOL 68.

ALGOL W (Wirth and Hoare, 1966) introduced the value-result method of parameter passing as an alternative to the inefficiency of pass-by-name and the problems of pass-by-reference.

In Pascal and Modula-2, the default parameter-passing method is pass-by-value, and pass-by-reference can be specified by prefacing formal parameters with the reserved word **var**. For example, the Pascal header for the ALGOL 68 ADDER example above could be

```
procedure adder (var a : integer;
                      b : integer;
                 var c : real);
```

The designers of Ada defined versions of the three semantics modes of parameter transmission: in, out, and inout. The three modes are appropriately named with the reserved words **in**, **out**, and **in out**, where **in** is the default method. For example, the ADDER example could have the following Ada header:

```
procedure ADDER (A : in out INTEGER;
                 B : in INTEGER;
                 C : in out FLOAT) is
```

Ada formal parameters declared to be **out** mode can be assigned but not referenced. Parameters that are **in** mode can be referenced but not assigned. Quite naturally, **in out** mode parameters can be both referenced and assigned. The issue of how Ada **in out** mode parameters are implemented is interesting and is discussed in Section 8.5.5.

8.5.4   Type-Checking Parameters

It is now widely accepted that software reliability demands that the types of actual parameters be checked for consistency with the corresponding formal parameters. Without such type checking, small typographical errors can lead to program errors that may be difficult to diagnose because they are not detected by the system. For example, in the function call

```
RESULT := SUB1(1)
```

the actual parameter is an integer constant. If the formal parameter of SUB1 is a floating-point type, no error will be detected without parameter type checking. Yet SUB1 cannot produce a correct result given an actual parameter that is not even similar to the expected value of a floating point 1.0.

FORTRAN 77 does not require parameter type checking; Pascal, Modula-2, FORTRAN 90, and Ada do require it.

The C languages require some special discussion in the matter of parameter type checking. In the original C, neither the number of parameters nor their types were checked. In ANSI C, the formal parameters of functions can be declared two ways. First, they can be as in the original C; that is, the names of the parameters are listed in parentheses and the type declarations for them follow, as in

```
double sin (x)
    double x;
    { ... }
```

Using this method in ANSI C avoids type checking, thereby allowing calls such as

```
double value;
int count;
...
value = sin (count);
```

to be legal but nonsense.

The alternative is called the **prototype method,** in which the formal parameter types are included in the list, as in

```
double sin (double x);
    { ... }
```

If this version of sin is called with the same call as above, that is,

```
value = sin (count);
```

it also is legal. The type of the actual parameter (**int**) is checked against that of the formal parameter (**double**). Although they do not match, **int** is coercible to **double**, so the conversion is done. If the conversion is not possible (for example, if the actual parameter had been an array), or if the number of parameters is wrong, then a syntax error is detected. So, in ANSI C, the user chooses whether he or she wants parameters to be type checked.

In C++, all functions must have their formal parameters in prototype form. However, type checking can be avoided by replacing the parameter list with an ellipsis, as in

```
double sin ( ... );
    { ... }
```

Any actual parameter list is legal in a call to this version of sin.

A C++ formal parameter list can have both typed parameters and an ellipsis, as is the case with printf, which is defined as

```
printf (const char* ...);
```

In this case, a call to printf must include at least one parameter, a pointer to a constant character string. Beyond that, anything (including nothing) is legal. The way printf determines whether there are additional parameters is by the presence of special symbols in the string. For example, the format code for integer output is %d. This appears as part of the string, as in

```
printf ("The sum is %d\n", sum);
```

The % tells the compiler there is one more parameter.

8.5.5   Implementing Parameter-Passing Methods

We now address the question of how the primary implementation models
of parameter passing are actually implemented.

In ALGOL 60 and its descendant languages, parameter communication
takes place through the run-time stack. In the following discussion we
assume that the stack is used for all parameter transmission.

Pass-by-value parameters have their values copied into stack locations.
Pass-by-result parameters are implemented as the opposite of pass-by-
value. The values assigned to the pass-by-result actual parameters are
placed in the stack, where they can be retrieved by the calling program unit
upon termination of the called subprogram. Pass-by-value-result parameters can be implemented directly from their semantics as a combination of
pass-by-value and pass-by-result. Recall that the decision as to when the
address of a pass-by-result actual parameter is computed takes place is
important.

Pass-by-reference parameters are perhaps the simplest to implement.
Regardless of the type of the actual parameter, only its address must be
placed in the stack. In the case of constants, the address of the constant is
transmitted. However, because of the potential problem with constant
actual parameters, as described in Section 8.5.2.4, a better method is to pass
the address of a temporary copy of such a constant. In the case of an expression, the compiler must build code to evaluate the expression just before
the transfer of control to the called subprogram. The address where that
code places the result of its evaluation is then placed in the stack. Access
to the formal parameters in the called subprogram is by indirect addressing
from the stack location of the address. The implementation of pass-by-
value, result, value-result, and reference, where the run-time stack is used,
is shown in Figure 8.2.

Pass-by-name parameters are usually implemented with parameterless
procedures or run-time-resident code segments, called **thunks.** A thunk
must be called for every reference to a pass-by-name parameter in the called
subprogram. The thunk evaluates the reference in the proper referencing
environment, which is that of the subprogram in which the passed subprogram (the one being executed) was declared, and returns the address of the
actual parameter. If the parameter reference is in an expression, the code of
the reference must include the necessary dereference to get the value from
the cell whose address was returned by the thunk. Altogether, this is a
costly process, relative to the simple indirect addressing used by pass-by-
reference parameters. Recall that for actual parameters that are scalar variables, pass-by-name and pass-by-reference are semantically equivalent. The
cost of implementing pass-by-reference is that of indirect addressing,
whereas pass-by-name requires a subprogram call—albeit without parameters—and its execution to accomplish the same thing.

The Ada language definition specifies that simple (nonstructured) parameters are to be passed by copy; that is, **in** and **in out** mode parameters

```
program main;
   var w, x, y, z : integer;
   procedure sub(a, b, c, d : integer);
     var l : integer;
     ...
     end;
   begin
   ...
   call sub (w, x, y, z); {pass w by value, x by result,
                              y by value-result, z by reference}
   ...
   end;
```

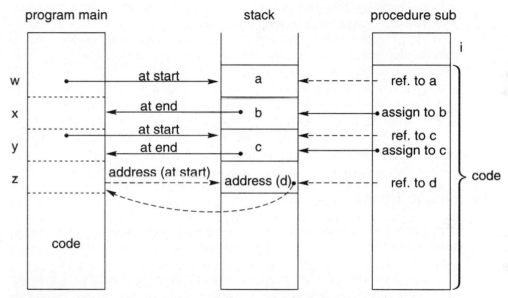

Figure 8.2
One possible stack implementation of the common parameter-passing methods

are to be local variables that are initialized by copying the value of the corresponding actual parameter. Simple parameters that are **out** or **in out** mode are to have their values copied back to the corresponding actual parameter at subprogram termination. The order of these copies, when there are more than one, is not defined by the language definition. The evaluation of **out** and **in out** mode parameters is done before the transfer of control to the called subprogram occurs.

In the case of formal parameters that are arrays, records, or tasks, implementors are given the choice between pass-by-value-result and pass-by-reference. By failing to specify the implementation method for passing structured parameters, the Ada designers left open the possibility of a subtle problem. The problem is that the two implementation methods can lead to different program results for certain program designs. This difference can occur because the pass-by-reference method provides access to a location in the calling program that can also be provided if the actual parameter is also available as a global, thereby creating an alias. If pass-by-value-result is used in place of pass-by-reference, this dual access to the actual parameter is not possible.

An additional problem is the following: Suppose the subprogram terminates abnormally (via an exception); the actual parameter in the pass-by-value-result implementation will be unchanged, whereas the pass-by-reference implementation may have changed the corresponding actual parameter before the error occurred. Once again, there can be a difference between the two implementation methods.

Ada programs that produce different results depending on how the **in out** method is implemented are termed **erroneous.** Despite this label, however, there is no way the compiler can detect the erroneous condition. So the error is usually detected only when the user moves the program from one implementation to another and realizes that it no longer produces the same result. The Ada design philosophy here is that programmers must guard against aliasing. If they create aliases, they must contend with the potential problems.

8.5.6   Design Considerations

Two important considerations are involved in choosing parameter-passing methods: efficiency and whether one-way or two-way data transfer is desired.

Contemporary software engineering principles dictate that access by subprogram code to data outside the subprogram be minimized. With this goal in mind, in-mode parameters should be used whenever no data is to be returned through a parameter to the caller. Out-mode parameters should be used when no data is transferred to the called subprogram, but the subprogram must transmit data back to the caller. Finally, inout-mode parameters should be used only when data must move in both directions between the caller and the called subprogram.

There is a practical consideration that is in conflict with this principle. Sometimes it is justifiable to pass access paths for one-way parameter transmission. For example, when a large array is to be passed to a subprogram that does not modify it, a one-way method may be preferred. However, pass-by-value would require that the entire array be moved to a local storage area of the subprogram. This would be costly in both time and space. In these situations, then, arrays are often passed by reference. This is precisely the reason why the Ada definition allows implementors to choose between the two for structured parameters. An even better approach would be to allow the user to choose between the methods.

The choice of a parameter-passing method for functions is related to another design issue: functional side effects. These two issues are discussed in Section 8.10.

8.6 Parameters That Are Subprogram Names

A number of situations occur in programming that are most conveniently handled if subprogram names can be sent as parameters to other subprograms. One of the more common of these occurs when a subprogram must sample some mathematical function. For example, a subprogram that does numerical integration estimates the area under the graph of a function by sampling the function at a number of different points. When such a subprogram is written, it should be usable for any given function—it should not need to be rewritten for every function that must be integrated. It is therefore natural that the name of a program function that evaluates the mathematical function to be integrated be sent to the integrating subprogram as a parameter.

Although the idea is natural and seemingly simple, understanding how it works can be difficult. If only the transmission of the subprogram code were necessary, it could be done by passing a single pointer. However, several complications arise.

First, the description of the subprogram's parameters must be sent, along with the subprogram name, assuming that the types of the actual parameters are to be checked at run time against the types of the formal parameters. The original definition of Pascal (Jensen and Wirth, 1974) allowed subprograms to be passed as parameters without including their parameter type information. If independent compilation is possible, the compiler is not allowed even to check for the correct number of parameters. In the absence of independent compilation, checking for parameter consistency is possible but is a very complex task, and it usually is not done. FORTRAN 77 suffers the same problem, but because parameter consistency is never checked in FORTRAN 77, it is not an additional problem.

When a subprogram name is passed as a parameter in ALGOL 68 or in the later versions of Pascal, the formal parameter types are included in the formal parameter list of the receiving subprogram, so parameter consistency in the actual call to the passed subprogram can be statically checked. For example, consider the following Pascal code:

```
procedure integrate (function fun (x : real) : real;
                     lowerbd, upperbd : real;
                     var result : real);

    ...
    var funval : real;
```

```
begin
...
funval := fun (lowerbd);
...
end;
```

The actual parameter in the call to `fun` in `integrate` can be statically checked for consistency with the type of `fun`'s formal parameter, which appears in the formal parameter list of integrate.

In Modula-2, procedure types are used to pass procedures as if they were variables. This method allows consistency checking of the parameters of passed subprograms, because the types of the parameters are part of the procedure type. FORTRAN 90 has a mechanism for providing types of parameters for subprograms that are passed as parameters, and they must be checked. Ada does not allow subprograms to be passed as parameters. The functionality of passing subprograms as parameters is instead provided by Ada's generic facility, which is discussed in Section 8.8.

A more difficult aspect of subprogram names that are passed as parameters is the question of what is the correct referencing environment for executing the passed subprogram. The three possibilities are (1) the environment of the subprogram that calls the passed subprogram, (2) the environment of the subprogram in which the passed subprogram is declared, or (3) the environment of the subprogram that includes the call statement that passed the subprogram as an actual parameter. The following example program illustrates these choices. Assume it is legal for SUB3 to call SUB4.

```
procedure SUB1;
   var x : integer;
  procedure SUB2;
    begin
    write('x=', x)
    end; {of SUB2}
  procedure SUB3;
    var x : integer;
    begin
    x := 3;
    SUB4(SUB2)
    end;    { of SUB3 }
  procedure SUB4(SUBX);
    var x : integer;
    begin
    x := 4;
    SUBX
    end;    { of SUB4 }
  begin    { of SUB1 }
  x := 1;
  SUB3
  end;    { of SUB1 }
```

The referencing environment of the execution of SUB2 (which is called from SUB4) for choice (1) is SUB4; for choice (2) it is SUB1; for choice (3) it is SUB3. The output of the program indicates the choice. If the referencing environment is that of SUB1, the output is x = 1; if the referencing environment is that of SUB3, the output is x = 3; if it is that of SUB4, the output is x = 4.

In some cases the subprogram that declares a subprogram also passes that subprogram as a parameter, so that choices (2) and (3) are the same. Choice (1) is called **shallow binding,** and choice (2) is called **deep binding.** Choice (3) has never been used because, one can assume, the environment in which the procedure appears as a parameter has no natural connection to the passed subprogram.

Shallow binding is not appropriate for block-structured languages because of static binding of variables. For example, suppose the procedure SENDER passes the procedure SENT as a parameter to the procedure RECEIVER. The problem is that RECEIVER may not be in the static environment of SENT, thereby making it very unnatural for SENT to have access to RECEIVER's variables. On the other hand, it is perfectly normal for any subprogram, including one sent as a parameter, to have its referencing environment determined by the lexical position of its definition. It is therefore more logical for block-structured languages to use deep binding. Some dynamic-scoped languages like SNOBOL use shallow binding.

8.7   Overloaded Subprograms

An overloaded operator is one that has multiple meanings. The meaning of a particular instance of an overloaded operator is determined by the types of its operands. For example, if the * operator has two floating-point operands in a Pascal program, it specifies floating-point multiplication. But if the same operator has two integer operands, it specifies integer multiplication.

An **overloaded subprogram** is a subprogram that has the same name as another subprogram in the same referencing environment. Every incarnation of an overloaded procedure must be unique in the types of its parameters. In the case of functions, the uniqueness can be either in the types of its parameters or in the type of the returned value. The meaning of a call to an overloaded subprogram is determined by the actual parameter list (and/or the type of the returned value, in the case of a function).

Ada allows both functions and procedures to be overloaded. For example, Ada programs often have several versions of the output function PUT available to them. The most common versions are those that accept string, integer, and floating-point type values as parameters. Because each version of PUT has a unique parameter type, the compiler can disambiguate occurrences of calls to PUT by the different type parameters.

Users are also allowed to write multiple versions of subprograms with the same name. Although it is not necessary for such subprograms to provide basically the same process, they usually do. For example, a particular program may require two sorting procedures, one for integer arrays and one for floating-point arrays. They both can be named SORT, as long as the types of their parameters are different. In the following skeletal Ada program, two procedures named SORT are included:

```ada
procedure MAIN is
    type FLOAT_VECTOR is array (INTEGER range <>) of FLOAT;
    type INT_VECTOR is array (INTEGER range <>) of INTEGER;
    ...
    procedure SORT(FLOAT_LIST  : in out FLOAT_VECTOR;
                   LOWER_BOUND : in INTEGER;
                   UPPER_BOUND : in INTEGER) is
    ...
    end SORT;
    procedure SORT(INT_LIST    : in out INT_VECTOR;
                   LOWER_BOUND : in INTEGER;
                   UPPER_BOUND : in INTEGER) is
    ...
    end SORT;
    ...
end MAIN;
```

C++ functions can be overloaded as long as the number or types of parameters of each version are unique.

8.8 Generic Subprograms

The Ada language provides a construct that supports the construction of multiple versions of program units to compute results from data of different data types. In the case of subprograms, this allows the construction of a subprogram whose parameters can not only have different values, but also different types. The different versions of the subprogram are constructed by the compiler upon request of the user program. Because the versions of the subprogram all have the same name, this provides the illusion that a single subprogram can process data of different types on different calls.

The same mechanism is used to allow different versions of a single subprogram to include uses of different subprograms. This is useful in providing the functionality of subprograms passed as parameters. Because program units of this sort are generic in nature, they are called **generic units.**

The following example illustrates a procedure that is generic in the type of its parameter. It is an exchange sort procedure that is designed to work on any array with elementary numeric type elements, using any ordinal type subscript range:

```
generic
 type ELEMENT is private;
 type INDEX is (<>);
 type VECTOR is array (INDEX) of ELEMENT;
 procedure GENERIC_SORT(LIST : in out VECTOR);
 procedure GENERIC_SORT(LIST : in out VECTOR) is
  TEMP : ELEMENT;
 begin
 for INDEX_1 in LIST'FIRST..INDEX'PRED(LIST'LAST) loop
   for INDEX_2 in INDEX'SUCC(INDEX_1)..LIST'LAST loop
     if LIST(INDEX_1) > LIST(INDEX_2)
       then
       TEMP := LIST(INDEX_1);
       LIST(INDEX_1) := LIST(INDEX_2);
       LIST(INDEX_2) := TEMP;
     end if;
     end loop;    -- for INDEX_1 ...
   end loop;    -- for INDEX_2 ...
 end GENERIC_SORT;
```

Parts of this generic procedure may appear rather odd if you are not familiar with Ada. However, it is not important to understand all the details of the syntax. The private type ELEMENT is the variable in this generic. Private types are discussed in Chapter 10. The array is declared to have any type subscript (that is, any type that is legal as a subscript) with any range.

This generic sort is nothing more than a template for a procedure; no code is generated for it by the compiler and it has no effect on a program, unless it is instantiated for some type. Instantiation is accomplished with a statement such as the following:

```
procedure INTEGER_SORT is new GENERIC_SORT (
                            ELEMENT => INTEGER,
                            INDEX => INTEGER,
                            VECTOR => INT_LIST_TYPE);
```

The compiler reacts to this statement by building a version of GENERIC_SORT named INTEGER_SORT that sorts INTEGER type variables.

The generic program units of Ada are a kind of poor cousin to a subprogram in which the types of the formal parameters are dynamically bound to the types of the actual parameters in a call. In this case only a single copy of the code is needed, whereas with the Ada method a copy must be created at compile time for each different type that is required.

Smalltalk and C++ support subprograms in which the calls are dynamically bound to the correct version of the subprogram, according to the types of the actual parameters. This capability is called polymorphism. These capabilities of Smalltalk and C++ are discussed in Chapter 15.

Recall that Ada does not allow subprograms to be passed as parameters to other subprograms. To provide that functionality, Ada allows generic formal subprograms. In a language such as Pascal, subprograms are passed as parameters so that a particular call of a subprogram can execute using the specific passed subprogram to compute its result. In Ada the same result is achieved by allowing the user to instantiate a generic subprogram any number of times, each with a different subprogram that can be used. For example, the procedure integrate, as defined in Section 8.6, can be written in Ada as

```
generic
  with function FUN(X : FLOAT) return FLOAT;
  procedure INTEGRATE (LOWERBD : in FLOAT;
                       UPPERBD : in FLOAT;
                       RESULT  : out FLOAT) is
    FUNVAL : FLOAT;
    begin
    ...
    FUNVAL := FUN (LOWERBD);
    ...
    end;
```

This could be instantiated for a user-defined function FUN1 with

```
INTEGRATE_FUN1 is new INTEGRATE (FUN => FUN1);
```

Now, INTEGRATE_FUN1 is a procedure for integrating the function FUN1.

8.9 Separate and Independent Compilation

The capability of compiling parts of a program without compiling the whole program is essential to the construction of large software systems. Thus, languages that are designed for such applications must allow this kind of compilation. With such a capability, only the modules of a system that are being changed need to be recompiled during development or maintenance. Newly compiled and previously compiled units are collected by a program called the linker, which is a part of the operating system. Without this capability, every change to a system requires a complete recompilation. In a large system, this is costly.

In this section, we discuss two distinct approaches to compiling parts of programs, called separate compilation and independent compilation. The parts of programs that can be compiled are sometimes called compilation units.

The term **separate compilation** means that compilation units can be compiled at different times, but their compilations are not independent of each other if either accesses or uses any entities of the other. This interdependence is required if interface checking is to be done. We first discuss separate compilation in the context of Ada.

To provide reliable separate compilation of a unit, the compiler must have access to information about program entities (variables, types, and subprograms, including their interfaces) that the unit uses but that are declared elsewhere. Information about the entities of an Ada package that can be visible in other units, which are called the exported entities, forms the interface of the package. The interface of a procedure includes the number, names, and types of its parameters, along with the order in which they appear. In the case of a function, the type of the returned value is also included. Ada implementations maintain these kinds of unit interface information in a library that is accessible to the compiler. Every compilation causes the interface information of that compilation to be placed in a library.

Libraries store library units, which are compiled compilation units. Compilation units in Ada are entities such as subprogram headers, package declarations (see Chapter 10), and subprogram bodies.

During compilation of an Ada program unit, all externally declared entities that are used are type checked against their local uses. In the case of subprograms, the whole interface is type checked. Not all library information is available to a particular program unit compilation. The names of those units that provide required external entities are listed on a **with** statement at the beginning of the unit being compiled. Using **with**, the programmer specifies the external units to which the code in the compilation must access. For example, the following procedure uses entities from two external units, GLOBALS and TEXT_IO, and thus specifies those two:

```
with GLOBALS, TEXT_IO;
procedure EXAMPLE is

   ...

   end EXAMPLE;
```

Modula-2 provides separate compilation that is similar to that of Ada. FORTRAN 90 also allows separate compilation of its subprograms and modules. Separate compilation in Modula-2 and Ada are discussed in greater detail in Chapter 10, after we have discussed the data abstraction facilities of those languages.

In some languages, most notably C and FORTRAN 77, independent compilation is allowed. With **independent compilation,** program units can be compiled without information about any other program units.

An important characteristic of independent compilation is that the interfaces between the separately compiled units are not checked for consistency. The interface of a FORTRAN 77 subroutine is its parameter list. When a subroutine is independently compiled, the types of its parameters are not stored with the compiled code or in a library. Therefore, when another program that calls that subroutine is compiled, the types of the actual parameters in the calls cannot be checked against the types of the formal parameters of the subroutine, even if the machine code for the called subroutine is available.

This is not surprising in FORTRAN 77. Even when the program that calls a subprogram and the subprogram are compiled from the same file, they are in effect, if not actually, compiled independently. So the parameter interface between FORTRAN 77 program units is never checked for type compatibility.

8.10 Design Issues for Functions

The following two design issues are specific to functions:

1. Are side effects allowed?
2. What types of values can be returned?

8.10.1 Functional Side Effects

Because of the problems of side effects of functions that are called in expressions, as described in Chapter 5, parameters to functions should always be in mode. Some languages, in fact, require this; for example, Ada functions can have only **in** mode formal parameters. This effectively prevents a function from causing side effects through its parameters, or through aliasing of parameters and globals. In Pascal, functions can have either pass-by-value or pass-by-reference parameters, thus allowing functions that cause side effects and aliasing. In C, the same is true.

8.10.2 Types of Returned Values

Most imperative programming languages restrict the types that can be returned by their functions. FORTRAN 77 functions allow only unstructured types to be returned. In Pascal and Modula-2, only simple types can be returned by functions. These are integer, real, char, Boolean, pointers, and enumeration types. The C language allows any type to be returned by its functions, except arrays and functions. Both of these can be handled by pointer type return values. The Ada language is alone among current imperative languages in that its functions can return values of any type.

8.11 Accessing Nonlocal Environments

Although much of the required communication between subprograms can be accomplished through parameters, most languages provide some other method of accessing variables from external environments.

The **nonlocal variables** of a subprogram are those that are visible within the subprogram but are not locally declared. **Global variables** are those that are visible in all program units. In Chapter 4, two methods of accessing nonlocal variables are discussed, static scoping and dynamic scoping. The problems with these designs are reviewed in the following paragraphs.

The primary problem of using static scoping as the means of nonlocal variable sharing is the following: A good deal of program structure in such languages may be dictated by the accessibility of procedures and nonlocal variables to other procedures, rather than dictated by well-engineered problem solutions. Additionally, in all cases, more access to nonlocals is provided than is necessary. Recall our examples of this problem in Chapter 4.

Two kinds of programming problems follow directly from dynamic scoping. First, during the time span beginning when execution of a subprogram begins and ending when that execution ends, all local variables of the subprogram are visible to any other executing subprogram regardless of its textual proximity. There is no way to protect local variables from this accessibility. Subprograms are always executed in the immediate environment of the caller. Because of this, dynamic scoping results in less reliable programs than static scoping.

A second problem that results from dynamic scoping is an inability to statically type check references to nonlocals. This results specifically from the inability to statically determine the declaration for a variable referenced as a nonlocal.

Implementation of accesses to nonlocal variables is discussed in detail in Chapter 9.

8.11.1 FORTRAN COMMON Blocks

FORTRAN provides access to blocks of global storage through its COMMON statement. There can be any number of these blocks, and all but one must be named. Any subprogram that wishes to access or create a common block has a COMMON statement that names the block and provides a list of the variables that it can use to access storage in the block. A common block is created when the first COMMON statement that mentions the block's name is found by the compiler.

The primary problem with using COMMON is that each of two subprograms can include a COMMON statement that specifies the same block name as the COMMON statement in the other, and thus refers to the same block. Further, each can specify a different list of variables, whose number and types can be unrelated to those in the other list. For example, it is perfectly legal to have the declarations

```
REAL A(100)
INTEGER B(250)
COMMON /BLOCK1/ A, B
```

in one subprogram and the declarations

```
REAL C(50), D(100)
INTEGER E(200)
COMMON /BLOCK1/ C, D, E
```

in another subprogram. The identifier delimited by slashes, BLOCK1, is the block name. The two views of the variables in BLOCK1 are shown in Figure 8.3. Note that we assume that integer and real variables take the same amount of space.

This can make sense only if BLOCK1 is merely used as shared storage, not shared data. In fact, storage sharing is the main reason for allowing this. In most cases, data in a COMMON block is to be shared using the same variable names and types. A simple ordering error in the list of variables on a COMMON statement in this situation can cause inadvertent storage sharing between variables of different types, which can cause an error that is difficult to locate.

Note that FORTRAN 90 states that COMMON is one of the "deprecated features," which means that it may be included in only one more version of FORTRAN. EQUIVALENCE is also a deprecated feature of FORTRAN 90.

Figure 8.3
Two views of a
COMMON block

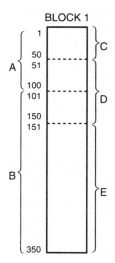

8.11.2 External Declarations and Modules

The Modula-2 and Ada languages use static scoping as a means of sharing data among program units. They both also provide an alternative method of data sharing by allowing units to specify the external modules to which access is required. Using this method, every module can specify exactly the other modules to which access is needed, no more and no less. In Modula-2, this access can be restricted to only specific procedures, variables, and data types from a given external module. Ada allows the user to specify only an external module's name, which then provides access to all of its types, variables, and procedures. This method is also possible in Modula-2. The approach of specifying each entity to which access is desired is certainly more tedious to use, because the lists of desired types, variables, and procedures can become long. It is, however, a safer method than simply specifying a module's name.

FORTRAN 90 also includes modules that can provide for selective and type-checked sharing of nonlocal data.

These language features are discussed more thoroughly in Chapter 10 in connection with data abstraction.

In C, there is no nesting of subprograms, so there is only a single level of scoping. Global variables can be created by placing their declarations outside function definitions. Access is provided to a variable in a function that declares the variable to be external with an **extern** statement. All functions whose definitions follow globally declared variables in a code file have access to those variables without declaring them to be external. This method is cumbersome and provides far more access than is usually needed.

Global variables that are defined in other files of C code that are included in a program can also be accessed by functions declaring them to be external. Thus separate, nonshared scopes can be introduced by separate compilation of modules. By this method, access to variables in those separately compiled modules is restricted to those other functions that declare the variables to be external.

8.12 User-Defined Overloaded Operators

Operators can be overloaded by the user in Ada and C++ programs. A popular example of this is the overloading of the asterisk operator for matrix multiplication, which can be done in Ada with the following:

```ada
function "*" (A, B : in MATRIX) return MATRIX is
   RESULT : MATRIX (A'FIRST(1)..A'LAST(1),
                    B'FIRST(2)..B'LAST(2))
   SUM : integer;
   begin
   for ROW in A'RANGE(1) loop
     for COL in B'RANGE(2) loop
       SUM := 0.0;
       for INNER in A'RANGE(2) loop
         SUM := SUM + A(ROW ,INNER) * B(INNER, COL):
         end loop;    -- for INNER ...
       RESULT(ROW, COL) := SUM;
       end loop;    -- for COL ...
     end loop;    -- for ROW ...
   end "*";
```

Note that this function does not check to see if the two input matrices are of dimensions that allow them to be multiplied, although the information to do that is available through the array attributes.

Matrix multiplication, as specified in this function definition, will be done whenever the asterisk appears with two operands of MATRIX type. The asterisk can be further overloaded any number of times, as long as the types or number of parameters differ or the return types are different.

The question naturally arises: How much operator overloading is good, or can you have too much? The answer is, to a large degree, a matter of taste. The argument against too much operator overloading is largely one of readability. In many cases, it is more readable to call a function to carry out an operation than to use an operator that is more frequently used for other type operands. Even in the case of matrix multiplication, it may be too easy to forget what is involved when a simple assignment statement, such as

```
C := A * B
```

is found in a program. It looks too much as though A, B, and C are simple scalars.

Another consideration is the process of building a software system from modules created by different groups. If the different groups overloaded the same operators in different ways, these differences obviously must be eliminated before putting the system together.

SUMMARY

Process abstractions are represented in programming languages by subprograms. A subprogram definition describes the actions represented by the subprogram. A subprogram call enacts those actions.

Formal parameters are the names that subprograms use to refer to the actual parameters given in subprogram calls.

Subprograms can be either functions, which model mathematical functions and are used to define new operations, or procedures, which define new statements.

Local variables in subprograms can be dynamically allocated from a stack, providing support for recursion, or statically allocated, providing efficiency and history-sensitive local variables.

There are three fundamental semantics models of parameter passing—in mode, out mode, and inout mode—and a number of implementation models that can be used to guide their implementation. The implementation models can actually be implemented in a variety of ways.

Aliasing can occur when pass-by-reference parameters are used, both among two or more parameters and between a parameter and an accessible nonlocal variable.

Access to nonlocal variables is provided in several different ways: through external declarations, global data blocks, external modules, and through static and dynamic scoping.

Parameters that are subprogram names provide a necessary service but are sometimes difficult to understand. The opaqueness lies in the referencing environment that is available when a subprogram that has been passed as a parameter is executing.

Ada and C++ allow both subprogram and operator overloading. Subprograms can be overloaded as long as the various versions can be disambiguated by the types of their parameters or returned values. Function definitions can be used to build additional meanings for operators.

Program units in Ada can be generic, so the desired types of their data objects can be passed to the compiler, which then can construct units for the requested types. Also, different instantiations of generic subprograms can use different subprograms, providing the functionality of subprograms passed as parameters.

PROBLEM SET

1. What are arguments for and against a user program building additional definitions for existing operators, as can be done in Ada? Do you believe such user-defined operator overloading is good or bad? Support your answer.

2. In most FORTRAN IV implementations, parameters were passed by reference, using access path transmission only. State both the advantages and disadvantages of this design choice.

3. Argue in support of the Ada designers' decision to allow the implementor to choose between implementing **in out** mode parameters by copy or by reference.

4. FORTRAN has two slightly different kinds of COMMON, blank and named. One difference between them is that blank COMMON cannot be initialized at compile time. See if you can determine the reason why blank COMMON was designed this way. *Hint*: This design decision was made early in the development of FORTRAN, when computer memories were quite small.

5. Suppose you wish to write a subprogram that prints a heading on a new output page, along with a page number that is 1 in the first activation and that increases by 1 with each subsequent activation. Can this be done without parameters and without reference to nonlocal variables in Pascal? Can it be done in FORTRAN?

6. FORTRAN allows a subprogram to have multiple entry points. Why is this sometimes a valuable capability?

7. Write a Pascal procedure ADDER that adds two integer arrays together. It must have only two parameters, which have the two arrays to be added. The second array also will hold the sum array on exit. Both parameters must be passed by reference. Test ADDER with the call

```
ADDER (A, A)
```

where A is an array to be added to itself. Explain the results of running this program.

8. Consider the program in Section 8.5.2.5. Change the two assignments to the LIST array to:

```
LIST[1] := 3
LIST[2] := 1
```

Hand execute the new program under the following assumptions and compare the resulting values in the array LIST in BIGSUB after the return from SUB:
   a. parameters are passed by value
   b. parameters are passed by reference
   c. parameters are passed by name
   d. parameters are passed by value-result

9. Present one argument against providing both static and dynamic local variables in subprograms.

10. Argue against the C design of providing only function subprograms.

11. From a textbook on FORTRAN, learn the syntax and semantics of statement functions. Justify their existence in FORTRAN.

12. Study the methods of user-defined operator overloading in C++ and Ada and write a report comparing the two, using our criteria for evaluating languages.

9

Implementing Subprograms

John Kemeny

John Kemeny and his colleague Thomas Kurtz at Dartmouth, developed compilers for several dialects of ALGOL and FORTRAN in the early 1960s. In 1963, Kemeny began the design of BASIC which became operational in 1964.

Key Concepts

- Subprogram linkage
- Activation records
- Static chains
- Displays

- Deep access versus shallow access
- Referencing environments for subprograms passed as parameters

The purpose of this chapter is to explore methods for implementing subprograms in the major imperative languages. The discussion will provide the reader with some insight into how such languages "work," and also why ALGOL 60 was a challenge to the unsuspecting compiler authors of the early 1960s. We begin with the simplest kind of subprograms—those in FORTRAN 77—and progress to the more complicated subprograms of the static-scoped languages, such as Pascal. The increased difficulty of implementing subprograms in these languages is caused by the need to include support for recursion and for mechanisms to access nonlocal variables.

Two methods of accessing nonlocals in static-scoped languages, static chains and displays, are discussed in detail and compared. Techniques for implementing blocks are covered briefly. Several methods of implementing nonlocal variable access in a dynamic-scoped language are discussed. Finally, a method is described for implementing parameters that are subprogram names.

9.1 The General Semantics of Calls and Returns

The subprogram call and return operations of a language are together called its **subprogram linkage.** Any implementation method for subprograms must be based on the semantics of subprogram linkage.

A subprogram call in a typical contemporary imperative language has numerous actions associated with it. The call must include the parameter-passing mechanism for whatever method is used. If local variables are not static, the call must cause storage to be allocated for the locals declared in the called subprogram and bind those variables to that storage. It must save the execution status of the calling program unit. It must arrange to transfer control to the code of the subprogram and ensure that control can return to the proper place when the subprogram execution is completed. Finally, if static scoping is used, the call must cause some mechanism to be created to provide access to nonlocal variables that are visible to the called subprogram.

The required actions of a subprogram return are also complicated. If the subprogram has parameters that are out mode and are implemented by copy, the first action of the return process is to move the local values of the associated formal parameters to the actual parameters. Next it must deallocate the storage used for local variables. Some action must then be taken to return the mechanism used for nonlocal references to the configuration it had before the call. Finally, control must be returned to the calling program unit.

9.2 Implementing FORTRAN 77 Subprograms

We begin with the relatively simple situation of FORTRAN 77 subprograms. All referencing of nonlocal variables in FORTRAN 77 is through COMMON. COMMON is not connected to the subprogram linkage mechanism, so it is not discussed here. Another simplifying characteristic of FORTRAN 77 is the fact that subprograms cannot be recursive. Furthermore, in most implementations, variables declared in subprograms are statically allocated.

The semantics of a FORTRAN 77 subprogram call requires the following actions:

1. Save the execution status of the current program unit.
2. Carry out the parameter-passing process.
3. Pass the return address to the callee.
4. Transfer control to the callee.

The semantics of a FORTRAN 77 subprogram return requires the following actions:

1. If pass-by-value-result parameters are used, the current values of those parameters are moved to the corresponding actual parameters.
2. If the subprogram is a function, the functional value is moved to a place accessible to the caller.
3. The execution status of the caller is restored.
4. Control is transferred back to the caller.

The call and return actions require storage for the following:

1. Status information about the caller
2. Parameters
3. Return address
4. Functional value for function subprograms

These, along with the local variables and the subprogram code, form the complete set of information a subprogram needs to execute and then return control to the caller.

A FORTRAN 77 subprogram consists of two separate parts: The actual code of the subprogram, which is static, and the local variables and data listed above, which can change when the subprogram is executed. Note that both of these parts have fixed sizes.

The noncode part of a subprogram is associated with a particular execution, or activation, of the subprogram, and is therefore called an **activation record.** Because FORTRAN 77 does not support recursion, there can be only one active version of a given subprogram at a time. Therefore, there can be only a single instance of the activation record for a subprogram. One possible layout for FORTRAN 77 activation records is shown in Figure 9.1. The saved execution status of the caller is omitted simply because it is not relevant to our discussion.

Because the activation record for a FORTRAN 77 subprogram has fixed size, it can be statically allocated. In fact, it could be attached to the code part of a subprogram.

Figure 9.2 shows a FORTRAN 77 program consisting of COMMON storage, a main program, and three subroutines: A, B, and C. Note that although Figure 9.2 shows all the code segments separated from all of the data areas, in some cases the data areas are attached to their associated code segments.

The construction of the complete FORTRAN 77 program shown in the figure is not done entirely by the compiler. In fact, because of independent compilation, the four program units—MAIN, A, B, and C—may have been compiled on different days or even in different years. At the time each unit is compiled, the machine code for it, along with a list of references to external subprograms and COMMON variables within the code, is written to a file. The executable program shown in Figure 9.2 is put together by the linker, which is part of the operating system. (Sometimes linkers are called loaders, linker/loaders, or link editors.) When the linker is called for a main program, its first task is to find the files that contain the translated subprograms referenced in that program, along with their data areas, and load them into memory. It also must determine the size of all COMMON blocks and allocate storage for them. Then the linker must set the target addresses of all calls to those subprograms in the main program to the entry addresses of those subprograms. The same must be done for all calls to subprograms in the loaded subprograms and all calls to FORTRAN library subprograms. In the example above, the linker was called for MAIN. The linker had to find the machine code programs for A, B, and C, along with their data areas, and load them into memory with the code for MAIN. Then it had to patch in the

Figure 9.1
A FORTRAN 77 activation record format

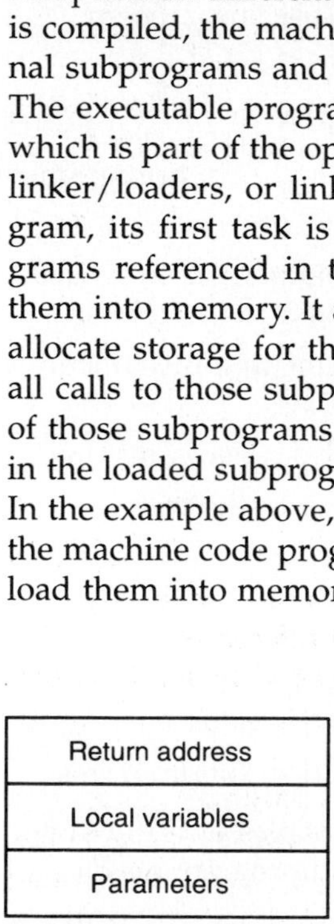

| Return address |
| Local variables |
| Parameters |

Figure 9.2
The code and activation records of a FORTRAN 77 program

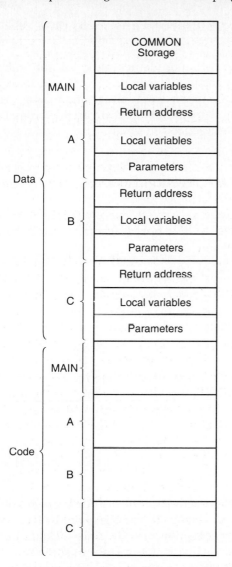

target addresses for all calls to A, B, C, and any library subprograms in A, B, C, and MAIN. Furthermore, all references to variables in COMMON had to be patched with the proper addresses. In many cases, references to COMMON variables are handled by offset addressing within the block, obviating the need for address patching.

FORTRAN 90 allows its subprograms to be both nested (using static scoping) and recursive, thereby requiring its implementation to be more like that of the block-structured languages. Implementation methods for these languages are discussed at length in the following section.

9.3 Implementing Subprograms in ALGOL-like Languages

We now examine the implementation of the subprogram linkage in ALGOL-like languages, focusing on the call and return operations required for increasingly complicated situations. Two related but different approaches to implementing nonlocal variable accesses, called static chains and displays, are described in detail.

9.3.1 More Complex Activation Records

Subprogram linkage in ALGOL-like languages is more complex than the linkage of FORTRAN 77 subprograms for the following reasons:

1. Parameters are usually passed by two different methods. For example, in Modula-2 they are passed by value or reference.

2. Variables declared in subprograms are often dynamically allocated.

3. Recursion adds the possibility of multiple simultaneous activations of a subprogram, which means there can be more than one instance (incomplete execution) of a subprogram at a given time, with one call from outside the subprogram and one or more recursive calls. Recursion, therefore, requires multiple instances of activation records, one for each subprogram activation that can exist at the same time. Each activation requires its own copy of the formal parameters and the dynamically allocated local variables, along with the return address.

4. Finally, ALGOL-like languages use static scoping to provide access to nonlocal variables. Support for these nonlocal accesses must be part of the linkage mechanism.

The format of an activation record for a given subprogram in a static-scoped language is known at compile time. In Pascal procedures, the size is also known for activation records, since all data local to a Pascal procedure is of fixed size. That is not the case in some other languages, in which the size of a local array can depend on the value of an actual parameter. In those cases, the format is static, but the size can be dynamic. An activation record format is a template for instances of the activation record. The form of the template is static; instances of it must be created dynamically. The typical activation record format for an ALGOL-like language is shown in Figure 9.3.

Local scalar variables are bound to storage within an activation record instance. Local variables that are structures are sometimes allocated elsewhere, and only their descriptors and a pointer to that storage are part of the activation record. The static link, which is sometimes called a static scope pointer, points to the activation record instance of an activation of the static parent. It is used for accesses to nonlocal variables. Static links are explained in detail in Section 9.3.4. The dynamic link is a pointer to an instance of the activation record of the caller. In static-scoped languages, this link is used in the destruction of the current activation record instance when the procedure completes its execution. The dynamic link is required because in some cases there are other allocations from the stack by a subprogram beyond its activation record. So, although the size of the activation record may be known, the size cannot simply be subtracted from the stack top pointer to remove the activation record. The return address often consists of a pointer to the code segment of the caller and an offset address in that code segment of the instruction following the call. The actual parameters in the activation record are the values or addresses provided by the caller.

Consider the following skeletal Pascal procedure:

```
procedure sub (var total : real; part : integer);
  var list : array [1..5] of integer;
  sum : real;
  begin
  ...
  end;
```

The activation record format for sub is shown in Figure 9.4.

Activating a procedure requires the dynamic creation of an instance of the activation record for the procedure. As stated earlier, the format of the activation record is fixed at compile time, although its size may depend on the call. (In the case of the example procedure, sub, the size of the activation record is fixed.) Because the call and return semantics specify that the subprogram last called is the first completed, it is reasonable to create instances of these activation records on a stack. Every procedure activation, whether recursive or nonrecursive, creates a new instance of an activation record on

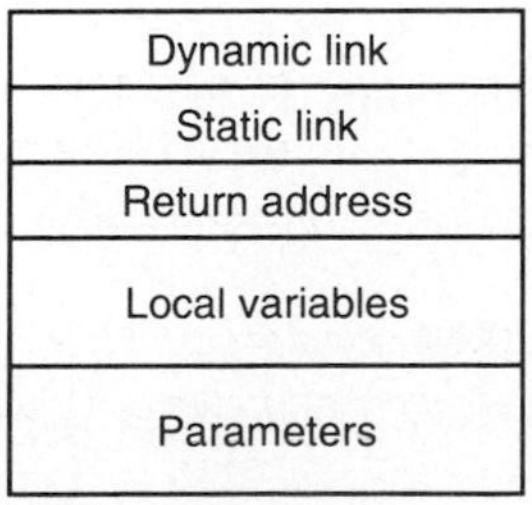

Dynamic link	
Static link	
Return address	
Local	list [1]
Local	list [2]
Local	list [3]
Local	list [4]
Local	list [5]
Local	sum
Parameter	total
Parameter	part

Dynamic link
Static link
Return address
Local variables
Parameters

Figure 9.3
A typical activation record format for an ALGOL-like language

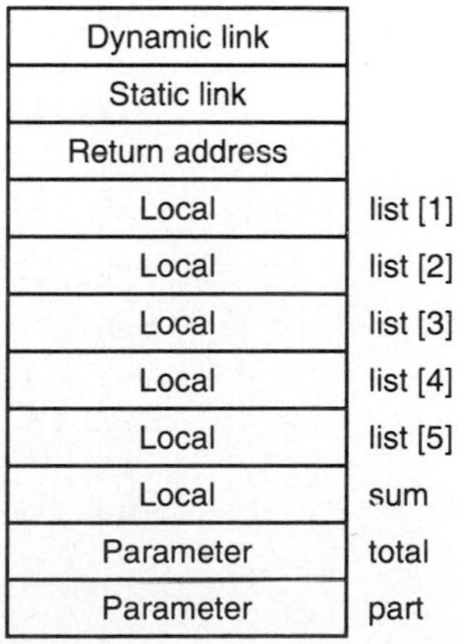

Figure 9.4
The activation record format for procedure sub

the stack. This provides the required separate copies of the parameters, local variables, and the return address.

Recall from Chapter 8 that a subprogram is **active** from the time it is called until the time that execution is completed. At the time it becomes inactive, its local scope is terminated and its referencing environment is no longer meaningful. So, at that time, its activation record instance is destroyed.

9.3.2   An Example Without Recursion and Nonlocal References

Because of the complexity of implementing subprogram linkage, we consider it in several stages. First we examine an example program that does not reference nonlocal variables and has no recursive calls. For this example, the static link is not used. We later consider how recursion and nonlocal referencing can be implemented.

Consider the following skeletal example program:

```
program MAIN_1;
  var P : real;
  procedure A (X : integer);
    var Y : boolean;
    procedure C (Q : boolean);
      begin
      ...        <---------------------------3
      end;   { of procedure C }
    begin
    ...          <---------------------------2
    C (Y);
    ...
    end;   { of procedure A }
  procedure B (R : real);
    var S, T : integer;
    begin
    ...          <---------------------------1
    A (S);
    ...
    end;   { of procedure B }
  begin   { MAIN_1 program body }
  ...
  B (P);
  ...
  end.   { of MAIN_1 program }
```

The sequence of procedure calls in this program is

```
MAIN_1 calls B
B calls A
A calls C
```

The stack contents for the points labeled 1, 2, and 3 are shown in Figure 9.5.

At point 1, only the activation record instances for program MAIN_1 and procedure B are on the stack. When B calls A, an instance of A's activation record is created on the stack. When A calls C, an instance of C's activation record is created on the stack. When C's execution ends, the instance of its activation record is removed from the stack, and the dynamic link is used to reset the stack top pointer. A similar process takes place when procedures A and B terminate. After the return from the call to B from MAIN_1, the stack has only the instance of the activation record of MAIN_1. Note that some

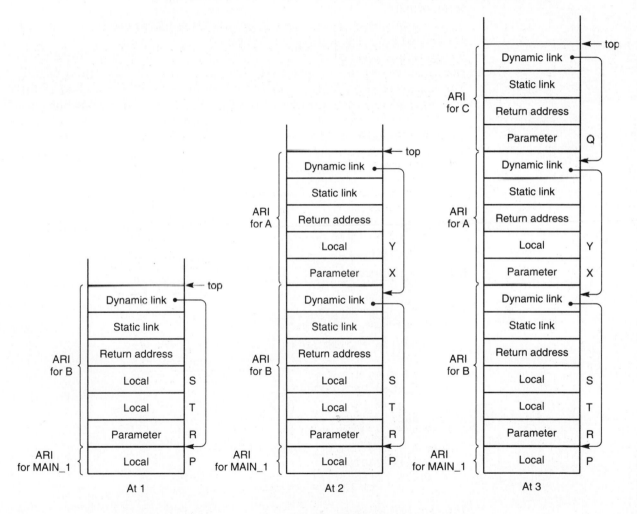

ARI = Activation Record Instance

Figure 9.5
Stack contents for three points in a program

implementations do not actually use an activation record instance on the stack for MAIN_1, such as the one shown in the figure. However, it can be done this way, and it simplifies both the implementation and our discussion.

The collection of dynamic links present in the stack at a given time is called the **dynamic chain,** or **call chain.** It represents the dynamic history of how execution got to its current position, which is always in the procedure code whose activation record instance is on top of the stack. References to local variables can be represented in the code as offsets from the beginning of the activation record of the local scope. Such an offset is called a **local_offset.**

The local_offset of a variable in an activation record can be determined at compile time, using the order, types, and sizes of variables declared in the procedure associated with the activation record. To simplify the discussion, assume that all variables take one position in the activation record. The first local variable declared in a procedure would be allocated in the activation record three positions from the top (the first three positions are for the dynamic and static links and the return address). The second local variable declared would be four positions from the top and so forth. For example, consider the preceding example program. In A, the local_offset of Y is 3. Likewise, in B, the local_offset of S is 3; for T it is 4.

9.3.3 Recursion

Consider the following example program, which uses recursion to compute the factorial function:

```
program TEST;
  var VALUE : integer;

  function FACTORIAL (N : integer);
    begin    <----------------------------1
    if N <= 1
      then FACTORIAL := 1
      else FACTORIAL := N * FACTORIAL (N - 1);
    end;      <--------------------------2

begin { beginning of body of TEST }
VALUE := FACTORIAL (3);
writeln ("factorial of 3 is:", VALUE)<----3
end.
```

The activation record format for the function FACTORIAL is shown in Figure 9.6. Notice that it has an additional entry for the returned value of the function.

Figure 9.6
The activation record
format for `factorial`

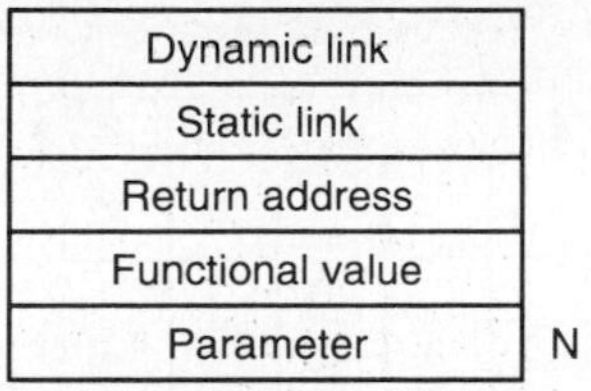

Dynamic link
Static link
Return address
Functional value
Parameter

N

Figure 9.7 on the following page shows the contents of the stack for the three times that execution reaches position 1 in the function FACTORIAL. Each shows one more activation of the function, with its functional value undefined. The first activation record instance has the return address to the calling program, TEST. The others have a return address to the function itself; these are for the recursive calls.

Figure 9.8 (p. 349) shows the stack contents for the three times that execution reaches position 2 in the function FACTORIAL. Recall that the code for the function multiplies the current value of the parameter, N, times the value returned by the recursive call to the function. The first return from FACTORIAL returns the value 1. The activation record instance for that activation has a value of 1 for its version of the parameter N. The result from that multiplication, 1, is then returned to the second activation of FACTORIAL to be multiplied by its parameter value for N, which is 2. This returns the value 2 to the first activation of FACTORIAL and multiplies it by its parameter value for N, which is 3, yielding the final functional value of 6, which is then returned to the first call to FACTORIAL in TEST.

9.3.4 Mechanisms for Implementing Nonlocal References

There are two major implementation mechanisms for creating accesses to nonlocal variables in a static-scoped language: static chains and displays. Both of these are examined in detail in the following sections.

A reference to a nonlocal variable requires a two-step access process. All variables that can be nonlocally accessed are in activation record instances and therefore are somewhere in the stack. The first step of the access process is to find the instance of the activation record in the stack where the variable was allocated. The second part is to use the local_offset of the variable (within the activation record instance) to actually access it.

Finding the correct activation record instance is the more interesting and more difficult of the two steps. First note that in a given subprogram, only variables that are declared in static ancestor scopes can be nonlocally accessed. Also, activation record instances of all of the static ancestors are guaranteed to exist on the stack when variables in them are referenced by a nested procedure. This is guaranteed by the semantic rules of the static-

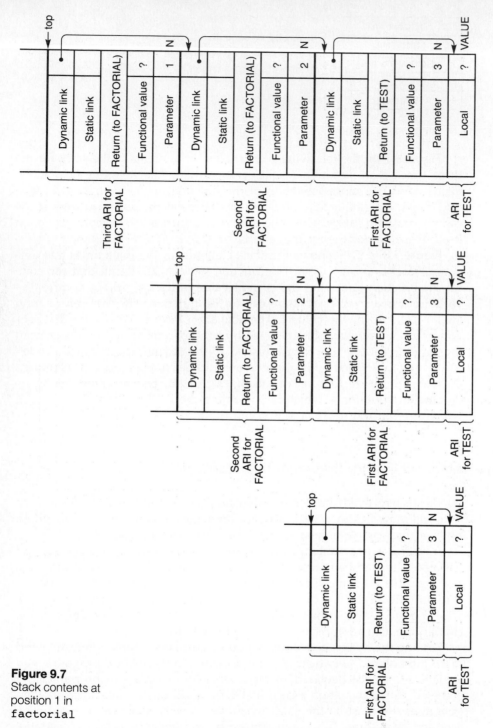

Figure 9.7
Stack contents at
position 1 in
`factorial`

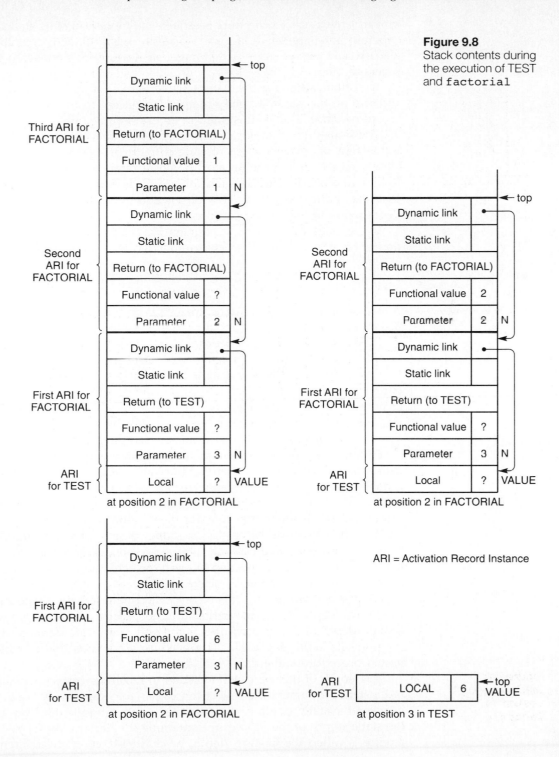

Figure 9.8
Stack contents during the execution of TEST and `factorial`

ARI = Activation Record Instance

scoped languages: A procedure is callable only when all of its static ancestor program units are active. If a static ancestor were not active, its local variables would not be bound to storage, so it would be nonsense to allow access to them.

Note that although the parent scope activation record must have an instance on the stack, it need not appear adjacent to the child's activation record instance. This is illustrated in an example below.

The semantics of nonlocal references dictate that the correct declaration is the first one found when looking through the enclosing scopes, most closely nested first. So to support nonlocal references, it must be possible to find all of the instances of activation records in the stack that correspond to those static ancestors. This observation leads to the two methods described in the following sections.

In the following sections, we assume we are dealing with languages that do not have blocks, so all scopes are defined by subprograms.

9.3.4.1   Static Chains

A **static chain** is a chain of static links that connect certain activation record instances in the stack.

During the execution of a procedure P, the static link of its activation record instance points to an activation record instance of P's static parent program unit. That instance's static link points, in turn, to P's static grandparent program unit's activation record instance, if there is one. So the static chain links all the static ancestors of an executing subprogram, in order of static parent first. This chain can obviously be used to implement the accesses to nonlocal variables in static-scoped languages.

Finding the correct activation record instance of a nonlocal variable using static links is relatively straightforward. When a reference is made to a nonlocal variable, the activation record instance containing the variable can be found by searching the static chain until a static ancestor activation record instance is found that contains the variable. However, it is much easier than that. Because the nesting of scopes is known at compile time, the compiler can determine not only that a reference is nonlocal, but also the length of the static chain needed to reach the activation record instance that actually contains the nonlocal object.

Let **static_depth** be an integer associated with a static scope that indicates how deeply it is nested in the outermost scope. The main program has a static_depth of 0. If procedure A is the only procedure defined in a main program, its static_depth is 1. If procedure A contains the definition of a nested procedure B, then B's static_depth is 2.

The length of the static chain needed to reach the correct activation record instance for a nonlocal reference to a variable X is exactly the difference between the static_depth of the procedure containing the reference to X and the static_depth of the procedure containing the declaration for X. This difference is called the **nesting_depth,** or **chain_offset,** of the reference. The actual reference can be represented by an ordered pair of integers (chain_offset, local_offset), where chain_offset is the number of links to the correct activation record instance (local_offset is described in Section 9.3.2). For example, consider the following skeletal program:

```
program A;
  procedure B;
    procedure C;
      ...
    end;  { of procedure C }
    ...
  end;  { of procedure B }
  ...
end;  { of program A }
```

The static_depths of A, B, and C are 0, 1, and 2, respectively. If procedure C references a variable declared in A, the chain_offset of that reference would be 2 (static_depth of C minus the static_depth of A). If procedure C references a variable declared in B, the chain_offset of that reference would be 1. References to locals can be handled using the same mechanism, with a chain offset of zero.

To illustrate the complete process of nonlocal accesses, consider the following skeletal program in Pascal:

```
program MAIN_2;
  var X : integer;
  procedure BIGSUB;
    var A, B, C : integer;
    procedure SUB1;
      var A, D : integer;
      begin
      A := B + C;        <---------------------1
      ...
      end;  { of procedure SUB1 }
    procedure SUB2;
      var B, E : integer;
      procedure SUB3;
        var C, E : integer;
        begin
        ...
        SUB1;
        ...
        E := B + A;        <------------------2
        end;  { of procedure SUB3 }
      begin
      ...
      SUB3;
      ...
      A := D + E;        <---------------------3
      end;  { of procedure SUB2 }
```

```
        begin   { BIGSUB }
        ...
        SUB2;
        ...
        end;    { of procedure BIGSUB }
      begin
      ...
      BIGSUB;
      ...
      end.   { of MAIN_2 }
```

The sequence of procedure calls is:

```
MAIN_2 calls BIGSUB
BIGSUB calls SUB2
SUB2 calls SUB3
SUB3 calls SUB1
```

The stack situation at this first arrival at point 1 in this program is shown in Figure 9.9.

At position 1 in procedure SUB1, the reference is to the local variable A, not to the nonlocal variable A from BIGSUB. This reference to A has the chain_offset/local_offset pair (0, 3). The reference to B is to the nonlocal B from BIGSUB. It can be represented by the pair (1, 4). The local_offset is 4, because a 3 offset would be the first variable, as explained above. Notice that if the dynamic link were used to do a simple search for an activation record instance with a declaration for the variable B, it would find the variable B declared in SUB2, which would be incorrect. If the (1, 4) pair were used with the dynamic chain, the variable E from SUB3 would be used. The static link, however, points to the activation record for BIGSUB, which has the correct version of B. The variable B in SUB2 is not in the referencing environment at this point and is (correctly) not accessible.

After SUB1 completes its execution, the activation record instance for SUB1 is removed from the stack, and control returns to SUB3. The reference to the variable E at position 2 in SUB3 is local and uses the pair (0, 4) for access. The reference to the variable B is to the one declared in SUB2, because that is the nearest static ancestor that contains such a declaration. It is accessed with the pair (1, 3). The reference to the variable A is to the A declared in BIGSUB, because neither SUB3 nor its static parent SUB2 has a declaration for a variable named A. It is referenced with the pair (2, 3).

After SUB3 completes its execution, the activation record instance for SUB3 is removed from the stack, leaving only the activation record instances for MAIN_2, BIGSUB, and SUB2. At position 3 in SUB2, the reference to the variable A is to the A in BIGSUB, which has the only declaration of A among the active routines. This access is made with the pair (1, 3). At this position, there is no visible scope containing a declaration for the variable D, so this reference to D is a static semantics error. The error would be detected when the compiler attempted to compute the chain_offset/local_offset pair. The reference to E is to the local E in SUB2.

Figure 9.9
Stack contents at position 1 in the program MAIN_2

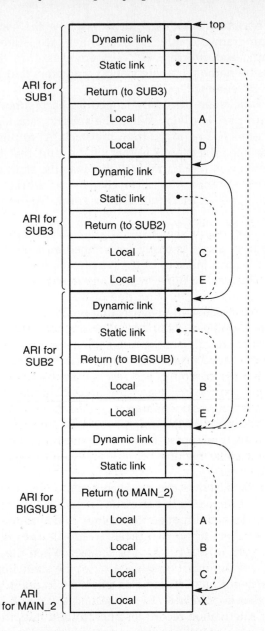

ARI = Activation Record Instance

In summary, the references to the variable A at points 1, 2, and 3 would be represented by the following points:

- (0, 3) (local)
- (2, 3) (two levels away)
- (1, 3) (one level away)

It is reasonable at this point to ask how the static chain is maintained during program execution. If its maintenance is too complex, the fact that it is simple and effective will be unimportant. In this section, we assume that pass-by-name parameters and parameters that are subprogram names are not implemented.

The static chain must be changed for each subprogram call and return. The return part is trivial: When the subprogram terminates, its activation record instance is removed from the stack. After this removal, the new top activation record instance is that of the unit that called the subprogram whose execution just terminated. Because the static chain from this activation record instance was never changed, it works correctly just as it did before the call to the other subprogram. Therefore, no other action is required.

The action required at a subprogram call is more complex. Although the correct parent scope is easily determined at compile time, the most recent activation record instance of the parent scope must be found at the time of the call. This can be done by looking at activation record instances on the dynamic chain until the first one of the parent scope is found. However, this search can be avoided by treating procedure declarations and references exactly as variable declarations and references. When the compiler encounters a procedure call, among other things, it determines the procedure that declared the called procedure, which must be a static ancestor of the calling routine. It then computes the nesting_depth, or the number of enclosing scopes between the caller and the procedure that declared the called procedure. This information is stored and can be accessed by the procedure call during execution. At the time of the call, the static link of the called procedure's activation record instance is determined by moving down the static chain of the caller the number of links equal to the nesting depth computed at compile time.

Figure 9.10 shows the stack contents of the example program above, MAIN_2, as it appeared in Figure 9.9, except before the call to SUB1 by SUB3. At the call to SUB1 in SUB3, the compiler determines the nesting_depth of SUB3 (the caller) to be two levels inside the procedure that declared the called procedure, SUB1, which is BIGSUB. When the call to SUB1 in SUB3 is executed, this information is used to set the static link of the activation record instance for SUB1. This static link is set to point to the activation record instance that is pointed to by the second static link in the static chain from the caller's activation record instance. In this case, the caller is SUB3, whose static link points to its parent's activation record instance (that of SUB2). The static link of the activation record instance for SUB2 points to the activation record instance for BIGSUB. So the static link for the new activation record instance for SUB1 is set to point to the activation record instance for BIGSUB. This method works for all procedure linkage, except when parameters that are subprogram names are involved. That situation is discussed in Section 9.6.

Figure 9.10
Stack contents just
before the call of SUB1
in SUB3 in program
MAIN_2

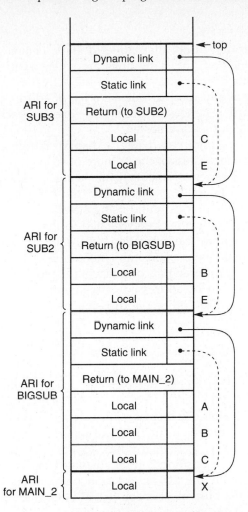

ARI = Activation Record Instance

One criticism of using the static chain to access nonlocal variables is that references to variables in scopes beyond the static parent are costly. The static chain must be followed, one link per enclosing scope from the reference to the declaration, to accomplish the access. Another criticism is that it is difficult for a programmer working on a time-critical program to estimate the costs of nonlocal references, since the cost of each reference depends on the depth of nesting between the reference and the scope of declaration. Further complicating this problem is the fact that subsequent code modifications may change nesting depths, thereby changing the timing of some references, both in the changed code and possibly in code far from the changes.

9.3.4.2 Displays

The only widely used alternative to static chains is the display method. With this method, the static links are collected in a single array called a **display,** rather than being stored in the activation records. The contents of the display at any specific time are a list of addresses of the accessible activation record instances in the stack—one for each active scope—in the order in which they are nested.

Accesses to nonlocals using a display requires exactly two steps for every access, regardless of the number of scope levels between the reference and the declaration of the variable being accessed. These two steps are accomplished as follows: The link to the correct activation record, which resides in the display, is found using a statically computed value called the display_offset, which is closely related to the static chain chain_offset. The local_offset within the activation record instance is computed and used exactly as with static chain implementations. A nonlocal reference is represented by an ordered pair of integers (display_offset, local_offset). A nonlocal variable can be addressed conveniently and quickly with two applications of an offset-indirect addressing mode, which many contemporary computers have.

Every subprogram call and return requires that the display be modified to reflect the new scope situation. We now investigate the actions required to maintain the display. Once again, we assume that parameters are not subprogram names and that pass-by-name parameters are not involved. The more complex case is considered in Section 9.6.

First, note that the display_offset depends only on the static_depth of the procedure in which the nonlocal reference appears. If the static_depth of procedure P is 2, then the link to P's activation record instance will always appear in position 2 in the display. Display entries begin at the subscript of 0, with the zeroth position being used for access to variables declared in the outermost scope (usually the main program).

In general, the pointer at position k of the display points to an activation record instance for a procedure with a static_depth of k. The display modification required for a call to procedure P, which has a static_depth of k, is

1. Save, in the new activation record instance, a copy of the pointer at position k in the display.
2. Place the link to the activation record instance for P at position k in the display.

Subprogram termination requires the saved pointer in the activation record instance of the terminating subprogram to be placed back in the display. Then the activation record instance is removed from the stack, as with the static chain implementation.

To see that the two simple steps of display modification for procedure calls are correct, we examine the three possible situations defined by considering a call to procedure P by procedure Q. Let Psd be the static_depth of P and Qsd be the static_depth of Q. The three cases are defined as follows:

1. Qsd = Psd
2. Qsd < Psd
3. Qsd > Psd

We use the following program, which is a skeletal version of the program of our earlier example, MAIN_2, to examine these three cases:

```
program MAIN_3;
  procedure BIGSUB;
    procedure SUB1;
      . . .
      end;  { SUB1 }
    procedure SUB2;
      procedure SUB3;
        . . .
        end;  { SUB3 }
      . . .
      end;  { SUB2 }
    . . .
    end;  { BIGSUB }
  end.  { MAIN_3 }
```

The first case would occur if SUB2 called SUB1, because they are both at a depth level of 2. The stack and display for the situation for just before and just after the call are shown in Figure 9.11.

The call, as always, requires that the new activation record instance for SUB1 be added to the stack. The new referencing environment includes only

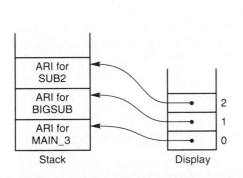

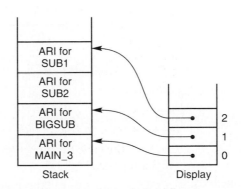

a. MAIN_3 calls BIGSUB; BIGSUB calls SUB2   **b.** SUB2 calls SUB1

ARI = Activation Record Instance

Figure 9.11
Display modification for callers and callees with equal depth values

SUB1, BIGSUB, and MAIN_3. Because the static_depth values of SUB1 and SUB2 are equal, their display links must occupy the same position in the display, that is, their display offsets must be equal. Because the display links are always saved in the new activation record instance, this is no problem. In this case, therefore, the display entry for SUB2 must be removed. The new display entry for SUB1 is then inserted into its proper position, which is position 2, the static_depth of SUB1. When SUB1 completes its execution and returns control to SUB2, the display entry for SUB2 must be restored. Just before the activation record instance for SUB1 is removed from the stack, the saved display entry is moved from the instance to the display.

The second case would occur if SUB2 called SUB3. The static_depth value of SUB2 is 2, and for SUB3 it is 3. The stack and display for the situations just before the call and just after the call are shown in Figure 9.12. In this case, the new activation record instance is created on the stack, as usual, but the referencing environment simply grows by one new scope, that of the called subprogram. Thus, the new pointer can be simply added to the display. This particular example does not require that the existing pointer in the display at the position of the new pointer be saved. However, this is not true in general. Other situations of the same case do require that the existing display pointer be saved. It is easier simply to save the existing pointer each time than it is to determine at every subprogram call whether it must be saved. As an example of a situation in which the pointer must

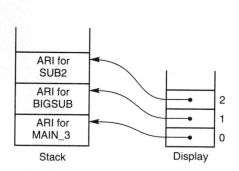

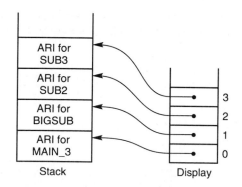

a. MAIN calls BIGSUB; BIGSUB calls SUB2   **b.** SUB2 calls SUB3

ARI = Activation Record Instance

Figure 9.12
Display modifications for callers with smaller depth values than the callee

be saved, suppose there were a subprogram, SUB4, defined in SUB1 in our example, as shown below:

```
program MAIN_4;
  procedure BIGSUB;
    procedure SUB1;
      procedure SUB4;
        . . .
        end; { SUB4 }
      . . .
      end;  { SUB1 }
    procedure SUB2;
      procedure SUB3;
        . . .
        end;  { SUB3 }
      . . .
      end;  { SUB2 }
    . . .
    end;  { BIGSUB }
  end.  { MAIN_4 }
```

Suppose execution produced the following sequence of subprogram calls:

```
MAIN_4 calls BIGSUB
BIGSUB calls SUB2
SUB2 calls SUB3
SUB3 calls SUB1
```

The result would be the stack and display contents shown in Figure 9.13.

Now suppose SUB1 calls SUB4. This is an example of a subprogram calling a subprogram with a larger static_depth. In this case, the display pointer for SUB3 is at the position where SUB4's pointer must be placed in the display. They both have a static_depth of 3. Therefore, the existing display

Figure 9.13
Stack and display before SUB1 calls SUB4 in MAIN_4. Dashed lines indicate inactive pointers

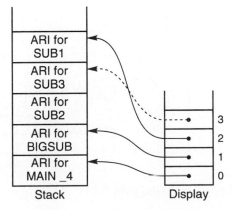

ARI = Activation Record Instance

pointer must be saved before the new pointer is placed in the display. The correct stack and display for the execution of SUB4 is shown in Figure 9.14.

The third case is illustrated by a call to SUB1 from SUB3. The procedure SUB3 has a static_depth of 3 and that of SUB1 is 2. The stack and display values for just before the call and just after the call are shown in Figure 9.15.

In this case, it appears that two display elements must be temporarily removed: those for SUB2 and SUB3, which are not in the referencing environment of SUB1. However, only one must actually be removed, the one for SUB2. The pointer for SUB3 can remain in the display. Variable references in

Figure 9.14
Stack and display after SUB1 calls SUB4 in program MAIN_4

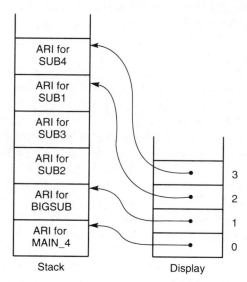

ARI = Activation Record Instance

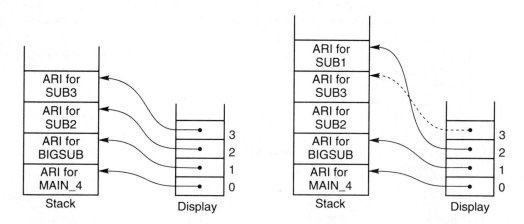

a. MAIN_4 calls BIGSUB; BIGSUB calls SUB2; SUB2 calls SUB3   **b.** SUB3 calls SUB1

Figure 9.15
Display modification for callers with larger depth values than their callees

SUB1 will not use the SUB3 display pointer because the SUB3 variables are not visible to SUB1; thus, leaving the pointer in the display is safe. The compiler cannot generate code that will access display entries above the entry for the current active subprogram.

The display can be stored as a run-time static array in memory. The maximum size of the display, which is the maximum static_depth of any subprogram in the program, can be determined by the compiler. Storing the display in memory works reasonably well as long as the machine has indirect addressing through memory locations. Nonlocal accesses, then, cost one more memory cycle than local accesses, which can use direct addressing. An alternative is to place the display in registers, assuming the machine has a sufficient number of registers. In this case, accesses do not require the extra memory cycle.

We can now compare the static chaining and display methods. In an implementation such as we have described, references to local variables would be slower with a display than with static chains if the display is not stored in registers, because all references must go through display entries—a process that adds a level of indirection. This indirection can easily be avoided when static chains are used. At a cost of slightly increased compiler complexity, however, the display method can also be made to avoid indirection for access to locals, so this is not a real difference.

References to nonlocals that are only one static level away take the same time for both methods, but if they are more than one static level away they will be faster with a display, since no chain needs to be followed. The task of estimating the time required for a nonlocal reference is trivial when a display is used—the time is equal for all nonlocal references. For time-critical code, this is an advantage of displays over static chains.

The maintenance at a procedure call is faster with static chains, unless the called procedure is more than a few static levels away. In that case, extra time is required to follow the static chain of the caller to the activation record instance of the declarer of the called procedure. The maintenance of a procedure return has fixed cost with both methods, with static chaining always being slightly faster. The display must be restored when the subprogram terminates.

Overall, displays are better if there is deep static nesting and many references to distant nonlocal variables. Static chaining is better if there are few nesting levels and few references to distant nonlocal variables, which is the more common situation. Note that experiments indicate that nesting levels rarely exceed three in practice.

9.4 Blocks

Recall from Chapter 4 that several languages, including Ada and C, provide for user-specified local scopes for variables called blocks. As an example of a block, consider the following C code segment:

```
    { int index;
    for (index = 0; index <= last; index++)
      {
        ...
      }
    }
```

A block is specified in C as a segment of code that begins with one or more data declarations and is enclosed in braces. The lifetime of the variable `index` in the block above begins when the **for** begins execution and ends when the loop terminates. This example creates a local counting variable, `index`, for the **for** statement. The advantage of using such a local is that it cannot interfere with any other variable with the same name that is declared elsewhere in the program.

Blocks can be implemented by using the process we described for implementing Pascal procedures. Blocks are treated as parameterless procedures that are always called from the same place in the program. One disadvantage of this is that as maximum nesting grows, required display size grows along with it. For a display to be stored in registers, it must be relatively small. So requiring display cells for blocks can cause the display to be stored in memory rather than in registers, causing considerable slowing of references to nonlocal variables.

Blocks can also be implemented in a different and somewhat simpler way. The maximum amount of storage required for block variables at any time during the execution of a program can be statically determined, because blocks are entered and exited in strictly textual order. This amount of space can be allocated next to the local variables in the activation record. Offsets for all block variables can be statically computed, so block variables can be addressed exactly as if they were local variables.

For example, consider the following skeletal program:

```
MAIN_5 ()
  { int x, y, z;
    while ( ... )
      { int a, b, c;
        ...
        while ( ... )
          { int d, e;
            ...
          }
      }
    while ( ... )
      { int f, g;
        ...
      }
    ...
  }
```

For this program, the static memory layout shown in Figure 9.16 could be used.

Figure 9.16
Block variable storage
when blocks are not
treated as parameter-
less procedures

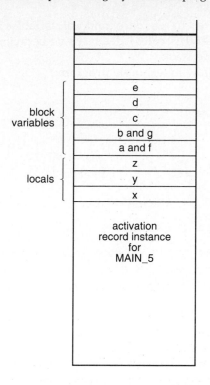

9.5 Implementing Dynamic Scoping

There are at least two distinct ways in which nonlocal references in a dynamic-scoped language can be implemented: deep access and shallow access. Note that deep and shallow accesses are not concepts related to deep and shallow binding. The most important difference is that deep and shallow bindings result in different semantics; deep and shallow accesses result in the same semantics.

9.5.1 Deep Access

When a program in a language that uses dynamic scoping refers to a nonlocal variable, the reference can be resolved by searching through the declarations in the other subprograms that are currently active, beginning with the one most recently activated. This concept is somewhat similar to that of accessing nonlocal variables in a static-scoped language, except that the dynamic—rather than the static—chain is followed. The dynamic chain links together all subprogram activation record instances in the reverse of the order in which they were activated. Therefore, the dynamic chain is exactly what is needed to reference nonlocal variables in a dynamic-scoped language. This method is called **deep access** because access may require searching deep in the stack.

Consider the following example program:

```
procedure A;
    integer v, w;
    begin
    ...
    end;
procedure B;
    integer w, x;
    begin
    ...
    end;
procedure C;
    integer x, z;
    begin
    x := u + v;
    ...
    end;
program MAIN_6;
    integer v, u;
    begin
    ...
    end;
```

Now suppose the following sequence of procedure calls occur:

```
MAIN_6 calls A
A calls A
A calls B
B calls C
```

Figure 9.17 shows the stack during the execution of procedure C after this calling sequence. Notice that the activation record instances do not have static links, which would serve no purpose in a dynamic-scoped language.

Consider the references to the variables x, u, and v in procedure C. The reference to x is found in the activation record instance for C. The reference to u is found by searching *all* the activation record instances on the stack, because the only existing variable with that name is in MAIN_6. This involves following four dynamic links and examining ten variable names. The reference to v is found in the most recent (closest on the dynamic chain) activation record instance for the procedure A.

There are two important differences between the deep access method for nonlocal access in a dynamic-scoped language and the static chain method for static-scoped languages. First, in a dynamic-scoped language, there is no way to determine at compile time the length of the chain that must be searched. Every activation record instance in the chain must be searched

Figure 9.17
Stack contents for a
dynamic scoped
program

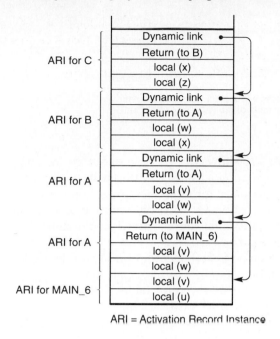

ARI = Activation Record Instance

until the first instance of the variable is found. This is one reason why dynamic-scoped languages typically have slower execution speeds than static-scoped languages. Second, activation records must store the names of variables, whereas in static-scoped language implementations, only the values are required. The names are needed for the search process.

9.5.2 Shallow Access

Shallow access is an alternative implementation method, not an alternative semantics. As stated above, the semantics of deep access and shallow access are identical. In the shallow access method, variables declared in subprograms are not stored in the activation records of those subprograms. Because with dynamic scoping there is at most one visible version of a variable of any specific name at a given time, a very different approach can be taken. One variation of shallow access is to have a separate stack for each variable name in a complete program. Every time a new variable with a particular name is created by a declaration at the beginning of a subprogram activation, it is given a cell on the stack for its name. Every reference to the name is to the variable on top of the stack, because it is the most recently created. When a subprogram terminates, the lifetime of its local variables ends and the stacks for those variable names are popped. This method allows very fast references to variables, but maintaining the stacks at the entrances and exits of subprograms is expensive.

Figure 9.18
One method of using shallow access to implement dynamic scoping

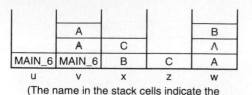

(The name in the stack cells indicate the program units of the variable declaration)

Figure 9.18 shows the variable stacks for the above example program in the same situation as shown with the stack in Figure 9.17.

Another option for implementing shallow access is to use a central table that has a location for each different variable name in a program. Along with each entry, a bit called **active** is maintained that indicates whether the name has a current binding or variable association. Any access to any variable can then be to an offset into the central table. The offset is static, so the access can be fast.

Maintenance of a central table is straightforward. A subprogram call requires that all of its local variables be logically placed in the central table. If the position of the new variable in the central table is already active— that is, if it contains a variable whose lifetime has not yet ended (which is indicated by the active bit)—that value must be saved somewhere during the lifetime of the new variable. Whenever a variable begins its lifetime, the active bit in its central table position must be set.

There have been several variations in the design of the central table and in the way values are stored when they are temporarily replaced. One variation is to have a "hidden" stack on which all saved objects are stored. Because subprogram calls and returns, and thus the lifetimes of local variables, are nested, this works well.

The second variation is perhaps the cleanest and least expensive to implement. A central table of single cells is used, and replaced variables are stored in the activation record of the subprogram that created the replacement variable. This is a stack mechanism, but one that already exists, so the new overhead is minimal.

9.6 Implementing Parameters That Are Subprogram Names

Parameters that are subprogram names were discussed at length in Chapter 8. Recall that static-scoped languages use a method called deep binding to associate a referencing environment with the activation of a subprogram that was passed as a parameter. We now investigate how deep binding can be implemented using the static chain and display methods.

9.6.1   Static Chaining

Suppose static chaining is used in the implementation. A subprogram that passes a subprogram name as a parameter must have in its static ancestry the unit in which that subprogram was declared; if it does not, the name of the subprogram to be passed will not be visible and the compiler will detect this as a syntax error. So, for syntactically correct calls, the compiler can simply pass the link to the static parent of the subprogram to be passed, along with the subprogram name. The activation record instance of the subprogram that is passed is then initialized with this link in its static link field, instead of a link derived in the usual way. Terminating the passed subprogram does not require any actions different from those for any other subprogram activation.

9.6.2   Displays

Now suppose a display, rather than static chaining, is used. Recall that we specifically stated that the display maintenance process described in Section 9.3.4.2 was correct only in the absence of subprogram name parameters (and some other features). Maintenance for calls without these involves the simple replacement of a single display pointer. When a parameter is a subprogram name, pointers to all the static ancestors of that subprogram must be placed in the display, thus requiring that that number of old display pointers be saved. Because the static environment of an activation of a subprogram that has been passed as a parameter may have little relationship to the static environment of the subprogram in which it is called, in many cases the entire display needs to be replaced. In many implementations, the entire existing display is saved for every call to a subprogram that has been passed as a parameter, often in the activation record instance of the subprogram in execution. When the passed subprogram terminates, the complete saved display replaces the display used for the passed subprogram's execution.

9.6.3   Referencing Environment Confusion Revisited

Now that activation records and implementation methods have been covered, we can expand somewhat on a problem introduced in Chapter 8: the possible misunderstanding concerning which referencing environment is correct when a subprogram that was passed as a parameter is executed. For example, consider the following skeletal program, which is a variation of one found in Ghezzi and Jazayeri (1987):

```
program MAIN_7;
  procedure SUB1;
    begin
    ...
    end;  { of procedure SUB1 }
  procedure SUB2 (procedure SUBX);
    var SUM : real;
    procedure SUB3;
      ...
      begin    { of procedure SUB3}
      SUM := 0.0;
      ...
      end;   { of procedure SUB3 }
    begin  { of procedure SUB2 }
    SUBX;
    SUB2 (SUB3);
    ...
    end;  { of procedure SUB2 }
  begin  { MAIN_7 }
  ...
  SUB2 (SUB1);
  ...
  end.   { MAIN_7 }
```

MAIN_7 calls SUB2, sending SUB1 as a parameter. SUB2 then calls the passed procedure, SUB1. Upon return from SUB1, SUB2 calls itself, sending its own procedure, SUB3, as a parameter. There are now two instances of the activation record for SUB2 on the stack, with the topmost being for the recursive call. The topmost activation of SUB2 then calls SUB3. When SUB3 uses the variable SUM, there are two versions of it, one for each activation of SUB2, where it is declared. Because the referencing environment of SUB3 is that of the caller that sent SUB3 as a parameter, it is the first activation of SUB2, not the most recent. This is indeed not apparent to the casual reader of the program.

This is admittedly a contrived example. However, the same kind of situation could occur in more realistic programs. The problem is that, although intuitively it may seem that the most recent activation should be the referencing environment, that is not always the case.

Figure 9.19 shows the stack during the execution of SUB3 of the preceding example program.

SUMMARY

Subprogram linkage semantics requires many actions by the implementation. In the case of FORTRAN 77, these actions are relatively simple for the following reasons: the lack of nonlocal references, other than through COM-

Figure 9.19
Stack contents for the
example program
MAIN_7, with a param-
eter that is a
subprogram

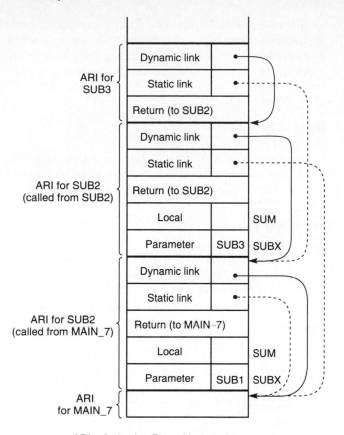

ARI = Activation Record Instance

MON; the fact that local variables are usually static; and the absence of recursion. In the ALGOL-like languages, subprogram linkage is far more complex. This follows from the requirements of nonlocal accesses through static scoping, semidynamic local variables, and recursion.

Subprograms in ALGOL-like languages have two components: the actual code, which is static, and the activation record, which is dynamic. Activation record instances contain the formal parameters and local variables, among other things.

Static chains and displays are the two primary methods of implementing accesses to nonlocal variables in static-scoped languages. In both methods, access paths can be statically established to variables in all static ancestor scopes.

Access to nonlocal variables in a dynamic-scoped language can be implemented by use of the dynamic chain or through some central variable table method. Dynamic chains provide slow accesses but fast calls and returns. The central table methods provide fast accesses but slow calls and returns.

Parameters that are subprograms provide a necessary service, but are sometimes difficult to understand. The opaqueness lies in the referencing environment that is available when a subprogram that has been passed as a parameter is executing. Subprograms that are passed as parameters can be implemented with either static chains or displays.

BIBLIOGRAPHIC NOTES

Implementation of both static and dynamic scoping is covered in Pratt (1984) and Ghezzi and Jazayeri (1987), but it is discussed more thoroughly in books on compiler design, such as Fischer and LeBlanc (1988).

PROBLEM SET

1. Write an algorithm to perform the display maintenance required upon entry to a subprogram in a language that uses static scoping and also allows subprogram names as parameters.

2. Write an algorithm to perform the display maintenance required upon exit from a subprogram in a language that uses static scoping and also allows subprogram names as parameters.

3. Show the stack with all activation record instances, including static and dynamic chains, when execution reaches position 1 in the following skeletal program:

```
procedure BIGSUB;
  procedure A;
    procedure B;
      . . .
      begin
      . . .      <-------------------1
      end;   { of procedure B }
    procedure C;
      . . .
      begin
      . . .
      B;
      . . .
      end;   { of procedure C }
    begin   { of procedure A }
    . . .
    C;
    . . .
    end;   { of procedure A }
  begin   { of BIGSUB }
  . . .
  A;
  . . .
  end;   { of procedure BIGSUB }
```

4. For the skeletal program in Problem 3, show the display that would be active at position 1, along with the activation record instances on the stack.

5. Show the stack with all activation record instances, including static and dynamic chains, when execution reaches position 1 in the following skeletal program:

```
procedure BIGSUB;
  procedure C; forward;
  procedure A;
   boolean flag;
   procedure B;
     ...
     A (false)
     end;   { of B}
   begin    { of A}
   if flag
     then B
     else C
   ...
   end;      {of A}
   procedure C;
      procedure D;
        ... <------------------1
        end;     {of D}
      ...
      D
      end;     { of C }
    begin { of BIGSUB }
    A (true);
    ...
    end;
```

The calling sequence for this program for execution to reach D is

BIGSUB calls A
A calls B
B calls A
A calls C
C calls D

6. For the skeletal program in Problem 5, show the display that would be active at position 1, along with the activation record instances on the stack.

7. Although local variables in Pascal procedures are dynamically allocated at the beginning of each activation, under what circumstances could the value of a local in a particular activation retain the value of the previous activation?

8. It is stated in this chapter that when nonlocal variables are accessed in a dynamic-scoped language using the dynamic chain, variable names must be stored in the activation records with the values. If this were actually done, every nonlocal access would require a sequence of costly string comparisons on names. Design an alternative to these string comparisons that would be faster.

9. Pascal allows gotos with nonlocal targets. How could such statements be handled if static chains were used for nonlocal variable access? [*Hint*: Consider the

way the correct activation record instance of the static parent of a newly enacted procedure is found (Section 9.3.4.1).]

10. Repeat Problem 9, using a display instead of static chains

11. How could the display mechanism described in this chapter be modified to make local variables accessible without indirect addressing?

12. The static chain method could be expanded slightly by using two static links in each activation record instance, where the second points to the static grandparent activation record instance. How would this affect the time required for subprogram linkage and nonlocal references?

10

Data Abstraction

George Radin

George Radin of IBM was one of the principle designers of both the PL/1 language and IBM's first compiler for PL/1. He was also a member of the design teams for OS/360 and TSS, IBM's first time-sharing system.

Key Concepts

- Abstraction in programming languages
- Data abstraction
- Encapsulation
- Information hiding
- Class hierarchies

- Transparent versus opaque export
- Name qualification
- Private types
- Generic packages

In this chapter, we explore the concept of data abstraction as a supported feature in programming languages, from its origins in SIMULA 67 to its more advanced form in contemporary languages. Among the new ideas of the last 25 years in programming methodologies and programming language design, data abstraction is one of the most profound.

We begin by discussing the general concept of abstraction in programming and programming languages. Data abstraction is then defined and illustrated with an example. We then briefly describe the partial support for data abstraction in SIMULA 67. Full linguistic support for data abstraction is discussed in terms of three specific languages: Modula-2, Ada, and C++. An implementation of the same example data abstraction is shown in each of these languages. This illuminates the similarities and differences in the design of the language facilities that support data abstraction.

10.1   The Concept of Abstraction

In general, the concept of abstraction holds that some category of processes or objects can be represented by only a subset of its attributes. These are the essential attributes of the category, with all the other attributes abstracted away or hidden. Abstraction is a weapon against the complexity of programming; its purpose is to simplify the programming process. It is an effective weapon because it allows programmers to concentrate on essential attributes and ignore subordinate attributes.

The two fundamental kinds of abstraction in contemporary programming languages are process abstraction and data abstraction.

The concept of **process abstraction** is among the oldest in programming language design. Even Plankalkül had a method for constructing subprograms. All subprograms are process abstractions: They are a way of allowing a program to specify that some process is to be done, without spelling out how it is to be done (at least in the calling program). For example, when a program needs to sort an array of numeric data objects of some type, it can use a subprogram for the process. Then, when the sorting process is required, a statement such as

```
SORT_INT (LIST, LENGTH)
```

is placed in the program. This call is an abstraction of the actual sorting process, whose algorithm is not specified. The call is independent of the algorithm implemented in the called subprogram.

Process abstraction is absolutely essential to the programming process. The ability to abstract away many of the details of procedures makes it possible to construct and comprehend large programs.

In the case of the subprogram SORT_INT, the only essential attributes are the name of the array to be sorted, the type of its elements, and the array's length. The particular algorithm that SORT_INT implemented is an attribute that was nonessential to the user.

All subprograms, including coroutines and concurrent subprograms (discussed in Chapter 11) and exception handlers (discussed in Chapter 12), are process abstractions.

10.2 Introduction to Data Abstraction

Data abstraction as a concept in programming methodologies was discovered much later than process abstraction. The idea of data abstraction is similar to that of process abstraction, as far as its usefulness to programming is concerned. It is a weapon against complexity, a means of making large and/or complicated programs more manageable.

In the last few years, a new paradigm for software development has become increasingly popular—object-oriented programming. Object-oriented programming, which is described in Chapter 15, is an outgrowth of the use of data abstraction in software development, and data abstraction is one of its most important components.

10.2.1 Floating-Point as an Abstract Data Type

The concept of data abstraction, at least in terms of built-in types, is not a recent development. All built-in data types, even those of FORTRAN I, are abstract data types. For example, consider the floating-point data type. Included in most languages, this type provides a means of creating variables for floating-point data and also provides a set of arithmetic operations for manipulating objects of the type.

Floating-point types in high-level languages often employ a key concept in data abstraction: information hiding. The actual format of the data value in a floating-point memory cell is usually hidden from the user. The only operations available are those provided by the system. The user is not allowed to create new operations on data of the type, except those that can be constructed using the built-in operations. In particular, the user is not allowed to directly manipulate the actual representation of floating-point objects. This makes it possible to have a flexible data representation, rather than one fixed in some particular format. It is this feature that allows program portability between implementations, even though the implementations may use different representations of floating-point values.

10.2.2   User-Defined Abstract Data Types

The concept of user-defined abstract data types is a relatively recent one. A user-defined abstract data type should provide the same characteristics provided by floating-point types: (1) a type definition that allows program units to declare variables of the type, but which hides the representation of these variables, and (2) a set of operations for manipulating objects of the type.

We now formally define an abstract data type, in the context of user-defined types. An **abstract data type** is a data type that satisfies the following two conditions:

1. The representation, or definition, of the type and the operations on objects of the type are described in a single syntactic unit.

2. The representation of objects of the type are hidden from the program units that use the type, so that the only direct operations possible on those objects are those provided in the type's definition.

The primary advantage of packaging the representation and operations in a single syntactic unit is that it cleanly localizes modifications. There are several advantages of hiding representation details. The most important of these is that program units that use the type are not able to "see" the representation details, and thus their code cannot depend on that representation. The result of this is that the representation can be changed at any time without affecting the program units that use the type.

Another distinct and important benefit of information hiding is increased reliability. Program units cannot change part of the underlying representations directly, either intentionally or by accident, thus increasing the integrity of such objects. These objects can be changed only through the provided operations. It is difficult to overstate the importance of hiding the representation details of an abstract data type.

10.2.3   An Example

Suppose an abstract data type is to be constructed for a stack, consisting of the following abstract operations:

create(stack)	Creates and/or initializes a stack object
destroy(stack)	Deallocates the storage for the stack
empty(stack)	A predicate function that returns true if the specified stack is empty and false otherwise
push(stack, element)	Pushes the specified element on the specified stack
pop(stack)	Removes the top element from the specified stack
top(stack)	Returns a copy of the top element from the specified stack

Note that some designs of abstract data types for stacks will not require the create operation. The same is true for the destroy operation.

Now suppose that a large program uses an implementation of this abstraction, having STK1 and STK2 as variables of the abstract stack type. Then there could be code sequences like the following:

```
...
push(STK1, COLOR1);
push(STK1, COLOR2);
...
if(not empty(STK1))
  then TEMP := top(STK1);
...
push(STK2, TEMP);
...
```

Further suppose that the original implementation of the stack abstraction uses an adjacency representation (one that implements stacks in arrays). At a later time, because of memory management problems with the adjacency representation, it is changed to a linked list representation. Because data abstraction was used, this change can be made in the code that defines the stack type, but no changes will be required in any of the program units that use the stack abstraction. In particular, the code sequence above does not need to be changed.

In the absence of data abstraction, such a change would require that all the program units that used the stack type be modified to conform to the new representation. Suppose, for example, that the stack operations had been implemented in Pascal to operate on arrays. The change to linked list representation would require that user programs be modified to send pointers instead of array names as parameters to the stack operation procedures.

In summary, the goal of data abstraction is to provide the facilities so that programs can be written that depend only on the abstract properties, not on the representation of data objects. In the stack example, the main abstract properties are the order of access, the operations create, push, top, pop, and destroy, and the predicate empty.

10.3 Design Issues

A complete facility for defining abstract data types in a language must provide a syntactic unit that can encapsulate the type definition and subprogram definitions of the abstraction operations. It must be possible to make the type names and subprogram headers visible to other program units that use the abstraction. Although the type names must have external visibility, the type definitions must be hidden.

Few, if any, operations should be provided for objects of abstract data types, other than those provided with the type definition. Assignment and comparison for equality are the only operations that should be built in. If assignment is not treated like an operator in the language, then users cannot overload it, so it must be built in. Comparison for equality should be built in because it is the same for all types.

The encapsulation requirement of abstract data types can be met in two distinct ways. First, an encapsulation construct can be designed to provide a single data type and its operations. This is the approach of Concurrent Pascal (Brinch Hansen, 1975), Smalltalk (Goldberg and Robson, 1983), and C++ (Ellis and Stroustrup, 1990). The alternative to this is to provide a more generalized encapsulation construct that can define a number of entities, any of which can be selectively specified to be visible outside the encapsulating unit. This is the approach of Modula-2 and Ada.

The primary design issues beyond this fundamental one of encapsulation include the following: First, restricting the kinds of types that can be abstract has some advantages. In particular, if only pointers can be abstract, a great deal of recompilation can be avoided in the software development process. On the other hand, some consider this a severe restriction because of its disadvantages. Another design issue is whether abstract data types can be generic. One final design issue is how imported types (or other entities if the encapsulation construct is generalized) can be qualified to prevent collisions between local and nonlocal names.

10.4 SIMULA 67 Classes

The first language facilities for the direct support of data abstraction, although incomplete by our definition, appeared in the class construct in SIMULA 67.

10.4.1 Encapsulation

A SIMULA 67 class definition is a template for a type. Instances of a class, sometimes called class objects, are created dynamically at the request of the user program and can be referenced only with pointer variables.

The general syntactic form of a class definition is

```
class class_name;
  begin
  -- class variable declarations --
  -- class subprogram definitions --
  -- class code section --
  end class_name;
```

The code section of a class instance is executed only once, at instance creation time. It is used only for initialization of class variables. After instantiation, the variables and procedures of a class instance can be used by any other unit in a program.

SIMULA 67's contribution to data abstraction is to have the class construct allow data declarations and the procedures that manipulate them to be syntactically encapsulated. Interestingly, the significance of this aspect of the class construct was not recognized until several years after the design of SIMULA 67 was completed. The importance of data abstraction was not generally realized until the early 1970s.

10.4.2 Information Hiding

The variables that are declared in a SIMULA 67 class are not hidden from other program units that allocate class objects using the class. These variables can be accessed through the operations provided by the class subprograms or directly through their names. This violates one of the two major characteristics of the definition of a data abstraction because multiple access paths are possible. The impact of the violation is that a class used as a data abstraction is far less reliable than a true abstraction. Furthermore, because program units that use the class can be designed to depend on the variable definitions in the class, changes to those variable definitions may require changes in the other program units. This makes such programs more difficult to modify.

10.4.3 Evaluation

As explained above, the SIMULA 67 class construct provides for the syntactic encapsulation of data objects and the procedures that manipulate them. However, it does not provide information hiding, which allows representation details to be kept from the program modules that use them.

SIMULA 67 was revolutionary in its development of the class construct. However, because the language never enjoyed widespread use, we discuss it primarily for its historic interest. We now turn our attention to three contemporary languages that implement a more complete form of data abstraction: Modula-2, Ada, and C++.

10.5 Abstract Data Types in Modula-2

Modula-2 provides facilities for data abstraction, including the ability to hide the representations of abstract data types.

10.5.1 Encapsulation

The program unit of Modula-2 that provides the facilities for data abstraction is the module. Like the SIMULA 67 class construct, the module is, at least in part, meant to break away from the limitations of static scoping. Both SIMULA 67 and Modula-2 retain static scoping, but they also offer other methods of sharing data among program units.

A Modula-2 module is a program unit that can include definitions of types, objects, and subprograms that may be accessed by other program units. Access by other units to the types, objects, and subprograms of a module is gained by specifically requesting it. The units that have access to a module are called **clients** of the module.

Modules can be either local or library modules. Local modules are not useful for designing abstract data types, so we focus on library modules here. A **library module** consists of two syntactic entities—the definition and implementation units, which are also called modules. The **definition module** contains at least partial specifications of the types and objects as well as the headers of the subprograms that are visible to client units. These specifications define the **interface** of the module. The **implementation module** contains the complete definitions of any types that were only partially defined in the corresponding definition module. Also, the implementation module contains the complete definitions of the subprograms whose headers appear in the corresponding definition module.

A definition module and its associated implementation module share the same name. The syntactic difference between the headers of these two lies in the appearance of the reserved words DEFINITION and IMPLEMENTATION.

Modules are separately compilable; even the two parts, the definition and implementation modules, can be separately compiled as long as the definition module is compiled first. When a definition module is compiled, its interface information is kept. This allows the facilities of precompiled modules to be referenced by a program, with complete interface checking possible. The interfaces are checked by the loader at the time the program is assembled for execution. This is a great advance over a language such as FORTRAN 77, in which no interface checking among units is done.

10.5.2 Information Hiding

The types that are declared in a definition module can have their representation, or complete definition, included in or excluded from the definition module. If the representation is included, the type is said to be **transparent,** and its representation is not hidden from the modules that import it. If the representation is not included but rather is placed in the associated implementation module, that type is said to be **opaque,** and its representation is not available to client units. An abstract data type obviously must be opaque.

An important aspect of the design of Modula-2 modules is that only pointer types can be opaque. The design decision to require this restriction is partially based on the efficiency of software development. If client modules are allowed to declare variables of an opaque type, they need to be able to determine the size of objects of that type. If they see only the type name, this can be a problem, unless all opaque types have the same size (of course, all pointers do have the same size). Perhaps more importantly, changes to the representation details of opaque types do not require recompilation of client modules if they are always pointers. If other types were opaque and exported, changes in their representation would require recompilation of client modules.

The restriction of opaque types to pointers is not a severe one from the user's point of view, because a pointer can point to any data structure. It does, however, create some problems, which are discussed in Section 10.5.5.

10.5.3 An Example

As an example of a specification module, consider the following:

```
DEFINITION MODULE stackmod;
  TYPE stacktype;
  PROCEDURE empty (stk : stacktype) : BOOLEAN;
  PROCEDURE push (VAR stk : stacktype;
                  element : INTEGER);
  PROCEDURE pop (VAR stk : stacktype);
  PROCEDURE top (stk : stacktype) : INTEGER;
  PROCEDURE create (VAR stk : stacktype);
END stackmod.
```

This definition module describes the external view of a stack type for integer elements. The type, stacktype, is opaque, so the details of its representation will be visible only in the implementation module; they will not be visible to any client modules. One of the results of restricting opaque types to pointers is that the stack in our example must be dynamically allocated before it can be used. Therefore, an initialization procedure must be included so the user can create a stack for use.

The implementation module for stacks is as follows:

```
IMPLEMENTATION MODULE stackmod;
  FROM InOut IMPORT WriteString, WriteLn;
  FROM Storage IMPORT ALLOCATE;
  CONST max = 100;
```

```
              TYPE stacktype = POINTER TO
                             RECORD
                             list : ARRAY [1..max] OF INTEGER;
                             topsub : [0..max]
                             END;
        PROCEDURE empty (stk : stacktype) : BOOLEAN;
          BEGIN
          RETURN stk^.topsub = 0
          END empty;

        PROCEDURE push (VAR stk : stacktype;
                        element : INTEGER);
          BEGIN
          IF stk^.topsub = max THEN
            WriteString ("ERROR - Stack overflow");
            WriteLn
          ELSE
            INC(stk^.topsub);
            stk^.list[stk^.topsub] := element
          END
          END push;

        PROCEDURE pop (VAR stk : stacktype);
          BEGIN
          IF empty (stk) THEN
            WriteString ("ERROR - Stack underflow");
            WriteLn
          ELSE
            DEC(stk^.topsub)
          END  (* of IF empty... *)
          END pop;

        PROCEDURE top (stk : stacktype) : INTEGER;
          BEGIN
          IF empty (stk) THEN
            WriteString ("ERROR - Stack underflow");
            WriteLn
          ELSE
            RETURN stk^.list[stk^.topsub]
          END  (* of IF empty ... *)
          END top;

        PROCEDURE create (VAR stk : stacktype);
          BEGIN
          NEW (stk);
          stk^.topsub := 0
          END create;
      END stackmod.
```

The second and third statements of the implementation module import the
necessary procedures for displaying error messages and for allocation of the

stack in the create procedure. The rest of the code should be self-explanatory.

The following skeletal module demonstrates how the facilities of stack-mod can be used:

```
MODULE usestacks;
  FROM InOut IMPORT WriteInt, WriteLn, WriteString;
  FROM stackmod IMPORT stacktype, empty, push, pop,
                        top, create;
  VAR stack : stacktype;
  VAR stuff : INTEGER;
  ...
  BEGIN
  ...
  create (stack);
  push (stack, 42);
  push (stack, 27);
  pop (stack);
  stuff := top (stack);
  ...
  END usestacks.
```

This code creates and initializes a stack, pushes two values, 42 and 27, on it, and pops the 27, leaving the stack with the value 42.

10.5.4 Name Qualification

An imported name is **qualified** in a client module if it indicates the source module of the name so that there are no conflicts with other entities of the same name that are either declared locally or imported from other modules. Client modules can qualify references to those imported entities in two ways: explicitly or implicitly.

If the client module needs all of the exported entities from a module, it can simply import the entire module by naming the module on an IMPORT statement. This obviates the need to list each entity to be imported. When a module is imported this way, every reference to the imported entities needs to be explicitly qualified by attaching the exporting module's name, as in

```
stackmod.push (stack, 22)
```

The alternative to this form of qualification is the method used in our module usestacks, in which we imported specific entities from stackmod. This method, called implicit qualification, requires no explicit qualification on references to the imported entities. Implicit qualification is better in the sense that it restricts access to entities that are not needed. However, the use of implicitly qualified references to imported entities has two drawbacks. First, it prevents the compiler from detecting some mistaken uses of variables, types, and processes. For example, suppose there was a local variable and an imported variable with similar names. A minor keying error might replace one with the other, leading to a subtle but serious program error, and the system would not be able to detect the error. Of course, this problem can occur with any use of similar names, not just imported names. Second, references to imported variables that are explicitly qualified with their source module names are obviously more precise. This advantage is lost when implicit qualification is used.

10.5.5   Evaluation

The restriction of opaque types to pointers in Modula-2 causes some problems. The first is related to the fact that Modula-2 pointer variables are not always automatically initialized to nil. If a user forgets to call the create procedure before using a pointer to an abstract data type, the error may not be detected until after some meaningless operations have taken place, possibly making the error difficult to find.

Another problem with the restriction to pointers is that it forces a good deal of unnecessary use of pointers, which are far less safe to use than nonpointer variables (recall our discussion in Chapter 5 of the problems related to pointers).

The fact that definition modules can be separately compiled has an important effect on constructing software systems in Modula-2. True topdown design can be used, and an entire system can be built initially with only definition modules (which include subprogram headers). All module interfaces can then be automatically checked for consistency by the compiler, before any implementation code is written.

10.6   Abstract Data Types in Ada

The method of constructing abstract data types in Ada is similar to that of Modula-2, although there are a few important differences.

10.6.1   Encapsulation

The encapsulating constructs, or modules, in Ada are called **packages.** As with Modula-2 modules, packages can have two parts, each of which is also called a package. In this case, they are called the specification package and the body package, although not all packages have body parts (some packages that contain only data do not have bodies).

A specification package and its associated body package share the same name. The reserved word **body** in a package header identifies it as being a body package. Specification and body packages may be compiled separately, provided the specification package is compiled first.

10.6.2 Information Hiding

Ada provides an effective mechanism for supporting information hiding. We describe that mechanism by contrasting it with that of Modula-2.

The most important difference between Modula-2 modules and Ada packages is that the types that are exported are not restricted to pointers in Ada. Any type that can be defined anywhere in an Ada program can be defined in a specification package and thus exported.

Recall that the advantage of the Modula-2 restriction that exported types can only be pointers is that client modules do not have to be recompiled when the representation of the exported type is changed. Because the client modules see only a pointer, whose size is fixed regardless of the structure to which it points, the modules do not depend in any way on that structure.

In Ada packages, these problems are partially overcome by allowing a kind of visible/invisible specification for types. A type that is to be exported from a package, but whose representation details are to be hidden, is declared twice in the specification package. The specification has two sections: one that is entirely visible to importers and one that is only partially visible outside the package. The part that is only partially visible is called the **private** part. It is introduced by the reserved word **private**.

Suppose a type named NODE_TYPE is to be exported by a package, but its representation is to be hidden. NODE_TYPE is declared in the visible part of the specification package without its representation details, as in

```
type NODE_TYPE is private;
```

In the private clause, the declaration of NODE_TYPE is repeated, but this time with the complete type definition, as in

```
package LINKED_LIST_TYPE is
  type NODE_TYPE is private;
  ...
  private
    type NODE_TYPE;
    type PTR is access NODE_TYPE;
    type NODE_TYPE is
      record
      INFO : INTEGER;
      LINK : PTR;
      end record;
end LINKED_LIST_TYPE;
```

The part of a specification before the private clause, which is always at the end of a specification package, is visible outside the package. However, the private clause declarations are hidden to all other program units except the matching implementation package.

When client program units are being compiled, the compiler can "see" enough of a private type specification to get the size of its objects, thus allowing such units to declare variables of the type. However, client units cannot access any of the entities described in the private part of the specification. Types that are declared to be private are called **private types.**

Private data types have built-in operations for assignment and comparisons for equality and inequality. Any other operation must be defined in the specification package that defined the type.

An alternative to private types is a more restricted form, limited private types. **Limited private types** are described in the private section of a specification package, just as private types are. The only syntactic difference is that limited private types are declared to be **limited private** in the visible part of the package specification.

Objects of a type that is declared limited private have no built-in operations. If assignment or equality comparisons are required, they must be provided by the specification package. The assignment operation needs to be in the form of a normal procedure, whereas the equal and not equal operators can be provided by overloading those operators for the new type.

10.6.3   An Example

To allow easy comparison with Modula-2, we have again chosen a stack to illustrate an Ada abstract data type.

```
package STACKPACK is
  type STACKTYPE is limited private;
  MAX_SIZE : constant := 100;
  function EMPTY (STK : in STACKTYPE) return BOOLEAN;
  procedure PUSH (STK    : in out STACKTYPE;
                  ELEMENT : in INTEGER);
  procedure POP (STK : in out STACKTYPE);
  function TOP (STK : in STACKTYPE) return INTEGER;
  private
    type LIST_TYPE is array (1..MAX_SIZE) of INTEGER;
    type STACKTYPE is
    record
      LIST   : LIST_TYPE;
      TOPSUB : INTEGER range 0..MAX_SIZE := 0;
    end record;
end STACKPACK;
```

The body package for the specification package for the stack type is as follows:

```
with TEXT_IO; use TEXT_IO;
package body STACKPACK is
  function EMPTY (STK: in STACKTYPE) return BOOLEAN is
    begin
    return STK.TOPSUB = 0
    end EMPTY;

  procedure PUSH (STK      : in out STACKTYPE;
                  ELEMENT : in INTEGER) is
    begin
    if STK.TOPSUB >= MAX_SIZE
      then
        PUT_LINE ("ERROR - Stack overflow");
      else
        STK.TOPSUB := STK.TOPSUB + 1;
        STK.LIST(TOPSUB) := ELEMENT;
    end if;
  end PUSH;

  procedure POP (STK : in out STACKTYPE) is
    begin
    if STK.TOPSUB = 0
      then PUT_LINE ("ERROR - Stack underflow");
      else STK.TOPSUB := STK.TOPSUB - 1;
    end if;
    end POP;

  function TOP (STK : in STACKTYPE) return INTEGER is
    begin
    if STK.TOPSUB = 0
      then PUT_LINE ("ERROR - Stack is empty");
      else return STK.LIST(S.TOPSUB);
    end if;
    end TOP;
  end STACKPACK;
```

The first line of the code of this package contains two statements: a **with**
and a **use**. The **with** statement imports external packages, in this case
TEXT_IO, that provide functions for input and output of text. The **use** statement eliminates the need for explicit qualification of the references to entities from the named package. Thus, in our package, we use the procedure
PUT_LINE from TEXT_IO without explicit qualification. The **use** statement
is, therefore, a means of creating implicit qualification for the entities in the
package it lists.

There must be subprogram definitions in the body package with headings that match the subprogram headings in the associated specification
package. The specification package, in a sense, promises that these subprograms will be defined in the associated body package.

The following procedure is an example of how the package STACKPACK
might be used. It is identical in effect to the Modula-2 module usestacks
shown in the previous section.

```
with STACKPACK, TEXT_IO;
use STACKPACK, TEXT_IO;
procedure USE_STACKS is
  TOPONE : INTEGER;
  STACK : STACKTYPE;
  begin
  ...
  PUSH (STACK, 42);
  PUSH (STACK, 17);
  POP (STACK);
  TOPONE := TOP (STACK);
  ...
  end USE_STACKS;
```

The only significant difference between this and the Modula-2 version is that here it was not necessary to create the stack; that was done automatically when we declared the variable stack to be of STACKTYPE. If an Ada package were used to implement an abstract type that exported only a pointer, it too would require a create operation.

10.6.4 Generic Packages

Generic procedures in Ada are discussed and illustrated in Chapter 8. Packages can also be generic, however, so we can also construct generic abstract data types.

The stack abstract data type example of the previous section suffers two restrictions: (1) Stacks of its type can store only integer type elements, and (2) the stacks can have only up to 100 elements. Both of these restrictions can be eliminated by using a generic package, which can be instantiated for other element types and any desirable size. The following specification package describes the interface of a generic stack abstract data type with these features:

```
generic
  MAX_SIZE : POSITIVE;
  type ELEMENT_TYPE is private;
package GENERIC_STACK is
  type STACKTYPE is limited private;
  function EMPTY (STK : in STACKTYPE) return BOOLEAN;
  procedure PUSH (STK : in out STACKTYPE;
                  ELEMENT : in ELEMENT_TYPE);
  procedure POP (STK : in out STACKTYPE);
  function TOP (STK : in STACKTYPE) return ELEMENT_TYPE;

private
  type LIST_TYPE is array (1..MAX_SIZE) of
                              ELEMENT_TYPE;
```

```
type STACKTYPE is
  record
  LIST : LIST_TYPE;
  TOPSUB : INTEGER range 0..MAX_SIZE := 0;
  end record;
end GENERIC_STACK;
```

The body package for GENERIC_STACK is the same as the body package for the STACKPACK body in the previous section, except that the type of the ELE-MENT formal parameter in PUSH and TOP is ELEMENT_TYPE instead of INTEGER.

To get the facilities available in STACKPACK from GENERIC_STACK, the following instantiation could be used:

```
package INTEGER_STACK is new GENERIC_STACK (100, INTEGER);
```

One could also build an abstract data type for a stack of length 500 for floating-point elements, as in

```
package FLOAT_STACK is new GENERIC_STACK (500, FLOAT);
```

The utility of generic packages in the construction of abstract data types is obvious.

10.6.5 Evaluation

There are several differences between the support for data abstraction in Modula-2 and that in Ada. Abstract data types in Ada are more flexible than those of Modula-2 because of Modula-2's restriction of opaque export to pointers only. Ada's design lessens the dependence on pointers, which introduce their own batch of insecurities.

Modula-2's design of allowing selected entities to be imported from a module is an advantage over Ada's design, wherein all or none of a package must be imported.

It may seem to be a disadvantage that Ada must recompile client modules when the representation of an exported type is changed. But this recompilation is necessary only when the exported type is not a pointer. When a pointer is exported from a specification package, the definition of the type to which the pointer points can be declared in the associated body package. Therefore, if Ada is used in the restricted fashion of Modula-2 and exports only pointers, neither it nor Modula-2 will require recompilation of client program units. Only when a nonpointer type is exported in Ada is recompilation of client program units necessary. Thus, the additional cost in Ada arises only from the additional flexibility of allowing any nonpointer type to be exported.

10.7   Abstract Data Types in C++

As stated in Chapter 2, C++ is a language that was created by adding facilities to support object-oriented programming to C, an imperative language. Because one of the primary components of object-oriented programming is data abstraction, C++ supports it.

One significant difference between C++ support for data abstraction and that of Modula-2 and Ada is that the unit that defines and exports the abstract data type in C++, the class, exports *only* a type and its operations. Classes are in fact types. Recall that Modula-2 and Ada export collections of types, objects, and constants. However, this is not as different as it sounds, for although the facilities of a C++ class are made available only through an object that has been declared to be an instance of the class, the class can include any number of data and function elements, and all of these elements are available through that object.

10.7.1   Encapsulation

The classes of C++ are based on the classes of SIMULA 67 and are an extension to the **struct** types of C. Because of its heritage, a C++ class is a template for a data type and therefore can be instantiated any number of times.

A class includes specifications of data members, like a C structure, and also member functions. All the instances of a class share a single set of member functions, but each instance gets its own set of the class's data members. Although class instances can also be static and explicit dynamic, we consider only semidynamic classes here. The instances of such classes are always created by elaboration of an object declaration. Furthermore, the lifetime of such a class instance ends when the scope of its declaration is reached. Classes can have explicit dynamic data members, so that even though a class instance is semidynamic, it can include data members that are explicit dynamic and allocated from free store.

C++ uses the **new** and **delete** operators to manage heap storage. Objects created with **new** are obviously explicitly dynamic.

Member functions can have just their headers in the class definition, in which case their bodies are separately compiled, or they can have both headers and bodies in it. When both the header and the body of a member function appear in the class definition, the member function is implicitly inlined. Recall that this means that their code is placed in the caller's code, rather than requiring the usual call and return linkage process.

10.7.2   Information Hiding

A C++ class can contain both hidden and visible entities. Hidden entities are written in a **private** clause, and visible, or public, entities are written in a **public** clause. The **public** clause therefore describes the interface to the class instances. There is also a third category of visibility, **protected,** which is discussed in the context of subclasses in Chapter 15.

C++ allows the user to include functions called **constructors,** in class definitions, which are used to initialize and provide parameters to the object creation process. A constructor has the same name as the class of which they are a part, which looks odd but is harmless. There can be more than one constructor for a class, in which case they are obviously overloaded. Of course, each must have a unique parameter profile. Constructors are implicitly called when an instance of the class type is created.

A C++ class can also include a function called a **destructor,** which is implicitly called when the lifetime of an instance of the class ends. Explicit dynamic objects live until explicitly deallocated with the **delete** operator. As stated above, semidynamic class instances can contain explicit dynamic data members. The destructor function for such an instance can include a **delete** operator on the explicit dynamic members to deallocate their free store space. Destructors are often used as a debugging aid, in which case they simply display or print values of some or all of the object's data members before they are deallocated.

The name of a destructor is the class's name, preceded by a tilde (~).

Neither constructors nor destructors have return types, and neither use **return** statements. Constructors cannot be explicitly called, although destructors can and sometimes are.

In some situations it is convenient to be able to grant nonmember functions, or even other whole classes, access to the private members of a class. This can be done by declaring them to be friends, with a statement of the form:

```
friend function_or_class_name
```

This declaration is placed in the class definition, usually at the beginning.

10.7.3 An Example

Our example of a C++ abstract data type is, once again, a stack.

```
#include <iostream.h>
class stack {
private:
  int *stack_ptr;
  int max_len;
  int top_ptr;
public:
  stack () { stack_ptr = new int [100];
             max_len = 99;
             top_ptr = -1};
  ~stack () {delete stack_ptr;};
```

```
    void push (int number)
      { if (top_ptr == max_len)
        cout << "Error in push--stack is full\n";
        else stack_ptr[++top_ptr] = number;
      }
    void pop ()
      {if (top_ptr == -1)
        cout << "Error in pop--stack is empty\n";
        else top_ptr--;
      }
    int top () {return (stack_ptr[top_ptr]);}
    int empty () {return (top_ptr == -1);}
  }
```

We will only discuss a few of the aspects of this class definition, since it is not necessary to understand all of the details of the code. The #include is used to provide visibility to a standard input and output package, iostream.h, which provides the simple output process used by the code, cout. The class has three data members, stack_ptr, max_len, and top_ptr, all of which are private. It also has four public member functions—push, pop, top, and empty—a constructor, and a destructor. The constructor uses the allocator function **new** to allocate an array of 100 integer elements. It also initializes max_len and top_ptr. The purpose of the destructor function is to deallocate the storage for the array used to implement the stack. Because the bodies of the member functions are included, they are all implicitly inlined. This is a recommended practice for relatively small member functions.

An example program that uses the stack abstract data type above is

```
main ()
  {int top_one;
   stack stk;
   ...
   stk.push (42);
   stk.push (17);
   stk.pop ();
   top_one = stk.top ();
   ...
  }
```

In this example, the data members max_len and top_ptr are semidynamic and are therefore allocated from the run-time stack.

To make the stack class generic in the stack size, only the constructor function needs to be changed, as in

```
stack (int size) {stk_ptr = new int [size];
                   max_len = size - 1;
                   top = -1;}
```

The declaration for a stack object now may appear as

```
stack (100) stk;
```

The class definition for `stack` can include both constructors, so users can use the default size stack or specify some other size.

10.7.4 Evaluation

C++ support for data abstraction, through its class construct, is similar in expressive power to that of Ada, through its packages. Both provide effective mechanisms for encapsulation and information hiding of general types. The primary difference is that classes *are* types, whereas packages are collections of program entities. Of course, the class was designed for more than data abstraction, as discussed in Chapter 15.

SUMMARY

The concept of data abstraction and its use in program design were milestones in the development of programming as an engineering discipline. Although the concept is relatively simple, its use did not become convenient and safe until languages were designed to support it.

The two primary features of data abstraction are encapsulation of data objects with their associated operations and information hiding.

SIMULA 67 provided the first construct for encapsulating data objects with their operations—the class. However, the class construct does not provide for information hiding.

Modula-2 and Ada provide forms of complete data abstraction. The main difference between the two designs is Modula-2's restriction of exported types with hidden representations to pointers. This restriction allows changes to representations that do not require recompilation of definition modules and their clients. The Ada language allows any type to be exported. When nonpointer types are exported, client program units must be recompiled when the representation is changed.

C++ data abstraction is provided by classes, which are loosely modeled on the classes of SIMULA 67. Classes are types, and instances can be created in all of the ways object instances of other types can be created.

PROBLEM SET

1. Design the example abstract stack type in Pascal, assuming that the stack definition, its operations, and the code that use it are all in the same program.

2. What critical part or parts of the definition of an abstract data type are missing from a Pascal implementation of the stack type, such as the one in Problem 1?

3. Design the example abstract stack type in FORTRAN 77, using a single subprogram with multiple entries for the type definition and the operations.

4. How does the FORTRAN implementation of Problem 3 compare with the Ada implementation in this chapter, in terms of reliability and flexibility?

5. Modify the Modula-2 implementation module for the abstract stack type to use a linked-list representation, and test it with the same code that appears in this chapter.

6. What operations are built in for the opaque types in Modula-2?

7. What is the main drawback of exporting transparent types in Modula-2?

8. Devise a situation in which it would be advantageous to define a type in a Modula-2 definition module that is not to be exported.

9. How is Modula-2's EXPORT different from FORTRAN's COMMON?

10. Some software engineers believe that all imported entities should be qualified by the name of the exporting program unit. Do you agree? Support your answer.

11. Design a matrix abstraction in a language that you know, including operations for addition, subtraction, and matrix multiplication.

12. Design a queue abstraction in a language you know, including operations for enqueue, dequeue, and empty.

13. Suppose someone designed a stack abstraction in which the function top returned an access path (or pointer), rather than returning a copy of the top element. This is not a true data abstraction. Why? Give an example that illustrates the problem.

14. Write an abstract data type for complex numbers, including operations for addition, subtraction, multiplication, division, extraction of each of the parts of a complex number, and construction of a complex number from two floating-point constants, variables, or expressions. Use either Modula-2, Ada, or C++.

15. Write an abstract data type for queues whose elements store ten-character names. The queue elements must be dynamically allocated from the heap. Queue operations are enqueue, dequeue, and empty. Use either Modula-2, Ada, or C++.

11

Symmetric and Concurrent Subprograms

Ole-Johan Dahl

Ole-Johan Dahl and Kristen Nygaard, then both at the Norwegian Computing Center, were both primarily interested in computer simulation. Driven by their needs in simulation, they designed and implemented the simulation languages SIMULA in 1964, and SIMULA 67 in 1967.

Key Concepts

- Physical and logical concurrency
- Symmetric unit control (coroutines)
- Competition and cooperation synchronization
- Semaphores

- Shared data buffers
- Monitors
- Message-passing model of concurrency
- Nondeterminancy in message receiving

Subprograms whose behavior is restricted by a small set of rules were discussed in Chapter 8. In particular, such a subprogram has a single entry point and returns control to the caller when its execution terminates normally. Also, the calling program unit is suspended during execution of the called subprogram, and therefore only a single program unit is executing at any given time. This results in what is referred to as a single thread of control.

Symmetric and concurrent subprograms have control semantics that do not follow all of these rules. Symmetric control allows an equal relationship between units, rather than the master-slave relationship between caller and called subprograms described above. Symmetric control also allows a unit to return control to the caller after partial execution; its execution is restarted later from the point where it earlier relinquished control. This provides a sequence of unit entry points.

Concurrent control allows more than one program unit to execute at the same time, either physically on separate processors or logically, in some time-sliced fashion on a single-processor computer system. Concurrent control results in having multiple threads of control. On the surface, this may appear to be a simple concept, but it presents serious design problems in a programming language.

Both symmetric and concurrent control methods increase programming flexibility. Both were originally devised for particular problems but can be used for a variety of other programming applications. Many software systems are designed to simulate actual physical systems, and many of these physical systems consist of multiple concurrent subsystems. For these applications, the more restricted form of subprogram control is inadequate.

In this chapter, we discuss the concepts underlying symmetric and concurrent unit control and the design choices for programming languages to support these concepts. Note that the intention of this chapter is to discuss the aspects of symmetric and concurrent unit control that are most relevant to language design issues. It is not our intent to present a definitive study of all of the issues of concurrency. That would clearly be inappropriate for a book on programming languages.

11.1 Introduction

11.1.1 Categories of Concurrency

There are several categories of concurrent unit control. One such category is called the symmetric unit model, in which a number of program units, called **coroutines,** can cooperate to intertwine their execution sequences, but only one can be in execution at any given time. The execution of symmetric units is sometimes called **quasi-concurrency.** The most general category of concurrency is that in which, assuming that more than one processor is available, several program units literally execute simultaneously. This is **physical concurrency.** A slight relaxation of this concept of concurrency allows the programmer and the application software to assume that there are multiple processors providing actual concurrency when, in fact, the actual execution of programs is taking place in interleaved fashion on a single processor. This is **logical concurrency.** It is similar to the illusion of simultaneous execution that is provided to different users of a multiprogrammed computer system. From the programmer and language designer points of view, logical concurrency is the same as physical concurrency. It is the language implementor's task to map the logical concurrency to the underlying hardware. Both logical and physical concurrency allow the concept of concurrency to be used as a program design methodology. For the remainder of this chapter, we will mean logical concurrency whenever we use the word **concurrency** without qualification.

One useful technique for visualizing the flow of execution through a program is to imagine a thread laid on the source text of the program. Every point reached on a particular execution is covered by the thread representing that execution. Visually following the thread through the source program parallels the execution flow through the executable version of the program. A **thread of control** in a program is the sequence of program points reached as control flows through the program.

Quasi-concurrent programs have a single thread of control. Programs executed with physical concurrency have multiple threads of control. Although logically concurrent program execution may actually have only a single thread of control, such programs can only be usefully designed and analyzed by imagining them as having multiple threads of control.

There are at least two reasons to study concurrency. First and foremost, it provides a method of conceptualizing about program solutions to problems. Many problem domains lend themselves naturally to concurrency, in much the same way that recursion is a natural way to design the solution to some problems. Much of computing involves simulating physical entities. In many cases, the system being simulated includes more than one entity, and the entities do whatever they do simultaneously—for example, aircraft in a control area, relay stations in a communications network, and the various machines in a manufacturing facility. To accurately simulate such systems with software, that software must be able to provide for concurrency.

The second reason to discuss concurrency is that multiple processor computers are now being widely used, thus creating the need for software to make effective use of that hardware capability.

There are similar, although far less compelling, reasons to consider symmetric unit control.

Because of the importance of concurrent and symmetric unit control, facilities to provide them must be developed and included in contemporary programming languages.

11.1.2 Fundamental Concepts

A **task** is a program unit that can be in concurrent execution with other program units. Each task in a program can provide one thread of control.

There are two characteristics of tasks that distinguish them from subprograms. First, a task may be implicitly started, whereas a subprogram must be explicitly called. Second, when a program unit invokes a task, it need not wait for the task to complete its execution before continuing its own execution.

A task can communicate with other tasks through shared nonlocal variables, through message passing, or through parameters. If a task does not communicate with or affect the execution of any other task in a program in any way, it is said to be **disjoint.** Because tasks often work together to create simulations or solve problems and therefore are not disjoint, they must use some form of communication to either synchronize their executions or share data or both.

Synchronization is a mechanism that controls the order in which tasks execute. Two kinds of synchronization are required when tasks share data: cooperation and competition. **Cooperation synchronization** is required between task A and task B when task A must wait for task B to complete some activity before task A can continue its execution. **Competition synchronization** is required between two tasks when both require the use of some resource that cannot be simultaneously used.

A simple form of cooperation synchronization can be illustrated by a common category of applications called the producer-consumer problem. This problem originated in the development of operating systems, in which one program unit produces some data value and another uses that value. Such data is usually placed in a storage buffer by the producing unit and removed from that buffer by the consuming unit. The sequence of stores to and removals from the buffer must be synchronized. The consumer unit must not be allowed to take a value from the buffer if the buffer is empty. Likewise, the producer unit cannot be allowed to place a new value in the buffer if the buffer is full. This is called the problem of cooperation synchronization because the users of the shared data structure must cooperate if the buffer is to be used correctly.

Note that the need for cooperation synchronization in the producer-consumer application is not restricted to the realm of concurrency. Cooperation synchronization is also required for a shared buffer when the producers and consumers are coroutines whose execution is only quasi-concurrent. This will be made clear in the examples of Section 11.2.

Competition synchronization prevents two tasks from accessing a shared data structure at exactly the same time—a situation that could destroy the integrity of that shared data. To provide competition synchronization, mutually exclusive access to the shared data must be guaranteed.

To clarify the competition problem, consider the following scenario: Suppose task A is in the process of adding 1 to the shared integer variable TOTAL. To do this, it fetches a copy of the current value of TOTAL to do the addition. Before A updates the value of TOTAL, task B begins to increment TOTAL by 1, using the same method. Task B fetches the old value of TOTAL, because A has not yet stored the new value. Then A writes its new value to TOTAL. Finally, B writes its new value to TOTAL. The result of this scenario is that after both A and B are finished incrementing TOTAL, the value of TOTAL is larger by only 1, although it should have been incremented twice, once by A and once by B. This scenario is shown in Figure 11.1.

Note that competition synchronization is not a problem with coroutines, because only one of them can be in execution at a given time. Furthermore, control cannot be switched from one coroutine to another in the middle of a data update operation (control can only be switched from a coroutine between the execution of source-level statements).

One general method for providing mutually exclusive access to a resource is to consider the resource to be something that a task can possess and then allow only a single task to possess a shared resource at a time. To gain possession of a shared resource, a task must request it. When a task is finished with a shared resource that it possesses, it must relinquish that resource so that the resource can be made available to other tasks.

Figure 11.1
The need for competition synchronization

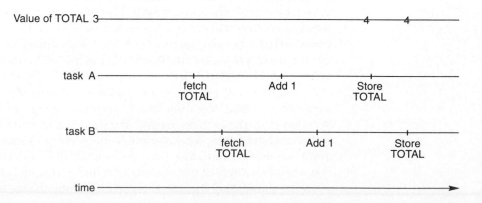

Three methods of providing mutually exclusive access to a shared data structure are semaphores, which are discussed in Section 11.3.2; monitors, which are discussed in Section 11.3.3; and message passing, which is discussed in Section 11.3.4.

Associated with the use of shared resources is the concept of **liveness.** In the environment of sequential programs, a program has the characteristic of liveness if it continues to execute, eventually leading to completion. In more general terms, liveness means that if some event—say program completion—is supposed to occur, it will occur, eventually. That is, progress is continually made. In the environment of concurrency and the use of shared resources, the liveness of a task can cease to exist, meaning that the program cannot continue and thus will never terminate.

For example, suppose task A and task B both need the shared resources X and Y to complete their work. Further suppose that task A gains possession of X and task B gains possession of Y. After some execution, task A needs resource Y to continue, so it requests Y but must wait until B releases it. Likewise, task B requests X but must wait until A releases it. Neither relinquishes the resource it possesses, and as a result both lose their liveness, guaranteeing that execution of the program will never complete normally. This particular kind of loss of liveness is called **deadlock.** Deadlock is a serious threat to the reliability of a program, and therefore its avoidance demands serious consideration in both language and program design.

We are now ready to discuss some of the mechanisms for providing symmetric and concurrent unit control.

11.2 Language Design for Coroutines

The actual origin of the concept of symmetric unit control is difficult to determine. One of the earliest published applications of coroutines was in the area of syntax analysis (Conway, 1963). The first high-level programming language to include facilities for coroutines was SIMULA 67. Recall that the original purpose of SIMULA was system simulation, which often requires the modeling of independent processes. This need was the motivation for the development of SIMULA 67's coroutines. Other languages that support coroutines are BLISS (Wulf et al., 1971), INTERLISP (Teitelman, 1975), and Modula-2 (Wirth, 1985).

A coroutine is a subprogram that has multiple entry points, which are controlled by the coroutine itself, and the means to maintain its status between activations. This means that coroutines must be history sensitive and thus have static local variables. Secondary executions of a coroutine often begin at points other than the beginning of the coroutine. Because of this, the invocation of a coroutine is called a **resume** rather than a call.

A coroutine may include a segment of code that is executed only at the time the coroutine is created. This code is called the coroutine's **initializa-**

tion code, and its purpose will become clear when coroutines are illustrated with an example.

One of the usual characteristics of subprograms is maintained in coroutines: Only one coroutine actually executes at a given time. There is only a single thread of control in a program with coroutines. Rather than executing to their ends, however, coroutines often partially execute and then transfer control to some other coroutine. When restarted, the first coroutine resumes execution just after the statement that was last active.

Typically, coroutines are created in an application by a program unit called the **master unit,** which is not a coroutine. When created, coroutines execute their initialization code and then return control back to that master unit. When all of a family of coroutines are constructed, the master program resumes one of the coroutines, and the family of coroutines then resume each other in some order until their work is completed, if in fact it can be completed. If the execution of a coroutine reaches the end of its code section, control is transferred to the master unit that created it. This is the mechanism for ending execution of the collection of coroutines, if that is desirable, which is not always the case.

One example of a problem that can be solved with this sort of collection of coroutines is the simulation of a card game. Suppose the game has four players who all use the same strategy for playing. Such a game can be simulated by having a master program unit create a family of coroutines, each with a collection, or hand, of cards. The master program could then start the simulation by resuming one of the player coroutines, which, after it had played its turn, could resume the next player coroutine, and so forth until the game ended.

The same form of resume statement can be used both to start and to restart the execution of a coroutine.

Suppose program units A and B are coroutines. Figure 11.2 on the following page shows two ways an execution sequence involving A and B might proceed.

In Figure 11.2a, the execution of coroutine A is started by the master unit. After some execution, A starts B. When coroutine B in Figure 11.2a first causes control to return to coroutine A, the semantics is that A continues from where it ended its last execution. In particular, its local variables have the values left them by the previous activation. Figure 11.2b shows an alternative execution sequence of coroutines A and B. In this case, B is started by the master unit.

Rather than have the patterns shown in Figure 11.2, a coroutine often has a loop containing a resume. Figure 11.3 on the following page describes the execution sequence of this scenario.

11.2.1 Design Issues

Because the actions of a coroutine are well defined, there are few important design issues. For example, coroutines must be history sensitive, and they

Figure 11.2
Two possible execution
control sequences for
two coroutines without
loops

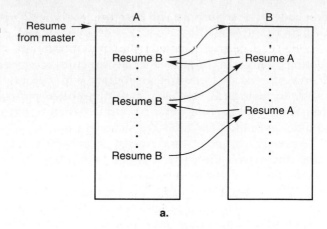

a.

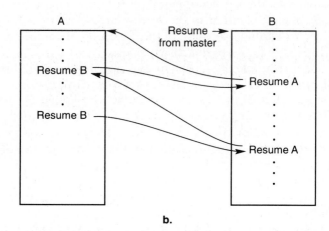

b.

Figure 11.3
Coroutine execution
sequence with loops

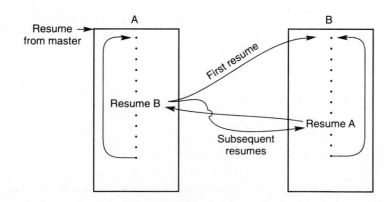

must have some means of resuming other coroutines. How such control is provided is one issue; it is primarily one of choosing between new language statements and relying on some external library of capabilities. Another issue is when and how coroutine execution begins and ends: Does a coroutine begin execution when it is created or only after it is invoked? Finally, there is the question of how and when coroutines are created: Are they static or dynamic?

The following summarizes these design issues for coroutines:

1. Are the coroutine control statements in the language or provided in a library?
2. How and when should coroutine execution begin and end?
3. Are coroutines created statically or dynamically?

11.2.2 Coroutines in SIMULA 67

SIMULA 67 classes were devised to implement coroutines. Although SIMULA 67 was the first programming language to include coroutines, our discussion of its coroutines will be relatively brief because of the obscurity of the language.

11.2.2.1 Design

The execution of SIMULA 67 coroutines is controlled, at least in part, by the **resume** and **detach** statements. The **detach** statement suspends the execution of a coroutine and returns control to the master unit that created it. A **detach** statement is usually placed immediately after the initialization code in a class body. Recall that the class body is executed when the class is instantiated through the execution of **new**.

The **resume** statement is similar to a procedure call, except that the execution of the called coroutine begins with the statement following the statement that was last executed. Because the initial execution of a SIMULA 67 coroutine occurs when it is created, a **resume** can never begin execution of a coroutine at its beginning. Instead, the first **resume** of a coroutine begins executing at the first statement after its first **detach**.

11.2.2.2 An Example

The producer-consumer problem described in Section 11.1 can be solved using coroutines, because coroutines provide the required cooperation synchronization. In the following skeletal SIMULA 67 program for a simple version of the producer-consumer problem, the entity being produced and consumed is a simple integer value. Note that the integer value is transferred between the producer and the consumer through a single-element global buffer named buf.

```
begin
COMMENT *** DEFINITION OF THE PRODUCER COROUTINE
  class producer;
    begin
    integer stuff;
    ref (consumer) cons;
    detach;
    while true do
      begin
      -- produce stuff --
      buf := stuff;
      resume (cons);
      end
    end;

COMMENT *** DEFINITION OF THE CONSUMER COROUTINE
  class consumer;
    begin
    integer value;
    ref (producer) prod;
    detach;
    while true do
      begin
      value := buf;
      -- consume value --
      resume (prod);
      end
    end;

COMMENT *** THE MASTER PROGRAM UNIT
    integer buf;
  ref (producer) prod1;
  ref (consumer) cons1;
  prod1 :- new producer;
  cons1 :- new consumer;
  prod1.cons :- cons1;
  cons1.prod :- prod1;
  resume (prod1)
  end;
```

The main program code area of this system, which begins with the declaration of the variable buf, creates the instances of the producer and consumer coroutines and then continues executing the producer with a **resume**, thereby beginning the action of the coroutines. Execution control then alternates between the producer and consumer coroutines. Notice that this program has no way of terminating gracefully. This is not uncommon for coroutine systems, although some are not designed to run forever. If execution is simply allowed to reach the end of any coroutine, control returns to the master program.

The cooperation synchronization of these two coroutines guarantees that the `producer` places a value in the buffer before the `consumer` removes it, and vice versa. This synchronization is accomplished by the use of the **resume** statements in the two coroutines.

11.2.3 Coroutines in Modula-2

The language design philosophy of Niklaus Wirth is centered on the concept that simplicity is an essential characteristic of a good programming language, and Modula-2 clearly reflects this. It is an attempt to design the simplest language possible that has powerful and flexible capabilities.

11.2.3.1 Design

There are no statements, data types, or operators in Modula-2 for either symmetric or concurrent control units. However, that does not disallow those capabilities. Most Modula-2 compilers supply a module, as suggested by Wirth (1985), that provides sufficient facilities for building and using coroutines. This technique allows support for coroutines without enlarging the language.

Two levels of abstraction for coroutine support are typically provided with a Modula-2 compiler: (1) a low-level module, usually called SYSTEM, that provides a data type and procedures for creating, starting, and resuming coroutines; and (2) a high-level module that uses the low-level module to provide a data type and procedures for dealing with coroutines, including synchronizing their execution sequences. The following is a brief description of one version of this higher-level module, called Processes.

The coroutines of Modula-2 are called processes. They are constructed from parameterless procedures using the facilities of the SYSTEM module, and they can be called only through other facilities of SYSTEM. Because they are actually just procedures, Modula-2 coroutines are statically created.

The Processes module can be designed for a variety of applications because it is not part of the language. For example, an abstract description of a version of Processes can be designed for use in building data abstractions for handling shared data buffers. The definition module for this version of Processes is as follows:

```
DEFINITION MODULE Processes;
   EXPORT SIGNAL, StartProcess, SEND, WAIT,
                   Awaited, Init;
   TYPE SIGNAL;
   PROCEDURE StartProcess (p : PROC; n : CARDINAL);
   PROCEDURE SEND (VAR s : SIGNAL);
   PROCEDURE WAIT (VAR s : SIGNAL);
   PROCEDURE Awaited (s : SIGNAL) : BOOLEAN;
   PROCEDURE Init (VAR s : SIGNAL);
END Processes.
```

The SIGNAL type is for objects that can be associated with a shared buffer, in order to allow cooperation synchronization to be managed for that structure. A SIGNAL type object consists of an integer counter and a queue for storing process descriptors. The actual form of a process descriptor is not important here. For our discussion, simply assume a processor descriptor is whatever it takes to be able to refer to a process.

11.2.3.2 An Example

The following description of the facilities of Processes is in terms of its intended purpose: management of a shared multiposition buffer. The problem of providing cooperation synchronization is somewhat more complex when the shared buffer has more than one position. Rather than simply keeping track of whether the buffer is full or empty, the module must have some way of recording both the number of empty positions and the number of filled positions. The counter component of a SIGNAL type variable can be used for this purpose. One SIGNAL type variable, say emptyspots, can be used to store the number of empty locations in a shared buffer, and another, say fullspots, can be used to store the number of filled locations in the buffer.

The buffer is designed as an abstract data type in which all data enters the buffer through the procedure deposit, and all data leaves the buffer through the procedure fetch. Then the deposit procedure only needs to check with the emptyspots SIGNAL to see if there are any empty positions in the buffer. If there are, it can go ahead with the deposit. If the buffer is full, the caller to deposit must be made to wait in the emptyspots queue for an empty spot to become available. When the deposit is complete, the deposit procedure can indicate to the fullspots SIGNAL that there is one more filled location in the buffer.

The fetch procedure has the opposite sequence of deposit. It checks the fullspots SIGNAL to see if the buffer contains at least one item. If it does, the item is removed and the emptyspots SIGNAL has its counter incremented by 1. If the buffer is empty, the calling process is put in the fullspots queue to wait until an item appears.

To clarify the purpose of the queue component of a SIGNAL type variable in terms of a shared buffer, consider the situation in which several coroutines attempt to place a data value in a shared buffer that is full. In this situation, the system must "remember" all coroutines that attempted to place a data value in the queue but were not allowed, so that when an empty position becomes available, one of the waiting coroutines can be resumed. In our example, references to coroutines waiting for empty positions in the buffer are stored in the queue of the emptyspots SIGNAL variable.

The operations on SIGNAL types are not direct but rather are done through the WAIT and SEND procedures in Processes. Before these procedures can be described, however, the concept of a ready queue for processes must be discussed. When there is a collection of processes, in this case coroutines, in quasi-concurrent execution and that execution must be synchronized, occasionally one or more of the processes will be suspended while they wait for some event. If more than one process is waiting for the same event, only one process can be resumed when that event occurs. The others must be stored somewhere until the executing process is suspended, at which time one of the others can be given the processor. The place where these waiting processes are stored is called the **process ready queue,** or simply ready queue. The WAIT and SEND procedures must be able to access the ready queue.

This use of a process ready queue is exactly like the method employed by multiprogramming operating systems. Modula-2 was designed so that such software systems could be written using it.

The WAIT procedure is used by a coroutine to test the counter of a given SIGNAL variable. If the value is greater than zero, the coroutine can carry out its operation. In this case, the counter value of the SIGNAL variable is decremented to indicate that it now has one fewer of whatever it had. If the value of the counter is less than or equal to zero, the coroutine must be placed on the waiting queue of the SIGNAL variable.

The SEND operation is used by a coroutine to allow some other coroutine to have one of whatever the counter of the specified SIGNAL variable counts. If the queue of the specified SIGNAL variable is empty, which means no coroutine is waiting, SEND increments its counter (to indicate there is one more of whatever is being controlled that is now available). If one or more coroutines are waiting, SEND moves one of them from the SIGNAL queue to the ready queue.

The following is a concise description of WAIT and SEND:

```
WAIT (signal1)
  IF signal1's counter > 0
    THEN decrement signal1's counter
    ELSE
      put the caller in signal1's queue
      attempt to transfer control to some ready process
          {If the ready queue is empty, deadlock occurs}
  END

SEND (signal1)
  IF signal1's queue is empty {no process is waiting}
    THEN increment signal1's counter
    ELSE
      put the calling process in the ready queue
      transfer control to a process from signal1's queue
  END
```

Now we can present our Modula-2 data abstraction for the shared buffer, which stores simple integers and has 100 locations in a logically circular structure:

```
DEFINITION MODULE Buffer;
  PROCEDURE deposit (newstuff: INTEGER);
  PROCEDURE fetch (VAR oldstuff: INTEGER)
END Buffer.

IMPLEMENTATION MODULE Buffer;
  FROM Processes IMPORT SIGNAL, SEND, WAIT, Init;
  CONST BUFSIZE = 100;
  VAR fullspots : SIGNAL;
    emptyspots : SIGNAL;
    in, out : [0..BUFSIZE-1];
    buf : ARRAY [0..BUFSIZE-1] OF INTEGER;
    counter : INTEGER;

  PROCEDURE deposit (newstuff : INTEGER);
    BEGIN
    WAIT (emptyspots);
    buf[in] := newstuff;
    in := (in + 1) MOD BUFSIZE;
    SEND (fullspots)
    END deposit;

  PROCEDURE fetch (VAR oldstuff : INTEGER);
    BEGIN
    WAIT (fullspots);
    oldstuff := buf[out];
    out := (out + 1) MOD BUFSIZE;
    SEND (emptyspots)
    END fetch;

  BEGIN   { code body for Buffer }
  in := 0;
  out := 0;
  Init (emptyspots);
  Init (fullspots);
  FOR counter := 1 TO BUFSIZE DO
    SEND (emptyspots)
  END
END Buffer.
```

The declarations of the Buffer implementation module create the buffer, the two signals for synchronizing its use, and the indices for storing the next available element and empty locations in it. The variable counter is used only in the module code body.

The code body of the Buffer implementation module first initializes the indices, in and out, to correspond to the first location in the buffer. Then the Init procedure, which was imported from Processes, initializes the two SIGNAL variables, emptyspots and fullspots. This empties their process queues and sets their counters to zero. SEND is then called with emptyspots as its parameter, once for each position in the new buffer. This simply sets the counter in emptyspots to that value, because initially the buffer is indeed empty. The loop is necessary because the only access to a SIGNAL is through SEND and WAIT; a SIGNAL's counter cannot simply be set to a value. After these initializing actions, the Buffer module is available for use by any number of coroutines that need to share its buffer.

The SIMULA 67 coroutine example given earlier manages a single-entry buffer, whereas the Modula-2 example manages a multiple-entry buffer. A SIMULA 67 program to manage the same multiple-entry buffer could have been written, but the program would have had to include the implementation of some form of the SIGNAL type and the SEND and WAIT operations, similar to those provided by the Modula-2 Processes module.

Keep in mind that the Processes module can be rewritten to make it convenient for other applications. The one given here was designed explicitly to support the shared buffer. The SIGNAL type and the WAIT and SEND procedures can be whatever the user wants them to be.

The following code shows a typical skeletal procedure for a producer coroutine that could use the Buffer module:

```
PROCEDURE Producer;
   VAR stuff : INTEGER;
   BEGIN
     LOOP
       --produce stuff--
       deposit(stuff)
     END
   END Producer;
```

Note that a coroutine is constructed and its execution is started by procedures provided by the SYSTEM module, the details of which are not discussed here.

11.2.3.3 Evaluation of the Modula-2 Coroutine Model

Use of the SIGNAL type variables to provide cooperation synchronization creates an unsafe programming environment: There is no way to statically check for the correctness of their use, which depends on the semantics of the program in which they appear. In the buffer example, leaving the WAIT (emptyspots) statement out of the deposit procedure would result in buffer overflow. Leaving the WAIT (fullspots) statement out of the fetch procedure would result in buffer underflow. Leaving out either of the SENDs would result in deadlock. These are cooperation synchronization failures. A more reliable method of providing cooperation synchronization is discussed in Section 11.3.4.

Another problem with the Modula-2 implementation of coroutines is that no means is provided for returning control to a master unit. To make it a viable system, some method must be devised to handle process termination in a less catastrophic way. One such method has been suggested in Sewry (1984a). Recall that in SIMULA 67, coroutines can return control to their master program units, either by execution of a **detach** statement or by executing to their ends.

Finally, the decision to relegate coroutine creation and control to a library has the following negative repercussion: There is no strong incentive for Modula-2 implementors to provide Processes modules that are identical to those in other implementations. Therefore, programs that use Processes must provide the Processes code themselves if they are to be portable. That is the price of the simplicity gained by leaving coroutine control out of the language.

We now turn our attention to concurrent unit control.

11.3   Language Design for Concurrency

One of the fundamental capabilities that are required to support concurrency is competition synchronization. In this section, three methods of providing this capability are discussed: semaphores, monitors, and the message-passing model. Of course, any linguistic mechanism that is meant to support concurrency must also provide for cooperation synchronization.

11.3.1   Design Issues

The most important design issues for language support for concurrency have already been discussed at length: competition and cooperation synchronization. In addition, there are the issues of how and when tasks start and end executions, and how and when they are created.

The following is a summary of the primary design issues for language support for concurrency:

1. How is competition synchronization provided?
2. How is cooperation synchronization provided?
3. How and when do tasks begin and end execution?
4. Are tasks statically or dynamically created?

There are several additional design issues for concurrent unit control. Prominent among them is how to provide for task scheduling. However, for simplicity's sake, our discussion of concurrency is intentionally incomplete, and several design issues are neither listed above nor discussed in this chapter.

The following sections discuss three alternative answers to the first design issue for concurrency, the question of how to provide competition synchronization. The three approaches are semaphores, monitors, and message passing.

Note that PL/I was the first programming language to include concurrent tasks. It allowed user programs to execute any subprogram concurrently with the unit that called it. Synchronization of these concurrent executions, however, was primitive. It consisted of only the ability to detect when a task had completed its execution. Because of the severe limitations of the PL/I design, it will not be discussed further in this chapter.

11.3.2 Semaphores

11.3.2.1 Semaphore Design Concepts

In an effort to provide for competition synchronization through mutually exclusive access to shared data structures, Edsger Dijkstra devised semaphores in 1965 (Dijkstra, 1968b). The concept of a semaphore is that, to provide limited access to a data structure, one simply places guards around the code that accesses the structure. A **guard** is a linguistic device that allows the guarded code to be executed only under a specified condition. A guard can be used to allow only one task to access a shared data structure at a time. An integral part of a guard mechanism is a technique for ensuring that all attempted executions of the guarded code actually take place, eventually. This is accomplished by having requests for access that occur when access cannot be granted be stored in a queue, from which they are later allowed to leave and execute the guarded code. Therefore, a semaphore must have both a counter and a process queue. This should all sound familiar because the SIGNAL data type exported by the Modula-2 module, Processes, is a form of semaphore. The SIGNAL data type is modeled after Dijkstra's semaphores. Since the use of semaphores to provide cooperation synchronization has already been discussed, the focus here is on the use of semaphores to provide competition synchronization.

The only two operations provided for semaphores were originally named *P* and *V* by Dijkstra, after the two Dutch words *passeren* (to pass) and *vrygeren* (to release) (Andrew and Sneider, 1983). These correspond to the WAIT and SEND operations of the SIGNAL data type and are called wait and release in the following discussion.

Suppose there is a shared data structure named STUFF, and access to it must be mutually exclusive. Access to the structure can be provided with a semaphore, which is named SEMASTUFF, if all processes that share STUFF have the following form:

```
process example
  begin
    . . .
```

```
wait (SEMASTUFF)
-- access STUFF --
release (SEMASTUFF)
...
end
```

The code in this process that accesses STUFF is called the **critical region,** which is protected by the semaphore SEMASTUFF. Whenever a process gets to its critical region, it uses **wait**. The **wait** statement allows access only if the SEMASTUFF counter has the value 1, which indicates that STUFF is not currently being accessed. If the SEMASTUFF counter has a value of 0, there is a current access taking place, and the process is placed on the queue of SEMASTUFF. Notice that SEMASTUFF's counter must be initialized to 1. The queues of semaphores must always be initialized to empty.

Figure 11.4 shows two processes using a semaphore to protect a critical region.

A semaphore that only requires a binary-valued counter, like the one used to control access to a critical region of code, is called a **binary semaphore.**

11.3.2.2 A Concurrently Accessed Shared Buffer with Semaphores

The example code below illustrates the use of semaphores to provide both competition and cooperation synchronization for a concurrently accessed shared buffer.

Figure 11.4
Two processes using a semaphore to synchronize access to shared data

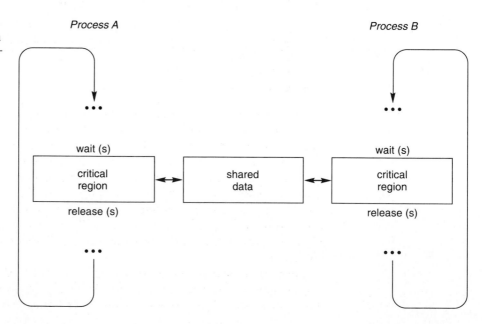

Two semaphores are used to ensure against buffer underflow or overflow, thus providing cooperation synchronization. A third semaphore is used to control access to the buffer, thereby providing competition synchronization. Assume that the buffer has length BUFLEN, and the routines that actually manipulate it already exist as REMOVE and ENTER. Accesses to the counter of a semaphore are specified by dot notation. For example, if access is a semaphore, its counter is referenced by access.count.

```
semaphore access, fullspots, emptyspots;
access.count := 1;
fullspots.count := 0;
emptyspots.count := BUFLEN;


process producer;
  loop
  -- produce VALUE --
  wait (emptyspots);   { wait for a space }
  wait (access);   { wait for access }
  ENTER (VALUE);
  release (access);   { relinquish access }
  release (fullspots);  { increase filled spaces }
  end loop;
end producer;

process consumer;
  loop
  wait (fullspots);   { make sure its not empty }
  wait (access);   { wait for access }
  REMOVE (VALUE);
  release (access);  { relinquish access }
  release (emptyspots);  { increase empty spaces }
  -- consume VALUE --
  end loop;
end consumer;
```

The semaphore fullspots records the number of filled locations in the buffer. It causes the consumer process to be queued to wait for a buffer entry if it is currently empty. The semaphore emptyspots stores the number of empty spaces in the buffer. It causes the producer process to be queued to wait for an empty space in the buffer if it is currently filled. These two semaphores are used in exactly the same way that the two SIGNAL type variables of the same names were used in the Modula-2 coroutine example: The access semaphore ensures mutually exclusive access to the buffer. Note that there may be more than one producer and more than one consumer.

There is one crucial aspect of semaphores that thus far has not been discussed here. Recall the earlier description of the problem of competition synchronization: Operations on shared data must not be overlapped. If a second operation can be begun while an earlier operation is still in progress, the shared data can become corrupted. A semaphore is a shared data object, so the operations on semaphores are also susceptible to the same problem. It is therefore essential that semaphore operations be uninterruptable. Many computers have uninterruptable instructions that were designed specifically for semaphore operations. If such instructions are not available, then using semaphores to provide competition synchronization is a serious problem with no simple solution.

11.3.2.3 Evaluation of Semaphores

Semaphores used to provide cooperation synchronization suffer the same problems faced by the `SIGNAL` type variables in Modula-2. Similar problems arise with using semaphores for competition synchronization. Leaving out the **wait** (access) statement in either process can cause insecure access to the buffer. Leaving out the **release** (access) statement in either process results in deadlock. These are competition synchronization failures. Lastly, semaphores cannot prevent accesses to shared data structures that are inadvertently placed outside the protected critical regions. Noting the danger in using semaphores, Brinch Hansen wrote "The semaphore is an elegant synchronization tool for an ideal programmer who never makes mistakes" (Brinch Hansen, 1973). Unfortunately, that kind of programmer is rare.

11.3.3 Monitors

11.3.3.1 Monitor Design Concepts

In retrospect, we can see that one relatively obvious solution to some of the problems of semaphores in a concurrent environment is to encapsulate shared data structures with their operations and hide their representations—that is, make shared data structures abstract data types. This solution can provide competition synchronization without semaphores by transferring responsibility for synchronization to the operating system.

When the concepts of data abstraction were being formulated, the people involved in that effort applied the same concepts to shared data in concurrent programming environments to produce monitors. According to Per Brinch Hansen (Brinch Hansen, 1977, page xvi), Edsger Dijkstra suggested in 1971 that all synchronization operations on shared data be gathered into a single program unit. Brinch Hansen formalized this concept in the environment of operating systems (Brinch Hansen, 1973). The following year, Hoare named these structures monitors (Hoare, 1974).

11.3.3.2 Monitors in Concurrent Pascal

The first programming language to incorporate monitors was Concurrent Pascal (Brinch Hansen, 1975). Modula (Wirth, 1976), CSP/k (Holt et al.,

1978), and Mesa (Mitchell et al., 1979) also provide monitors. The following discussion of monitors is based on their incarnation in Concurrent Pascal.

Concurrent Pascal is Wirth's Pascal with three important kinds of constructs added: classes from SIMULA 67, processes, and monitors. Our concern here is with the features that support concurrent programming: processes and monitors. Note that some of the concepts underlying the design of the Modula-2 coroutine mechanism originated in the processes and monitors of Concurrent Pascal.

A Concurrent Pascal process has a syntactic form that is similar to that of a procedure, but the semantics is quite different. All processes are types, so they are defined in **type** statements of the form

```
type process_name = process (formal parameters)
   --local declarations--
   --process body--
end
```

Because they are types, process definitions are merely templates for actual processes, and because variable declarations are used to create processes, they can be created either statically or dynamically. Declaring a variable to be of a process type creates the code for the process but does nothing else. To cause the allocation of its local data and to begin its execution, an **init** statement that includes actual parameters is used, as in

```
init process_variable_name (actual parameters)
```

After execution of the **init**, the process remains in the execution state for the duration of the program, except when it is put to sleep by delayed access to the shared data in a monitor.

Before an example of a process can be of value, Concurrent Pascal monitors must be briefly discussed. Monitors are abstract data types for shared data resources. Their general form is

```
type monitor_name = monitor (formal parameters)
   --declarations of shared variables--
   --definitions of local procedures--
   --definitions of exported procedures--
   --initialization code--
end
```

The exported procedures of a monitor are syntactically different from local procedures only in that they contain the reserved word **entry** in their **procedure** statements.

Like process types, monitor types are templates. The **init** statement, with actual parameters, is used to create instances of monitors. This causes dynamic allocation of storage for the variables of the process and execution of the initialization code. The lifetime of monitor variables, except those in monitor procedures, begins with the **init** and terminates with the program.

Figure 11.5
A program using a
monitor to control ac-
cess to a shared buffer

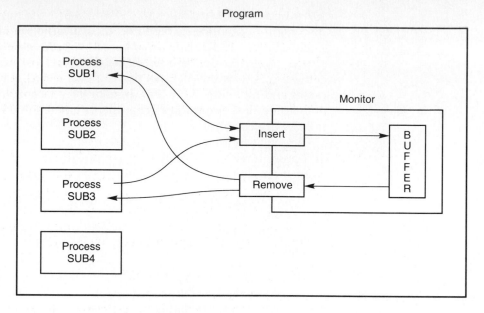

Their scope is only the monitor itself. The exported procedures of a monitor can be called by either processes or procedures in other monitors.

One of the most important features of monitors is that shared data is resident in the monitor rather than in any of the client program units. Thus the programmer does not synchronize mutually exclusive access to shared data through the use of semaphores or other mechanisms. Because all accesses are resident in the monitor, the monitor implementation can be made to guarantee synchronized access by simply allowing only one access at a time. Calls to monitor procedures are queued if the monitor is busy at the time of the call.

Although mutually exclusive access to shared data is intrinsic with a monitor, cooperation between processes is still the task of the programmer. In particular, the programmer must guarantee that a shared buffer does not underflow or overflow. For this purpose, Concurrent Pascal has a special data type, **queue**, and two operations on it, **delay** and **continue**. The queue type is a form of semaphore, and the two operations are related to the send and release semaphore operations.

A variable of queue type stores processes that are waiting to use a shared data structure. This waiting, as we saw, is caused by the need for cooperation synchronization: Either a process tries to place a value in a full storage structure, or a process tries to remove a value from an empty structure.

The **delay** operation takes a queue type variable as a parameter. Its action is to place the process that calls it in the specified queue and remove its exclusive access rights to monitor data structures. Thus the process that executes **delay** has its execution suspended. The monitor is then available to other processes.

The **continue** operation also takes a queue type parameter. Its action is to disconnect the process that calls it from the monitor, thus freeing the monitor to access by other processes; **continue** then examines the specified queue. If the queue contains a process, that process is removed and its execution, which had been suspended by a **delay** operation, is restarted.

A program containing four processes and a monitor that provides synchronized access to a concurrently shared buffer is shown in Figure 11.5.

11.3.3.3 A Monitor Implementation of a Concurrently Accessed Shared Buffer

Using the **queue** data type and the **delay** and **continue** operations, a monitor can be constructed that controls a shared buffer, thus providing both competition and cooperation synchronization. In the following example, the shared buffer is the same as that implemented in the Modula-2 coroutine example: a logically circular list of 100 integers.

```
type databuf =
  monitor
    const bufsize = 100;
    var buf : array [1..bufsize] of integer;
      next_in,
      next_out      : 1..bufsize;
      filled        : 0..bufsize;
      sender_q,
      receiver_q    : queue;

  procedure entry insert (item : integer);
    begin
    if filled = bufsize
      then delay (sender_q);
    buf[next_in] := item;
    next_in := (next_in mod bufsize) + 1;
    filled := filled + 1;
    continue (receiver_q)
    end;

  procedure entry remove (var item : integer);
    begin
    if filled = 0
      then delay (receiver_q);
    item := buf[next_out];
    next_out := (next_out mod bufsize) + 1;
    filled := filled - 1;
    continue (sender_q)
    end;

  begin
  filled := 0;
  next_in := 1;
  next_out := 1
  end;
```

An instance of type `databuf` is an abstraction of a particular kind of buffer for storing integers. Besides storing integers, a `databuf` type buffer coordinates the activities of adding and removing its values by concurrent processes. The integrity of this buffer is guaranteed by the mechanisms used to construct it. It is protected against underflow and overflow, and concurrent processes using it cannot destructively interfere with each other.

An example of declarations for processes that can use the `databuf` monitor is as follows:

```
type producer = process (buffer : databuf);
  var stuff : integer;
  begin
    cycle
    -- produce stuff --
    buffer.insert (stuff);
    end
  end;

type consumer = process (buffer : databuf);
  var stored_value : integer;
  begin
  cycle
  buffer.remove (stored_value);
  -- consume stored_value --
  end
end;
```

Note that **cycle** . . **end** is an infinite loop.

The type declarations of the monitor `databuf` and the two processes `producer` and `consumer` can be included in the declaration section of a program in which they are to be used, as in

```
--type declarations--

var new_producer : producer;
    new_consumer : consumer;
    new_buffer : databuf;
begin
init new_buffer, new_producer (new_buffer),
        new_consumer (new_buffer);
end;
```

This may appear a bit odd to the reader not familiar with concurrent programs, because it is not obvious how the program either begins or terminates. Our example program begins when the **init** is executed, creating a buffer and two processes, at which time the processes begin execution. It never ends.

11.3.3.4 Evaluation of Monitors

Monitors, as implemented in Concurrent Pascal, provide the same capabilities as the coroutines of Modula-2. In addition, they also provide for the mutually exclusive access to shared data structures that is required in a language that supports tasks. Monitors are a better way to provide competition synchronization than semaphores, primarily because of the problems of semaphores, as discussed in Section 11.3.2.3. The use of **queue** type variables to provide cooperation synchronization are, however, subject to the same problems as semaphores used in other languages for this same purpose.

11.3.4 Concurrency through Message Passing

11.3.4.1 Design Concepts of the Message-Passing Model

The monitor construct is a dependable and safe method for providing competition synchronization for shared data access in concurrent units that share a single memory. However, consider the problem of synchronizing the units in a distributed system, in which each processor has its own memory rather than a single shared memory. Obviously, the monitor construct cannot be used effectively in this situation. Synchronization in a distributed system must be achieved by some kind of message passing among the nodes. Message passing, it turns out, can be used to provide synchronization for concurrent systems, whether distributed or not.

The first efforts to design languages that provide the capability for message passing among concurrent tasks were those of Brinch Hansen (1978) and Hoare (1978). The pioneer developers of message passing also developed a technique for handling the problem of what to do when multiple simultaneous requests were made by other tasks to communicate with a given task. It was decided that some form of nondeterminism was required to provide a kind of fairness in choosing among those requests. This fairness can be defined in various ways, but in general it means that all requesters are provided an equal chance of communicating with a given task. Nondeterministic constructs for statement-level control, called guarded commands, were introduced by Dijkstra (1975). (Guarded commands are discussed in Chapter 7.) Guarded commands are the basis of the construct designed for controlling message passing.

In the following, the process of message passing between tasks is briefly explored. The basic concept of message passing is that tasks are often busy and, when busy, are unwilling to be interrupted by other units. Suppose task A and task B are both in execution, and A wishes to send a message to

B. Clearly, if B is busy, it is not desirable to allow another task to interrupt it. That would disrupt B's current processing. Furthermore, messages usually cause associated processing in the receiver, which may not be sensible if other processing is incomplete. The alternative is to provide a linguistic mechanism that allows a task to specify to other tasks when it is ready to receive messages. This is somewhat like an executive who instructs his or her secretary to hold all incoming calls until an important activity, perhaps another telephone conversation, is completed. Later, the executive tells the secretary he or she is now willing to receive one of the callers who has been placed on hold.

A task can be designed so it can suspend its execution at some point, either because it is idle or because it needs information from another unit before it can continue and is waiting to receive a message. This is like a person who is waiting for an important call. In some cases, there is nothing else to do but sit and wait. In this situation, if task A wants to send a message to B, and B is willing to receive a message, the message can be transmitted. This actual transmission is called a **rendezvous.** Note that a rendezvous can occur only if both the sender and receiver want it to happen. Note also that the information of the message can be transmitted in either or both directions.

Both cooperation and competition synchronization of tasks can be conveniently handled with the message-passing model.

11.3.4.2   The Ada Message-Passing Model

The Ada design for tasks is partially based on the work of Brinch Hansen and Hoare, in that message passing is the design basis and nondeterminism is used to choose among competing message-sending tasks.

The full Ada tasking model is complex and the following discussion of it must be limited. The focus here will be on the Ada version of the message-passing mechanism.

Ada tasks can be more active than monitors. Monitors are passive entities that provide management services for the shared data they store. They provide their services, however, only when those services are requested. When used to manage shared data, Ada tasks can be thought of as managers that can reside with the resource they manage. They have several mechanisms, some deterministic and some nondeterministic, that allow them to choose among competing requests for access to their resources.

The form of Ada tasks is similar to that of Ada packages. There are two parts, a specification part and a body part, each with the same name. The interface of a task is its entry points, or locations where it can accept messages from other tasks. It is natural that these be listed in the specification part of a task. Because a rendezvous can involve an exchange of information, messages can have parameters; therefore, task entry points must also allow parameters, which must also be described in the specification part. In appearance, a task specification is very similar to the package specification for an abstract data type.

As an example of an Ada task specification, consider the following, which includes a single entry point named ENTRY_1:

```
task TASK_EXAMPLE is
  entry ENTRY_1 (ITEM : in INTEGER);
  end TASK_EXAMPLE;
```

A task body must include some syntactic form of entry points that correspond to the **entry** clauses in that task's specification part. In the Ada language, these are specified by **accept** clauses, which are introduced by the **accept** reserved word. An **accept** clause is defined as the range of statements beginning with the **accept** reserved word and ending with the matching **end** reserved word. **Accept** clauses are themselves relatively simple, but other constructs in which they can be embedded can make their semantics quite complex. A simple **accept** clause has the form

```
accept entry_name (formal parameters) do
  . . .
  end entry_name;
```

The **accept** entry name matches the name in an **entry** clause in the associated task specification part. The optional parameters provide the means of communicating data between the caller and the called tasks. The statements between the **do** and the **end** define the operations that take place during the rendezvous. These statements are together called the **accept clause body.** During the actual rendezvous, the sender task is suspended.

Ada tasks communicate with other tasks using the rendezvous mechanism. Whenever a task entry point, or **accept** clause, receives a message that it is not ready to accept, for whatever reason, the sender task must be suspended until the entry point in the receiver task is ready to accept the message. For this purpose, each **accept** clause in a task has a queue associated with it. The queue records a list of other tasks that have attempted to communicate with the associated entry point.

The following is the skeletal body of the task whose specification was given above:

```
task body TASK_EXAMPLE is
  begin
  loop
    accept ENTRY_1 (ITEM : in INTEGER) do
      . . .
      end ENTRY_1;
    end loop;
  end TASK_EXAMPLE;
```

The **accept** clause of this task body is the implementation of the entry named ENTRY_1 in the task specification. If the execution of TASK_EXAMPLE begins and reaches the ENTRY_1 **accept** clause before any other task sends a message to ENTRY_1, TASK_EXAMPLE is suspended. If another task sends a message to ENTRY_1 while TASK_EXAMPLE is suspended at its **accept**, a rendezvous occurs and the **accept** clause body is executed. Then, because of the loop, execution proceeds to the **accept** again. If no additional calling task has sent a message to ENTRY_1, execution is again suspended to wait for the next message.

A rendezvous can occur in two basic ways in this simple example. First, the receiver task, TASK_EXAMPLE, can be waiting for another task to send a message to the ENTRY_1 entry. When the message is sent, the rendezvous occurs. This is the situation described above. Second, the receiver task can be busy with one rendezvous, or with some other processing not associated with a rendezvous, when another task attempts to send a message to the same entry. In that case, the sender is suspended until the receiver is free to accept that message in a rendezvous. If several messages arrive while the receiver is busy, the senders are queued to wait their turn for a rendezvous.

The two rendezvous just described are illustrated with the time line diagrams in Figure 11.6.

Tasks need not have entry points. Such tasks are called **actor tasks** because they do not wait for a rendezvous in order to do useful work. Actor

Figure 11.6
Two ways a rendezvous with TASK-EXAMPLE can occur

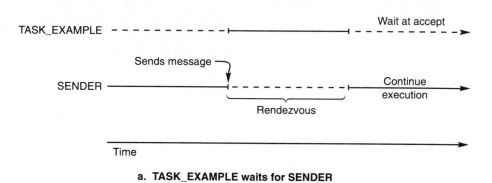

a. **TASK_EXAMPLE waits for SENDER**

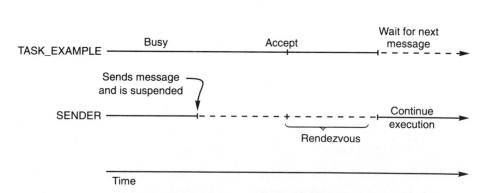

b. **SENDER waits for TASK_EXAMPLE**

tasks can rendezvous with other tasks by sending them messages. In contrast to actor tasks, a task can have entry points but little or no code other than that associated with accepting messages, so it can only react to other tasks. Such a task is called a **server task.**

An Ada task that sends a message to another task must know the entry name in that task. However, the opposite is not true: A task entry need not know the name of the task from which it will accept messages. This asymmetry is in contrast to the design of the language known as CSP (Communicating Sequential Processes) (Hoare, 1978). In CSP, which also uses the message-passing model of concurrency, tasks accept messages only from explicitly named tasks. The disadvantage of this is that libraries of tasks cannot be built for general use.

The usual graphical method of describing a rendezvous in which task A sends a message to task B is shown in Figure 11.7.

Ada tasks are types, and as such they can be either anonymous or named. An Ada task with a named type can be dynamically created using the **new** operator and referenced through a pointer. For example, consider the following:

```
task type BUFFER is
  entry DEPOSIT (STUFF : in INTEGER);
  entry REMOVE (STUFF : in INTEGER);
  end;
type BUF_PTR is access BUFFER;
...
BUF_PTR := new BUFFER;
```

Figure 11.7
Graphical representation of a rendezvous caused by a message sent from task **A** to task **B**

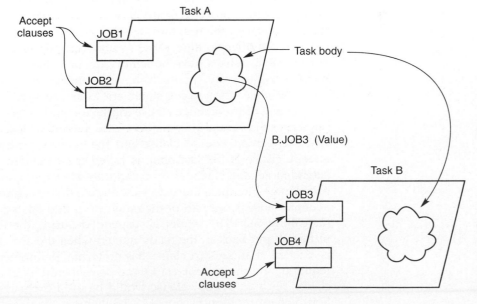

Tasks are declared in the declaration part of a package, subprogram, or block. They begin executing at the same time as the statements in the code to which that declarative part is attached. For example, a task declared in a main program begins execution at the same time as the first statement in the code body of the main program. Task termination is a complex issue; therefore, it will not be discussed here.

A task that has more than one entry point uses a **select** statement to enclose the entries, as in the following:

```
task body TASK_EXAMPLE is
  loop
    select
      accept ENTRY_1 (formal parameters) do
      ...
      end ENTRY_1;
      ...
    or
      accept ENTRY_2 (formal parameters) do
      ...
      end ENTRY_2;
      ...
    end select;
  end loop;
end TASK_EXAMPLE;
```

In this task, there are two entry points, or **accept** clauses, each of which has an associated queue. The action of the **select**, when it is executed, is to examine the queues associated with the two **accept** clauses. If one of the queues is empty but the other contains at least one waiting message, the **accept** clause associated with the waiting message has a rendezvous with the task that sent the first message that was received. If both **accept** clauses have empty queues, the **select** waits until one of the entries is called. If both **accept** clauses have nonempty queues, one of the **accept** clauses is nondeterministically chosen to have a rendezvous with one of its callers. The loop forces the **select** statement to be executed repeatedly, forever.

The **end** of the **accept** clause marks the end of the code that assigns or references the formal parameters of the **accept** clause. The code, if there is any, between an **accept** clause and the next **or** (or the **end select** if the **accept** clause is the last one), is called the **extended accept clause**. The extended **accept** clause is executed only after the associated (immediately preceding) **accept** clause is executed. This execution of the extended **accept** clause is not part of the rendezvous and takes place in parallel with the calling task. The sender is suspended during the rendezvous, but it is restarted (put back in the ready queue) when the end of the **accept** clause is reached. If an **accept** clause has no formal parameters, the **do-end** is not required, and the **accept** clause can consist entirely of an extended **accept** clause. Such an **accept** clause would be used exclusively for synchronization. The example in Section 11.3.4.3 includes extended **accept** clauses.

Each **accept** clause can have a guard attached, in the form of a **when** clause, that can delay rendezvous. For example,

```
when not FULL (BUFFER) =>
  accept STORE_NEW (NEW_VALUE) do
```

An **accept** clause with a **when** clause can be either open or closed. If the Boolean expression of the **when** clause is currently true, that **accept** clause is called **open;** if the Boolean expression is false, the **accept** clause is called **closed.** An **accept** clause that does not have a guard is always open. An open **accept** clause is available for rendezvous; a closed **accept** clause cannot rendezvous.

Suppose there are several guarded **accept** clauses in a **select** clause. Such an **accept** clause is usually placed in an infinite loop. The loop causes the **select** clause to be executed repeatedly, with each **when** clause evaluated on each repetition. Each repetition causes a list of open **accept** clauses to be constructed. If exactly one of the open clauses has a nonempty queue, a message from that queue is taken and a rendezvous takes place. If more than one of the open **accept** clauses have nonempty queues, one queue is chosen nondeterministically, a message is taken from that queue, and a rendezvous takes place. If the queues of all open clauses are empty, the task waits for a message to arrive at one of those **accept** clauses, at which time a rendezvous will occur. After each rendezvous, the **select** execution is repeated. If, on a particular repetition, every **accept** clause is closed, a run-time exception, or error, results. This possibility can be avoided, either by making sure one of the **when** clauses is always true or by adding an **else** clause in the **select**.

An **else** clause can include any sequence of statements, except an **accept** clause. When an **else** clause execution completes, the loop causes the **select** to be executed again.

The features described so far provide for cooperation synchronization and communication among tasks. We next discuss how mutually exclusive access to shared data structures can be enforced.

If access to a data structure is to be controlled by a task, then mutually exclusive access can be achieved by declaring the data structure within a task. The semantics of task execution usually guarantees mutually exclusive access to the structure, because only one **accept** clause in the task can be active at a given time. The only exceptions to this occur when tasks are nested in procedures or other tasks. For example, if a task that defines a shared data structure has a nested task, that nested task can also access the shared structure, which could destroy the integrity of the data. Thus, tasks that are meant to control access to a shared data structure should not define procedures or tasks.

11.3.4.3 A Concurrently Accessed Shared Buffer using Ada Tasks

The following is an example of an Ada task to provide synchronized access to a buffer. It is very similar in effect to our monitor example.

```
task BUF_TASK is
  entry INSERT (ITEM : in integer);
  entry REMOVE (ITEM : out integer);
 end BUF_TASK;

task body BUF_TASK is
BUFSIZE : constant integer := 100;
BUF     : array (1..BUFSIZE) of integer;
FILLED  : integer range 0..BUFSIZE := 0;
NEXT_IN,
NEXT_OUT : integer range 1..BUFSIZE := 1;
begin
  loop
    select
      when FILLED < BUFSIZE =>
        accept INSERT (ITEM : in integer) do
          BUF (NEXT_IN) := ITEM;
          end INSERT;
        NEXT_IN := (NEXT_IN mod BUFSIZE) + 1;
        FILLED := FILLED + 1;
    or
      when FILLED > 0 =>
        accept REMOVE (ITEM : out integer) do
          ITEM := BUF (NEXT_OUT);
          end REMOVE;
        NEXT_OUT := (NEXT_OUT mod BUFSIZE) + 1;
        FILLED := FILLED - 1;
    end select;
  end loop;
end BUF_TASK;
```

In this example, both **accept** clauses have extended **accept** clauses. These
allow concurrent execution of BUF_TASK with the calling tasks.

The tasks for the producer and consumer that could use the BUF_TASK
task have the following form:

```
task PRODUCER;
task CONSUMER;
task body PRODUCER is
  STUFF : integer;
  begin
    loop
    -- produce STUFF --
    BUF_TASK.INSERT (STUFF);
    end loop;
  end PRODUCER;

task body CONSUMER is
  STORED_VALUE : integer;
  begin
```

```
      loop
      BUF_TASK.REMOVE (STORED_VALUE);
      -- consume STORED_VALUE --
      end loop;
   end CONSUMER;
```

If access to a data structure is to be controlled and it is not encapsulated in a task, another means must be used to provide mutually exclusive access. One way is to build a binary semaphore task to use with the task that references the data structure. Such a binary semaphore task could be defined as follows:

```
task BINARY_SEMAPHORE is
   entry WAIT;
   entry RELEASE;
end BINARY_SEMAPHORE;

task body BINARY_SEMAPHORE is
   begin
   loop
     accept WAIT;
     accept RELEASE;
   end loop;
   end BINARY_SEMAPHORE;
```

The purpose of this task is to guarantee that the WAIT and RELEASE operations occur alternatively. Note that synchronization, in this case, is identical to that used in the SIMULA 67 example in Section 11.2.2.2, in which coroutine access to a shared single-element buffer is provided.

The BINARY_SEMAPHORE task illustrates the simplifications that are possible when Ada messages are passed only for synchronization, rather than to also pass data. Specifically, notice the simple form of **accept** clauses that do not need bodies.

Use of the BINARY_SEMAPHORE task to provide mutually exclusive access to a shared data structure would take place exactly as with the use of semaphores in the example program in Section 11.3.2.2. Of course, this use of semaphores suffers all of the potential problems discussed in Section 11.3.2.3.

Like semaphores, monitors can be simulated with the Ada tasking capability. So the Ada tasking model includes both semaphores and monitors.

11.3.4.4 Evaluation of the Message-Passing Model of Concurrency

In the absence of distributed processors with independent memories, the choice between monitors and message passing as means of providing competition synchronization is somewhat a matter of taste. Cooperation synchronization in message passing is less dependent than semaphores (which are required with monitors) on correct usage. Overall, therefore, message passing is slightly better, even in a shared memory environment.

For distributed systems, however, message passing is a clearly superior model for concurrency, because it naturally supports the concept of separate processes executing in parallel on separate processors.

SUMMARY

There are different categories of concurrency, two of which are of great concern to language design and evaluation: symmetric unit control and concurrent unit control. We use the phrase physical concurrency when multiple processors are actually used to execute concurrent units. If concurrent units are executed on a single processor, we term it logical concurrency. The underlying conceptual model of all concurrency can be referred to as logical concurrency.

Two of the primary facilities that concurrent languages must provide are mutually exclusive access to shared data structures (competition synchronization) and cooperation among tasks.

A coroutine provides quasi-concurrency in the same sense that multiprogramming operating systems provide the illusion of concurrency by executing several users' programs "simultaneously." SIMULA 67 classes serve well as implementations of coroutines.

The Modula-2 language provides no facilities for symmetric or concurrent unit control. However, a module commonly provided with Modula-2 compilers provides a few low-level facilities for support of coroutines. These facilities can be used to build higher-level abstractions to implement coroutines.

Semaphores can be used to provide both competition and cooperation synchronization among concurrent tasks. Semaphores can easily be used incorrectly, and these errors cannot be detected by the compiler, linker, or run-time system.

Monitors are data abstractions that provide a natural way of allowing mutually exclusive access to data shared among tasks. They are included in several programming languages. Cooperation synchronization in languages with monitors must be provided with some form of semaphores.

Ada provides complex but effective constructs, based on the message-passing model, for concurrency. The basic concurrent units are tasks, which communicate with each other through the rendezvous mechanism. A rendezvous is the action of a task accepting a message sent by another task. Ada includes both simple and complicated methods of controlling the occurrences of rendezvous among tasks.

BIBLIOGRAPHIC NOTES

The general subject of concurrency is discussed at great length in Andrews and Schneider (1983), Holt et al. (1978), and Ben-Ari (1982).

The first work on coroutines appears in Conway (1963). Coroutines are also discussed in Knuth (1968b). The SIMULA 67 version of coroutines is described in Birtwistle et al. (1973). The implementation of coroutines in Modula-2 is discussed by Wirth (1985). Methods for using Modula-2 for logically concurrent control were developed by Sewry (1984a and 1984b).

The monitor concept is developed and its implementation in Concurrent Pascal is described by Brinch Hansen (1977).

The early development of the message-passing model of concurrent unit control is discussed by Hoare (1978) and Brinch Hansen (1978). An in-depth discussion of the development of the Ada tasking model can be found in Ichbiah et al. (1979).

PROBLEM SET

1. Describe two problems in which it is most natural to program the solution using coroutines.

2. Explain clearly why competition synchronization is not a problem in a programming environment that has symmetric unit control but no concurrency.

3. Compare the wait and release operations on semaphores with the SEND and WAIT operations in our Modula-2 Processes module.

4. What is the best action a system can take when deadlock is detected?

5. Write an Ada task to implement general semaphores.

6. Write an Ada task to manage a shared buffer such as the one in our example, but using the semaphore task from Problem 5.

7. Busy waiting is a method of having a task wait for a given event by continuously checking for that event to occur. What is the main problem with this approach?

8. In the producer-consumer example of Section 11.3.2.2, suppose that we incorrectly replaced the release(access) in the consumer process with wait(access). What would be the result of this error on execution of the system?

9. From a book on VAX assembly language programming, determine what instructions the VAX architecture includes to support the construction of semaphores.

10. From a book on assembly language programming for a computer that uses an Intel 80286 processor, determine what instructions are provided to support the construction of semaphores.

11. Why do coroutines require local static storage?

12

Exception Handling

Niklaus Wirth

Niklaus Wirth of ETH in Zurich has been continuously involved in language design since the mid-1960s. He left the ALGOL 68 design team in the mid-1960s to develop ALGOL-W. He also designed Euler and PL/360 in the 1960s. Since then he has been responsible for the development of the Pascal, Modula, Modula-2, and Oberon languages.

Key Concepts

- Error and nonerror exceptions
- Exception handlers
- Static and dynamic binding of exceptions to handlers

- Exception propagation
- Execution continuation

Some programming languages have facilities for users to handle run-time errors and other special events that occur during program execution. Designers of these languages face difficult decisions involving trade-offs between complexity, safety, and flexibility.

We first define the fundamental concepts of exception handling, and then we describe some of the basic design alternatives. The design choices of three of the programming languages that include such facilities—PL/I, CLU, and Ada—are described and evaluated. More widely used contemporary languages are not included because none of them, except Ada, includes exception-handling mechanisms.

12.1 Introduction to Exception Handling

Most computer hardware systems are capable of detecting certain run-time error conditions, such as arithmetic overflow. Many programming languages are designed and implemented in such a way that the user program can neither detect nor attempt to deal with such errors. In these languages, the occurrence of such an error simply causes the program to be terminated and control to be transferred to the operating system. The typical operating system reaction to a run-time error is to print a diagnostic message, which may be very meaningful or highly cryptic, and then terminate the program.

In the case of input and output operations, however, the situation is sometimes different. For example, a FORTRAN READ statement can intercept input errors and end-of-file conditions, both of which are detected by the hardware. In both cases, the READ statement can specify a statement label of user code that deals with the condition. In the case of the end-of-file, it is clear that the condition is not always to be considered an error. In most cases, it is nothing more than a signal that one kind of processing is completed and a new kind should be started. In spite of the obvious difference between end-of-file and events that are always errors, such as failed input processes, FORTRAN handles both situations with the same mechanism. Consider the following FORTRAN READ statement:

```
READ (UNIT=5, FMT=1000, ERR=100, END=999) WEIGHT
```

The ERR clause specifies that control is to be transferred to the statement
labeled 100 if an error occurs in the read operation. The END clause specifies
that control is to be transferred to the statement labeled 999 if the read operation encounters the end of the file. So FORTRAN uses the all-powerful
unconditional branch for both input and output errors and end-of-file.

12.1.1 Basic Concepts

We term both the errors detected by hardware, such as disk read errors, and
unusual conditions, such as end-of-file (which are also detected by hardware), as exceptions. We further extend the concept of an exception to
include errors or unusual conditions that are software detectable. Accord-
ingly, we define an **exception** to be any unusual event, erroneous or not,
that is detectable either by hardware or software and that may require special processing.

The special processing that may be required by the detection of an
exception is called **exception handling.** This processing is done by a code
unit called an **exception handler.** An exception is **raised** when its associated
event occurs. Exception handlers are usually different for different exception types. Detection of end-of-file nearly always requires some specific program action. But, clearly, that action would not also be appropriate for an
arithmetic overflow exception. In some other cases, the only action may be
the generation of an error message and an orderly termination of the
program.

In some situations, it may be desirable to ignore certain exceptions for
a time. This would be done by disabling the exception. A disabled exception
could be enabled again at a later time.

The absence of separate or specific exception-handling facilities in a language does not preclude the handling of a user-defined, software-detectable
exception. Such an exception detected within a program unit is often handled by the unit's caller, or invoker. One possible design is to send an auxiliary parameter, which is used as a status variable. The status variable is
assigned a value in the called unit according to the correctness and/or nor-
malness of its computation. Immediately upon return from the called unit,
the caller tests the status variable. If the value indicates that an exception
has occurred, the handler, which may reside in the calling unit, can be
enacted.

Another possibility is to pass a label parameter to the subprogram. This
allows the called unit to return to a different point in the caller if an exception has occurred. As in the first alternative, the handler is often a segment
of the calling unit's code. This is a common use of label parameters in
FORTRAN. This technique is distinctly unattractive for static-scoped languages because of the difficulty of managing the run-time stack when
returns are to different places in the calling program unit.

A third possibility is to have the handler as a separate subprogram that is passed as a parameter to the called unit. In this case, the handler subprogram is provided by the caller, but the called unit calls the handler when an exception is raised. One problem with this approach is that one is required to send a handler subprogram with *every* call, whether it is desirable or not. Furthermore, to deal with several different kinds of exceptions, several different handler routines would need to be passed, complicating the code.

If it is desirable to handle an exception in the unit in which it is detected, the handler is simply a segment of code in that unit. This kind of handler is raised by a selection statement.

12.1.2 Design Issues

We now explore some of the design issues for an exception-handling facility that is built into a programming language. In such a language, users are allowed to create software-detectable exceptions and also write exception handlers for both language- and user-defined exceptions.

Consider the following skeletal procedure that includes an exception handling mechanism:

```
procedure example;
  ...
  average := sum / total;
  ...
  return;
;-- Exception handlers
  ...
  when zero_divide do
    average := 0;
    print ('Error--cannot compute average');
    print (' total is zero')
    end;
  ...
  end example;
```

In this procedure, the exception of division by zero is intercepted by the program, which then transfers control to the appropriate handler, which is then executed.

The first design question for user-defined exception handlers is their form. This is, essentially, a choice between having handlers that are complete program units or handlers that are code segments. In the latter case, they may be embedded in the units that raise the exceptions they are to handle, as in the above example, or they may be embedded in a different unit, such as the unit that called the one in which the exception is raised.

If the handler is a separate unit, it can be in the same scope as the code that can cause it to be raised. This simplifies communications between the two units. If the handler is a separate unit outside the scope of the unit that can raise its associated exception, communication can be through parameters.

Another important design issue for exception handling is how an exception occurrence is bound to an exception handler. This issue occurs on two different levels. On the unit level, there is the question of how the same exception being raised in different points in a unit can be bound to different handlers within the unit. For example, in the example procedure above, there is a handler for a division-by-zero exception that appears to be written to deal with an occurrence of division by zero in a particular statement (the one shown). But suppose the procedure includes several other expressions with division operators. For those operators, this handler is probably not appropriate. So, it should be possible to bind the exceptions that can be raised by particular statements to particular handlers, even though the same exception can be raised by many different statements.

At a higher level, the binding question arises when there is no exception handler local to the unit in which the exception is raised. In this case, the design requires the choice of whether to propagate the exception to some other unit. How this propagation takes place and how far it goes have an important impact on the writability of exception handlers. For example, if handlers must be local, then many handlers must be written, which complicates both the writing and reading of the program. On the other hand, if exceptions are propagated, a single handler might handle the same exception raised in several program units, which may require the handler to be less specific than is desirable.

Another important factor is whether the binding of exceptions to handlers is static or dynamic; that is, whether binding depends on the syntactic layout of the program or on its execution sequence. As it is in other language constructs, static binding of exceptions is easier to understand and implement than dynamic binding.

After an exception handler executes, control can either transfer to somewhere in the program outside of the handler code, or program execution can simply terminate. We term this the question of control continuation after handler execution, or simply **continuation.** Termination is obviously the simplest choice, and in many error exception conditions, it is the best. However, in other situations, particularly those associated with unusual but not erroneous events, it is desirable to continue execution. In these cases, some conventions must be chosen to determine where execution is to continue. It might be the statement that raised the exception, the statement after the statement that raised the exception, or possibly some other unit. The choice to return to the statement that raised the exception may seem like a good one, but in the case of an error exception, it is only useful if the handler is able to somehow modify the values or operations that caused the exception to be raised. Otherwise, the exception will simply be reraised. The required modification for an error exception is often very difficult. Even when possible, however, it may not be a sound practice. It allows the program to remove the symptom of a problem without removing the cause.

The two issues of binding of exceptions to handlers and continuation are illustrated in Figure 12.1.

Another design issue is the following: If users are allowed to define exceptions, how are these exceptions specified? The usual answer is to require that they be declared in the specification parts of the program units in which they can be raised. The scope of a declared exception is usually the scope of the program unit that contains the declaration.

When a language includes built-in exceptions, several other design issues follow. For example, should the language run-time system provide default handlers for the built-in exceptions, or should the user be required to handle all exceptions? Another question is whether built-in exceptions can be explicitly raised by the user program. This can be convenient if there are software-detectable situations in which the user would like to use a built-in handler.

Finally, there is the question of whether exceptions, either built-in or user-defined, can be temporarily or permanently disabled. This question is somewhat philosophical, particularly in the case of built-in error conditions. For example, suppose a language has a built-in exception that is raised when a subscript range error occurs. Many believe that subscript range errors should always be detected, and therefore it should not be possible

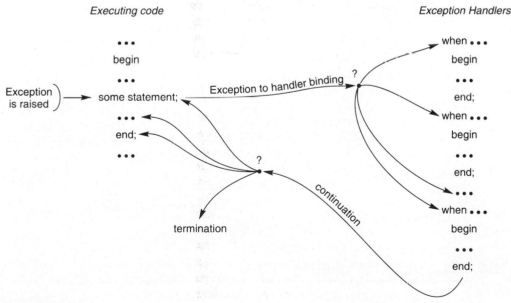

Figure 12.1
Exception-handling control flow

for the program to disable detection of these errors. Others argue that sub-script range checking is too costly for production software, where, presumably, the code is sufficiently proven that range errors cannot occur.

12.1.3   Summary of Design Issues

1. How and where are exception handlers specified, and what is their scope?
2. How is an exception occurrence bound to an exception handler?
3. Where does execution continue, if at all, after an exception handler completes its execution (the question of continuation)?
4. How are user-defined exceptions specified?
5. Should there be default exception handlers for programs that do not provide their own?
6. Can built-in exceptions be explicitly raised?
7. How can exceptions be disabled, if at all?

12.1.4   History

PL/I (ANSI, 1976) pioneered the concept of allowing user programs to be directly involved in exception handling. The language allows the user to write exception handlers for a long list of language-defined exceptions. Furthermore, PL/I introduced the concept of user-defined exceptions, which allow programs to create software-detected exceptions. These exceptions use the same mechanisms that are used for the built-in exceptions.

Since PL/I was designed, a substantial amount of work has been done to design alternative methods of exception handling. In particular, CLU (Liskov et al., 1981), Mesa (Mitchell et al., 1979), and Ada (Goos and Hart-manis, 1983) include exception-handling facilities. More recently, ML (Milner et al., 1990) includes exception handling, and there is an experimental exception-handling mechanism under development for C++ (Stroustrup, 1991). Neither of these two designs include significantly different fundamental characteristics than the exception-handling design of Ada.

We are now prepared to examine the exception-handling facilities of three of these programming languages.

12.2   Exception Handling in PL/I

In still another pioneering effort, the designers of PL/I tackled the problem of providing users with the first linguistic mechanisms for exception handling. As was their style in other areas, they provided facilities that are very powerful and highly flexible. But, as with some other PL/I constructs, the exception-handling facilities are difficult to understand, implement, and use reliably.

Twenty-two standard conditions cause exceptions in the execution of a PL/I program. These range from arithmetic errors, such as ZERODIVIDE, to programming errors, such as SUBSCRIPTRANGE.

12.2.1 Exception Handlers

User-defined exception handlers have the form of executable code blocks. They can appear anywhere an executable statement can appear, and have the form

```
ON condition [SNAP] BEGIN;
               ...
             END;
```

where condition is the name of the associated exception. In place of the block, the single keyword, SYSTEM, can be used to specify that the system-supplied handler is to be used. The keyword SNAP, when included, specifies that the dynamic chain of the program at the time the exception was raised is to be printed when the exception occurs. This provides the traceback information that allows the programmer to determine how execution got to the point of the exception. Such information is an obvious aid to debugging.

The referencing environment of a PL/I exception handler is that of the code in which it is embedded. Because exception handlers do not have parameters, it is common to place handlers near the places where their exceptions are likely to be raised.

12.2.2 Binding Exceptions to Handlers

The binding of exceptions to handlers in PL/I is dynamic. The ON statement specifies the binding of an exception to an exception handler. Since it is executable, its position in the program has a critical impact on its effect. If ON were a declarative statement, there could be only one per exception per block. In fact, however, there can be more than one ON statement for a given exception, even within the same block. The ON binding stays in effect until either a new ON statement for the same exception is executed or the block in which it occurs is exited.

12.2.3 Continuation

In PL/I, built-in exception handlers for different exceptions provide different continuation actions. For some exceptions, execution returns to the statement that caused the exception; other conditions cause program termination. User-defined handlers can cause control to go to any part of the program they wish after handling an exception, but there is no mechanism that provides the address of the statement that caused the exception, so it is often impossible to return to it. The choice between the two actions in system handlers was made on the basis of whether it was deemed possible for a handler to fix the cause of the problem and continue successfully. In some cases, such as some arithmetic errors, it was believed that successful continued processing was not possible. In other cases, such as the CONVERSION exception (for errors in converting strings to numerics), it was thought possible to recover, so control returned to the statement that caused the exception after the handler completed its execution. The PL/I design for continuation is often confusing for program readers and writers alike.

12.2.4   Other Design Choices

User-defined exceptions are created in PL/I programs by using a simple declaration with the form

    CONDITION exception_name

All built-in exceptions have built-in handlers. These handlers can be preempted by user-defined exception handlers. User-defined exceptions must be raised explicitly, which is done with a statement of the form

    SIGNAL CONDITION (exception_name)

Any condition can be explicitly raised with a SIGNAL statement, although the built-in exceptions are normally raised implicitly by hardware or software conditions. A SIGNAL of an exception that is currently disabled does nothing.

Built-in exceptions are divided into three categories: (1) those that are always enabled, (2) those that are enabled by default but can be disabled by user code, and (3) those that are disabled by default but can be enabled by user code.

The process of enabling and disabling exceptions is accomplished by prefixing a statement, block, or procedure with the exception name or names, as in

    (SUBSCRIPTRANGE, NOOVERFLOW):
       BEGIN;
       ...
       END;

In this case, the SUBSCRIPTRANGE exception is enabled and the OVERFLOW exception is disabled. (The default values for these are the opposite, NOSUBSCRIPTRANGE and OVERFLOW.) The prefix NO can be attached to any exception that is not permanently enabled (to disable it).

12.2.5 An Example

The following example program illustrates two simple but common uses of exception handlers in PL/I. The program computes and prints a distribution of input grades by using an array of counters. There are ten categories of grades (0–9, 10–19, . . . , 90–100). The grades themselves are used to compute indices into an array of counters, one for each grade category. Invalid input grades are detected by trapping indexing errors in the counter array. A grade of 100 is special in the computation of the grade distribution, because the categories all have ten possible grade values, except the highest, which has eleven (90, 91, . . . , 100). The grade of 100 is also handled in the same exception handler that is used for invalid input data.

```
GRADE_DISTRIBUTION: PROCEDURE OPTIONS (MAIN);
 DECLARE FREQ(1:10) FIXED INIT ((10) 0),
         NEW_GRADE FIXED,
         LIMIT_1 FIXED,
         LIMIT_2 FIXED,
         INDEX FIXED;
/* Exception Handlers */
ON ENDFILE (SYSIN) GOTO FINISH;
ON SUBSCRIPTRANGE
  BEGIN;
  IF NEW_GRADE = 100
   THEN FREQ(10) = FREQ(10) + 1;
   ELSE
     DO;
     PUT LIST ('INPUT GRADE:' || NEW_GRADE ||
                       'NOT IN RANGE') SKIP;
     GOTO INPUT_LOOP;
     END;
   END;
/* Main program body */
 INPUT_LOOP:
   DO;
   GET LIST (NEW_GRADE);
   INDEX = NEW_GRADE / 10 + 1;
 (SUBSCRIPTRANGE):
   FREQ(INDEX) = FREQ(INDEX) + 1;
   END INPUT_LOOP;

 FINISH:
  PUT LIST (' LIMITS FREQUENCY') SKIP(2);
   DO INDEX = 0 TO 9;
   LIMIT_1 = 10 * INDEX;
   LIMIT_2 = LIMIT_1 + 9;
   IF INDEX = 9
    THEN LIMIT_2 = 100;
   PUT LIST (LIMIT_1, LIMIT_2, FREQ(INDEX+1));
   END;
 END GRADE_DISTRIBUTION;
```

Three different events trigger exception handling in this program. Among these three, only one is an error; the other two simply signal that something special has happened. In one case, it is a grade of 100; in the other, the end of the input data has been reached.

Notice that the handler for the SUBSCRIPTRANGE exception allows execution to continue for illegal grades, even though the built-in handler for that exception would cause program termination.

12.2.6   Evaluation

In summary, PL/I offers a powerful and flexible facility for exception detection and handling. The high level of flexibility, however, is not without cost. One of the primary problems with PL/I's exception-handling design is the dynamic binding of exceptions to handlers.

The dynamic nature of this binding causes a problem in writability and readability that is related to the problems of dynamic scoping. Indeed, it is the identical problem: The scope of the exception handler is dynamic, so it is very difficult to determine from a program listing which binding is in effect at any given point in the program. Because of dynamic binding, it is easy to have a handler unintentionally used for an exception that is in fact syntactically far from the exception and also completely inappropriate for that exception in that situation. For example, consider the following simple code segment:

```
(SUBSCRIPTRANGE):
  BEGIN;
  ...
  ON SUBSCRIPTRANGE
    BEGIN;
    PUT LIST ('ERROR - BAD SUBSCRIPT IN ARRAY SUBSUM');
    GO TO FIXIT;
    END;
  ...
  ON SUBSCRIPTRANGE
    BEGIN;
    PUT LIST ('ERROR - BAD SUBSCRIPT IN ARRAY BLK');
    GO TO QUIT;
    END;
  ...
LABEL1:;
  ...
  BLK(I, J, K) = SUM;
  ...
  END;
```

If the code between the two handlers for the exception SUBSCRIPTRANGE happened to include a GO TO LABEL1, then the first handler would be executed if the exception was raised by the assignment to BLK. This would enact the wrong handler, causing at the very least a good deal of confusion for the user.

Another serious problem is posed by the flexibility of the continuation rules of PL/I exceptions. They are difficult to implement, harmful to readability in the same way that the goto is, and also difficult to learn to use effectively.

12.3 Exception Handling in CLU

Because PL/I's mechanisms for exception handling were thought to be too complex, they were not copied by other language designers. A major problem with PL/I exception handling is that exceptions are dynamically bound to exception handlers. A more restricted model was proposed in 1975 by Goodenough (1975), in which exceptions are statically bound to exception handlers. An even more constrained model was designed into the CLU language in the mid-1970s (Liskov et al., 1981).

A CLU procedure definition can include a list of exceptions that the procedure may raise. These are simply listed at the top of the procedure definition, as in the following:

procedure_name = **proc** (formal parameters)
                        signals (exception_1 (parameters),
                                ...
                          exception_n (parameters))
-- procedure body --
end procedure_name

Note that exceptions can have parameters, which are sent to the handlers.

12.3.1 Exception Handlers

The CLU designer's view was that exceptions are raised in procedures and are normally handled in the calling unit. Therefore, a procedure definition, say sub1, includes exception handlers for those exceptions that can be raised in the procedures called by sub1. This design seems to disallow the handling of exceptions in the unit in which they are raised. This is not true, though, because in CLU, all operators are treated as if they were subprogram calls. For example, if a and b are integer variables, a + b is really just shorthand for int$add(a, b). Therefore, if this addition causes overflow, it can be handled in the routine that contains the expression. As we shall see in Section 12.3.2, this does not mean arithmetic exceptions must be handled locally; they can be propagated to other units for handling.

Exception handlers can be attached to any statement in a CLU procedure. When attached to a statement, they handle only exceptions raised by subprograms called by that statement. The general form of an exception handler is

statement **except** handler-list **end**

Because the placement of handlers on individual statements can reduce code readability, they are collected at the end of the procedure whenever possible. They are placed at locations other than the end only if two or more handlers are supplied for the same exception, in which case they are attached to the code segment for which they are to handle exceptions.

The form of the exception handler list is

when exception_name_1 (parameters): statement_1
. . .
when exception_name_n (parameters): statement_n

The parameters are used to pass information about the exception to the handler.

There is only one built-in exception handler in CLU, **failure**, which is described below.

12.3.2 Bindings of Exceptions to Handlers

Exceptions are always bound to the appropriate handler in the nearest enclosing static scope. If a statement calls a procedure that raises an exception, but that statement has no attached handler for that exception, then the exception is propagated to progressively larger static scopes within the procedure. If no handler is found in the procedure, the built-in default exception **failure** is raised.

The **failure** exception is always handled by the system. If **failure** is raised by the lack of a handler for an exception, its handler prints the name of the unhandled exception. If it is raised explicitly, which is possible, the handler prints a message passed through the raising statement, as discussed in Section 12.3.4. In both cases, program execution is terminated.

12.3.3 Continuations

CLU procedures that raise exceptions are normally terminated. If a handler is found in the static environment of the calling statement, it is executed. In the case of a handler that is attached to a statement, control simply flows to the following statement after the handler is executed. In the case of a handler that appears at the end of a procedure, continuation is to the caller of the procedure that contains the exception handler.

For exceptions that are attached to statements (rather than appearing at the end of the code), a special kind of exception signaling can be used to transfer control to the end of the procedure. To clearly illustrate that an exception is to be handled locally, it is raised with a different statement, **exit**, which has the form

```
exit exception_name
```

The **exit** statement is similar to an unconditional branch statement, transferring control to the named exception handler. CLU has no goto statement.

The following example illustrates the use of **exit** and multiple handlers for the same exception. The block has separate overflow handlers for two occurrences of integer division.

```
begin
  a := b / c
    except when overflow:
      ...
      exit done
    end
  b := d / e
    except when overflow:
      ...
      exit done
    end
  ...
end   % end of block
  except when done:
    ...
  end
```

Both handlers for the overflow exception raise the local exception, done. In both cases, the done handler is executed.

12.3.4 Other Design Choices

Except for **failure**, CLU does not include default exception handlers; therefore, most handlers must be provided by the user.

CLU exceptions can be explicitly raised with the **signal** statement, which is syntactically somewhat like a procedure call and includes optional parameters that can be used to pass information to the handler. Handlers can themselves raise exceptions. A handler can use this capability to reraise an exception that it is handling, thereby passing the problem of handling an exception to a higher level in the dynamic chain.

Because the designers thought that one would rarely guarantee that an exception would not occur, CLU does not include a mechanism for disabling an exception condition.

12.3.5 An Example

The following complete procedure example, which appears in Liskov and Snyder (1979), shows the form and use of the CLU exception-handling mechanisms. The purpose of this procedure is to get an integer from an input file. To do this, it uses another procedure, get_field, to get a string of nonblank characters from the input file, and then another procedure, s2i, to convert the string representation of an integer to the corresponding integer value. Both get_field and s2i can raise exceptions that get_number can either handle or propagate to its caller.

```
get_number = proc (s: stream) returns (int)
                signals (end_of_file,
                          unrepresentable_integer (string),
                          bad_format (string))
        field: string := get_field (s)
          except when end_of_file:
                  signal end_of_file
          end
        return (s2i (field))
          except when unrepresentable_integer:
                  signal unrepresentable_integer (field)
                when bad_format, invalid_character (*):
                  signal bad_format (field)
          end   % end of exception clause
        end get_number
```

The definition statements for get_field and s2i are as follows:

```
get_field = proc (s: stream) returns (string)
                                signals (end_of_file)
s2i = proc (s: string) returns (int)
                signals (invalid_character(char),
                          bad_format,
                          unrepresentable_integer)
```

The get_field procedure can raise but one exception, end_of_file, which is simply reraised by the **signal** statement in the handler attached to the call to get_field in get_number. The s2i procedure can raise three different exceptions: unrepresentable_integer, which means the integer gotten from the string was too large to be represented in the form of an integer; bad_format, which means that there was more than one minus sign, or a minus sign followed a digit; and invalid_character, which means the string contained a character that was neither a digit nor a minus sign (plus signs are not allowed).

The handler in get_number for the bad_format and invalid _character exceptions, which can be raised in s2i, uses the * parameter form to indicate that the two have either no parameters or parameters that do not have the same names among the exception conditions; in either case, none of the parameters are used in the handler. This may seem to be odd syntax, but it is quite appropriate. It specifies that the parameters are not important, either in number or name. Both of these exceptions are propagated to the caller as the single exception, `bad_format`.

12.3.6 Evaluation

CLU's exception-handling design has neither of the main difficulties of PL/I—that is, dynamic binding of handlers to exceptions and continued execution nearly anywhere after an exception has been handled.

CLU's static binding of exceptions to handlers is a great advantage over the dynamic binding of PL/I. A program reader can easily determine the exception bindings in a CLU program, whereas that can be extremely difficult in a PL/I program.

12.4 Exception Handling in Ada

The facilities in Ada for exception handling are partially based on those of CLU.

The Ada language includes five built-in exceptions, which are actually categories of exceptions. For example, the exception CONSTRAINT_ERROR is raised when an array subscript is out of range, when there is a range error in a numeric variable with a range restriction, when a reference is made to a record field that is not present in a discriminated union, and in a few additional situations.

12.4.1 Exception Handlers

Ada exception handlers are usually local to the code in which the exception can be raised. Because this provides them with the same referencing environment, parameters for handlers are not necessary and are not allowed.

Exception handlers have the general form

    when exception_choice {| exception_choice} =>
        statement_sequence

where exception_choice has the form

    exception_name | **others**

The exception name indicates the particular exception or exceptions that this handler is meant to handle. The statement sequence is the handler body. The reserved word **others** indicates that the handler is meant to handle exceptions not named elsewhere locally.

Exception handlers can be included in blocks or in the bodies of subprograms, packages, or tasks. Regardless of the block or unit in which they appear, handlers are gathered together in an **exception** clause, which must be placed at the end of the block or unit. For example, the usual form of an exception clause is shown in the following:

```
begin
   -- the block or unit body --
   exception
     when exception_name =>
       -- first handler --
     when exception_name =>
       -- second handler --
       -- other handlers --
end;
```

Any statement that is legitimate in the block or unit in which the handler is placed is also legal in the handler.

12.4.2   Binding Exceptions to Handlers

When the block or unit that can raise the exception includes a handler for that exception, the exception is (statically) bound to that handler. If an exception is raised in a block or unit that does not have a handler for that particular exception, the exception is propagated to some other block or unit. The way in which exceptions are propagated depends on the program entity in which the exception occurs.

When an exception is raised in a procedure, whether in the elaboration of its declarations or in the execution of its body, and the procedure has no handler for it, an exception is implicitly propagated to the calling program unit at the point of the call. This policy is reflective of the philosophy that exception propagation should trace back through the control path, not through static ancestors.

If the calling unit to which an exception has been propagated also has no handler for the exception, it is again propagated to that unit's caller. This continues, if necessary, to the main program. If an exception is propagated to the main unit and still does not have a handler, execution is terminated.

In a discussion of exception handling, Ada blocks are considered to be parameterless procedures that are "called" by their parent blocks when execution control reaches their beginnings. When an exception is raised in a block, in either its declarations or executable statements, and the block has no handler for it, the exception is implicitly propagated to the next larger enclosing scope, which is the code that "called" it. The point to which the exception is propagated is just after the end of the block in which it occurred, which is its "return" point. In this case, the Ada design of statically binding an exception to a handler is identical to that of CLU.

When an exception is raised in a package body and the package body has no handler for the exception, the exception is implicitly propagated to the declaration section of the unit containing the package declaration. If the package happens to be a library unit (separately compiled), the program is terminated.

If an exception occurs in a task body and the task contains a handler for the exception, that handler is executed and the task is marked as being completed (meaning, among other things, that it can no longer communicate with other tasks). If the task does not have a handler for the exception, the task is simply marked as being completed; the exception is not propagated. The control mechanism of a task is too complex to lend itself to a reasonable and simple answer to the question of where its unhandled exceptions should be propagated.

Exceptions can also occur during the elaboration of the declarative sections of subprograms, blocks, packages, and tasks. For example, suppose that a function is called to initialize a variable in its declaration statement, as in the following:

```
procedure RIVER is

    . . .
    CURRENT_FLOW : FLOAT := GET_FLOW;
    ...
    begin
    ...
    end RIVER;
```

If the function GET_FLOW raises and propagates an exception to its caller, the exception is reraised in this declaration. Storage allocation during declaration elaboration can also raise an exception.

In the cases of procedures, packages, and blocks, exceptions that occur in declaration elaborations are propagated exactly as if the exception were raised in the code section. In the case of a task, the task is marked as being completed, no further elaboration takes place, and the built-in exception, TASKING_ERROR, is raised at the point of activation for the task.

12.4.3 Continuation

The block or unit that raises an exception, along with all units to which the exception was propagated but which did not handle it, is always terminated. Control never returns implicitly to the raising block or unit after the exception is handled. Control simply continues after the exception clause, which is always at the end of a block or unit. This causes an immediate return to a higher level of control.

When deciding where execution would continue after exception handler execution was completed, the Ada design team had little choice, because the requirements specification (Department of Defense, 1980a) clearly states that program entities that raise exceptions cannot be continued or resumed.

However, in the case of a block, a statement can be retried after it raises an exception and that exception is handled. For example, suppose a statement that can raise an exception and a handler for that exception are both enclosed in a block, which is itself enclosed in a loop. The following example coded segment, which gets four integer values in the desired range from the keyboard, illustrates this kind of structure:

```
...
type AGE_TYPE is 0..125;
type AGE_LIST_TYPE is array (1..4) of AGE_TYPE;
package AGE_IO is new INTEGER_IO(AGE_TYPE);
use AGE_IO;
AGE_LIST : AGE_LIST_TYPE;
...
begin
for AGE_COUNT in 1..4 loop
   loop
EXCEPT_BLK:
      begin
      PUT_LINE ("Enter an integer in the range 0..125");
      GET (AGE_LIST(AGE_COUNT));
      exit;
      exception
        when DATA_ERROR =>
          PUT_LINE ("Illegal numeric value");
          PUT_LINE ("Please try again");
        when CONSTRAINT_ERROR =>
          PUT_LINE ("Input number is out of range");
          PUT_LINE ("Please try again");
      end EXCEPT_BLK;
   end loop;
end loop;
...
```

Control stays in the inner loop, which contains only the block, until a valid input number is received.

12.4.4   Other Design Choices

User-defined exceptions can be defined with the following declaration:

```
exception_name_list : exception
```

Such exceptions are treated exactly as built-in exceptions, except that they must be raised explicitly.

There are default handlers for the built-in exceptions, all of which result in program termination.

Exceptions are explicitly raised with the **raise** statement, which has the general form

```
raise [exception_name]
```

The only place a **raise** statement can appear without naming an exception is within an exception handler. In that case, it reraises the same exception that caused execution of the handler. This has the effect of propagating the exception according to the propagation rules stated above. A **raise** in an exception handler is useful when one wishes to print an error message when an exception is raised but handle the exception elsewhere.

An Ada pragma is a directive to the compiler. Exception conditions can be disabled in Ada programs by use of the SUPPRESS pragma, which has the form

```
pragma SUPPRESS (exception_list)
```

and can only appear in declaration sections. When it appears, all listed exceptions are ignored in the associated block or program unit of which the declaration section is a part. Explicit raises are not affected by SUPPRESS.

12.4.5   An Example

The following example has the same intent and use of exception handling as the PL/I program shown earlier in this chapter. It produces a distribution of input grades by using an array of counters for ten categories. Illegal grades are detected by checking for invalid subscripts used in incrementing the selected counter.

```
with TEXT_IO;  use TEXT_IO;
procedure GRADE_DISTRIBUTION is
 package INTEGER_TEXT_IO is new INTEGER_IO (INTEGER);
 use INTEGER_TEXT_IO;
 FREQ: array (1..10) of INTEGER;
 NEW_GRADE,
 INDEX,
 LIMIT_1,
 LIMIT_2 : INTEGER;
 begin
   loop
   GET (NEW_GRADE);
   INDEX := NEW_GRADE / 10 + 1;
    begin
    FREQ(INDEX) := FREQ(INDEX) + 1;
    exception
     when CONSTRAINT_ERROR =>
      if NEW_GRADE = 100
      then FREQ(10) := FREQ(10) + 1;
      else
```

```
                    PUT ("ERROR -- new grade: ");
                    PUT (NEW_GRADE);
                    PUT (" is out of range");
                    NEW_LINE;
                  end if;
                end;
             end loop;
          exception
            when END_OF_FILE =>
             PUT ("Limits   Frequency");
             NEW_LINE; NEW_LINE;
             for INDEX in 0..9
              loop
              LIMIT_1 := 10 * INDEX;
              LIMIT_2 := LIMIT_1 + 9;
              if INDEX = 9
               then LIMIT_2 := 100;
              end if;
              PUT (LIMIT_1);
              PUT (LIMIT_2);
              PUT (FREQ(INDEX));
              NEW_LINE;
              end loop;
          end GRADE_DISTRIBUTION;
```

Notice that the code to handle invalid input grades is in its own local block. This allows the program to continue after such exceptions are handled, as in our earlier example involving a tape read.

12.4.6 Evaluation

As in some other language constructs, Ada's design of exception handling represents something of a consensus of, at least at the time of its design, ideas on the subject. Many believe that it is superior to any previous design in a nonexperimental imperative language. It is doubtful, however, that this design is the ultimate one. Rather, one should expect that exception handling in programming languages will continue to evolve. For example, exception handling facility is currently being developed for C++. This design may include some new innovation.

As with most other language constructs, later designs of exception handling are cleaner and safer than earlier designs.

SUMMARY

Exception handling has been incorporated in few widely used languages, although many experimental languages designed since the mid-1970s have had such facilities.

PL/I has powerful and flexible exception-handling capabilities, but there are a number of difficulties with the design. Overall, PL/I exception handling is sometimes too complex to be easily used and understood. The dynamic binding of exceptions to their handlers is one of the major causes of these problems.

CLU includes a much more restricted form of exception handling than PL/I. One of the main features of CLU's design is that the binding of exceptions to exception handlers is static.

Ada provides extensive exception-handling facilities and a small but comprehensive collection of built-in exceptions. The handlers are attached to the program entities, although exceptions can be implicitly or explicitly propagated to other program entities if no local handler is available.

BIBLIOGRAPHIC NOTES

One of the most important papers on exception handling that is not connected with a particular programming language is the work by Goodenough (1975). The problems with the PL/I design for exception handling are covered in MacLaren (1977). The CLU exception-handling design is clearly described by Liskov and Snyder (1979). Exception-handling facilities of the Ada language are described by Goos and Hartmanis (1983).

PROBLEM SET

1. What run-time errors or conditions, if any, can Pascal programs detect and handle?

2. From textbooks on the PL/I and Ada programming languages, look up the respective sets of built-in exceptions. Do a comparative evaluation of the two, considering both completeness and flexibility.

3. Write a CLU or Ada code segment that retries a call to a procedure, `tape_read`, that reads input from a tape drive and can raise the `tape_read_error` exception.

4. Why does CLU need the built-in exception, **failure**, which is implicitly raised when no handler is found for some other exception, and Ada does not?

5. From *The Programming Language Ada Reference Manual* (Goos and Hartmanis, 1983), determine how exceptions that take place during rendezvous are handled.

6. In languages without exception-handling facilities, it is common to have most subprograms include an "error" parameter, which can be set to some value representing "OK" or some other value representing "error in procedure." What advantage does a linguistic exception-handling facility like that of CLU have over this method?

7. From a textbook on COBOL, determine how exception handling is done in COBOL programs.

8. In a language without exception-handling facilities, one could send an error-handling procedure as a parameter to each procedure that can detect errors that must be handled. What disadvantages are there to this method?

9. Compare the methods suggested in Problems 6 and 8. Which do you think is better and why?

10. Compare the experimental exception-handling facilities of C++ (Stroustrup, 1991) with those of Ada. Which design, in your opinion, is the most flexible? Which makes it possible to write more reliable programs?

11. Suppose you are writing an Ada procedure that has three alternative methods for accomplishing its requirements. Write a skeletal version of this procedure so that if the first alternative raises any exception, the second is tried, and if the second alternative raises any exception, the third is executed. Write the code as if the three methods were procedures named ALT1, ALT2, and ALT3.

12. Write an Ada program that inputs a list of integer values in the range of -100 to 100 from the keyboard and computes the sum of the squares of the input values. This program must use exception handling to ensure that the input values are in range and are legal integers, to handle the error of the sum of the squares becoming larger than a standard INTEGER variable can store, and to detect end-of-file and use it to cause output of the result. In the case of overflow of the sum, an error message must be printed and the program terminated.

13

Functional Programming Languages

John McCarthy

John McCarthy and Marvin Minsky formed MIT's Artificial Intelligence Project in 1958. In 1958–59, McCarthy designed LISP, which became operational in 1959. McCarthy also served on the ALGOL design team.

Key Concepts

- Mathematical functions
- Functional forms
- Lambda notation
- Symbolic computation
- Conditional expressions

- Mapping functional forms
- Run-time code construction
- The functional argument problem
- Scheme
- COMMON LISP

The first 12 chapters of this book have been concerned primarily with the imperative programming languages. This chapter is the first to focus on a category of nonimperative languages.

The high degree of similarity among the imperative languages arises in part from one of the common bases of their design: the von Neumann architecture, as discussed in Chapter 1. One can think of the imperative languages collectively as a progression of developments to improve the basic model, which was FORTRAN I. All have been designed to make efficient use of von Neumann architecture computers. Although the imperative style of programming has been found acceptable by most programmers, its heavy reliance on the underlying architecture is an unnecessary restriction on the process of software development.

Other bases for language design exist, many of them oriented more to particular programming paradigms than to efficient execution on a particular computer architecture. Thus far, however, the reduced efficiency in executing programs written in these languages has prevented them from dominating the software business.

The functional programming paradigm, which is based on mathematical functions, is the design basis for one of the most important nonimperative styles of languages. This style of programming is supported by functional, or applicative, programming languages.

LISP began as a purely functional language, but it soon acquired some important imperative features that increased its execution efficiency. It is still the most important of the functional languages, at least in the sense that it is the only one to achieve widespread use. Scheme is a small, static-scoped descendant of LISP. COMMON LISP is an amalgam of several early 1980s dialects of LISP.

The objective of this chapter is to introduce the concept, but not the process, of functional programming. We also will describe one way in which a language can be designed to provide convenient facilities for functional programming. Our method is to discuss mathematical functions and functional programming and then to introduce a subset of purely functional LISP to illustrate the functional programming style. Brief descriptions of the primary features of Scheme and COMMON LISP are also included in this chapter.

Sufficient material on LISP and Scheme is included to allow the reader to write some simple but interesting programs. It is difficult to acquire an actual feel for functional programming without some actual programming experience, so that is strongly encouraged.

13.1   Mathematical Functions

A mathematical function is a **mapping** of members of one set, called the **domain set,** to another set, called the **range set.** A function definition specifies the domain and range sets, either explicitly or implicitly, along with the mapping. The mapping is described by an expression. Functions can be applied to a particular element of the domain set. Note that the domain set may be the cross-product of several sets. A function yields, or returns, an element of the range set.

One of the fundamental characteristics of mathematical functions is that the evaluation order of their mapping expressions is controlled by recursion and conditional expressions, rather than by the sequencing and iterative repetition that are common to the imperative programming languages.

Another important characteristic is that mathematical functions do not produce side effects. Therefore, given the same set of arguments, a mathematical function always yields the same value.

13.1.1   Simple Functions

Function definitions are often written as a function name, followed by a list of parameters in parentheses, followed by the mapping expression. For example:

$$\text{cube}(x) \equiv x * x * x, \text{ where } x \text{ is a real number}$$

The domain and range sets are the real numbers. The symbol $\equiv$ is used to mean "is defined as." The parameter, x, can represent any member of the domain set, but it is fixed to represent one specific element during evaluation of the function expression.

Function applications are specified by pairing the function name with a particular element of the domain set. The range element is obtained by evaluating the function mapping expression with the domain element substituted for the occurrences of the parameter. For example, cube(2.0) yields the value 8.0. It is important to note that during evaluation, the mapping of a function contains no unbound variables, where a bound variable is a name for a particular value. Every occurrence of a parameter is bound to a value from the domain set and is considered a constant during evaluation.

Early theoretical work on functions separated the task of defining a function from that of naming the function. Lambda notation, as devised by Alonzo Church (Church, 1941), provides a method for defining nameless functions. A **lambda expression** specifies the parameter and the mapping of a function. The value of a lambda expression is the function itself. For example, consider

$\lambda(x)x * x * x$

The parameter of a lambda expression is sometimes called a bound variable. As stated above, before evaluation, a parameter represents any member of the domain set, but during evaluation it is bound to a particular member. When a lambda expression is evaluated for a given parameter, the expression is said to be applied to that parameter. The mechanics of such an application are the same as for any function evaluation. Application of the lambda expression above is denoted as in the following example:

$(\lambda(x)x * x * x) (2)$

which results in the value 8.

Lambda expressions, like other function definitions, can have more than one parameter.

13.1.2 Functional Forms

Complex functions in mathematics are defined in terms of other functions. A higher-order function, or **functional form,** is one that either takes functions as parameters or yields a function as its result, or both. One common kind of functional form is **function composition,** which has two functional parameters and yields a function whose value is the first actual parameter function applied to the result of the second. Function composition is written as an expression, using ° as an operator, as in

$h \equiv f \circ g$

For example, if

$f(x) \equiv x + 2$
$g(x) \equiv 3 * x$

then h is defined as

$h(x) \equiv f(g(x))$, or $h(x) \equiv (3 * x) + 2$

Construction is a functional form that takes a list of functions as parameters. When applied to an argument, a construction applies each of its functional parameters to that argument and collects the results in a list or sequence. A construction is syntactically denoted by placing the functions in brackets, as in [f, g]. Consider the following example:

let

$$g(x) \equiv x * x$$
$$h(x) \equiv 2 * x$$
$$i(x) \equiv x / 2$$

then

$[g, h, i]$ (4) yields (16, 8, 2)

Apply-to-all is a functional form that takes a single function as a parameter. If applied to a list of arguments, apply-to-all applies its functional parameter to each of the values in the list argument and collects the results in a list or sequence. Apply-to-all is denoted by α. Consider the following example: let

$$h(x) \equiv x * x$$

then

$\alpha(h, (2, 3, 4))$ yields (4, 9, 16)

There are many other functional forms, but these examples should illustrate their characteristics.

13.2 Functional Programming Languages

The objective of the design of a functional programming language is to mimic mathematical functions to the greatest extent possible. This results in an approach to problem solving that is fundamentally different from methods used with imperative languages. In an imperative language, an expression is evaluated and the result is stored in a memory location, which is represented as a variable in a program. This necessary attention to memory cells results in a relatively low-level programming methodology. A program in an assembly language often must also store the results of partial evaluations of expressions. For example, to evaluate

$$(x + y) / (a - b)$$

the value of $(x + y)$ is computed first. That value must then be stored while $(a - b)$ is evaluated. To help alleviate this problem, the storage of intermediate results of expression evaluations in high-level languages are handled by the compiler. The storage for intermediate results is still required, but the details are hidden from the programmer.

A purely functional programming language does not use variables or assignment statements. This frees the programmer from concerns about the memory cells of the computer on which the program is executed. Programs are function definitions and function application specifications, and executions consist of evaluating the function applications. Although functional languages are often implemented with interpreters, they can also be compiled.

A functional language provides a set of primitive functions, a set of functional forms to construct complex functions from those primitive functions, a function application operation, and some structure or structures for storing data. A well-defined functional language requires only a few primitive functions.

Imperative languages provide some support for functional programming. Most, for example, include some kind of function definition and enactment facilities. The most serious drawback to using an imperative language to do functional programming is that functions in imperative languages have strong restrictions on the types of values that can be returned. In many languages, such as FORTRAN and Pascal, only simple type values can be returned. More importantly, they cannot return a function. Such restrictions limit the kinds of functional forms that can be provided. Another serious problem with the functions of imperative languages is the possibility of functional side effects.

13.3 An Introduction to Pure LISP

A number of functional programming languages have been developed. The oldest and most widely used is LISP. Studying functional languages through LISP is somewhat akin to studying the imperative languages through FORTRAN: LISP was the first functional language, but some now believe that, although it has steadily evolved over the last 30 years, it no longer represents the latest design concepts for functional languages. In addition, with the exception of the first version, all LISP dialects include imperative language features, such as imperative-style variables, assignment statements, and iteration. (Imperative-style variables are used to name memory cells whose values can change many times during program execution.) Despite this and its somewhat odd form, however, LISP still represents well the fundamental concepts of functional programming and is therefore worthy of study. Our discussion of the original language is relatively brief and does not touch on its imperative features. Because of this deliberate omission, we call the subset we discuss pure LISP.

To investigate LISP as a functional language, we first discuss its fundamental features and then see how it fulfills the needs of functional programming. Because LISP was designed to deal with data in a particular and unusual (for imperative language programmers) form, we also discuss the development of that form.

13.3.1 Data Types and Structures

There are only two types of data objects in pure LISP: atoms and lists. They are not types in the sense that imperative languages have types. Atoms, which have the form of identifiers, are the symbols of LISP. Numeric constants are also considered atoms.

Recall from Chapter 2 that LISP originally used lists as its data structure because they were thought to be an essential part of list processing. As it eventually developed, however, LISP rarely requires the operations of insertions and deletions.

Lists are specified by delimiting their elements with parentheses. The elements of simple lists are restricted to atoms, as in

(A B C D)

Nested list structures are also specified by parentheses. For example, the list

(A (B C) D (E (F G)))

is a list of four elements. The first is the atom A; the second is the sublist (B C); the third is the atom D; the fourth is the sublist (E (F G)), which has as its second element the sublist (F G).

Internally, lists are usually stored as single-linked list structures, in which each node has two pointers and represents an element. A node for an atom has its first pointer pointing to some representation of the atom, such as its symbol or numeric value. A node for a sublist element has its first pointer pointing to the first node of the sublist. In both cases, the second pointer of a node points to the next element of the list. A list is referenced by a pointer to its first element.

The internal representations of the two lists given above are shown in Figure 13.1. Note that the elements of a list are shown horizontally. The last

Figure 13.1
Internal representation of two LISP lists

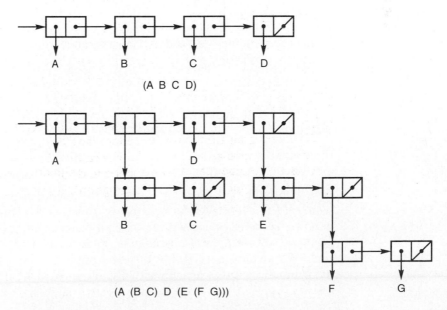

(A B C D)

(A (B C) D (E (F G)))

element of a list has no successor, so its link is NIL. Sublists are shown with the same structure.

13.3.2   The First LISP Interpreter

The original intent was to have a notation for LISP programs that would be as close to FORTRAN's as possible, with additions when necessary. This notation was called M-notation, for meta-notation. There was to be a compiler that would translate programs written in M-notation into semantically equivalent machine code programs for the IBM 704.

Early in the development of LISP, McCarthy decided to write a paper that would promote list processing as a general symbolic processing method. McCarthy believed that list processing could be used to study computability, which at the time was usually studied using Turing machines. McCarthy thought that the processing of symbolic lists was a more natural model of computation than Turing machines. One of the common requirements of the study of computation is that one must be able to prove certain computability characteristics of the whole class of whatever model of computation is being used. In the case of the Turing machine model, one can construct a universal Turing machine that can mimic the operations of any other Turing machine. From this concept came the idea of constructing a universal LISP function that could evaluate any other function in LISP.

The first requirement for the universal LISP function was a notation that allowed functions to be expressed in the same way data was expressed. The parenthesized list notation described in Section 13.3.1 had already been adopted for LISP data, so it was decided to invent conventions for function definitions and function calls that could also be expressed in list notation. Function calls were specified in a prefix list form called Cambridge Polish, as in the following:

(function_name   argument_1 . . . argument_n)

The lambda notation described in Section 13.1.1 was chosen to specify function definitions. It had to be modified, however, to allow the binding of functions to names so that functions could be referenced by other functions and by themselves. This name binding was specified by a list consisting of the function name and a list containing the lambda expression, as in

(function_name (LAMBDA (arg_1 . . . arg_n) map_expression))

If you have had no prior exposure to functional programming, it may seem odd to even consider a nameless function. However, nameless functions are sometimes useful in functional programming (as well as in mathematics). An example of one is given in Section 13.3.8.

LISP functions specified in this new notation were called S-expressions, for symbolic expressions. Eventually, all LISP structures, both data and code, were called S-expressions. An S-expression can be either a list or an atom.

McCarthy successfully developed a universal function that could evaluate any other function that was in the form of an S-expression. This function was named EVAL and was itself in the form of an S-expression. Two of the people in the AI Project, Stephen B. Russell and Daniel J. Edwards, noticed that an implementation of EVAL could serve as a LISP interpreter, and they promptly constructed such an implementation (McCarthy et al., 1965).

There were several important results of this quick, easy, and unexpected implementation. First, all early LISP systems copied EVAL and were therefore interpretive. Second, the definition of M-notation was never completed or implemented, so S-expressions became LISP's only notation. The use of the same notation for data and code has important consequences, one of which will be discussed in Section 13.3.9. Third, much of the original language design was effectively frozen, keeping certain odd features in the language, such as the conditional expression form and the use of zero for both the NIL address and logical false.

Another feature of early LISP systems that was apparently accidental was the use of dynamic scoping. Functions were evaluated in the environments of their callers. No one at the time knew much about scoping, and it is doubtful that much thought was given to the choice. We further discuss the scoping rules of LISP in Section 13.3.10.

As stated earlier, EVAL is often implemented as an interactive interpreter. Such an implementation produces a prompt, such as

```
EVAL>
```

and then waits for the user to ask it to evaluate some function for which a definition has previously been given. When a function name and the appropriate parameters are typed in, EVAL applies the requested function to the parameter values and prints the result of the application. Any parameters that are themselves function calls must be evaluated before the function is applied. These evaluations are identical to that of the other function and are accomplished by recursive calls to EVAL. We discuss this process in the following section.

13.3.3 LISP as a Functional Language

As pointed out in Section 13.2, a functional programming language consists of a set of primitive functions, a set of functional forms, a function application operator, and some structures for storing data. The LISP function application operator is EVAL, and its data structures are atoms and lists. In the following sections we describe the primitive LISP functions. We also describe LISP's one functional form and how others can be added through LISP's extensibility capability.

13.3.4 Primitive LISP Functions

Computer programs manipulate data whether the language is imperative or functional. Because lists are the primary data structure of LISP, the language must include primitives for manipulating lists. In particular, it must provide operations for selecting parts of a list, which in a sense dismantle the list, and an operation for constructing lists. Because the primary operations of functional languages are provided by functions, LISP includes primitive functions for these operations.

The first LISP primitive we describe is neither a selector nor a constructor. Rather, it is a utility function required by the nature of the LISP function application operation, EVAL. When called, EVAL first evaluates the parameters of the given function. This action is necessary when the actual parameters in a function call are themselves function calls, which is frequently the case. In some calls, however, the parameters are data elements, either atoms or lists, rather than function references. When a parameter is not a function reference, it obviously should not be evaluated.

For example, suppose we have a function that has two parameters, an atom and a list, whose purpose is to determine whether the given atom is in the given list. Neither the atom nor the list should be evaluated; they are literal data to be examined. To avoid evaluating parameters, they are first given as parameters to the primitive function QUOTE, which simply returns them as they are, as in this example:

```
(QUOTE A)   returns A
(QUOTE (A B C))   returns (A B C)
```

In the remainder of this chapter, we will use the abbreviation of the call to QUOTE, as provided by most LISP systems: The S-expression parameter to QUOTE is preceded by an apostrophe symbol ('). Thus, instead of (QUOTE A), we will use 'A.

There are two primitive list selectors in LISP: CAR and CDR (read "could-er"). The CAR function returns the first element of a given list. The following examples illustrate CAR:

```
(CAR '(A B C))   returns (A)
(CAR '((A B) C D))   returns (A B)
(CAR 'A)   is undefined (A is not a list)
(CAR '(A))   returns A
(CAR '())   is undefined (the list has no first element)
```

The CDR function returns the remainder of a given list after its CAR is removed:

```
(CDR '(A B C))   returns (B C)
(CDR '((A B) C D))   returns (C D)
(CDR 'A)   is undefined
(CDR '(A))   returns () or NIL
(CDR '())   is undefined
```

Notice that an empty list can be written either as () or as NIL. NIL is, in effect, both an atom and a list.

The names of the CAR and CDR functions are peculiar at best. The origin of these names lies in the first implementation of LISP, which was on an IBM 704 computer. The 704's memory words had two fields, named decrement and address, that were used in various operand addressing strategies. Each of these fields could store a machine memory address. The 704 also included two machine code instructions, named CAR (contents of address register) and CDR (contents of decrement register), that extracted the associated fields. It was natural to use the two fields to store the two pointers of a list node, so that a memory word could neatly store a node. Using these conventions, the CAR and CDR instructions of the 704 provided efficient list selectors. The names carried over into the LISP primitives and were never changed.

CONS is the LISP primitive list constructor. It builds a list from its two arguments, the first of which can be either an atom or a list; the second is usually a list. Consider the following examples:

```
(CONS 'A '())   returns (A)
(CONS 'A '(B C))  returns (A B C)
(CONS '() '(A B))  returns (() A B)
(CONS '(A B) '(C D))  returns ((A B) C D)
```

The results of these CONS operations are shown in Figure 13.2 (p. 464).

Note that CONS is, in a sense, the inverse of CAR and CDR. CAR and CDR take a list apart, and CONS constructs a new list from given list parts. The two parameters to CONS become the CAR and CDR of the new list. Thus, if lis is a list, then

```
(CONS (CAR lis) (CDR lis))
```

is the identity function.

There are three predicate functions among LISP's primitive functions: EQ, ATOM, and NULL. A predicate function is one that returns a Boolean value (either true or false). In LISP, the two Boolean values are T and NIL.

The EQ function takes two parameters. It returns T if both parameters are atoms and the two are the same; otherwise, it returns NIL. Consider the following examples:

```
(EQ 'A 'A)   returns T
(EQ 'A 'B)   returns NIL
(EQ 'A '(A B))   returns NIL
(EQ '(A B) '(A B))   may return either NIL or T
```

As the last case indicates, the result of comparing lists with EQ is implementation dependent—some yield T and some yield NIL. The reason for this difference is that EQ is often implemented as a pointer comparison, and two lists that are exactly the same are often not duplicated in memory. At the time the LISP system creates a list, it checks to see if there is already

Figure 13.2
The results of several
CONS operations

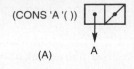

(A)   A

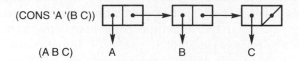

(A B C)   A   B   C

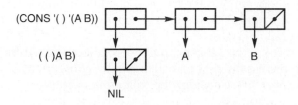

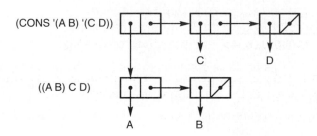

such a list. If there is, the new list is nothing more than a new pointer to the existing list. In these cases, the two lists are judged equal by EQ. However, in some cases, it may be difficult to detect the presence of an identical list, in which case a new list is created. In this scenario, EQ yields NIL.

The ATOM predicate function returns T if its single argument is an atom and NIL otherwise, as in the following examples:

```
(ATOM '(X Y))   returns NIL
(ATOM 'X)   returns T
```

The NULL function tests its parameter to determine whether it is the empty list and returns T if it is. Consider the following examples:

```
(NULL '(A B))   returns NIL
(NULL '())   returns T
(NULL 'A)   returns NIL
(NULL '(()))   returns NIL
(NULL NIL)   returns T
```

The second to the last case is NIL because the parameter is not the empty list. Rather it is a list containing a single element, an empty list. The last case is T because NIL represents both an atom and the empty list.

Functional composition is the only primitive functional form provided by the original LISP. Functions are simply applied to the results of other function calls. Inner function calls, like outer function calls, are parenthesized. The following examples illustrate function composition:

```
(CDR (CDR '(A B C)))  returns (C)
(CAR (CAR '((A B) B C)))  returns A
(CDR (CAR '((A B C) D)))  returns (B C)
(ATOM (CAR '(A B)))  returns T
(NULL (CAR '(() B C)))  returns T
(CONS (CAR '(A B)) (CDR '(A B)))  returns (A B)
```

Notice that inner function names are not quoted, because they must be evaluated rather than treated as literal data. Additional functional forms can be constructed by the LISP system implementor and the user. We describe one of the more common of these in Section 13.3.8.

13.3.5 Functions for Constructing Functions

As stated earlier, LISP uses lambda notation in list form to define functions. For example, the lambda expression list

```
(LAMBDA (L) (CAR (CDR L)))
```

is a function that returns the second element of its given parameter, which must be a list. This function can be applied in the same way that named functions are: by placing it in the beginning of a list that contains the actual parameters. For example, we could have

```
((LAMBDA (L) (CAR (CDR L))) '(A B C))
```

which yields B. Notice that actual parameters to LISP functions that are defined as parameters of the lambda expression are not quoted; an example is the parameter L in the call to CDR in the expression above. L is called a bound variable within the lambda expression. A bound variable is not evaluated in the expression after being bound to an actual parameter value at the time the lambda expression is first evaluated.

It is often necessary to bind a function definition to a name, so it can be easily applied to various arguments and also so it can be recursive. This is done in LISP with the DEFINE function, whose one parameter is a list of "labeled" lambda expressions. The label on each lambda expression is bound to that expression and serves as its function name. The following example call to DEFINE has only a single element in its argument list:

```
(DEFINE (
  '(second (LAMBDA (L)
    (CAR (CDR L))
  ))
))
```

Once this function has been evaluated, the function second can be used, as in

```
(second '(A B C))
```

which yields B.

Our function second uses CDR to create a list in which the second element of the given list is the parameter list's first element. If parameters were passed by reference, this would change the actual parameter list. However, LISP parameters are passed by value, so this does not happen. Regardless of what a function does to its formal parameters, the actual parameters are not affected.

13.3.6 Control Flow

The control flow mechanisms of LISP are modeled after those of mathematical functions. Control flow in mathematical function definitions is quite different from that in functions in imperative programming languages. Whereas functions in imperative languages are defined as collections of statements that may include several kinds of sequence control flow, mathematical functions do not have multiple statements and use only recursion and conditional expressions for evaluation flow. For example, the factorial function can be defined with these two operations as:

$$f(n) \equiv \left\{ \begin{array}{ll} 1 & \text{if } n = 0 \\ n * f(n - 1) & \text{if } n > 0 \end{array} \right.$$

Note that a mathematical conditional expression is in the form of a list of pairs, each of which is a guarded expression. Each guarded expression has a predicate guard and an expression. The value of such a conditional expression is the value of the expression associated with the predicate that is true. Only one of the predicates is true for a given parameter or parameter list.

The LISP conditional expression is in the form of a call to a function, which in this case is named COND. COND is a slightly generalized version of the mathematical conditional expression that allows more than one predicate to be true at the same time. Because different mathematical conditional expressions have different numbers of parameters, COND does not require a fixed number of actual parameters. Each parameter to COND is a pair of S-expressions in which the first is a predicate.

The semantics of COND is as follows: The predicates of the parameters are evaluated, one at a time, in order from the first, until one evaluates to true. The S-expression that is the right component of the first parameter whose predicate is found to be true is then evaluated and returned as the yield of COND. Note that the atom T can and often is used as a constant predicate in a COND, in which case T's S-expression component is always evaluated and returned as COND's value. Of course, it only makes sense to use T as the predicate of the last parameter of COND.

As an example of a COND call, assume that LISP allows numeric atoms and has primitives for arithmetic (which all contemporary dialects do), and consider the following function for factorial:

```
(DEFINE (
  '(factorial (LAMBDA (n)
     (COND
       ((EQ n 0) 1)
       (T (TIMES n (factorial (SUB1 n))))) 
   )
  ))
))
```

TIMES is a built-in function that takes a variable number of numeric atoms as parameters and returns their product. SUB1 is also a built-in function. It returns a value one less than its numeric parameter. Note the close resemblance of the LISP factorial function to the mathematical version.

If no parameter to COND has a predicate that evaluates to true, COND returns NIL. To prevent this, COND often has T as the predicate of its last parameter. Notice the similarity between a COND and the multiple selection statement with an "otherwise" clause at the end, such as the Ada **case** statement.

13.3.7 Example LISP Functions

This section contains several examples of functional programs using LISP. These programs solve simple list-processing problems.

Consider the problem of membership of a given atom in a given simple list. A simple list is one without sublists. If the function is named member, it could be used as follows:

```
(member 'B '(A B C))    returns T
(member 'B '(A C D E))   returns NIL
```

Thinking in terms of iteration, the membership problem is simply to compare the given atom and the individual elements of the given list, one at a time in some order, until either a match is found or there are no more elements in the list. A similar process can be accomplished using recursion. The function can compare the given atom with the CAR of the list. If they match, the value T is returned. If they do not match, then the atom can only be found in the remainder of the list, so the function should call itself with the CDR of the list as the list parameter. In this process, there are two ways out of the recursion: either the list is empty on some call and NIL is returned, or a match is found and T is returned.

Altogether, there are three cases that must be handled in the function: an empty input list, a match between the atom and the CAR of the list, or a mismatch between the atom and the CAR of the list, which causes the recursive call. These three cases are exactly the three parameters to COND, with the last being the default case that is triggered by a T predicate. The complete function follows:

```
(DEFINE (
  '(member (LAMBDA (atm lis)
    (COND
      ((NULL lis) NIL)
      ((EQ atm (CAR lis)) T)
      (T (member atm (CDR lis)))
    )
  ))
))
```

This form is typical of simple LISP functions. LISP is a list-processing language, and the data in lists are usually processed one element at a time. The individual elements may be gotten by CAR, and the process is continued using recursion on the CDR of the list.

As another example, consider the problem of determining whether two given lists are equal. If the two lists are simple, the solution is relatively easy, although some unfamiliar techniques are involved. A predicate function for comparing simple lists is shown here:

```
(DEFINE (
  '(equalsimp (LAMBDA (lis1 lis2)
    (COND
      ((NULL lis1) (NULL lis2))
      ((NULL lis2) NIL)
      ((EQ (CAR lis1) (CAR lis2))
              (equalsimp (CDR lis1) (CDR lis2)))
      (T NIL)
    )
  ))
))
```

The first case, which is handled by the first parameter to COND, is for when the first list parameter is the empty list. This can occur in an external call if the first list parameter is initially empty. Because a recursive call uses the CDRs of the two parameter lists as its parameters, the first list can be empty if the first list has had all of its elements removed by previous recursive calls. When the first list is empty, the second list must be checked to see if it is also empty. If so, they are equal, and NULL correctly returns T. If the second list is not empty, it is larger than the first list and NIL should be returned, as it is by NULL. Note that any non-empty list that is returned by a predicate function is interpreted as T.

The next case deals with the second list being empty when the first list is not. This situation occurs only when the second list is larger than the first. Only the second list must be tested, because the first case catches all instances of the first list being empty.

The third case is the recursive step that tests for equality between corresponding elements in the two lists. It does this by comparing the CARs of the two nonempty lists. If they are equal, then the two lists are equal up to this point, so recursion is used on the CDRs of both. This case fails when two unequal atoms are found. When this occurs, we obviously do not want to continue, so the default case, which is last, takes effect and causes the functional value to be NIL without further comparisons.

Note that equalsimp expects lists as parameters and does not operate correctly if either or both parameters are atoms.

The problem of comparing general lists is slightly more complex than this, because sublists must be traced completely in the comparison process. This is a situation where the power of recursion is uniquely appropriate, since the form of sublists is the same as that of the given lists. Anytime the corresponding elements of the two given lists are lists, they are separated into their two parts, CAR and CDR, and recursion is used on them. This is a perfect example of the usefulness of the divide and conquer approach. If the corresponding elements of the two given lists are atoms, they can simply be compared using EQ.

The definition of the complete function follows:

```
(DEFINE (
  '(equal (LAMBDA (lis1 lis2)
    (COND
      ((ATOM lis1) (EQ lis1 lis2))
      ((ATOM lis2) NIL)
      ((equal (CAR lis1) (CAR lis2))
                      (equal (CDR lis1) (CDR lis2)))
      (T NIL)
    )
  ))
))
```

The first two cases of the COND handle the situation where either of the parameters is an atom instead of a list. The third COND case is the most interesting. The predicate is a recursive call with the CARs of the lists as parameters. If this call returns T, then recursion is used again on the CDRs of the lists.

This definition of equal works on any pair of S-expressions, not just lists.

Another commonly needed list operation is that of constructing a new list that contains all of the elements of two given list arguments. This is usually implemented as a LISP function named append. It can be constructed by repeated use of CONS to place the elements of the first list argument into the second list argument. To clarify the action of append, consider the following examples:

```
(append '(A B) '(C D R)) returns (A B C D R)
(append '((A B) C) '(D (E F))) returns ((A B) C D (E F))
```

The definition of append is:

```
(DEFINE (
  '(append (LAMBDA (lis1 lis2)
    (COND
      ((NULL lis1) lis2)
      (T (CONS (CAR lis1) (append (CDR Lis1) lis2)))
    )
  ))
))
```

Consider the following LISP function, named funfun, that uses the member function described in this section. Try to determine what it does before reading the description that follows it. Assume that the parameters are simple lists.

```
(DEFINE (
  '(funfun (LAMBDA (lis1 lis2)
    (COND
      ((NULL lis1) ())
      ((member (CAR lis1) lis2)
        (CONS (CAR lis1) (funfun (CDR lis1) lis2)))
      (T (funfun (CDR lis1) lis2))
    )
  ))
))
```

The two parameters of funfun are assumed to be simple lists that represent lists. funfun yields a simple list that contains the common elements of its two parameters. So, if the parameter lists represent sets, funfun computes a list that represents the intersection of those two sets.

13.3.8 Another Functional Form

Because of its ease of extensibility, LISP need not provide many primitive functional forms. Implementors and users can add their own. The most common functional forms added by implementors are variations of mathematical apply-to-all functional forms. The simplest of these is mapcar, which has two parameters, a function, and a list. mapcar applies the given function to each element of the given list, and it returns a list of the results of these applications. A definition of a mapcar function follows:

```
(DEFINE (
  '(mapcar (LAMBDA (fun lis)
    (COND
     ((NULL lis) ())
     (T (CONS (fun (CAR lis))
                        (mapcar fun (CDR lis))))
    )
  ))
 ))
```

Note the simple form of the LISP function mapcar, which expresses a complex functional form. This is testament to the great expressive power of LISP.

As an example of the use of mapcar, suppose we want all of the elements of a list cubed. We can accomplish this with

```
(mapcar (LAMBDA (num) (TIMES num num num))· (3 4 2 6)
```

This call returns (27 64 8 216).

Note that the first parameter to mapcar is a lambda expression. It defines the nameless function that is to be applied to each element of the second parameter.

The paucity of functional forms in LISP can be viewed in at least two different ways. On the one hand, it is unsatisfactory to have only composition as a primitive functional form. On the other, it is good that LISP allows users to construct their own functional forms. Some users believe, however, that this kind of extensibility leads to chaos. They feel that the best functional language design should include a rich set of functional forms and disallow users from adding their own. It should be noted that this view is held by a minority of interested people.

13.3.9 LISP Functions That Build LISP Code

The fact that programs and data have the same structure can be exploited in constructing programs. Combined with access to the function EVAL, this fact allows user programs to construct other programs and immediately evaluate them.

One of the simplest examples of this process involves numeric atoms. Most LISP systems include a function for numeric atoms named PLUS, which takes any number of numeric atoms as arguments and returns their sum. For example, (PLUS 3 7 10 2) returns 22.

Our problem is as follows: Suppose that in a program we have a list of numeric atoms and need the sum. We cannot apply PLUS directly on the list, because PLUS can take only atomic parameters, not a list of numeric atoms. We could, of course, write a function that repeatedly adds the CAR of the list to the sum of its CDR, using recursion to go through the list. Such a function follows:

```
(DEFINE (
  '(adder (LAMBDA (lis)
    (COND
      ((NULL lis) 0)
      (T (PLUS (CAR lis) (adder (CDR lis))))
    )
  ))
))
```

An alternative solution to the problem is to write a function that builds a call to PLUS with the proper parameter forms. This can be done by using CONS to insert the atom PLUS into the list of numbers. This new list can then be submitted to EVAL for evaluation, as in the following:

```
(DEFINE (
  '(adder (LAMBDA (lis)
    (COND
      ((NULL lis) 0)
      (T (EVAL (CONS 'PLUS lis)))
    )
  ))
))
```

For example, the call

```
(adder '(3 4 6))
```

causes adder to build the list

```
(PLUS 3 4 6)
```

This list is then submitted to EVAL, which invokes PLUS and returns the result, 13.

Note that complete functions can be built and evaluated by LISP programs.

13.3.10 The Functional Argument Problem

Until the late 1970s, most LISP systems were interpretive and implemented dynamic scoping, following the lead of the first LISP system, as discussed in Section 13.3.2. The disadvantages of dynamic scoping are discussed in Chapter 4.

When functions are sent as actual parameters in a language that uses dynamic scoping, some unusual and often unexpected results can occur. Consider the following scenario. Suppose that function P references a non-local variable X, and that P is sent as a parameter to function Q. The problem arises if Q happens to have another formal parameter, and it happens to be named X. When Q calls P, Q's parameter X will be used in P, rather than the X that was in the environment of P at the time Q was called. Two instances of this situation are shown and further explained with the following skeletal program:

```
(DEFINE (
  '(funa (LAMBDA (...)
     ... (CAR X) ...
  ))

  '(funb (LAMBDA (FUN X)
     ... FUN ...
  ))

  '(func (LAMBDA (X Z)
     ... funa ...
     ... (funb funa Z) ...
  ))
))
```

```
(func '(I J) '(K L M))
```

func's direct call to funa causes funa to reference the X that is a formal parameter in func. func is bound to the list (I J), so the call (CAR X) in funa yields I. Then func calls funb, passing funa and Z, the latter being bound to the list (K L M). Then funb calls the passed function, funa. This execution of funa references the X that is the formal parameter in funb, which is then bound to (K L M). So this time, (CAR X) in funa yields K. This will likely be unexpected by the programmer and will yield odd and probably incorrect results.

This problem, called the functional argument problem or simply the funarg problem, can be solved by adding a new function, named FUNCTION, to LISP's primitives. FUNCTION takes a function as a parameter and returns both the function and some representation of the current referencing environment (for example, a pointer into the stack). It is used on a function being sent as an actual parameter in order to provide that function with its proper referencing environment and to avoid the possibility of a later binding that would hide the reference to a variable that was in the environment of the sender.

In the example above, the call to funb in func could be changed to

```
(funb (FUNCTION funa) Z)
```

which would cause funa to use func's referencing environment. Both calls to funa in this program would then use the same X reference.

Note that this solution is precisely what is done when subprogram names are passed as parameters in imperative languages (Chapter 9) to ensure that correct variable bindings can be done.

An alternative solution to the funarg problem would have been to simply change the semantics of LISP to use static scoping. This solution was rejected at the time because some programmers had become accustomed to dynamic scoping, and there was a desire to maintain backward compatibility with earlier implementations of LISP.

Note that the use of FUNCTION does not provide static scoping in the same sense as in Pascal, where bindings of nonlocal references can be made at compile time. The binding of a nonlocal is still dynamic with FUNCTION; it is just earlier in execution time. In fact, the result of using FUNCTION is very similar to the effect of passing parameters by name. The address evaluation procedures for parameters passed by name are evaluated in the referencing environment of the caller, not that of the called procedure.

Recent dialects of LISP, such as COMMON LISP (Steele, 1984), abandon backward compatibility and adopt static scoping, which not only solves the funarg problem but also slightly simplifies compilation. Furthermore, as argued in Chapter 4, programs in static-scoped languages are easier to read because the execution sequence does not determine nonlocal variable bindings.

The problem of choosing the correct environment for execution of a subprogram that has been passed as a parameter was discussed in Chapter 8. Recall that the static-scoped languages employ a method comparable to one that results from the use of FUNCTION. That is, subprograms passed as parameters execute in the referencing environment of the subprogram that sent them as actual parameters. This is called **deep binding.** Passing a LISP function in the dynamic-scoped versions of LISP without using FUNCTION results in **shallow binding.** Users of dynamic-scoped LISP are thus given the choice between deep and shallow binding.

13.4   Two Contemporary Dialects of LISP: Scheme and COMMON LISP

The LISP language features described in Section 13.3 reflect the development of the language of the mid-1960s. The evolution of LISP has been continuous over its more than 30-year history. In the following sections, a few important features of two contemporary dialects of LISP, Scheme and COMMON LISP, are briefly discussed.

13.4.1   Scheme

The Scheme language emerged from MIT in the mid-1970s (Sussman and Steele, 1975). It is characterized by its small size, its exclusive use of static scoping, and its treatment of functions as first-class entities. As first-class entities, Scheme functions can be the values of expressions and elements of lists, and they can be assigned to variables, passed as parameters, and returned as the values of function applications. Early versions of LISP did not provide all of these capabilities.

As a small language with simple syntax and semantics, Scheme is well suited to educational applications, such as courses in functional programming and also general introductions to programming.

13.4.1.1 Some Functional Features of Scheme

A great deal of the syntax and semantics of Scheme are the same as those of the pure LISP described in Section 13.3. In this section some differences and some new features of Scheme are described.

Names in Scheme can consist of letters, digits, and special characters; they are case insensitive but must not begin with a digit.

The usual arithmetic operator symbols can be used in the same Cambridge Polish notation as used in pure LISP, as shown here:

Expression	Value
(* 3 7)	21
(− 5 6)	−1
(− 24 (* 4 3))	12

COND in Scheme uses ELSE for the last predicate, rather than T, which is often used in pure LISP in that position, as in

```
(COND
   (predicate_1     expression_1)
   (predicate_2     expression_2)
   ...
   (ELSE expression)
)
```

Scheme also includes a two-way conditional with the form

(IF predicate then_expression else_expression)

Functions can be defined and bound to names in two ways: with or without LAMBDA.

```
(DEFINE (circle_area radius)
   (* 3.14159 (* radius radius))
   )

(DEFINE (circle_area (LAMBDA (radius)
   (* 3.14159 (* radius radius))
))))
```

DEFINE is also used to bind a name to a value, as in

(DEFINE pi 3.14159)

Lambda expressions, such as

```
(LAMBDA (radius) (* 3.14159 (* radius radius)))
```

are simply unnamed functions and can appear in the operator position of any S-expression.

Scheme includes a few simple output functions, such as

```
(DISPLAY expression)
```

and

```
(NEWLINE)
```

with the obvious semantics.

LET is a function that allows names to be temporarily bound to the values of subexpressions. These names can then be used in the evaluation of another expression. Its general form is

```
(LET (
   (name_1  expression_1)
   (name_2  expression_2)
   . . .
   (name_n  expression_n))
   body
)
```

The semantics of LET is that the first n expressions are evaluated and the resulting values are bound to their associated names. Then the expressions in the body are evaluated. The result of LET is the value of the last expression in its body. The following example illustrates the use of LET:

```
(DEFINE (quadratic_roots a b c)
   (LET ((root_part_over_2a
            (/ (SQRT (- (* b b) (* 4 a c))) (* 2 a)))
         (minus_b_over_2a (/ (- 0 b) (* 2 a))))
   (DISPLAY (+ minus_b_over_2a root_part_over_2a))
   (NEWLINE)
   (DISPLAY (- minus_b_over_2a root_part_over_2a))
))
```

LET creates a new local static scope, much the same as Ada's **declare**. New variables can be created, used, and then discarded when the end of the new scope is reached. The named components of LET are like assignment statements, but they can be used only in LET's new scope. Furthermore, they are not rebound to new values in LET.

In the following section, a Scheme function is described that provides a method of doing precisely what the imperative language assignment statement does.

13.4.1.2 Imperative Features of Scheme

Scheme is a descendent of pure LISP that is not so pure: It includes several features that are borrowed from the imperative languages. Pure LISP has no imperative-style variables and no assignment statements. In Scheme, however, names can be bound to values, and those bindings can be changed later. This is done with the function SET!, as in the following:

```
(DEFINE pi 3.14159)
(SET! pi 3.141593)
```

In pure LISP, lists cannot be changed. They can be taken apart with CAR and CDR, but a given list cannot be changed, for that would require an imperative language feature, a side effect, of a function call. Scheme includes two functions that create such side effects, SET-CAR! and SET-CDR!. Consider the following examples:

```
(DEFINE lst (LIST 'a 'b))
(SET-CAR! lst 'c)
(SET-CDR! lst '(d))
```

The SET-CAR! changes the list bound to lst from (a b) to (c b). The SET-CDR! changes the list (c b) to (c d).

The imperative features of Scheme described above were put in Scheme for the sake of efficiency, but these strayings from functional programming also have their costs. Programs become harder to debug and maintain because of the possibility of aliasing and the fact that side effects allow identical function calls to produce different results at different times. For example, consider the following:

```
(DEFINE count 0)

(DEFINE (inc_count number)
   (SET! count (+ count number))
 )
```

Although the following two calls to inc_count are identical, they produce different results.

```
 (inc_count 1)
1
(inc_count 1)
2
```

13.4.2 COMMON LISP

COMMON LISP (Steele, 1984) was created in an effort to combine the features of several early 1980s dialects of LISP, including Scheme, into a single language. Being a combination, it is a quite large and complex language. Its basis, however, is pure LISP, so its syntax, primitive functions, and fundamental nature come from that language.

Recognizing the occasional flexibility provided by dynamic scoping as well as the simplicity of static scoping, COMMON LISP allows both. The default scoping for variables is static, but by declaring a variable to be "special," that variable becomes dynamically scoped.

The list of features of COMMON LISP is long: a large number of data types and structures, including such things as records, arrays, complex numbers, and character strings; powerful input and output operations; a form of packages for modularizing collections of functions and data, and also providing access control; the imperative features of Scheme—specifically functions that do what Scheme's SET!, SET-CAR!, and SET-CDR! do, plus more of its own.

COMMON LISP, along with most dialects of LISP except Scheme, includes a function named PROG that allows statement sequencing, as is common in imperative languages. Labels and the two functions, GO and RETURN, are included to provide iteration control. GO is used to transfer control to a label within the scope of PROG. RETURN is a means of exiting the PROG. The general form of PROG is

```
(PROG (local variables)
   expression_1
   ...
   expression_n
)
```

The local variables are initialized to NIL, have the scope of the PROG and exist only during execution of PROG. If there are global names that are the same as the locals, the globals are unaffected (and hidden) in PROG. Expressions in PROG that are atoms are treated as labels. GO transfers control to its parameter, which must be a label within the PROG expression list. RETURN has a parameter, which becomes the value of PROG.

Note that PROG is included in contemporary versions of LISP only to provide backward compatibility with older dialects. COMMON LISP has better constructs to provide the capabilities of PROG. For example, COMMON LISP has DOTIMES and DOLIST constructs for iteration and PROG1, PROG2, and PROGN for building sequences.

SETQ is the COMMON LISP function that corresponds to Scheme's SET!, and DEFUN is its version of DEFINE. Consider the following iterative version of the list membership function. The iterative version is followed by a recursive version similar to one that appeared in Section 13.3.7.

```
(DEFUN iterative_member (atm lst)
  (PROG ()
    loop_1
    (COND
      ((NULL lst) (RETURN NIL))
      ((EQUAL atm (CAR lst)) (RETURN T))
    )
    (SETQ lst (CDR lst))
    (GO loop_1)
))
```

```
(DEFUN recursive_member (atm lst)
  (COND
    ((NULL lst) NIL)
    ((EQUAL atm (CAR lst)) T)
    (T (recursive_member atm (CDR lst)))
))
```

As another example, consider the following interative and recursive functions that compute the length of a list:

```
(DEFUN iterative_length (lst)
  (PROG (sum)
    (SETQ sum 0)
    again
    (COND
      ((ATOM lst (RETURN sum)))
    )
    (SETQ sum (ADD1 sum))
    (SETQ lst (CDR lst))
    (GO again)
))

(DEFUN recursive_length (lst)
  (COND
    ((NULL lst) 0)
    (T ADD1 (recursive_length (CDR lst)))
  )
)
```

In a sense, Scheme and COMMON LISP are opposites. Scheme is far smaller and somewhat cleaner, in part because of its exclusive use of static scoping. COMMON LISP was meant to be a commercial language and has succeeded in being a widely used language for AI applications. Scheme, on the other hand, is much more often used in college courses on functional programming. It is also more likely to be studied as a functional language because of its relatively small size. An important design criterion of COMMON LISP that caused it to be a very large language is the desire to make it compatible with several earlier dialects of LISP.

13.5 Applications of Functional Languages

Over the past 35 years in the history of high-level programming languages, only a few functional languages have gained widespread use. Most prominent among these is LISP. In spite of its heavy use of the assignment statement, APL also is often considered a functional language, partly because of its functional forms.

APL has been used for a wide variety of applications, ranging from hardware description to management information systems. Because of the great difficulty in reading a typical APL program, its most natural place in contemporary computing is in the category of throwaway programming. With its powerful collection of array operations, it is an excellent vehicle for quick but dirty solutions to problems involving many array manipulations.

LISP is a versatile and powerful language. For its first 15 years, it was thought of, mostly by nonusers, as a strange language that was very costly to use. Indeed, it was common in the 1960s and early 1970s to think of two categories of languages, one containing LISP and one with all of the other programming languages.

As described in this chapter, LISP was developed for symbolic computation and list-processing applications, which lie mainly in the AI area of computing. In AI applications, LISP and its derivative languages are still the standard languages.

Within AI, a number of areas have been developed, primarily through the use of LISP. Although other kinds of languages can be used—primarily logic programming languages—most existing expert systems, for example, were developed in LISP. LISP also dominates in the areas of knowledge representation, machine learning, natural language processing, intelligent training systems, and the modeling of speech and vision.

Outside AI, LISP has also been successful. For example, the EMACS text editor is written in LISP, as is the symbolic mathematics system, MACSYMA, which does symbolic calculus, among other things. The LISP machine is a personal computer whose entire systems software is written in LISP. LISP has also been successfully used to construct experimental systems in a variety of application areas.

A collection of other functional languages, such as HOPE (Burstall et al., 1980), ML (Milner et al., 1990), and FQL (Buneman et al., 1981) have been used for a variety of both experimental and practical applications.

13.6   A Comparison of Functional and Imperative Languages

A brief discussion of the advantages—some widely accepted and some only widely conjectured—of functional programming and functional programming languages is now in order.

It is natural to compare functional programming with programming in imperative languages. Because imperative languages are based directly on the von Neumann architecture, programmers using them must deal with the management of variables and assignment of values to them. The results of this are increased efficiency of execution but laborious construction of programs. In a functional language, the programmer need not be concerned with variables, because memory cells need not be abstracted into the language. One result of this is decreased efficiency of execution. Another result, however, is a higher level of programming, which should require less labor than programming in an imperative language. Many believe that this is the case and that it is a definite advantage of functional programming.

Functional languages can have a very simple syntactic structure. The list structure of LISP is an example. The syntax of the imperative languages is much more complex. The semantics of functional languages can also be simple in comparison with that of the imperative languages.

Concurrent execution in the imperative languages is difficult to design and difficult to use. For example, consider the tasking model of Ada, in which cooperation among concurrent tasks is the responsibility of the programmer. Functional programs can be executed by first translating them into graphs. These graphs can then be executed through a graph reduction process, which can be done with a great deal of concurrency that was not specified by the programmer. The graph representation naturally exposes many opportunities for concurrent execution. Cooperation synchronization in this process is not the concern of the programmer.

In an imperative language, the programmer must make a static division of the program into its concurrent parts, which are then written as tasks. This can be a complicated process. Programs in functional languages can be divided into concurrent parts dynamically by the execution system, making the process highly adaptable to the hardware on which it is running. Understanding concurrent programs in imperative languages is much more difficult.

These factors make concurrency simple for the programmer. Much of the responsibility for concurrency is placed on the execution system, making programs easy to write and to read. Furthermore, although functional programs may be less efficient than imperative programs on uniprocessor machines, they may be more efficient on multiprocessor machines, which are now becoming more widely available.

SUMMARY

Mathematical functions are named or unnamed mappings that use only conditional expressions and recursion to control their evaluations. Complex functions can be built using functional forms, in which functions are used as parameters, returned values, or both.

Functional programming languages are modeled on mathematical functions. In their pure form, they do not use variables or assignment statements to produce results; rather they use functional applications, conditional expressions, and recursion for execution control, and functional forms to construct complex functions. LISP began as a purely functional language but has since had a number of imperative language features added in order to increase its efficiency and ease of use.

The first version of LISP grew out of the need for a list-processing language for AI applications. LISP is still the most widely used language for that area.

LISP is used primarily to process symbolic data stored in lists, as opposed to numeric data stored in arrays, which is the case for most imperative languages. Therefore, LISP's primary primitives include functions for list selection and construction. LISP also includes primitives for conditional expressions and simple list predicates. Function definitions can be named or unnamed. Pure LISP's only primitive functional form is for composition, but other functional forms can and have been added by implementors and users.

The first implementation of LISP was serendipitous: The original version of EVAL was developed solely to demonstrate that a universal LISP function could be written.

Because LISP data and LISP programs have the same form, it is possible to have a program build another program. The availability of EVAL allows such programs to be executed immediately.

Scheme is a small but powerful static-scoped dialect of LISP. COMMON LISP is a large LISP-based language that was designed to include most of the features of the LISP dialects of the early 1980s. It allows both static- and dynamic-scoped variables.

Although LISP's primary area of application is AI, it has been successfully used for a number of different areas of problem solving.

Although there may be advantages to purely functional languages over their imperative relatives, their lower efficiency of execution on von Neumann machines has prevented them from being considered by many as replacements.

BIBLIOGRAPHIC NOTES

The first published version of LISP can be found in McCarthy (1960). A widely used version from the mid-1960s until the late 1970s is described in McCarthy et al. (1965) and Weissman (1967). The somewhat standardized contemporary version is called COMMON LISP and is described in Steele (1984). The Scheme language, along with some of its innovations and advantages are discussed in Rees and Clinger (1986).

A rigorous discussion of functional programming in general can be found in Henderson (1980). A thorough discussion of the funarg problem can be found in Moses (1970). The process of implementing functional languages through graph reduction is discussed in detail in Peyton Jones (1987).

PROBLEM SET

1. Write a LISP function that returns the reversal of its simple list parameter.
2. Write a LISP predicate function that tests for the structural equality of two given lists. Two lists are structurally equal if they have the same list structure, although their atoms may be different.

3. Write a LISP function that returns the union of two simple list parameters that represent sets.

4. Write a LISP function that returns the set intersection of two simple list parameters that represent sets.

5. Write a LISP function with two parameters, an atom and a list, that returns the list with all occurrences, no matter how deep, of the given atom deleted. The returned list cannot contain anything in place of the deleted atoms.

6. Read John Backus's paper on FP (Backus, 1978) and compare the features of LISP discussed in this chapter with the corresponding features of FP.

7. Find definitions of the LISP functions EVAL and APPLY, and explain their actions.

8. One of the most modern and complete programming environments for any language is the INTERLISP system for LISP, as described in "The INTERLISP Programming Environment," by Teitelmen and Masinter (*IEEE Computer*, Vol. 14, No. 4, April 1981). Read this article carefully and compare the difficulty of writing LISP programs on your system with that of using INTERLISP (assuming that you do not normally use INTERLISP).

9. Refer to a book on LISP programming and determine what arguments support the inclusion of the PROG feature in LISP.

10. A functional language could use some data structure other than the list. For example, it could use sequences of symbols. What primitives would such a language have in place of the CAR, CDR, and CONS primitives of LISP?

14

Logic Programming Languages

Robert Kowalski

Robert Kowalski of the University of Edinburgh is a researcher in artificial intelligence. Kowalski, along with Alain Colmerauer and Phillippe Roussel of the University of Aix-Marseille, developed the first logic programming language, Prolog.

Key Concepts

- Predicate calculus
- Propositions
- Clausal form
- Resolution

- Unification
- Logic programming
- Forward versus backward chaining

Chapter 13 discusses the functional programming paradigm, which is significantly different from that typically employed by users of imperative languages. In this chapter, we describe a different programming methodology. In this case, the programming paradigm is to express programs in a form of symbolic logic and use a logical inferencing process to produce results. Logic programs are declarative rather than procedural, which means that only the specifications of the desired results are stated, rather than detailed procedures for producing them.

Programming that uses a form of symbolic logic as a programming language is often called **logic programming,** and languages based on symbolic logic are called **logic programming languages** or **declarative languages.** The example logic programming language we have chosen to describe is Prolog, primarily because it is the most widely used logic language.

Logic programming languages are remarkably different from the imperative languages and are even quite different from functional languages. The semantics of logic programs bears little resemblance to that of imperative language programs. These observations should lead the reader to some curiosity about the nature of logic programming and declarative languages.

The objectives of this chapter are to introduce the concepts of logic programming and logic programming languages, including a brief description of a subset of Prolog. We begin with an introduction to predicate calculus, which is the basis for logic programming.

14.1 A Brief Introduction to Predicate Calculus

Before we can discuss logic programming, we must briefly investigate its basis, which is formal logic.

A **proposition** can be thought of as a logical statement that may or may not be true. It is made up of objects and their relationships to each other. Formal logic was developed to provide a method for describing propositions, with the goal of allowing those formally stated propositions to be checked for validity.

Symbolic logic can be used for the three basic needs of formal logic: to express propositions, to express the relationships between propositions, and to describe how new propositions can be inferred from other propositions that are assumed to be true.

There is a great deal of similarity between formal logic and mathematics. In fact, much of mathematics can be thought of in terms of logic. The fundamental axioms of number and set theory are the initial set of propositions, which are assumed to be true. Theorems are the additional propositions that can be inferred from the initial set.

The particular form of symbolic logic that is used for logic programming is called **predicate calculus.** In the following sections, we present the highlights of predicate calculus. Our goal is to lay the groundwork for a discussion of logic programming and the logic programming language Prolog.

14.1.1 Propositions

The objects in logic programming propositions are represented by simple terms, which are either constants or variables. A constant is a symbol that represents an object. A variable is a symbol that can represent different objects at different times, although in a sense that is far closer to mathematics than to the imperative programming language.

The simplest propositions, which are called **atomic propositions,** consist of single compound terms. A **compound term** is one element of a mathematical relation, written in a form that has the appearance of mathematical function notation. A compound term is composed of two parts: **functor,** which is the function symbol that names the relation, and an ordered list of parameters. A compound term with a single parameter is a 1-tuple; one with two parameters is a 2-tuple, and so forth. For example, we might have the two propositions

    man(jake)
    like(bob, redheads)

which state that {jake} is a 1-tuple in the relation named man, and that {bob, redheads} is a 2-tuple in the relation named like. If we added the proposition

    man(fred)

to the two propositions above, then the relation man would have two distinct elements, {jake} and {fred}. All of the simple terms in these propositions—man, jake, like, bob, and redheads—are constants. Note that these propositions have no intrinsic semantics. They mean whatever we want them to mean. For example, the second example above may mean that bob likes redheads, or that redheads like bob, or that bob is in some way similar to a redhead.

Propositions can be stated in two modes: one in which the proposition is defined to be true, and one in which the truth of the proposition is something that is to be determined. The example propositions above could be either.

Propositions can contain a kind of variable that may become bound. For example,

man(X)

refers to some element of the man relation; for example, man(jake) or man(bob). Propositions with variables are used extensively as queries in logic programming, as discussed in later sections.

Compound propositions have two or more atomic propositions, which are connected by logical connectors, or operators, in the same way compound logic expressions are constructed in imperative languages. The names, symbols, and meanings of the predicate calculus logical connectors are as follows:

Name	Symbol	Example	Meaning
negation	$\neg$	$\neg\, a$	not a
conjunction	$\cap$	$a \cap b$	a and b
disjunction	$\cup$	$a \cup b$	a or b
equivalence	$\equiv$	$a \equiv b$	a is equivalent to b
implication	$\supset$	$a \supset h$	a implies b
	$\subset$	$a \subset b$	b implies a

The following are examples of compound propositions:

$a \cap b \supset c$
$a \cap \neg b \supset d$

The operator $\neg$ has the highest precedence, followed by $\cap$, $\cup$, and $\equiv$ at the same level, followed by $\supset$ and $\subset$. So the second example above is equivalent to

$(a \cap (\neg b)) \supset d$

Variables can appear in propositions, but only when introduced by special symbols called quantifiers. Predicate calculus includes two quantifiers, as described below, where X is a variable and P is a proposition:

Name	Example	Meaning
universal	$\forall X.P$	For all X, P is true
existential	$\exists X.P$	There exists a value of X such that P is true

For example, consider the following:

$\forall X. (\text{woman}(X) \supset \text{human}(X))$
$\exists X. (\text{mother}(\text{mary}, X) \cap \text{male}(X))$

The first of these propositions means that for any value of X, if X is a woman, then X is a human. The second means that there exists a value of X such that mary is the mother of X and X is a male, in other words, mary has a son. The scope of the universal and existential quantifiers is the atomic propositions to which they are attached. This scope can be extended using parentheses, as in the two compound propositions just described. So the universal and existential quantifiers have higher precedence than any of the operators.

14.1.2 Clausal Form

One problem with predicate calculus as we have described it thus far is that there are too many different ways of stating propositions that have the same meaning. To simplify matters, a standard form for clauses is desirable. Clausal form, which is a relatively simple form of propositions, is one such standard form. Without loss of generality, all propositions can be restricted to clausal form. A proposition in clausal form has the following general syntax:

$$B_1 \cup B_2 \cup \ldots \cup B_n \subset A_1 \cap A_2 \cap \ldots \cap A_m$$

in which the As and Bs are terms. The meaning of this clausal form proposition is as follows: If all of the As are true, then at least one B is true. The primary characteristics of clausal form propositions are the following: Existential quantifiers are not required; universal quantifiers are implicit in the use of variables in the atomic propositions (as explained later); and no operators other than conjunction and disjunction are required. Also, conjunction and disjunction need appear only in the order shown in the general clausal form: disjunction on the left side and conjunction on the right side. All predicate calculus propositions can be algorithmically converted to clausal form. The fact that this can be done and a simple conversion algorithm for doing it is given by Nilsson (1971).

The right side of a clausal form proposition is called the **antecedent.** The left side is called the **consequent** because it is the consequence of the truth of the antecedent. As examples of clausal form propositions, consider the following:

likes(bob, mary) $\subset$ likes(bob, redhead) $\cap$ redhead(mary)
father(louis, al) $\cup$ father(louis, violet) $\subset$
    father(al, bob) $\cap$ mother(violet, bob) $\cap$
      grandfather(louis, bob)

The English version of the first of these states that if bob likes redheads and mary is a redhead, then bob likes mary. The second states that if al is bob's father and violet is bob's mother and louis is bob's grandfather, then louis is either al's father or violet's father.

14.2 Predicate Calculus and Proving Theorems

Predicate calculus provides a method of expressing collections of propositions. One use of collections of propositions is to determine whether any interesting or useful facts can be inferred from them. This is exactly analogous to the work of mathematicians, who strive to discover new theorems that can be inferred from known axioms and theorems.

The early days of computer science (the 1950s and early 1960s) saw a great deal of interest in automating the theorem-proving process. Perhaps the most significant breakthrough in automatic theorem-proving was the discovery of the resolution principle by Alan Robinson at Syracuse University (Robinson, 1965).

Resolution is an inference rule that allows inferred propositions to be computed from given propositions, thus providing a method with potential application to automatic theorem proving. Resolution was devised to apply to propositions in clausal form. The concept of resolution is the following: Suppose there are two propositions with the forms

$$P_1 \subset P_2$$
$$Q_1 \subset Q_2$$

Their meaning is that P_2 implies P_1, and Q_2 implies Q_1. Further suppose that P_1 is identical to Q_2, so that we could rename P_1 and Q_2 as T. Then, we could rewrite the two propositions as

$$T \subset P_2$$
$$Q_1 \subset T$$

Now, because P_2 implies T and T implies Q_1, it is logically obvious that P_2 implies Q_1, which we could write as

$$Q_1 \subset P_2$$

This process of inferring this proposition from the original two propositions is called resolution.

As another example, consider the following two propositions:

older(joanne, jake) ⊂ mother(joanne, jake)
wiser(joanne, jake) ⊂ older(joanne, jake)

From these propositions, the following proposition can be constructed using resolution:

wiser(joanne, jake) ⊂ mother(joanne, jake)

The mechanics of this resolution construction are simple: The terms of left sides of the two propositions are ANDed together to make the left side of the new proposition. Then the same thing is done to get the right side of the new proposition. Then, the term that appears on both sides of the new proposition is removed from both sides. The process is exactly the same when the propositions have multiple terms on either or both sides. The left side of the new inferred proposition initially contains all of the terms of the left sides of the two given propositions. The new right side is similarly constructed. Then the term that appears in both sides of the new proposition is removed. For example, if we have

father(bob, jake) ∪ mother(bob, jake) ⊂ parent(bob, jake)
grandfather(bob,fred) ⊂ father(bob,jake) ∩ father(jake,fred)

resolution says that

mother(bob,jake) ∪ grandfather(bob, fred) ⊂
                    parent(bob, jake) ∩ father(jake, fred)

which has all but one of the atomic propositions of both of the original propositions. The one atomic proposition that allowed the operation, father(bob, jake) in the left side of the first and in the right side of the second, is left out. In English, we would say:

if: bob is the parent of jake implies that bob is either
        the father or mother of jake
  and:
        bob is the father of jake and jake is the father of
            fred implies that bob is the grandfather of fred
  then: if bob is the parent of jake and jake is the father
            of fred
        then: either bob is jake's mother or bob
            is fred's grandfather

Resolution is actually more complex than these simple examples illustrate. In particular, the presence of variables in propositions requires resolution to find values for those variables that allow the matching process to succeed. This process of determining useful values for variables is called **unification.** The temporary assigning of values to variables to allow unification is called **instantiation.**

It is common for the resolution process to instantiate a variable with a value, fail to complete the required matching, and then be required to backtrack and instantiate the variable with a different value. We will discuss unification and backtracking more extensively in the context of Prolog.

A critically important property of resolution is its ability to detect any inconsistency in a given set of propositions. This property allows resolution to be used to prove theorems, which can be done as follows: We can envision a theorem proof in terms of predicate calculus as a given set of pertinent propositions, with the negation of the theorem itself stated as a new proposition. The theorem is negated so that resolution can be used to prove the theorem by finding an inconsistency. This is proof by contradiction. Typically, the original propositions are called the **hypotheses** and the negation of the theorem is called the **goal.**

Theoretically, this is a valid and useful process. The time required for resolution, however, can be a problem. Although resolution is a finite process when the set of propositions is finite, the time required to find an inconsistency in a large database of propositions may be huge.

Theorem proving is the basis for logic programming. Much of what is computed can be couched in the form of a list of given facts and relationships as hypotheses, and a goal to be inferred from the hypotheses, using resolution.

When propositions are used for resolution, only a restricted kind of clausal form is required, which further simplifies the resolution process. The special kinds of propositions, called **Horn clauses,** can be in only two forms: They have either a single atomic proposition on the left side or an empty left side. [Horn clauses are named after A. Horn, who studied clauses in this form (Horn, 1951).] The left side of a clausal form proposition is sometimes called the head, and Horn clauses with left sides are called headed Horn clauses. Headed Horn clauses are used to state relationships, such as

likes(bob, mary) $\subset$ likes(bob, redhead) $\cap$ redhead(mary)

Horn clauses with empty left sides, which are often used to state facts, are called headless Horn clauses. For example,

father(bob, jake)

14.3 An Overview of Logic Programming

Languages used for logic programming are called declarative languages because programs written in them consist of declarations rather than assignments and control flow statements. These declarations are actually statements, or propositions, in symbolic logic.

One of the essential characteristics of logic programming languages is their semantics, which is called **declarative semantics.** The basic concept of this semantics is that there is a simple way to determine the meaning of each statement, and it does not depend on how the statement might be used to solve a problem. Declarative semantics is considerably simpler than the semantics of the imperative languages. For example, the meaning of a given proposition in a logic programming language can be concisely determined from the statement itself. In an imperative language, the semantics of a simple assignment statement requires examination of local declarations, knowledge of the scoping rules of the language, and possibly even examination of programs in other files just to determine the types of the variables in the assignment statement. Then, assuming the expression of the assignment contains variables, the execution of the program prior to the assignment statement must be traced to determine the values of those variables. The resulting action of the statement, then, depends on its run-time context.

Comparing this with the simple examination of a single statement, with no need to consider textual context or execution sequences, it is clear that declarative semantics is vastly simpler than that of imperative languages. Thus, declarative semantics is often stated as one of the advantages declarative languages have over imperative languages (Hogger, 1984, pp. 240–241).

Programming in both imperative and functional languages is primarily procedural, which means that the programmer knows *what* is to be accomplished by a program and instructs the computer on exactly *how* the computation is to be done. In other words, the computer is treated as a simple device that obeys orders. Everything that is computed must have every detail of that computation spelled out. Some people believe that this is the essence of the difficulty of programming computers.

Programming in some kinds of nonimperative languages, and in particular in logic programming languages, is nonprocedural. Programs in such languages do not state exactly *how* a result is to be computed, but rather describe the form of the result. The difference is that we assume the computer system can somehow determine *how* the result is to be gotten. What is needed to provide this capability for logic programming languages is a concise means of supplying the computer with both the relevant information and a method of inference for computing desirable results. Predicate calculus supplies the basic form of communication to the computer, and the proof method developed first by Robinson provides the inference technique.

An example commonly used to illustrate the difference between procedural and nonprocedural systems is the process of rearranging a list of data into some particular order, otherwise known as sorting. In a procedural language like Pascal, sorting is done by explaining in a Pascal program all the details of some sorting algorithm to a computer that has a Pascal compiler. The computer, after translating the Pascal program into machine code or some interpretive intermediate code, follows the instructions and produces the sorted list.

In a nonprocedural language, it is necessary only to describe the characteristics of the sorted list: It is some permutation of the given list such that for each pair of adjacent elements, a given relationship holds between the two elements. This can be stated formally as follows: Suppose the list to be sorted is in an array named list that has a subscript range $1 .. n$. Then the concept of sorting the elements of the given list, named old_list, and placing them in a separate array named new_list can be expressed as follows:

$$\text{sort(old\_list, new\_list)} \subset \text{permute(old\_list, new\_list)} \cap \text{sorted(new\_list)}$$
$$\text{sorted(list)} \subset \forall j \text{ such that } 1 \leq j < n, \text{list(j)} \leq \text{list(j+1)}$$

where permute is a predicate that returns true if its second parameter array is a permutation of its first parameter array.

From this description, the nonprocedural language system could produce the sorted list. That makes nonprocedural programming sound like the mere production of concise software requirements specifications, which is a fair assessment. Unfortunately, however, it is not that simple. Logic programs face serious problems of machine efficiency. Furthermore, the best form of a logic language has not yet been determined, and good methods of creating programs in logic programming languages for large problems have not yet been developed.

14.4 The Origins of Prolog

As stated in Chapter 2, Alain Colmerauer and Phillippe Roussel at the University of Aix-Marseille and Robert Kowalski at the University of Edinburgh developed the fundamental design of Prolog. The collaboration between the University of Aix-Marseille and the University of Edinburgh continued until the mid-1970s. Since then, research on the development and use of the language has progressed independently at those two locations, resulting in, among other things, two syntactically different dialects of Prolog.

The development of Prolog and other research efforts in logic programming received limited attention outside of Edinburgh and Marseille until the announcement in 1981 that the Japanese government was launching a large research project called the Fifth Generation Computing Systems (FGCS) (Fuchi, 1981; Moto-oka, 1981). One of the primary objectives of the project is to develop intelligent machines, and Prolog was chosen as the basis for this effort. The announcement of FGCS aroused in researchers and the governments of the United States and several European countries a sudden strong interest in artificial intelligence and logic programming. Although Prolog changed little during its first decade, the recent resurgence of interest in it is likely to lead eventually to a variety of modifications and additions.

Prolog is a logic programming language whose syntax is a modified version of predicate calculus. Its inferencing method is a restricted form of resolution.

14.5 The Basic Elements of Prolog

There are now a number of different dialects of Prolog. These can be grouped into three categories: those that grew from the Marseille group, those that came from the Edinburgh group, and micro-Prolog, a version developed for Z80-based microcomputers, which is described by Clark and

McCabe (1984). The syntactic forms of these three are somewhat different. Rather than attempt to describe all three or some hybrid of them, we have chosen one particular, widely available dialect, which is the one developed at Edinburgh. This form of the language is sometimes called Edinburgh syntax. It is specifically that of the DEC System-10 implementation (Warren et al., 1979), which is also available for PDP-11 and VAX computer systems.

14.5.1   Terms

As with programs in other languages, Prolog programs consist of collections of statements. There are only a few kinds of statements in Prolog, but they can be complex. All Prolog statements are constructed from terms.

A Prolog **term** is a constant, a variable, or a structure. A constant is either an **atom** or an integer. Atoms are the symbolic values of Prolog and are similar to their counterparts in LISP. In particular, an atom is either a string of letters, digits, and underscores that begins with a lowercase letter, or a string of any printable ASCII characters delimited by apostrophes.

A variable is any string of letters, digits, and underscores that begins with an uppercase letter. Variables are not bound to types by declarations. The binding of a value, and thus a type, to a variable is called an **instantiation.** Instantiation occurs only in the resolution process. A variable that has not been assigned a value is called uninstantiated. Instantiations last only as long as it takes to satisfy one complete goal, which involves the proof or disproof of one proposition. Prolog variables are only distant relatives, in terms of both semantics and use, to the variables in the imperative languages.

The last kind of term is called a structure. Structures represent the atomic propositions of predicate calculus, and their general form is the same:

   functor(parameter list)

functor is any atom and is used to identify the structure. The parameter list can be any list of atoms, variables, or other structures. As discussed at length in the following section, structures are the means of specifying facts in Prolog. They can also be thought of as objects, in which case they allow facts to be stated in terms of several related atoms. In this sense, structures are relations, for they state relationships among terms. A structure is also a predicate when its context specifies it to be a query.

14.5.2   Fact Statements

Our discussion of Prolog statements begins with those statements used to construct the hypotheses, or database of assumed information—the statements from which new information can be inferred.

Prolog has two basic statement forms; these correspond to the headless and headed Horn clauses of predicate calculus. The simplest form of the headless Horn clause in Prolog is a single structure, which is interpreted as an unconditional assertion, or fact. Logically, facts are simply propositions that are assumed to be true.

The following examples illustrate the kinds of facts one can have in a Prolog program. Notice that every Prolog statement is terminated by a period.

```
female(shelley).
male(bill).
female(mary).
male(jake).
father(bill, jake).
father(bill, shelley).
mother(mary, jake).
mother(mary, shelley).
```

These simple structures state certain facts about `jake`, `shelley`, `bill`, and `mary`. For example, the first states that `shelley` is a `female`. The last four connect their two parameters with a relationship that is named in the functor atom; for example, the fifth proposition might be interpreted to mean that `bill` is the `father` of `jake`. Note that these Prolog propositions, like those of predicate calculus, have no intrinsic semantics. They mean whatever the programmer wants them to mean. For example, the proposition

```
father(bill, jake).
```

could mean `bill` and `jake` have the same `father`, or that `jake` is the `father` of `bill`. The most common and straightforward meaning, however, is that `bill` is the `father` of `jake`.

14.5.3 Rule Statements

The other basic form of Prolog statement for constructing the database corresponds to a headed Horn clause. This form can be related to a known theorem in mathematics from which a conclusion can be drawn if the set of given conditions is satisfied. The right side is the antecedent, or **if** part, and the left side is the consequent, or **then** part. If the antecedent of a Prolog statement is true, then the consequent of the statement must also be true. Because they are Horn clauses, the consequent of a Prolog statement is a single term, while the antecedent can be either a single term or a conjunction.

Conjunctions contain multiple terms that are separated by logical AND operations. In Prolog, the AND operation is implied. The structures that specify atomic propositions in a conjunction are separated by commas, so one could consider the commas to be AND operators. As an example of a conjunction, consider the following:

```
female (shelley), child (shelley).
```

The general form of the Prolog headed Horn clause statement is

structure_1 :− antecedent_expression.

It is read as follows: "structure_1 can be concluded if the antecedent expression is true or can be made to be true by some instantiation of its variables." For example,

```
ancestor(mary, shelley) :- mother(mary, shelley).
```

states that if mary is the mother of shelley, then mary is an ancestor of shelley. Headed Horn clauses are called **rules** because they state rules of implication between propositions.

As with clausal form propositions in predicate calculus, Prolog statements can use variables to generalize their meaning. Recall that variables in clausal form provide a kind of implied universal quantifier. The following demonstrates the use of variables in Prolog statements:

```
parent(X, Y) :- mother(X, Y).
parent(X, Y) :- father(X, Y).
grandparent(X, Z) :- parent(X, Y) , parent(Y, Z).
sibling(X, Y) :- mother(M, X) , mother(M, Y),
                 father(F, X) , father(F, Y).
```

These statements give rules of implication among some variables, or universal objects. In this case, the universal objects are X, Y, Z, M, and F. The first rule states that if there are instantiations of X and Y such that mother(X, Y) is true, then for those same instantiations of X and Y, parent(X, Y) is true.

14.5.4 Goal Statements

So far, we have described the Prolog statements for logical propositions, which are used to describe both known facts and rules that describe logical relationships among facts. These statements are the basis for the theorem-proving model. The theorem is in the form of a proposition that we want the system to either prove or disprove. In Prolog, these propositions are called goals, or queries. The syntactic form of Prolog goal statements is identical to that of headless Horn clauses. For example, we could have

```
man(fred).
```

to which the system will respond either yes or no. The answer yes means that the system has proved the goal was true under the given database of facts and relationships. The answer no means that either the goal was proved false, or the system was simply unable to prove or disprove it.

Conjunctive propositions and propositions with variables are also legal goals. When variables are present, the system not only asserts the validity of the goal but also identifies the instantiations of the variables that make the goal true. For example,

```
father(X, mike).
```

can be asked. The system will then attempt, through unification, to find an instantiation of x that results in a true value for the goal.

Because goal statements and some nongoal statements have the same form (headless Horn clauses), a Prolog implementation must have some means of distinguishing between the two. Interactive Prolog implementations do this by simply having two modes, indicated by different interactive prompts: one for entering fact and rule statements and one for entering goals. The mode can be changed by the user at any time.

14.5.5 The Inferencing Process of Prolog

This section examines Prolog resolution. Efficient use of Prolog requires that the programmer know precisely what the Prolog system does with his or her program.

Queries are called **goals.** When a goal is a compound proposition, each of the structures is called a **subgoal.** To prove that a goal is true, the inferencing process must find a chain of inference rules and/or facts in the database that connect the goal to one or more facts in the database. For example, if Q is the goal, then either Q must be found as a fact in the database, or the inferencing process must find a sequence of propositions P_1, P_2, ..., P_n such that

$$P_1 :- P_2$$
$$P_2 :- P_3$$
$$...$$
$$P_n :- Q$$

and P_1 is a fact. Of course, the process can and often is complicated by compound right sides of rules and the presence of variables in rules. The process of finding the P's, when they exist, is basically a comparison, or matching, of terms with each other.

Because the process of proving a subgoal is done through a proposition-matching process, it is sometimes called matching. In some cases, proving a subgoal is called **satisfying** that subgoal.

Consider the following query:

```
man(bob).
```

This goal statement is the simplest kind. It is relatively easy for resolution to determine whether it is true or false: the pattern of this goal is compared with the facts and rules in the database. Suppose the database includes the fact

```
man(bob).
```

In this case, proof is trivial. If, however, the database contains the following fact and inference rule,

```
father(bob).
man(X) :- father(X).
```

Prolog would be required to find these two statements and use them to infer the truth of the goal. This would necessitate unification to instantiate X temporarily to bob.

Now consider the goal

```
man(X).
```

In this case, Prolog must match the goal against the propositions in the database. The first proposition that it finds that has the form of the goal, with any object as its parameter, will cause X to be instantiated with that object's value. X is then displayed as the result. If there is no proposition having the form of the goal, the system indicates that the goal cannot be satisfied by displaying "no."

There are two opposite approaches to attempting to match a given goal to a fact in the database. The system can begin with the facts and rules of the database and attempt to find a sequence of matches that lead to the goal. This approach is called bottom-up resolution, or **forward chaining.** The alternative is to begin with the goal and attempt to find a sequence of matching propositions that lead to some set of original facts in the database. This approach is called top-down resolution, or **backward chaining.** In general, backward chaining works well when there is a reasonably small set of candidate answers. The forward chaining approach is better when the number of possibly correct answers is large; in this situation, backward chaining would require a very large number of matches to get to an answer. Prolog implementations use backward chaining for resolution, presumably because its designers believed backward chaining was suitable for a larger class of problems than forward chaining.

Consider again the example query:

```
man(bob).
```

Assume the database contains

```
father(bob).
man(X) :- father(X).
```

Forward chaining would first search for and find the first proposition. The goal is then inferred by matching the first proposition with the right side of the second rule (father(X)), through instantiation of X to bob, and then matching the left side of the second proposition to the goal. Backward chaining would first match the goal with the left side of the second proposition (man(X)), through instantiation of X to bob. As its last step, it would match the right side of the second proposition (now `father(bob)`) with the first proposition.

The next design question arises whenever the goal has more than one structure, as in our example above. The question then is whether the solution search is done depth first or breadth first. A **depth-first** search finds a complete sequence of propositions—a proof—for the first subgoal before working on the others. A **breadth-first** search works on all subgoals of a given goal in parallel. The depth-first approach was chosen by Prolog's designers, primarily because it can be done with fewer computer resources. The breadth-first approach is a parallel search that can take a large amount of memory.

The last feature of Prolog's resolution mechanism that must be discussed is backtracking. When a goal with multiple subgoals is being processed and the system fails to show the truth of one of the subgoals, the system abandons the subgoal it could not prove. Instead, the system reconsiders the previous subgoal, if there is one, and attempts to find an alternative solution to it. This backing up in the goal to the reconsideration of a previously proven subgoal is called **backtracking.** A new solution is found by beginning the search where the previous search for that subgoal stopped. Multiple solutions to a subgoal result from different instantiations of its variables. Backtracking can require a great deal of time and space because it may have to find all possible proofs to every subgoal. The fact that these subgoal proofs are not organized to minimize the time required to find the one that will result in the final complete proof exacerbates the problem.

To solidify your understanding of backtracking, consider the following example. Assume that there is a set of facts and rules in a database and that Prolog has been presented with the following compound goal:

```
male(X), parent(X, shelley).
```

This goal asks whether there is an instantiation of `X` such that `X` is a `male` and `X` is a `parent` of `shelley`. Prolog first finds the first fact in the database with `male` as its functor. It then instantiates `X` to the parameter of the found fact, say `mike`. Then it attempts to prove that a `parent(mike, shelley)` is true. If it fails, it backtracks to the first subgoal, `male(X)`, and attempts to resatisfy it with some alternative instantiation of `X`. The resolution process may have to find every `male` in the database before it finds the one that is a `parent` of `shelley`. It definitely must find all `males` to prove that the goal cannot be satisfied. Note that our example goal might be processed more efficiently if the order of the two subgoals were reversed. Then, only after resolution had found a `parent` of `shelley` would it try to match that person with the `male` subgoal. This is more efficient if `shelley` has fewer `parents` than there are `males` in the database, which seems like a fair assumption. Section 14.6.1 discusses a method of limiting the backtracking done by a Prolog system.

Subgoals are always satisfied left to right, and the database searches always proceed in the direction of beginning to end.

The following two sections describe Prolog examples that further illustrate the resolution process.

14.5.6 Simple Arithmetic

Prolog supports integer variables and integer arithmetic. Originally, the arithmetic operators were functors, so that the sum of 7 and the variable x was formed with

```
+(7, X)
```

Prolog now allows a more abbreviated syntax for arithmetic with the **is** operator. This operator takes an arithmetic expression as its right operand and a variable as its left operand. All variables in the expression must already be instantiated, but the left-side variable cannot be already instantiated. For example, in

```
X is Y / 17 + Z.
```

if Y and Z are instantiated, but X is not, then this clause will cause X to be instantiated with the value of the expression. When this happens, the clause is satisfied. If either Y or Z are not instantiated or X is instantiated, the clause is not satisfied and no instantiation of X can take place. The semantics of an **is** proposition is considerably different from that of an assignment statement in an imperative language. This difference can lead to an interesting scenario. Because the **is** operator makes the clause in which it appears look like an assignment statement, a beginning Prolog programmer may be tempted to write a statement such as

```
Sum is Sum + Number.
```

which is never useful, or even legal, in Prolog. If Sum is not instantiated, the reference to it in the right side is undefined and the clause fails. If Sum is already instantiated, the clause fails because the left operand cannot have a current instantiation when **is** is evaluated. In either case, the instantiation of Sum to the new value will not take place.

Prolog does not have assignment statements in the same sense as imperative languages do. They are simply not needed in most of the programming for which Prolog was designed. The usefulness of assignment statements in imperative languages depends on the capability of the programmer to control the execution control flow of the code in which the assignment statement is embedded. Because this type of control is not always possible in Prolog, such statements are far less useful.

As a simple example of the use of numeric computation in Prolog, consider the following problem: Suppose we know the average speeds of several automobiles on a particular racetrack and the amount of time they are on the track. This basic information can be coded as facts, and the relationship between speed, time, and distance can be written as a rule, as in the following:

```
speed(ford, 100).
speed(chevy, 105).
speed(dodge, 95).
speed(volvo, 80).
time(ford, 20).
time(chevy, 21).
time(dodge, 24).
time(volvo, 24).
distance(X, Y) :- speed(X, Speed),
                  time(X, Time),
                  Y is Speed * Time.
```

Now, queries can request the distance traveled by a particular car. For example, the query

```
distance(chevy, Chevy_Distance).
```

instantiates Chevy_Distance with the value 2205. The first two clauses in the right side of the distance computation statement simply instantiate the variables Speed and Time with the corresponding values of the given automobile functor. After satisfying the goal, Prolog also displays the name Chevy_Distance and its value.

At this point it is instructive to take an operational look at how a Prolog system produces results. Prolog has a built-in structure named trace that displays the instantiations of values to variables at each step during the attempt to satisfy a given goal. Trace is used to understand and debug Prolog programs. To understand trace, it is best to introduce a different model of the execution of Prolog programs, called the **tracing model.**

The tracing model describes Prolog execution in terms of four events: Call, which occurs at the beginning of an attempt to satisfy a goal; Exit, which occurs when a goal has been satisfied; Back to, which occurs when backtrack causes an attempt to resatisfy a goal; and Fail, which occurs when a goal fails. Call and Exit can be related directly to the execution model of a subprogram in an imperative language if processes like append are thought of as subprograms. The other two events are unique to logic programming systems. In the following trace example, the goal requires no Back to or Fail events.

The following is a trace of the computation of the value for Chevy_Distance:

```
trace.
distance(chevy, Chevy_Distance).

(1) 1 Call: distance(chevy, _0)?
(2) 2 Call: speed(chevy, _5)?
(2) 2 Exit: speed(chevy, 105)
(3) 2 Call: time(chevy, _6)?
(3) 2 Exit: time(chevy, 21)
(4) 2 Call: _0 is 105*21?
```

```
(4) 2 Exit: 2205 is 105*21
(1) 1 Exit: distance(chevy, 2205)
```

```
Chevy_Distance = 2205
```

Symbols in the trace that begin with the underscore character (_) are internal variables used to store instantiated values. The first column of the trace indicates the subgoal whose match is currently being attempted. For example, in the above trace, the first line with the indication (3) is an attempt to instantiate the temporary variable _6 with a time value for chevy, where time is the third term in the statement that describes the computation of distance. The second column indicates the depth of the matching process. The third column indicates the current action.

To illustrate backtracking, consider the following example database and traced compound goal:

```
likes(jake, chocolate).
likes(jake, apricots).
likes(darcie, licorice).
likes(darcie, apricots).

trace.
likes(jake, X), likes(darcie, X).

(1) 1 Call: likes(jake, _0)?
(1) 1 Exit: likes(jake, chocolate)
(2) 1 Call: likes(darcie, chocolate)?
(2) 1 Fail: likes(darcie, chocolate)
(1) 1 Back to: likes(jake, _0)?
(1) 1 Exit: likes(jake, apricots)
(3) 1 Call: likes(darcie, apricots)?
(3) 1 Exit: likes(darcie, apricots)

X = apricots
```

One can think about Prolog computations graphically as follows: Consider each goal as a box with four ports—call, fail, exit, and redo. Control enters a goal in the forward direction through its call port. Control can also enter a goal from the reverse direction through its redo port. Control can also leave a goal in two ways: if the goal succeeded, control leaves through the exit port; if the goal failed, control leaves through the fail port. A model of the example above is shown in Figure 14.1. In this example, control flows through each subgoal twice. The second subgoal fails the first time, which forces a return through redo to the first subgoal.

14.5.7   List Structures

So far, the only Prolog data structure we have discussed is the atomic proposition, which looks more like a function call than a data structure. Atomic propositions, which are also called structures, are actually a form of records.

Figure 14.1
Control flow model for
the goal likes (jake, X),
likes (darcie, X)

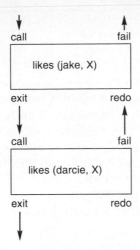

The other basic data structure supported is the list, which is similar to the list structure used by LISP. Lists are sequences of any number of elements, where the elements can be atoms, atomic propositions, or any other terms, including other lists.

Prolog uses a conventional syntax to specify lists. The list elements are separated by commas and the entire list is delimited by square brackets, as in

```
[apple, prune, grape, kumquat]
```

The notation [ ] is used to denote the empty list. Instead of having explicit functions for constructing and dismantling lists, Prolog simply uses a special notation. [X | Y] denotes a list with head X and tail Y, where head and tail correspond to CAR and CDR in LISP. This is in keeping with the nonprocedural nature of the language. Rather than describing how to manipulate lists, we need only describe the characteristics of the result.

A list can be created with a simple structure, as in

```
new_list([apple, prune, grape, kumquat]).
```

which states that the constant list [apple, prune, grape, kumquat] is a new element of the relation named new_list (a name we just made up). This statement does not bind the list to a variable named new_list; rather, it does the kind of thing that the proposition

```
male(jake)
```

does. That is, it states that [apple, prune, grape, kumquat] is a new element of new_list. Therefore, we could have a second proposition with a list argument, such as

```
new_list([apricot, peach, pear])
```

In query mode, one of the elements of new_list can be dismantled into head and tail with

```
new_list([New_List_Head | New_List_Tail]).
```

If new_list has been set to have the two elements as above, this statement instantiates New_List_Head with the head of the first list element (in this case apple) and New_List_Tail with the tail of the list (or [prune, grape, kumquat]). If this were part of a compound goal and backtracking forced a new evaluation of it, New_List_Head and New_List_Tail would be reinstantiated to apricot and [peach, pear], respectively, because [apricot, peach, pear] is the next element of new_list.

The notation used to dismantle lists can also be used to create lists from given instantiated head and tail components, as in

```
[Element_1 | List_2]
```

If Element_1 has been instantiated with pickle and List_2 has been instantiated with [peanut, prune, popcorn], the notation above will create, for this one reference, the list [pickle, peanut, prune, popcorn].

As stated above, the list notation that includes the | symbol is universal: It can specify either a list construction or a list dismantling. Note further that the following are equivalent:

```
[apricot, peach, pear | []]
[apricot, peach | [pear]]
[apricot | [peach, pear]]
```

When dealing with lists, certain basic operations are often required, such as those found in LISP. As an example of such operations in Prolog, we examine an append function, which is related to such a function in LISP. In this example, the differences and similarities between functional and declarative languages can be seen. We need not specify how Prolog is to construct a new list from the given lists; rather, we need only specify the characteristics of the new list in terms of the given lists.

In appearance, the Prolog version of append is very similar to the LISP version, and a kind of recursion in resolution is used in a similar way to produce the new list. In the case of Prolog, the recursion is caused and controlled by the resolution process.

The first two parameters to the append operation in the following code are the two lists to be appended, and the third parameter is the resulting list:

```
append([ ], List, List).
append([Head | List_1], List_2, [Head | List_3]) :-
        append(List_1, List_2, List_3).
```

The first proposition specifies that when the empty list is appended to any other list, that other list is the result. This statement corresponds to the recursion-terminating step of the LISP append function. Note that the terminating proposition is placed before the recursion proposition. This is done because we know that Prolog will match the two propositions in order, starting with the first (because of its use of the depth-first order).

The second proposition specifies several characteristics of the new list. It corresponds to the recursion step in the LISP function. The left-side predicate states that the first element of the new list is the same as the first element of the first given list, because they are both named Head. Whenever Head is instantiated to a value, all occurrences of Head in the goal are, in effect, simultaneously instantiated to that value. The right side of the second statement specifies that the tail of the first given list (List_1) has the second given list (List_2) appended to it to form the tail (List_3) of the result list.

One way to read the second statement of append is as follows: Appending the list [Head | List_1] to any list List_2 produces the list [Head | List_3], but only if the list List_3 is formed by appending List_1 to List_2. In LISP, this would be

```
(CONS (CAR FIRST) (APPEND (CDR FIRST) SECOND))
```

In both the Prolog and LISP versions, the resulting list is not constructed until the recursion produces the terminating condition; in this case, the first list must become empty. Then, the result list is built using the append function itself; the elements taken from the first list are added, in reverse order, to the second list. The reversing is done by the unraveling of the recursion.

To illustrate how the append process progresses, consider the following traced example:

```
trace.
append([bob, jo], [jake, darcie], Family).

(1) 1 Call: append([bob, jo], [jake, darcie], _10)?
(2) 2 Call: append([jo], [jake, darcie], _18)?
(3) 3 Call: append([], [jake, darcie], _25)?
(3) 3 Exit: append([], [jake, darcie], [jake, darcie])
(2) 2 Exit: append([jo], [jake, darcie],
                                    [jo, jake, darcie])
(1) 1 Exit: append([bob, jo], [jake, darcie],
                               [bob, jo, jake, darcie])
Family = [bob, jo, jake, darcie]
yes
```

The first two Calls, which represent subgoals, have List_1 nonempty, so they create the recursive calls from the right side of the second statement. The left side of the second statement effectively specifies the arguments for the recursive calls, or goals, thus dismantling the first list one element per step. When the first list becomes empty, in a Call, or subgoal, the current instance of the right side of the second statement succeeds by matching the first statement. The effect of this is to return as the third parameter the value of the empty list appended to the second original parameter list. On successive Exits, which represent successful matches, the elements that were removed from the first list are appended to the result list, `Family`. When the Exit from the first goal is accomplished, the process is complete, and the result list is displayed.

The append propositions can also be used to create other list operations, such as the following, whose effect we invite the reader to determine. Note that `list_op_2` is meant to be used by providing a list as its first parameter and a variable as its second, and the result of `list_op_2` is the value to which the second parameter is instantiated.

```
list_op_2([], []).
list_op_2([Head | Tail], List) :- list_op_2(Tail, Result),
                          append(Result, [Head], List).
```

As the reader may have been able to determine, `list_op_2` causes the Prolog system to instantiate its second parameter with a list that has the elements of the list of the first parameter, but in reverse order. For example, ([apple, orange, grape], Q) instantiates Q with the list [grape, orange, apple].

Once again, although the LISP and Prolog languages are fundamentally different, similar operations can use similar approaches. In the case of the reverse operation, both Prolog's `list_op_2` and LISP's reverse function include the recursion terminating condition, along with the basic process of appending the reversal of the CDR or tail of the list to the CAR or head of the list to create the result list.

The following is a trace of this process, now named `reverse`:

```
trace.
reverse([a, b, c], Q).

(1)  1 Call: reverse([a, b, c], _6)?
(2)  2 Call: reverse([b, c], _65636)?
(3)  3 Call: reverse([c], _65646)?
(4)  4 Call: reverse([], _65656)?
(4)  4 Exit: reverse([], [])
(5)  4 Call: append([], [c], _65646)?
(5)  4 Exit: append([], [c], [c])
(3)  3 Exit: reverse([c], [c])
(6)  3 Call: append([c], [b], _65636)?
(7)  4 Call: append([], [b], _25)?
(7)  4 Exit: append([], [b], [b])
(6)  3 Exit: append([c], [b], [c, b])
(2)  2 Exit: reverse([b, c], [c, b])
(8)  2 Call: append([c, b], [a], _6)?
(9)  3 Call: append([b], [a], _32)?
(10) 4 Call: append([], [a], _39)?
(10) 4 Exit: append([], [a], [a])
(9)  3 Exit: append([b], [a], [b, a])
(8)  2 Exit: append([c, b], [a], [c, b, a])
(1)  1 Exit: reverse([a, b, c], [c, b, a])

Q = [c, b, a]
```

Suppose we need to determine whether a given symbol is in a given list. A straightforward Prolog description of this is

```
member(Element, [Element | _]).
member(Element, [_ | List]) :- member(Element, List).
```

The underscore indicates an "anonymous" variable; it is used to mean that we do not care what instantiation it might get from unification. The first statement above succeeds if the Element is the head of the list, either initially or after several recursions through the second statement. The second statement succeeds if the Element is in the tail of the list. Consider the following traced examples:

```
trace.
member(a, [b, c, d]).
(1) 1 Call: member(a, [b, c, d])?
(2) 2 Call: member(a, [c, d])?
(3) 3 Call: member(a, [d])?
(4) 4 Call: member(a, [])?
(4) 4 Fail: member(a, [])
(3) 3 Fail: member(a, [d])
(2) 2 Fail: member(a, [c, d])
(1) 1 Fail: member(a, [b, c, d])
no


member(a, [b, a, c]).
(1) 1 Call: member(a, [b, a, c])?
(2) 2 Call: member(a, [a, c])?
(2) 2 Exit: member(a, [a, c])
(1) 1 Exit: member(a, [b, a, c])
yes
```

14.6 Deficiencies of Prolog

Several problems arise in using Prolog as a logic programming language. Although it is a useful tool, it should not be considered the perfect logic programming language.

14.6.1 Resolution Order Control

Prolog, for reasons of efficiency, allows the user to control the ordering of pattern matching during resolution. In a pure logic programming environment, the order of attempted matches that take place during resolution could be nondeterministic, or all matches could be attempted concurrently. However, because Prolog always matches in the same order, starting at the beginning of the database and at the left end of a given goal, the user can profoundly affect efficiency by ordering the database statements to optimize a particular application. For example, if the user has knowledge that certain rules are much more likely to succeed than the others during a particular "execution," then the program can be made more efficient by placing those rules first in the database.

In addition to allowing the user to control database and subgoal ordering, Prolog, in another concession to efficiency, allows some explicit control of backtracking. This is done with the cut operator, which is specified by an exclamation point (!). The cut operator is actually a goal, not an operator. As a goal, it always succeeds immediately, but it cannot be resatisfied through backtracking. Thus, a side effect of the cut is that subgoals to its left in a compound goal also cannot be resatisfied through backtracking. For example, in the goal

```
a, b, !, c, d.
```

if both a and b succeed, but c fails, the whole goal fails. This goal would be used if it were known that whenever c fails, it is a waste of time to resatisfy b or a.

The purpose of the cut, then, is to allow the user to make programs more efficient by telling the system when it should not attempt to resatisfy subgoals that presumably will not result in a complete proof.

As an example of one use of the cut operator, consider the member rules from Section 14.5.7, which are repeated below:

```
member(Element, [Element | _]).
member(Element, [_ | List]) :- member(Element, List).
```

If the list argument to member represents a set, then it can be satisfied only once (sets contain no duplicate elements). Therefore, if member is used as a subgoal in a multiple subgoal goal statement, there can be a problem. The problem is that if member succeeds but the next subgoal fails, backtracking will attempt to resatisfy member by continuing a prior match. But because the list argument to member had only one copy of the element to begin with, member cannot possibly succeed again, which eventually causes the whole goal to fail, in spite of any additional attempts to resatisfy member. The solution to this inefficiency is to add a right side to the first statement of the member definition, with the cut operator as the sole element, as in

```
member(Element, [Element | _]) :- !.
```

Backtracking will not attempt to resatisfy member, but instead it will cause the entire subgoal to fail.

There is a programming strategy in Prolog, called **generate and test,** in which cut is particularly useful. In these programs, the goal consists of subgoals that generate potential solutions, which are then checked by later "test" subgoals. Rejected solutions require backtracking to "generator" subgoals, which generate new potential solutions. As an example of a "generate and test" program, consider the following, which appears in Clocksin and Mellish (1984):

```
divide(N1, N2, Result) :-
  is_integer(Result),
  Product1 is Result * N2,
  Product2 is (Result + 1) * N2,
  Product1 =< N1, Product2 > N1, !.
```

This program performs integer division, using addition and multiplication. Because most Prolog systems provide division as an operator, this program is not actually useful, other than to illustrate a simple generate and test program.

The predicate is_integer succeeds as long as its parameter is not instantiated to some value that is not a non-negative integer. If its argument is not instantiated, is_integer instantiates it to the value 0. If the argument is instantiated to an integer, is_integer instantiates it to the next larger integer value.

So, in divide, is_integer is the generator subgoal. It generates elements of the sequence 0, 1, 2, ..., one each time it is satisfied. All of the others are the testing subgoals they check to determine whether the value produced by is_integer is, in fact, the quotient of the first two parameters, N1 and N2. The purpose of the cut as the last subgoal is simple: It prevents divide from ever trying to find an alternative solution once it has found *the* solution. Although is_integer can generate a huge number of candidates, only one is the solution, so the cut here prevents useless attempts to produce secondary solutions.

Use of the cut operator has been compared to the use of the goto in imperative languages (Van Emden, 1980). Although it is sometimes needed, it is possible to abuse it. Indeed, it is sometimes used to make logic programs have a control flow that is inspired by imperative programming styles.

The ability to tamper with control flow in a Prolog program is a deficiency because it is directly detrimental to one of the important advantages of logic programming—the fact that programs do not specify how solutions are to be found. Rather, they simply specify what the solution should look like. This makes programs easier to write and easier to read. They are not cluttered with the details of how the solutions are to be determined and, in particular, the precise order in which the computations are done to produce the solution. So, while logic programming requires no control flow directions, Prolog programs use them frequently, mostly for the sake of efficiency.

14.6.2   The Closed World Assumption

The nature of Prolog's resolution sometimes creates misleading results. The only truths, as far as Prolog is concerned, are those that can be proved using its database. It has no knowledge of the world other than its database. Any query about which there is insufficient information in the database to prove absolutely is assumed to be false. Prolog can prove that a given goal is true, but it cannot prove that a given goal is false. It simply assumes that, because it cannot prove a goal true, the goal must be false.

Actually, the closed world assumption should not be at all foreign to you—our judicial system operates the same way. Suspects are innocent until proven guilty.

The problem of the closed world assumption is related to the negation problem, which is discussed in the following section.

14.6.3   The Negation Problem

Another problem with Prolog is its difficulty with negation. Consider the following database of two facts and a relationship:

```
parent(bill, jake).
parent(bill, shelley).
sibling(X, Y) :- (parent(M, X), parent(M, Y).
```

Now, suppose we typed the query

```
sibling(X, Y).
```

Prolog responds with

```
X = jake
Y = jake
```

Thus, Prolog "thinks" jake is a sibling of himself. This happens because the system first instantiates M with bill and X with jake, to make the first subgoal, parent(M, X), true. It then starts at the beginning of the database again to match the second subgoal, parent(M, Y), and arrives at the instantiations of M with bill and Y with jake. Because the two subgoals are satisfied independently, with both matchings starting at the database's beginning, the response above results. To avoid this, X must be specified to be a sibling of Y only if they have the same parents *and* they are not the same. Unfortunately, stating that they are not equal is not straightforward in Prolog, as we discuss below. The most exacting method would require adding a fact for every pair of atoms, stating that they were not the same. This can, in general, cause the database to become very large, for there is often far more negative information than positive information. For example, most people have 364 more unbirthdays than they have birthdays.

A simple alternative solution is to state in the goal that X must not be the same as Y, as in

```
sibling(X, Y) :- parent(M, X), parent(M, Y), not(X = Y).
```

In other situations, the solution is not so simple.

The Prolog not operator is satisfied in this case if resolution cannot satisfy the subgoal x = y. Therefore, if the not succeeds, it does not necessarily mean that x is not equal to y; rather, it means that resolution cannot prove from the database that x is the same as y. Thus, the Prolog not operator is not equivalent to a logical NOT operator, in which NOT means that its operand is provably true. This nonequivalency can lead to a problem if we happen to have a goal of the form

```
not(not(some_goal)).
```

which would be equivalent to

```
some_goal.
```

if Prolog's not operator were a true logical NOT operator. In some cases, however, they are not the same. For example, consider again the member rules:

```
member(Element, [Element | _]) :- !.
member(Element, [_ | List]) :- member(Element, List).
```

To discover one of the elements of a given list, the following goal could be used:

```
member(X, [mary, fred, barb]).
```

which would cause x to be instantiated with mary, which would then be printed. But if we used

```
not(not(member(X, [mary, fred, barb]))).
```

the following sequence of events would take place: First, the inner goal would succeed, instantiating x to mary. Then Prolog would attempt to satisfy the next goal:

```
not(member(X, [mary, fred, barb])).
```

This would fail because member succeeded. When this goal failed, x would be uninstantiated because Prolog always uninstantiates all variables in all goals that fail. Next, Prolog would attempt to satisfy the outer not goal, which would succeed, because its argument had failed. Finally, the result, which is x, would be printed. But x would not be currently instantiated, so the system would indicate that. Generally, uninstantiated variables are printed in the form of a string of digits that begins with an underscore. So the fact that Prolog's not is not equivalent to a logical NOT can be, at the very least, misleading.

The fundamental reason why logical NOT cannot be an integral part of Prolog is the form of the Horn clause:

$$A :- B_1 \cap B_2 \cap \ldots \cap B_n$$

If all the *B* propositions are true, it can be concluded that *A* is true. But regardless of the truth or falseness of any or all of the *B*s, it cannot be concluded that *A* is false. From positive logic, one can only conclude positive logic. Thus, the use of the Horn clause form prevents any negative conclusions.

14.7   Applications of Logic Programming

In this section we briefly describe a few of the larger classes of present and potential applications of logic programming in general and Prolog in particular.

14.7.1   Relational Database Management Systems

Relational database management systems (RDBMSs) store data in the form of tables. Queries on such databases are often stated in relational calculus, which is a form of symbolic logic. The query languages of these systems are nonprocedural in the same sense that logic programming is nonprocedural. The user does not describe how to retrieve the answer; rather, he or she only describes the characteristics of the answer. The connection between logic programming and RDBMSs should be obvious. Simple tables of information can be described by Prolog structures, and relationships between tables can be conveniently and easily described by Prolog rules. The retrieval process is inherent in the resolution operation. The goal statements of Prolog provide the queries for the RDBMS. Logic programming is thus a natural match to the needs of implementing an RDBMS.

One of the advantages of using logic programming to implement an RDBMS is that only a single language is required. In a typical RDBMS, a database language includes statements for data definitions, data manipulation, and queries, all of which are embedded in a general-purpose programming language, such as COBOL. The general-purpose language is used for processing the data and input and output functions. All of these functions can be done in a logic programming language.

Another advantage of using logic programming to implement an RDBMS is that deductive capability is built in. Conventional RDBMSs cannot deduce anything from a database other than what is explicitly stored in them. They contain only facts, rather than facts *and* inference rules. The primary disadvantage of logic programming compared with conventional RDBMSs is its lower level of efficiency. Logical inferences are simply much slower than ordinary table look-up methods using imperative programming techniques.

14.7.2 Expert Systems

Expert systems are computer systems designed to emulate human expertise in some particular domain. They consist of a database of facts, an inferencing process, some heuristics about the domain, and some friendly human interface that makes the system appear much like an expert human consultant. In addition to their initial knowledge base, which is provided by a human expert, expert systems learn from the process of being used, so their databases must be capable of growing dynamically. Also, an expert system should include the capability of interrogating the user to get additional information when it detects that such information is needed.

One of the central problems for the designer of an expert system is dealing with the inevitable inconsistencies and incompleteness of the database. Logic programming appears to be well suited to deal with these problems. For example, default inference rules can help deal with the problem of incompleteness.

Prolog can and has been used to construct expert systems. It can easily fulfill the basic needs of expert systems, using resolution as the basis for query processing, using its ability to add facts and rules to provide the learning capability, and using its trace facility to inform the user of the "reasoning" behind a given result. Missing from Prolog is the automatic ability of the system to query the user for additional information when it is needed.

One of the most widely known uses of logic programming in expert systems is the expert system construction system known as APES, which is described in Sergot (1983) and Hammond (1983). The APES system includes a very flexible facility for gathering information from the user during expert system construction. It also includes a second interpreter for producing explanations to its answers to queries.

APES has been successfully used to produce several expert systems, including one for the rules of a government social benefits program and one for the British Nationality Act, which is the definitive source for rules of British citizenship.

14.7.3 Natural Language Processing

Certain kinds of natural language processing can be done with logic programming. In particular, natural language interfaces to computer software systems, such as intelligent databases, and other intelligent knowledge-based systems can be conveniently done with logic programming. For describing language syntax, forms of logic programming have been found to be equivalent to context-free grammars. Proof procedures in logic programming systems have been found to be equivalent to certain parsing strategies. In fact, backward chaining resolution can be used directly to parse sentences whose structures are described by context-free grammars.

It has also been discovered that some kinds of semantics of natural languages can be made clear by modeling the languages with logic programming. In particular, research in logic-based semantics networks has shown that sets of sentences in natural languages can be expressed in clausal form (Deliyanni and Kowalski, 1979). Logic-based semantic networks are also discussed by Kowalski (1979).

14.7.4 Education

In the area of education, there have been extensive experiments in teaching children as young as seven how to use the logic programming language micro-Prolog (Ennals, 1980). Researchers claim a number of advantages in teaching Prolog to young people. First, it is possible to introduce computing using this approach. It also has the side effect of teaching logic, which can result in clearer thinking and expression. This will help students in learning a variety of subjects, such as solving equations in mathematics, dealing with grammars for natural languages, and understanding the rules and order of the physical world.

The experiments in teaching logic programming to the very young have produced the interesting result that it is easier to teach logic programming to a beginner than to a programmer with a significant amount of experience in an imperative language.

14.8 Conclusions

Many believe that Prolog is, at least at this point, still a grand experiment. It has a growing number of proponents, however, as many other languages have had, and some believe it can be at least a part of the solution to the software crisis, in which the imperative languages currently in use simply cannot cope with the problems that need to be solved by computers (Cuadrado and Cuadrado, 1985).

Some of the reasons why adherents believe that Prolog is better than imperative languages are the following, as originally stated by Jacques Cohen (1985), one of Prolog's boosters:

1. Because Prolog is based on logic, Prolog programs are likely to be more logically organized and written, which should lead to fewer errors and less maintenance.

2. Prolog processing is naturally parallel, making Prolog interpreters particularly able to take advantage of multiple-processor machines.

3. Because of the conciseness of Prolog programs, development time is decreased, making it a good tool for prototyping.

Of course, there are people who do not agree. Many computer scientists are skeptical of Prolog's usefulness outside a few small areas of artificial intelligence. Some believe Prolog will replace LISP as the main language of artificial intelligence, although that is certainly not clear at this time. A comparison of the two languages has been made by Warren et al. (1977).

SUMMARY

Symbolic logic provides the basis for logic programming and logic programming languages. The approach of logic programming is to use as a database a collection of facts and rules that state relationships between facts, and to use an automatic inferencing process to check the validity of new propositions, assuming the facts and rules of the database are true. This approach is the one developed for automatic theorem proving.

Prolog is the most widely used logic programming language. The origins of logic programming lie in Robinson's development of the resolution rule for logical inference. Prolog was developed primarily at Marseille and Edinburgh.

Logic programs are nonprocedural, which means that the characteristics of the solution are given, but the complete process of getting the solution is not.

Prolog statements are either facts, rules, or goals. Most are made up of structures, which are atomic propositions, and logic operators, although arithmetic expressions are also allowed.

Resolution is the primary activity of a Prolog interpreter. This process, which uses backtracking extensively, involves mainly pattern matching among propositions. When variables are involved, they can be instantiated to values to provide matches. This instantiation process is called unification.

Logic programming has been used in a number of different areas, primarily in relational database systems, expert systems, and natural language processing.

BIBLIOGRAPHIC NOTES

The Prolog language is described in several books. Edinburgh's form of the language is covered in *Programming in Prolog* by W.F. Clocksin and C.S. Mellish. The microcomputer implementation is described in *Micro-PROLOG: Programming in Logic* by K.L. Clark and F.G. McCabe.

Introduction to Logic Programming by Christopher Hogger is an excellent book on the general area of logic programming. It is the source of the material in this chapter's section on logic programming applications.

PROBLEM SET

1. Explain the connection between automatic theorem proving and Prolog's inferencing process.

2. Explain the difference between procedural and nonprocedural languages.

3. Describe how a multiple-processor machine could be used to implement resolution. Could Prolog, as currently defined, use this method?

4. Explain why Prolog systems must do backtracking.

5. Compare the concept of data typing in Ada with that of Prolog.

6. What is the relationship between resolution and unification in Prolog?

7. Under what circumstances is the variable that is the left operand of the **is** operator instantiated?

8. Write a Prolog description of your family tree (based only on facts) going back to your grandparents and including all descendants. Be sure to include all relationships.

9. Write a set of rules for family relationships, including all relationships from grandparents through two generations. Now, add these to the facts of Problem 8 and eliminate as many of the facts as you can.

10. Write a Prolog program that succeeds if the intersection of two given list parameters is empty.

11. Write a Prolog program that returns a list containing the union of the elements of two given lists.

15

Object-Oriented Programming Languages

Adele Goldberg

Adele Goldberg spent 14 years at Xerox's Palo Alto Research Center, leading the design team for Smalltalk and its implementation. She was instrumental in the development of not only Smalltalk, but of the window- and icon-based user interface paradigm.

Key Concepts

- Object-oriented programming
- Objects and classes
- Message passing
- Message expressions and methods
- Control structures using message passing
- Class hierarchies and inheritance
- Dynamic binding
- Polymorphism

There are several distinct categories of object-oriented programming languages. First, there are the so-called pure object-oriented languages in which all computation is based on message passing. The pure object-oriented languages can be further divided into those that use dynamic type binding, such as Smalltalk, and those that are statically typed, such as Eiffel (Meyer, 1988). Second, there are hybrid languages, which use procedure calls rather than message passing, and a mixture of both static and dynamic type binding. Examples of these are CLOS (Bobrow et al., 1988) and C++ (Stroustrup, 1991).

In this chapter, we examine two languages, Smalltalk and C++, that represent the dynamically typed pure category and the hybrid category of object-oriented languages, respectively. These two languages are dramatically different, and the styles of programming that they support and promote are quite different.

We begin with a brief discussion of object-oriented programming. This is followed by an overview of Smalltalk. We then describe in detail a subset of Smalltalk and illustrate it with several complete Smalltalk programs. C++ support for object-oriented programming is then described. Finally, the two languages, Smalltalk and C++, and their respective approaches, pure and hybrid, are compared.

15.1 Object-Oriented Programming

The concept of **object-oriented programming** has its roots in SIMULA 67 but was more fully developed in the evolution of the Smalltalk language.

Data-oriented programming focuses on abstract data types. Recall that an abstract data type is defined as a data structure in which the data and its operations are defined together in a single syntactic unit. Furthermore, the structural definition and process implementation are hidden from the program units that use them. These program units are called clients. Focusing on data is the opposite from the traditional procedural programming approach that focuses on processes and their implementation in subprograms. The data-oriented programming paradigm was popular in the 1980s, and it is well served by the data abstraction facilities of Modula-2 and Ada.

One fundamental restriction of abstract data types is that, once defined, they cannot be conveniently modified for slightly different applications. There is also no way to collect the common characteristics of families of closely related types. Object-oriented programming languages extend data abstraction with inheritance to provide these capabilities. Neither Ada nor Modula-2 include inheritance, although Ada 9x probably will.

Inheritance began in a limited form in SIMULA 67, whose classes can be defined in hierarchies. In static typed languages such as SIMULA 67 and C++, inheritance is a generalization of the idea of subtypes. An Ada subtype of the built-in type INTEGER inherits all of the operations of INTEGER. Inheritance allows both user and system classes to be created that inherit characteristics from existing classes. The result is that new programs often are constructed as variations of existing program units, which in this case are classes. This provides an effective technique for software reuse.

Dynamic binding couples with inheritance to provide a specific kind of code genericity. This is not a general kind of dynamic binding, such as that of types in APL. Rather it is the dynamic binding of requests for services to specific code that can properly provide those services for a specific type of data object.

15.2 Fundamental Concepts of Smalltalk

15.2.1 The Message-Passing Model of Computation

A program in Smalltalk consists entirely of objects, and the concept of an object is truly universal. Virtually everything, from items as simple as the integer constant 2 to a complex file-handling system, are objects. As objects, they are treated uniformly. They all have local memory, inherent processing ability, the capability to communicate with other objects, and the ability to inherit characteristics from ancestors. Objects do not have names; they are anonymous and can be referenced only by pointers. However, they can be treated as first-class entities in the sense that they can be passed as parameters and returned from other objects as the results of received messages.

All objects are faithful data abstractions, meaning that the definitions of their data structures and the operations on those structures can be hidden from the objects that send messages to request information or processing. In this sense, objects are similar to Ada packages.

Objects communicate with other objects by sending messages. A message is used by an object to request an operation that another object (or itself) provides.

The operation definitions in objects are called **methods**. A method specifies the reaction of the object when it receives a message that is directed to that method. The binding of a message to a method is dynamic. The entire collection of methods of an object is called the **message protocol**, or **message interface**, of the object.

One can think of objects as having sockets into which other objects can place messages, but only if the message fits the socket. Ada task communication is based on the same message-passing model that pure object-oriented languages use. Tasks have message sockets, called **accept** clauses, to which messages from other tasks may be sent. Furthermore, messages are sent to tasks to request services, exactly as if they were objects in an object-oriented language.

Messages can be parameterized with object names, thus providing flexibility in fixed messages. Replies to messages have the form of objects and are used to return requested information or to confirm that the requested service has been completed.

All computing in Smalltalk is done by the same uniform technique: sending a message to an object to invoke one of its methods. A reply to a message is an object that returns the requested information or simply notifies the sender that the requested processing has been completed.

Smalltalk can be described as a simulation of a collection of computers (objects) that communicate with each other (through messages). Each object is an abstraction of a computer in the sense that it stores data and provides processing capability for manipulating that data. In addition, objects can send and receive messages. In essence, those are the fundamental capabilities of computers: to store and manipulate data and to communicate.

The essence of object-oriented programming using a pure object-oriented language is solving problems by identifying the real-world objects of the problem and the processing required of those objects, and then creating simulations of those objects, their processes, and the required communications between the objects using existing classes whenever possible. Abstract data types, dynamic type binding, and inheritance are the concepts that make object-oriented problem solving not only possible but convenient and effective.

15.2.2   Classes

In Smalltalk, object abstractions are **classes**, which are similar to the classes of SIMULA 67. The common characteristics of a category of objects is captured by a class definition. Instances of the class can be created and are the objects of the program. Each object has its own local data and represents a different instance of its class. The only difference between two objects of the same class is the state of their local variables.

As in SIMULA 67, class hierarchies can be formed in Smalltalk. Subclasses of a given class are refinements of it, inheriting the functionality and local variables of the parent class, or **superclass**. Subclasses can add new local memory and functionality, and they can modify or hide inherited functionality. Inheritance is further discussed in Section 15.3.8.

The interface of an object is completely defined by the class of which it is an instance (and that class' ancestor classes).

It is easy to relate the concepts of a pure object-oriented language to the abstract data types of Ada. Classes are similar to abstract data type definitions. Objects correspond to instances of data abstractions. A message is like a statement that calls a subprogram that is defined in a data abstraction, and the process of message passing corresponds to that of calling that subprogram. It is inheritance and dynamic type binding that distinguishes object-oriented programming from just programming with abstract data types.

15.2.3 The Smalltalk Environment

As stated earlier in this chapter, Smalltalk's environment is quite different from that of a typical imperative language. The Smalltalk system integrates a program editor, compiler, the usual features of an operating system, and a virtual machine into a single system. The interface to this system is highly graphical, making use of multiple overlaid windows and pop-up menus, a mouse pointing device, and a high-resolution, bit-mapped monitor.

An important aspect of the Smalltalk environment is that it is written almost entirely in Smalltalk, and it can be modified by the user to fit his or her particular needs. Therefore, the source version of the Smalltalk system must be available to the user.

To reiterate, Smalltalk is far more than just a programming language; it is also a programming methodology and a programming environment.

15.3 The Smalltalk Language

15.3.1 Expressions

Smalltalk programs consist primarily of objects and messages. Objects are instances of classes, which consist largely of methods that correspond to possible messages to which those instances can respond. Methods are in turn constructed from expressions. An expression specifies an object, which happens to be the value of the expression.

Smalltalk has four kinds of expressions: literals, variable names, message expressions, and block expressions. Literals, variables, and message expressions are discussed in the following three sections. Block expressions are described in Section 15.3.4.1.

15.3.1.1   Literals

The most common literals are numbers, strings, and keywords. Numbers are literal objects that represent numeric values. They are quite different from the numeric literals of the common imperative languages, which act somewhat like named constants because they are associated with memory locations that contain their values. In Smalltalk, numeric literals are objects that are characterized by their message protocol and by the results that are produced when messages are received. The message protocol of numeric literals, as is the case with other objects, is defined in the class definition along with its inherited class definitions. In the case of an integer literal, the parent class is `Integer`; it provides methods for the usual arithmetic operators, among other things.

Syntactically, a string literal is a sequence of characters delimited by apostrophes. Semantically, a string literal is an object that is capable of responding to messages that access individual characters, replace substrings, and perform comparisons with other strings.

A keyword is an identifier, which may be user-defined, with a trailing colon. The use of keywords is discussed in Section 15.3.1.3.

15.3.1.2   Variables

A Smalltalk variable name is syntactically similar to those of other programming languages: a sequence of letters and/or digits that begins with a letter. Smalltalk variables come in two varieties: private, which means they are local to an object, and shared, which means they are visible outside the object in which they are "declared." Names of private variables must begin with lowercase letters. Names of shared variables must begin with uppercase letters.

All Smalltalk variables are pointers; they can only refer to objects or classes. In a sense, they are typeless because any variable can point to any object. The only shared variables discussed here are those that refer to classes.

15.3.1.3   Message Expressions

Messages have the form of expressions. They provide the means of communication among objects and are the way the operations of an object are requested.

Message expressions have two parts, a specification of the object that is to receive the message and the message itself. The message itself specifies a selector entry, or method, in the receiver object and possibly one or more parameters. Parameters are, like other variables, pointers to other objects. When a message is evaluated, it is sent to the specified receiver object. Methods are discussed in Sections 15.3.2 and 15.3.6.

For the remainder of the chapter, we will refer to message expressions simply as messages. Messages correspond in many ways to procedure calls in languages like Pascal and C.

There are three categories of messages: unary, binary, and keyword. Unary messages are the simplest kind, having no parameters. They have only two parts, the object to which they are to be sent and the method in that receiving object. The first symbol of a unary message specifies a receiver object; the last symbol specifies the method of that object that is to be executed. For example, the message

```
firstAngle sin
```

sends a parameterless message to the `sin` method of the object `firstAngle`. Recall that all objects are referenced by pointers, so `firstAngle` is really a pointer to an object.

Binary messages have a single parameter, an object, that is passed to the specified method of the specified receiver object. Among the most common binary messages are those for arithmetic operations, such as the following:

```
21 + 2
sum / count
```

In the first message, the receiver object is the number 21, to which is sent the message + 2. This message passes the parameter object 2 to the + method of the object 21. The code of that method uses the object 2 to build a new object, in this case, 23. If the system already contains the object 23, then the result is a reference to it, rather than to a new object.

It may seem odd to consider the number 21 an object, but in Smalltalk it is perfectly natural for numbers to be objects with operations. This allows them to inherit all their operations from the class `Integer`, of which they are instances.

In the second message above, the message "/ count" is sent to the object referred to by `sum`, which results in the object referenced by the variable `count` being passed as a parameter to the / method of the object referenced by `sum`.

Keyword expressions specify one or more keywords to organize the correspondence between the actual parameters in the message and the formal parameters in the method. That is, the keywords act in concert to select the method to which the message is directed. The interspersion of keywords and parameters in messages enhances their readability. Methods that accept keyword messages are not named. Such methods are identified instead by the keywords themselves. Consider the following example:

```
firstArray at: 1 put: 5
```

This message sends the objects 1 and 5 to a particular method of the object `firstArray`. The keywords at: and put: identify the formal parameters of the method to which 1 and 5, respectively, are to be sent. The method to which this message is sent includes the keywords of the message. In fact, keyword methods do not have names; rather they are identified by their keywords. This catenation—in this case, at:put:—is called a **selector.**

Message expressions can consist of any number of any combination of the three kinds of expressions, as in

```
total - 3 * divisor
firstArray at: index - 1 put: 77
```

To determine how these are evaluated, the precedence and associativity of expression operators must be known. Unary expressions have the highest precedence, followed by binary expressions, followed by keyword expressions. Both unary and binary expressions associate left to right. Note that this is quite different from the precedence rules commonly used in languages such as Pascal and C.

Expressions can be parenthesized to force any order of operator evaluation. The first expression above, parenthesized to illustrate but not alter its normal evaluation order, is

```
(total - 3) * divisor
```

This expression sends 3 to the – method of the object total. The value of the variable divisor is then sent to the * method of the object that resulted from the first operation.

The expression

```
firstArray at: index - 1 put: 77
```

sends 1 to the – method of the object index. The result of this operation, along with 77, are then sent to the at:put: method of the object firstArray.

Messages can be cascaded, which means that multiple messages can be sent to the same object without duplicating the receiver object's name. This is done by separating the selector-parameter groups, or messages, by semicolons. The messages are sent sequentially, as they appear, left to right. For example,

```
ourPen home; up; goto: 500@500; down; home
```

is equivalent to the following:

```
ourPen home.
ourPen up.
ourPen goto: 500@500.
ourPen down.
ourPen home
```

This sequence draws a line on the display, assuming that ourPen is an instance of the Pen class. An object of class Pen is illustrated in Section 15.3.11.

Notice that periods are used to separate messages that are sent to different methods and appear on adjacent lines. This is similar to the use of semicolons to separate statements in Pascal programs.

15.3.2 Methods

A method of a class defines the operations an instance of the class will execute when a message corresponding to the method is received. In a sense, methods are like function definitions, complete with parameters and the capability of returning values.

The general syntactic form of a Smalltalk method is

message_pattern [| temporary variables |] statements

where the brackets are meta-symbols that indicate that what they enclose is optional. Because Smalltalk has no type declarations, temporary variables, when present, need only be named in a list. Temporary variables exist only during execution of the method in which they are listed. There is no punctuation at the end of a method.

The message pattern corresponds to the procedure statement in a language such as Pascal. Message patterns, which are prototypes for messages, can be in one of two basic forms. For unary or binary messages, only the method's name is included. For keyword messages, the keywords and the names of the formal parameters form the message pattern.

A value to be returned by a method is indicated by preceding the expression that describes it with an up arrow (^). In many cases, this is the last expression that appears in the method. If no return value is specified in a method, the receiver object itself is the return value.

A message pattern for a unary message is simply the method name. An example of a unary method is

```
currentTotal
^(oldTotal + newValue)
```

This method returns the value of the expression

```
oldTotal + newValue.
```

Binary methods are used primarily for arithmetic operations, which are predefined, so they are not discussed here.

The general form of the message pattern for keyword message methods is

key_1: parameter_1 key_2: parameter_2 ... key_n: parameter_n

Consider the following example keyword method, which does not specify a value to be returned:

```
x: xCoord y: yCoord
   ourPen up; goto xCoord @ yCoord; down.
```

In this method, which matches the x:y: message selector, the object ourPen is sent the messages "up", "goto" (which uses the two parameters xCoord and yCoord), and "down". The message pattern is simply a list of the keyword/formal parameter name pairs in the method.

An example message for this method is

```
ourPen x: 300 y: 400
```

Additional features of methods, including temporary variables, are discussed in Section 15.3.6.

15.3.3 Assignment Statements

Smalltalk has assignment statements that are similar, at least in appearance, to those of languages such as Pascal and C. Any message expression, literal object, or variable name can be the right side of an assignment statement. The left side is a variable name, and the operator is specified with a left arrow, as in

```
total ← 22
sum ← total
```

The particular object referenced by a variable is changed when that variable's name appears on the left side of an assignment. In the above example, the variable total is set to refer to the object 22. Then the variable sum is set to refer to the same object. This operation is closely related to the assignment of pointer variables in Pascal or Ada.

Recall that all methods transmit information back to the senders that sent the messages. To save that returned information, the message expression is placed on the right side of an assignment to a variable. The variable is then set to refer to the returned information, as in the following:

```
index ← index + 1
salesTax ← deducts grossPay: 350.0 dependents: 4
```

In the first assignment, the message "+ 1" is sent to the object referenced by index. The variable index is set to reference the new object that results from executing the + method. In the second, the keyword message "grossPay: 350.0 dependents: 4" is sent to the grossPay:dependents: method of the object deducts. The variable salesTax is set to refer to the object returned by deducts.

It should be obvious that Smalltalk is, by our definition, an imperative language—computation is through expression evaluation and assignment statements, and results are stored in variables.

15.3.4 Blocks and Control Structures

One of the most unusual aspects of Smalltalk is that the control structures are not provided by statements in the language. Instead, they are formed with the fundamental object-oriented paradigm: message passing.

Blocks provide a way to collect expressions into groups. These groups can be used to build execution control constructs.

15.3.4.1 Blocks

A block is an unnamed literal object that contains a sequence of expressions. Blocks are instances of the class Block. A message can be sent to a block by placing the message immediately after the block.

A block is specified in brackets, with its expression components separated by periods, as in

```
[index ← index + 1. sum ← sum + index]
```

The expressions in a block are deferred actions because they are not executed when encountered; rather they are executed only when the block is sent the unary message **value**. For example,

```
[sum ← sum + index] value
```

sends the message **value** to the block, causing its execution. When a block execution is completed, the value of the last expression in the block is returned.

Blocks can be assigned to variables and executed by sending the "**value**" message to the variable. For example, given the expression

```
addIndex ← [sum ← sum + index]
```

the message expression

```
addIndex value
```

causes index to be added to sum. This message expression could also be assigned to a variable as follows:

```
addIndex ← [sum + index]
sum ← addIndex value
```

Blocks are always executed in the context of their definition, even when they are sent as parameters to a different object. Thus, they are semantically related to the pass-by-name parameters of ALGOL 60.

Blocks can be thought of as procedure declarations that may appear anywhere. Like procedures, blocks can have parameters. Block parameters are specified in a section at the beginning of the block that is separated from the remainder of the block by a vertical bar (|). The formal parameter specifications require a colon to be attached to the left end of each parameter. Because there are no declared types, the specifications include only the formal parameter names, which are listed without any separating punctuation. As an example of a block with parameters, consider the following:

```
[:x :y | sum ← x + 10. total ← sum * y]
```

Blocks provide a means of collecting expressions, so they are a natural way to form control structures in Smalltalk.

15.3.4.2   Iteration

Blocks can contain relational expressions, in which case they return one of the predefined Boolean objects, **true** or **false**. Such blocks are sometimes called conditional blocks. The two objects, **true** and **false**, have methods that provide some of the facilities for building control structures.

Logical pretest loops can be formed by using the keyword method `whileTrue:`, which the class `Block` provides, to send the block to be controlled to a second block that contains the loop condition. This method is defined for all blocks that return Boolean objects. The `whileTrue:` method is defined to send **value** to the object that contains the method (either **true** or **false**), thereby causing its parameter block to be executed, as in the following:

```
count ← 0.
sum ← 0.
[count <= 20]   "The block with the loop condition"
    whileTrue: [sum ← sum + count.
                count ← count + 1]     "The loop body"
```

Although this code may have a somewhat conventional appearance, and in fact accomplishes a rather conventional operation, the process by which it does it is significantly different from that used by imperative languages.

The loop control is realized as follows: The block containing the code to add count to sum and increment count, which is the code segment whose execution is to be controlled, is sent as the parameter to the `whileTrue:` method of the conditional block `[count <= 20]`. The `whileTrue:` method sends **value** to the conditional block, thus causing that block to be evaluated. The result of this evaluation is a Boolean object, either **true** or **false**. If the result is **true**, the `whileTrue:` method causes the parameter sent by the `"whileTrue:"` message to be evaluated. Its parameter is the block that contains the expressions of the iteration. After they are evaluated, the process is repeated by sending the block of expressions to `[count <= 20]` again. The repetition stops when an evaluation of `[count <= 20]` produces **false** as a result object.

Suppose the control block in the above example were `[count <= 1]`, rather than `[count <= 20]`. The following is a trace of the actions that occur when the modified code is executed. Note that " " indicates a message being sent.

```
count ← 0
sum ← 0
[sum ← sum+count. count ← count+1]   [count<=1] WhileTrue
value  [count<=1]     "sent by WhileTrue"
[count<=1] returns true
WhileTrue evaluates [sum ← sum+count. count ← count+1]
     (sum ← 2; count ← 1)     "results of the evaluation"
[sum ← sum+count. count ← count+1]   [count<=1] WhileTrue
value  [count<=1]        "sent by WhileTrue"
```

```
[count<=1] returns true
WhileTrue evaluates [sum ← sum+count. count ← count+1]
    (sum ← 4; count ← 2)      "results of the evaluation"
[sum ← sum+count. count ←count+1]   [count<=1] WhileTrue
value   [count<=1]
[count<=1] returns false
```

Another common loop control structure is simple repetition with a counter control. For this, there is a method for integers named `timesRepeat:`. When `timesRepeat:` is sent to an integer with a block as the parameter, the block is executed that many times. For example,

```
xCube ← 1.
3 timesRepeat: [xCube ← xCube * x]
```

computes the cube of x by a rather lengthy process.

Control structures similar to ALGOL 68's **for** loops can be built with some of the methods of integers. The two most useful of these are `to:do:` and `to:by:do:`. First consider the method `to:do:`. The `to:` parameter is an integer expression whose value serves as the terminal value. The `do:` parameter is a block that is to be executed by the integer method. The `to:do:` method generates, internally, a sequence of values, beginning with the integer literal to which the message is sent and ending with the `to:` parameter value. For example, consider the following message:

```
1 to: 5 do: [sum ← sum + x]
```

The block is executed five times. The internal values produced and returned by the object 1 are 1, 2, 3, 4, and 5.

The block that forms a loop body can have a parameter. Such a parameter is implicitly assigned the internal values created by the message. The internal values are those returned by the numeric object to which the whole message is sent. For example, consider the following message:

```
2 to: 10 by: 2 do: [:even | sum ← sum + even]
```

This message causes the block to be executed five times, but in this case even the block parameter takes on the internal values, which in this case are 2, 4, 6, 8, and 10.

15.3.4.3 Selection

Selection constructs also have a conventional appearance, but they operate in an unconventional way. The method `ifTrue:ifFalse:` is provided for the **true** and **false** objects. The two arguments of the "ifTrue:ifFalse:" message represent the then and else clauses of the selection construct. The message is sent to a Boolean expression. If the expression evaluates to **true**, then the message is sent to **true**. In this case, the `ifTrue:ifFalse:` method sends **value** to its first argument and ignores its second argument. If sent to **false**, the opposite takes place. For example, consider the following message:

```
total = 0
  ifTrue: [average ← 0]
  ifFalse: [average ← sum // total]
```

The Boolean expression `total = 0` causes the message "`= 0`" to be sent to the object `total`, which returns either **true** or **false**. The resulting object (either **true** or **false**) is then used as the receiver for the message, which is sent to the `ifTrue:ifFalse:` method. The two parameters to this method are the then and else blocks, one of which is to be executed. The `//` operator specifies integer division.

Four different messages can be sent to the **true** and **false** objects. In addition to `ifTrue:ifFalse:`, there are `ifTrue:`, `ifFalse:`, and `ifFalse:ifTrue:`.

The semantics of the control structures we have just discussed may seem rather odd, but they are really quite natural to experienced Smalltalk users. Furthermore, the ability to handle control structures within this framework is a tribute to the power and flexibility of the message-passing model. It also simplifies Smalltalk by obviating the need for any structure outside the world of objects and message passing.

15.3.5   Classes

All Smalltalk objects are instances of classes. A class has four parts:

1. A class name.
2. The superclass name, which specifies the new class's position in the hierarchy of classes in the system.
3. A declaration of the local variables, called instance variables, that will be available to the instances of the class.
4. The methods that define how instances of the class will respond to messages. (Recall that an object inherits the methods of all ancestor classes, too.)

Messages to an object normally cause the class to which the object belongs to be searched for a corresponding method. If the search fails, it is continued in the superclass of that class, and so forth, up to the system class, `Object`, which has no superclass. If no method is found anywhere in that chain, an error occurs. It is important to remember that this method search is dynamic—it takes place when the message is sent.

For example, consider the following situation: Class C has a method named z; class B has a method named y; class A has a method named x. The superclass of C is B, and B's superclass is A. Now, let `ball` be an object of class C. Then the message

```
ball z
```

uses the method z from class C. If C includes no method named y, then

```
ball y
```

uses the method y from class B. If neither C nor B include a method named x, then the message

```
ball x
```

uses the method x from class A.

The private memory of an instance of a class contains its instance variables. Instance variables are not visible to other objects. Each instance variable refers to one object, called its value. The values of all of an instance's variables together represent that instance's current state.

Instance variables are either named or indexed. Named variables correspond to pointers to nonarray types in an imperative language. Indexed instance variables are accessed not by name but by messages that have integers as parameters. Most indexed variables are used in a way that corresponds to arrays in conventional imperative languages, although indexing itself is done through message passing. The integer parameter in a message to reference an indexed instance variable corresponds to the subscript in a reference to an array element in a conventional imperative language.

Instances of classes are created by sending the message **new** to the class in an assignment, which sets the left-side variable to reference the newly created object. For example,

```
ourPen ← Pen new
```

creates an instance of the class Pen (by sending the message **new** to the class Pen) and sets the variable ourPen to reference it. This example demonstrates that messages can be sent to classes as well as to objects.

15.3.6 More About Methods

In this section we examine some features of methods that were not covered in Section 15.3.2.

The following method illustrates the use of temporary variables:

```
first: x second: y | temp |
  temp ← x + y.
  temp > 1000
    ifTrue: [y ← 1000].
  ^ y
```

This method adds the values of its two parameters together and places the sum in the temporary variable temp. If the value of temp is greater than 1000, the second parameter, y, is set to 1000. The value of y is the returned object.

The pseudovariable **self** is an object name that refers to the object in which it appears. Therefore, **self** is used for recursive messages, or messages to the object itself. The object name **self** is often used for error message display, as in

```
total = 0
  ifTrue: [self error: 'Error- cannot compute average']
  ifFalse: [^ sum // total]
```

If `total` is equal to zero, this code sends the message "error: 'Error – cannot compute average'" to the object in which the code resides. Otherwise, it returns the value of the expression `sum // total`.

The message "error", like other messages, is directed to a superclass of the object to which it is sent if that object does not include a method for it. If no other ancestor class has a method for the "error" message, the system object, `Object`, which does include an `error` method, receives the message. `Object`'s method for `error` prints the message parameter and terminates the program.

For a somewhat more familiar example of recursion, consider the following method, which is understood by integers. It is taken from Goldberg and Robson (1983).

```
factorial
  self = 0
    ifTrue: [^1].
  self < 0
    ifTrue: [self error 'Factorial not defined']
    ifFalse: [^ self * (self - 1) factorial]
```

This is a binary method for integer objects. It can be invoked by a message such as

```
5 factorial
```

The first Boolean expression, **self** = 0, sends the parameter 0 to the = method of the integer to which the factorial message was sent. The message "ifTrue: [^1]" is then sent to the result of the = method execution. If the result is the object **true**, as it would be for the message "0 factorial", the value 1 is returned to the sender of factorial. If the result of the = method execution is **false**, no action is taken because the ifTrue: method in **false** is defined to do nothing.

The next Boolean expression, **self** < 0, sends the parameter 0 to the < method of the integer to which factorial was sent. The rest of the factorial message (the entire "ifTrue:ifFalse:" message) is then sent to the result of the < method execution. If the resulting object is **true**, the error message is sent to the object to which factorial was sent. If the result of the < method is **false**, then the block on the ifFalse: part of the ifTrue:ifFalse: method is executed, and the result is returned to the sender of factorial.

To understand the "ifFalse:" message, you must understand the precedence rules of message evaluation. In this expression, there are two binary expressions (those with * and -) and one unary expression (factorial). Recall that unary expressions take precedence over binary expressions, unless the binary expression is parenthesized. Also, all expressions have left associativity. Now the order of evaluation is clear: First, "- 1" is sent to **self**, producing an object that is smaller by 1 than the object to which the message was sent. Then factorial is sent to this new object. The final result of this message, after all recursion, is sent with * to **self**, which is the original object to which factorial was sent. The result of this message is the factorial value.

Once again, the similarity in recursion across widely differing language semantics is illustrated in this example.

15.3.7 Type Checking and Generics

Smalltalk variables are not typed; any name can be bound to any object. The only type checking that is done occurs dynamically when a message is sent to an object. If the object or one of its ancestor classes has a method for the message, the message is legal and the object reacts to it. If there is no method that corresponds to a message, either in the object or in one of its ancestor classes, it is a run-time error. This is a significantly different concept of type checking than that of the imperative languages. Smalltalk type checking has the simple form of ensuring that a message matches a method.

All Smalltalk code is generic in the sense that the types of the variables are irrelevant, as long as they are consistent. For example, consider the expression

```
a * b - c
```

Evaluation of this expression begins by sending the message "* b" to the object referenced by a. Then the message "- c" is sent to the result of the first. If a, b, and c reference any numeric type objects, this process is all predefined.

If we define a class for complex numbers to have methods for * and -, then the expression above is also legal for variables a, b, and c that refer to objects of the class complex numbers. This is, in essence, the overloading of the * and - operators.

The point of this discussion is not overloading, however. It is, rather, that as long as the objects referenced in an expression have methods for the messages of the expression, the types of the objects are irrelevant. This means that all code is generic; none is tied to a particular type. A sort method, for example, could be written for a class. Then all new classes that needed that sort capability can simply be made subclasses of that class. This is precisely how the Smalltalk system itself is constructed—as a hierarchy of classes, where the hierarchy is designed to maximize reuse through inheritance of fundamental capabilities.

15.3.8   Inheritance

As should be obvious from the previous sections of this chapter, inheritance is naturally a central concept in Smalltalk. The Smalltalk system includes a large hierarchy of classes. Programming in Smalltalk consists, to a large degree, in creating subclasses of existing classes. It is this potential reuse of existing code that is the most interesting and valuable result of inheritance. In fact, inheritance is perhaps the most important advance of object-oriented languages over imperative languages.

Specifically, a subclass inherits all of the instance variables, instance methods, and class methods of its superclass. The subclass can also have its own instance variables, which must have different names than the variable names in its ancestor classes. Finally, the subclass can define both new methods and methods that already exist in an ancestor class. When a subclass has a method whose name or protocol is the same as an ancestor class, the subclass method hides that of the ancestor class. Access to such a hidden method is provided by prefixing the message with the pseudovariable **super**. This causes the method search to begin in the superclass, rather than locally.

15.3.9   Polymorphism and Dynamic Binding

Polymorphism denotes the particular kind of dynamic binding that occurs in a language that incorporates inheritance. Specifically, **polymorphism** is a typing concept in which a specific message may be sent to different instances of different classes at different times. Such a message is dynamically bound to a method in a particular object.

Consider the following situation: A class named shape has been defined, along with a collection of subclasses for different kinds of shapes, such as circles, rectangles, and so forth. If objects of these subclasses need to be displayed, the display method must be defined within the class of the particular kind of shape, for each kind of shape will require different display code. Suppose that a linked list of objects of various shapes is constructed, and code is written to display each object on the list. Then the message to display_shape is the same for each object on the list, but it must be dynamically bound to the display_shape method in the proper object. This message is obviously polymorphic.

Languages that provide this sort of dynamic binding are called polymorphic languages. Smalltalk is obviously a polymorphic language.

All Smalltalk messages are dynamically bound to methods through the method search process, which operates as follows: Every class has a method dictionary. When a message is received by an object, its method dictionary is searched to determine whether there is a matching local method. If none is found, the search continues in the superclass, and so forth, until Object's dictionary has been searched. If no method is found anywhere in the hierarchy, a run-time error is signaled. The important point is, of course, that the method search is done during execution, at the time a message is sent. This allows code to be polymorphic, with messages being bound to methods in the correct class only during execution.

15.3.10 A Simple Table Handler

The example class of this section demonstrates that simple table management problems typically implemented in common imperative languages can also be implemented easily in Smalltalk. The problem is to build a program that creates and does look-ups in a table of department names and their code numbers. Because of the lack of static typing, the resulting system could be used for any table consisting of two parallel arrays of data, where the look-ups are based on the data elements in the first array.

One of the interesting features used in the program is the dynamic binding of index range to array. The two arrays are always exactly the size of the stored data. Each addition to the table simply increases the size of the table. Note that while this may be interesting and space efficient, it is highly inefficient in terms of execution time. Each addition causes the creation of two new arrays and a move of the contents of the old arrays to the new arrays—a very time-consuming process.

One of the omissions of the program is the lack of a method for removing an entry.

Note that quoted strings in the program are comments.

```
class name                    DeptCodes
superclass                    Object
instance variable names       names
                              codes


"Class methods"
"Create an instance"
new
      ^ super new

"Instance methods"
"Number of table entries"
size
      ^ names size

"Fetch the code for a department"
at: name | index |
      index ← self indexOf: name.
```

```
          index = 0
            ifTrue: [self error: 'Error--Name not in table']
            ifFalse: [^codes at: index]

   "Install a new code; create entry if necessary"
   at: name put: code |index|
          index ← self indexOf. name.
          index = 0
            ifTrue: [index ← self newIndexOf: name].
          ^ codes at: index put: code

   "Look-up index of a given department name"
   indexOf: name
          1 to: names size do:
            [:index | (names at: index) = name ifTrue: [^index]].
          ^ 0

   "Create a new entry with the given name and return index"
   newIndexOf: name
          self grow.
          names at: names size put: name.
          ^ names size

   "Stretch table by one element and put in new name"
   grow | oldNames oldCodes|
          oldNames ← names.
          oldCodes ← codes.
          names ← Array new: names size + 1.
          codes ← Array new: codes size + 1.
          names replaceFrom: 1 to: oldNames size with: oldNames.
          codes replaceFrom: 1 to: oldNames size with: oldCodes

   "Test for inclusion of a given name"
   includes: name
          ^ (self  indexOf: name) ~= 0

   "Test for empty"
   isEmpty
          ^ names isEmpty

   "Create initial empty arrays"
   initialize
          names ← Array new: 0.
          codes ← Array new: 0
```

Because it has not been previously discussed, we now briefly describe the action of the `replaceFrom:` method. The first `replaceFrom:` method used in the grow method operates by moving the elements of the array `oldNames` indexed with the range 1..size of `oldNames` to the array named `names`.

The following expressions and the computed results illustrate how an instance of `DeptCodes` behaves. Note that `isEmpty:` is a unary method inherited from `Object`.

EXPRESSION	RESULT
`Codes ←DeptCodes new`	creates new instance
`dCodes initialize`	creates empty arrays
`dCodes isEmpty`	true
`dCodes at: 'Physics' put: 100`	100
`dCodes at: 'Chemistry' put: 110`	110
`dCodes at: 'Biology' put: 120`	120
`dCodes isEmpty`	false
`dCodes size`	3
`dCodes at: 'Chemistry'`	110
`dCodes includes 'Physics'`	true
`dCodes includes 'Computing'`	false

15.3.11 LOGO-Style Graphics

In this section, an example program is presented that illustrates the Smalltalk class that provides the kind of drawing that originated in the turtle graphics of LOGO. This class, named `Pen`, is a subclass of another system class, `BitBlt`, which we will not discuss.

An instance of `Pen` is very much like a ball point pen under computer control, writing on a screen rather than paper. A `Pen` object has three primary parameters: direction, position, and frame. The position is either up or down, where up means it does not write when moved, and down means it does. Direction is measured counterclockwise in degrees from the direction to 0, with 0 being toward the right on the screen. The frame of a `Pen` object is the region of the screen in which it can draw, measured in bits. When a `Pen` instance is outside its frame, it cannot draw.

The initial condition of an instance of `Pen` is that it is pointing at 270 degrees, which is straight up on the screen; it is located at the coordinates (300,400); and it is in the up position. The (300,400) position is the center of the assumed screen size, which is 600 bits wide and 800 bits high.

The current parameters of a Pen instance can be gotten from the methods direction, location, and frame. The frame method returns the upper-left corner and the lower-right corner coordinates of the area in which the pen can draw.

The frame can be set by a second frame message:

```
frame: (aPoint extent: aPoint)
```

where `aPoint` is a pair of bit positions separated by an "at" sign (@). The parentheses are required in order to force the desired precedence in the message expression. The first occurrence of `aPoint` in this message indicates the upper-left corner of the frame. The second indicates the distance the frame will extend in the x and y directions from the upper-left corner. For example, the message

```
frame: (50@50 extent: 300@300)
```

sets the `frame` to have an upper-left corner at (`50,50`) and a lower-right corner at (`350,350`).

The message protocol for moving and drawing with objects of the class `Pen` is as follows:

down	Sets the pen in the drawing position.
up	Sets the pen in the nondrawing position.
turn: degrees	Changes the direction of the pen by the number of degrees specified in the parameter.
go: distance	Moves the pen in its current direction by the number of bits specified in the parameter.
goto: aPoint	Moves the pen to the position specified by the parameter point. If the pen is currently down, it draws a line.
place: aPoint	Sets the pen at the position specified in the parameter. No lines are drawn.
home	Sets the pen at the center of the frame.
north	Sets the direction of the pen to 270, which is straight up on the screen.

The color of the lines drawn by instances of `Pen` have a default value of black. The shape of the pen tip defaults to 1 bit by 1 bit. Both can be changed.

Simple geometric shapes can be easily drawn with instances of `Pen`. First, an instance of `Pen` must be created:

```
OurPen ← Pen new defaultNib : 2.
OurPen up; goto: 800@300; down
```

Now a triangle can be drawn with

```
OurPen go: 100; turn: 120; go: 100; turn: 120; go: 100
```

Figure 15.1 shows the result of executing this code. It also shows the rest of the screen at the time, which illustrates the flavor of the Smalltalk user interface.

The message above can be simplified somewhat with a block, as in

```
3 timesRepeat: [OurPen go: 100. OurPen turn: 120]
```

This message can be generalized to draw any equilateral polygon by repeating the block a number of times equal to the number of sides and turning

Figure 15.1
Smalltalk screen with
output of a triangle

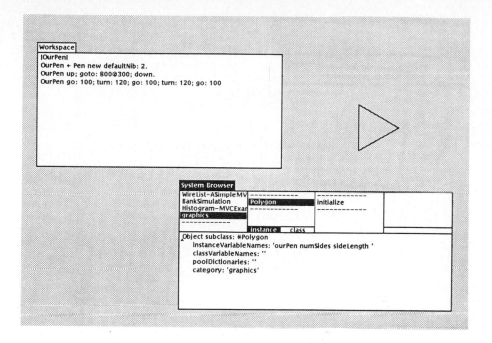

by an amount equal to 360 divided by the number of sides, as in the
following:

```
numSides timesRepeat: [ourPen go: 100. ourPen turn: 360 //
                          numSides]
```

Using this method, a general equilateral polygon-drawing class can be built.
The following example is similar to one in Goldberg and Robson (1983):

```
class name                Polygon
superclass                Object
instance variable names   ourPen
                          numSides
                          sideLength

"Class methods"
"Create an instance"
new
    ^ super new getPen

"Instance methods"
"Get a pen for drawing polygons"
getPen
    ourPen ← Pen new defaultNib: 2

"Draw a polygon"
draw
    numSides timesRepeat: [ourPen go: sideLength;
                            turn: 360 // numSides]
```

```
"Set length of sides"
length: len
    sideLength ← len

"Set number of sides"
sides: num
    numSides ← num
```

Notice that the variable ourPen in the class definition above does not begin with an uppercase letter, as it did when it was used outside a class. This is the case because it is a local, private variable here, but it had to be a global variable when it was used outside the class definition.

With this class, a sequence of polygons with various numbers of sides can be drawn, as with

```
|MyPoly|
MyPoly ← Polygon new.
MyPoly length: 60.
3 to: 8 do: [:sides | MyPoly sides: sides. MyPoly draw]
```

This code draws the figure shown in Figure 15.2. The lines in the figure can be made wider by changing the shape of the pen tip, which is done by sending the message inside the class definition:

```
ourPen defaultNib: 4
```

Figure 15.2
Concentric polygons
from the object
Polygon

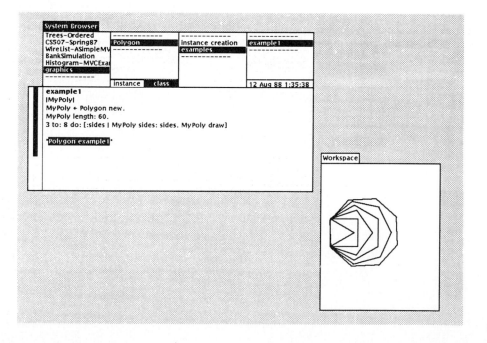

This changes the shape of the tip to 4 bits by 4 bits. The result of drawing the same polygons as above with this new tip is shown in Figure 15.3.

15.3.12 Evaluation

Smalltalk is important as a programming language. In addition, it is significant because of its connections to object-oriented programming and graphical user interface systems, both of which are rapidly becoming prominent in software development.

Smalltalk is really a small language, although the Smalltalk system is large. The syntax of the language is simple and very regular. It is a fine example of the power that can be provided by a small language, if that language is built around a simple but powerful concept. In the case of Smalltalk, that concept is that all programming can be based on simulation, using only objects and message passing.

In comparison with conventional compiled imperative language programs, equivalent Smalltalk programs are, at least at this point, significantly slower. Therefore, efficiency will clearly be an issue in most discussions of the practical applicability of Smalltalk. This was also the case for all of the early implementations of LISP that were interpreted. It is also the case with Prolog.

Figure 15.3
Concentric polygons
with **nib** set to 4

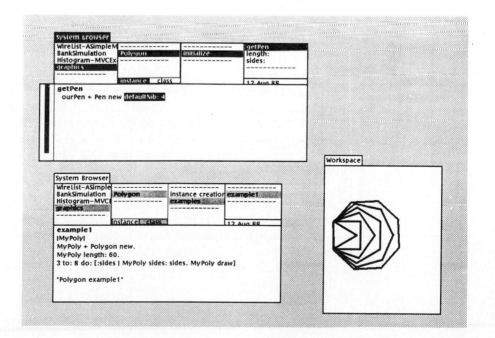

The Smalltalk user interface has already had an important impact on computing: It is difficult to escape the integrated use of windows, mouse pointing devices, and pop-up or pull-down menus in new software applications systems.

Perhaps the greatest impact of Smalltalk thus far is the advancement of object-oriented programming. Object-oriented programming is being vigorously touted as the next significant step in the evolution of programming, after the structured programming revolution of the 1970s. It has enjoyed rapid acceptance as a design and coding methodology.

In the following section, the features of C++ that support inheritance and dynamic type binding are described.

15.4   Support for Object-Oriented Programming in C++

Chapter 2 describes how C++ evolved from C and SIMULA 67, with the design goal of support for object-oriented programming. C++ features to support abstract data types are discussed in Chapter 10. C++ support for the other essentials of object-oriented programming is explored in the following sections.

15.4.1   Inheritance

A C++ class can be defined to be a subclass of an existing class, which is then its parent, or base, class. Subclasses are called derived classes in C++. A C++ class can also be stand-alone, without any superclasses.

Some or all of the data members and member functions of the base class may be inherited by the derived class, which can also add new data members and member functions. (Recall that a C++ class can include data members, which are the data part of the class objects, and member functions, which are the operations on the data members.) Accessibility of the members of subclasses can be different than that of the corresponding members of the base class.

Recall (from Chapter 10) that class members can be private, protected, or public. Private members are accessible only by member functions and friends of the class where they are declared. Public members are accessible by any function. Protected members are like private members, except in derived classes, whose access is described below. Derived classes can modify accessibility for their inherited members. The syntactic form of a derived class is

    class derived_class_name : access_mode base_class_name
        {data member and member function declarations};

The access_mode can be either public or private. The public and protected members of a base class are also public and protected, respectively, in a public derived class. In a private derived class, both the public and protected members of the base class are private. So, in a class hierarchy, a private derived class cuts off access to all members of all ancestor classes to all successor classes, and protected members may or may not be accessible to subsequent subclasses (past the first). Private members of a base class are never inherited by a derived class. Consider the following example:

```
class base_class {
  private:
    int a;
  protected:
    int b;
  public:
    int c;
};

class subclass_1 : public base_class { ... };
class subclass_2 : private base_class { ... };
```

In subclass_1, b is protected and c is public. In subclass_2, both b and c are private. No derived class of subclass_2 can have members with access to any member of base_class. The data member a in base_class is not accessible in either subclass_1 or subclass_2.

The accessibility of an inherited member can be modified in a derived class, but we will not discuss why or how this is done.

Consider the following example of C++ inheritance, in which a general linked list class is defined and then used to define two useful subclasses:

```
class single_linked_list {
    class node {
      friend class single_linked_list;
     private:
      node* link;
      int contents;
     };
  private:
    node *head;
  public:
    single_linked_list () {head = 0};
    void insert_at_head (int);
    void insert_at_tail (int);
    int remove_at_head ();
    int empty ();
};
```

The nested class, node, defines a cell of the linked list to consist of an integer location and a pointer to a cell. It lists single_linked_list as a friend, thus granting objects of class `single_linked_list` access to its two data members. This is necessary because enclosing classes have no special access rights to members of their nested classes.

The enclosing class, `single_linked_list`, has just a single data member, a pointer to act as the list's header. It contains a constructor function, which simply sets `head` to the null pointer value. The four member functions allow nodes to be inserted at either end of a list object, nodes to be removed from one end of a list, and lists to be tested for empty.

The following definitions provide stack and queue classes, both based on the `single_linked_list` class:

```
class stack : public single_linked_list {
  public:
    void push (int value) {single_linked_list ::
                      insert_at_head (int value);}
    int pop () {return single_linked_list ::
                      remove_at_head ();}
};
class queue : public single_linked_list {
  public:
    void enqueue (int value) {single_linked_list ::
                      insert_at_tail (int value);}
    int dequeue () {single_linked_list ::
                      remove_at_head ();}
};
```

The double colon (::) in these two class definitions is a scope operator. It specifies the class where its following parameter is defined. Note that objects of both the stack and queue subclasses can access the empty function defined in the base class, `single_linked_list`.

15.4.2 Dynamic Binding

In some cases, the derived classes must redefine a member function in the base class. This, coupled with the fact that a pointer to a derived class object can also point at the base class, leads to situations in which some function calls can be bound to functions only at run time. The code that contains such a call is polymorphic because it can cause computations on objects of different classes. In a strongly typed language, where function calls are normally bound to functions at compile time, polymorphism poses a problem. The C++ solution is to allow the programmer to define member functions to be **virtual**, which means that calls to them are to be dynamically bound. So a C++ function call can be either statically or dynamically bound to a function.

Consider again the situation of having a base class named `shape`, along with a collection of subclasses for different kinds of shapes, such as circles, rectangles, and so forth. If these shapes need to be displayed, then the display member function must be unique for each subclass, or kind of shape. When a call to this function is made with a pointer to an object of one of the subclasses as its parameter, that call must be dynamically bound to the correct member function. This is implemented by the following method: At the time an object is created, a list of pointers to virtual functions is created, which is then used in the dynamic binding of function calls to functions. Therefore, calls to virtual functions are handled by indirect addressing. Contrast this with the dynamic binding of messages to methods in Smalltalk, where every message requires a method search.

15.4.3 Abstract Classes

Recall that in Chapter 10 we mentioned abstract classes in conjunction with data abstraction support in C++. We can now describe abstract classes.

In a strict sense, an abstract data type is one that cannot have concrete objects but rather is used only to represent the concepts of a type. Subclasses of such a type can, of course, have objects. C++ provides abstract classes, which model these truly abstract types.

An abstract class has one or more pure virtual member functions. A pure virtual function is denoted by initialization to the value 0, as in

```
virtual void mover (int, int) = 0;
```

No object of an abstract class can be created. The purpose of a pure virtual function is to provide the interface of a function without revealing any of its implementation.

If a subclass of an abstract class does not redefine a pure virtual function of its parent class, that function remains as a pure virtual function.

Abstract classes and inheritance together support a powerful technique for software development. They allow types to be hierarchically defined, so that related types can be subclasses of truly abstract types that define their common abstract characteristics.

15.5 Comparing Smalltalk and C++

Our comparison of Smalltalk and C++ is organized into several topics, each of which is discussed in a separate section.

15.5.1 Programming Environments

As discussed earlier in this chapter, Smalltalk is a language that is part of an integrated software development system. The user interface to the tools in this system is graphical; in fact, Smalltalk is one of the first systems to use multiple windows, menus, and a mouse pointing device. Owing largely to the common graphical interface to all system tools, Smalltalk is pleasant to use. The negative side of the graphical interface is its significant consumption of resources. A side effect of this is that, at least until recently, Smalltalk ran effectively only on relatively powerful workstations. The advent of powerful personal computers has, of course, alleviated this problem.

C++ is a conventional compiled programming language. It can run under any conventional operating system, and C++ programs can be linked easily to programs written in other languages. C++ compilers are efficient and can be implemented on relatively small computers without difficulty.

15.5.2 Control Structures and Data Structures

As discussed in Section 15.2.1, Smalltalk uses the message-passing model to provide control structures. Simple data structures such as arrays are also provided through message passing. This universal use of message passing is elegant but costly in terms of execution efficiency. In contrast, C++ provides the usual collection of data structures and control structures that one expects to find in an imperative language. Because these imperative features were originally developed for efficiency, they are much faster than their counterparts in Smalltalk. Although it is theoretically interesting that array indexing and loops can be provided within the message-passing model, efficiency is an important factor in the evaluation of programming languages.

15.5.3 Dynamic Versus Static Binding

Recall from Section 15.4.2 that C++ function calls can be either statically or dynamically bound to functions (dynamic if virtual; otherwise static). Virtual functions may appear to provide the same flexibility as the dynamic binding of Smalltalk, but that is not entirely the case.

One problem is that virtual functions in C++ that have the same name must also have the same type protocols. That is, every one must return the same type and have the same number and types of parameters. This is a significant restriction, and it means that part of Smalltalk's power is not available in C++. For an example of this deficiency, see Kamin (1990, pages 335–336).

The trade-off here is efficiency versus flexibility. Although Smalltalk's dynamic binding is more flexible, the cost in efficiency is significant. Calls to C++ virtual functions cost only slightly more than a statically bound call, whereas all Smalltalk calls are costly by comparison. More importantly, many if not most C++ functions can be statically bound.

Another problem with Smalltalk's dynamic binding is that type errors are not detected until run time. A program can be written and compiled that includes messages to nonexistent methods. Such errors are detected by a C++ compiler. Recall that compiler-detected errors are less expensive to repair than those detected at run time.

When parameterized types are added to the current C++ language, nearly all of the flexibility of Smalltalk's dynamic binding will be available in C++, with the added advantage of static type checking, which is not possible in Smalltalk.

15.5.4   Should Classes be Types?

As noted by Liu (1991), perhaps one of the most fundamental differences between C++ and Smalltalk in their support for object-oriented programming is that C++ classes are types, but Smalltalk classes are not. This naturally leads to a number of differences between the languages. One of these differences is that a C++ object can access the private members of another object of the same class, because C++ uses only type checking to prevent such accesses and all objects of a class are of the same type. This is a small loophole in the information hiding of C++ objects. For an example of this phenomenon, see Liu (1991).

Another result of classes being types, at least in the current version of C++, is that it is less elegant to provide genericity, or polymorphism. For example, one cannot easily define a generic data structure in C++, as can be done in Smalltalk. To define a generic stack in C++, for example, one must define a stack base class with virtual member functions. Then a subclass must be defined for each different stack type desired. The stack operations must be defined in each of these subclasses. This is clearly less elegant than the single stack class that can be defined in Smalltalk, in the absence of strong typing. Note that this will no longer be a problem with future versions of C++, which will include parameterized types to provide an easy technique for creating such a generic stack.

15.5.5   Overall Efficiency

We have already discussed the fact that message passing for control structures, array indexing, and method enactment is significantly less efficient than the techniques used by conventional languages. Another efficiency advantage of non-message-passing object-oriented languages is that small subprograms can be inlined, thereby completely eliminating the overhead of linkage. This is not possible in a pure object-oriented language because the compiler cannot determine the method to which a given message is to be bound.

According to Chambers and Ungar (1991), Smalltalk ran a particular set of small C-style benchmarks at only 10% the speed of optimized C. C++ programs require only a bit more time than equivalent C programs. Only virtual functions take more time to call, and such calls require only five more memory references than statically bound calls (Stroustrup, 1988).

Finally, Smalltalk programs require more memory than do equivalent programs in C++.

Given the great efficiency gap between Smalltalk and C++, it is little wonder that the commercial use of C++ is growing far more rapidly than that of Smalltalk. Of course, there are other factors in this difference, but efficiency is clearly a strong argument in favor of C++.

SUMMARY

Object-oriented programming involves three fundamental concepts: abstract data types, dynamic type binding, and inheritance. The so-called pure object-oriented programming languages support the paradigm with objects, classes, and message passing.

Smalltalk programs consist primarily of objects and messages. Objects are instances of classes, which consist largely of methods that correspond to possible messages to which those instances can respond. Methods are in turn constructed from expressions. An expression describes an object, which happens to be the value of the expression.

Control structures in Smalltalk, like everything else, are constructed using objects and messages. While they have a somewhat conventional appearance, their semantics are very different from that of corresponding structures in the imperative languages.

C++ provides support for data abstraction, inheritance, and a form of dynamic typing, along with all of the conventional features of C. C++ classes are types, which results in several differences between object-oriented programming in C++ and in Smalltalk.

While Smalltalk's dynamic binding provides somewhat more programming flexibility than the hybrid language, C++, it is far less efficient.

PROBLEM SET

1. What purpose does the pseudovariable **super** serve?
2. Explain what the message protocol of a Smalltalk object defines.
3. What is the relationship between Smalltalk objects and classes?
4. What are methods?
5. In essence, all Smalltalk variables are of a single type. What is that type?
6. How many parameters are there in a binary message?

7. Explain the precedence rules of Smalltalk expressions.

8. How can one force a block to be executed?

9. What purpose does the pseudovariable **self** serve?

10. Write the following Pascal loop structure in Smalltalk:

```
while count < 100 do
  begin
  sum := sum div (2 * count - 1);
  count := count + 1
  end
```

11. Write the following Pascal **for** loop in Smalltalk:

```
for index := 10 downto 1 do
  sum := sum + index
```

12. Write the following Pascal selection construct in Smalltalk:

```
if count < 10 then
  answer := 1
else
  begin
  answer := 0;
  count := 0
  end
```

Bibliography

ACM. (1979) "Part A: Preliminary Ada Reference Manual" and "Part B: Rationale for the Design of the Ada Programming Language." *SIGPLAN Notices*, Vol. 14, No. 6.

Ambler, A.L., D.I. Good, J.C. Browne, W.F. Burger, R.M. Cohen, C.G. Hoch, and R.E. Wells. (1977) "Gypsy: A Language for Specification and Implementation of Verifiable Programs." Proceedings of the ACM Conference on Language Design for Reliable Software. *ACM SIGPLAN Notices*, Vol. 12, No. 3, pp. 1–10.

Andrews, G.R., and F.B. Schneider. (1983) "Concepts and Notations for Concurrent Programming." *ACM Computing Surveys*, Vol. 15, No. 1, pp. 3–43.

Aho, A.V., R. Sethi, and J.D. Ullman. (1986) *Compilers: Principles, Techniques, and Tools.* Addison-Wesley, Reading, MA.

Amoroso, S., P. Wegner, D. Morris, and D. White. (1977) "Language Evaluation Coordinating Committee Report to the High Order Language Working Group." January.

ANSI. (1974) *American National Standard Programming Language COBOL.* ANSI X3.23–1974, American National Standards Institute, New York.

ANSI. (1976) *American National Standard Programming Language PL/I.* ANSI X3.53–1976. American National Standards Institute, New York.

ANSI. (1978a) *American National Standard Programming Language FORTRAN.* ANSI X3.9–1978. American National Standards Institute, New York.

ANSI. (1978b) *American National Standard Programming Language Minimal BASIC.* ANSI X3.60–1978. American National Standards Institute, New York.

ANSI. (1985) *American National Standard Programming Language COBOL.* ANSI X3.23–1985, American National Standards Institute, New York.

ANSI. (1989) *American National Standard Programming Language C.* ANSI X3.159–1989. American National Standards Institute, New York.

ANSI. (1990) *American National Standard Programming Language FORTRAN 90.* ANSI X3.198 (draft). American National Standards Institute, New York.

Arden, B.W., B.A. Galler, and R.M. Graham. (1961) "MAD at Michigan." *Datamation*, Vol. 7, No. 12, pp. 27–28.

Backus, J. (1954) "The IBM 701 Speedcoding System." *J. ACM*, Vol. 1, pp. 4–6.

Backus, J. (1959) "The Syntax and Semantics of the Proposed International Algebraic Language of the Zurich ACM-GAMM Conference." *Proceedings International Conference on Information Processing*, UNESCO, Paris, pp. 125–132.

Backus, J. (1978) "Can Programming Be Liberated from the von Neumann Style? A Functional Style and Its Algebra of Programs." *Commun. ACM*, Vol. 21, No. 8, pp. 613–641.

Backus, J., F.L. Bauer, J. Green, C. Katz, J. McCarthy, P. Naur, A.J. Perlis, H. Rutishauser, K. Samualson, B. Vauquois, J.H. Wegstein, A. van Wijngaarden, and M. Woodger. (1962) "Revised Report on the Algorithmic Language ALGOL 60." *Commun. ACM*, Vol. 6, No. 1, pp. 1–17.

Ben-Ari, M. (1982) *Principles of Concurrent Programming*. Prentice-Hall, Englewood Cliffs, NJ.

Birtwistle, G.M., O-J. Dahl, B. Myhrhaug, and K. Nygaard. (1973) *Simula BEGIN* . Van Nostrand Reinhold, New York.

Bobrow, D.G., L. DeMichiel, R. Gabriel, S. Keene, G. Kiczales, and D. Moon. (1988) "Common Lisp Object System Specification X3J13 Document 88-002R," *ACM SIGPLAN Notices*, Vol. 23, September.

Bodwin, J.M., L. Bradley, K. Kanda, D. Litle, and U.F. Pleban. (1982) "Experience with an Experimental Compiler Generator Based on Denotational Semantics." *ACM SIGPLAN Notices*, Vol. 17, No. 6, pp. 216–229.

Bohm, C., and G. Jacopini. (1966) "Flow Diagrams, Turing Machines, and Languages with Only Two Formation Rules." *Commun. ACM*, Vol. 9, No. 5, pp. 366–371.

Booch, G. (1987) *Software Engineering with Ada*, 2nd ed., Benjamin/Cummings, Redwood City, CA.

Brinch Hansen, P. (1973) *Operating System Principles*. Prentice-Hall, Englewood Cliffs, NJ.

Brinch Hansen, P. (1975) "The Programming Language Concurrent-Pascal." *IEEE Transactions on Software Engineering*, Vol. 1, No. 2, pp. 199–207.

Brinch Hansen, P. (1977) *The Architecture of Concurrent Programs*. Prentice-Hall, Englewood Cliffs, NJ.

Brinch Hansen, P. (1978) "Distributed Processes: a Concurrent Programming Concept." *Commun. ACM*, Vol. 21, No. 11, pp. 934–941.

Buneman, P., et al. (1981) "A Practical Functional Programming System for Databases." *Proc. ACM/MIT Conf. on Functional Programming and Computer Architecture*, Portsmouth, MA.

Burstall, R.M., D.B. MacQueen, and D.T. Sannella. (1980) "HOPE: An Experimental Applicative Language." *Conf. Record of the 1980 LISP Conference*, pp. 136–143

Chambers, C. and D. Ungar. (1991) "Making Pure Object-Oriented Languages Practical," *SIGPLAN Notices*, Vol. 26, No. 1, pp. 1–15.

Chomsky, N. (1956) "Three Models for the Description of Language." *IRE Transactions on Information Theory*, Vol. 2, No. 3, pp. 113–124.

Chomsky, N. (1959) "On Certain Formal Properties of Grammars." *Information and Control*, Vol. 2, No. 2, pp. 137–167.

Church, A. (1941) *Annals of Mathematics Studies. Volume 6: Calculi of Lambda Conversion*. Princeton Univ. Press, Princeton, NJ. Reprinted by Klaus Reprint Corporation, New York, 1965.

Clark, K.L., and F.G. McCabe. (1984) *Micro-PROLOG: Programming in Logic*. Prentice-Hall, Englewood Cliffs, NJ.

Clarke, L.A., J.C. Wileden, and A.L. Wolf. (1980) "Nesting in Ada Is for the Birds." *ACM SIGPLAN Notices*, Vol. 15, No. 11, pp. 139–145.

Cleaveland, J.C., and R.C. Uzgalis. (1976) *Grammars for Programming Languages: What Every Programmer Should Know about Grammar*. American Elsevier, New York.

Clocksin, W.F. and C.S. Mellish. (1984) *Programming in PROLOG*. 2nd ed. Springer-Verlag, New York.

Cohen, J. (1981) "Garbage Collection of Linked Data Structures." *ACM Computing Surveys*, Vol. 13, No. 3, pp. 341–368.

Cohen, J. (1985) "Describing Prolog by Its Implementation and Computation." *Commun. ACM*, Vol. 28, No. 12, pp. 1311–1324.

Conway, M.E. (1963) "Design of a Separable Transition-Diagram Compiler." *Commun. ACM*, Vol. 6, No. 7, pp. 396–408.

Conway, R., and R. Constable. (1976) "PL/CS—A Disciplined Subset of PL/I." Technical Report TR76-293, Department of Computer Science, Cornell University, Ithaca, NY.

Cornell University. (1977) *PL/C User's Guide, Release 7.6*. Department of Computer Science, Cornell University, Ithaca, NY.

Cox, B.J. (1986) *Object-Oriented Programming: An Evolutionary Approach*, Addison-Wesley, Reading, MA.

Cuadrado, C.Y., and J.L. Cuadrado. (1985) "Prolog Goes to Work." *BYTE*, August 1985, pp. 151–158.

Dahl, O.-J., E.W. Dijkstra, and C.A.R. Hoare. (1972) *Structured Programming*. Academic Press, New York.

Dahl, O.-J., and K. Nygaard. (1967) "SIMULA 67 Common Base Proposal." Norwegian Computing Center Document, Oslo.

Deliyanni, A., and R.A. Kowalski. (1979) "Logic and Semantic Networks." *Commun. ACM*, Vol. 22, No. 3, pp 184–192.

Department of Defense. (1960) "COBOL, Initial Specifications for a Common Business Oriented Language."

Department of Defense. (1961) "COBOL—1961, Revised Specifications for a Common Business Oriented Language."

Department of Defense. (1962) "COBOL—1961 EXTENDED, Extended Specifications for a Common Business Oriented Language."

Department of Defense. (1975a) "Requirements for High Order Programming Languages, STRAWMAN," July.

Department of Defense. (1975b) "Requirements for High Order Programming Languages, WOODENMAN," August.

Department of Defense. (1976) "Requirements for High Order Programming Languages, TINMAN," June.

Department of Defense. (1977) "Requirements for High Order Programming Languages, IRONMAN," January.

Department of Defense. (1978) "Requirements for High Order Programming Languages, STEELMAN," June.

Department of Defense. (1980a) "Requirements for High Order Programming Languages, STONEMAN," February.

Department of Defense (1980b) "Requirements for the Programming Environment for the Common High Order Language, STONEMAN," Department of Defense, Washington, D.C.

Deutsch, L.P., and D.G. Bobrow. (1976) "An Efficient Incremental Automatic Garbage Collector." *Commun. ACM*, Vol. 11, No. 3, pp. 522–526.

Dijkstra, E.W. (1968a) "Goto Statement Considered Harmful." *Commun. ACM*, Vol. 11, No. 3, pp. 147–149.

Dijkstra, E.W. (1968b) "Cooperating Sequential Processes." In *Programming Languages*, F. Genuys (ed.). Academic Press, New York, pp. 43–112.

Dijkstra, E.W. (1972) "The Humble Programmer." *Commun. ACM*, Vol. 15, No. 10, pp. 859–866.

Dijkstra, E.W. (1975) "Guarded Commands, Nondeterminancy, and Formal Derivation of Programs." *Commun. ACM*, Vol. 18, No. 8, pp. 453–457.

Dijkstra, E.W. (1976). *A Discipline of Programming*, Prentice-Hall, Englewood Cliffs, NJ.

Ellis, M.A. and B. Stroustrup (1990) *The Annotated C++ Reference Manual*, Addison-Wesley Publ. Co., Reading, MA.

Ennals, J.R. (1980) "Logic as a Computer Language for Children." Logic Programming Research Reports. Theory of Computing Research Group, Dept. of Computing, Imperial College of Science and Technology, London.

Farrow, R. (1982) "LINGUIST 86: Yet Another Translator Writing System Based on Attribute Grammars." *ACM SIGPLAN Notices*, Vol. 17, No. 6, pp. 160–171.

Feuer, A., and N. Gehani. (1982) "A Comparison of the Programming Languages C and Pascal." *ACM Computing Surveys*, Vol. 14, No. 1, pp. 73–92.

Fischer, C.N., G.F. Johnson, J. Mauney, A. Pal, and D.L. Stock. (1984) "The Poe Language-Based Editor Project." *ACM SIGPLAN Notices*, Vol. 19, No. 5, pp. 21–29.

Fischer, C.N., and R.J. LeBlanc. (1977) "UW-Pascal Reference Manual." Madison Academic Computing Center, Madison, WI.

Fischer, C.N., and R.J. LeBlanc. (1980) "Implementation of Runtime Diagnostics in Pascal." *IEEE-TSE*, SE-6, No. 4, pp. 313–319.

Fischer, C.N., and R.J. LeBlanc. (1988) *Crafting a Compiler*, Benjamin/Cummings, Menlo Park, CA.

Floyd, R.W. (1967) "Assigning Meanings to Programs." *Proceedings Symposium Applied Mathematics*, in *Mathematical Aspects of Computer Science*, ed. J.T. Schwartz. American Mathematical Society, Providence, RI.

Frege, G. (1892) "Über Sinn und Bedeutung," *Zeitschrift fur Philosophie und Philosophisches Kritik*, 100, pp. 25–50.

Friedman, D.P. and D.S. Wise. (1979) "Reference Counting's Ability to Collect Cycles is Not Insurmountable," *Inf. Processing Letters*, Vol. 8, No. 1, pp. 41–45.

Fuchi, K. (1981) "Aiming for Knowledge Information Processing Systems." *Proceedings of the International Conference on Fifth Generation Computing Systems*, Japan Information Processing Development Center, Tokyo. Republished (1982) by North-Holland Publishing, Amsterdam.

Gehani, N. (1983) *Ada: An Advanced Introduction*. Prentice-Hall, Englewood Cliffs, NJ.

Ghezzi, C., and M. Jazayeri. (1987) *Programming Language Concepts*. 2d ed. Wiley, New York.

Gilman, L., and A.J. Rose. (1976) *APL: An Interactive Approach*. 2d ed. J. Wiley, New York.

Goldberg, A. and D. Robson. (1983) *Smalltalk-80—The Language and its Implementation*, Addison-Wesley, Reading, MA.

Gordon, M. (1979) *The Denotational Description of Programming Languages, An Introduction*, Springer-Verlag, Berlin-New York.

Goodenough, J.B. (1975) "Exception Handling: Issues and Proposed Notation." *Commun. ACM*, Vol. 18, No. 12, pp. 683–696.

Goos, G., and J. Hartmanis. (eds.) (1983) *The Programming Language Ada Reference Manual*. American National Standards Institute, ANSI/MIL-STD-1815A-1983, Lecture Notes in Computer Science 155. Springer-Verlag, New York.

Gries, D. (1981) *The Science of Programming*, Springer-Verlag, New York.

Griswold, R.E., and M.T. Griswold. (1983) The *ICON Programming Language*, Prentice-Hall, Englewood Cliffs, NJ.

Griswold, R.E., F. Poage, and I.P. Polonsky. (1971) *The SNOBOL4 Programming Language*. 2d ed. Prentice-Hall, Englewood Cliffs, NJ.

Hammond, P. (1983) *APES: A User Manual*. Dept. of Computing Report 82/9. Imperial College of Science and Technology, London.

Henderson, P. (1980) *Functional Programming: Application and Implementation*. Prentice-Hall, Englewood Cliffs, NJ.

Hoare, C.A.R. (1969) "An Axiomatic Basis of Computer Programming." *Commun. ACM*, Vol. 12, No. 10, pp. 576–580.

Hoare, C.A.R. (1972) "Proof of Correctness of Data Representations." *Acta Informatica*, Vol. 1, pp. 271–281.

Hoare, C.A.R. (1973) "Hints on Programming Language Design." *Proceedings ACM SIGACT/SIGPLAN Conference on Principles of Programming Languages*. Also published as Technical Report STAN-CS-73-403, Stanford University Computer Science Department.

Hoare, C.A.R. (1974) "Monitors: An Operating System Structuring Concept." *Commun. ACM*, Vol. 17, No. 10, pp. 549–557.

Hoare, C.A.R. (1978) "Communicating Sequential Processes." *Commun. ACM*, Vol. 21, No. 8, pp. 666–677.

Hoare, C.A.R. (1981) "The Emperor's Old Clothes." *Commun. ACM*, Vol. 24, No. 2, pp. 75–83.

Hoare, C.A.R., and N. Wirth. (1973) "An Axiomatic Definition of the Programming Language Pascal." *Acta Informatica*. Vol. 2, pp. 335–355.

Hogger, C.J. (1984) *Introduction to Logic Programming*. Academic Press, London.

Holt, R.C., G.S. Graham, E.D. Lazowska, and M.A. Scott. (1978) *Structured Concurrent Programming with Operating Systems Applications*. Addison-Wesley, Reading, MA.

Horn, A. (1951) "On Sentences Which Are True of Direct Unions of Algebras." J. Symbolic Logic, Vol. 16, pp. 14–21.

Huskey, H.K., R. Love, and N. Wirth. (1963) "A Syntactic Description of BC NELIAC." *Commun. ACM*, Vol. 6, No. 7, pp. 367–375.

IBM. (1954) "Preliminary Report, Specifications for the IBM Mathematical FORmula TRANslating System, FORTRAN." IBM Corp., New York.

IBM. (1956) "Programmer's Reference Manual, The FORTRAN Automatic Coding System for the IBM 704 EDPM." IBM Corp., New York.

IBM. (1964) "The New Programming Language." IBM UK Laboratories.

Ichbiah, J.D., J.C. Heliard, O. Roubine, J.G.P. Barnes, B. Krieg-Brueckner, and B.A. Wichmann. (1979) "Rationale for the Design of the Ada Programming Language." *ACM SIGPLAN Notices*, Vol. 14, No. 6, Part B.

IEEE. (1985) "Binary Floating-Point Arithmetic," IEEE Standard 754, IEEE, New York.

Ingerman, P.Z. (1967). "Panini-Backus Form Suggested," Commun. ACM, Vol. 10, No. 3, p. 137.

ISO. (1982) *Specification for Programming Language Pascal*. ISO7185-1982. International Organization for Standardization, Geneva, Switzerland.

Jensen, K., and N. Wirth. (1974) *Pascal Users Manual and Report*. Springer-Verlag, Berlin.

Johnson, S.C. (1975) "Yacc—Yet Another Compiler Compiler." Computing Science Report 32, A.T.& T. Bell Laboratories, Murray Hill, NJ.

Jones, N.D. (ed.) (1980) *Semantic-Directed Compiler Generation*. Lecture Notes in Computer Science, Vol. 94. Springer-Verlag, Heidelberg, FRG.

Kamin, S.N. (1990) *Programming Languages—An Interpreter-Based Approach*, Addison-Wesley, Reading, MA.

Kay, A. (1969) "The Reactive Engine." Ph.D. Thesis, University of Utah, September.

Kernighan, B.W., and R. Pike. (1984) *The UNIX Programming Environment*. Prentice-Hall, Englewood Cliffs, NJ.

Kernighan, B.W., and D.M. Ritchie. (1978) *The C Programming Language*. Prentice-Hall, Englewood Cliffs, NJ.

Knuth, D.E. (1967) "The Remaining Trouble Spots in ALGOL 60." *Commun. ACM*, Vol. 10, No. 10, pp. 611–618.

Knuth, D.E. (1968a) "Semantics of Context-Free Languages." *Mathematical Systems Theory*, Vol. 2, No. 2, pp. 127–146.

Knuth, D.E. (1968b) *The Art of Computer Programming*. Vol. 1. Addison-Wesley, Reading, MA.

Knuth, D.E. (1974) "Structured Programming with GOTO Statements." *ACM Computing Surveys*, Vol. 6, No. 4, pp. 261–301.

Knuth, D.E., and Luis Trabb Pardo. (1977) "Early Development of Programming Languages." In *Encyclopedia of Computer Science and Technology*, Vol. 7. Dekker, New York, pp. 419–493.

Kowalski, R.A. (1979) *Logic for Problem Solving*. Artificial Intelligence Series, Vol. 7. Elsevier-North Holland, New York.

Lampson, B.W., J.J. Horning, R.L. London, J.G. Mitchell, and G.J. Popek. (1977) "Report on the Programming Language Euclid." *ACM SIGPLAN Notices*, Vol. 12, No. 2. (Revised Report, XEROX PARC Technical Report CSL78-2.)

Laning, J.H., Jr., and N. Zierler. (1954) "A Program for Translation of Mathematical Equations for Whirlwind I." Engineering memorandum E-364, Instrumentation Laboratory, Massachusetts Institute of Technology, Cambridge, MA.

Ledgard, H.F. (1984) *The American Pascal Standard*. Springer-Verlag, New York.

Ledgard, H.F., and M. Marcotty. (1975) "A Genealogy of Control Structures." *Commun. ACM*, Vol. 18, No. 11, pp. 629–639.

Liskov, B.H., R. Atkinson, T. Bloom, E. Moss, J.C. Schaffert, R. Scheifler, and A. Snyder. (1981) *CLU Reference Manual*. Springer-Verlag, New York.

Liskov, B.H., and A. Snyder. (1979) "Exception Handling in CLU." *IEEE Transactions on Software Engineering*, Vol. SE-5, No. 6, pp. 546–558.

Liu, C. (1991) "On the Object-Orientedness of C++," *ACM SIGPLAN Notices*, Vol. 26, No. 3, pp. 63–67.

Lomet, D. (1975) "Scheme for Invalidating References to Freed Storage." *IBM J. of Research and Development*, Vol. 19, pp. 26–35.

MacLaren, M.D. (1977) "Exception Handling in PL/I." *ACM SIGPLAN Notices*, Vol. 12, No. 3, pp. 101–104.

Marcotty, M., H.F. Ledgard, and G.V. Bochmann. (1976) "A Sampler of Formal Definitions." *ACM Computing Surveys*, Vol. 8, No. 2, pp. 191–276.

Mather, D.G., and S.V. Waite (eds.) (1971) *BASIC*. 6th ed. University Press of New England, Hanover, NH.

McCarthy, J. (1960) "Recursive Functions of Symbolic Expressions and Their Computation by Machine, Part I." *Commun. ACM*, Vol. 3, No. 4, pp. 184–195.

McCarthy, J., P.W. Abrahams, D.J. Edwards, T.P. Hart, and M. Levin. (1965) *LISP 1.5 Programmer's Manual*, 2d ed. MIT Press, Cambridge, MA.

McCracken, D. (1970) "Whither APL,", *Datamation*, Sept. 15, pp. 53–57.

Meyer, B. (1988) *Object-Oriented Software Construction*, Prentice-Hall, Englewood Cliffs, NJ.

Milner, R. M. Tofte, and R. Harper. (1990) *The Definition of Standard ML*, MIT Press, Cambridge, MA.

Milos, D., U. Pleban, and G. Loegel. (1984) "Direct Implementation of Compiler Specifications." *ACM Principles of Programming Languages 1984*, pp. 196–202.

Mitchell, J.G., W. Maybury, and R. Sweet. (1979) *Mesa Language Manual, Version 5.0*, CSL-79-3. Xerox Research Center, Palo Alto, CA.

Moses, J. (1970) "The Function of FUNCTION in LISP." *ACM SIGSAM Bulletin*, July, pp. 13–27.

Moto-oka, T. (1981) "Challenge for Knowledge Information Processing Systems." *Proceedings of the International Conference on Fifth Generation Computing Systems.*

Japan Information Processing Development Center, Tokyo. Republished (1982) by North-Holland Publishing, Amsterdam.

Naur, P. (ed.) (1960) "Report on the Algorithmic Language ALGOL 60." *Commun. ACM*, Vol. 3, No. 5, pp. 299–314.

Newell, A., and H.A. Simon. (1956) "The Logic Theory Machine—A Complex Information Processing System." *IRE Transactions on Information Theory*, Vol. IT-2, No. 3, pp. 61–79.

Newell, A., and F.M. Tonge. (1960) "An Introduction to Information Processing Language V." *Commun. ACM*, Vol. 3, No. 4, pp. 205–211.

Nilsson, N.J. (1971) *Problem Solving Methods in Artificial Intelligence*. McGraw-Hill, New York.

Pagan, F.G. (1981) *Formal Specifications of Programming Languages*. Prentice-Hall, Englewood Cliffs, NJ.

Papert, S. (1980) *MindStorms*: *Children, Computers and Powerful Ideas*. Basic Books, New York.

Perlis, A., and K. Samelson. (1958) "Preliminary Report—International Algebraic Language." *Commun. ACM*, Vol. 1, No. 12, pp. 8–22.

Peyton Jones, S.L. (1987) *The Implementation of Functional Programming Languages*. Prentice-Hall, Englewood Cliffs, NJ.

Polivka, R.P., and S. Pakin. (1975) *APL: The Language and its Usage*. Prentice-Hall, Englewood Cliffs, NJ.

Pratt, T.W. (1984) *Programming Languages*: *Design and Implementation*. 2d ed. Prentice-Hall, Englewood Cliffs, NJ.

Rees, J. and W. Clinger. (1986) "Revised Report on the Algorithmic Language Scheme," *ACM SIGPLAN Notices*, Vol. 21, No. 12, pp. 37–79.

Remington-Rand. (1952) "UNIVAC Short Code." unpublished collection of dittoed notes. Preface by A.B. Tonik, dated October 25, 1955 (1 p.); Preface by J.R. Logan, undated but apparently from 1952 (1 p.); Preliminary exposition, 1952? (22 pp., where pp. 20–22 appear to be a later replacement); Short code supplementary information, topic one (7 pp.); Addenda #1, 2, 3, 4 (9 pp.).

Richards, M. (1969) "BCPL: A Tool for Compiler Writing and Systems Programming." *Proc. AFIPS SJCC*, Vol. 34, pp. 557–566.

Robinson, J.A. (1965) "A Machine-Oriented Logic Based on the Resolution Principle" *Journal of the ACM*, Vol. 12, pp. 23–41.

Roussel, P. (1975) "PROLOG: Manual de Reference et D'utilisation," Research Report, Artificial Intelligence Group, Univ. of Aix-Marseille, Luming, France

Rutishauser, H. (1967) *Description of ALGOL 60*. Springer-Verlag, New York.

Sammet, J.E. (1969) *Programming Languages*: *History and Fundamentals*. Prentice-Hall, Englewood Cliffs, NJ.

Sammet, J.E. (1976) "Roster of Programming Languages for 1974-75." *Commun. ACM*, Vol. 19, No. 12, pp. 655–669.

Schorr, H., and W. Waite. (1967) "An Efficient Machine Independent Procedure for Garbage Collection in Various List Structures." *Commun. ACM*, Vol. 10, No. 8, pp. 501-506.

Sergot, M.J. (1983) "A Query-the-User Facility for Logic Programming." In *Integrated Interactive Computer Systems*, ed. P. Degano and E. Sandewall. North-Holland Publishing, Amsterdam.

Sewry, D.A. (1984a) "Modula-2 Process Facilities." *ACM SIGPLAN Notices*, Vol. 19, No. 11, pp. 23–32.

Sewry, D.A. (1984b) "Modula-2 and the Monitor Concept." *ACM SIGPLAN Notices*, Vol. 19, No. 11, pp. 33–41.

Scott, D.S., and C. Strachey. (1971) "Towards a Mathematical Semantics for Computer Language." *Proceedings Symposium on Computers and Automation*, ed. J. Fox. Polytechnic Institute of Brooklyn Press, New York, pp. 19–46.

Shaw, C.J. (1963) "A Specification of JOVIAL," *Commun. ACM*, Vol. 6, No. 12, pp. 721–736.

Sommerville, I. (1989) *Software Engineering*, 3rd ed., Addison-Wesley, Reading, MA.

Steele, G.L., Jr. (1984) *Common LISP*. Digital Press, Burlington, MA.

Stoy, J.E. (1977) *Denotational Semantics*: *The Scott-Strachey Approach to Programming Language Semantics*, MIT Press, Cambridge, MA.

Stroustrup, B. (1983) "Adding Classes to C: An Exercise in Language Evolution," *Software—Practice and Experience*, Vol. 13.

Stroustrup, B. (1984) "Data Abstraction in C,", AT & T Bell Laboratories Technical Journal, Vol. 63, No. 8.

Stroustrup, B. (1986) *The C++ Programming Language*. Addison-Wesley, Reading, MA.

Stroustrup, B. (1988) "What is Object-Oriented Programming," *IEEE Software*, May 1988, pp. 10–20.

Stroustrup, B. (1991) *The C++ Programming Language*, 2nd ed., Addison-Wesley, Reading, MA.

Sussman, G.J. and G.L. Steele, Jr. (1975) "Scheme: An Interpreter for Extended Lambda Calculus," MIT AI Memo No. 349 (December, 1975).

Suzuki, N. (1982) "Analysis of Pointer 'Rotation'," *Commun. of ACM*, Vol. 25, No. 5, pp. 330–335.

Tenenbaum, A.S. (1978) "A Comparison of Pascal and ALGOL 68." *Computer Journal*, Vol. 21, pp. 316–323.

Tenenbaum, A.S., Y. Langsam, and M.J. Augenstein (1990) *Data Structures using C*, Prentice-Hall, Englewood Cliffs, NJ.

Taylor, W., L. Turner, and R. Waychoff. (1961) "A Syntactic Chart of ALGOL 60." *Commun. ACM*, Vol. 4, p. 393.

Teitelbaum, T., and T. Reps. (1981) "The Cornell Program Synthesizer: A Syntax-Directed Programming Environment." *Commun. ACM*, Vol. 24, No. 9, pp. 563–573.

Teitelman, W. (1975) *INTERLISP Reference Manual*, Xerox Palo Alto Research Center, Palo Alto, CA.

Turner, D. (1990) (ed) *Research Topics in Functional Programming*, Addison-Wesley, Reading, MA.

Van Emden, M.H. (1980) "McDermott on Prolog: A Rejoiner." *SIGART Newsletter*, No. 72, August, pp. 19–20.

van Wijngaarden, A. B.J. Mailloux, J.E.L. Peck, and C.H.A. Koster. (1969) "Report on the Algorithmic Language ALGOL 68," *Numerische Mathematik*, Vol. 14, No. 2, pp. 79–218.

Warren, D.H.D., L.M. Pereira, and F.C.N. Pereira. (1977) "Prolog: The Language and Its Implementation Compared to LISP." *ACM SIGPLAN Notices*, Vol. 12, No. 8, and *ACM SIGART Newsletter*, Vol. 6, No. 4.

Warren, D.H.D., L.M. Pereira, and F.C.N. Pereira. (1979) "User's Guide to DEC System-10 Prolog." Occasional Paper 15. Dept. of Artificial Intelligence, Univ. of Edinburgh, Scotland.

Watt, D.A. (1979) "An Extended Attribute Grammar for Pascal." *ACM SIGPLAN Notices*, Vol. 14, No. 2, pp. 60–74.

Weissman, C. (1967) *LISP 1.5 Primer*. Dickenson Press, Belmont, CA.

Welsh, J., M.J. Sneeringer, and C.A.R. Hoare. (1977) "Ambiguities and Insecurities in Pascal." *Software-Practice and Experience*, Vol. 7, No. 6, pp. 685–696.

Wegner, P. (1972) "The Vienna Definition Language." *ACM Computing Surveys*, Vol. 4, No. 1, pp. 5–63.

Wexelblat, R.L. (ed.) (1981) *History of Programming Languages*. Academic Press, New York.

Wheeler, D.J. (1950) "Programme Organization and Initial Orders for the EDSAC." *Proc. R. Soc.* London, Ser. A, Vol. 2, pp. 573–589.

Wilkes, M.V. (1952) "Pure and Applied Programming." In *Proceedings of the ACM National Conference*, Vol. 2, Toronto, pp. 121–124.

Wilkes, M.V., D.J. Wheeler, and S. Gill. (1951) *The Preparation of Programs for an Electronic Digital Computer, with Special Reference to the EDSAC and the Use of a Library of Subroutines*. Addison-Wesley, Reading, MA.

Wilkes, M.V., D.J. Wheeler, and S. Gill (1957) *The Preparation of Programs for an Electronic Digital Computer*. 2d ed. Addison-Wesley, Reading, MA.

Wirth, N. (1971) "The Programming Language Pascal." *Acta Informatica*, Vol. 1, No. 1, pp. 35–63.

Wirth, N. (1973) *Systematic Programming: An Introduction*. Prentice-Hall, Englewood Cliffs, NJ.

Wirth, N. (1975) "On the Design of Programming Languages." *Information Processing 74* (Proceedings of IFIP Congress 74), North Holland, Amsterdam, pp. 386–393.

Wirth, N. (1976) "Modula: A Language for Modular Multi-programming," *Software—Practice and Experience*, Vol. 7, pp. 3–35.

Wirth, N. (1985) *Programming in Modula-2*. 3rd ed. Springer-Verlag, New York.

Wirth, N., and C.A.R. Hoare. (1966) "A Contribution to the Development of ALGOL." *Commun. ACM*, Vol. 9, No. 6, pp. 413–431.

Wulf, W.A., D.B. Russell, and A.N. Habermann. (1971) "BLISS:A Language for Systems Programming." *Commun. ACM*, Vol. 14, No. 12, pp. 780–790.

Zuse, K. (1972) "Der Plankalkül." Manuscript prepared in 1945, published in *Berichte der Gesellschaft fur Mathematik und Datenverarbeitung*, No. 63 (Bonn, 1972); Part 3, 285 pp. English translation of all but pp. 176–196 in No. 106 (Bonn, 1976), pp. 42–244.

INDEX

About the Author

Robert Sebesta is an Associate Professor and Chairman of the Computer Science Department at the University of Colorado, Colorado Springs. Professor Sebesta received his Ph.D. in Computer Science from the Pennsylvania State University and has been teaching computer science for over 20 years. His research interests are in programming languages, compiler design, and software testing methods and tools. He has been a consultant to Federal Express, Hewlett-Packard, Ford Microelectronics, Paramax, and Labtek. Professor Sebesta is the author of several books, including texts on structured assembly language programming for the PDP-11 and VAX minicomputers. He is a member of the ACM and the IEEE Computer Society.